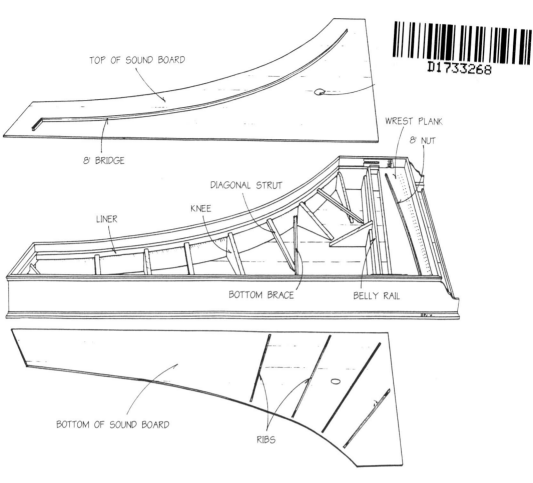

TOP OF SOUND BOARD

8' BRIDGE

WREST PLANK

8' NUT

DIAGONAL STRUT

KNEE

LINER

BOTTOM BRACE

BELLY RAIL

BOTTOM OF SOUND BOARD

RIBS

ITALIAN HARPSICHORD
EXPLODED VIEW

D1733268

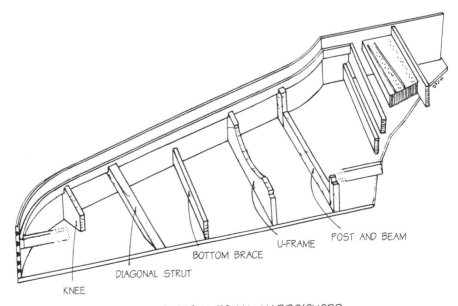

KNEE

DIAGONAL STRUT

BOTTOM BRACE

U-FRAME

POST AND BEAM

INTERNATIONAL HARPSICHORD
TYPICAL BRACING SCHEMES

A HISTORY

OF THE

Harpsichord

A HISTORY

OF THE

EDWARD L. KOTTICK

INDIANA UNIVERSITY PRESS

Bloomington and Indianapolis

This book is a publication of

INDIANA UNIVERSITY PRESS
Office of Scholarly Publishing
Herman B Wells Library 350
1320 East 10th Street
Bloomington, Indiana 47405 USA

iupress.indiana.edu

The paper used in this publication meets the minimum requirements of American National Standard for Information Sciences—Permanence of Paper for Printed Library Materials, ANSI Z39.48-1984.

MANUFACTURED IN THE UNITED STATES OF AMERICA

Library of Congress Cataloging-in-Publication Data

Kottick, Edward L.
A history of the harpsichord / Edward L. Kottick.
p. cm.
Includes bibliographical references (p.) and index.
ISBN 0-253-34166-3 (alk. paper)
1. Harpsichord—History. I. Title.
ML650 .K68 2003
786.4'19'09—dc21
2002006385

ISBN 978-0-253-02347-6 (cloth)

1 2 3 4 5 21 20 19 18 17 16

For Gloria

WITHOUT WHOM THIS

OR ANYTHING ELSE

WOULD HAVE BEEN IMPOSSIBLE

Contents

PART III THE SEVENTEENTH CENTURY

Plates and Illustrations

Acknowledgments

There may be those whose knowledge of the harpsichord encompasses the whole of its six-hundred-year history, but I am not among them. I have had to rely on the research of other scholars for much of the detailed information in this book, and it is important that I acknowledge my debt to them for the many articles and books I have consulted. Grant O'Brien, John Koster, and Denzil Wraight have my particular gratitude for their careful and detailed work on Ruckers, the early history of the harpsichord, and Italian harpsichords in general. Merely remarking that Charles Mould's edition of Donald Boalch's *Makers of the Harpsichord and Clavichord* (*Boalch III*) was an invaluable resource is to understate the extent to which I relied on it, and the same can be said of Denzil Wraight's dissertation, "The Stringing of Italian Keyboard Instruments c. 1500–c. 1650," the second part of which is a detailed register of all the extant Italian harpsichords. Sheridan Germann has been my mentor in all things decorative, through both her writing and our personal and epistolary interactions. I would like to express special admiration for the work of Frank Hubbard, whose *Three Centuries of Harpsichord Making*, though at this writing more than thirty years old, remains a fount of fact and wisdom that this book cannot supplant.

R. Dean Anderson, Peter Bavington, Sheridan Germann, John Koster, Laurence Libin, George Lucktenberg, and David Sutherland all took on the task of reading an earlier draft of this book, and all contributed immensely to its accuracy and readability. Larry Palmer, John Phillips, Malcolm Rose, and Darryl Martin were kind enough to read sections of the manuscript dealing with their own areas of expertise. I need to thank all of these scholars, builders, and performers, not only for their invaluable assistance, but for the willingness with which they gave it as well. Whatever the merits of the book, it would be a far poorer work without their assistance. Nevertheless, the interpretation I place on the information contained herein is mine alone, and any criticism for faulty reasoning or misunderstanding of material must be directed to me alone.

I particularly want to recognize the support and assistance of George Lucktenberg. He was responsible for my first exposure to the antique harpsichords in the museums of Europe, he spurred my growing interest in the instrument's history, he was my coauthor for *Early Keyboard Instruments in European Museums,* and his close reading of the manuscript of the present book helped rid it of many grammatical gaffes, stylistic infelicities, wrong-headed statements, and blatant stupidities. His friendship and support for the past twenty years have meant a lot to me.

My thanks also go to the museum directors, curators, conservators, and private collectors who allowed the use of illustrations of instruments in their care and in many cases also provided photographs.

I would like to thank my editors at Indiana University Press, for their unending support, their constant stream of technical advice, and their everlasting patience. The drawings on the endpapers are by David Jensen. Other drawings are by the author unless otherwise noted.

A HISTORY
OF THE
Harpsichord

INTRODUCTION

*W*RITING CA. 1460, the cleric, astronomer, physician, and encyclopedist Paulus Paulirinus noted, "The harpsichord is an instrument of wonderful sweetness for making music. . . . It provides a means of introduction to the musical arts, and of comprehending all species of modes and pitches. Its attack is like that of the clavichord, except that it sounds sweeter and louder."[1] Paulirinus was one of the first to describe the sound of the harpsichord, which had been invented some sixty years before, and his characterization of it as an inclusive instrument, one that could not only encompass all of music but also do it beautifully, was an observation echoed by writers through succeeding centuries. Almost two hundred years later, in 1650, the Parisian organist and harpsichord maker Jean Denis lavished his praise on the instrument, amplifying Paulirinus's pithy definition:

> Our ancestors, having recognized that the human voice produced beautiful melodies, took pleasure in fashioning, for greater convenience, an instrument that could imitate the voice, or come as close to it as possible. All things considered, they could have taken up no instrument more appropriate than the harpsichord. . . . The harpsichord is the most perfect instrument of all instruments, for since it has many strings, each of which produces its own pitch, one can sound all the notes of music, pitch by pitch. The harpsichord with its keyboard can realize everything in written music, that which other instruments cannot accomplish unless there are several people and several instruments.[2]

Even as late as 1791, when the harpsichord's first existence was essentially over, the author of the article "Clavecin" in the *Musique* volume of the *Encyclopédie méthodique* recognized its lasting utility:

> The undoubted resources of the harpsichord in harmony, and the ease with which it represents on the keyboard the effect of the diverse instruments which make up the orchestra, have assigned it the first rank among the instruments of music. It has become the instrument of composers because it renders them better account of their intentions than any other instrument. It has become that of singing masters because its fixed sounds guide the irresolutions of the voice, always likely to sharp or flat when it is not sustained, and because it accustoms the person who sings to feel all the parts which must accompany him. This use and these advantages of the harpsichord have put it in the position of directing the orchestra in the theater and in concerts.[3]

Invented in the closing years of the fourteenth century and developed in the fifteenth, from the sixteenth through eighteenth centuries the harpsichord was found in the palatial dwellings of royalty and nobility, the boudoirs and music rooms of the wealthy, the homes of middle-class merchants, the studios of the maestros, and the pits of theaters and opera houses. Its extensive solo literature ranged from simple dances and variation sets to the virtuoso sonatas of Scarlatti and the lofty, complex suites of Rameau, Bach, and Handel. Everything from folk songs to opera overtures was arranged for it. Aside from its solo uses and didactic purposes, it became essential for the accompaniment of singers and instrumentalists, as the continuo foundation of ensembles, and ultimately as a solo instrument for concertos. It came in a variety of shapes and sizes, from petite triangular octave spinets, to bentside spinets, to virginals, to modest single-manual $1 \times 8'$ or $2 \times 8'$ harpsichords, to large, double-manual instruments, some with $16'$ choirs. If space was lacking, there were clavicytheria, or upright versions. Some types, such as virginals or bentside spinets, were the equivalent of the modern console piano; nevertheless, they were capable of making deeply satisfying music. Larger instruments, with their additional resources, were capable of majestic sonorities and a wide variety of effects.

The harpsichord's tonal appeal was often matched by the splendor of its appearance. Cases of even the smallest instruments were frequently decorated with a richness transcending their modest musical function, and larger ones could be even more ornate. Professional musicians, whose practical needs took precedence over decor, probably owned plainer models; but the royal, titled, and moneyed classes required that their musical instruments match the elegant decor of their drawing rooms and boudoirs. Accordingly, some of the finest harpsichords were made for the wealthy, those with elevated taste and the means to indulge it. Not surprisingly, the specimens from this last category are the ones most likely to have survived into our time. If workaday versions were frequently found in more humble surroundings, their association nevertheless was with majesty, royalty, nobility, property, affluence, and power. Like the automobile today, it is likely that these instruments were among the major status symbols of the household.

The history of the harpsichord was studied extensively in the years following World War II. Raymond Russell's *The Harpsichord and Clavichord,* written in 1959, and Frank Hubbard's monumental *Three Centuries of Harpsichord Making,* in 1965, both built their narratives around the concept of national schools, a principle certainly not ignored in this present account. However, since the 1960s hundreds of new instruments have been discovered and studied,[4] generating a flood of publications from writers such as John Barnes, Wilson Barry, Sheridan Germann, John Koster, Jeannine Lambrechts-Douillez, John Henry van der Meer, Charles Mould, Grant O'Brien, Edwin Ripin, Michael Thomas, and Denzil Wraight, among many others. In some cases their work has eroded paradigms that seemed obvious to earlier scholars, such as the perception that Italy developed the harpsichord a century before the Flemish. This view has been challenged, primarily by Koster, who was also among the first to articulate the existence of a third, International style which, although it seemed to share characteristics of both, was distinct from Russell's and Hubbard's Northern and Southern groupings. We have also come to realize that few antique instruments are in their original states, and that earlier scholars, misreading the evidence before them, drew erroneous conclusions about building practices and dispositions. It is now evident that some of our prior assumptions about the harpsichord's history are wanting.[5]

Recent scholarship has made it necessary to further modify Russell's and Hubbard's geographical approach, which divided harpsichord building into schools in the South of Europe (Italy and Iberia), and the North (Flanders, France, England, and Germany), but did not account for the profound differences between earlier and later instruments. Although the surviving sixteenth-century harpsichords from the various regions of Europe differ from each other, most of them nevertheless appear to have been created for royalty, wealth, and power, which influenced the way in which they were built and decorated. A century later these market forces seemed to have undergone a fundamental transformation, and changes in musical style also engendered modifications in the instruments. The development of continuo playing affected the seventeenth-century Italian harpsichord, whereas the popularity of the lute in France influenced the tonal qualities of harpsichords built there. Germany, apparently still under the influence of the colorful Renaissance instrumentarium, continued to favor an organlike variety of sound, a tradition found in England as well. In the next century harpsichord building changed dramatically almost everywhere, as Ruckers-inspired concepts of building and tone quality took hold. Hence, although one-hundred-year divisions may be even more artificial than geographic ones, there is a virtue in defining our areas of study along both lines.[6]

One of the most problematical questions about harpsichords concerns the pitch levels at which they were intended to sound. A quick answer is that nobody really knows. Grant O'Brien, for example, assigns a reference pitch "R" to the standard Ruckers harpsichord and suggests that R might have been about a semitone below modern pitch.[7] John Koster, on the other hand, arrives at a value for R of *two* semitones below modern pitch.[8] The question of pitch is a thorny thicket, which this book does not attempt to penetrate; instead, I use the term "normal pitch" for an instrument sounding at what we would recognize as 8′ pitch. Where two instruments stand at a relationship of a semitone or so apart, one will be designated as above or below normal pitch, depending on which is closest to that elusive yardstick. For larger relationships the instrument will be described in terms of the operative interval, as in "a fourth above normal pitch," or "a fifth below normal pitch." Such terminology is vague, but unavoidably so.

This book utilizes the commonly used modern system of octave designations. "Middle C" is indicated as c^1. The notes of the octave below run upward from c to b, and below that from C to B. Below that, doubled letters are used, from CC to BB (but few harpsichords descend lower than FF). The octave above middle C is designated c^1 to b^1, the octave above that, c^2 to b^2, and above that, c^3 to b^3 (but few harpsichords ascend higher than g^3). As illustrations, the standard Flemish four-octave compass is designated C/E–c^3 (C/E signifies short octave, with the apparent E sounding C), while the common five-octave compass of the late French harpsichord is designated as FF–f^3. Accidentals not present are indicated by a comma; thus, a compass of F–a^2 in which there is no low F♯ nor high g♯^{2} would be given as F,G–g^2,a^2. In discussing octave instruments and those at other pitch levels, notes are designated by their appearance; hence, the C in the middle of the keyboard will be called c^1, regardless of its "absolute" pitch.

Another convention is the designation of registers and choirs of strings. A harpsichord with a single set of strings at normal pitch is said to be disposed 1×8′, meaning that it has one set of strings, and that they sound at normal, or 8 foot, pitch (a term borrowed from the organ world). A 2×8′ harpsichord has two sets of 8′ strings, and a 2×8′, 1×4′ has a third set of strings sounding an octave higher than the other two. A choir (or single set) of suboctave strings is identified as 1×16′. A further addition of "plus buff" or "plus lute" indicates that those stops are also present.

The word "harpsichord" itself requires something of an explanation. In the generally accepted meaning, any stringed keyboard instrument making plucked sounds by means of a jack action is called a harpsichord. The most common form today is the wing-shaped *grand*—the "harpsichord-shaped" harpsichord. But there is also the *clavicytherium,* in upright form; the *virginal,* in polygonal or rectangular shape with its bass strings in the front; and the *spinet,* in rectangular, trapezoidal, or bent-side configuration, with its bass strings at the rear of the case. Smaller versions exist, sounding at pitch levels up to an octave above normal pitch, and larger, deeper-sounding designs were built as well. Finally, there are combined instruments, such as the *mother and child* virginal. All of these are referred to as harpsichords, so that the statement "the Ruckers family made harpsichords" is intended to include virginals, octave instruments, and combined instruments, as well as those in grand shape. The text will clarify any finer distinctions.

Even in the eighteenth century the spelling of names was not standardized. Cristofori's name, for example, could appear as Cristofai, Cristofani, Christofani, or Cristofali, and his first name, Bartolomeo, was often spelled Bartolommeo. Ruckers was also spelled Ruyckers, Rueckers, Rueckaers, Ruquers, Rycardt, Rickaert, Ruckeerts, Ruckaert, Ricaert, Rickers, and Ruykers. The Italian builder Trasuntino's first name was variously spelled Guido, Giulio, Vito, and Vido. It was the custom in many places, particularly in Italy, to Latinize names; thus Giovanni Antonio Baffo, a Venetian builder, signed his instruments JOANNES ANTONIVS BAFFO VENETVS. To avoid confusion I have taken *Boalch III* as the ultimate authority for standardizing names of builders.

Dates for builders, players, composers, and other personages mentioned are almost always given. Exceptions occur only for figures so well known (like Beethoven) that dates are superfluous, when tracking them down would have required heroic efforts, or where the personages are so minor that the data are pointless.

In writing this book I felt somewhat like the elephant in one of Gary Larson's *Far Side* cartoons. The pachyderm is seated at a grand piano, in front of an audience, about to poise his enormous forelimbs over impossibly tiny keys. Staring down at the instrument the poor fellow is saying to himself, "What am I doing here? I can't play this thing. I'm a *flutist,* for crying out loud." Readers, I am not a flutist, but I had my start in music playing the trombone. Earlier in my life I made my living with the instrument, and I still think of myself as a trombonist, although I have not played in decades. But in writing this history of the harpsichord, the instrument that long ago captured my musicological heart, I understand how that elephant felt.

PART I

The Fourteenth and Fifteenth Centuries

[1]

FROM PSALTERY AND MONOCHORD
TO HARPSICHORD AND VIRGINAL

IN 1356, during the Hundred Years' War, John the Good—the misnamed ne'er-do-well who ruled France from 1350 to 1364—was captured by the English at the battle of Poitiers and spent his next four years in ignominious captivity.[1] The royal prisoner did not lack amenities, and a 1360 account book from the French court notes that he was given an *eschequir* by Edward III, the English monarch.[2] This is the first documentation we have for the existence of a new instrument called the *chekker* (also known as the *eschequir, eschiquir, eschaquier, eschiquier,* etc.), which is generally conceded to have been a stringed keyboard instrument of some sort.[3]

The chekker is mentioned soon again, ca. 1367, by the poet and composer Guillaume de Machaut (ca. 1300–1377), at the end of a passage in his long poem *La Prise d'Alexandrie* enumerating all the musical instruments known to the mid–fourteenth century. The last few lines read as follows:

> Trompes, buisines & trompettes,
> Guiges, rotes, harpes, chevrettes,
> Cornemuses & chalemelles,
> Muses d'Aussay, riches & belles,
> Et la fretiaus, & monocorde,
> Qui à tous instrumens s'acorde,
> Muse de blé, qu'on on prent en terre,
> Trepié, **l'eschaquier d'Engletere**,
> Chifonie, flaios de saus.[4]

Interestingly, Machaut identifies the instrument as an *eschaquier d'Engletere,* or an English chekker. Given that John the Good received his chekker from Edward III, this could indicate that the instrument was associated with England in its early days; but this is scant evidence, and subsequent mentions in French, Spanish, and Burgundian sources make it clear that its presence was widespread shortly thereafter. For example, a letter written in 1388 by John I of Aragon to Philip the Bold, duke of Burgundy, refers to an instrument "resembling an organ but sounded by strings" (semblant dorguens que sona ab cordes).[5] Since John's purpose was to obtain the services of a musician who could play the *organetto,* a small, lap-held upright organ, the stringed instrument in question may possibly have been a *clavicytherium,* or upright harpsichord, which in octave form could also be played on the lap;[6] but scholarly opinion holds that it was probably a chekker.[7] Records, letters, and literary sources up through the beginning of the sixteenth century continue to mention the elusive chekker,[8] although by this late date the name was likely applied in an archaic sense to the harpsichord.

HERMANN POLL AND THE CLAVICEMBALUM

A letter from Padua, dated 1397, speaks specifically of the *clavicembalum,* one of the early terms for harpsichord.[9] The message indicates that the instrument's maker was the physician Hermann Poll, who has the signal honor of being the earliest named builder of harpsichords and may actually have been the instrument's inventor.[10]

Prior to the eighteenth century new musical instruments seem to have been generated by some mysterious process to which names of originators could rarely be attached. Until that time, perhaps the earliest known inventor of a musical instrument was John Rose, who in 1562 created the bandora, a wire-strung plucked bass instrument. Consequently, it is difficult to believe that we can point to someone who lived six hundred years ago and say, even without absolute proof, "He was the inventor of the harpsichord"; yet growing evidence suggests that we may indeed be able to make such a claim. Born in Vienna during the 1360s, Hermann Poll attended the University of Vienna from 1388 to 1393, earning bachelor's and master's degrees. In 1397 he went to Italy to study medicine at the University of Pavia and on his way met a gentleman named Lodovico Lambertacci. It may have been no more than a chance encounter, but Lambertacci asked Poll to deliver a cup to his son-in-law, who was already in Pavia. He wrote to his son-in-law that Poll was "a young man of good conversation and good manners, a very ingenious man and inventor of an instrument that he calls the clavicembalum."[11]

Ordinarily, one would not lend credence to what could have been only an idle boast—the history of musical instruments is full of similar claims known to be false. But Poll was no ordinary physician. He was a medical astrologer whose diagnoses depended heavily on reading his patients' horoscopes. To do so properly required a precise knowledge of the positions of the planets, which in turn depended on accurate observations of the heavenly bodies, which in turn relied on the availability of mechanically reliable astronomical instruments. Since ordinary craftsmen would lack the knowledge of mechanics, geometry, and mathematics needed to build such devices, it is thought that these medical astrologers were forced to construct them themselves. Hence, these physicians had unique skills in mechanical invention and were among the few able to design and build not only astrolabes and clocks, but *trebuchets,* stage machinery, and musical instruments. Standley Howell calls them "the leading innovators in machine technology in the fourteenth and fifteenth centuries."[12]

Poll was awarded a doctorate after only a year and a half in Pavia, and furthermore was awarded the degree not by the University of Pavia but the University of Vienna; thus, Howell suggests that he had already completed his studies before sojourning to Pavia and went there for an internship. That he was hired as the personal physician to Rupert, a minor German king (who nevertheless reigned as emperor of the Holy Roman Empire between 1400 and 1410), indicates that he had the advanced qualifications of a medical astrologer. Hence, he was perfectly capable of inventing a new music-making machine such as the harpsichord, particularly since he was known to be an accomplished organist.

The putative inventor of our glorious instrument met a gruesome end. He somehow became involved in a plot to poison Rupert, was discovered, and condemned to die in a most horrible manner: his limbs and back were broken, and he was tied to a wheel. There he stayed, undoubtedly in absolute agony, until death claimed him. He was thirty-one years old.

THE PSALTERY AND THE MONOCHORD

The clavicembalum is unequivocally mentioned in a poem of 1404 from Eberhard Cersne's *Minne Regal* (Rules of Love). Like

Machaut's *La Prise d'Alexandrie,* the passage lists musical instruments:

> Noch cymbel mid geclange,
> Noch harffe edil flegil,
> Noch schachtbret, monocordium,
> Noch stegereyff, noch begil,
> Noch rotte, clavicordium
> Noch medicinale
> Noch portitiff, psalterium,
> Noch figel sam cannale
> Noch lûte, **clavicymbolum**
> Noch dan quinterna, gyge, videle, lyra, rubeba,
> Noch pfife, floyte noch schalmey,
> Noch allir leye horner lûd.[13]

Both Machaut and Cersne mention several plucked stringed instruments in their poems, including the psaltery (*psalterium, micanon*), the lyre (*rotte*), the monochord (*monocordium*), and the chekker (*schachtbret*). The psaltery, the most common of the wire-strung group, came in a variety of shapes, but the one that interests us looked like a small, wide harpsichord with bent-sides on both left and right. It was known by several names, but the most common was *canon.* The version that looked like half a *canon*—the *micanon*—served as the paradigm for the harpsichord, Cersne's *clavicymbolum.* But someone needed to wed a small organ keyboard[14] to the psaltery, and to work out an action—a mechanism whereby individual keys could activate devices to pluck the strings. That someone may have been Hermann Poll, although like many great ideas, it may have occurred simultaneously to several people.

1-1. *The Fountain of Life,* school of van Eyck (early fifteenth century). The *micanon* and the lute are both played with plectra. Both instruments are fairly large examples of their types. Madrid, Museo del Prado.

A sound box with a single string, the monochord was also wire strung and plucked, although strictly speaking it was not an instrument at all. With its moveable bridge it was a useful tool for tuning, finding intervals, and giving pitches. Evidently, it was thought that the monochord could be transformed into a viable maker of music with the addition of a few more strings, and a keyboard with tangents (such as those found in the hurdy-gurdy) to both strike the strings and act as bridges. The result was the clavichord (Cersne's *clavicordium*). Hence, just prior to the appearance of stringed keyboard instruments there was the plucked-stringed psaltery, whose strings could be excited by plucking, and the monochord, which, though also plucked, when mechanized would have a touching action in which a tangent both strikes a string and demarcates its sounding length.[15] Then at some time before the end of the fourteenth century—although probably not at the same time—both were provided with keyboards and transformed into the instruments we now know as the harpsichord and the clavichord.[16]

ICONOGRAPHICAL EVIDENCE OF THE HARPSICHORD

An early representation of a harpsichord is found in a carving from 1425 from the Cathedral at Minden, in northern Germany.[17] Its details present some problems. It is a tiny instrument, probably no larger than 18″ or so in length, and its bentside is on the left, rather than the right; moreover, the carving shows neither bridge nor strings. But to question such details implies that the carver should have known something about harpsichords. Indeed, he knew enough to get the essentials correct: regardless of its size or the location of its bentside, it is a harpsichord-shaped instrument with some sort of jackrail, it has a keyboard, and it is played with both hands. From the position of the player's wrists, it seems to be placed on a horizontal surface.[18] The carver neglected to show strings, but he did equip the instrument's soundboard with two rose holes (with perhaps a third, at the tail), prominent embellishments to the layperson's eye. From the artisan's point of view he supplied all the important features of a harpsichord.

Most other paintings and carvings between 1425 and 1500 also show small instruments, although perhaps not as tiny as the one played by the Minden angel, so it is

1-2. Guido of Arezzo and his pupil Theobaldus at the monochord (anonymous drawing, twelfth century). The soundboard is marked off by string divisions. Any pitch can be obtained by using the moveable bridge (on the left) and plucking the string. Vienna, Österreichische Nationalbibliothek.

1-3. A keyed psaltery in an anonymous French Book of Hours (ca. 1450). With the longest strings in the middle, some sort of mechanical means (such as an organ-builder's roller board) must have been used to link the keys to their appropriate strings. It is possible, however, that the instrument was a figment of the artist's imagination. London, Conway Library, Courtault Institute of Art.

likely that the first harpsichords were high-pitched instruments. As with the Minden carving, some of the other representations also show bentsides on the left, which might indicate that to the artisans the fundamentals of the shape were more important than the details, but which might also mean there were at least some early harpsichords in which bass and treble were reversed.[19] The variety of other elements exhibited in these fifteen or so representations from England, France, Sweden, Spain, and Austria also suggests that the harpsichord was not yet standardized. In some of these depictions keyboards are inset, and in others they project. Two English instruments—one in stained glass from before 1450, the other a carving from the late 1460s—both lack roses, and the carving has a jackrail, whereas the example in stained glass does not.[20] A harpsichord in a fresco done in the 1470s, in a church in what is now Yugoslavia, displays three truly enormous roses in its soundboard, while another fresco, in a Swedish church, dating from ca. 1475, features five small roses.[21] A large box-shaped jackrail is a prominent peculiarity on an example in a French manuscript illustration of 1468.[22]

Whatever its characteristic features, there seems to be no question that the harpsichord was an established member of the musician's instrumentarium by the mid-1400s. Judging from the iconography, it was found all over Europe: as far north as Sweden, as far south as Italy, as far east as Croatia, and as far west as England. But its growth was certainly a Northern European phenomenon, perhaps particularly connected with Burgundy,[23] whose court, under the reign of Philip the Good, was second to none in its support of the arts.[24] More important than where the instrument was invented and first developed, however, is the rapidity of its acceptance. It is likely that European musicians welcomed a plucked instrument capable of playing one or more voices of the complex secular polyphony of composers such as Baude Cordier (died ca. 1398), John Dunstable (ca. 1390–1453), and Guillaume Dufay (ca. 1400–1474). In fact, it was while these masters were writing that instrumental music began to come into its own.[25] Another possible explanation for the harpsichord's rapid acceptance is that it was an independent home instrument, one on which organists could practice during winter months and avoid freezing their fingers, toes, noses, and backsides in unheated churches. The instrument also had no need for warm-bodied bellows pumpers. Other uses of these proto-harpsichords would have been to play monophonic dances and, like the organetto, take a part in an ensemble.

Furthermore, the many types of materials needed for the construction of harpsichords were readily at hand. Good iron and brass wire, used for making chain mail and decorative items, were available in a variety of gauges; the finest, made specifically for the needs of musical instruments, soon became known as "music wire."[29] Metallurgy was sufficiently advanced so that cutting tools and blades could take and hold sharp edges. Thus, harpsichord soundboards, bridges, nuts, wrest-planks, and case parts could be shaped and planed smoothly and accurately; and action parts, made to rather close toler-ances, would hardly daunt medical astrologers and mechanics who could build intricate clock mechanisms. Woven cloth, to ensure quiet actions, was another common item, and animal glue had been in constant use since the days of the Egyptians.[30] It is also likely that musical instrument making, a new profession that emerged in the fourteenth century, was well established by this time.[31]

A DIGRESSION ON PITCH AND SCALE

Pitch and scale are closely interrelated concepts crucial to the understanding of the design of stringed keyboard instruments. *Pitch* is determined by four factors. First, the *sounding length,* the por-tion of the string found between the nut and bridge, excluding the sec-tions between bridge and hitch-pins, and nut and wrestpins (tuning pins). Second, the *material* from which the strings are constructed, traditionally iron or brass. Third, the *thickness* or *diameter* of the wire, whose significance will be discussed shortly. Finally, one of the most im-portant elements affecting pitch is the *tension* that can be placed on a string. Since iron is inherently harder than brass, strings of the for-mer can stand higher tensions and can be drawn up to a higher pitch than the latter without breaking.

For centuries conventional wis-dom has dictated that for the best sound a string should be drawn up to just below its breaking point;[32] in practice, greater leeway has been al-lowed. Given that strings can rise in

1-4. A carving of a harpsichord from the Cathedral at Minden, 1425. Note the small psaltery on the left. The compass of this harpsichord is probably no more than two octaves. Berlin, Bodenmuseum.

pitch as much as a whole tone in conditions of high temperature and humidity,[33] builders have wisely designed their harpsichords with that sort of safety margin built in. But generally speaking, a string will give a good sound when it is no more than three semitones beneath its breaking point, although subjective judgment plays a part in determining what is "good." Below that, it may start to sound false.

Aside from the material from which it was made, another element in the strength of a string has to do with a phenomenon of wire drawing. Clearly, a thicker wire is stronger than a thinner one; but if the sounding length of both is the same, the thicker wire needs more tension to bring it to the same pitch. The two wires would indeed break at about the same point if it were not for the phenomenon called *tensile pickup,* in which the wire, as it is drawn thinner, develops additional strength,[34] acting as if it were made of a slightly stronger material (the effect is greater in iron than it is in brass).[35] Hence, the thinner wire can be pulled up to a somewhat higher breaking point than the thicker one.

The word *scale* is used to describe several different but closely related phenomena. It can apply to the *length* of a particular string, to the *name* of the string's note, to the *relationship* of other strings to that string, and to the *material* from which the string is made. In modern stringed keyboard design the length of one particular string, c^2, defines the *pitch scaling* of that instrument, although both it and f^1 (and possibly other standards as well) were used in earlier times.[36] Thus, the pitch scaling of a particular harpsichord can be described in terms of the nominal pitch of the string and its length, as in "the c^2 scale of this instrument is $14'''$" or, more succinctly, "this instrument has a $14''$ scale."

The relationship of the other strings to c^2 is another aspect of scale. The physics of vibrating strings tells us that other things being equal ("other things" being material, thickness, and tension), if two notes are an octave apart, the lower one has twice the sounding length of the upper. Accordingly, if c^2 is $14''$, c^3 would have a sounding length of $7''$, and c^1 would be $28''$

THE EARLIEST KEYBOARD MUSIC

The only keyboard compositions we have from the fourteenth century—and most of the fifteenth as well—are arrangements of dance pieces and secular songs such as chansons and motets. The earliest source containing keyboard music, actually predating the appearance of the harpsichord, is the *Robertsbridge Codex* from ca. 1320,[26] which consists of some arrangements of medieval dances (*estampies*), a few adaptations of motets from the *Roman de Fauvel* (one of the best-known French manuscripts of the early fourteenth century), and half a hymn. The *Faenza Codex,*[27] one of the largest and most comprehensive collections of keyboard arrangements in the early fifteenth century, contains arrangements of vocal music by Machaut and Landini, among others. It is not until the short preludes found in the *Ileborgh Tablature*[28] of 1448 that we begin to see original keyboard pieces. This does not mean, however, that such pieces were not improvised before this time. Undoubtedly intended primarily for organ, all these works would have just as readily been played on harpsichord and clavichord.

long. The other notes in those octaves would be halved or doubled accordingly. The designation of *just* or *Pythagorean*[37] *scale* is given to a series of string lengths that demonstrate this precise integer relationship. In practice, almost all harpsichords have Pythagorean scales in the treble, but not in the bass. Italian harpsichords, with shorter scales, have them down to around c, whereas in longer-scaled Northern instruments the Pythagorean portion of the scale may descend only to c^1. Below those limits, for lack of room if nothing else, the lower strings are foreshortened; that is, they are shorter than a Pythagorean doubling would suggest. Even if a harpsichord were extremely long, one would expect the bass notes to be non-Pythagorean, since with a 14″ scale a Pythagorean C string would have a sounding length of more than 9′.

Another way of compensating for a non-Pythagorean scale in the bass is to change the material of the string. Harpsichords with 14″ scales are usually strung in iron, but down in the bass, where the foreshortening begins, a switch is made to brass, which can be appropriately stressed at a higher tension than iron. Despite the brass bass strings, such a scheme is known as an *iron scale*. Harpsichords with shorter scales — say, 11″ — generally have a *brass scale* and are strung throughout in that weaker metal. In practice, the scales of the extant antiques do not fit so easily into these two classifications, and many harpsichords have scales intermediate to these two extremes. If such instruments were strung in brass their pitch would be lower, since the weaker brass strings could not be tensioned as much as iron; and conversely, if strung in iron, the pitch could be as much as a fourth or even a fifth higher, depending on how closely one adhered to the dictum to stress the strings close to their breaking points. Instruments with scales longer than 14″ and shorter than 11″ are also found, suggesting that they were designed for even lower and higher pitches; in fact, aside from the "normal" levels implied by those scales, the longer and shorter scales group themselves into classes a fourth or fifth above and below normal 8′ pitch.

Had there been a more consistent standard in use from the fifteenth throughout the eighteenth centuries, we could more easily relate the pitch level of one instrument to another. But pitch standards varied in place and time, and even when the standard of a particular place and time is known, instruments at different pitch levels were not uncommon. Clearly, even when scale and stringing material are known, the pitch of an antique harpsichord can only be estimated. To make this situation even more complex, there is evidence that throughout much of the harpsichord's history two different pitch standards were in use concurrently, one tone apart.[38]

Despite the written and pictorial accounts, our knowledge of the harpsichord would be far the poorer were it not for one of the most significant organological resources of the fifteenth century, an extraordinary manuscript written around 1440 by Henri Arnaut of Zwolle.[39] Arnaut, who was the medical astrologer to the court of the Burgundian duke Philip the Good, assembled a compendium of information about mechanics, astronomy, and astronomical instruments; but he also described and drew detailed plans of a number of musical instruments, including the harpsichord (*clavisimbalum*),[40] the clavichord (*clavicordum*), and another keyboard instrument, looking like a clavichord but with a hammer action, that he called the *dulce melos*.[41] In these drawings the sizes of the various parts were determined by proportion: the harpsichord, for example, is eight units wide and thirteen units long. Clearly, these are plans for working instruments.[42]

To anyone familiar with the craft of harpsichord construction, Arnaut's drawing yields enough information to build the instrument. True, he says nothing about the kinds of woods to use for soundboard, bridge, nut, wrestplank, case, and so on; he is silent about details of the case, such as thickness of the walls, depth of the sides, and type and placement of the interior bracing; and he does not furnish a stringing schedule. Nevertheless, these are details that could be supplied by any knowledgeable maker. What Arnaut does give is the crucial information, such as the location of the bridge and the nut, the placement of the soundboard bars and the five roses, and a plan of the keyboard. He does tell us that the instrument can be single or double strung, but with one string above the other, rather than alongside.[43] Hence, for the first time we have information about the shape of the bentside (an arc of a circle, also seen in many of the iconographical examples), the placement of the bridge (whose shape is also an arc of a circle), how the soundboard was barred (four bars running across the width of the soundboard, all passing under the bridge), the range of its keyboard (a thirty-five note compass of B–a^2),[44] and the string scaling (the relationship of one string length to another). In Arnaut's harpsichord drawing the string scaling more than halves every octave ascended, a scheme known as a *rising scale*.[45]

Arnaut presented different actions for the harpsichord, three of which functioned by plucking the strings. These are heavy, complex affairs, quite unlike the standard jack sliding vertically in one or two registers now associated with all forms of plucked keyboards, and one suspects that lightness of touch and

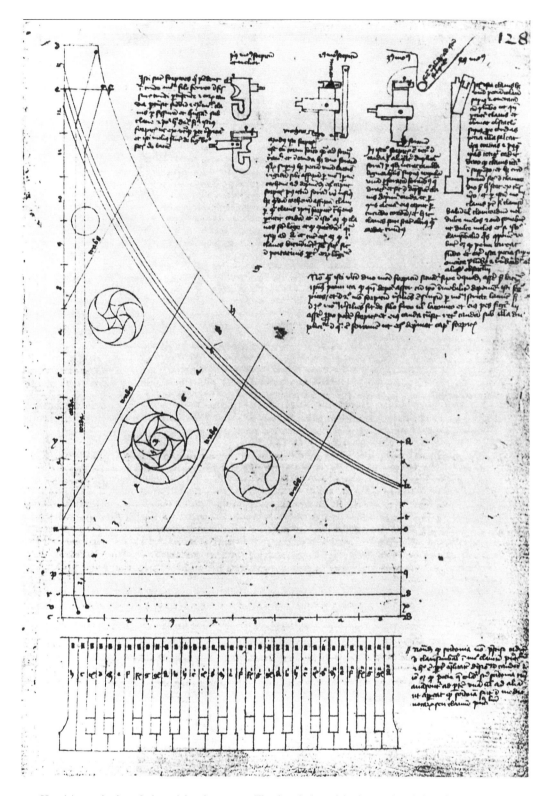

1-5. Henri Arnaut's plan of a harpsichord, ca. 1440. The description of the four actions is found across the top of the page. The first three are plucking mechanisms, although none is like the conventional jack action. The instrument is laid out by means of proportions, rather than fixed measurements. Paris, Cliché Bibliothèque Nationale de France.

1-6. Woodcut of a harpsichord from the *Weimarer Wunderbuch*. Thought to have dated from ca. 1440, this German manuscript is now placed in the sixteenth century. Nevertheless, like Arnaut's harpsichord, the bentside appears to be an arc of a circle. Weimar, Herzogin Anna Amalia Bibliothek.

surety of repetition might not have been expected.[46] Furthermore, there is no indication that any of these actions used dampers: Arnaut's harpsichord would have allowed every played note to sound until it decayed to inaudibility, and other strings would ring sympathetically. Although at first we might consider this effect somewhat primitive, it should not surprise us. All plucked instruments, whether gut-or wire-strung—harps, lyres, psalteries, lutes, guitars, and citterns, to name just a few—ring in this undamped manner, a characteristic not at all considered objectionable. It is likely that the *clavisimbalum* was still regarded as a mechanized psaltery, and dampers would have created a change in sound alien to its nature (of course, dampers will eventually be used, but probably not until the next century). Arnaut also stated that the quilling material was usually metal, although bird feather was also a possibility. This comes as something of a surprise, since the handheld plectrum for all the plucked strings was a bird quill. That some sort of metal was preferred suggests that there may have been a desire to produce sounds of a sharper character.

The fourth apparatus was a hammer action, and he asserted that when this mechanism was used with the harpsichord it would sound like a *dulce melos* (he also indicated that this same hammer action could be applied to the clavichord). Hence, supplied with hammers, a *clavisimbalum* would become a *dulce melos;* or in modern terms, a harpsichord could be turned into a piano.[47]

What we infer from Arnaut, therefore, is that by the middle of the fifteenth century, stringed keyboard instruments came in two shapes with three possible actions. One shape was the winglike grand harpsichord, in horizontal and perhaps upright (clavicytherium) form as well,[48] with plucking or striking action. The second was the oblong box, which could be either a harpsichord, a clavichord, or a *dulce melos,* since the three means of exciting the strings of this instrument were plucking, touching, and striking. Hence, the harpsichord, the clavichord, and the instrument that later became known as the piano existed side by side almost at the very beginning of the history of stringed keyboard instruments. Provided it was not a figment of Arnaut's imagination, which is unlikely, the striking mechanism must have fallen into immediate disuse; but there was some cross-fertilization between the other two shapes and actions.

CLAVICHORDS AND VIRGINALS

Arnaut noted that a clavichord could become a harpsichord if the strings were plucked instead of touched;[49] in other words, a harpsichord could be built into a clavichord-like oblong box, with its projecting keyboard and strings parallel to the spine. It would then be a virginal, although he did not use that word.[50] Arnaut's design (oblong box, projecting keyboard, strings parallel to the spine)[51] is found as far back as the 1430s,[52] and the two earliest surviving clavichords, both anonymes (unsigned instruments) from ca. 1540 (Leipzig, Musikinstrumenten-Museum der Universität Leipzig) are also of that type. It was a design that persisted through most of the fifteenth century; in fact, a woodcut of a virginal answering to just that description — oblong, projecting keyboard, parallel strings — is found in Virdung's

1-7. Adriaen van Wesel, *Adoration of the Magi* (1475–77). A carving of a clavichord of the type described by Arnaut. The case is oblong, and the strings are parallel to the spine and at right angles to the projecting keyboard. The soundboard is under the key levers. Amsterdam, Rijksmuseum.

The first mention of the term "virginal" for the oblong harpsichord is found in a 1459–63 encyclopedic dictionary of the arts and sciences, the *Liber viginti artium*, written by a Czech physician and minor cleric named Paulus Paulirinus.[55] He characterized the virginal (*virginale*) as an instrument with metal strings, shaped like a clavichord (*clavicordium*), but sounding like a harpsichord (*clavicimbalum*).[56] In addition to the clavichord and the virginal Paulirinus also described an [*i*]*nnportile*, an instrument that appears to be a *claviorganum*, or combined organ-harpsichord. He commented that the harpsichord was an "instrument of wonderful sweetness" (but he thought that the dulcimer, the psaltery, the sistrum, the virginal, the [*i*]*nnportile*, and a few other nonstring instruments as well, also had that quality). Giving voice to an aphorism to be repeated often in centuries to come, Paulirinus noted that the instrument he describes "is called a virginal because, like a virgin, it soothes with a sweet and gentle voice."[57]

Paulirinus is one of the more bizarre authorities associated with the harpsichord. Jewish-born in Prague, he was kidnapped at an early age, raised by heretical Hussites, baptized, educated in Vienna, Padua, Bologna, and Kraków, became an orthodox Catholic and a canon, was persecuted by Hussites, imprisoned and exiled for Hussite activity, and eventually ended up as an advisor to George of Podebrad, the Hussite king of Bohemia. Howell believes that, like Hermann Poll and Henri Arnaut, Paulirinus was also a medical astrologer and may have served George as a physician; and in fact, most of his *Liber viginti artium* dictionary was devoted to medical matters and astronomical observations, with only one surviving page dealing with musical instruments.[58]

1511 *Musica getutscht*,[53] although there are no known examples surviving from this early date.[54]

Extrapolating from the evidence of other early clavichords, it is likely that the next development in the virginal was the creation of the polygonal shape. It must have been merely a question of time before the unused right- and left-hand corners at the back of the case came to be considered superfluous and were simply "removed" for a more elegant shape. A clavichord exactly answering to that description (Leipzig, Musikinstrumenten-Museum der Universität Leipzig) was built by Dominicus Pisaurensis in 1543, and there is also a large, undated, anonymous example from sometime in the next century (Brussels, Musée Instrumental).[59]

The final step in this process of refinement, which again took place in both clavichords and virginals, was the angling of the strings. In virginals this provided for a less steeply sloped row of jacks and resulted in some lengthening of the short bass key levers. Since the difference in length between a virginal's long treble and short bass keys is fairly pronounced, any attempt to minimize this discrepancy and even out the touch would have been seen as an advantage. At the same time, the case of the Northern virginal was reconfigured so that the keyboard was inset, rather than projecting.[60]

THE ROYAL COLLEGE OF MUSIC CLAVICYTHERIUM

Hermann Poll may have been building harpsichords as early as 1397, but it is only around 1470 that an actual instrument emerges from the mists of the past. It is an anonymous clavicytherium, probably made in Ulm,[61] in southern Germany, and now in London's Royal College of Music (RCM; see Plate 1).[62] It has a curious feature, a partial soundboard, that is, a soundboard that ends where one might otherwise expect to find a 4′ bridge. But otherwise, the resemblance between this instrument and the Arnaut drawing is striking. Both have rose holes proceeding down the soundboard in the large area on the left of the bridge: the Arnaut shows five holes; the RCM has one circular hole and two peaked Gothic "windows." Both have arclike bentsides and bridges, although the RCM, with seven additional low notes, straightens out in the bass and lacks a tail: the bentside is joined directly to the spine. The Arnaut drawing shows a very small tail, and if it had seven more notes in the bass, it would probably have disappeared, like the RCM's. Both have rising scales.[63] Both instruments are fairly small: the Arnaut is presumed to be so, and the RCM is little more than 4½′ high. The ranges are similar, although not identical: the Arnaut drawing shows a thirty-five-note compass, B–a²; the RCM's forty-note keyboard has been altered, but the consensus is that it was probably E,E♯,F,G–g².[64] The E and E♯ could well have been tuned to C and D; and if the G♯ was tuned to E, a nearly conventional short-octave tuning would result: C/E, D/E♯, E/G♯. Finally, both

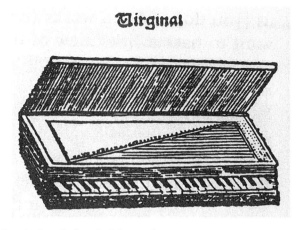

1-8. The virginal from Virdung's *Musica getutscht* (1511). The woodcut is crude, but the oblong shape, strings parallel to the spine, and the projecting keyboard are obvious.

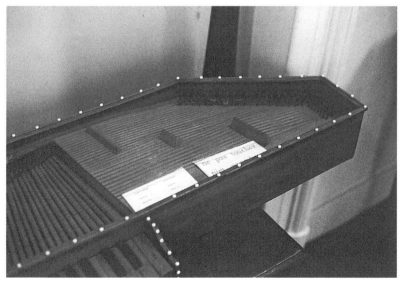

1-9. The soundboard end of a large, anonymous early-seventeenth-century Italian clavichord. The polygonal shape, sloping soundboard, multiple straight bridges, and string band parallel to the spine are characteristics typical of clavichords of the sixteenth century. © IRPA-KIK, Brussels.

THE KEYED HARP

The RCM instrument is important not only because of its age, but also because, unlike most other clavicytheria, it has a partial soundboard. This instrument may relate to the harp as well as the harpsichord, and, in fact, with its partial-soundboard construction, it does somewhat resemble the favored instrument of angels. Only two other upright harpsichords with partial soundboards are known: one is another anonyme (Oslo, Norsk Folkmuseum), and the other is signed Henning Hake 1657 (Stockholm, Musikmuseet). These three instruments are dealt with in some length by van der Meer in his article "A Contribution to the History of the Clavicytherium."[65] After tracing tantalizing hints of such an instrument through Paulus Paulirinus, Virdung (*Musica getutscht*, 1511), Agricola (*Musica instrumentalis deudsch*, 1528), Luscinius (*Musurgia seu praxis musicae*, 1536), Zacconi (*Prattica di musica*, 1592), Mersenne (*Harmonie universelle*, 1636–37), and Kircher (*Musurgia universalis*, 1650), van der Meer finally arrives at a description of an upright harpsichord as either a "normal" harpsichord but with case, strings, and soundboard in vertical position, or one similar but with a partial soundboard. This second type, says van der Meer, has a resemblance to the harp and may have represented a keyed version of that instrument.

This is still not the end of the story of the keyed harp. In his *Harmonie universelle*[66] the French theorist Marin Mersenne pictures an upright harpsichord with an open framework holding the strings and a small horizontal soundboard under which the key levers pass. There is no vertical soundboard at all, partial or otherwise, and this instrument is a more convincing-looking keyed harp than the three exemplars just described. It is likely that Mersenne, who called it "a new form of spinet in use in Italy" (une nouvelle forme d'Epinette dont on use en Italie), never actually saw such an instrument but was relying on someone else's description.

There are other depictions of the keyed harp, possibly inspired by Mersenne's engraving. Filippo Bonanni included one — with a soundboard area at least twice that of Mersenne's — in his 1723 *Gabinetto armonico*,[67] although Bonanni is known for his inventiveness with instruments unfamiliar to him. One of the most impressive portrayals of the instrument is in a ca. 1640 painting by the Roman artist Andrea Sacchi, *Apollo Crowning the Singer Marc Antonio Pasqualini*.[68] This clavicytherium may be even more fanciful than Bonanni's. The painting is redolent with classical symbolism (see Plate 2), and the similarities between the lyre tucked under Apollo's arm and Pasqualini's upright instrument are too strong to be ignored.[69] It is likely that the keyed harp in its several forms will forever remain a mystery instrument, one which may or may not have existed.

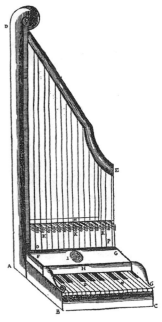

1-10. This clavicytherium, from Mersenne's 1636 *Harmonie universelle,* shows yet another type of upright harpsichord, with a small, horizontal soundboard directly behind the keys.

instruments would produce the undamped sounds characteristic of their hand-plucked cousins. The similarities are clear enough for us to say that both instruments seem to share a common building style.

	Arnaut's Drawing	RCM Clavicytherium
Date	ca. 1440	ca. 1470
Type	Grand harpsichord	Clavicytherium
Compass	35 notes: B–a^2	40 notes: E,E♯,F,G–g^2
Size	Not given, but presumed small	Small — 4½′ high
Pitch level	Presumed high	Presumed high
Bentside and bridge	Arc of a circle	Arc of circle, straight in the bass
Case walls	Not indicated, but probably thick cased	Thin-case with outer case
Number of roses	Five	Three
Soundboard barring	Five bars, under bridge	No barring
String scaling	Rising	Rising
Action	Early obsolete action	Jack action
Plectrum material	Unknown	May have been metal
Damping	None	None
Other		Partial soundboard

All this detail should not hide the fact that the RCM clavicytherium is a refined and sophisticated instrument, which suggests that it represents a mature tradition. Its thin sides are less than ¼″ thick, and it is protected by an outer case (with a painted decoration from a later date) that still exists, a combination known today as "inner-outer." It is single strung (although Arnaut allows for the possibility of single or double stringing, from his description one surmises that single stringing was the norm). Light and resonant, it has a soundboard of spruce or fir.[70] There are no bars under the soundboard, but in any case it has so little area that bars would not be needed for structural reasons. When a key is released, its jack returns by gravity — the vertical stickers rising from the ends of the keys to the horizontal jacks are simple and effective. The instrument's thin sides overlap a heavier bottom (actually, the back), and the case is unpainted. A landscape is carved in relief in the recessed area of the case, which is also outlined with delicate carvings. The thin cheeks were scroll sawn in a simple pattern. Further ornamentation is found in a row of ivory buttons following the line of the soundboard cutout, paralleling the bridge. A molding is cut into the front of the wrestplank. The middle rose hole, one of the peaked Gothic windows, still has its carved wooden device backed by painted and gilded paper. Its half-round bridge is meticulously carved to suggest a slender tree branch with new shoots emerging, perhaps evoking the spirit of the tree from which the bridge was made. It is now quilled in bird feather, although there is some evidence that it once had metal plectra.[71] Its jacks are without dampers, and with its brief sustain (that is to say, the brief sustain of its facsimile) it sounds much like a psaltery or small harp.[72] In short, it is a carefully designed and skillfully executed instrument, with sculptural, architectural, and painted decoration.

SUMMING UP

The ca. 1470 RCM clavicytherium is the world's oldest extant harpsichord, and by comparing it to Henri Arnaut's ca. 1440 drawing and description, we can draw some tentative conclusions about building practices relatively early in the instrument's history. It appears that by the end of the fifteenth century, well over a hundred years after its birth, the harpsichord was still a smallish, high-pitched instrument, probably used in ensembles, for dances, and to play organ music. Although some of its development may have taken place in Burgundy and probably elsewhere, by this time there seems to have been strong Germanic activity.[73]

The range of its keyboard is not much wider than Guido's gamut (G–e^2), since the eleventh century the theoretical limits for the human voice. Except for the extreme bass, it is a chromatic instrument, with all the usual naturals and accidentals. At some time between Arnaut's drawing and the construction of the RCM clavicytherium the conventional jack action was developed. The sound of the instrument would have been undamped. And finally, from as far back as we can tell, harpsichords were graced with multiple holes cut into the soundboard, intended to accommodate pierced ornamental roses.

The early representations show rather heavy cases, but there are others with thin case walls. The RCM clavicytherium is thin walled and set in a protective outer case. This thin-walled style of construction lasted for another sixty or seventy years in Northern Europe, and much longer in the South.[74]

PART II

The Sixteenth Century

[2]

THE EMERGENCE OF THE
NORTHERN HARPSICHORD

*W*ERE IT NOT for a stray instrument or two, some pictorial evidence, the serendipitous survival of a record here and there, or the discovery of an archive documenting the existence of builders in other localities, one could easily believe that almost all sixteenth-century harpsichord building in the North of Europe took place in Flanders, with little or no activity in France, Germany, England, the Baltic countries, Scandinavia, and other regions. Nothing could be farther from the truth, although once again we must rely on documents, rather than instruments, for our sources of information — and admittedly even these are extremely rare in some of these areas. War, natural disaster, civil disruption, vagaries of fashion, wear and tear, and undoubtedly cannibalization for parts by builders themselves have conspired to destroy the evidence. Thus, outside Flanders, we know of only two instruments to have survived the century: a 1537 grand harpsichord by Hans Müller of Leipzig, and a 1579 claviorganum, built in London by the transplanted Flemish builder Lodewijk Theewes.[1]

Still, the harpsichord seemed to thrive in the Renaissance.[2] As a mature instrument it came to be associated with royalty, nobility, wealth, and power, regarded not only as a music-making tool of incomparable worth, but also as a visual and sculptural expression of rank and privilege. As such it was often ornately decorated inside and out with painted patterns, decorated soundboards, edifying mottoes, elaborate roses, inlays, veneers, and finely cut moldings. It appears that more of these opulent harpsichords were produced in the sixteenth century—particularly in Italy—than at any other time, and some of these instruments are breathtaking in their ornamentation. One possible explanation may be found in the law of the "survival of the fanciest," which holds that highly decorated instruments have always had a disproportionately greater chance of survival than the workaday versions; the former are apt to be conserved as works of art, whereas the latter get used up and discarded as useless, outmoded tools. Hence, our samples of harpsichord building almost everywhere are likely to be heavily skewed in the direction of the highly decorated examples.

Harpsichords on both sides of the Alps continued to evolve, although in different ways. In the 1560s, for example, Flemish virginals were transformed from thin-walled pentagonal instruments with protective outer cases to oblong-shaped, thick-walled, integral-case models. Perhaps this was an effort to make them a little easier to build, a little less expensive, a little less elegant, and therefore a little more accessible to rich burghers eager to purchase and display symbols of their wealth. Shortly after that date the disposition of Italian harpsichords began to change from 1×8′, 1×4′ to 2×8′, possibly in an attempt to meet the specific requirements of continuo playing; and before the end of the century integral-case Italian instruments began to appear. It would be misleading to suggest that this evolution proceeded in a straight line. Although the RCM clavicytherium, the Arnaut drawing, and the available fifteenth-century iconography all show bentside instruments with strings running in the same direction as key levers, almost all the sixteenth-century survivors from the North of Europe are cross-strung virginals. It is not until the end of the 1500s that we begin to see grand harpsichords in the North. Italy, on the other hand, seems to have been producing both grands and virginals right from the beginning of the century.

ARCHIVAL RECORDS

It is likely that hundreds, possibly even thousands, of harpsichords were created between ca. 1470, the date of the RCM clavicytherium, and 1537, the date of the next extant Northern harpsichord, a 1537 grand by Hans Müller. Sadly, from this span of history, only these two have survived. Nevertheless, archival evidence suggests that harpsichord building was practiced all over Europe. Like Machaut in 1367 and Cersne in 1404, in 1506 the Englishman Stephen Hawes, in a poem entitled *Passetyme of Pleasure,* cataloged the instruments in common use. The harpsichord, which he called the *claricimbale,* is prominently mentioned, as is the clavichord (*clarycorde*):

There sat dame Musyke with all her mynstrasy;
As tabors trumpettes with pipes melodious,
Sakbuttes, organs, and the recorder swetely,
Harpes, lutes, and crouddes ryght delycyous:
Cymphans, doussemers, wyth **claricimbales** gloryous
Rebeckes, clarycordes, eche in theyr degre,
Did sytte aboute theyr ladyes mageste.[3]

As early as 1505 passages in the Antwerp city archives point to an active community of organ builders, all or most of whom presumably made harpsichords (as did organ builders elsewhere).[4] Hans van Cuelen (Hans of Cologne, also known as Hans Suys or Süss; before 1500–ca. 1560), who came to Antwerp from Germany in 1509 and who became an influential builder, is often mentioned as the "father of the Flemish school."[5] He made a *clavicenon* for Eleanor of Austria in 1512.[6] Antonius Moors (fl. 1514–1652), one of a distinguished family of organ makers, was another Antwerp builder who provided Eleanor with a keyboard instrument, a clavichord, for which he received payment in 1516.[7] Ioes Karest (before 1500–ca. 1560), also formerly from Cologne, moved to Antwerp and became a citizen in 1516–17. In his early twenties he joined the Guild of St. Luke, the painter's guild to which harpsichord makers also belonged.[8] Karest must have been highly respected, since it was he who led the 1557 delegation of Antwerp builders requesting that the guild reclassify them as instrument makers rather than painters. The names of another thirty or so sixteenth-century Flemish makers are known to us through archival records, most often guild documents.[9]

Almost twenty builders lived in London and elsewhere in England in the sixteenth century, some of them, like Thomas Browne in Cambridge, active as early as 1508.[10] Another, William Lewes (fl. 1518–31), is known to have supplied instruments to the court of Henry VIII.[11] Interestingly, some, like Sir Michael Mercator (1491–1544), John de John (fl. 1526–31), Gregory Estamproy (fl. 1526), and Lodewijk Theewes (fl. 1560–85), came from Flanders or elsewhere in the Low Countries.[12] At least one, William Treasorer (before 1521–ca. 1584), who made instruments for Edward VI, was of German origin. The *Bristol Apprentice Register,* which recorded the details of the indenture of the apprentices for all that city's trades, reveals that a number of "virginallsmakers" and their masters worked there between 1536 and 1643.[13] The 1547 inventory of the instruments owned by Henry VIII lists fifteen plucked keyboards, probably originating in England, Italy, Flanders, and perhaps Germany and France.[14] A little later, a 1566 inventory of the instruments of the Augsburg arts patron Raymund Fugger (1528–69) indicates that he owned harpsichords made in England, the Netherlands, Germany, and Italy.[15] Thus, archival evidence points to a thriving international community of builders, including many who left their native countries to practice their trade on foreign shores. Apparently, harpsichord building in Northern Europe in the sixteenth century was anything but insular.

Nevertheless, these are records, not instruments, and time is the pitiless enemy of artifacts deemed to have lost their value.[16] North of the Alps, until 1537 the only surviving witnesses to those lost instruments are a few carvings and paintings.[17] Still, adding up the records, the pictures and carvings, and the few instruments themselves, it is clear that at the dawn of the sixteenth century harpsichords on both sides of the Alps were thin-case instruments set into heavier, protective outer boxes. Applied moldings surrounded the top and bottom of the case, soundboard, namebatten, and jackrail. The inner cases were unpainted, relying on complex moldings to impart an architectural quality to their restrained decor. Virginals were also thin cased and polygonal in shape. Furthermore, it is also clear that at some point after the construction of the RCM clavicytherium, harpsichord making took two paths — a Northern and a Southern, both departing somewhat from the earlier iconographical representations. At first the differences between them were subtle, dealing more with concepts of sound and the increasing of resources than with building practices that might have been of secondary importance; but those differences would grow during the course of the century.

GERMANY AND THE
MÜLLER HARPSICHORD

Over the centuries Germany has been a frequent battleground. The Thirty Years' War (1618–48), for example, was fought mainly on German soil, and many cities lost from half to two-thirds of their civilian populations in the devastation. It has been suggested that the dearth of harpsichords from the sixteenth and seventeenth centuries, as well as the constant exodus of German artisans to other lands, is best explained by those difficult circumstances; nevertheless, German expatriate artisans often ended up in places just as bloody as their homeland,

and a great deal of instrument building of specific sorts — brass instruments and organs, for example — remained in Germany.

Another interpretation of the paucity of harpsichords in Germany in the sixteenth century (and the seventeenth and eighteenth as well) is simply that the Germans excelled at organ building, and string-keyboard making was considered a sideline, perhaps something to pursue between commissions. For whatever reason, Germany did not have centers of harpsichord building like those found in major cities such as Antwerp, Venice, Paris, or London. Although *Boalch III* identifies nearly forty builders active in France in the sixteenth century, and more than sixty in Italy, it lists only seventeen in Germany, and none of these are from locales we could identify as harpsichord-building centers.[18] Hence, whereas Flemish, Italian, and French builders worked in strong, guild-dominated traditions, German makers labored in a less structured environment.[19] Nevertheless, one cannot lightly dismiss the German-speaking lands, particularly in light of the central importance of the ca. 1470 RCM clavicytherium. Furthermore, treatises by Virdung (1511) and Agricola (1528) describe — or at least mention — jack-action instruments early in the sixteenth century, indicating that these instruments were known in Germany.[20]

The earliest extant German harpsichord, built in 1537 by Hans Müller (Rome, Museo Nazionale degli Strumenti Musicali),[21] is the first Northern exemplar to which we can attach a maker's name. It is younger than the RCM clavicytherium by two-thirds of a century; nevertheless, there are many similarities between them. The Müller's range of forty-four notes, C,D–g^2,a^2, is only slightly wider than the RCM's forty.[22] Its sides are nearly as thin as the RCM's; therefore, it was almost certainly an inner-outer, although its presumed outer case has not survived. Its only internal bracing is a single diagonal strut and some small upright reinforcements or stiffeners glued to the interior of the spine and bentside case walls between the bottom and the liners.[23] Like the RCM, its projecting keyboard has scroll-sawn cheeks, although they are cut in a more complex pattern. Both instruments are small, under 5′ in length.

Otherwise, the two harpsichords are more notable for their differences. The Müller is more elegant and refined in its decoration. Its case sides sit on, rather than overlap, the bottom. The bottom itself is in two pieces: the larger section, under the body of the instrument, has its grain running parallel to the spine, while the grain of the shorter piece, under the keyboard, runs at right angles to it. Both of these features — which will become the norm for Flemish and, later, French and English harpsichords — are seen here for the first time. The Müller is also the earliest known example of a harpsichord with a transposing keyboard: moving it to the left effected the transposition of a whole tone.[24] And the Müller is signed, with the moralizing motto GOTTES WORT BLEIBT EWICK BEISTAN DEN ARMEN ALS DEN REICHEN DVRCH HANS MVLLER CV LEIPCIK IM 1537 (The word of God remains forever to help the poor [as much] as the rich. [Made] by Hans Müller in Leipzig in 1537)[25] appearing on gilded paper glued to the nameboard.

In contrast to the single-strung Arnaut and RCM instruments, the Müller has two sets of unison strings[26] and three sets of jacks, one of which runs close to and roughly parallel to the nut. This close-plucking register produces a distinctly nasal sound. The other two sets slant across the width of the instrument, allowing the jacks to pluck deeper into the strings, and even deeper into the bass than the treble. Obviously, two sorts of tone qualities were desired: a nasal sound, with the quills plucking the strings close to the nut; and a more rounded quality, with the strings plucking farther from the nut. The Müller's soundboard is made of slab-sawn cypress,[27] with a cutoff bar and some ribs underneath.[28] The instrument has a geometric rose, but rather than the usual separate glued-in device, it is carved directly into the soundboard.

On most harpsichords the soundboard extends from tail to bellyrail, ending at the gap. Additional soundboard wood, if seen, is usually a veneer of about ⅛″ in thickness glued to the top of the wrestplank. The Müller's soundboard, however, extends across the gap, right up to the back of the nameboard. The wrestplank (a so-called "hollow" wrestplank) underneath is narrow, just wide enough to accept the two rows of wrestpins. The nut is therefore glued to unencumbered soundboard wood. In contrast to the RCM's rounded bridge, both bridge and nut have parallel sides with molded tops. Cut into the soundboard are oversized slots for three sets of jacks, which are supported by movable upper guides set just under the board, and by stationary lower guides. However, it is likely that the original scheme was just the opposite: fixed upper guide slots in the soundboard and moveable lower guides.[29] The present jacks, with

2-1a. The 1537 Hans Müller harpsichord. The slanting jackrail covers the two sets of deep-plucking jacks, and the one close to the nut covers the jacks, producing the nasal sound. Rome, Museo Nazionale degli Strumenti Musicali.

dampers, are not original. A set of buffs is mounted on a narrow, moveable batten placed between the two angled registers, but this feature is probably not original, since buff pads in this position act as dampers. More than likely, the rail had been fitted with iron hooks for an *arpichordum* stop:[30] the hooks would vibrate against the strings, creating a nasal, buzzing sound perhaps derived from the Renaissance harp, with its brays vibrating against the strings. The three registers and the "buff stop" are controlled by extensions—now longish slips of wood, but likely originally knobs—exiting through the wall of the cheek.

The Müller's bentside, more a Pythagorean curve than an arc of a circle, is shaped differently from the RCM clavicytherium's. The Müller's case sides also have outside top and bottom moldings and a cap molding to provide strength, visual balance, and a more substantial appearance to the case. Finely cut moldings grace the two jackrails and the nameboard as well.[31] The case is veneered with Hungarian ash, a highly figured wood in use for furniture and room paneling at that time.[32]

2-1b. A view of the jacks of the 1537 Müller harpsichord. It is likely that the buff pads mounted on the batten between the two sets of jacks are replacements for the metal hooks of an arpichordum stop. Note the ripple molding on the jackrail. Rome, Museo Nazionale degli Strumenti Musicali.

Current opinion holds that the Müller's bridge was originally in another position, about as far in from its present location as it now is from the bentside;[33] in fact, the marks of this putative inner placement are still faintly visible in Illustration 2-1a. Had the bridge been in that position and the instrument strung in iron, it would have sounded something like an octave higher than normal pitch. It is believed that some years—perhaps even centuries—after it was built, the bridge was moved to its present position, toward the bentside, in order to increase the lengths of the strings,[34] and that by changing to brass stringing, it would now sound at approximately modern pitch.

But John Koster proposes an alternate notion. Based mainly on his study of the arrangement of the strings, he concludes that the instrument was originally built with two bridges, one for each of the string choirs, thus placing its two sets of all-brass strings a fourth apart.[35] Koster's argument, though persuasive, is not in itself convincing enough to abandon the more conventional view that the bridge had been moved, and he himself regards this conclusion as tentative. However, there is a further piece of evidence that seems to have escaped notice until now. With the bridge in its present location, the rose is now centered on the soundboard between bridge and spine — but it would not be so with the bridge in its inner, supposedly original position. This presents an interesting dilemma: if the bridge has been moved, it was from an original location in which the position of the rose was out of balance, to one in which it is now centered. If Koster's view is adopted, the rose position balances with the larger of the two bridges (the inner bridge would have to have been smaller, so that the strings going to the outer bridge could pass over it). This can be seen clearly in Illustration 2-1a. Although it is true that in later instruments with 4′ strings the rose balances in the space between the spine and the 4′ bridge, there is at least one example, the 1579 Theewes, in which the rose is centered on the outer, 8′ bridge. Such a centering of the rose — and thus the presence of two bridges — is likely to have been original on the Müller. Hence, with its transposing keyboard and its two sets of strings a fourth apart, the Müller would have been capable of playing at four different pitch levels. Like Koster, I must view this conclusion as tentative; still, it now seems that his theory is not at all unlikely. But either way, through a rebuilding, an old and essentially worthless instrument was turned into a useable, if flawed tool, an act that more than likely contributed to its survival.

Clearly, the Müller is a startlingly different sort of harpsichord. Even if it were possible to ignore Koster's theory of four possible pitch levels, its design indicates that tonal variety was a paramount consideration. It has two sets of strings; but with three registers, one can be made to sound (although not at the same time) with two different tonal qualities by plucking it in different locations. The Müller provides for the nasal sound of a close-plucking register; a rounded, single-string sound with one of the two angled registers: a more powerful sound, with both angled registers; and the snarling tone of the arpichordum stop. This characteristically Germanic desire for variety or mutation of tone quality is in direct contrast to single-strung, single-register, single-sound instruments like the Arnaut and the RCM clavicytherium. But it also resonates with what may have been an early Northern predilection for the sharper sounds that could be produced by the metal plectra mentioned in connection with the Arnaut and RCM instruments. Aside from mutation stops and its small size, the Müller is built very much like later Northern instruments and can be presumed to be a mature example of an established tradition.

THE RCM CLAVICYTHERIUM AND THE MÜLLER HARPSICHORD AT A GLANCE		
	RCM Clavicytherium	*Müller Harpsichord*
Size	Small	Small
Pitch level	High	High
Compass	40 notes: E,E♯,F,G–g² [36]	44 notes: C,D–g²,a²
Bentside and bridge	Arc of a circle	Pythagorean
Case walls	Thin	Thin
Case bracing	None	One diagonal strut, small uprights
Number of roses	Three	One
Soundboard barring	None	Cutoff bar
Stringing	Single strung	Double strung
Damping	None	Jacks with dampers
Case moldings	Little	Complex applied moldings
Mutation stops	None	Nasal and arpichordum stops

Finally, by the time of the 1537 Müller two important innovations in harpsichord design had taken place: first, the jack mechanism with tongue and spring escapement became the standard, superseding the quill-holding devices of Arnaut, and perhaps other contrivances of which we have no knowledge. And second, dampers had become universal, forever removing the harpsichord from its association with the psaltery.

ANTWERP AND THE VIRGINALS OF IOES KAREST

In an intriguing quirk of fate the next pair of Northern survivors, from 1548 (Brussels, Musée Instrumental) and 1550 (Rome, Museo Nazionale degli Strumenti Musicali), are both polygonal virginals with angled string bands and inset keyboards and were both built by Ioes Karest of Cologne (ca. 1500–ca. 1560). These fascinating instruments exhibit some of the German characteristics of the Müller harpsichord, as well as many of the attributes soon to be identified as Flemish. In fact, they are the first extant examples of the Flemish school, a style related to, but quite distinct from, later Germanic instruments.[37] And as the first virginals we have encountered, they set a benchmark for those that follow.

In common with the Müller harpsichord, both Karests are thin-walled inner-outer instruments (both outers still exist). Both have maple case sides that sit on, rather than overlap, the bottom.[38] Both are braced internally by inner extensions of the cheek that extend back to the spine (few virginals of any type have any more case bracing than this). Both have the same sort of applied cap and upper moldings, as well as a complex and rather substantial molding running around the bottom, decorative in nature but also intended to hide the sides-to-bottom joint. The touch plates of the naturals of both are made of a wood resembling box.[39] Like the Müller's set of close-plucking jacks, those of the virginals closely follow their left bridges, so both these instruments would make a somewhat nasal sound. They also use an upper guide of a strip of leather glued to the soundboard with jack slots pierced through it, and a lower consisting of a piece of soundboard wood the width of the keyboard, with another strip of slotted leather glued in the appropriate position to accept the jacks.[40] In a gesture of economy to become associated with virtually all Northern virginals, two jacks occupy each slot.

The 1548 instrument is the smaller of the two, sounding a third or fourth higher.[41] The 1550 seems to be "full sized" — that is, sounding somewhere near normal pitch. The 1548 may have been a holdover from the era of higher-pitched harpsichords, but as we will see, Ruckers virginals were also made in a variety of pitch levels. The keyboard of the 1548 comprises forty-five notes, C/E–c³, the compass that becomes the Flemish standard in the next century; but the 1550 has a compass of C,D–f³, more typical of contemporaneous Italian harpsichords. Evidently, elements such as keyboard compass had not yet become firmly established. It may well have been the practice to go as high as the scale and stringing material would permit; or less likely, the appearance of the keyboard — the manner it which it balanced visually against the case — might have been a factor in determining compass.

The Müller has but a single rose, although the Arnaut harpsichord, the RCM clavicytherium, and most iconographical representations all suggest that until now multiple roses had been the rule. The Karests each have two (on the 1548 the smaller rose is in the shape of a peaked Gothic window, similar to the RCM's two larger roses),[42] and all four rose holes still have their geometrically derived pierced paper or parchment roses.

2-2. The 1548 Ioes Karest virginal. The shallow tool box on the left becomes a feature of almost all Northern virginals. © IRPA-KIK, Brussels.

The Karest instruments also have characteristics connecting them with the mature Flemish style to emerge later in the century. The larger 1550 has a long scale, almost identical to the standard 14″ scale of the typical Flemish harpsichord or virginal.[43] Because both pluck so close to the left bridge, their keyboards are positioned on the left side of the case, a

2-3. The 1550 Karest virginal in its outer case (the front is missing). Notice the painted decoration on the exterior of the inner case. Rome, Museo Nazionale degli Strumenti Musicali.

configuration known as the *spinett* in Flemish style. The keyboards are inset, typical of Flemish instruments to come. The forty-five-note C/E–c³ compass of the 1548 instrument foreshadows the standard range of Flemish instruments after 1580, a few notes wider than the C/E–a² found until then. The soundboards are of quarter-sawn spruce or fir.

Although their cases have applied moldings, including the massive one running around the bottom of the case, the jackrails of both Karest virginals have their moldings cut into the wood, a feature that will become part of the emerging Flemish style. In profile, the bridges are neither half-round as on the RCM clavicytherium nor parallel-sided as on the Müller; instead, their backs are slanted, their fronts concave, and their tops molded. This elegant cross section will remain a distinctive characteristic of Flemish bridges up to and including early Ruckers virginals. Like Flemish instruments to come, the cases are decorated inside and out. A soundboard painting, similar to those that will appear later in the century, can still be made out on the 1550, and there are faint remains of one on the 1548. The 1548 has mottoes ringing both the interior and exterior of the case; the interior walls of the 1550 are painted blue above the soundboard and encircled with a motto, while the natural-wood exterior is painted with an arabesque design featuring dolphins.[48] This painted external decoration is similar to the designs printed on the papers later used to cover Flemish instruments. The keys are also decorated: the naturals have two lines scribed at the

2-4. The paper or parchment rose of the 1548 Karest virginal is glued to the underside of the soundboard. © IRPA-KIK, Brussels.

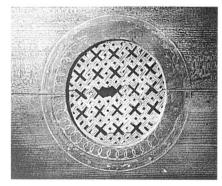

THE SHORT OCTAVE

The term "short octave" describes both a physical element of the extreme bass notes of keyboard instruments and the method of tuning them. In a C/E short-octave tuning scheme, the bottom note of the keyboard, an E, is tuned so that it sounds C, a third lower. The accidental that appears to be F♯ is tuned to D, and the apparent G♯ is tuned to either E or E♭, depending on the requirements of the music. Thus, from the lowest note up, the keyboard's bottom octave sounds C (by playing the apparent E), D (by playing the apparent F♯), E or E♭ (by playing the apparent G♯), then F, G, A, and B♭. From this point on the keyboard is chromatic. The GG/BB short octave is similar, and the extension of the keyboard is down to GG, rather than the apparent BB.

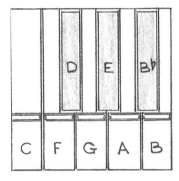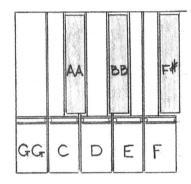

2-5. C/E and GG/BB short octaves.

The use of the short octave was widespread during the harpsichord's early years, appearing on clavichords and organs as well. Its earliest appearance was on the RCM clavicytherium, with its probable C/E, D/E♯, F, and E/G♯ scheme. It lasted far into the seventeenth century, and examples can still be found in the eighteenth.[44] There were good reasons for its long life, since it extended the bass register from F down to C with only a slight enlargement of the case (the apparent E had to be fitted in). That the low F♯ and G♯ (or C♯ and E♭ on a GG/BB short octave) were "missing" was of little consequence to composers who practically never required them (although it could be argued that they were never written for because the instruments lacked them). A reason for the short octave's continued existence may have had to do with the expense of the largest pipes on the organ. On that instrument it was a real economy to use the short octave, thereby avoiding the purchase of large, costly metal pipes for accidentals that would never be used anyway. In any event, since harpsichordists, clavichordists, and organists were the same people (amateurs aside), the stratagem presented no problem.[45]

Composers sometimes used the idiosyncrasies of short-octave tuning to both their and the player's advantage. In Illustration 2-6, from a *Pavane* by Peter Philips (1561–1628), the left hand is asked to play a series of alternating tenths and octaves. On a keyboard with chromatic bass it can be played only with unsatisfyingly awkward stretches; but on a keyboard with a short octave the kinesthetic sensation is that of successive octaves, since the low D's and E's are played on the F♯ and G♯ keys. The sensuality of effortlessly achieving tenths is so strong, so delightful, that one cannot really claim to know the piece unless it has been played on a short-octave keyboard.[46] Other passages are extremely difficult, if not impossible, on an instrument without short-octave tuning.[47]

(continued on next page)

(continued from previous page)

2-6a. An excerpt of a
Pavane by Peter Philips.
With a C/E short-octave
keyboard, the left hand
can be played with ease
as "octaves."

2-6b. Another excerpt
from Philips's *Pavane*.
Without a short-octave
keyboard the left hand
cannot be played
satisfactorily.

2-7. Key coverings of the 1550 Karest virginal. The decorative scoring on the natural and sharps can be clearly seen. The 1550s two roses are also visible. Rome, Museo Nazionale degli Strumenti Musicali.

joint of the heads and tails, with a notch centered between them on either side. The sharps have the same decorative gesture at the half-point of their length. Finally, there are painted touches of light and dark on the moldings, suggesting a rope pattern.[49]

We noted that both Karest instruments are polygonal—hexagonal, to be more precise. The right side of the 1550 is attractively curved, corresponding to a bentside; however, the gesture was undoubtedly more visual than anything else, since the only things curved are the outside of the wrestplank and the case wall next to it. The polygonal shape will be seen in only one other extant Flemish virginal, a thick-case 1591 Hans Ruckers; but thin-case polygonal Northern virginals similar to the two Karests can be seen in a number of contemporary paintings. One of these, *Girl at a Spinet* by Catharina de Hemessen (Cologne, Wallraf-Richartz Museum), was done in 1548, making it exactly contemporary with the smaller Karest. Ripin notes that the similarity between them is "striking," even down to the shapes of the two rose holes.[50] The Hemessen virginal has the same style of painted grotesque decoration with dolphins on the exterior, a motto running around the interior of the sound-well,[51] a soundboard painting, and a large molding surrounding the bottom part of the instrument. The two virginals could have come from the same workshop.

An instrument with comparable characteristics is also seen in a 1561 painting by Frans Floris, *The van Berchem Family* (Lier, Museum Vuyts–van Campen and Baron Caroly), although here the exterior case painting is of floral swags and birds. Another virginal, appearing in *Pierre Moucheron and His Family,* painted in 1563 by Cornelis de Zeeuw (Amsterdam, Rijksmuseum), clearly shows a circular geometric rose with a surrounding

DOLPHINS AND MUSIC

The dolphin has a strong connection to music, particularly through the Greek myth of Arion, who was said to have lived around 700 B.C. A master poet and singer to the lyre, Arion entered a music contest in Sicily and won a rich prize. As he was returning to his home in Corinth, the sailors on his vessel conspired to take his treasure and kill him. Confronted by his imminent demise, Arion asked to be allowed to sing to his beloved lyre once more before he died. He was granted his wish, then flung into the sea. But a school of dolphins, attracted by the ravishing beauty of his music, surrounded him and bore him safely to shore. Appearing not only on the papers that covered Flemish instruments, dolphins were often the subject of lid and case paintings, depicting Arion, playing his lyre, astride one of his rescuers (see Plate 3 for an example of an "Arion and the Dolphins" lid painting). Arion's story epitomized not only the power of music, but also music's ability to restore order and harmony to the world.

2-8. The instrument seen in Catharina de Hemessen's *Girl at a Spinet,* painted in 1548, is similar to the 1548 Karest virginal in size and shape, and its external decoration is similar to that of the 1550. Cologne, Wallraf-Richartz Museum.

wreath, a motto around the interior of the soundwell, and the blue borders, scallops, and arabesques associated with later Flemish soundboard painting. A polygonal virginal partially pulled from its plain, oblong outer case is pictured in De Zeeuw's *Family Portrait* of 1564 (England, private collection). Richly decorated, the exterior of the inner case is covered with dolphin grotesques, and the decorative touches of paint on the moldings can be plainly seen. The instrument even has a "bentside" comparable to that of the 1550 Karest.[52]

Such pictorial evidence tends to confirm the assumption that thin-case Flemish polygonal virginals were the rule around the middle of the sixteenth century.[53] Like the 1548, some are small, perhaps indicating that the tradition of high-pitched instruments had not yet ended, or that there was another tradition, as yet unknown, of virginals in several sizes (such as those of the Ruckerses).

FRANCE

As in the Low Countries, the production of virginals seems to have been the major activity of sixteenth-century string-keyboard makers in France, with grand harpsichords becoming more plentiful only after the middle of the next century. The earliest reference in France to a harpsichord builder (or, for that matter, to a customer) is to a Victor Cothen, from Tours, who made an *espinète* in 1496 for the Comtesse d'Angoulême.[54] Virtually no other signs of harpsichord activity can be found in France in the remaining years of the fifteenth century; but for the sixteenth, *Boalch III* lists nearly forty known builders.[55] Applying the "Koster formula," which assumes a productive life of twenty years for a maker, and that with apprentices and journeymen he was capable of producing five instruments a year,[56] it is likely that some four thousand virginals and perhaps a few harpsichords would have been generated in sixteenth-century France. But no extant instruments have been discovered. Nevertheless, we do have references, such as one in 1561 to Jean Potin, "faiseur d'espinettes du roy" (royal maker of espinettes).[57] Judging from the sparse evidence available, virginals (*espinettes*) were probably made at a much higher rate than grand harpsichords (*clavecins*). Marin Mersenne, writing in 1635, noted that there were no clavecins in the previous century,[58] and not until 1600 do we find one mentioned, in an inventory of the instruments belonging to the deceased Paris organist and harpsichordist Pierre Chabanceau de la Barre;[59] until then, all references are to espinettes. There is some confusion, though, since the French tended to use the word espinette to refer to grand harpsichords as well as virginals, and did so even in the eighteenth century.

A rare representation of a pre-seventeenth-century virginal is found in a manuscript from the 1580s by the organist Jacques Cellier.[60] Not surprisingly, the instrument appears to be oblong and thin cased, but the spine is heavier, to support a lid. This is probably an instrument in International style, a term for a loose collection of characteristics of sixteenth- and seventeenth-century instrument building common to England and Germany as well as France. Apart from what will shortly be identified as Flemish and Italian practices, International style, which included the use of unpainted hardwoods, integral-case construction, case sides of moderate thickness, heavy spines with lids, applied moldings, cross-bridge soundboard barring, "hollow" wrestplanks, jacks plucking close to the nut, metal plectra, mutation stops, and decorative papers, essentially defined European harpsichord building at this time.[61]

The lid of the Cellier virginal is coffered, that is, formed to suggest a chest, or coffer. A 1568 Flemish virginal (the "Duke of Cleves," to be described in the next chapter) also has a coffered lid, and nearly every extant seventeenth-century English virginal has one as well, although the manner of coffering differs. The

2-9. This sixteenth-century drawing of a French virginal, from Jacques Cellier's 1583–87 *Fantasie sur orgue ou espinette faicte par Monsieur Costelley*, shows an integral-case instrument with a coffered lid. Paris, Cliché Bibliothèque Nationale de France.

French example is rounded, whereas the central portion of the Duke of Cleves's lid is raised with panels and moldings. The English style, though a century later, was different still, with two angled pieces at the back and front of the lid raising the center section.[62] It seems likely, therefore, that coffered lids were not uncommon on Northern virginals in the sixteenth century and may have been the rule. Another decorative element, most likely either paint or papers, can be seen on the back wall of the case and on top of the jackrail of the Cellier virginal. Otherwise, the instrument looks somewhat austere, with neither a rose nor a soundboard painting.

Some care is necessary in accepting Illustration 2-9, since the keyboard is not depicted realistically. Its range would undoubtedly have been greater than the little more than three octaves shown, and the extra sharp in the bass and the squeezed-in d^3 in the treble confuse the issue. The right bridge does not appear to have been carefully drawn, and there is no sign of a left bridge, although that could be hidden by the jackrail. One also wonders about the shallowness of the case and the longer-than-necessary jackrail, but a confirmation of those two features will appear in Chapter 8.

ENGLAND AND THE THEEWES CLAVIORGANUM

Henry VIII (he of the six wives), king of England from 1509 to 1547, broke with papal authority in 1529 to found the Church of England because he was thwarted in his efforts to divorce Catherine of Aragon. He closed the Catholic monasteries and executed many of those who refused to recognize him as head of the new church. His unnecessary wars with France squandered England's resources. Henry was something of a cruel despot, but he was also a music lover. An accomplished keyboard player, he had a sizeable array of virginals, harpsichords, clavichords, claviorgana, organs, and regals at his disposal. When he died, Philip van Wilder, the court musician who looked after his instruments, drew up an inventory of the collection, and it is that document that forms the basis of our scant knowledge of harpsichord making in sixteenth-century England.[63] As an accumulation of expensive instruments, many of which undoubtedly came from foreign shores as diplomatic gifts, the inventory cannot be truly indicative of the state of English harpsichord building; nevertheless, it does offer some clues.

Ambiguous as to the identification of actual types of instruments and places of origin, the inventory nevertheless indicates that the Westminster court referred to all its plucked keyboard instruments as *paires of virginalles,*[64] with the word *paire* presumably used in the same manner in which we identify "a pair of pants" or "a pair of scissors."[65] And just as the French used the term *espinette,* it was the English custom to call any jack-action instrument a *virginalles,* consistently using the plural form of the word[66] (although in the next century sometimes the grand was identified as a *harpsicon* or *harpsycon*). But a distinction was also made between single and double virginals. It is doubtful that these were instruments with two keyboards, since there is little evidence that these existed before the end of the sixteenth century,[67] and it is even less likely that they were 2×8′ virginals—although such were made, they were extremely rare and in any case not found until a century later. They could have been virginals in the style of the Flemish mother and child, but as far as we know, at this early date they were not found even in Antwerp. It is possible that the *double virginalles* were 2×8′ harpsichords;

nevertheless, as Barry points out, it is more likely that the word *double* referred to the notes below C, which we still designate as AA or BB—"doubled" notes. Accordingly, double virginalles were likely jack-action instruments with extended rages below C.[68] In fact, either single or double virginalles could have been either virginals or harpsichords, but by the process of elimination one suspects that they really were the former,[69] since one of the inventory items consisted of two *longe virginalles made harpe fashion*, and those were likely to have been in grand harpsichord shape.[70]

Some of the virginalles may have been Italian imports, since the document notes that they were made of cypress, but that wood is also seen on at least one native English instrument. The inventory also lists an item (found in Hampton, rather than Westminster), likely a clavicytherium, called *a paire of Virginalles facioned like a harp.* Henry also had claviorgana, as in *a paire of single Virgynalles with pipes underneath.* And he had an automatic *ottavino,* likely a gift or import from Germany. Finally, there are references to cases decorated in leather and fabric, and it is difficult to know if these are integral-case instruments or inner-outers. We might suspect either.

In sixteenth-century England, as in Italy, Antwerp, France, and Germany, virginals must have been far more numerous than grand harpsichords; but there are no survivors, no descriptions in books and treatises, and few woodcuts, drawings, or paintings.[71] The earliest harbinger we have of the attributes of sixteenth-century English virginals comes from a ca. 1560–70 painting attributed to the "Master of the Countess of Warwick," which shows only a small portion of the instrument. Darryl Martin, who has examined an illustration of the painting, notes that "the casework is clearly dark, and the soundwell decorated with a gold, presumably embossed, finish."[72] Another representation is the virginal in the woodcut that graces the title page of *Parthenia, or the Maydenhead of the First Musicke that was ever printed for the Virginalls* (1612–13).[73] Although the illustration is lacking in detail, it does show an oblong case with thin walls, with a (presumably) heavier spine supporting a rounded coffered lid, differing little from the sixteenth-century French examples discussed earlier in this chapter. There is no hint of any decorative detail such as moldings or embossed paper. Whether this instrument represents an indigenous virginal or one made in France or Germany—or even elsewhere—is impossible to tell.[74]

Henry's inventory does not identify a single fifteenth- or sixteenth-century builder, foreign or domestic. Still, we do know of a small handful of makers who worked in England, eighteen of them, almost all in London;[75] but these are virtually unknown

2-10. The title page of *Parthenia*. The virginal shows little of the decorative style of the surviving seventeenth-century English virginals.

except for William Lewes, who supplied virginals to the court on several occasions, and Lodewijk Theewes (fl. 1560–85),[76] the maker of the only jack-action keyboard instrument built in England to have survived the sixteenth century. If we somewhat arbitrarily assume that we are aware of only half of the builders who were working there, and apply to this number the Koster formula, we arrive at the tentative conclusion that at the very least, some thirty-five hundred plucked keyboards were built during this time.[77] Nevertheless, from all those years only the Theewes harpsichord has survived. As always, fashion and musical requirements often relegated older instruments to the status of junk, to be discarded, razed, and cannibalized for parts. And once again, we face the realities of the harshness of earlier times: between 1642 and 1649 the British Isles endured three civil wars, and undoubtedly instruments were lost then. The Commonwealth that followed was biased against music in the church, and nearly all the service organs in England were destroyed. Many jack-action instruments may have been demolished as well. But far more devastating was the 1666 Great Fire of London, a five-day conflagration that reduced most of London to ashes.

Theewes, who immigrated to London sometime before 1571, when his name is to be found in its parish records, came from a family of Antwerp builders. His father Jacob (fl. 1533–57) made both lutes and harpsichords, and a namesake relative, possibly his uncle, was one of the signatories to Ioes Karest's 1557 petition to the Guild of St. Luke. Lodewijk had been a guild member himself, admitted in 1561. It may have been the unsettled conditions in Antwerp that prompted him to leave the security of his home for an unknowable future in London; but apparently he was successful in his new environment, since his only extant work bears the armorial symbols of a noble English family.

Theewes's 1579 instrument (London, Victoria and Albert

Museum) is part of a claviorganum, or combined harpsichord-organ. The narrow-tailed single-manual plucked instrument, nearly 7′ long, sits on top of the large, oblong organ chest, both strings and pipes activated from the harpsichord's keyboard. It is not in good condition: the keys are missing, bridges have been poorly replaced, only one jack survives, and the rose is gone. Nevertheless, there is much that the instrument can tell us.[78] The case is built of oak, with sides about ½″ thick, substantial enough to support the existing lid. Moldings are applied to the interior of the case, above the soundboard. Two tall bottom braces run from spine to bentside. The exterior of the case is covered with embossed leather, and the keywell, jackrail, and soundwell are faced with gold-embossed paper. The lid is painted with a strapwork design and a cartouche of Orpheus serenading the beasts. The rose hole balances visually with the 8′ rather than the 4′ bridge. The soundboard painting is almost all gone. A light 4′ hitchpin rail is on the underside of the soundboard. As in the Müller, the spruce soundboard does not end at the upper bellyrail, but extends across the gap to the back of the nameboard—another "hollow wrestplank." Unlike the Müller, however, the instrument had three sets of strings, 2×8′, 1×4′ (the 4′ strings passing through holes in the 8′ nut on their way to the wrestpins), the earliest known harpsichord with this disposition. In the section over the gap the soundboard has three rows of leathered slots, intended for three sets of jacks. Moveable lower guides allowed the registers to be turned on or off by hand stops, in the form of draw knobs, that project

2-11. This 1579 combined harpsichord and organ by Lodewijk Theewes, a transplanted Fleming, is the earliest extant harpsichord from the British Isles. London, Victoria and Albert Museum.

through the front of the case. The compass is C–c³.[79] The long ca. 13½″ scale rises in the treble, in the manner seen in early Flemish instruments.[80]

In addition to the full chromatic bass and the 2×8′, 1×4′ disposition, there are a few other surprising things about this instrument. First, it is quite wide in relation to its compass: generous amounts of soundboard wood are found on either side of the register slots, and the extra space in the keywell was filled with boxlike affairs on either side of the keyboard. Although it is possible that Theewes had acoustical reasons for wanting all that extra soundboard, it is perhaps more likely that he made the instrument wider so that it would fit more harmoniously with the wider organ case.[81] Second, one jack has survived, and Koster has noted that the mortise for the plectrum is too narrow for bird quill, and furthermore contains a fragment of metal.[82] Hence, if the jack indeed belongs to the instrument, it would seem possible that at least one register was quilled with metal. Finally, each of the bridge pins for the shorter of the two 8′ strings is accompanied by a curious inverted L-shaped pin screwed into the bridge. Although those pins have suffered much bending and abuse, it is fairly certain that they were intended to touch the strings and act as an arpichordum stop.[83] Accordingly, it is likely that the back 8′ choir was a mutation stop.[84]

SUMMING UP

Some intriguing changes in harpsichord design took place in the century between the ca. 1470 RCM clavicytherium and the Theewes claviorganum of 1579. The 1537 Müller revealed the emergence of a Teutonic appetite for pungent, nasal sounds and mutation stops, preferences that relate to International style and will resonate in German, Scandinavian, and English harpsichords for the next 250 years. With its fancy-grain wood and applied ripple moldings, the Müller also demonstrates a significant increase in the refinement of harpsichord design and decor. Of paramount importance was the adoption of the "standard" jack and the introduction of dampers to stop the strings from ringing. Finally, the Müller represents harpsichord building just at, or perhaps slightly before, the time when Flemish and International styles were beginning to sort themselves out. Hence, characteristics of both can be seen in it, as well as some native German traits such as inner-outer construction and the use of ripple molding. International traits include the light internal bracing, the presence of three registers with a 2×8′ disposition, a separation of tone colors into a deep-plucking sound and a nasal one, a hollow wrestplank, a natural-wood finish, and the use of gilded paper on the nameboard. Flemish features are presaged by the placement of the case sides on, rather than around, the bottom, the employment of upper and lower guides, and the two-piece bottom board.

The Karest virginals of 1548 and 1550 still exhibit some German properties — the thin-walled inner-outer construction and the applied moldings; but the Flemish features are more insistent: upper and lower guides, a long scale (in the 1550 instrument), inset keyboards in the spinett position, quarter-sawn soundboards of spruce or fir, jackrails with cut-in moldings, soundboard paintings, and exterior grotesque designs featuring dolphins (the 1550). The Karest instruments represent the first physical evidence we have of the establishment of a Flemish school of virginal building, one in which graceful polygonal shapes, thin cases, inset keyboards, cut-in as well as applied moldings, soundboard paintings, elaborate roses, nicely shaped bridges, embellished naturals and sharps, and detailed external painted decoration provided an elegance that is only dimly reflected in the instruments' present condition.

Lodewijk Theewes was born in Antwerp, but the harpsichord he built in London in 1579 is an early representative of International style. Its hardwood case walls of intermediate thickness, light internal bracing, integral-case construction, "hollow" wrestplank, possible use of metal plectra, use of embossed and gilded papers, and the advanced disposition of 2×8′, 1×4′ are not characteristics we will find in Flemish instruments.

All of this could leave an impression that the harpsichord evolved in neat, straight lines, from North European origins as a keyed psaltery, to the development of the proto-harpsichord in

Germany, to a splitting off into Northern and Southern practices, with the Northern itself branching into the new Flemish style, and a continuation of the Germanic into the International. Although this orderly family tree is not exactly wrong, it is misleading. There were too many countercurrents in the instrument's development to fit these categories quite so neatly. Koster suggests that sixteenth-century Northern harpsichord building was more of an international affair, with ideas crossing boundaries of time as well as space. He notes, for example, that the influences might have been just as strong from Flanders to Germany as they were the other way around. His words are worth quoting:

> Certainly the situation should not be viewed as one in which there was an immutable standard practice that was strictly observed . . . in all of France, England, the German-speaking lands, Eastern Europe, and Scandinavia. Rather, the International style should be understood as a group of somewhat variable local traditions that (to use a modern analogy) drew upon the same gene pool originating from a Gothic lineage.[87]

Whatever their pedigrees, these virginals and harpsichords were valued tools of organists, who used them to work out the many ricercars, canzonas, and toccatas of Paul Hofhaimer (1459–1537), Johannes Buchner (1483–ca. 1540), Nikolaus Ammerbach (ca. 1530–97), Mark Antonio Cavazzoni (ca. 1490–ca. 1560), Claudio Merulo (1533–1604), Antonio de Cabezón (1500–66), and Thomas Tallis (ca. 1505–85). But both they and nonprofessional players also must have delighted in playing fantasies, preludes, dances, variations sets, and arrangements of motets, madrigals, and solo songs by Hans Kotter (ca. 1485), Leonhard Kleber (ca. 1495–1556), Andrea Gabrieli (ca. 1533–86), William Byrd (1543–1623), and John Bull (ca. 1562–1628).

[3]

ANTWERP HARPSICHORD BUILDING
BETWEEN KAREST AND RUCKERS

T HE PREVIOUS chapter began with speculation about how many harpsichords might have been built between the times of the ca. 1470 Royal College of Music clavicytherium and the 1537 Müller harpsichord. The same question could be asked about instruments produced by the Flemish school, particularly in Antwerp,[1] in the years between the 1550 Karest virginal and 1581, the date of the first extant Ruckers virginal. We could attribute the disappearance of hordes of harpsichords to the vicissitudes of fashion, but natural and man-made disasters also played a role. Undoubtedly, many were demolished during the sacking of Antwerp in 1576—the "Spanish Fury" that resulted in an extraordinary destruction of property as well as thousands of deaths. Many more harpsichords may have been destroyed, perhaps even burned as firewood, during the 1585 siege of Antwerp by the Spanish. It is also possible that builders recycled obsolete instruments, reusing case parts, keyboards, pins, jacks, and perhaps even strings. Nevertheless, a small but significant group of Antwerp virginals survived those turbulent years. Together, they demonstrate the presence of a mature Flemish style as well as a typically sixteenth-century predilection for opulence of decoration. Three pre-Ruckers grands are also extant, suggesting that the art of building bentside instruments was also well established during those years.

ANTWERP

A flourishing commercial city in the sixteenth century, Antwerp grew rapidly when its harbor on the Scheldt River replaced the seaport of Bruges as Flanders's principal outlet to the North Sea.[2] By 1550 it had become the chief financial and trade center of Northern Europe, as well as the locus of the international diamond trade.[3] By then its population, only twenty thousand in 1500, had exploded to 100,000. With unparalleled prosperity and a merchant class with disposable income, Antwerp was a Mecca for artists and craftsmen for most of the century. Tielman Susato (d. 1561), Christophe Plantin (1520–89), and other publishers established profitable printing businesses. Painters Quentin Metsys (1465–1530), Jan Metsys (1505–75), Frans Floris (1516–70), Joachim Patinir (1480–1524), Peter Bruegel

---

THE GUILD OF ST. LUKE

The history of the Guild of St. Luke goes back to the end of the fourteenth century. It was the painter's guild, but it also included "sculptors, engravers, printers, gold- and silversmiths, potters, chest makers, craftsmen in glass, etc."[5] It is generally thought that harpsichord makers were originally included because of the decorative aspects of their instruments. If so, it might tell us something about the way harpsichords were viewed in Antwerp. Although we might assume it was a musical instrument built by someone who was mainly a cabinetmaker, they may have considered its decorative aspects at least as important as the musical ones.[6] But it is equally likely that the builders belonged to the guild because of the similarity of harpsichord building to chest making.

Before 1557, guild membership for harpsichord builders was apparently discretionary, and only Ioes Karest, his brother Goosen, and a few other makers belonged. But in that year, ten Antwerp builders (among them one with the descriptive name of Hans der Orgelmakere, who was probably the Hans Bos to be mentioned shortly), a few of whom were already members, petitioned the Guild of St. Luke to assume authority for the regulation of harpsichord building. Those petitioners who were already masters, but not guild members, asked to be admitted without examination. Their idea, of course, was to limit competition and control the standards of workmanship. Anyone in Antwerp wishing to make harpsichords would have to apply to the guild, which would also judge the work—the "masterpiece"—of apprentices seeking entrance. The piece was to be inspected and tested by two or three designated makers. If it passed muster, it then became the property of the apprentice's master, who had provided him with tools, training, and materials; but if it was rejected, the apprentice had to pay his master for the materials and the use of his tools. The process was not quite as democratic as it now seems, however, since children of masters were admitted to membership without examination.

The petition was accepted in 1558; thereafter, only members could make or sell harpsichords in Antwerp. The decree, spelling out the rights and obligations of harpsichord builders and the requirements for admission to the guild by future makers, evidently had the force of law, stipulating a fine for violating the "ordinance." Also on pain of a fine, the document stated that each harpsichord maker should apply a distinctive emblem to his work.[7] The gilded lead or pewter rose on the soundboard is generally considered to be the device by which the Flemish builders signed their instruments, although they also used the namebattens of harpsichords and the jackrails of virginals for that purpose.

---

the Elder (1525–69), Jan Bruegel (1568–1625), and Peter Paul Rubens (1577–1640), all members of the Guild of St. Luke (the same guild to which the harpsichord makers belonged), had outstanding careers there. Some of Europe's most celebrated musicians either were born, or spent time, in Antwerp: Jacques Barbireau (ca. 1408–91) headed the cathedral choir from 1447 until his death, and his student Johannes Ockeghem (ca. 1410–97) was a youthful singer in the cathedral in 1443–44; Jacob Obrecht (ca. 1450–1505) was at Antwerp from 1491 to 1503; and the English composer John Bull (ca. 1562–1628) became organist

GOOSEN KAREST THE APPRENTICE

The archives of Antwerp's City Hall contain a document dated February 1538 stating the conditions for the apprenticeship of Goosen Karest to his elder brother, Ioes. For a period of three years Ioes was to provide Goosen with all materials necessary to build and decorate harpsichords; teach him the art of building, voicing, and playing them; and pay him a stipend. Goosen, in return, had to furnish his own tools and work twelve hours a day, with an hour off for lunch. He had to pay Ioes for food and was obliged to pay for any missed time. Interestingly, at this time Goosen was already a member of the Guild of St. Luke, but as a journeyman painter.[10] Goosen's first apprenticeship was undertaken when he was a teenager, but he was in his thirties when he decided to become a *clavecimbel* maker.[11]

at the cathedral in 1617. Harpsichord makers also flourished amid this wealth and activity. Ioes Karest was admitted to the Guild of St. Luke in 1523, and an additional nineteen makers entered the organization before 1579, the year Hans Ruckers's name appears.[4] Thus, although we have only four virginals remaining from that period, it is obvious that a strong tradition of harpsichord building was present in Antwerp long before the Ruckerses.

Antwerp's fortunes suffered a reversal later in the century, when it became embroiled in the revolt of the Dutch against the Spanish. In 1576 it was ravaged by Spanish mutineers, and in 1585, after undergoing a year-long siege, it fell to Spanish troops. With hard times and a shrinking population, a number of Antwerp builders emigrated to the Dutch republic, among them guild members Marten van der Biest, who became a citizen of Amsterdam in 1587, and Johannes Grouwels, who moved to Middelburg in 1593.[8] Nevertheless, by the end of the century the city had recovered some of its former economic viability. If there was not enough work for van der Biest and Grouwels, there seemed to be more than enough for Hans Ruckers and his progeny.[9]

THE SURVIVING VIRGINALS

After the two virginals of Ioes Karest, the next to survive is a Flemish anonyme of 1568 known as the Duke of Cleves virginal (London, Victoria and Albert Museum).[12] Its rectangular case is made of walnut, with walls about ⅞″ thick. Resembling a sarcophagus, or stone coffin, the instrument has convex sides, ornately carved on the exterior with instruments, weapons, armor, vines, and leaf patterns. This is a unique decoration, probably created specifically for its eponymous owner, William, Duke of Cleves, otherwise known as William the Rich, whose coat of arms is found on the lid. The interior of the lid is painted a light blue and is adorned with gold strapwork bordered by two Latin mottoes, all surrounded by molding. The narrow soundwell is also painted blue, as is the fallboard. The top of the lid is raised with moldings and contains more carving, with "Orpheus serenading the beasts" portrayed in relief in the center. Lions' heads guard the keyboard at both ends. The effect is one of great richness.

Its extraordinary decor should not obscure the fact that much about this instrument is consonant with both earlier and later Flemish style.[13] Similar to the 1550 Karest in size, its scale is consistent with a Flemish virginal at normal pitch or a tone above.[14] It also has a rising scale,[15] a soundboard painting, a recessed keyboard, upper and lower guides, double-length jack slots (two per slot), and a forty-five-note $C/E-c^3$ compass.[16] Mottoes around the base of the exterior, as well as on the lid, fallboard, and jackrail, resonate with the richness of decor of the Karest instruments and the few later sixteenth-century virginals.

The position of the keyboard is significant. In the Karest virginals, as well as the contemporaneous representations of virginals in paintings cited in the last chapter, it was placed to the left, so that the strings would be plucked fairly close to the nut; but the Duke of Cleves's keyboard is set in the center of the case. Consequently, its strings would be plucked farther from the nut, producing a more rounded, less nasal tone than the Karest instruments. Only one other extant Flemish virginal has this central keyboard placement, the 1580 by Johannes Grouwels, to be discussed shortly; but it is likely that there were other examples of center-keyboard virginals that have not survived.[17] The sides of the Duke of Cleves are heavier than those found in subsequent Flemish virginals, but necessarily so because of the sarcophagus shape and the carving. The case material—walnut—is also unique, since Flemish builders almost always used poplar. But if the exterior was to be carved in natural wood, poplar would not have done nearly as well as the harder and showier walnut. (The Duke of Cleves virginal is seen in Plate 4.)

The two most obvious elements linking the Duke of Cleves to later Flemish virginals are the oblong shape and the heavy case construction. These changes from earlier practice did not occur simultaneously. An engraving by Cornelis Cort published in 1565 (New York, Metropolitan Museum of Art), but supposedly based on a decade-old (but no longer extant) painting by Frans Floris, clearly shows an oblong but thin-case instrument.[18] Not surprisingly, it is decorated in a manner similar to that of the virginals described in the last chapter, has no lid, and displays the usual heavy bottom molding. With the exception of a 1591 instrument by Hans Ruckers, Flemish builders will henceforth make their virginals in this oblong form, although builders in Italy and Germany will continue to produce polygonal instruments.

Clearly, sometime between 1550 and 1568 Flemish harpsichord building separated itself forever from the thin-case inner-outer designs that had characterized harpsichord building since the beginning of the century. Ripin cloaked the moment in a bit of drama: "The emergence of the thick-cased design is an event shrouded in at least as much mystery as the development of the preceding thin-cased type, except that there seems no doubt as to the date—about 1565—and very little doubt as to the place—Flanders."[19] The heavy case of the Duke of Cleves, with enough heft to allow the attachment of hinges, also permitted the instrument to have a lid. Actually, it is ironic that this particular virginal should be the first survivor in heavy-case oblong style, since it is likely that the switch was designed to simplify the construction process. Only one case need be built for the heavier instrument, and with sturdier sides the structure is simpler and perhaps a little more forgiving; and an oblong instrument with only four sides and right angles, rather than five or six sides and skewed angles, is certainly easier to deal with.[20] Flemish instruments were still meticulously and painstakingly decorated with paint inside and out, but an element of elegance, derived from its form and the application of complex moldings, was now missing.

A ca. 1570–80 spinett virginal by Hans Bos (Tordesillas, Monastario de Santa Clara) was one of many artifacts exported to Spain when Flanders was under its control.[21] Bos (fl. 1543–78) entered the Guild of St. Luke in 1558 and was listed as an organ builder, but obviously he also made harpsichords.[22] Ac-

3-1. Aside from the shape, the virginal portrayed by Cornelis Cort in 1565 is similar in almost every respect to those of Karest as well as those illustrated in the paintings discussed in the last chapter. New York, Metropolitan Museum of Art.

cording to Ripin, the Santa Clara instrument resembles Ruckers spinett virginals "in virtually every detail" except for a slightly longer scaling in the treble.[23] The case is oblong and of heavy construction, with sides of about ⅝″. The compass is C/E–c³. The front of the virginal, the fallboard, and the soundwell are covered with block-printed Flemish papers, either black on white or the reverse, with motifs derived from stock books of patterns. Although designs of grotesques featuring dolphins were common,[24] they were by no means the only ones used.[25] This is the first instrument known to use papers to this extent: in effect, rather than using paint to produce those or similar designs, Bos glued patterned paper to the case, inside and out. With few exceptions—the instruments by van der Biest and Ruckers, to be discussed shortly, are among them—Flemish paper will be seen on subsequent virginals (and harpsichords too, for that matter). Like heavy cases and oblong shapes, its use must reflect another attempt on the part of builders to save time and labor, since it was far easier to glue on paper than to painstakingly paint patterns. Evidently, the virginal was changing roles in Antwerp and probably in the Low Countries in general. It was no longer an instrument intended primarily for royalty and nobility; instead, there was likely a growing market in the affluent middle class—people who would be comfortable with a fancy instrument, but perhaps not with an elegant one.

But while modifying the older opulent style, Flemish builders were by no means abandoning it. The Bos's lid interior is decorated with a courtly pastoral,[26] a genre scene of stylized Renaissance balance, portraying well-to-do burghers and courtiers enjoying music, games, dancing, hunting, boating, and other pleasurable activities.[27] Three roses adorn the decorated soundboard. The leftmost hole has lost its rose, the middle hole has a geometric rose, but the rightmost hole has a gilded metal device, a tiny organ, with the initials "HB." This is the first appearance of a nongeometric cast-metal rose carrying the builder's initials.[28] There are "gilt masks in relief on the far end of the sharp key-plates,"[29] a decorative touch not found on any other extant Flemish instruments.

The third virginal, by Johannes Grouwels, ca. 1580 (Brussels, Musée Instrumental), is also oblong and heavy cased. A generation younger than Bos, Grouwels (fl. 1579–93) joined the Guild of St. Luke in 1579, but moved to Middelburg, a ferry ride from Antwerp across the Scheldt River.[30]

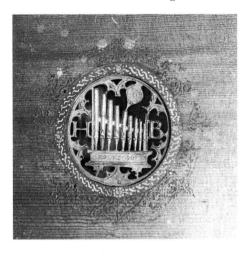

3-2. This rose, from the ca. 1578 Hans Bos spinett virginal, is the earliest extant example of the use of a gilded lead or pewter rose. Tordesillas, Monasterio de Santa Clara.

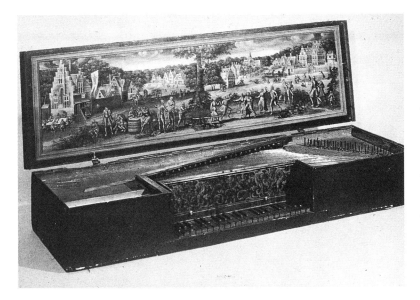

3-3. Like the Duke of Cleves, this ca. 1580 virginal by Johannes Grouwels has its keyboard centered on the case. Although now black, it is likely that the virginal was originally decorated in the traditional manner, with its case front covered with papers and the sides and lid painted to resemble porphyry. © IRPA-KIK, Brussels.

Like the Duke of Cleves virginal, the keyboard of Grouwels's ca. 1580 instrument is centered on the case, and it is the only other extant Flemish virginal to have that configuration, although there may have been many others like them, now lost. Otherwise, it is quite similar to the Bos virginal, but with a shorter, forty-one-note C/E–g^2,a^2 compass (the present $g\sharp^2$ is a later addition). As with the Karest virginals, its lower guide is a piece of soundboard wood the width of the keyboard.[31] Flemish paper covers the keywell and the interior surfaces above the soundboard, but at present not the front of the case; more than likely, it was removed and the surfaces were painted black. There is a soundboard painting and a single geometric parchment rose. At first glance the Grouwels's lid painting seems similar to the stylized genre scene found on the Bos, but the subject matter deals with simple pleasures of villagers rather than the genteel disporting of the courtly pastoral.[32] It is a lid decoration that would have pleased a burgher who was perhaps better acquainted with the peasant scenes of Peter Bruegel than with the formalized early Renaissance tableaus of someone like Joachim Patinir.

The last of the extant pre-Ruckers virginals, a mother and child spinett of 1580, is by Marten van der Biest (Nuremberg, Germanisches Nationalmuseum). Although he is survived only by this one instrument, van der Biest (fl. 1557–84) is a fairly well-known builder. He was one of the ten masters who petitioned the Guild of St. Luke to enroll harpsichord makers as members, although thirty years later he would leave Antwerp and become a citizen of Amsterdam. He was also a witness at

Hans Ruckers's wedding in 1575. His strikingly decorated virginal is similar to the Bos and Grouwels instruments in construction, scale, and compass (originally $C/E-c^3$, now $C-c^3$), except, of course, that it has a cutout for storage of the child to the right of the keyboard. Rather than a covering of Flemish paper, however, the case is delicately painted with colored, repetitive patterns. There are two raised medallions on the nameboard, one on the front of the case to the left, two to the right (on the "door" that closes in the child), and two on the child's nameboard, each with a portrait of a royal or political figure, one of whom is Allesandro Farnese, the governor of the Netherlands, for whom the instrument was made. The mother's decorated soundboard has two geometric parchment roses; the child's has one.[33] The lid painting is another colorful courtly pastoral, similar to the one on the Bos.[34] The effect of this instrument is one of great visual richness and is matched by the richness of its sound.[35] Intended for nobility, it eschewed the new practice of using printed papers in favor of the older, more labor-intensive convention of patterned painting on the case. With its multiple roses, seven raised medallions, and the colorful genre scene on the lid, it marks something of a return to the opulent style of earlier days.

A VIRGINAL BY HANS RUCKERS

Because of its unique relationship to the instruments just discussed, a 1581 mother and child (New York, Metropolitan Museum of Art), the first extant instrument of Hans Ruckers, is worth some attention.[38] The most obvious distinction is in the position of the keyboard. Where two locations have now been seen — in the center and to the left of center — this instrument has its keyboard to the right, with the child ensconced in a compartment to the left. This placement allows the strings to be plucked far from the left bridge, at a point somewhere between two-thirds to one-half of their sounding length. A string plucked around these locations tends to vibrate strongly at its fundamental and odd partials, but like the spectrum of a clarinet tone in the *chalumeau* register, its even partials are weak. This lends an attractive quality of "hollowness" to the sound that is quite distinct, and quite different from the more penetrating tone of the close-plucking spinett virginal. This is the first extant example of such an arrangement, which was called a *muselar*, and which would become more popular than the spinett.[39]

Plucking points aside, there are similarities to the other virginals discussed in this chapter that should be noted. The

THE MOTHER AND CHILD VIRGINAL

The mother and child, or as the Flemish called it, *de moeder met het kind,* consisted of a spinett, or more commonly a muselar virginal, whose case front was left open, as if to accept a drawer. An octave virginal—the child—was slid into the exposed recess. A separate fallboard usually closed the child's compartment, giving the instrument the appearance of an ordinary spinett or muselar; but with the fallboard down the child's keyboard would be exposed, and pulled out partially, it could be played. It could also be completely removed from its mother, and even taken elsewhere.[36]

Another mode of playing was also possible, where the mother's jackrail was removed and the child mounted on top of her case. The child had a diagonal slot cut in its bottom, under the ends of its key levers, and when properly placed on top of the mother the jacks of the larger instrument were positioned just below the bottoms of the backs of the child's keys. Playing the mother's keyboard pushed up the backs of the corresponding keys on the child, thereby activating its jacks. Thus, the combination would sound normal and octave pitches simultaneously, adding brilliance to the sound, and the child could still be played by itself. When disposed in this manner the mother and child had resources similar to that of a 1×8′, 1×4′ harpsichord.

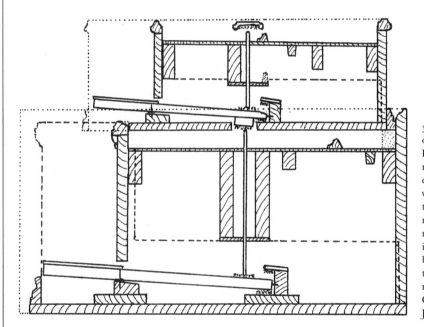

3-4. Cross section of the Hans Ruckers 1581 mother and child muselar virginal. With the child mounted on the mother, both instruments can be played from the lower manual. Courtesy of John Koster.

The reasons—musical or otherwise—for combining these two instruments escape us. Although certainly possible, duet playing would not seem appropriate, since the smaller instrument would sound an octave higher than the larger. The combination might have been built simply because it was possible to do so; or, perhaps it was specifically intended as a teaching tool for a mother and her child. (Plates 5a and b show the van der Biest mother and child spinett virginal, with the child in its compartment and mounted on top of the mother.)[37]

Ruckers is oblong, of heavy-case construction, with cut-in moldings, a $C/E–c^3$ compass, and a soundboard painting. It has many characteristics in common with the van der Biest mother and child: a colorful but refined, repetitive painted decoration on the front, the keywell, and the interior case walls, and two raised medallions on the mother's nameboard, portraying King Philip II and his fourth wife, Anne of Austria (coincidentally, both of these personages also appear on the medallions in the van der Biest virginal). Two geometric parchment roses appear in the mother's soundboard, whereas the child has one. The courtly pastoral painted on its lid is similar in theme and style to those on both the Bos and the van der Biest. Like the van der Biest, the 1581 mother and child muselar is a rich and handsome instrument (see Plate 6).

Similar to the scale of the van der Biest's child, that of the 1581 Ruckers child is also rising, but the treble of the mother's scale is Pythagorean.[40] Koster believes that a change in scale from rising to Pythagorean occurred in Flemish instruments around this time, and that this also led to — or may have been caused by — a change in stringing practices. Hence, it is thought that while the child was strung with the same sort of thin wire as the other rising-scale instruments discussed here, the mother was strung with wire of a heavier gauge.[41] This deduction is based on Grant O'Brien's contention that the Ruckerses used strings that were considerably thicker than those used by other builders and traditions,[42] raising the remote possibility that Hans Ruckers may have been responsible for the rigorously Pythagorean trebles normally found from now on.

THE SURVIVING GRANDS

Three pre-Ruckers grand harpsichords have survived, a 1584 1×8′, 1×4′ single-manual instrument by Hans Moermans, and two double-manual instruments from the last ten or twenty years of the century. Moermans (fl. 1570–1610) became a guild member in 1570, and little is assumed to be original in his one extant instrument (Sudbury, Maine, private ownership).[43] Nevertheless, the heavy case with moldings cut into the sides has a divided bellyrail, and the sides sit on the two-piece bottom. The bentside has a gentle curve, resembling a section of a parabola. The scale is a long 14″. The painted soundboard (although not original) bears the typical Flemish 4′ hitchpin rail, cutoff bar, and ribs. Case framing consists of upper and lower braces. Registers project through the cheeks. These are all hallmarks of seventeenth-century Flemish style, even if their authenticity is questionable in this particular instrument. Its compass is the common pre-1600 C/E–a².

The other two grands (both in Brussels, Musée Instrumental) are anonymous nonaligned doubles. Neither two-manual harpsichords nor nonaligned keyboards have been seen before, and these concepts will be dealt with in detail in Chapter 5; but the appearance of these instruments at this early date requires some discussion. The first (usually referred to by its museum number, 2394), from ca. 1580, has the same typical Flemish constructional characteristics as the Moermans.[44] The upper manual has a compass of C/E–a², and the bottom is a fourth lower, C/E–d³. But it is unique in that it has only three registers, in contrast to the four always found on Ruckers nonaligned doubles.[45] The second double (museum number 2510), from about the same time, also appears to have been Flemish in origin (but not by Hans Ruckers, despite the appearance of an "HR" rose on the soundboard) and has keyboards with the same compasses as number 2394, pitched a fourth apart. But it is also unique, in that in addition to its 8′ and 4′ choirs it has a set of strings at 16′ pitch, with its own bridge on a raised section of soundboard. It is the only Flemish instrument known with suboctave strings, and they appear to be genuine, even though the instrument itself has been extensively rebuilt. But Koster points out that suboctave instruments of all sorts were made in the sixteenth century, a practice mostly discontinued in the seventeenth.[46] At any rate, number 2510 was not disposed in the manner of eighteenth-century German doubles with 16′ stops, and the deep-sounding strings would have been employed in an entirely different way.

These harpsichords also raise the issue of the 4′ register, something not seen before in surviving Flemish harpsichords; but this choir was available on Italian harpsichords since early in the sixteenth century, and it was quite likely known on earlier Flemish instruments as well.[47] With so many Flemish artists and musicians visiting Italy, the fruits of the Italian Renaissance were not unknown in the Low Countries.

SUMMING UP

The five virginals and three harpsichords dealt with in this chapter exhibit obvious differences. The Duke of Cleves and the Grouwels both have their keyboards placed in the center of the case; the Bos and the van der Biest have their keyboards in the usual spinett position, on the left; and the 1581 Ruckers has it in the muselar position, on the right. The Duke of Cleves, the Bos, and the Grouwels are single virginals, but the van der Biest and the Ruckers are both mother and child virginals, a new configuration. Yet, taken together, the virginals conform to fairly rigorous standards of construction, scale, pitch level, compass, and decoration, all obviously based on, yet different from, the thin-case models of Müller and Karest. In the grand harpsichords, moldings were cut into the thicker sides, to lighten their appearance; but in the virginals, cap moldings still appear on the front of the case, although these are concealed when the front flap is closed. In general, it can now be said that applied moldings are no longer used in a three-dimensional, architectural manner designed to add an appearance of substance. All these instruments have soundboard and lid paintings.

In terms of case thickness, it is evident that both virginals and grands have already passed through two stages and have arrived at a third. The earliest examples, as seen in the Minden carving (1425), the *Weimarer Wunderbuch* (ca. 1440), and other iconography, apparently had cases with heavy sides; but the RCM clavicytherium, the Müller harpsichord, the two Karest virginals, and the virginals portrayed in the de Hemessen painting and in other contemporary art all make it clear that from some time prior to ca. 1470, for something like one hundred years harpsichords were thin-walled instruments, housed in heavier, protective outer cases. Now, another shift in case design is seen, back to heavy cases. The two Karest virginals are the last inner-outers to be found in Flanders and, with few exceptions, the last to be seen outside of Italy. After about 1565 all Flemish instruments will be built this way.

Along with the move to heavy-case construction comes the reappearance of the oblong virginal and the simplified construction allowed by its shape. Toward the end of the century we see the substitution of printed paper, much cheaper and easier to apply, for painted decoration on case exteriors, keywells, and soundwells. The 1580 van der Biest, the 1581 Ruckers, and a few other instruments may represent the last vestiges of the earlier, more elegant style of decoration. All of these changes bear witness to the hypothesis that a social realignment was taking place in the manner in which the Flemish harpsichord was perceived and marketed. Whereas earlier it had been a product frequently intended for those of royal or noble blood, people whose tastes were highly developed and to whom objects of elegance and refined beauty were worth owning, no matter what the cost, it seemed that it was now produced for an affluent but less discerning clientele of middle-class burghers. That so many of these surviving instruments are virginals might be considered fortuitous, but it is more likely that before the seventeenth century the virginal, rather than the grand harpsichord, was by far the more common of the two. One can assume that the same sort of decorative shifts occurred in the grand instrument as well, but that would be no more than a supposition. What we do know is that by the end of the sixteenth century virginals were colorful and eye-catching, but usually no longer elegant.

Finally, we have noted the transition from rising to Pythagorean scales in the treble of Flemish instruments from around 1580 and have proposed that with his introduction of thicker strings, Hans Ruckers may have been responsible for this change.

[4]

EARLY ITALIAN STYLE

*C*URSED WITH the burden of the Italian Wars, Italy was under foreign domination from the end of the fifteenth century to the middle of the eighteenth. Nevertheless, it not only survived, but after a fashion it even thrived. One reason was that many of its major cities were ruled by the great *signori:* the Medicis in Florence, the Sforzas in Milan, the d'Estes in Ferrara, the Gonzagas in Mantua — men of extraordinary affluence and privilege, virtual dictators with hereditary powers. They displayed their riches ostentatiously, dispensing patronage to the best artists, painters, sculptors, poets, writers, composers, performers, and craftsmen from all over Europe. In Florence alone, for example, artists such as Leonardo da Vinci (1452–1519),[1] Michelangelo (1475–1564),[2] Raphael (1483–1520), and Benvenuto Cellini (1500–1571), madrigalists like Philippe Verdelot (ca. 1475–ca. 1535) and Luca Marenzio (ca. 1553–99), and singer-composers like Giulio Caccini (ca. 1545–1618) were all recipients of state patronage.

A prodigious amount of the *signori*'s wealth went into patronage of artists and artisans, and they also provided work for armies of skilled craftsmen through the construction of monuments, palaces, and churches. But many other artisans produced products such as paper, firearms, silk thread, violins, lutes, and harpsichords. Much of this activity took place not in the major centers, but in the hinterlands; not in factories, but in small shops. It is an exaggeration to portray sixteenth-century Italy as a landscape dotted with thousands of Gepettos in picturesque cottages, fabricating all sorts of useful artifacts, but the image contains some truth. Thus, while Italian harpsichord manufacturing took place in metropolitan centers, it was also carried out in many other locations, and few craftsmen were able to dominate the field. The guild system operated in Italy, as it did throughout Europe; but it does not seem to have been as strong, or have played as central a role, as in Antwerp and other Northern locations.

Surviving Italian harpsichords—*clavicembali*, or often, just *cembali*—vastly outnumber those from other countries, particularly from the early years of the sixteenth century when, as we have seen, few Northern harpsichords escaped destruction. Hence, it seems somewhat paradoxical that the first extant Italian harpsichord, by Vincentius Livigimeno (dates unknown; Siena, Accademia Chigiana), was built in 1515 or 1516, some forty years after the construction of the RCM clavicytherium.[3] But from that date to 1600 we have a veritable flood of extant Italians: about fifty grand harpsichords, more than one hundred virginals,[4] and a smattering of *ottavini* (octave virginals and spinets).[5] Compared to the handful of Flemish survivors from this period—most of which are from after 1580 (half of them by Hans or Ioannes Ruckers), and all but a few of which are virginals—the Italian survivors constitute a substantial sample, enabling us to describe sixteenth-century Italian building practices in some detail.

There may be several reasons why so many early Italian instruments are still with us. It could have been the sheer numbers produced—*Boalch III* lists thirteen builders working in the Italian states before 1500,[6] but only one name from all the Low Countries.[7] Also, there may be more survivors because originally they were dispersed so widely: as export items, Italian harpsichords, virginals, and spinets were found in halls, theaters, opera pits, studios, drawing rooms, boudoirs, and palaces throughout Europe.[8] It is also possible that so many survived because rebuilding and modernizing an Italian harpsichord could be done by simply shifting its compass, removing the 4′ bridge and nut, and supplying another set of 8′ bridge pins, nut pins, jacks, and strings, rather than having to enlarge or alter its case. (On the other hand, rebuilding a Northern instrument was usually a more complex process, often calling for an expanded compass, added choirs of strings, transforming two-manual transposing instruments into aligned doubles, and later, even adding wood to enlarge the case.)

Italian instruments changed—or evolved, depending on one's point of view—during the course of three hundred years, but in ways differing from their Northern counterparts. At the beginning of the sixteenth century, 1×8′, 1×4′ choirs were customary, with some 1×8′ and 2×8′ instruments as exceptions; but in the next, the ratio had been reversed, and the 1×8′ and the 1×8′, 1×4′ dispositions were generally abandoned by ca. 1630.[9] By that time the 2×8′ was regarded as the Italian standard, and it remained so to the end of the eighteenth century. By 1587 we see the appearance of some false inner-outer instruments: harpsichords and virginals with heavy-case construction, painted on the exterior, but with unpainted cypress veneers and moldings on the interior, giving the appearance of a true inner-outer.[10] Clearly, just before the turn of the seventeenth century, the Italian harpsichord was quite different from the typical Flemish instrument, with its heavy case, 1×8′, 1×4′ stringing, and dual keyboards. In fact, it is this simplicity—a faithfulness to a single keyboard and the purity of two sets of strings—that characterizes Italian harpsichord building from its earliest survivors to its last practitioners and sets it apart from its more complex Northern counterparts.

THE EARLIEST ITALIAN HARPSICHORDS

There are hints that harpsichord makers were active in Italy from as early as 1419,[11] but the first mention of the instrument was in 1461, when on November 15 of that year a Modenese builder named Sesto Tantini wrote to Duke Borso d'Este, requesting that he pay for the harpsichord Sesto had built for him.[12] Although we have no instruments from that time, a harpsichord depicted in an intarsia from ca. 1520, in the San Lorenzo Cathedral in Genoa, is assumed to represent a version of the instrument from the end of the quattrocento.[13] It has several interesting features: a thin-case instrument with a deeply curved bentside, it has cap moldings on the case walls and the nameboard,[14] and two rose holes on the soundboard. The projecting keyboard shows a compass of F,G,A–f²,g²—Virdung's 1511

4-1a. Intarsia of a harpsichord from ca.1520, Genoa, San Lorenzo Cathedral. The doubly curved bentside, a feature of at least some fifteenth-century instruments, had disappeared by the sixteenth.

gamut[15] — and the cheek pieces are gracefully scrolled.[16] In short, it is an instrument that shares many characteristics with the ca. 1470 RCM clavicytherium (compass, thin-case construction, multiple rose holes, scrolled cheeks, and the deep bentside), as well as with the 1537 Müller (thin case, cap moldings, projecting keyboard, and scrolled cheeks). In general appearance, there is little to distinguish the instrument in this intarsia from what we have come to understand as early Northern harpsichord building, except for a doubly curved bentside.

4-1b. Intarsia of a virginal in the Stanza della Segnatura in the Vatican, early sixteenth century. The "bentside" is similar to the one on the 1550 Karest virginal. Vatican, Monumenti Musei e Gallerie Pontificie.

This last characteristic of the instrument has been called unique,[17] but there is another intarsia, a virginal, also from early in the sixteenth century, found on a door of the Stanza della Segnatura in the Vatican,[18] that exhibits the same peculiarity. That the right side of the case is curved at all reminds us of the similar configuration of the 1550 Karest virginal, as well as the instrument portrayed in Cornelius de Zeuuw's 1564 *Family Portrait*.[19] The Vatican virginal's back corners are rounded off so that the left side and spine form a continuous curve, and its keyboard is projecting; but

otherwise, the shape of the case is quite similar to the Karest, which might indicate that early virginals with bentsides were not unique to either Northern or Southern traditions. The Vatican virginal also shares virtually the same range with the 1548 Karest, C/E–f³. With so few instruments from which to draw inferences, one can only speculate about the variety of shapes that were produced in the fifteenth century; but there certainly are indications that both Northern and Southern instruments shared some of them.[20]

HARPSICHORDS, ITALIAN STYLE

The essential features of the Italian harpsichord seem to have been set by the time Vincentius made his 1515–16 instrument. The next survivor, a 1521 by the Roman builder Hieronymus Bononiensis (London, Victoria and Albert Museum), differs little in elements of construction, disposition, and compass; the same could be said of most Italian instruments built in the 1500s. They were thin-case inner-outers, with projecting keyboards, and with cheeks scroll-sawn in elaborate geometric patterns or sometimes carved in three dimensions. The square cheeks of the outer case would extend beyond the projecting keyboard, enclosing it and the scrolled or carved cheeks, thus forming a keywell that, at a casual glance, was similar to the front of a Flemish case. Length was not standardized, but except for octave instruments, few were shorter than 6′ or longer than 8′.

Italian makers refined the concept of thin-case construction, reducing the walls of their instruments to thicknesses of a mere 3/16″ or so. The sides were usually made of Mediterranean cypress, a close-grain coniferous wood which, though classified with the softwoods, is harder and stiffer than the poplar used in the North. The bottom was in one piece, with the grain running the long way. The sides overlapped the bottom. One or more battens glued to the interior of the bottom countered the wood's tendency to expand or contract when the humidity changed. The thin sides were held in place by knees glued to both bottom and sides, and diagonal struts were often used to direct the thrust of the bentside to the rigid joint of bottom and spine. Bellyrails were one piece, or two pieces overlapping each other, rather than the separate upper and lower rails used by the Flemish and later Northern builders. Frank Hubbard noted that "The Ruckers harpsichords are charming, but their naïve crudity is to the sophisticated Italian harpsichord as a cuckoo clock is to Brunelleschi's Duomo."[21] To equate this simple internal structure to the brilliant engineering of Brunelleschi's dome may be a bit disingenuous, but it provided the thin case with the strength that Flemish instruments accomplished by means of heavy sides and upper and lower braces.

Rather than the rising scales favored in the North, Italian builders employed Pythagorean relationships, normally carrying the doubling of the scale down to the bass c. Bentsides closely followed the deep Pythagorean curve of the bridges, adding to the graceful, slender, narrow-waisted appearance of the instruments. The tail was mitered, sometimes square to the spine, but usually at an angle, sometimes fairly acute. The bass section of the bridge was also mitered, normally following the angle of the tail. The cases were not as deep as those in the North, and the soundboard was set farther down into them. A wide, finely cut molding completely surrounded the bottom of the case exterior, and a similar, but smaller, molding did the same at the top. Another molding often encircled the top of the interior surface of the soundwell. A cap molding sat astride the rim of the case and the exterior and (if present) interior top moldings. More moldings were used to outline the soundboard, the jackrail, and the nameboard. All this molding strengthened the thin case sides, gave them a more substantial appearance, and contributed to the three-dimensional, architectural character of the instruments.[22] Small ornamental ivory studs were often placed at regular intervals on the cap molding, the top of the jackrail, and on the cheeks, outlining the instrument's plan view.

Sixteenth-century Italian harpsichords were normally disposed 1×8′, 1×4′, commonly with a fifty-note compass of C/E–f³; but some survivors were single-strung at 8′ pitch, usually with a smaller forty-five-note C/E–c³ compass,[23] and about an equal number were disposed 2×8′.[24] That Italian harpsichords and virginals should ascend to f³ seems strange, since little written music calls for notes above c³. Nevertheless, the 1550 Karest virginal ascended to the same note, and since transposition of a fourth or fifth was common practice, the f³ may have been far more useful than we suspect. Furthermore, improvisation, an essential part of a keyboardist's skills, undoubtedly utilized those notes, and it is likely that neither builder nor player saw any reason to limit the upper portion of the compass.[25]

In contrast to Flemish practice, where the 8′ jacks would be placed in front of the 4′, plucking closer to the nut and thereby emphasizing the more colored aspects of the basic sound, the Italians regularly located the 4′ in that front position.[26] Also contrary to Flemish harpsichords, the gap often slanted away from the wrestplank, causing the bass strings to be plucked farther from the nut (nevertheless, the 1537 Müller's gap also

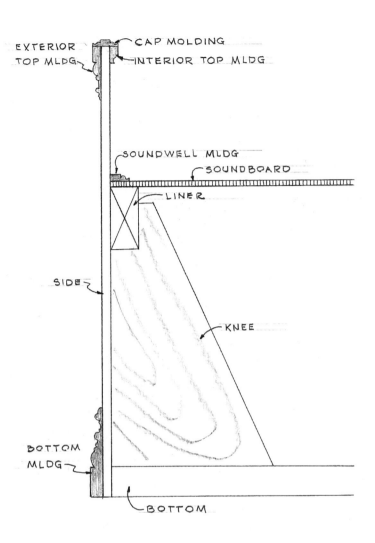

EXTERIOR
TOP MLDG

CAP MOLDING

INTERIOR TOP MLDG

SOUNDWELL MLDG

SOUNDBOARD

LINER

SIDE

KNEE

BOTTOM
MLDG

BOTTOM

4-2. A section through the side of a typical Italian harpsichord showing the thin side, and external and internal moldings.

angled, and we will see angling on some other German and English instruments too, so this characteristic is certainly not exclusively Italian). Clearly, the Italians did not share the Northern affinity for the more colored and distinctive aspects of harpsichord tone.

Italian jacks normally had two slots for dampers, and their tongues were returned by thin, flat, brass springs. Each set of jacks was supported in the gap by a box guide — a rail about 2″ deep, with slots for each of the jacks. On most 1×8′, 1×4′ harpsichords, nicely turned knobs of metal, wood, or ivory were attached to the ends of the guides, which projected through holes in the cheek. Thus, each register could be turned on or off by reaching around to the exterior of the cheek and pulling or pushing its knob, moving the entire guide slightly to the left or right. (This is, of course, identical to the manner of changing registers found on the Müller, and it will be seen again on Flemish harpsichords.) Outer cases normally had little doors or flaps in that area, so that the stops could be reached without taking the instrument out of its protective box. The cases of single-strung instruments did not have these external knobs — since there was no need to silence the one choir, its register was fixed in place. Undoubtedly, it was intended that 2×8′ harpsichords be played with both sets of strings on, since provision was rarely made for turning a register off (although a player could do so, for tuning purposes, by inserting a finger under the jackrail and pushing on the guide).

Soundboards were usually made of slab-sawn cypress,[27] and 4′ strings were normally hitched to pins merely driven through the board, and reinforced from below only with a drop of glue. Separate, thin 4′ hitchpin rails were used in the rare cases of the combination of a 4′ with a spruce board.[28] Soundboard barring was of two types. In one, three to six bars ran across the width of the board, from spine to bentside, approximately perpendicular to the bridge. Little cutouts were usually made in the bars where they crossed the bridge, assuredly to allow bridge and board to vibrate freely at those points. In the other type a cutoff bar was used, sometimes alone and sometimes with one or more additional bars perpendicular to it. Bridges and nuts were narrow, with parallel sides and a molded top. Usually, the ends of these members terminated with a neatly carved scroll. On the wrestplanks of 1×8′, 1×4′ harpsichords, the two nuts were placed close to each other in the treble, making it impossible to

4-3. Cross section from a sixteenth-century Italian harpsichord. After crossing their nut the 4′ strings pass through holes drilled in the 8′ nut.

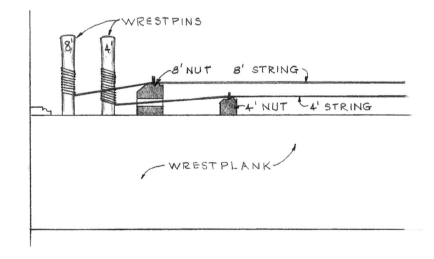

ITALIAN ROSES

The geometric roses in sixteenth-century Italian stringed keyboards are particularly beautiful and seem to have been strongly influenced by Moorish designs. Made of paper, parchment, leather, wood, ivory, or combinations of these materials, they were often at least nominally three-dimensional, with the rim of the rose on top of the soundboard and the body below. These elements were frequently built up from layers of material, and sometimes, in the manner of an upside-down wedding cake, they receded into the soundboard, in tiers of ever-decreasing diameter.[30] Roses in the next century would not be as elaborate or interesting; but that is commensurate with the general decline in the ornateness of harpsichords and virginals after 1600.

4-4a. The elements in this Moorish dome are often found in Italian roses.

4-4b. The ornate rose on this anonymous 1540 virginal owned by Eleanor d'Este shows a distinct Moorish influence. New York, Metropolitan Museum of Art.

4-5a. The geometric rose from this sixteenth-century Flemish virginal is less complex than contemporaneous Italian examples. New York, Metropolitan Museum of Art.

4-5b. Rose from a 1666 Girolamo Zenti harpsichord. Seventeenth-century Italian roses were generally simpler. New York, Metropolitan Museum of Art.

(continued on next page)

(continued from previous page)

It appears that some builders made their own roses, while others purchased them. Denzil Wraight notes that there is one particular rose, quite elaborate, whose pattern appears in instruments by Giovanni Baffo, Giovanni Celestini, Guido Trasuntino, Benedetto Floriani, and some anonymes as well.[31] These builders must have purchased their roses from a specialist—either another maker who crafted particularly nice roses and was willing to sell them, or someone who made a living supplying roses to the trade. Such an artisan could also have supplied roses to the luthiers who made guitars and other plucked-string instruments using glued-in roses. Wraight cites accounts of Cristofori, in which on two occasions he billed Prince Ferdinand's treasury "for a Cypress rose" to put into instruments he was constructing.[32] Finally, Wraight indicates that some of the roses of Dominicus Pisaurensis are identical and not found elsewhere, suggesting that Dominicus might have made his own.

4-6a. The beautiful rose in Guido Trasuntino's 1606 harpsichord was purchased from a craftsman who supplied the same device to other builders. Bologna, Musei Civici d'Arte Antica.

4-6b. A beautiful and complex Italian upside-down wedding-cake rose.

place 4' wrestpins between them. Consequently, after traversing their pins and nut, the 4' strings passed through holes drilled through the 8' nut, and both 4' and 8' strings were wound on two rows of wrestpins between the 8' bridge and the interior face of the nameboard. An elaborate geometric rose was normally placed in the center of the triangular area bounded by the nearest bridge, the spine, and the edge of the gap. Some of the earlier instruments had more than one rose.[29]

The natural keys were usually overlaid with boxwood touch plates, although some of the more sumptuous instruments were given ivory or bone coverings. Sharps were normally made of black-dyed fruitwood, sometimes topped with ebony. Note

4-7. This simple anonymous instrument from ca. 1580 was valued enough to have been rebuilt several times in the seventeenth century. Originally 1×8′, C/E–c³, it is now 2×8′, C,D–d³. London, Royal College of Music, Museum of Instruments. Harpsichord, ca. 1580, RCM 175.

names were often inked on the rear of the natural touch plates, between the sharps, and traces of these markings can still be seen on some instruments. The fronts of the naturals were normally decorated with arcades — thin pieces of wood with semicircles incised into their faces. Two or three lines were scored into the natural touch plates where the heads and tails butted together, and the edges of the plates were rounded up to the first of these lines. Nameboards were removed by pulling straight up; consequently, most Italians did not use namebattens. The builder's cognomen, when present, was inked into the nameboard itself.

VIRGINALS AND SPINETS

The earliest extant virginal (*spinetta,* in Italian),[42] dated 1523, is by the Veronese builder Francesco de Portalupi (Paris, Musée de la Musique); but from iconography described earlier, it is clear that Italians were building them in the previous century as well. Virginal construction was similar to the harpsichord in materials, thin cases, and action parts. During the sixteenth century almost all virginals were inners, normally intended to be placed in a heavier outer case. Like their Flemish counterparts, the only internal bracing was a continuation of the cheeks through the case to the spine. But unlike Flemish virginals, where jacks ran in upper and lower guides, two to a slot, here jacks passed through individual slots in a box guide glued to the bottom of the soundboard. C/E–f³ was the most common compass. Cases were usually five-sided, but six-sided and oblong versions are also found, and there are even some seven-sided virginals, from Milan.[43] As with the harpsichords, the keyboards of these virginals normally projected from the case; but in some examples — again, mostly those from Milan — they were half-recessed, and in a few cases (like the Flemish models), fully recessed. Rather than the extreme left or right locations found in Flemish spinetts and muselar virginals, Italian builders preferred a more central placement for their keyboards. Thus, while Flemish and Northern builders generally pursued more distinctive sounds, Italians seemed to prefer a more neutral tone. Still, the left bridge on most Italian virginals sweeps away from the jacks in the tenor and bass, gradually deepening the plucking points of these registers.

Sixteenth-century Italian builders also made spinets (no relation to the Flemish "spinett virginal"), but seemingly only in octave versions (called *ottavini*). The cases were triangular in shape and, like virginals, also strung perpendicular to the keys; but their bass strings were at the back, rather than the front, of the case. The box guide for the jacks was set in the gap between the wrestplank and the soundboard, and the keyboard projected from the case. Octave spinets were certainly minimal machines for making music, but they seemed to have found particular favor in Italy, where they were sometimes ornately decorated (see Plate 3). Charles Burney, who traveled through Europe in the late eighteenth century surveying the musical scene, reported that these ottavini were still in use then. Burney was puzzled by what he considered to be the ultra-conservatism of Italian keyboard players and thought their instruments were next to useless. He wrote that "Throughout Italy they have generally little octave spinets to accompany singing, sometimes in a triangular form, but more frequently in the shape of our old virginals; of which the keys are so noisy, and the tone so feeble, that more wood is heard than wire."[44]

ITALIAN SCALES

The material with which these instruments were strung (brass or iron), their scales (long or short), and their pitch levels (normal pitch or lower) are all related, and all are points of contention. Most extant sixteenth-century Italians are now disposed 2×8′, with scales of 10–11″, and with GG/BB–c³ (or something similar) keyboards. Lacking the hard-won knowledge we now possess, these characteristics were accepted as original by early post–World War II scholars, and only later was it realized that they had been converted from 1×8′, 1×4′ dispositions by removing the 4′ bridge and nut and adding another set of 8′ strings.[45] It was also discovered their original compasses had been C/E–f³ but had been shifted down a fourth to GG/BB–c³, either by supplying a new keyboard or by rebuilding the old one. Shifting the compass also converted the scale from 13–14″ to 10–11″, allowing brass stringing at normal pitch.[46]

Since the 14″ scale was standard on Ruckers instruments, it was assumed by some that with iron stringing, sixteenth-century Italians originally would have had a similar scale and stand at normal pitch. Thus, when rebuilt with keyboards shifted down by a fourth and with brass stringing, the instruments would still

PULLDOWNS, PEDALBOARDS, AND PEDAL DIVISIONS[33]

When Denzil Wraight examined the 1515 Vincentius harpsichord, he found that it had been changed from a 1×8′ to a 2×8′, the bridge had been moved, the compass changed from (a probable) C/E–f³ to C,D–d³, a new wrestplank and nut had been put in, the scale had been shortened, and the stringing changed from iron to brass. In other words, the instrument had been modernized to accommodate contemporary music, and it is likely that it went through the process more than once (at some point it was shortened by cutting off part of its tail). But Wraight also found holes bored in the bottom of the instrument, under the front portion of the key levers.[34] These holes, drilled at one of the intermediate stages of the rebuilding, were there for pulldowns to pedals.

As early as the mid–fifteenth century Paulus Paulirinus commented that the clavichord could have a pedalboard.[35] Virdung alluded to it again, in 1511, and noted that although clavichords had become larger, pedals could still be added to them.[36] Indeed, to the end of the eighteenth century, many harpsichords, virginals, and clavichords were so equipped, making practice on a nonwinded keyboard instrument possible for organists. As noted earlier, churches were unheated in the winter, and organs required someone to pump the bellows; thus, for an organist, it was vitally important to have some other keyboard on which to practice, and even a small, fretted clavichord was better than nothing. Hence, the practice of fitting pedalboards to stringed keyboard instruments was found everywhere. Pedalboards were almost never mentioned in connection with virginals and harpsichords, but in instrument after instrument, the telltale slot or holes in the bottom board, and the holes in the bottoms for the lowest octave of keys suggest that the practice was widespread.

The usual way of providing a pedal division was to provide pulldowns. Hooks or staples were anchored to the key bottoms in front of the balance pin, and cords fastened to them; or, a hole could simply be drilled through the key and a knotted cord inserted through it. Passing through holes in the instrument's bottom, the cords went through a collector, then fanned out to a small pedalboard normally attached to the base or stand. Pressing a pedal pulled down the front of the attached key, thus sounding the string.

Another, more complex way of providing a pedalboard was to make a completely independent instrument. Although none has survived, there is ample evidence that they existed, particularly in France, where organs with separate pedal divisions were much more common than in Italy or England. For example, the 1686 inventory of the French builder Jean Denis II's workshop lists "a harpsichord with one keyboard . . . with a pedalboard harpsichord."[37] Another mention from 1684,

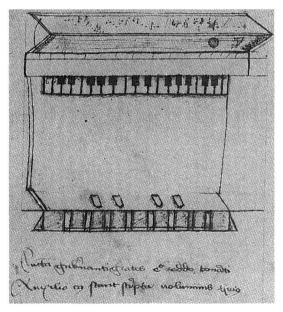

4-8. This illustration of a clavichord with pedals comes from a sketch drawn in the fifteenth century on a copy of a treatise written in 1332. The pedals could either be pulldowns or a separate pedal division. Stuttgart, Württembergische Landesbibliothek.

(continued on next page)

(continued from previous page)
in connection with a pedalboard harpsichord owned by the organist Jean Lebègue, notes that his two-manual harpsichord, part of the ensemble, had been sold.[38] As late as 1758 the German theorist Jacob Adlung talked about such special pedal instruments (*Pedalkörper*), and he described one disposed 2×8′, 1×16′, with overwound strings used for the 16′.[39] With such a pedal division beneath a two-manual harpsichord an organist would certainly be fully equipped.[40] But elsewhere, Adlung noted that the simplest way to get pedal notes is by using pulldowns, and he said that "These are common and for them one need only drive staples or screws into the key levers of the two lowest octaves."[41] A number of twentieth-century builders have made harpsichords with separate pedal divisions.

stand at normal pitch, but with a short scale, and with the apparent compass lowered by a fourth.[47] The opposite view maintains that this ignores evidence for a wide variety of pitches in the sixteenth century, and holds that the long-scaled 1×8′, 1×4′ harpsichords were originally strung in brass, not iron, and sounded a fourth or fifth below normal pitch.[48] If this view is correct, it means that what we have been calling a 1×8′, 1×4′ Italian harpsichord might better be described as an instrument with two choirs of strings, one a fourth or fifth below "normal" pitch, and another a fifth or fourth above. This makes the independent use of the higher-pitched choir much more comprehensible and puts an entirely different light on the ways it might have been used. With such an ensemble of strings, both together would produce a much fuller sound than an 8′ and a 4′ at the higher, normal pitch. Separately, the lower set of strings could be used for works of a grave nature, while the upper set might have been considered more appropriate for sprightlier pieces. Since there are many examples of a sixteenth-century Italian penchant for low sounds — ranging from an affinity for bass voices that could reach down to BB♭, to the extravagant use of low trombones, to the invention of the theorbo as a means of adding low strings to the lute — this view makes sense, and more and more builders and players have come to accept it.[49] On the other hand, most virginals do seem to have been intended for iron stringing at normal pitch.[50]

DECORATION

The Italian harpsichord described so far was a much more conventional reflection of Renaissance ideals than the few surviving Flemish instruments. Next to marbled cases, printed papers, decorated soundboards, and moralizing mottoes, an Italian harpsichord, with its graceful shape, unadorned cypress case, and delicate moldings, embodied restrained dignity.[62] True,

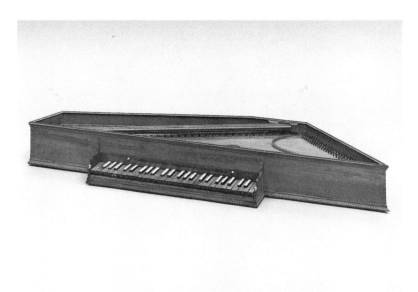

4-9a. Most Italian virginals looked like this 1574 example by Joseph Salodiensis: a plain, unadorned cypress case, strengthened and enlivened by cypress moldings. The soundboard is also cypress. The natural touch plates are boxwood, and the blackened pearwood sharps are capped with ivory (but may originally have been topped with ebony). The rose is made of parchment. Despite the simplicity, its shape, projecting keyboard, complex moldings, and scroll-sawn cheeks give it an elegant appearance. Museum of Fine Arts, Boston. Reproduced with permission. © 2000 Museum of Fine Arts, Boston.

with an asymmetrical configuration and foreshortened bass strings, no harpsichord could reflect ideal concepts of balance and harmony; but with its deep, gracefully curved, beautifully proportioned bentside and pleasing width-to-length ratio, the Italian instrument was a tangible abstraction of Pythagorean principles, and its complex moldings, scroll-sawn cheeks, and other three-dimensional features recalled the balanced shapes of classical architecture. Rather than a soundboard painting, a Gothic- or Moorish-derived geometric rose provided a visual focal point. Of course, all of this was surrounded by an outer case and lid, usually painted but sometimes covered with leather or fabric. Most outers were cruder than the instrument itself, and decorated in a less than tasteful manner; but others, undoubtedly meant for the wealthy, were handsomely appointed. The instruments themselves were unfailingly elegant.

Legends of classical antiquity involving music, or characters associated with music, were favorite subjects for paintings on lids and sometimes on the instruments themselves. A lovingly decorated 1593 Giovanni Celestini virginal (London, Royal College of Music) has three cartouches containing miniatures on the nameboard: the contest of Pan and Apollo, Orpheus serenading the beasts (a favorite, perhaps because it gave artists the opportunity to paint a variety of animals), and Apollo pursuing Daphne. Apollo is flaying Marsyas on the lid of an undated, anonymous virginal (Milan, Museo degli Strumenti Musicali), and Apollo and the muses (another favorite, perhaps because it gave artists the opportunity to paint nubile women in various stages of undress) is found in a cartouche on the lid of a

1574 Giovanni Antonio Baffo (London, Victoria and Albert Museum). Arion and the dolphins, another popular motif, can be seen on the lid of the anonymous, ornate triangular octave spinet (London, Victoria and Albert) pictured in Plate 3. A nude Venus of Rubenesque proportions, with her son Cupid, graces the lid of a 1531 harpsichord by Alessandro Trasuntino (London, Royal College of Music). Biblical scenes were also used, but were not as common.[63] More mundane paintings were simply landscapes or pastoral scenes; others were variations on grotesques, such as the lid of the 1574 Giovanni Antonio Baffo. External case decoration ranged from solid colors to garlands of flowers, dancing putti, grotesques, vine patterns, and moresques. Although the best Italian artists rarely, if ever, seem to have painted harpsichord lids, their work was sometimes copied or adapted by lesser lights. The ultimate source of the "Apollo and the Muses" on the 1574 Baffo, for example, was a ca. 1511 painting by Raphael.[64]

Describing the decoration of outer cases is problematical, since they were frequently redecorated, sometimes many times over, and often were not original to the instrument. It is also possible that some cases were not painted at all, receiving their decoration years later. The same is true of stands, the most ephemeral aspect of harpsichords. Nevertheless, the typical Italian stand usually consisted of two parts: a front bench with two legs (often lathe-turned), connected by a stretcher, with a platform upon which the front of the instrument rested; and sup-

4-9b. The outer case (but not the stand) of the 1574 Salodiensis virginal is thought to be original, although much of its painted decoration, including the dancing putti on the front faces, is modern. Museum of Fine Arts, Boston. Reproduced with permission. © 2000 Museum of Fine Arts, Boston. All rights reserved.

porting the rear, a pedestal with one leg and a smaller platform. Normally, there was no connection between the two sections. Trestle stands were also sometimes used.

VENICE AND THE TRADITION OF OPULENCE

The major centers of harpsichord building in sixteenth-century Italy were in the North. Milan and nearby Brescia had active builders who left a meaningful body of work, and other cities also had harpsichord builders, but more than half the instruments extant from that epoch were made in Venice, which seems to have been the undisputed leader in the production of harpsichords and virginals.

If the most influential city in Italy was Rome, the most formidable was Venice, known as the "queen of the seas." As a mercantile power its mighty port was the conduit for continuous trade between the Orient and Western Europe. Strong in arms, Venice's imposing naval presence played a critical role in the battle of Lepanto, a famous naval engagement of 1571 in which the heretofore invincible Turkish fleet was destroyed,[65] and the superiority of its vaunted infantry has already been mentioned in connection with the battle of Marignano. Commercially vigorous, it was a cultural crossroads, enriched by a veneer of Eastern exotica dating back to Marco Polo's voyage to Beijing in 1275. Removed from Rome by geography and custom, Venice followed its own path and experienced a glorious sixteenth-century golden age.[66]

The city was as rich in cultural pursuits as it was in trade and arms. Along with nearby Padua, it was home to a group of influential German lute makers. Its school of painting, which emphasized light and color over line and sculptural effects, was practiced by artists such as Titian (ca. 1488–1576) and Tintoretto (1518–94). Important churches by Andrea Palladio (1508–80), the most influential architect of the cinquecento, left their mark on the municipality. The printer Ottaviano Petrucci (1466–1539) opened his shop in Venice and in 1501 produced the *Odhecaton,* the first printed collection of part songs. The greatest musicians in Europe were employed at the basilica of St. Mark's, including the Netherlanders Adrian Willaert (ca. 1490–1562) and Cipriano de Rore (ca. 1516–65), native Italians Gioseffo Zarlino (1517–90) and Andrea Gabrieli (ca. 1533–86), and Andrea's illustrious nephew, Giovanni Gabrieli (ca. 1553–1612).

Like the paintings of Titian and Tintoretto, the music of the famed Venetian school, with its massed polychoral effects involving voices and instruments, emphasized the coloristic elements of late Renaissance musical style. This exuberant fascination for

---

ITALIAN HARPSICHORDS AND THEIR "SPECIOUS UNIFORMITY"

"The Specious Uniformity of Italian Harpsichords" was the title of a 1971 article by John Barnes, in which the author put to rest the notion, hitherto held by post–World War II historians, that the Italian harpsichord sprang forth fully formed, exhibiting little in the way of evolutionary change from the sixteenth through the eighteenth centuries.[57] The article contradicted Frank Hubbard, who was persuaded that he saw a "degree of standardization" in Italian instruments not found in the Flemish.[58] Raymond Russell's chapter on Italian harpsichords conveys the same understanding as Hubbard: he saw two compasses for Italian instruments, GG/BB–c^3 and C/E–f^3; but he failed to realize that the presence of a keyboard with the lower compass in an earlier instrument most likely indicated that it originally had the higher range but had been transformed through a rebuilding process.[59] Hubbard, Russell, and others had been misled by the continuous, thorough, and frequently quite skillful modernizing to which Italian harpsichords were subjected, often over and over again for hundreds of years, to extend their useful life. What appeared to be uniformity was indeed specious, imposed on the instruments through centuries of changing scales, stringing, pitch standards, compasses, and materials. When it was realized that 1×8′, 1×4′ dispositions were reconstituted into 2×8′s with modified compasses, it became easier to understand why all Italian harpsichords appeared to have been cut from the same cloth.[60]

Nevertheless, Italian harpsichords did not go through a Ruckers-inspired upheaval in design as Northern instruments did; hence, there is a kernel of truth in the original assumption that Italian instruments changed little over the years. Essentially, Italians makers built their harpsichords with one manual and, beginning with the seventeenth century, with a 2×8′ disposition. Earlier instruments, disposed 1×8′, 1×4′ or infrequently 1×8′, were rebuilt into 2×8′s. Although there are exceptions, builders south of the Alps showed little interest in exploiting the resources of two keyboards, or the common Northern disposition of 2×8′, 1×4′. Writing in a French *encyclopédie* at the end of the eighteenth century, one observer noted that "The Italians did not profit by the new progress of the harpsichord and continued to make theirs with two unisons and one keyboard."[61]

4-10. Orpheus serenading the beasts, on the nameboard of a 1593 virginal by Giovanni Celestini. In common with many instruments in the opulent style, the natural touch plates are ivory, and the sharps are ebony or some blackened wood. London, Royal College of Music, Museum of Instruments. Virginal, Giovanni Celestini, Venice, 1593, RCM 176.

color is sometimes seen in harpsichords as well, and there is no question that some of the most intricately decorated instruments produced in the sixteenth century originated in Venice and nearby Padua. Venetian roses are among the most elaborate found in Italy. Their builders used more veneer, inlays, marquetry, parquetry, ivory, ebony, mother-of-pearl, paint, and sculptural elements than any other builders except for some from Milan; in fact, outside of Venice, Padua, Milan, and Brescia, applied substances other than moldings are conspicuously absent from Italian harpsichords.

The name Trasuntino must have been an honored one among sixteenth-century builders. There seem to have been four of them—Alessandro (ca. 1485–ca. 1545, worked in Venice), Giovanni Francesco (if he existed, fl. 1532, worked in Naples), Bernardinus de (fl. 1574, location unknown), and Guido (or Vido or Vito, fl. ca. 1522, worked in Venice). What the relationship was between them—or if they were related at all, or even if they were all real—is unknown. Giovanni has only one extant virginal, which may not have been made by him;[67] hence, Giovanni may never have existed. The 1531 harpsichord by Alessandro (London, Royal College of Music; see Illustration 4–12) is known for the nude Venus painted on the lid of its outer case; but more to the point, its soundwell, cheeks, nameboard, and jackrail are embellished with complex painted and inlaid moresque flatwork. A profusion of ivory studs outline the instrument, and the soundboard contains three ornate roses. The naturals are of ivory and the sharps of ebony or a black-dyed wood. Clearly, this instrument received decoration where it would be seen, since the outer surfaces of the inner case, normally concealed, are unadorned except for the usual moldings. Alessandro is survived by at least two other harpsichords (1530, Italy, private collection; 1538, Brussels, Musée Instrumental), and perhaps a few others, including a 1604 virginal (Halle, Händel-Haus). The late date of this last, however, makes it suspect, since Alessandro would have to have been in his nineties when it was built.

Two ornate instruments are signed by Guido. The older, a 1571[68] harpsichord (Milan, Museo degli Strumenti Musicali), is covered with a rich combination of tooled leather and contrasting woods in the soundwell and on the nameboard, cheeks, and jackrail. The natural keys are inlaid with ebony, the sharps are topped with ivory, and the cheek pieces are carved. Although the case decor differs strikingly from Alessandro's instrument, it is the same surfaces — those not covered by the outer case — that received the decoration. However, the earlier 1560 harpsichord (Berlin, Staatliches Institut für Musikforschung, seen in Plate 7) has a different scheme. It is also outlined in ivory studs, but this time the soundwell is undecorated; instead, the exterior of the inner case is painted in eye-catching red, green, black, and gold moresque patterns. The nameboard, cheeks, and jackrail are similarly treated, and natural touch plates of ivory contrast with inlaid rosewood sharps. This is almost a reversal of the decorative scheme of Guido's 1571 and Alessandro's 1531 harpsichords and suggests that the 1560 may have been designed to

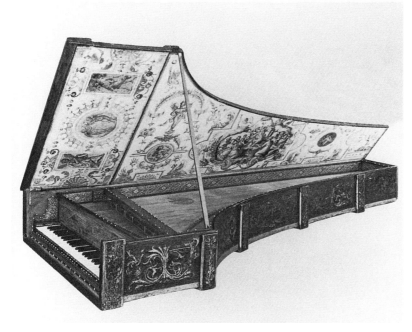

4-11. The visible surfaces of the inner case of this 1574 Giovanni Antonio Baffo are inlaid with rosewood, boxwood, and ebony. The cartouche on the lid, with its Apollo and the Muses, is surrounded by grotesques. London, Victoria and Albert Museum.

be removed from its outer case when played, or even that it was never intended to be housed in a protective case at all.[69] But it is also possible that the decoration was placed where it would not normally be seen because Alfonso d'Este II, Duke of Ferrara, for whom the instrument was made, was willing to pay for—and might even have delighted in—the hidden ostentation. Whatever the scheme, both instruments were surely built for people of wealth.[70]

Guido was also the maker of an extraordinary harpsichord, a single-strung *archicembalo* dated 1606 (Bologna, Museo Civico Medievale) whose thirty-one notes to the octave ostensibly allowed the performer to play in the diatonic, chromatic, and enharmonic genera described by the fourth-century B.C. Greek theorist Aristoxenus. Its four-octave keyboard is a marvel, with naturals and accidentals arranged in tiers, with each key lever describing a graceful curved path to its distal end, there to be met perpendicularly by its jack. On the nameboard, Guido called it a *clavemusicum omnitonum.*[71]

There may be as many as four more instruments by this builder, but except for a 1601 virginal (Paris, Musée de la Musique) they are in private collections and little is known about them.

4-12. This 1531 inner-outer by Alessandro Trasuntino is decorated with moresque patterns, closely spaced ivory studs, and three roses; but the focus of attention is the nude Venus on the lid. London, Royal College of Music, Museum of Instruments. Harpsichord, Alessandro Trasuntino, Venice, 1531, RCM 2.

A handsome 1561 harpsichord (Munich, Deutsches Museum) by Franciscus Patavinus (fl. 1527–62) is very long, nearly 8′, one of the low-pitched instruments discussed earlier. Although not as ornate as some of the instruments described so far, its black and white contrasts are nonetheless striking. The case is veneered in ebony, with ebony-ivory-ebony sandwiches for cheek brackets. The inside layer of each cheek is fret-carved, so that one sees the ebony on an ivory ground. Black and white vine patterns surround the soundwell, and four roses grace the cypress soundboard.[83] The natural touch plates are mother-of-pearl, and the sharps are ebony. As a foil to the pervasive black and white, the wrestpins were gilded, undoubtedly to match the warm tones of the brass strings. Franciscus signed his instrument *Francisci Patavini Dicti Ongaro,*

Flemish	Italian
Thin case, then thick	Thin case
With thick case, cut-in moldings	Finely cut applied moldings
With thick case, no suggestion of inner-outer	Inner-outer; later, false inner-outer
Poplar the common case wood	Cypress the common case wood
Upper and lower braces	Knees, diagonal struts, bottom braces
Sides sit on the bottom	Bottom overlaps sides
Bentside resembles a section of a parabola	Bentside is Pythagorean for most of its length
Two-piece bottom	One-piece bottom
Soundboards of spruce or fir	Soundboards of spruce, fir, or cypress
1×8′, 1×4′	1×8′, 1×4′; later, 2×8′
Upper and lower guides	Box guides
Registers project through cheek	Registers project through cheek
Gap parallel to nameboard	Gap sometimes parallel, sometimes angles away from nameboard
Bridges and nuts basically triangular	Bridges and nuts have parallel sides with a molded top
Bass portion of the bridge is curved	Bass portion of the bridge is mitered
Rising scale for most of century	Pythagorean scale down to c, then Pythagorean scale down to c′
14″ scale, strung in iron	14″ probably strung in iron, but possibly brass
Sounded at normal pitch	Probably sounded at many pitches
Inset keyboard	Projecting keyboard
Painted case, decorated soundboard	Natural wood, no soundboard decoration
Geometric rose for most of century; cast, gilded metal at end of century	Geometric rose based on Gothic and Moorish designs

indicating that he was called "the Hungarian," although he was from Pavia and worked in Venice. Either he was born in Hungary, or he came from a Hungarian lineage, and once again, one wonders if a foreign origin was not considered desirable for a builder. Franciscus is also survived by two virginals, a 1527 (Brussels, Musée Instrumental) and a 1552 (Venice, Conservatorio Benedetto Marcello).

Two harpsichords by Giovanni Antonio Baffo (fl. 1570–81) are decorated in one of the two previously described patterns. The soundwell, nameboard, jackrail, and scrolled cheeks of a 1574 are veneered in rosewood, inlaid with boxwood and ebony, and covered with gilded arabesques. Closely spaced ivory studs dot the rosewood moldings (see Illustration 4-11). Unfortunately, long after it was built, almost 10″ were cut from its tail, perhaps because it was too long for a wall against which it stood. This instrument has a soundboard extending over the gap to the nameboard, with a narrow wrestplank at the front

HARPSICHORDS WITH MORE THAN TWELVE NOTES TO THE OCTAVE

Prior to the Renaissance, fifths and octaves were considered to be the building blocks of music, and thirds and sixths were regarded as unstable combinations that required resolution to those consonances. This was not merely a philosophical distinction, since it is almost certain that before the end of the fifteenth century most keyboard instruments were tuned according to Pythagorean principles, by pure, beatless fifths and octaves. In such a tuning, many of the thirds and sixths were even wider than they are in equal temperament. Since they beat harshly, they were considered dissonances (though mild ones). The major problem with Pythagorean tuning, however, is that the gamut is not a closed system, and a cycle of perfect fifths will always end up with a bit left over, about a quarter of a semitone, called a "Pythagorean comma." Hence, an octave set by tuning pure fifths and octaves will contain a wildly dissonant interval. In practice, this comma was placed where it would be least offensive — say, B–F♯ — and it was simply avoided.

This system experienced a major stylistic transformation in the Renaissance. Now thirds and sixths were recognized as consonances, albeit imperfect ones, and played a much more important role in the musical fabric. As a consequence, a new method of tuning was adopted in which fifths were tempered: that is, tuned a little less than perfect, so that thirds could be tuned pure. The most commonly used of these temperaments was *quarter-comma meantone*, or simply *meantone*, which prevailed during the sixteenth century and for a good deal of the seventeenth as well.[72] The fifths were somewhat dissonant, but in triadic playing the purity of beatless thirds made so strong an impact that the beating of less-than-perfect fifths was scarcely noticed. Like every temperament, this one also had musical consequences. For one thing, the accidentals were not enharmonic; that is, the key between F and G could serve as either F♯ or G♭, but not as both (the five accidentals were normally tuned to C♯, E♭, F♯, G♯, and B♭). For another, triads involving "missing" accidentals, such as the D♯ (which would be tuned E♭) in a B-major triad were so dissonant as to be useless for normal purposes.

This system worked well as long as three restrictions were observed: first, composers (and, one assumes, improvisers) avoided forbidden triads. Rather than a problem, this was simply viewed as a constraint to be worked around; and if a B-major triad, for example, was absolutely indispensable to a piece, the accidental in each octave normally tuned to E♭ could easily be retuned to the needed D♯. The second restriction was that the music could not modulate, since traversing the circle of fifths inevitably would lead to keys involving forbidden triads. Again, this did not present difficulties, since the system of keys and the concept of functional tonality — the tonal milieu in which modulation takes place — was not fully developed until well into the seventeenth century[73] (when, of course, it did become a problem). Finally, a piece could ask for either the flat or sharp version of an accidental — say, A♭ rather than G♯ — but not both.

In practice, these stratagems were adequate for harpsichord solos, and when confronted with the need to transpose, perhaps in order to accompany a singer or an instrument at something other than normal pitch level, one could either retune an accidental or two, or use an instrument supplied with extra keys in the form of split sharps. Retuning a few notes on the fly was a simple enough process on the harpsichord, annoying though it might be; but on the organ, of course, it was not possible. Hence, starting in the fifteenth century, Italian organs occasionally were supplied with one or two additional notes to the octave, usually a D♯ and/or an A♭. Although the need was not as crucial, harpsichords nevertheless followed suit after a while.[74] Accordingly, plucked instruments with thirteen or fourteen notes to the octave, and even a few more, were not uncommon in the sixteenth century.[75] Hardly any such instruments exist today; most were rebuilt into harpsichords and virginals with conventional keyboards. Curiously, almost all such instruments were virginals, perhaps intended for ensemble playing and accompaniment, rather than solos. In a large-scale piece such as an opera or oratorio, retuning accidentals would not have been feasible, and the alternate notes would have been useful.[76]

A second type of split-key instrument, sometimes called the *cimbalo cromatico*, carried the notion of providing alternate accidentals even farther.[77] Split notes were supplied for all the

(continued on next page)

(continued from previous page)

accidentals, along with extra keys between B–C and E–F, for B♯ and E♯. With seven extra accidentals, the number of notes per octave totaled nineteen. The logic behind such instruments was not so much that of ease of transposition, although that certainly must still have been a consideration, but of providing a keyboard that could overcome the restrictions of meantone temperament. It allowed an instrument of fixed pitch to play in the same manner in which voices could sing the chromatic madrigals of de Rore, Luzzasco Luzzaschi (ca. 1545–1607), and Carlo Gesualdo (ca. 1561–1613), pieces in which all triads were considered useable (voices, which had no pitch restrictions, were of course able to make the necessary minute adjustments for pure thirds and fifths). Thus, like voices, a cimbalo cromatico could play a C♯-major triad as in-tune as a C-major triad (although both chords would still have impure fifths). In addition, both the sharp and flat versions of any accidental could be called for in the same piece.[78] Nineteen-note-per-octave instruments must have been somewhat common in Italy: music written for them by Asciono Mayone (ca. 1565–1627), Giovanni Maria Trabaci (ca. 1580–1647), Gioanpietro del Buono (fl. 1641), and Adriano Banchieri (1568–1634) still exists.[79] All the extant "chromatic harpsichords" were rebuilt into conventional instruments long ago; but from ca. 1550 to the middle of the next century, they provided the slithery sounds demanded by those impatient with meantone temperament's restrictions.

There was a third type of split-key harpsichord, called the *arcicembalo* or *archicembalo*, with thirty-six notes to the octave and probably inspired more by the humanistic application of classical Greek music theory than by any concerns for transposition or chromaticism. Such an instrument was described and possibly built by the composer and theorist Nicola Vicentino (1511–ca. 1576).[80] Vicentino, who had written a book of madrigals for five voices that called for the microtone tunings of the Greek genera, was challenged to a debate on the practice by a respected colleague and was judged to have lost. To defend himself, Vicentino wrote his *L'antica musica ridotta alla moderna prattica* (Rome, 1555), in which he explained how the ideas of Greek music theory could be applied to modern (that is, sixteenth-century) music. His archicembalo was a harpsichord capable of producing Aristoxenus's diatonic, chromatic, and enharmonic genera[81] and hence provided sonic "proof" of his theories.

Guido Trasuntino built his 1606 thirty-one-note-per-octave version in *clavemusicum omnitonum* in 1606 for Camillo Gonzaga, count of Novellara, whose name appears on the instrument along with the information that it was intended for the playing of the three genera. Each accidental is represented by four keys, plus sharp and flat keys between B–C and E–F. Even thirty-one keys were not enough to close the system so that all chords could be played in just intonation, with pure fifths as well as thirds, but it comes fairly close.[82] Truly, the world of the archicembalo was a narrow one; nevertheless, it did occupy the efforts of a few Italian makers and composers who hoped to return the Greek genera to what they perceived as their previously exalted position.

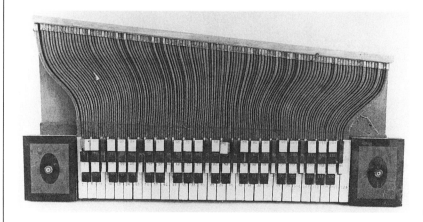

4-13. The keyboard of Guido Trasuntino's 1606 archicembalo. This four-octave keyboard with thirty-one notes to the octave could not have been easy to construct. Bologna, Musei Civici d'Arte Antica.

and slots for the jacks cut through the soundboard — a hollow wrestplank.[84] The second Baffo, a 1579 (Paris, Musée de la Musique) is adorned in the same areas, but in intricately tooled and tinted leather. The compass of the 1574 was originally the usual sixteenth-century $C/E–f^3$, but that of the 1579 went up to c^4, a quite unusual five-octave fifty-seven-note range. Both instruments have long scales, indicating the possibility of pitch levels a fourth or fifth below normal pitch.[85]

Like Trasuntino, mystery surrounds the Venetian master Dominicus Pisaurensis (fl. 1533–75). The confusion begins with his name: are Dom*i*nicus Pisaurensis, Dom*æ*nicus Pisaurensis, Dom*i*nicus Venetus, and Dom*æ*nicus Venetus one and the same, or are they two, three, or even four different people?[86] In Italy the builder's second name, if not a patronymic, usually referred to the city of his birth; but it was sometimes used to indicate the place in which he worked, so it is possible he could change his signature from time to time, depending on which geographical element of his life — his place of birth or of work — he wished to emphasize.[87] One wonders why Dominic, who usually signed his harpsichords [*born in*] *Pesaro* would sign some instruments Dominic [*works in*] *Venice,* but the lack of further evidence makes it impossible to draw any conclusions. Almost twenty-eight harpsichords, virginals, and clavichords bear his name, although Wraight maintains that only fifteen can reliably be ascribed to him;[88] but either number represents a remarkable survival rate, exceeding that of any other Italian maker at any time.

Dominicus made some unusual instruments. He is particularly famous for the 1548 chromatic harpsichord (which no longer exits) with twenty-four notes to the octave he built for Gioseffo Zarlino, theorist and choir conductor at Saint Mark's.[89] A 1533 harpsichord (Leipzig, Musikinstrumenten-Museum der Universität Leipzig), like the 1574 Baffo, has a hollow wrestplank, and this seems to be the first appearance of that feature. Two of Dominicus's survivors are octave harpsichords, a 1543 (Paris, Musée de la Musique) and a 1546 (Vienna, Kunsthistorisches Mu-

4-14. Veneered in ebony and nearly 8′ long, the 1561 Patavinus harpsichord is an imposing study in black and white. Munich, Deutsches Museum.

seum), both disposed 2×4′. Dominicus was also one of the earliest builders we know of to make a 2×8′ harpsichord (Nice, private ownership), a disposition that would become the normal one in Italy in the next century.[90] Other than his jack-action instruments, Dominicus is survived by an extremely important artifact from 1543: the earliest-known signed and dated clavichord (Leipzig, Musikinstrumenten-Museum der Universität Leipzig), a thin-case pentagonal inner with projecting keyboard. Visually, none of Dominicus's instruments equal the more sumptuous examples discussed here. Nevertheless, it is worth remembering that except for a select group of ornate instruments produced primarily for rich courts, most Italian harpsichords looked very much like those of this builder. They were viewed as excellent music-making devices, rather than as musical objects made primarily to captivate the eye.

At least three virginals are signed Dominicus (or Domenicus) Venetus, and a fourth is attributed to him. Three are oblong in shape, with recessed keyboards, rare in Italian instruments. The earliest, dated 1556 (New Haven, Yale Collection), is a thin-case instrument,[91] but two others, a 1562 (Hamburg, private collection) and a 1566 (Nuremberg, Germanisches National Museum) are both early examples of false inner-outers.[92]

Harpsichords appear in many seventeenth- and eighteenth-century paintings, but almost never with an indication of the name of the maker. Such is not the case with Giovanni Celestini, one of the best-known Venetian builders. He and one of his instruments were immortalized by the artist Saverio della Rosa,

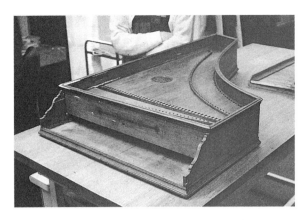

4-16. The 1543 Pisaurensis octave harpsichord in the conservation atelier of the Musée de la Musique in Paris. A portion of the keyboard can be seen on the right. Paris, Musée de la Musique.

4-17. The earliest extant clavichord, dated 1543, by Pisaurensis. Leipzig, Musikinstrumenten-Museum der Universität Leipzig.

in a 1770 painting showing a youthful Mozart seated at the keyboard of a harpsichord bearing the legend *Joannes Celestini Veneti MDLXXIII.* Unfortunately, that instrument is not among the three extant Celestinis, two of which (1596, Toronto, Royal Ontario Museum; 1608, Hamburg, Museum für Kunst und Gewerbe) show some interesting characteristics. Both have 2×8′ dispositions and C/E–f³ compasses. Shorter than normal Italians, and with shorter scales, they were designed to sound a minor third or so above normal pitch.[93] Most unusual, however, is the strange configuration of the back ends of their key levers, which Wraight calls "S-shaped."[94] The unison strings of 2×8′ harpsichords are spaced apart, so that a jack can fit between them. Each of the unison strings is close to its half-step neighbor, thus creating the appearance of wide and narrow pairs. Ordinarily, both jacks of a unison (a wide pair) sit on the end of the same key lever, one behind the other and facing in opposite directions: the jack pointing right plucks the shorter of the two strings, while the one facing left plucks the longer. The difference in length between the strings of a unison pair is quite small in the extreme treble, where the bridge steeply curves toward the cheek; but in the tenor, the differences can be as much as several inches. Hence, the longer of the two unisons will be at a noticeably greater tension than the shorter; and since one is longer than the other, and the plectra of the two jacks are only about ¾″ apart, the ratio of length to plucking point will also differ. All these factors conspire to ensure that the tone quality of the two strings will differ somewhat. But by going to the trouble of sawing the ends of his keys in an "S shape," Celestini could tune his *close* pairs as unisons, thereby minimizing the tonal distinction between the two strings.[95] This is yet another indication of the concern with which Italian builders (and presumably, players, composers, and listeners) viewed the purity of harpsichord sound. Northern makers, on the other hand, seemed to take virtually an opposite view, both isolating and combining the various colors of plucked strings.

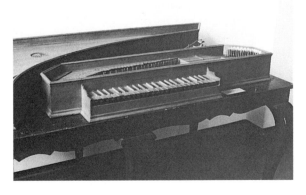

4-18. A 1566 virginal by Dominicus Venetus. A fully inset keyboard is rare among Italian virginals. New Haven, Yale University Collection of Musical Instruments.

This same concern for purity of sound is seen in yet another of Celestini's instruments, a 1610 oblong virginal (Brussels, Musée Instrumental) that the builder called an *arci spineta* and that Wraight describes as a harpsichord in virginal form.[96] The strings are spaced at equal intervals, as they would be on a single-strung harpsichord, and the jacks all face in the same direction. To accomplish this, Celestini had to forgo placing his strings in alternating close and wide pairs, a space-saving device on virginals. This resulted in a wider instrument, but each string was as close as possible to its Pythagorean correctness. A 1594 Celestini virginal (Hamburg, Museum für Kunst und Gewerbe), similar in concept to the 1610, has two strings per note.[97] The builder Donatus Undeus (fl. 1590–1622), from nearby Bergamo, also built a 2×8′ virginal, dated 1623 (Brussels, Musée Instrumental), and a 1569 virginal by Annibale dei Rossi (Hamburg, Museum für Kunst und Gewerbe) is another.

Examples of small, highly decorated home instruments are found among the surviving virginals of Celestini. The exterior of his 1587 (Hamburg, private collection) with fully recessed keyboard — one of the first extant Italian virginals in oblong shape — is covered with elaborate marquetry. The 1593 (London, Royal College of Music), a true inner-outer, pentagonal in shape, with a half-recessed keyboard, displays a colorful moresque treatment involving various woods, paint, mother-of-pearl, and gold (see Illustration 4-10).[100] The soundwell, keywell, and cheeks of the 1594 2×8′ pentagonal inner-outer discussed above (also with a half-recessed keyboard) were given gold arabesques on a black ground. The entire face of the case received the same treatment, indicating that the front of its outer case (now miss-

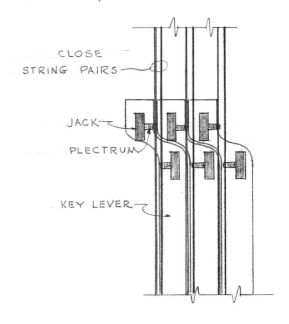

4-19. By cutting the end of his keys in an "S shape," Giovanni Celestini made it possible for the jacks to pluck close pairs, thus minimizing the timbral differences between unison strings.

CLOSE STRING PAIRS

JACK

PLECTRUM

KEY LEVER

ing) was probably meant to open completely when it was played.

This is almost certainly what was intended with the anonymous ca. 1570 instrument known as "Queen Elizabeth's virginal" (London, Victoria and Albert Museum), whose exterior is sumptuously enriched with red, blue, and gold arabesque decoration. It retains an outer case, which, although of a later date, may well be a copy of the original. It opens completely in front, so that all the decorated surfaces of the inner instrument are visible.[101] A similar decorative style is found on a 1571 virginal (Leipzig, Musikinstrumenten-Museum der Universität Leipzig) by Benedetto Floriani (fl. 1568–72). The case walls are made of ebony or some ebonized wood,[102] with gold arabesque patterns laid on the soundwell, jackrail, cheeks, nameboard, and front faces. A nearly identical treatment of gold on ebony is found on a 1568 virginal (London, Victoria and Albert Museum) by Marco Jadra (fl. 1552–68), but it is suspected that it might have been built by someone else, and that Jadra, whose place of business is as yet obscure, was merely a dealer.[103]

2×8′ VIRGINALS

In an interesting quirk of fate, both the 1569 Rossi and the 1594 Celestini virginals are in Hamburg's Museum für Kunst und Gewerbe. Both are ornate (although the front faces of the Celestini are undecorated, suggesting that it was intended to be covered by an outer case), with arabesque decoration on ebonized wood, two roses, and half-recessed keyboards. However, the really intriguing commonality is not their decoration, but their dispositions. These are two of the three known extant 2×8′ virginals.[98]

Not without good reason, virginals are normally single strung. Because the strings are perpendicular to the keys, the front-to-back dimension of the case should be as narrow as possible, since the keys that operate on the treble strings, at the top right, are much longer than those serving the bass strings, at the bottom left. Double-strung virginals must have wider cases, with greater discrepancies in the length of bass and treble keys. Then the difference in touch between highest and lowest keys could become troublesome.

On the Celestini instrument both sets of jacks sit on little ramps mounted on the ends of the keys. When the keyboard is pulled forward, the jacks in the back slide down the ramp, and their plectra are unable to reach the strings when the key is struck; but Wraight thinks that this refinement was a later addition, and that the instrument was originally intended to sound 2×8′ all the time.[99]

Paralleling the fortunes of Venice itself, the sixteenth century was its heyday for harpsichord building, and it is not at all clear why the city's preeminence in that craft declined. Instruments continued to be built there, no doubt of high quality; but while the names of fifteen Venetian builders survive from the 1500s, only five are known to us from the 1600s, and a mere six from the following century.[104] And none have reputations equaling those of Dominicus, Baffo, Floriani, and Trasuntino.

MILAN

Milan also had a rich history of instrument building in the cinquecento (Brescia, twenty-five miles to the east, is considered to

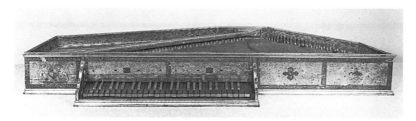

4-20. The anonymous ca. 1570 instrument known as "Queen Elizabeth's virginal." London, Victoria and Albert Museum.

have been part of Milan's artistic and creative orbit). Dominated by the Visconti family until 1477, and the Sforzas for most of the next century, it was one of Italy's greatest city-states. Like the rest of the peninsula, it was involved in the Italian Wars and from 1535 on was ruled by Spain; but that seems to have affected neither the artistic climate of the city nor the beautiful instruments that flowed from the workshops of its builders.

Annibale dei Rossi (fl. 1542–77) and his son Ferrante (fl. 1580–97) were prominent Milanese makers, with a half dozen virginals extant from the former and three from the latter. Most of these are apparently normal, plain-looking examples, such as Annibale's 1542 (St. Paul, Minn., Schubert Club), his first surviving instrument, and the 1597 (Boston, private ownership), his last. However, like the 1594 Celestini and the two Donatus instruments, Annibale's 1569 (Hamburg, Museum für Kunst und Gewerbe) is another rare 2×8′ virginal.

Annibale's other remaining virginals are among the most ornate known.[105] All the decoration on the soundwell, name-board, and cheeks of his 1555 vir-

4-21. A detail of the carving of the cheek piece of Annibale dei Rossi's 1555 virginal. London, Victoria and Albert Museum.

ginal with half-recessed keyboard (London, Victoria and Albert Museum) consists of relief carving. A sumptuous geometric rose of carved wood is centered in the soundboard. Figures carved in the round—one holding a lute and the other a *lira da braccio*—grace the cheeks, which in turn are carved with trophies of musical instruments. At the bass end of the case the jackrail is captured in the mouth of a ferocious serpent or dragon. The carving, beautifully done in miniature, imparts an effect of restrained richness. It is also quite Italian in character, unlikely to be found in any other tradition.[106]

As striking as Rossi's 1555 work

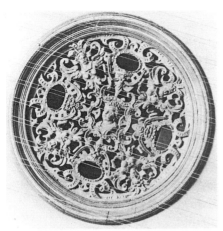

4-22. The rose of the 1577 Rossi virginal. London, Victoria and Albert Museum.

is, however, for sheer ostentation even it pales before his 1577 heptagonal opus (also London, Victoria and Albert Museum), whose soundwell, keywell, and exterior front face are covered with delicate cypress moldings framing filigreed ivory escutcheons containing precious jewels, all set against the ebony of the case walls.[107] The carved geometric rose, though relating to neither Gothic nor Moorish motifs, is one of the most exquisite examples to be found on an Italian instrument. A lion's head, guided by a putto, receives the bass end of the jackrail into its mouth. The natural touch plates of its half-recessed keyboard are covered with a colorful variety of stones, each edged in ivory. The sharps, also ivory-trimmed, are covered with lapis lazuli. Superbly carved figurines stand guard at the cheeks: a mother and child at one end, and a man at the other, regard each other across the expanse of the keyboard. The effect is of such overwhelming richness that one forgets the object also has a musical purpose. Rossi's jeweled virginal (see Plate 8) needs to be seen to be appreciated.

A final example of this extravagant style is an elaborate anonymous Milanese virginal (New York, Metropolitan Museum) made in 1540 for Eleanor d'Este, the duchess of Urbino. Its exterior and interior surfaces are covered with delicate fretwork, inlays of ebony and ivory, mother-of-pearl, veneers, and intarsia. Its large rose is intricately carved and pierced in a Gothic pattern. Its cheek blocks are sculpted and painted, its naturals and arcades are ivory, and its sharps are ebony. Across the namebatten, where the builder's signature would ordinarily go, is the motto "Riccho son doro / et riccho son di suono /

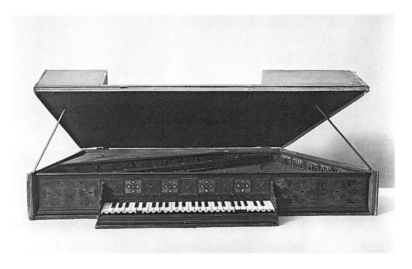

4-23. This anonymous virginal, made for Eleanor d'Este in 1540, is stunningly decorated. Its rose is shown in Illustration 4-4b. New York, Metropolitan Museum of Art.

Non mi sonar / si tu non ha del buono," warning the viewer that *I am rich in gold and rich in sound; do not play me if you cannot play me well.*

NAPLES AND ELSEWHERE

A somewhat different style of harpsichord building was practiced in Naples, a southern city which, though far removed from the metropolitan centers of the North, was hardly a cultural backwater.[108] Visually, little distinguished Neapolitan instruments from those made in other areas, but the primary building material was maple, rather than the usual cypress, and even the soundboard was sometimes made from that wood.[109] John Koster, who is primarily responsible for recognizing the existence of this tradition, identified a small group of sixteenth-century Neapolitan instruments.[110] The first two, both anonymous clavichords (Leipzig, Musikinstrumenten-Museum der Universität Leipzig), are known as "Leipzig Numbers 2 and 3" because of their position in the museum's catalog.[111] Third is a ca. 1520–40 anonymous oblong octave virginal (Vermillion, S.D., Shrine to Music Museum), the earliest known plucked keyboard from that region;[112] and the fourth is a ca. 1550 anonymous harpsichord (Boston, Museum of Fine Arts), a classic sixteenth-century 1×8′, 1×4′ Italian, but with case and soundboard of quarter-sawn maple.[113] Next is another anonymous harpsichord, ca. 1530 (Milan, Museo degli Strumenti Musicale), a 1×8′ that has been turned into a crude clavichord. Two others are harpsichords, anonymous and undated (Halle, Händel-Haus; New York, Metropolitan Museum of Art). The last, the only signed and dated instrument in the group, is a 1598 oblong virginal (Bologna, private collection) by Alessandro Fabri (ca. 1636–91).[114] This instrument and the Shrine to Music octave virginal are also the two earliest examples of a unique type of Neapolitan virginal to be discussed in Chapter 6.

Aside from maple construction, and in some instances maple soundboards as well, the Neapolitan origin of these instruments is revealed by a study of their moldings, their dovetail joinery, and their raised bottoms. The existence of this Neapolitan tradition (and its continuation in the next century as a distinctive school of virginal making) confirms what has been implied throughout much of this chapter: sixteenth-century Italian builders seem to have had a remarkable agreement on the general principles of harpsichord design — thin-case sides, single manual, projecting keyboard, architectural use of moldings, and so on — but they often differed in the details.

4-24. The case and soundboard of this anonymous 1550 Neapolitan harpsichord are constructed entirely from maple. Museum of Fine Arts, Boston. Reproduced with permission. © 2000 Museum of Fine Arts, Boston. All rights reserved.

Fine builders were active in other Italian cities during the cinquecento: Hieronymus Bononiensis in Rome is one whose sole surviving instrument was briefly discussed earlier; but for the most part the known makers of Bologna, Mantua, Florence, Ferrara, and other cities are little more than names to us. The few instruments extant from these locations are of the more mundane variety — thin-case cypress instruments whose shape and complex moldings lend an air of beauty and dignity to simple, bare wood. It should not be forgotten that it was instruments like these, rather than the opulent style, that typified Italian harpsichord making in the sixteenth century.

SUMMING UP

The "classic" Italian style was established early in the 1500s, possibly even at the close of the previous century. It was an inner-outer instrument whose thin case walls and soundboard were normally made of Mediterranean cypress. Complex, refined moldings both strengthened the case walls and gave them a more substantial appearance. The keyboard, flanked by scroll-sawn or carved cheeks, normally projected from the case. Internal bracing usually consisted of a batten or two across the bottom boards, knees, and diagonal struts. The scale was Pythagorean down to c. The bentside followed this curve closely and, combined with the intricate moldings and the pleasing width-to-length ratio of the case, gave the instruments an elegant appearance without the aid of paint, paper, or inlays. The normal disposition was $1 \times 8'$, $1 \times 4'$ with a fifty-note compass of C/E–f^3. The jacks operated in box guides. Virginals and spinets were constructed from the same materials in much the same way.

Instruments such as the ones just described undoubtedly constituted the vast majority of the harpsichords, virginals, and spinets made in sixteenth-century Italy. At the same time, there was a strong tradition of building opulent instruments, particularly in Venice. Using accoutrements such as ebony, ivory, rosewood, and boxwood inlays, painted and inlaid Moresque patterns, carvings and tooled leather, ornate roses and even precious stones, builders created some of the most breathtaking harpsichords and virginals ever made. Since such instruments were inherently more valuable than the plainer ones, it is inevitable that the latter literally got used up or discarded when fashion no longer valued them. But lavishly decorated instruments always retained value and have survived in numbers that wildly exaggerate their actual importance to contemporary building practices. The stunning Venetian and Milanese instruments were well able to match the beauty of the best of sixteenth-century Flemish virginals, such as the 1548 and 1550 Karest instruments, the 1658 Duke of Cleves, the 1580 van der Biest, and the 1581 Hans Ruckers; but their beauty is of an entirely different sort. Flemish products derived their aesthetic from illusionistic strategies, the Italians more from the inherent beauty of their materials and their sculptural and architectural techniques. Nevertheless, it should be stressed once again that most Italian builders — even including those whose fancy instruments have been discussed here — achieved their effects by simpler means. Frank Hubbard noted that the Italian harpsichord's unity of form and function allowed it to be examined as closely as a violin.[115] Sheridan Germann likened an Italian harpsichord to a violin, as an object that takes its beauty from its form.[116] Perhaps these are better measures of comparison than the mighty dome of Brunelleschi.

Nevertheless, both Flemish and Italian instruments exhibited a predilection toward elaborate decoration and an attention to time-consuming detail that became much rarer after 1600. This may have been because of changing ideas of craftsmanship, or perhaps the demise of a uniquely Renaissance regard for musical instruments. That harpsichords were becoming items of necessity to working musicians was a consideration, since these buyers could scarcely afford what must have been outrageously expensive decoration. Although instruments would continue to be built for royalty and nobility, it appears that in the seventeenth century a much larger share of the market would be middle-class merchants, artists, and artisans, with disposable income and the urge to emulate elegance.

PART III

The Seventeenth Century

[5]

THE RUCKERS-COUCHET DYNASTY

*T*HE BLANCHET-TASKIN dynasty, the Kirkmans, the Shudis, and the Silbermanns are among the great families of builders known to students of the harpsichord; but the Ruckerses and the Couchets, with reputations as exalted as the celebrated Italian violin master Antonio Stradivari, were the most famous of all time. The variety of harpsichords and virginals they produced exceeds that of any other, and except for the Kirkmans, more of their instruments survive than those of any other builders.[1] By the middle of the seventeenth century their instruments were found everywhere harpsichords were played, prized by their owners. The authority of their building practices was so strong that it would effectively wipe out the International style in France and England. Other than in Italy, which in the main appears to have ignored it, Northern European harpsichord building was never the same after the Ruckerses and the Couchets; from the end of the seventeenth century on, their work would define harpsichord building in much of Western Europe.

How they accomplished this is not readily explained. Certainly, they paid careful attention to the construction of their soundboards, jacks, guides, keys, and other action parts; but there were other fine Antwerp builders too, and their products were also well built. By 1579, the year that Hans Ruckers became a member,[2] there were at least nineteen harpsichord builders in the Guild of St. Luke. Some of their names—Hans Bos,[3] Johannes Grouwels, and Martin van der Biest—still have some luster today, but it was Hans Ruckers, not his colleagues, who achieved great prominence.[4] One also wonders why Hans's sons garnered such reputations of their own, while builders like Cornelius and Simon Hagaerts and Joris Britsen labored in what appears to have been relative obscurity. Both O'Brien and Koster[5] suggest that the Ruckerses used a shorter scale (that is, a scale that was Pythagorean rather than rising in the treble) and substantially heavier stringing than their colleagues. This might explain, at least in part, why their instruments were so prized.

THE RUCKERS-COUCHET FAMILY[8]

Of German origin,[9] Hans Ruckers, the family patriarch, was born ca. 1550 in Mechelen (Mechlin), a city about ten miles south of Antwerp. We do not know who his master was, or even if he learned the trade of harpsichord making there or in Antwerp, since it is not until 1575, when he married Adriana Knaeps in the cathedral at Antwerp, that his name first surfaces in any public records.[10] He joined the Guild of St. Luke in 1579, and from then on his name appears regularly.[11] One document notes payments to Hans for tuning and maintaining the cathedral organ, indicating that if he was not actually an organ builder, at least he had some experience with that instrument. Like van der Biest, Bos, and Johannes Grouwels, we have no idea how many harpsichords Hans Ruckers built in his lifetime; but unlike the single instruments by which these other builders are known today,[12] there are five survivors of Hans's work. Four are virginals: 1581 and 1591 mother and child muselars (New York, Metropolitan Museum; New Haven, Yale Collection), a 1583 spinett at quint pitch (Paris, private ownership), and a 1591 spinett in polygonal form (Bruges, Gruuthuse Museum). The remain-

---

INHARMONICITY

A taut string vibrates in predictable ways, based on integer multiples of its fundamental. For example, if the frequency of a string's fundamental is 200 Hz (Hz = Hertz, or one cycle per second), then its next partial will be 400 Hz, its next 600 Hz, its next 800 Hz, and so on, to a virtual infinity of partials (frequencies above 20,000 Hz are relatively unimportant to human hearing). All these frequencies are present as that string vibrates, although the relative strength of each depends in part on where the string is plucked.

However, this describes the behavior of an "ideal" string, one with neither mass nor thickness. In a real-life string, partials are usually slightly higher than integer multiples, and this departure from ideal behavior is known as "inharmonicity." To some extent, inharmonicity can be controlled: the thinner the string and the tighter it is drawn up, the more it approximates an ideal string; conversely, the thicker the string or the slacker its tension, the more the resulting sound departs from those neat integer multiples. Hence, the new stringing practices of the Ruckerses would have introduced more inharmonicity into the sound. Additionally, thicker strings would call for somewhat heavier plectra, producing sounds that were louder, more aggressive, and less "sweet" than the tone of instruments produced by the other builders.[6] This may have been among the innovations giving Hans Ruckers and his progeny an edge over their competitors.[7]

---

ing instrument, his last signed work, is the earliest extant Ruckers grand harpsichord (although the meaning of the word "grand" has been stretched here), a 1594 single-manual harpsichord/virginal combination (Berlin, Schloss Köpenick). Hans died in 1598.[13]

Hans and Adriana had eleven children, five of whom survived early childhood. The two eldest, Ioannes (born 1578) and Andreas I (born 1579), followed their father's trade. Adriana died in 1604, and Ioannes, then twenty-six, inherited his father's house and business. He married that same year, to Maria Waelrant, the daughter of the cathedral organist, and was admitted to the Guild of St. Luke in 1611. Three years later he received the prestigious appointment as harpsichord and clavichord builder to the court. Ioannes also maintained the cathedral organ, as well as the instruments of some of the other churches in town.[14] He must have been one of the more substantial denizens of Antwerp since later in life, along with the painters Peter Paul Rubens (1577–1640) and Jan Bruegel (1568–1625), he was excused from civic guard duty, an obligation that otherwise befell all citizens. He died in 1642.

Andreas I apparently worked with his older brother Ioannes from 1604, the year of Adriana's death, until 1608, when his share of the business was bought out by Ioannes. Andreas set up his own shop nearby. He and his wife had seven children, but only one, Andreas II (born 1607), became a harpsichord builder. Following the now familiar path, Andreas II began his apprenticeship with his father at the age of twelve, gained Guild membership in 1637, and married in the same year. It is almost impossible to distinguish between the work of the two Andreases, and it is likely that the son never had his own shop, but worked with his father until the latter's death somewhere between 1651 and 1653. In his seventies by that time, Andreas I was the only member of the family to reach old age. Andreas II died soon after his father, in 1654 or 1655.

Catherina Ruckers, a sister of Ioannes and Andreas I, married a surgeon named Carolus Couchet. Their one son, Ioannes[15] Couchet (born 1615), began his apprenticeship with Ioannes at the usual age of eleven. He continued working for his uncle long after his apprenticeship was over, not entering the Guild until his master's death in 1642. He married in 1643, an event that often seemed to accompany membership in the Guild. Like his uncle, he tuned and repaired the cathedral organ as well as those in other Antwerp churches. He died in 1655, with a reputation perhaps even greater than that of his grandfather Hans, his uncles Ioannes and Andreas I, and his cousin Andreas II. The great Dutch humanist, poet, and musician Constantijn Huygens, for example, praised him as a builder of double-manual harpsichords second to none.[16]

Ioannes Couchet had four sons, Ioannes II, Petrus Ioannes, Ioseph Ioannes, and Abraham, but little is known of any of them. Ioannes II entered the Guild in 1655–56, at age eleven, and became a builder. Petrus Ioannes was apprenticed to the harpsichord maker Simon Hagaerts but does not seem to have joined the Guild, and we know of no instruments made under his name. Ioseph Ioannes became a Guild member in 1666–67, and a few of his harpsichords survive. Abraham is known to have joined the Guild in 1666–67 as a painter as well as a harpsichord maker, but nothing signed by him remains. When Ioseph Ioannes died in 1706, suffering from mental illness, the incomparable Ruckers-Couchet dynasty came to an ignominious conclusion.[17] Actually, however, it had really ended around 1655, with the deaths of Andreas, Andreas II, and Ioannes Couchet all coming within a period of three or four years.

Coincidentally, Antwerp was dealt another severe economic blow at that time. In 1648, as a condition of the Peace of Westphalia, the Scheldt River was closed (actually, the Dutch had blocked it earlier), cutting off Antwerp's access to the sea. Harpsichords continued to be built in Antwerp, but never again at the heady rate or with the economic success enjoyed by the Ruckerses and Couchets.[18] Moreover, by the latter half of the century makers had become more and more engaged in rebuilding earlier instruments, extending their ranges and converting nonaligned to aligned doubles. This process, called *ravalement* by the French, will be dealt with in some detail in Chapter 13.

We do not know how many instruments were made by these men. Grant O'Brien reports about one hundred authenticated Ruckers or Couchet instruments extant—some sixty harpsichords, and the rest virginals—but they represent only a fraction of what must have been an extraordinary production.

Studying the numbering systems found on many of the surviving instruments, O'Brien estimates that the shops of Ioannes (with his work continued by Ioannes Couchet) and Andreas I and II each produced thirty-five to forty instruments a year.[19] Assuming that each shop maintained that rate for approximately forty-five years, their estimated total output would be somewhere between three thousand and thirty-six hundred virginals and harpsichords, not even including the unknown production of Hans Ruckers and Ioseph Ioannes Couchet. This astonishingly large number was exceeded only in the nineteenth century, when piano building became a mass-production enterprise.[20] Of course, the Ruckerses and Couchets did not build all these instruments with their own hands. Given that their harpsichords and virginals were finished at the prodigious rate of nearly one per week, Ioannes and Andreas I could better be described as factory owners, rather than harpsichord builders in the traditional sense. One might imagine that the masters did some work on every instrument—perhaps they thinned the soundboards, and almost certainly they checked every one before it went out the door—but the acquisition, stacking, drying, cutting, and thicknessing of lumber, the case work, keyboard, hardware, and jack making, the stringing, quilling, and decoration must have been done by a sizeable crew of hard-working employees, apprentices, and subcontractors.[21]

VIRGINALS

Except for some elements of decoration, to be discussed later, almost all the characteristics found in the earlier Flemish virginals are present in those of the Ruckerses and the one extant Couchet. They have heavy, ⅝″-thick case walls of poplar, recessed keyboards,[22] with the standard forty-five-note $C/E-c^3$ compass. The only internal bracing is a continuation of the cheeks through the case, across the bottom to the spine, and a support underneath the wrestplank. Moldings were cut into the sides of the case walls. The soundboards were made of spruce,[23] with (except for the octave instruments) a lidded box to the left for tuning key, strings, quills, and knife—the tools and supplies the player would need to keep the instrument maintained. The bridges were roughly triangular in shape (gone now is the refinement of the concave front face found on pre-1600 virginals), with a narrow top portion slanting downward toward the active segment of the strings, so that the wire would contact the bridge pins before touching wood.

The virginals had no separate jack guides; instead, slots were cut into the soundboard, and into a lower guide of the same wood that was glued to the internal bracing. As in the two Karest virginals, both surfaces were covered with leather into which slightly smaller openings were incised. Thus, the jacks, two to a slot, touched only the leather (and each other), helping to quiet the action. The jacks themselves were tapered in both width and thickness, so that at rest, they fit in the guides without much play; but when raised, they became looser, ensuring smooth operation. Tongues were returned by a spring made of boar's bristle, rather than the flat brass used by Italians. "Mouse-ear" dampers, two to a jack, fit into oval slots cut into the tops (child jacks had only one damper). The Ruckers scale, in iron, was just about 14″ for both virginals and harpsichords at normal pitch, with the scales of instruments at higher or lower pitches proportional to that. The scale was Pythagorean above c^1.

The Ruckerses built virginals and grand harpsichords for export and local consumption, but there is no question that the virginals figured more widely in domestic music making.[24] It was the instrument of choice for the many well-to-do burghers of the major metropolitan centers of the Low Countries, and paintings such as Jan Vermeer's *Woman at the Virginal* portray them mainly with young ladies, since the ability to play a keyboard instrument was considered an appropriate activity for women.[25] Nevertheless, grand harpsichords were also owned by amateurs and proudly displayed in paintings like Giles von Tilborgh's *Family Group*.[26]

Because the bass section of the right bridge of the muselar was straight, it was possible to place a thin wooden batten next to it, under the strings, with metal staples driven into it. By sliding the rail forward a fraction of an inch, the staples of this arpichordum stop would contact the bass strings, producing a buzzing sound possibly inspired by the brayed harp, and contrasting with the clear, bell-like tone of the treble.[27] The spinett did not have any tone-altering devices and also differed from muselars in that their left bridges were rendered inactive by virtue of a large piece of wood glued under the soundboard at that point.

Since the keyboards of octave virginals were almost as wide as the cases themselves, they were perforce centrally placed. Otherwise, there is no evidence that the Ruckerses ever made larger virginals with centered keyboards even though this placement was seen on the 1568 Duke of Cleves and the 1580 Johannes Grouwels.[31] Other Flemish builders may also have made virginals with centrally placed keyboards, but judging from its negligible survival rate, this sort of virginal seems to have been the least popular of the three designs.

Virginals were made in six sizes, falling into three well-defined groups. The first consisted of both muselars and spinetts at normal 8′ pitch and a step higher. In the second, both types were pitched a fourth (quart) higher than normal pitch, with spinetts only at a fifth (quint) higher. The third group consisted of two spinetts, each an octave above those in the first.[32] Only the three largest sizes could be muselars, since the position of the keyboards and jacks of the smaller sizes were determined by the size of the case: there are choices when fitting a forty-five-note C/E-c³ keyboard into a 5′ 6″ case, but not when the case is 3′ 9″ or smaller.

The Ruckerses — perhaps all Flemish builders — identified

5-2. Giles von Tilborgh, *Family Group* (1625–28). One of the daughters sits at a typical Flemish harpsichord, a prized possession of the family. The one-piece lid indicates that it is not by one of the Ruckers, whose lids were always in two sections. Note also that the lid leans against the wall, rather than being propped open by a stick. © IRPA-KIK, Brussels.

their virginals not by pitch class, but by length. The largest measure about 5′ 7″, those a step higher about 4′ 8″, the quarts 4′ 3″, the quints 3′ 9″, the octaves 2′ 8″, and the octaves plus a step 2′ 4″. Obviously, though, the builders did not use English measurements when making their instruments; they used the unit called the Flemish foot, or the *voet*.[33] Measured in these units, the instruments are nominally 6, 5, 4½, 4, 3, and 2½ *voeten* in length.[34] Builders even marked their instruments in this way, using the symbols 6, 5, 4½, and 4 to differentiate the first four sizes. They used the symbol "k" for the larger of the octave virginals: since the mother and child was called *de moeder met het kind,* the "k" obviously stood for *kind,* or child. In a reference to their high, sharp, piercing sound, Douwes identified the little octave instruments by the descriptive name of *Scherpen;*[35] and in an admirable display of efficiency, the smaller of these received no designation at all. With its diminutive size, what else could it be but a 2½-*voet Scherp?*

Extant 3-*voet* octave virginals by the Ruckerses and Couchets all seem to have been part of the mother and child combination. Some Ruckers children exist independently, but they are orphans, separated from their mothers, like the 1639 Andreas (The Hague, Gemeentemuseum).[36] On the other hand, the 2½-*voet* octave virginals were never intended to be part of a mother and child combination. Their key levers were compressed inward at the tails to accommodate a forty-five-note C/E–c³ keyboard in a narrow 2′ 4″ width, and they would not match up with the conventionally spaced keys of a 5-*voet* mother.[37]

The mother and child combination came in only two configurations, the 6-*voet* muselar and the 6-*voet* spinett; and to judge by surviving instruments, the former far outweighed the latter in popularity.

The question of why Flemish builders would combine two instruments in this manner was raised in Chapter 3, and several reasons were suggested—for duet playing, or to supply a teaching tool to a mother and child, or simply because it was possible; but other explanations come to mind, such as the North-

---

SPINETTS, MUSELARS, AND THE 1537 MÜLLER HARPSICHORD

One cannot help wondering if the desire for the contrasts between spinetts and muselars was influenced by the tonal concepts of instruments such as the 1537 Müller harpsichord. Although it is the earliest of its type to have survived, the two very different sounds produced by the Müller's close- and deep-plucking registers, along with its (probable) arpichordum stop represented a sound ideal that might have been customary for German harpsichords of the sixteenth century. This assumption is not unreasonable: contrasting registers are common on surviving seventeenth-century instruments from that region (see Chapter 9). Thus, what the Germans accomplished on one harpsichord by widely separating the registers, the Flemish accomplished with different types of virginals.[28] However, it appears that with one exception (to be discussed shortly), the Ruckerses and their colleagues never considered following Germanic practice by incorporating a wide variety of sounds into one instrument.

ern European proclivity for combining instruments with themselves: woodwinds like the bassoon, that doubles on itself, and the rankett, that turns on itself nine times, are prime examples. Another possible indication can be found in the seventeenth-century Flemish propensity for filling available spaces, a cultural trait that can be seen in paintings of homes, where walls are covered with pictures and tapestries, as well as the decoration on virginals and harpsichords, where there is little area not imbued with paint or paper. The mother and child, then, could represent a clever means of filling the empty space under the virginal's soundboard. Mounting the child on top of the mother gave the combination something of the resources of a 1×8′, 1×4′ harpsichord, with 1×8′, 1×4′ on the lower manual and 1×4′ on the upper, and the combination might have been particularly useful for playing popular echo pieces.

VAN BLANKENBURG, REYNVANN, AND MUSELARS

It is interesting to note that judging from the survival rate, muselars and muselar mother and child virginals were far more popular than the spinett versions; but even more interesting is the judgment of a later generation, which evidently had formed a contrary opinion. Writing in 1739, Quirinus van Blankenburg, a Dutch organist and theorist, stated that muselars sounded fine in the right hand, "but grunt in the bass like young pigs."[29] In 1795 the Dutch theorist Joos Verschuere Reynvann, under the entry "Harpsichord" in his dictionary of music, noted that muselar virginals made an unpleasant rumbling in the bass.[30] If an explanation is required for their remarks, it can only be that tastes change. By the middle of the eighteenth century virginals were long out of favor (the 1650 by Ioannes Couchet [Antwerp, Vleeshuis Museum] is the latest extant example), and the deep-plucking sound of the muselar, so different in tone quality and touch from the instruments they knew, probably struck van Blankenburg and Reynvann as the height of keyboard folly.

SINGLE-MANUAL HARPSICHORDS

The Ruckers shops seemed to produce four basic models of grand harpsichords—two singles and two doubles—and a variety of less frequently called-for or made-to-order designs. The harpsichords, like the virginals, were built of heavy poplar walls, with moldings cut in. Like the 1537 Müller harpsichord, the bottom was in two pieces and the sides sat on, rather than overlapped, the bottom. The internal structure consisted of upper and lower braces, with separate upper and lower bellyrails, rather than the knees, diagonal struts, and one-piece bellyrails favored in Italy. The nameboard was glued in place, and only the namebatten was removeable. Soundboards were made of quarter-sawn spruce, and glued to their underside was a cutoff bar, ribs, and a 4′ hitchpin rail between the cutoff bar and the bentside. Bridges and nuts were given the same shape as those found on virginals. The upper guides were made of beech, and the lower guides were covered with leather pierced for the jacks, similar to the slotted leather strip mounted on the soundboards of virginals. A box for tools and supplies was provided in the spine by putting a roof over the bottom belly-rail and the first lower brace, adding a back wall, and providing the ensuing chamber with a door.

The standard Ruckers single was a 6-*voet* instrument, about 6′ in length, with a C/E–c³ keyboard, a 1×8′, 1×4′ disposition with the 8′ plucking closest to the nut, and a divided buff stop with the rail split between f¹ and f♯¹ (where the arpichordum stop ended on muselars). The Ruckerses never made any other disposition (although the Couchets did). Like 1×8′, 1×4′ Italian harpsichords, the upper guides projected from the cheek, allowing the player to turn registers off or on by pushing or pulling these extensions. Unlike the elegantly turned knobs on Italian instruments, however, the Flemish simply ran the registers through the cheeks and capped the extensions with slips of bone. The treble end of the buff rail also projected through the cheek, to turn that section on or off (the bass end was controlled by a finger grip at the spine).

A variant of the standard single had a chromatic, rather than a short-octave bass. Three such instruments survive, although the Ruckerses undoubtedly built more.[38] No longer than the short-octave versions, they are a few inches wider to accommo-

5-3a. The gilded papier-maché rose in this ca. 1614 Ioannes Ruckers muselar virginal says HR, but Hans was long dead by this date. © IRPA-KIK, Brussels.

5-3b. Originally built with the normal C/E– c³ compass, this 1598 Hans and/or Ioannes Ruckers spinett virginal has been extensively altered and now has a range of GG/BB–c³. Paris, Musée de la Musique.

date four extra notes. O'Brien suggests that these instruments were built for export to England, since chromatic basses were the rule there, rather than the short octaves common on the Continent,[39] and the Flemish evidently identified these chromatic singles as built "in the English way."[40] Other sorts of singles were built, although they do not appear to have been standard models. A 1639 Ioannes (London, Victoria and Albert Museum) is a chromatic instrument ascending to d³, suggesting that the Ruckerses were willing to fulfill special requests. Perhaps the most unusual single made by a Ruckers is the 1627 Andreas (The Hague, Gemeentemuseum), with standard C/E– c³ keyboard and 1×8′, 1×4′ disposition; but at 4′ 6″ in length it is the harpsichord equivalent of the 4-*voet*, or quint, virginal and was even marked that way by the builder. We probably shall never know if this instrument is unique — perhaps built to special order — or the last remaining example of yet another standard Ruckers model; even so, that it exists at all is an additional verification of the diversity of instruments offered by those shops.[41]

Harpsichord jacks were identical to those utilized in virginals, also using mouse-ear dampers, two to a jack in the 8′ registers. Flemish mouse ears contacted the strings only when the register was turned "on." In its "off" position, that choir of

strings was free to vibrate sympathetically, as either the $4'$ or the $8'$ would have done when the other was being played alone. Thus, the $8'$ sound would be enhanced by sympathetic resonance from the $4'$ strings, and a faint halo of sound would remain when the keys were released. We have no direct evidence, musical or otherwise, that the $4'$ would be used alone, but there are indirect indications. One is the widespread existence of octave instruments, both in the North and in the South, a suggestion that $4'$ sound was known and appreciated for its own sake. More to the point, if the $4'$ register was intended only as an addition to the $8'$, the $8'$ would likely have been fixed permanently in its "on" position (in fact, this was normally the case with the second $8'$ of $2\times8'$ Italian harpsichords, where it was intended as an addition, not an alternative, to the first).

5-5. A lid, cheeks, and extended bottom board were constructed for this much-altered 1639 Andreas Ruckers motherless child virginal. The Hague, Gemeentemuseum.

To our jaded tastes these instruments appear small and simply disposed, but they were extremely good for the tasks demanded of them—accompanying voices and instruments, and playing a solo literature of dances, variation sets, fantasias, and arrangements of popular and folk songs. The pungent tone of the Ruckers instruments was powerful, and when the $4'$ was added the additional brilliance created quite a different quality. And, of course,

THE RUCKERS AND COUCHET VIRGINALS AT A GLANCE		
Name	*Nominal Size*	*Pitch Relationship*
1. 6-*voet* muselar	5′7″	
2. 6-*voet* muselar mother and child	5′7″	
3. 6-*voet* spinett	5′7″	
4. 6-*voet* spinett mother and child	5′7″	
5. 5-*voet* muselar	4′8″	Step higher
6. 5-*voet* spinett	4′8″	Step higher
7. 4½-*voet* muselar	4′3″	Fourth higher
8. 4½-*voet* spinett	4′3″	Fourth higher
9. 4-*voet* spinett	3′9″	Fifth higher
10. 3-*voet* Scherp	2′8″	Octave higher
11. 2½-*voet* Scherp	2′4″	Ninth higher

the 4′ could be used alone, as it undoubtedly was. Finally, with a split buff stop the player could damp the entire compass, or by buffing only the bass, provide a pizzicato accompaniment to a singing melody or running divisions in the treble.

DOUBLE-MANUAL HARPSICHORDS

The standard Ruckers double-manual harpsichord, although longer than the single by almost 1½′, also had a 1×8′, 1×4′ disposition; but the two keyboards stood a fourth apart. The upper manual was like the normal single, with the same scalings and the same forty-five-note C/E–c^3 range, and the keyboard ended at the left with a molded block of wood three naturals wide. The fifty-note lower manual, displaced to the left by a fourth, had a nominal compass of C/E–f^3, sounding GG/BB–c^3.[42] There were four rows of jacks, 8′, 4′, 8′, 4′, with each manual controlling its own set of 1×8′, 1×4′. As with the singles, a divided buff stop was provided; but the f^1–$f\sharp^1$ break was on the lower, transposed manual; the split on the upper was at c^1–$c\sharp^1$. The keyboards were not connected or coupled, so that only one manual's jacks could pluck the strings at any given time. Hence, the 8′ and 4′ jacks closest to the player were operated from the upper manual; but to play on the lower manual these had to be turned off and the rearmost rows of 8′ and 4′ jacks engaged, by pushing or pulling the register extensions at the cheek. Not only would the pitch of the two keyboards differ by a fourth, but their tone quality would differ as well. Plucking closer to the nut, the upper manual would produce a somewhat nasal sound; but the lower manual, plucking the strings farther back, would have a smoother, less pungent sound. Thus, like the mother and child

5-6. An echo piece by Jan Pieterszoon Sweelinck. The mother and child virginal would lend itself to pieces of this nature.

and the harpsichord/virginal combination, the unaligned double was really two harpsichords in one case.[43]

Analogous to the chromatic singles, the Ruckerses also made some chromatic-bass nonaligned doubles, but with the lower manual at normal pitch and a compass of GG–c³, and the upper a fourth higher with a compass of four chromatic octaves, F–f³. Four such instruments are extant, all in France, which suggests to O'Brien that they were intended for export to that country and made chromatic for that reason.[44] There is one extant example of a nonstandard double, a 1612 Ioannes (London, Fenton House), in which the keyboards seem to have been separated by a tone.[45]

Keyboards at different pitch levels imply transposition, and that is exactly what was going on.[46] For example, pressing the c¹ key on the upper manual sounded the normal c¹ pitch. The lower-manual key that lined up with it looked like an f¹, but it also would sound c¹. And if one played the nominal c¹ on the lower manual, it would pluck the actual g string. The short-octave basses on both keyboards presented a complicating factor: tuning the appropriate short-octave strings for the lower manual was not a problem, because the upper manual would never play those strings—it lacked both keys and jacks for them.

5-7. Cross section of a Ruckers single-manual harpsichord. Notice the compartment formed by the lower bellyrail and the first lower brace, likely used to store tools and supplies. Reprinted from *O'Brien 1990*, with the permission of Cambridge University Press.

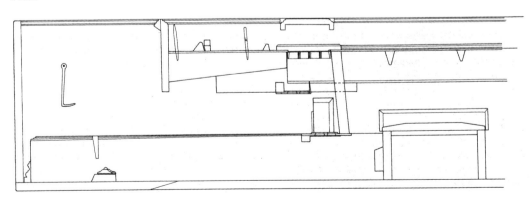

But the upper manual had a potential drawback: if its strings (the same strings used by the lower manual) were tuned to the usual short-octave scheme, then the apparent E (for example) would be tuned to C. But if that string was played from the lower manual by striking a nominal A, it would sound a nominal F, a third lower than desired. Hence that key, and the ones controlling the nominal F♯ and G♯ keys, were cranked to the left so that their jacks could pluck the appropriate strings. Some attention to Illustration 5-10 will make this and the relationship between the keyboards clear. The solution to this short-octave problem, though it may seem elementary, was well thought out, well executed, and typical of the Ruckerses' practical and business-like approach to harpsichord building.

One other nonaligned Ruckers double still exists, a 1612 by Ioannes whose two keyboards originally seem to have been a fifth and fourth below normal pitch. The manuals were probably nominally C/E–c^3 and C/E–d^3, a tone apart, certainly an unusual combination of keyboards, although O'Brien points out that organs were known to have this sort of transposition,[47] and that the 1537 Hans Müller was capable of transposition by a tone. Compounding the enigma is the fact that this instrument appears to have had only three sets of jacks, rather than the four normal for a double.[48] It could have had either a 4′ in front, a dogleg 8′ in the middle, and another 4′ behind that, with the dogleg 8′ doing duty for both keyboards, or else the back 8′ and 4′ were on the lower manual while the front 8′ was on the upper.

A double with an "HR" rose and the name of Hans Ruckers on the jackrail (Nuremberg, Germanisches Nationalmuseum) is dated 1658, long after the master's death. Until recently it was accepted as a product of a Ruckers workshop, but both O'Brien and Koster believe it to be a non-Ruckers "Flemish" harpsichord, probably built in the Low Countries, north of Antwerp, and it is so recorded in *Boalch III*.[49] Its compass is the normal forty-five-note C/E–c^3, and as with Ruckers doubles, it was originally strung 1×8', 1×4', with four sets of jacks. In its details it differs from the Ruckers instruments: perhaps most startling is the lack of any internal bracing. Equally startling, however, are its *aligned* keyboards. Furthermore, its choir of 8' strings could be plucked from two positions on the lower manual (the two sets of 8' jacks are separated by the 4') and one on the upper, the latter by means of a set of jacks in a gap in the wrestplank between the 4' and 8' nuts—in other words, a lute stop. Hence, all three sets of jacks plucked the single 8', but without coupler, they could only do so one at a time. In essence, this unknown builder combined two different-sounding instru-

5-9. A 1659 single-manual harpsichord by Gommaar van Everbroek. This sole surviving harpsichord by this less-well-known Antwerp builder is similar to the Ruckers instruments made at the same time. Vermillion, America's Shrine to Music Museum.

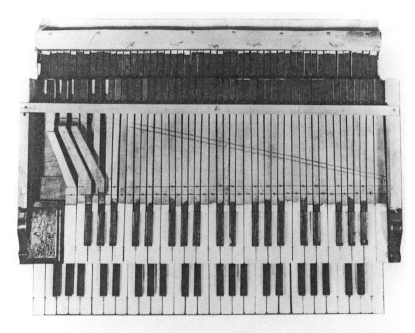

5-10. A set of nonaligned keyboards. The lower manual is a fourth lower than the upper, and both have short-octave basses. The block of wood on the left side of the upper manual simply fills in the unused space. Note that the short-octave keys on the upper manual reach over to the left so that their jacks can pluck the proper strings. Edinburgh, Russell Collection of Early Keyboard Instruments, University of Edinburgh.

ments into one case: a three-jack harpsichord with two slightly differing 8′ sounds (front and back 8′s), either of which could be combined with the 4′; and a nasal-sounding upper-manual instrument.[50] One wonders if the Germanic heritage on which the Flemish tradition was founded might not have had a stronger presence outside Antwerp, away from the overwhelming domination of the Ruckers family.[51]

Meantone temperament, with its nonenharmonic accidentals, introduced another complexity. On single-manual harpsichords the "forbidden" triads were simply avoided in the music; or, if used, a few strings could be retuned, the work of a few seconds. But avoidance was not always feasible on nonaligned keyboards. An upper-manual E♭, sounding at normal pitch, would sound a nominal A♭ when played on the lower keyboard, making an intolerable E-major triad. Retuning accidentals every time a player changed manuals was possible, but hardly a viable option.[52]

The Ruckerses solved this problem cleverly. Since it was obviously impossible for one string to sound at two different pitches, they supplied two strings at each 8′ and 4′ E♭/G♯ position, separated from each other at the nut by means of small, thin brass plates about 9⁄32″ wide and 5⁄8″ long. First, a shallow section was cut from the nut at that string position, and the plate was driven halfway into it. On the 8′ nut the top of the plate, now standing about 5⁄16″ above the nut, supported the E♭ string in a little notch. The G♯ string ran about 1⁄4″ below it, in

5-11. Although the exterior of this nonaligned 1638 Ioannes Ruckers harpsichord has been extensively redecorated, it is the only extant double with its original transposing configuration. Edinburgh, Russell Collection of Early Keyboard Instruments, University of Edinburgh.

the cut-out section of the nut, and slightly to the left, with the plate acting as the nut pin. The E♭ jack, on the upper manual, was a little longer than the others and was given a longer-than-usual quill, which reached over the G♯ string to pluck the E♭. The lower-manual G♯ jack was shorter than the others, with a shorter quill that lay under the G♯ string. A similar arrangement was used on the 4′ nut. On the normal short-octave nonaligned double only six of these plates were required, three for the 8′ strings and three for the 4′, while a fourth set was needed for the doubles with chromatic basses.[53]

THE HARPSICHORD/VIRGINAL COMBINATION

In addition to the mother and child virginal and the nonaligned double, the Ruckerses also built another combined instrument: a large rectangle, consisting of a normal harpsichord with an octave virginal occupying the space at the bentside. The harpsichord's bentside is the virginal's spine, and they share that member as a hitchpin rail. Each has a rose, and they are as inseparable as Siamese twins. Only three of these strange constructions have survived, all of an early date (one is undated but is assumed to have been built soon after 1600), leading us to surmise that it was not a particularly popular model and may have been phased out soon after its invention. Two of them, a 1594 Hans (Berlin, Schloss Köpenick) and the undated Ioannes (Berlin, Staatliches Institut für Musikforschung), are single-manual harpsichords, corresponding to the standard 6-*voet* instrument in range, disposition, and scale, but with an octave virginal built into the bentside. As already noted, the 1594 is of considerable interest, since it is the only extant harpsichord in grand shape (if that term can be stretched here to include this combination) by the patriarch of the Ruckers dynasty. The third, a 1619 Ioannes (Brussels, Musée Instrumental), is a nonaligned double whose virginal, an octave above the lower manual, sounds a fifth above normal pitch, like a 4-*voet* spinett. To call these extraordinary instruments would be an understatement.

As with the mother and child and the nonaligned double, we would like to know the purpose for this combination. Again, there are few hard answers. Duets for two harpsichords were certainly a possibility, although as with the mother and child, one of the instruments would be at octave pitch. Another is that the harpsichord would be reserved for music of a more serious nature, while the octave virginal would be used for dances or other light pieces. Finally, it must also be admitted that Hans and Ioannes may have done it simply because it was doable, an imaginative way to utilize the negative space of the bentside.

THE LATE COUCHET INSTRUMENTS

Ioannes Couchet worked in his uncle's shop until the latter's death in 1642, at which time he took over the business and began putting his own name on instruments. Between 1645 and 1680 there are some ten survivors by Ioannes, Ioannes II, or Ioseph Ioannes, and most of them show that while they continued the Ruckers tradition, they modified their practices to suit current conditions. The upper manual of a 1646 Ioannes nonaligned double (Brussels, Musée Instrumental) was given a GG/BB short octave, the first known appearance of that dis-

5-12. The arrangement of the strings on the E♭/G♯ transposing plates in the normal Ruckers double-manual harpsichord. Reprinted from *O'Brien 1990*, with the permission of Cambridge University Press.

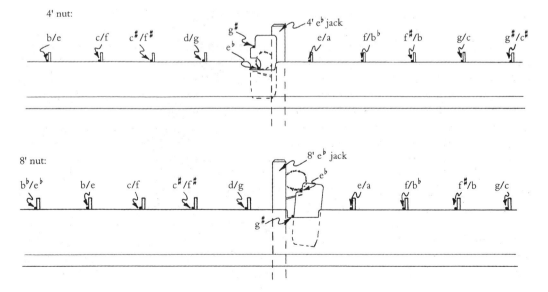

A DIGRESSION ON NONALIGNED KEYBOARDS

Why did the Ruckerses and Couchets—and presumably other Flemish builders as well—make instruments with nonaligned keyboards at all? Attempts to answer this question have led to some interesting conjecture. At first it was assumed that the keyboards were intended for transposition. Quirinus van Blankenburg, the Dutch organist whose reference to the porcine qualities of muselar basses was cited earlier, assumed that Flemish makers were forced to cater to the ineptitude of keyboard players and was appalled that the rudimentary level of their skills required them to use a special instrument to perform the easiest of all transpositions: "At that time they were so inexperienced in transposing that, in order to be able to transpose a piece a fourth lower, they made expressly a special second keyboard in the clavecimbel. This seems unbelievable."[54]

The transposition theory was reinforced in modern times by Sibyl Marcuse in 1952,[55] Raymond Russell in 1959,[56] and Frank Hubbard in 1965.[57] This view remained unchallenged until a 1976 international colloquium, when Nicolas Meeùs suggested that rather than allowing merely for the transposition of a fourth, by utilizing both manuals it facilitated transposition by many other intervals.[58] Richard Shann offered a different explanation in 1984. Rejecting the view that players contemporary to Hans Ruckers were unable to transpose at sight, he suggested that the purpose of the two keyboards was to provide echo effects and changes in timbre: since the lower manual's jacks plucked deeper into the string, its sound, along with its deeper tessitura, would have provided a desired contrast.[59] In the following year John Shortridge suggested that the normal E♭ on the upper manual could have been tuned to D♯, producing a good triad on B, and the G♯ on the lower manual to A♭, to allow a good triad on A♭,[60] thus making more tonalities available. Writing in 1990, O'Brien dismissed these later explanations and argued that double-manual harpsichords were indeed intended to facilitate transposition.[61] Reid Byers disavowed all of the above, suggesting that the lower keyboard was intended to allow performers to play music written and arranged for the lute, an instrument quite popular during the years nonaligned doubles were being produced. The lower manual would put the music in a more appropriate register, and since it plucked the strings farther from the bridge, would sound more lutelike, particularly if buffed.[62] At an international conference held in 1996 at Halle's Handel-Haus, Meeùs reiterated his earlier position but tied transposition to Renaissance modal theory.[63] At the same conference, Koster firmly suggested that the transposing argument was so persuasive as to make all others "too clever by half."[64] John Henry van der Meer, also at the Halle conference, joined those firmly on the side of the transposition theory.[65]

All these explanations are possible, and perhaps at one time or another some or all of them provided the rationale for the purchase of a nonaligned double. On the other hand, if it is true that performers learned these transpositions as they learned to play, then builders could much more easily have allowed for the E♭–G♯ problem by supplying a single-manual instrument with split accidental and two strings for every E♭ and G♯. Such keyboards were well known in Italy. Finally, perhaps they combined the two instruments—one at normal pitch and the other a fourth lower—into one for no other reason than that it could be done, leaving the players to find uses for it. All this suggests that we do not fully understand why they continued to make and sell these instruments for almost fifty years.

position in Antwerp on the nontransposing keyboard of a double. A 1652 Ioannes (private ownership, France) was a 2×8′ with three registers. In this disposition one of the 8′ choirs could be plucked by either the closest or the farthest set of jacks, permitting three contrasting 8′ sounds plus the unison, an arrangement reminiscent of the 1537 Müller and early German practice. Furthermore, the movement of the registers seems to have been operated by some mechanical means—pedals or knee levers—rather than through the normal extension of the upper guides through the cheek. Similarly, a 1679 Ioseph Ioannes (Washington, D.C., Smithsonian Institution), with 1×8′, 1×4′ had three sets of jacks, again allowing for two contrasting 8′ sounds on a single choir of strings, the 4′ alone, and the 8′ and 4′ together. A 1671 Ioseph Ioannes (private ownership, France) was probably also disposed 2×8′, but with two sets of jacks—the normal disposition in Italy by this time, but still a novelty in Antwerp. A ca. 1650 by Ioannes (Antwerp, Vleeshuis Museum), a 1680 Ioseph Ioannes (Boston, Museum of Fine Arts), and an undated instrument, also thought to be ca. 1680 (Stockholm, Stiftelsen Musikkulturens främjande) and also by Ioseph Ioannes, both have extended basses down to FF. The last of these is also very long, in its original one-manual state probably about 8′ 6″.[67] Quite likely, by the middle of the seventeenth century the standard models that served the family so well for more than

5-13. Undated Ioannes Ruckers harpsichord-virginal combination. This imposing instrument has been extensively rebuilt, with new keyboards and other parts. Neither the lid nor its canvas painting of the conversion of St. Paul is original. © Bildarchiv Preussischer Kulturbesitz, Berlin, Musikinstrumenten Museum.

fifty years began to appear old-fashioned and outdated; but by that time Antwerp had lost its position as a leading producer of harpsichords.

THE DECORATION OF HARPSICHORDS AND VIRGINALS[68]

Like many of their Italian counterparts, pre-1600 Ruckers virginals were lavishly and expensively decorated. The 1581 mother and child muselar by Hans, discussed in Chapter 3, was completely and painstakingly covered with painted patterns rather than paper and was given an impressive courtly pastoral lid painting. A ca. 1600 mother and child spinett by Ioannes (Milan, Museo degli Strumenti Musicali), while papered, is graced with a lid painting similar to Hans's 1581. In fact, with the exception of the ca. 1580 Grouwels, whose subject matter deals with peasants, and the 1591 Hans Ruckers polygonal spinett (Bruges, Gruuthuse Museum), whose lid is papered and has a motto, all the extant virginals between Hans Bos's ca. 1570 spinett and the ca. 1600 Ioannes have detailed, formal, stylized lid paintings. But subsequent decoration, while still elaborate and stereotypical, was far less expensive, and by the beginning of the seventeenth century Ruckers harpsichords and virginals were decorated in as standard a manner as the way in which they were built.

After ca. 1600, lids were usually covered with papers instead of paintings.[69] Lid paintings that do exist are fine-art pictures, undoubtedly commissioned by the purchasers, with subjects something other than courtly pastorals. In virginals, the keywell and the frontal areas to the left and right (both of which are concealed by the fallboard when raised) were papered. With both virginals and harpsichords the inner walls of the soundwell were covered with more papers, but of a narrower design. The builder's name and city were lettered in Roman capitals on the unpainted namebatten: for example, IOANNES RVCKERS FECIT ANVERPIÆ. On virginals the

ANOTHER HARPSICHORD/VIRGINAL COMBINATION

One other harpsichord/virginal combination exists, but dating from 1735, more than a century after Hans and Ioannes made theirs. The builder was Johannes Josephus Coenen, organist at the cathedral of the Dutch city of Roermond. It appears to have been modeled after the 1619 Ioannes instrument, although not as it was originally constructed, since by Coenen's time Ioannes's harpsichord had been rebuilt to a 2×8', 1×4' with aligned keyboards, while still retaining the quint virginal in the bentside. Coenen copied the rebuilt version, and it may well be that he was attempting to make what we would call today a historical copy.[66] The instrument is in the Plantin-Moretus Museum in Antwerp, where it is said to have resided since it was built. Unlike the more colorful decoration Ioannes would have supplied, its exterior is painted black; but it does have a lid painting, after Rubens, of St. Cecilia playing a small organ.

name and city were found on the top of the unpainted jackrail. The moldings cut into the top of the case were varnished, rather than painted, and the narrow case tops were painted black. Virginal exteriors were normally painted in an imitation green porphyry marble, except for the child virginals, which were entirely covered with paper. Although almost all extant virginals have been redecorated, only one other original external decorative scheme has ever been discovered.[70] Like Henry Ford's black model T automobile, the customer could have any color virginal he wanted as long as it was green porphyry.

Natural keys were covered with bone, with the same two pairs of scored lines and notches found on the touch plates of the Karest virginals. Note names were lettered in red on the rear of each natural touch plate, between the sharps, although almost all traces of this have long disappeared. Key fronts were covered with pierced, embossed paper. Except for some early instruments of Hans's, the sharps, made of a dark oak found in bogs or moors (bog oak), were no longer scored and notched.[71] Endblocks were molded and painted black.

The exteriors of most of the harpsichords, whether singles or doubles, were painted in a brownish-red faux marble,[72] with narrow grayish-green bands at the top and bottom of the case sides. In a casual attempt at trompe l'oeil, a dark line separated the band from the marble at the top, and a similar lighter line was placed at the bottom. The marbling and the bands often went all around the instrument, including the closed fallboard, the spine, and the lid. An alternate decorative scheme, no doubt more expensive than marbling, consisted of iron strapwork and brass studs painted over a red ground, with enormous jewels painted where the straps crossed.[73] The marbling of both virginals and harpsichords was not realistic, and probably deliberately so; the builders wanted an allusion to marble, not instruments that could be mistaken for rectangular blocks of porphyry or harpsichord-shaped blocks of red marble.

With their flowers, birds, insects, fruit, shrimp, snowflakes, angels, monkeys, and humans, it was undoubtedly the soundboard paintings of harpsichords and virginals that most attracted attention.[74] The soundboard, bridges, and nuts were all outlined in blue borders with scallops, from which sprang complex arabesques to slow down the eye and organize the motifs. A single gilded lead or pewter rose[75] with the maker's initials was surrounded by a wreath of some sort, ranging from a simple circle of foliage with tiny red and white flowers to a complex bouquet, depending on the decorator. Tulips seemed to be a specially favored flower, which was not surprising in view of the tulip mania then rampant in the Low Countries.[76] The soundboard painting was done in a rather naive style resembling crewel work, and not at all like the ravishing flower painting so beautifully executed by seventeenth-century Flemish artists such as Jan Bruegel. Like the papers, the flora and fauna on the soundboard seem to have been taken from pattern books, some of which may already have been more than a century old. Devices such as the wreaths surrounding the maker's rose, sometimes supported by angels, hark back to armorial symbols found in fifteenth-century illuminated manuscripts.[77] Nevertheless, with the colorful motifs, the gilded rose and its wreath, and the blue borders, scallops, and arabesques crowded onto the board in a spectacular display of a Flemish "love of profusion,"[78] the effect is extraordinary.

As noted earlier, stylized lid paintings were found on virginals prior to 1600.[79] After that date lids might get a fine painting, even by one of the better-known Antwerp artists,[80] but more often they were covered by papers printed to look like wood grain. Hiding wood with a paper designed to resemble wood is one of the stranger aspects of Flemish decoration, but the poplar from which the lids were made was a close-grained wood with no figure. Furthermore, the "grain" on the paper was supposed to remind one of Hungarian ash, the same wood veneer that

5-14. This 1615 Andreas double is one of the few Ruckers instruments still retaining its original marbling. A nonaligned double, at some time in the past the keyboards were aligned and one of the four sets of jacks discarded. Note the extension of the upper guides and the buff rail through the cheek. The lid motto, SIC TRANSIT GLORIA MVNDI, was a common one. Antwerp, Vleeshuis Museum.

covered the 1537 Müller harpsichord, and often used then as wall paneling.[81] But like the marbling on the exterior of the case, the effect was a little on the crude side.

Edifying Latin mottoes like SIC TRANSIT GLORIA MVNDI (Thus passes the glory of the world), SOLI DEO GLORIA (Glory to God alone), MVSICA MAGNORVM SOLAMEN DVLCE LABORVM (Music is the sweet solace of great toils), and MVSICA LAETITAE COMES MEDICINA DOLORVM (Music is the companion of joy, the medicine of sorrows) were inked on the lid papers in large Roman capitals. Lid flaps and fallboards could also receive mottoes.[82] Borders, scallops, and arabesques, like those on the soundboard, were repeated on the lid, but in red. Both decorators who worked for Andreas repeated some of the soundboard flora and fauna on the lid, surrounding — and sometimes threatening to overpower —

5-15. The 1637 Andreas single, another rare Ruckers instrument with its original decoration, although at some point the corners were cut off the case. The matching stand is not original. Nuremberg, Germanisches Nationalmuseum.

the lettered motto.[83] Like the marbling, soundboard painting, and wood-grain paper, the lettering was not particularly polished, and lines were not always straight. This was also true of the smaller lettering on the namebatten. In contrast, lettering on pre-1600 instruments was more elegantly executed and used a more classically oriented alphabet

The stands upon which the harpsichords and virginals rested were not part of the instruments. Made in trestle form with turned legs, they resembled the heavy oak furniture then in style; in fact, it is possible they were made by craftsmen in the furniture trade rather than by harpsichord builders. Few original stands are extant, but some indications of their shapes can be gleaned from the many paintings of Flemish instruments. One thing the paintings show is that the instruments were raised higher than we have them today. This means that either players sat on a stool or a higher-than-normal chair — a necessity in any case, since the fallboard was not detachable and would bump the knees at a normal sitting position — or they stood, which, for the diminutive women portrayed in the paintings, was a perfectly comfortable playing height.

In the sixteenth century it was not unusual for decoration to re-flect allegorical and mythological significance.[84] This was es-pecially true of musical instruments, and particularly so with stringed keyboards, whose size and complexity marked them as objects symbolizing wealth and power.[85] When ornately adorned, they were viewed as works of art as much as musical instruments. This was not a coincidence: their visual elements were intended to delight the eye, just as their sounds were ex-pected to enrapture the ear. Supplying them with moralizing mottoes instructed the mind and gave them an intellectual com-ponent that made them even more valuable. One, giving voice to this sentiment, is RENDO LIETI IN VN TEMPO GLI OCCHI E'L CORE (I make happy at one time the eyes and the heart). Through their strings, keyboard instruments were associated with Apollo's lyre and King David's harp; but they also resonated with the Pythagorean world of order and harmony, where distances be-tween planets were expressed in terms of the ratios of a vibrating string.[86] That parallel between the harmony of music and the harmony of the spheres was expressed in mottoes such as CON-SENTV LAETENTVR EO SUPER ASTRA LOC[ATO] (Let them rejoice in that harmony beyond the stars), and CONCORDIA MVSIS AMICA (Harmony is a friend to the Muses). Underscoring all was the fundamental belief that a musical instrument was a symbol of resurrection, a miraculous rebirth of a tree which, though felled and made into lumber, lived again as a music-making device through the mysterious skills of the builder. A motto posing the riddle DUM VIXI TACVI MORTVA DVLCE CANO (While alive I was silent; now dead, I sweetly sing) was the unwritten companion to all harpsichords. Similarly, Flemish soundboard paintings often included a caterpillar and a moth, symbols of the liberation of the spirit from the body, and a goldfinch, a resurrection symbol found in contemporary *vanitas* paintings as well.[87]

All these elements are harmoniously balanced in the 1581 Hans Ruckers mother and child muselar virginal discussed briefly in the last chapter. It is an exquisitely wrought instru-ment, with beautifully and delicately painted patterns on its front faces, keywell, and soundwell. A garden of delights ap-pears on the soundboard. The lid painting, a courtly pastoral, offers a model for appropriate and harmonious behavior. Two raised medallions, with portraits of Philip II of Spain and Anne of Austria, connect the instrument to royalty, wealth, position, and power. The moralizing motto on the fallboard, MVSICA

DVLCE LABORVM LEVAMEN (Music is the sweet lightener of labors), offers edifying instruction. A hundred little details, such as the crenelated top molding, the elaborate multicolored painted patterns, and the graceful, carefully spaced Roman alphabet of the motto, mark it as a rare and expensive musical instrument, truly a treat for eye and ear as well as a symbol of the harmonious universe.

Yet, in just a few years Flemish decoration would enter a new and different stage. Patterned paper was substituted for meticulously painted designs. Moldings with crenelations were no longer used, and raised medallions were never seen again. The marbling, though charming, was crude. A less formal alphabet was used for the mottoes and the maker's name and location. In short, from one-of-a-kind works of art, Flemish virginals and harpsichords became less expensive mass-produced items, with a seeming avoidance of the elegance previously lavished on them.[88] It would not have been difficult for the makers to marble their instruments more convincingly; the technique is relatively simple and was well known. They could have hired better painters to decorate their soundboards—artists who could paint flowers closer to the manner of Jan Bruegel or Jacob Jordaens, rather than like fifteenth-century manuscript illuminators. Nevertheless, if one accepts the conceit that the instrument is a block of green porphyry, or a harpsichord-shaped piece of red marble, there is no question that these instruments make an effect. Opening the lid reveals the blazing light of the black-on-white papers, the garden of delights on the soundboard, and the moralizing message of the motto. But with the unrealistic marbling, the archaic flower painting, and the faux grain patterns on the lid papers, there was no attempt to convince the viewer that it was anything more than a conceit.

Grant O'Brien is undoubtedly correct in ascribing the use of cheaper materials to changing fashion,[89] but the trend toward a more affordable "bourgeois" harpsichord is also seen at about that time in Italy. O'Brien further states that the Ruckerses were competing with their fellow builders for the Antwerp trade, attempting to price their product within the reach of middle-class burghers; but perhaps builders also thought it necessary to produce an instrument with which an Antwerp or Amsterdam merchant could feel comfortable, one that would not be out of place in his affluent, but not opulent, home. That merchant, though more prosperous than the rest of Europe's diminutive middle class, still had bourgeois tastes. The impulse may not have been so different from the Biedermeier movement in Germany, two centuries later.[90]

Without question, the Ruckers-Couchet dynasty dominated Antwerp harpsichord building. Their output was enormous, particularly when it is considered that in addition to a staggering number and variety of virginals and harpsichords, they probably built clavichords, and possibly organs as well; and all the while they were repairing, tuning, and maintaining the city's organs. It is clear that their rate of production was of an entirely different magnitude from that of other builders in Antwerp or elsewhere in seventeenth-century Europe. They must have employed many journeymen and apprentices, and it is likely that they kept a fairly sizeable group of subcontractors busy supplying jacks and sharps, and probably other parts as well. That level of production also suggests that acquiring, processing, seasoning, and cutting wood for cases, keyboards, and soundboards were never-ending tasks that must have taken the attention of several people in each shop. Clearly, the Ruckerses had the ability to organize and control large-scale production.

Many unexplained questions about the Ruckerses remain. Why did they (and others) build combined instruments—mother and child virginals, harpsichord/virginal combinations, and nonaligned doubles, and what uses were intended for them? Another unanswered question deals with all the other Antwerp builders: where are their instruments today? Hans Moermans is survived by two harpsichords, Cornelius and Simon Haegerts by two virginals and a harpsichord, Joris Britsen by two harpsichords and two octave virginals, and Gommaar van Everbroek by a single harpsichord. It may well be that instruments from these makers simply did not survive; but it is also likely that at least some of their work were given Ruckers roses and namebattens, and passed off as genuine Ruckers harpsichords.[91] By the end of the seventeenth century a harpsichord by Artus Gheerdinck might not have been worth much; but with the Ruckers name attached to it, it would be a valued artifact, to be enlarged and redecorated. That may have been the fate of a great number of non-Ruckers Antwerp instruments.

Finally, we still do not know why Ruckers instruments were so much in demand. It might have been the different sound of the shorter scale and heavier strings, but that could easily have been imitated by their competitors. It would be difficult to imagine that the Ruckers workmanship was superior to that of their colleagues, or that their instruments were more reliable, or better decorated. There is no evidence for it, but it could be that Ioannes and Andreas I had superior marketing skills, able to convince the buying public—and those to whom that public turned for advice — that their harpsichords were somehow better, more precious, more valuable, and more connected to the Muse of Music than the instruments of their colleagues in the Guild of St. Luke. But beyond that, it is likely that the Ruckerses and Couchets built instruments that were acoustically superior, so much so that in the final analysis their reputations were based more on the enduring qualities of their sound, rather than craftsmanship or marketing. The real mystery is how they achieved that sonic superiority.

Aside from all this, the instruments were superbly functioning music-making devices. They may have been rough inside, where prying eyes could not see the coarseness of unplaned wood, and their decoration may have been naive, perhaps even like Flemish cuckoo clocks; but their musical parts — jacks, guides, keyboards, soundboards — were beautifully made, demonstrating expert craftsmanship and an understanding of friction, leverage, and acoustics. If they were building instruments with which their fellow burghers would feel comfortable, those same instruments were equally prized by those with title and wealth. Whatever mysteries surround the Ruckerses and Couchets, there is no question that by the end of the seventeenth century their instruments were treasured. No knowledgeable owner would dream of discarding a Ruckers or a Couchet, and when the precious possession could no longer meet the demands of current taste and musical requirements, it was modernized and redecorated. Even more remarkable, however, was the effect these instruments had on makers in the late seventeenth and eighteenth centuries. As will be seen, the Ruckerses and Couchets literally changed the course of harpsichord building north of the Alps.

[6]

LATER ITALIAN STYLE

*I*TALY'S PRODUCTIVE power suffered in the seventeenth century. It still endured the devastating consequences of the Italian Wars and Spanish domination; it faced formidable competition from Holland, England, and France in the manufacture of silk and wool, in ship-building, and in the arena of international finance; and it withstood an eruption of plague. Nevertheless, as it had previously, Italy's cottage-industry structure helped to mitigate the worst consequences of hard times, and its artistic and cultural life continued to affect the rest of Europe. To cite only two examples, the revolutionary chiaroscuro techniques of Michelangelo Caravaggio (1573–1610), with his dramatic manipulation of light and dark, influenced generations of painters on both sides of the Alps. Claudio Monteverdi (1567–1643) not only transformed the madrigal from a polyphonic piece into a solo song, but also almost single-handedly established the newly invented genre of opera as a viable and compelling musico-dramatic form. Italian ideas led Europe into the seventeenth century and into the artistic revolution sweeping the Continent.

Based on a soloistic vocal style combined with a firm harmonic bass, the musical forces that initiated this stylistic change were visible in published music as early as ca. 1560, and twenty years after that were fairly widespread in northern Italy. Driving one of these currents was the humanistic desire for expression of emotion, and composers and theorists found inspiration in Plato, who stated in his *Republic* that all elements of music should be subservient to the expression of the words. Humanists also invoked the skills of the orators of ancient Greece and Rome, whose words were said to arouse the passions of their listeners. The crucible in which this new style was developed seems to have been the Florentine Camerata, a confederation of humanists at the Medici court, one of whom was the singer, teacher, and composer Giulio Caccini. It is believed that Caccini was responsible for the evolution of the monodic style—solo singing capable of expressing emotion and passion, with an accompaniment realized from a figured bass line by harpsichord, organ, lute, harp, or any other instrument capable of chordal playing.[1] The accompaniment soon came to be known as *basso continuo,* and it may well have been the catalyst that persuaded Italian harpsichord players and builders to abandon the 1×4′, 1×8′ disposition in favor of the 2×8′, a sound more preferable for continuo playing.

NEW DEVELOPMENTS IN THE SEVENTEENTH CENTURY

The 2×8′ disposition was first seen shortly before 1560 in a harpsichord by Bortolus (Naples, private collection), although it may not have caught on immediately, since the next surviving exemplar, by Dominicus Pisaurensis (Nice, private ownership), is dated 1570.[2] But after 1600 the 2×8′ became the common disposition for Italian harpsichords, and remained so until they were no longer built. With a few exceptions, by 1630 the 4′ register and the 1×8′ disposition had become virtually obsolete. Some instruments still ascended to f^3, but most only went up to c^3 or sometimes d^3. Basses commonly commenced with C/E, although others descended to GG/BB.[3]

One of the major activities of seventeenth-century Italian builders was the modernizing of earlier harpsichords; in fact, rebuilding seemed to go on continuously, as 1×8′ instruments received a second set of strings, and 1×8′, 1×4′ harpsichords lost their 4′ bridges and nuts in the conversion. By the end of the sixteenth century many Italian instruments had already experienced fairly substantial transformations. New keyboards were built—or, more likely, old ones rebuilt—as compasses changed and scales were transformed from iron to brass (or from low-pitched to normal-pitched brass scales, depending on one's assumptions). The 1531 Trasuntino (London, Royal College of Music), for example, originally had a compass of C/E–f^3, a scale of 14″, and a disposition of 1×8′, 1×4′. Later, its compass was changed to GG/BB–c^3,[4] its scale to 10″, and its disposition to

2×8′. This reclamation process ensured that almost all the older instruments began to resemble their younger siblings.[5] Examining these harpsichords early in the twentieth century, scholars assumed that the Italian harpsichord had sprung forth fully grown, like Jason's dragon-teeth men, around 1500. On the other hand, because of the difficulties involved in rebuilding, virginals were seldom subjected to such transformations.

The change in disposition was accompanied by a basic shift in attitude toward these instruments. With a 1×8′, 1×4′ harpsichord the two sets of strings could be used together or as solo stops. However, on a 2×8′, plucking points are so close that there is little distinction in tone color between the two choirs, and hence, no reason to play one *or* the other. It is likely that both 8′s were intended to be on almost all the time, since there was no easy provision for turning one on or off (for tuning purposes, one choir could be silenced by reaching under the jackrail and moving the register directly). With no need to change registers, there were no longer extension knobs protruding through the cheeks. Those instruments that now have shift levers mounted on the wrestplank or extending through the nameboard were probably retrofitted with these devices.

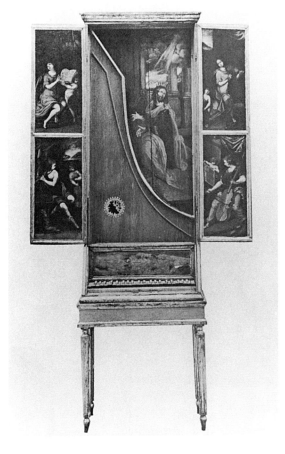

6-1. An anonymous seventeenth-century Italian clavicytherium. Upright harpsichords were never plentiful, in Italy or elsewhere. This unique example was built into a cabinet. New York, Metropolitan Museum of Art.

The construction of Flemish harpsichords shifted from thin-case to thick-case design after 1565, but in Italy that "advance" seems to have been ignored until the end of the sixteenth century, when a number of false inner-outer oblong virginals began to appear (false inner-outer harpsichords came somewhat later). The earliest extant is a 1587 Celestini (Hamburg, private collection). Builders attempted to fool the eye into thinking that a heavy-case instrument was actually a thin-walled virginal in a heavy box. The outside of the case and lid interior were decorated, normally with paint, just as a normal outer was; but the soundwell was veneered — usually with cypress, and supplied with a "cap molding" — a piece of molding set into a slot cut into the case just above the veneer. Carved or scroll-sawn cheeks were glued to the insides of the square case cheeks. In other words, where unpainted wood and molding would normally be seen on a true inner-outer, so they would be found on a false inner-outer. To a casual glance, the effect was quite convincing.

Softwoods ½″ or more were commonly used for heavy-case sides. Bracing still normally consisted of bottom battens and knees, and sometimes diagonal struts, although since these members were no longer required to provide the strength needed for thin-wall construction, fewer interior braces were found. Some instruments had only battens, some only knees, and a few nothing at all.[6] Spruce or fir became more frequent alternatives to cypress for soundboards. The rose was sometimes omitted and, even when present, was likely to be simpler than those used in the sixteenth century. Hence, although these modifications did not occur simultaneously, by the last few decades of the seventeenth century, the Italian harpsichord, with 2×8′ disposition, heavy, softwood, false inner-outer case, spruce or fir soundboard, short scale, and C/E–c³ compass, was quite different from its sixteenth-century predecessor. Nevertheless, the true inner-outer never died out and remained viable through the eighteenth century. Finally, the instrument's basic sound remained unchanged.

6-2. An anonymous seventeenth-century false inner-outer Italian harpsichord. Rome, Museo Nazionale degli Strumenti Musicali.

ROME

Fine jack-action instruments continued to be made in Italy as new makers rose to prominence, but the center of building seems to have shifted from Venice to Rome. Whereas only a handful of artisans are known to have practiced there in the sixteenth century, some forty-five have been identified in the seventeenth,[7] although many are just names, or known for one or two instruments. In the latter category is the builder Valerius Peres (or Perius), survived by an instrument and a memory. His 1625 harpsichord (New Haven, Yale Collection of Musical Instruments) is a conservative 2×8′ inner-outer with a C/E–c³ compass. Its only departure from normal Italian practice is a keyboard of bone naturals and ebony sharps. His sewing-box octave spinet, lost in World War II (and now only a memory), had a compartment for needles and a mirror on the inside of the lid.

Giovanni Battista Boni (fl. 1619–41) was born in Cortona but spent his productive years in the Holy City. If there is more information on Boni than on other Italian builders, it is because he is mentioned prominently in the archival records of the Barberini family.[8] Pope Urban VIII (Maffeo Barberini, pope from 1623 to 1644) had three nephews, Cardinal Francesco, Don Taddeo, and Cardinal Antonio, who provided munificent support of artistic endeavors in Rome. Boni was a frequent recipient of their patronage. The Barberini records show that Boni not only built harpsichords and organs, but also spent a great deal of his time restoring, repairing, maintaining, tuning, and renting instruments for the trio of nephews and their musicians.[9] Seven harpsichords either bear his name or are ascribed to him, but only four, all from 1619, seem to be genuine (Cambridge, Fitzwilliam Museum; Brussels, Musée Instrumental; Bristol, private collection; Miami, Dade County Museum of Art).[10] The first was originally strung 3×8′, but the others were single strung, beginning with a short-octave arrangement, ascending to c³, with split sharps on the tenor and alto D♯/E♭s and G♯/A♭s. They are not peas in a pod, however: the Brussels and

6-3. A 1625 harpsichord by the obscure maker Valerius Peres. By this time heavy-case instruments had been built in Italy for more than thirty years, but the true inner-outer always remained a viable form. New Haven, Yale University Collection of Musical Instruments.

Miami instruments are true inner-outers, whereas the Bristol is a false inner-outer. The Brussels and Miami begin on C/E, but the Bristol, with its second and third naturals divided front and back, probably had a bass sounding FF,GG/BB,C/AA.[11] Also, the division of the split sharps differs somewhat on all three instruments. Boni was known for making instruments with augmented keyboards — they may have been his specialty.

At Boni's death, Girolamo Zenti (ca. 1609–ca. 1666), perhaps the best-known seventeenth-century Roman builder, succeeded him as maker, tuner, and technician for the pope's nephews.[12] Zenti was born in Viterbo, but by 1638 he was registered as a harpsichord builder in nearby Rome.[13] Arguably the most peripatetic Italian harpsichord builder of all time, he did not tarry there long. In 1653 he went to Stockholm, in the service of Queen Christina of Sweden. He returned to Rome in 1660 to fulfill an organ-building commission, but left for Paris (the instrument unfinished), where he stayed until 1662. Hired away by the English court in 1664, he went to London with the title of the king's virginal maker. He was back in Rome again before that year was out, but in 1666 went to Paris once again. He died there that year or the next. It is thought that Zenti might also have served the Medicis in Florence, since an inventory made there in 1700, shortly after Cristofori's arrival, lists six of his instruments.[14] Unfortunately, we have no Zenti instruments from his Swedish, French, and English years; it would have been interesting to see how he built when working in traditions other than his own.[15]

Almost a dozen instruments either bear his name or are attributed to him, but we have precious few authenticated Zentis.

A 1666 (New York, Metropolitan Museum of Art), seen in Plate 9, is a simple cypress inner-outer with brass scaling and GG,AA–c³ compass that was restored almost a century after it was built by Giovanni Ferrini, Cristofori's student and successor at the Florentine court. Its original compass was enlarged to AA–f³, although probably not by Ferrini. The Metropolitan Museum also has an undated ebony inner-outer triangular octave spinet attributed to Zenti; its two-and-a-half-octave G–c² compass and diminutive keys suggest that it was made for a child. A harpsichord from 1658 (Munich, Deutsches Museum) has a strange history: it is now a three-manual instrument bearing the name of "Bartolomeo Cristofari," dated 1702, and disposed 1×16', 1×8', 1×4', but after an examination of the moldings, Wraight believes it was made by Zenti, and that it began life as a large single 2×8' descending to the 16' region.[16] It was transformed into its present configuration sometime between 1895 and

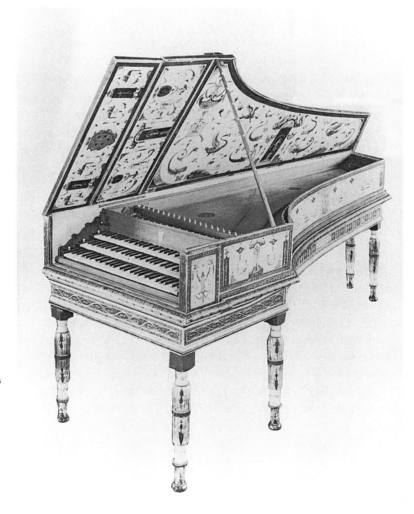

6-5. This 1658 Zenti was built as a large single-manual 2×8' descending to CC. It was turned into a three-manual harpsichord by Leopoldo Franciolini, who put Cristofori's name on it. Munich, Deutsches Museum.

1898 by Leopoldo Franciolini,[17] an unscrupulous Florentine antique dealer we will meet again, many times.

Today Zenti is probably best known for his earliest surviving instrument, a 1631 inner-outer bentside spinet (Brussels, Musée Instrumental) of thin-walled cypress, with a projecting keyboard and an outer case. This is the first-known spinet in bentside form, and the design has been credited to Zenti. The configuration is more harpsichord-like than square or trapezoidal spinets; in fact, it could be thought of as a harpsichord bent over to the right at the jackrail, putting the string band at an angle but leaving the keyboard and action facing straight ahead. The jacks operated in a box guide fitted into the gap, and like all spinets and virginals, the jack pairs pluck in opposite directions. A few bentside spinets by other Italian builders followed, so the idea did find some acceptance in the country of its birth. Bentsides were also built in France (where it was called *espinette à l'italienne*), Germany, and the Low Countries, but the shape achieved its greatest popularity in England.[18]

Giovanni Battista Giusti (ca. 1624–ca. 1693) was a student of Boni, then Zenti. Nearly twenty instruments have been attributed to him, but probably half are authentic.[19] Two, a 1679 (Bologna, private ownership) and a ca. 1681 (Basel, Historisches Museum), are 2×8′, 1×4′ harpsichords, an uncommon disposition for Italians.[20] The others are 2×8′. Two of his survivors, both from 1681 (Nuremberg, Germanisches Nationalmuseum; Vermillion, private ownership), are heavy-cased; the others are true inner-outers. The compasses of half the confirmed Giustis are C/E–c^3, but GG/BB–c^3 is found on a 1676 (Leipzig, Musikinstrumenten-Museum der Universität Leipzig). Another three commence with GG,AA, with two from 1679 and 1693 ascending to c^3 (Bologna, private ownership; Washington, D.C., Smithsonian Institution), and a 1681 to d^3 (Basel, Historisches Museum). This short recitation demonstrates that, other than a general faithfulness to the 2×8′ disposition and thin-case construction (either in reality or in appearance), even for a single builder there were often few discernable standards of compass and use of the short octave in seventeenth-century Italian harpsichord building. The Antwerp instruments were far more uniform.

Giacomo Ridolfi (fl. 1650–82) probably also studied with Zenti, since both names appear on a 1650 harpsichord (New York, private ownership), and Zenti is cited as his mentor on the nameboard of a 1665 (Washington, D.C., Smithsonian Institution). Ridolfi's six known instruments are mainly 2×8′, C/E–c^3, true inner-outer harpsichords, and hence conform more to the "standard" seventeenth-century Italian model.[21] A 1662 instrument (Nuremberg, Germanisches Nationalmuseum), however, originally had a compass of GG,AA–c^3.

Visitors to the musical instrument galleries of New York's Metropolitan Museum of Art are invariably impressed by one of its crowning glories, the "golden harpsichord" attributed to Michelle Todini (1625–after 1681).[22] It is a long 2×8′ inner-outer, almost 9′ in length, originally with a compass of GG,AA–c^3. The inner case is rarely seen, but the outer is part of an ensemble that bears analogy to an opera scene. Akin to an elaborate aria, the gilded case is carved in bas-relief depicting the triumph of Galatea. The base of the stand, carved and tinted green to represent the sea, is supported on a series of lion's feet. Three muscular tritons, rising from the sea, strain to support the case on their shoulders, while two naiads urge them on. A putto, seated on a seashell borne by a pair of ferocious-looking dolphins, oversees the operation. Placed at the keyboard end

6-7. A 1679 harpsichord by Giovanni Battista Giusti. This is one of the few 2×8′, 1×4′ harpsichords made by an Italian builder. Bologna, Tagliavini Collection. Photo by Antonio Guerra.

TODINI'S *GALLERIA ARMONICA*

Todini is known to have made organs, clavichords, lutes, clockworks, and mechanically bowed strings as well as harpsichords, and he was also a player of the violone, the trumpet, and the musette; but he is particularly famous for his *galleria armonica*, several rooms in a Roman palazzo in which he had placed a group of interconnected instruments. A woodcut from 1673, in Athanasius Kircher's *Phonurgia nova*, shows someone playing a fanciful clavicytherium which somehow also controls three other instruments in the background, causing music to emanate from them as well.[25] Beyond these is an organ without a visible keyboard, suggesting that it also was played by remote control. Todini himself described a conglomeration of seven instruments—four with jack action, two with bowed action (*Geigenwerk*), and one organ—all controlled from one keyboard.[26] The *galleria* remained in place until well after Todini's death. Filippo Bonanni, in his *Gabinetto armonico* of 1722, included a woodcut of another of Todini's combinations, four instruments in one L-shaped cabinet, all presumably controlled from the console of what seems to be a claviorganum.[27] Charles Burney visited the *galleria* in 1771 and described a harpsichord that also operated an organ, two spinets, a virginal, and three stringed instruments.[28]

6-8. By means of levers, stickers, and trackers, Michelle Todini created a fantastic gallery of remotely controlled instruments.

According to Todini himself, the golden harpsichord was displayed in one of the rooms of the palazzo.[29] He wrote a book about the *galleria*, and in chapter 3, devoted to a description of the *"machina di Polifemo e Galatea,"* he indicated that the instrument and all its appurtenances were part of a larger tableau, filling the entire room.[30] Hence, there is little doubt that Todini owned the instrument, although there is no absolute proof that he built it himself.

of the instrument is a free-standing statue of the cyclops Polyphemus, who, sitting on a rock and playing a bagpipe, is undoubtedly composing a love song to the sea nymph Galatea,[23] whose statue, also free-standing, occupies a complementary position at the tail.[24] This mélange contradicts earlier statements about the end of the era of opulence, but only the outer case receives the treatment, not the plain, undecorated inner. Nevertheless, the golden harpsichord, seen in Plate 10, is a spectacular sight.

Judging by the number of names that have come down to us, Florence had a flourishing circle of active builders in the seventeenth century,[32] but our knowledge of Florentine makers differs little from what we have found in other places in Italy, and most have not been survived by any of their work. Harpsichords made in Florence seem no different from those built elsewhere in Italy. Its artisans may have produced more virginals than Roman builders, but that speculation is based on surviving examples. As in Rome, most of the extant Florentine instruments are relatively plain cypress inner-outers, and that certainly is true of the seven surviving virginals of Francesco Poggio (d. 1634). Little is known of this builder other than that he worked for a while in Venice and spent most of his productive years in Florence, where he was a member of the guild. Like so many Italian builders, Poggio did not seem to have a standard model. Fourteen of his virginals ascend to f^3, while the other three reach c^3, although all commence with the short octave C/E. Eight virginals are polygonal (one of these, in Brussels, Musée Instrumental, is a trapezoidal ottavino), and nine are oblong. Most are true inner-outers.

Vincentius Pratensis (not to be confused with Vincentius Livigimeno) was a harpsichord maker and luthier from Prato, a small town near Florence. His 1612 inner-outer (Leipzig, Musikinstrumenten-Museum der Universität Leipzig) reminds us of the opulent Venetian harpsichords of the previous century; indeed, it is a late example of that sort of instrument. Originally a $1\times8'$, it is now a $2\times8'$, but it retained its conservative C/E–c^3 compass. The case sides are lacquered in black inside and out, with gilded vine and flower patterns in the soundwell and keywell. The nameboard is particularly well done, with birds and lions flanking a centrally placed heraldic device, and the cheek pieces are flatly carved cor-

---

THE MODEL FOR TODINI'S "GOLDEN HARPSICHORD"

In his book *Musical Instruments and Their Symbolism in Western Art,* Emanuel Winternitz, then curator of the New York Metropolitan Museum of Art's collection of musical instruments, relates a surprising sequel to the instrument's history.[31] Before World War II, Evan Gorga, the Romanian-born tenor who sang the first Rodolfo in Puccini's *La Bohème,* amassed a large collection of musical instruments. Hearing of this private cache, Winternitz visited Gorga at his home in Rome in 1949. He found that Gorga had sold his collection to the Italian government some years earlier (it subsequently formed the basis of the collection in Rome's Museo Nazionale degli Strumenti Musicali), but the tenor showed him photographs of the many treasures he once owned. To Winternitz's great excitement, among them was a picture of something that looked like a model for the golden harpsichord. Gorga recalled that he had owned such a model, made of clay, but had no idea of its present whereabouts. A little later Winternitz, rooting about in the storerooms of the Palazzo Venezia in Rome, accidentally discovered the pieces of the model and, since he had the original back home in New York, was able to reconstruct it. The model is now on display in Rome's Museo Nazionale degli Strumenti Musicali.

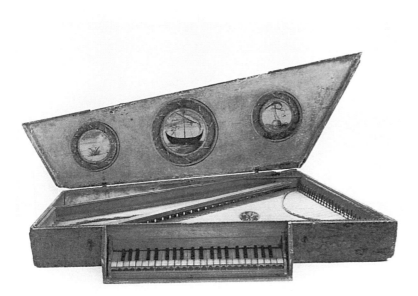

6-9. This 1586 inner-outer is Francesco Poggio's earliest extant virginal. The plain but refined inner instrument gains its loveliness from its elegant moldings and its interesting shape. Stuttgart, Württembergisches Landesmuseum.

nucopias. Vincentius's name is found on the back, rather than the front of the nameboard. An undated polygonal virginal is ascribed to "Baffo, 1791" (London, Fenton House), but attributed to Vincentius by Wraight on the evidence of the moldings.[33] With black lacquer and gold vines, and flat-carved cornucopia cheek blocks, this virginal has similarities to the 1612 harpsichord described above. The builder is survived by two other instruments, a 1610 octave virginal (also Leipzig, Musikinstrumenten-Museum der Universität Leipzig), and a harpsichord from 1610 (Poughkeepsie, N.Y., Vassar College). The last is particularly interesting, since it is the only known Italian harpsichord with a close-plucking lute stop. One immediately suspects the intervention of a Franciolini, but the stop seems genuine.

The Florentines Pasquino (fl. 1610–25) and Vincenzio Querci (fl. 1634) were father and son, but only three harpsichords (1613, Washington, D.C., Smithsonian Institution; ca. 1625, Leipzig, Musikinstrumenten-Museum der Universität Leipzig; Nuremberg, Germanisches Nationalmuseum), four polygonal virginals (1610, location unknown; 1624, Geneva, Musée d'Instruments Anciens de Musique; ca. 1625, Hamburg, private ownership; undated, Brussels, Musée Instrumental), and two octave spinets (1625, New York, Metropolitan Museum of Art; undated, private ownership) by Pasquino have survived.[34] It is possible that the son spent his entire career as a builder working for his father.

6-10. A harpsichord in opulent style, the case of the 1612 Vincentius Pratensis is lacquered in black, with gilded vine and flower patterns. The cheek pieces are flat-carved cornucopias. Leipzig, Musikinstrumenten-Museum der Universität Leipzig.

Clearly, other than what we glean through examination of their extant instruments, we know little about the lives of most seventeenth-century Italian harpsichords makers; but, like Boni and Zenti, Giuseppe Mondini is an exception. He was born in Imola in 1631, died in Florence in 1718, and is survived by two instruments. However, like Antonio Vivaldi (1678–1741), who was both priest and composer, Mondini was both priest and harpsichord maker and was so described in a 1741 Vatican manuscript listing famous seventeenth-century builders.[37] He is known to have supplied two harpsichords and a spinet for Ferdinand de' Medici, an indication that he was well thought of.[38] He also made a three-register harpsichord for Cardinal Pietro Ottoboni, the patron of both Alessandro Scarlatti (1660–1725) and Arcangelo Corelli (1653–1713), and a 1701 3×8′ inner-outer harpsichord by Mondini (Hamburg, private collection), nearly 9′ long, may well be that instrument.[39] The third choir of strings is on a separate nut close to the jacks, thus producing the nasal sound also found on the 1537 Müller and some seventeenth-century German and English instruments. There are a few other 3×8′ Italian harpsichords, but a concern for the more colorful possibilities of plucked-string tone was unusual in Italy, where even the buff stop was largely ignored. His other surviving harpsichord (New York, private ownership) is a more conventional 2×8′. Mondini may also have invented the folding harpsichord (an achievement usually attributed to the Parisian builder Jean Marius around 1700) and was so credited in a ca. 1732 publication listing famous Italian inventors and harpsichord makers.[40]

Other Florentine builders could be mentioned — Stefano Bolcioni, Giovanni de Pertici, and Antonio Migliai are a few — but reciting the statistics of their one or two surviving instruments would not add to our knowledge of seventeenth-century Florentine harpsichord building.[41] It was conservative, middle-of-the-road harpsichord building, much like that practiced in the rest of Italy.[42]

NAPLES AND ELSEWHERE

Rather like the city itself, Neapolitan builders continued to go their own way in the seventeenth century, producing virginals that, while certainly Italian in concept and execution, were nev-

THE DE QUOCOS

From the widespread dates of the instruments bearing the name, it has been assumed that the Florentine builder Nicolaus de Quoco could have been two men, perhaps father and son. The elder is known for two harpsichords, dated 1612 and 1615 (both in Copenhagen, Musikhistorisk Museum), while four are ascribed to the presumed younger de Quoco, a 1690 (Lisbon, Museu de Música), two from 1694 (Brussels, Musée Instrumental; Washington, D.C., Smithsonian Institution), and a 1697 (Milan, private ownership). But Denzil Wraight claimed that the 1612 bears little resemblance to other instruments attributed to the de Quoco name and hence called it a forgery. The 1615, he noted, shows closer ties to the Querci instruments than to the de Quocos, and the 1690 is probably a fabrication made by Franciolini. The 1694 in Brussels, Wraight demonstrated, was made by Giuseppe Solfanelli of Pisa. Wraight also casts doubts on the inscription to the 1694 de Quoco in the Smithsonian, since it would have been the only instrument even possibly made by a builder of that name. Wraight finally concluded that it is unlikely that Nicolaus de Quoco ever existed, except as a name that forgers put on nameboards.[35] Thus, like the smile on Alice's Cheshire cat, as a builder, de Quoco slowly fades from view, until only a faint memory remains of his once tangible presence. With continued research, and with previously unknown instruments still turning up, it is entirely possible that future discoveries will either confirm Wraight's assessment or return the de Quoco name to the realm of the corporeal.

No matter who made it, the 1612 has an interesting device on the soundboard that at first glance looks like a 4′ bridge; but it is a moveable rail upon which are mounted little hard felt wedges, one for each string. When the rail is moved by means of a stop knob at the front of the case, the wedges contact the strings of one of the 8′ choirs, dividing them in the middle. This creates a node, like lightly pressing a finger in the middle of a guitar string, so that strings contacted by the wedges would sound at 4′ pitch when plucked. Hence, this harpsichord could sound 2×8′, or 1×8′, or 1×4′, or 1×8′, 1×4′. This stop, sometimes called a *cornett zug*, was probably not original to the instrument, but may have been added early in its life.[36]

6-11. A 2×8′ harpsichord by "Nicolaus de Quoco." The strangely shaped rail occupying the position of a 4′ bridge is a *cornett zug*, a device with felt wedges that contact one of the choirs of 8′ strings to give it 4′ pitch. Copenhagen, Musikhistorisk Museum og Carl Claudius' Samling.

ertheless unique in several aspects. The Neapolitan virginal is an oblong inner-outer of cypress whose wrestplank is found behind the jacks, in the upper left portion of the case, rather than on the right. The wrestpins, of course, are also behind the jacks, rather than clustered on the right. Thus, the left bridge sits on a wrestplank, effectively deadening the portion of the sound-board to the left of the box guide.[44] Also contrary to usual Italian practice, the half-projecting keyboard is placed at the extreme left of the case, like a Flemish spinett, and the straight left bridge does not curve away from the bass jacks. Accordingly, a large part of the tonal difference of these Neapolitan instruments can be ascribed to close plucking points in the bass — much closer to the left bridge than normal in Italian virginals. Finally, Neapolitan virginals are usually a little more elaborate looking than those from the North of Italy.

The above description almost exactly fits the 1598 virginal by Alessandro Fabri mentioned in Chapter 4. Its cheek blocks are nicely carved, and its front faces are enlivened with additional moldings forming frames. Its bone naturals and ebony sharps contrast with the smooth brown color of the cypress inner case. The painted outer case (presumably original), with a "David playing his harp" lid painting, extends forward to enclose the projecting keyboard.

The principal representative of the Neapolitan school of virginal making is Honofrio Guarracino (1628–after 1698). Little is known of him, beyond the dates of his extant instruments, of which there may be as many as a dozen.[45] A 1651 (Italy, private collection) and an undated and unsigned (Berlin, Staatliches Institut für Musikforschung) are harpsichords, but al-

6-12. This long 1701 instrument by Giuseppe Mondini is disposed 3×8′, with one of the 8′ choirs acting as a nasal stop. The silk on the lid and outer case is old, but not original. Hamburg, Museum für Kunst und Gewerbe, Sammlung Beurmann.

BOLCIONI'S THREE-MANUAL HARPSICHORD

Stefano Bolcioni's fame rests on a harpsichord bearing his name with a 2×8′, 1×4′ disposition, three manuals, a C/E–g³ compass, and a date of 1627 (Edinburgh, Russell Collection). The instrument, an inner-outer, is indeed by Bolcioni but was originally a rather deep-case single-manual 2×8′, probably with a C/E–c³ disposition with some split accidentals. It was "converted" to its present form by Franciolini, who took its three keyboards from elsewhere. The painting of the outer case, which is finished in an attractive *vernis martin,* postdates Franciolini's "improvements."[43] Bolcioni is also survived by a 1631 harpsichord (New Haven, Yale Collection of Musical Instruments) and a half dozen oblong virginals.

6-13. Stefano Bolcioni's three-manual harpsichord was originally a modest single. The attractive *vernis martin* finish probably dates from this century, and the elaborate stand was likely supplied at the same time. Edinburgh, Russell Collection of Early Keyboard Instruments, University of Edinburgh.

most all the rest are virginals.[46] These include a 1661 (Berlin, Staatliches Institut für Musikforschung), a 1663 (Bologna, private collection), a 1667 (Milan, La Scala), a 1668 (Goudhurst, Finchcocks Collection), a 1677 (Rome, Museo Nazionale), a 1678 (London, private collection), a 1683 (whereabouts unknown), and a 1692 (Rome, Museo Nazionale). A 1694 octave virginal is also extant (Vermillion, Shrine to Music Museum),[47] as well as a 1668 bentside spinet (Rome, Museo Nazionale).

All surviving Guarracino virginals are cypress inner-outers with dovetailed case joints, C/E–c^3 compasses, half-projecting keyboards with natural touch plates of ivory or bone and sharps of dark wood (the exception to this last is the 1692; but its keys, or at least the touch plates, are not original), and two tool boxes (left front and left rear). Close to each other in size, and in scale as well, they could represent another exception to our observation that Italian builders most likely relied on commissions, and that the variety of their instruments reflected the tastes and requirements of their customers. Judging from the extant examples, Guarracino seems to have produced a "standard" model that changed little over thirty years.

The Bolognese builder Pietro Faby is yet another shadowy Italian harpsichord maker. His dates may be 1639–1703, or those may be the dates of an unrelated "Fabio of Bologna." There are unconfirmed reports that he worked in France. He is, however, survived by five instruments: a 1658 harpsichord (Milan, private ownership), two more harpsichords, from 1677 and 1681 (or 1691), an octave spinet of unknown date (all three in Paris, Musée de la Musique), and a 1684 octave spinet (Trondheim, Ringve Museum). The harpsichords of 1677 and 1681 and the 1684 spinet are elaborately embellished instruments, recalling the opulent style of the previous century. Made for Count Hercole Pepoli, Louis XIV's godson, the 1677 is par-

6-14. The 1598 virginal by Alessandro Fabri, the first known Neapolitan virginal at 8′ pitch. Unlike later examples, Fabri's instrument has a fully projecting keyboard. Bologna, Tagliavini Collection. Photo by Antonio Guerra.

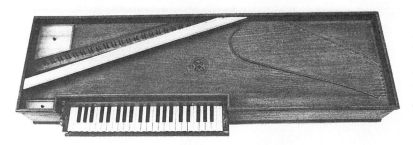

6-15. A 1663 Neapolitan virginal by Honofrio Guarracino. All Guarracino's virginals are cypress inner-outers with the wrestplank and wrestpins behind the jacks. Bologna, Tagliavini Collection. Photo by Antonio Guerra.

ticularly elegant, and it is likely that this "French connection" is responsible for the suggestion that he worked there.

Wherever it was made, the 1677 is thoroughly Italian in concept and looks. Once again we see a conservative inner-outer with 2×8′ disposition and a C/E–c³ compass.[50] The two lowest sharps are split, so that the fronts of the keys sound the notes of the short octave (D and E), while the back sections sound the nominal pitch of the accidentals (F♯ and G♯). The sharps themselves are sandwiches of ivory in ebony. The heads of the natural touch plates are ivory, and both the tails and the arcades are ivory embellished with a complex and beautifully executed black-on-white *sgraffito*.[51] The inner case is made of ebony (or some ebonized wood), and the soundwell and jackrail are inlaid with complex patterns of ivory and mother-of-pearl. The keywell is decorated in a similar manner, with fierce-looking lion heads and a coat of arms on the nameboard. The same theme is carried out on the wide cheek blocks. Natural wood moldings with a thin ebony inset, graced with exquisitely turned ivory buttons, provide a rich brown contrast to the black and white of the case and keywell. The cypress soundboard contains a black and gold rose, perhaps the only gilded rose known on an Italian harpsichord.

The instrument and its stand present an ensemble different from the usual Italian practice. Inner and outer cases are both much deeper than normal, the outer case has slanting cheeks, and the outer case decoration is dazzling. It is painted on all sides in large rope patterns in three different types of faux *marbre*, with exterior gilded moldings, and with a lid painting of a woodland scene. An apron stand with turned balustrades and a turned bottom stretcher, and even a turned lid stick, match the various faux *marbres* of the case. The harpsichord is also tonally unusual. Although its disposition is the usual 2×8′, it has two closely spaced nuts, the nearer taking the shorter strings and the other (next to the gap) the longer. Faby must have done this to

ANOTHER NEAPOLITAN OCTAVE VIRGINAL AND A MOTHER AND CHILD?

An unsigned and undated inner-outer octave cypress virginal (Bad Krozingen, Neumeyer-Junghanns-Tracey Collection) has its wrestplank and wrestpins behind the jacks, in the manner of all the known seventeenth-century Neapolitan virginals. It looks nothing like the 1694 octave virginal in Vermillion, and its star-shaped sunken rose looks nothing like the circular roses normally used by Guarracino, so it is probably not by that maker. But the placement of the wrestplank and wrestpins is so typically Neapolitan that it would not be incorrect to tentatively ascribe its origin to that city or its vicinity.[48]

6-16a, 6-16b. The octave virginal above, a 1694 by Guarracino, bears little physical resemblance to the undated anonyme below; still, the Neapolitan-style placement of the wrestplank behind the jacks might indicate a common place of origin. a: Vermillion, America's Shrine to Music Museum; b: Bad Krozingen, Neumeyer-Junghanns-Tracey Collection.

(continued on next page)

(continued from previous page)
Francesco Nocerino cites a document in which Guarracino, acting as an appraiser, valued an instrument by the otherwise unknown Giovanni Rispolo, which he described as a "large virginal joined to another small one, which could be played one above the other or separately, with an ivory keyboard and its own separate outer case."[49] This sounds suspiciously like a mother and child virginal, and even though we have no evidence that these were built outside of the Low Countries, they were certainly known. It would have been particularly easy to adopt a Neapolitan virginal to mother-and-child construction, since their keyboards are typically placed at the extreme left of the case, leaving sufficient room on the right for a child's compartment. There is evidence that such instruments were produced in England as well (see Chapter 10).

equalize the string lengths of each unison, thereby ensuring an otherwise unobtainable purity of sound. Faby's 1677 harpsichord is another throwback to the ornate style of sixteenth-century Venice and Milan, proving once again that despite the production of an overwhelming number of everyday harpsichords, Italy had many builders with the willingness and the ability to try something different.

ANONYMOUS INSTRUMENTS

An enormous number of anonymous harpsichords and virginals dating from sixteenth- and seventeenth-century Italy still exist. Undoubtedly, some did not begin life as anonymes, but were made so by accident or design: nameboards are easy to lose and easy to interchange. Nevertheless, it is clear that many Italian artisans labored with no expectation of recognition other than payment for an honest product. In this, their attitude differed little from the shoemaker's, whose shop may have been next door. Most Italian instruments of unknown origin are average looking, either false or true inner-outers with 2×8′ dispositions. Although they all differ in one way or another, together they testify to the inherent conservatism of Italian building.

Fortunately for the historian of early keyboard instruments, the number of anonymes is shrinking, mainly through the efforts of scholars like Denzil Wraight, who match unknown moldings, arcades, and fret-sawn cheek pieces with examples from known builders. As Wraight describes it, every builder had his own cutters, giving these decorative components a character akin to fingerprints. By matching these elements he and others have been able to ascribe many hitherto unnamed harpsichords to known builders.

The technique has also been used to correct false attributions. A large 2×8′ inner-outer with the extremely wide compass of GG,AA–f³ (The Hague, Gemeentemuseum), ostensibly signed by Giovanni Celestini and dated 1605, had long been accepted as a genuine member of that maker's oeuvre. But Wraight's examination discovered that (1) although the nameboard was signed with a Venetian alphabet similar to other examples of Celestini's work, the part itself was made of a wood other than cypress, and therefore could not be genuine; (2) the soundboard is made of spruce, a wood not used for that purpose by Celestini or any other Venetian builder at that time; (3) although the compass is original, the keyboard itself is not; (4) the three roses were unlike any used by Celestini; and

6-17a. The outer case of the 1677 Pietro Faby, with its faux *marbre* surfaces. Paris, Musée de la Musique.

6-17b. The keyboard
and the elaborately
decorated nameboard
of the 1677 Faby. Note
the split-sharp short
octave. Paris, Musée de
la Musique.

(5) the moldings were entirely different from those on Celestini's other instruments. Finally, the lid painting was identified as a copy based on an etching done in 1622; accordingly, the instrument is now identified as an anonyme, not from Venice at all, probably built around the middle of the seventeenth century.[52]

Sometimes attributions are made by the simple expedient of a strong, raking light, or an ultraviolet light, to reveal a signature. Other times, long-standing assumptions are challenged merely by examining an instrument more thoroughly. The detective work of Wraight and others eventually not only may provide more attributions, but will also tell us more about regional practices in Italy.[53] The history of the harpsichord in Italy, particularly in the seventeenth century, remains a work in progress.

6-17c. The jackrail and
wrestplank of the 1677
Faby. The two closely
spaced nuts can be
clearly seen. Paris,
Musée de la Musique.

Large numbers of harpsichords and virginals were produced in seventeenth-century Italy, for both domestic and foreign consumption. The advent of a new style of music, requiring a simple harpsichord with excellent continuo properties, made the 2×8′ Italian, with its incisive attack, the instrument of choice. As the market for harpsichords shifted partly from noble and royal households to theaters, opera houses, studios, and practice rooms, the opulent styles of Venice and Milan declined in favor of much plainer instruments. Nevertheless, with their graceful shapes and complex moldings, even the most ordinary Italian harpsichords and virginals nearly always achieved a classically elegant look. If sixteenth-century Italian harpsichords could withstand the sort of loving scrutiny one might give to violins, the same could be said of Italian harpsichords of the seventeenth.

Despite their loyalty to the 2×8′ disposition and the single

SEVENTEENTH-CENTURY FLEMISH AND ITALIAN HARPSICHORDS AT A GLANCE

Flemish	*Italian*
Thick case	Thin or thick case
Cut-in moldings	Finely cut applied moldings
No suggestion of inner-outer	Inner-outer and false inner-outer
Poplar the common case wood	Cypress the common case wood
Upper and lower braces	Knees, diagonal struts, bottom braces
Sides sit on the bottom	Bottom overlaps sides
Bentside resembles a section of a parabola	Bentside is Pythagorean for most of its length
Two-piece bottom	One-piece bottom
Soundboards of spruce or fir	Soundboards of spruce, fir, or cypress
1×8′, 1×4′	2×8′
Upper and lower guides	Box guides
Registers project through cheek	Normally no projections or levers to change registers
Gap parallel to nameboard	Gap sometimes parallel, sometimes angled away from nameboard
Bridges and nuts basically triangular	Bridges and nuts have parallel sides with a molded top
Bass portion of the bridge is rounded	Bass portion of the bridge is mitered
Pythagorean scale down to c′	Pythagorean scale down to c
Long scale, strung in iron	Short scale, strung in brass
Sounded at normal pitch	Sounded at normal pitch
Inset keyboard	Projecting keyboard
Painted case, decorated soundboard	Natural wood, no soundboard decoration
Gilded cast-metal rose	Parchment and wood geometric rose

keyboard, Italian makers nevertheless built with much more variety than the Flemish masters. The C/E–c^3 compass may have been the de facto standard, but GG/BB–c^3 and other schemes were not uncommon, and keyboards that ascended to f^3 never entirely went out of favor. The short octave was sometimes discarded, although the lowest accidentals were most often omitted, as in GG,AA,BB,C. While most keyboards started on C or GG, some started as low as FF. Split-sharp short octaves were found, as well as keyboards with split sharps for G♯/A♭ and E♭/D♯.[54]

False inner-outers began to supplant true inner-outers in the 1560s, but that innovation merely introduced a new option, and the true inner-outer never became obsolete. The same could be said of the oblong virginal: its shape was introduced — or rather, reintroduced — at the end of the previous century; but rather than replace the polygonal version, it served as an alternative. Accordingly, throughout the seventeenth century virginals continued to be built in polygonal or oblong shape, the former as either true or false inner-outers. The choice of soundboard wood — spruce, fir, or cypress — was another option. This lack of standardization may reflect the way these instruments were sold. The Ruckerses seemed to produce their standard models in a seventeenth-century version of assembly line methods, although they almost certainly filled special requests. It is more likely that Italian builders worked on commission, according to the requirements and desires of the buyer.

[7]

SEVENTEENTH-CENTURY
INTERNATIONAL STYLE

*E*VEN IF NOT in the quantities of the extant Italian and Flemish instruments, a respectable number of English, French, and German examples survived the seventeenth century. England is represented by twenty virginals and probably twice as many bentside spinets, but only a small handful of grand harpsichords. Some thirty-five harpsichords and ten spinets survived in France. Germany has fared the worst, with fewer than ten harpsichords and some octave virginals.

These numbers are sufficient to establish that the instruments built in these three regions have much in common. Similar in their use of hardwoods, methods of case construction, soundboard barring, scales, stringing, decoration, and tonal proclivities, they are quite different from Italian and Flemish practices. Collectively, they constitute a third, or International, style, one representing a continuation of European building practices of the fifteenth and sixteenth centuries.

Superficially, these harpsichords appear to stand in an intermediate relationship to the Italian (similarity of internal construction) and Flemish (similarity of decorative elements) schools and have often been characterized as hybrids. But the perception that International style instruments partake of the characteristics of these two dominant styles is misleading: it is Italian and Flemish practices that grew out of the International ones, not the other way around. Thin-case, short-scaled Italian inner-outers were a refinement on the somewhat thicker-case,[1] intermediate-scaled instruments common to most of the other regional building practices, and the heavy-case, long-scaled Flemish instruments, which arose around 1565, represented a move to the other extreme. Although these two regions may have dominated seventeenth-century harpsichord building, the rest of Europe continued to make the sort of instruments common since before the 1537 Müller, albeit with each area interpreting the style slightly differently.

CHARACTERISTICS OF INTERNATIONAL STYLE

The sides of a harpsichord or virginal case built in France, England, or Germany were usually made of a hardwood. Thicknesses varied considerably but were intermediate—neither as heavy as on Flemish instruments, nor as thin as on Italians. A variety of thicknesses was used: the spine, generally of a softer wood, was almost always heavier, up to twice as thick as the bentside, cheek, and tail, in order to take the stress of a hinged lid. The instrument's sides were assembled either around or on the bottom. Bentside curves varied from deep to shallow, depending on how closely they followed the curve of the 8′ bridge. Tails and the bass section of bridges were either mitered or rounded.

Internally, the harpsichords used bottom braces, knees, and diagonal struts; but the most commonly found structural member was the U-brace, which combined the functions of all of these. "Post and beam" was another means of internal construction. By the seventeenth century nearly all Italian harpsichords were short scaled and strung in brass. Flemish instruments had long scales and, except for the bass, were strung in iron. On the other hand, International-style scales were generally around 12–13″ long—that is, intermediate to scales used in Flemish and Italian instruments—strung either in brass at low pitch, or in iron at high pitch.[2]

Soundboards were normally made of spruce or fir, and frequently cross-barred, with the bracing passing under the bridges. Since these boards were often given a cutoff bar as well, their bracing tended to be more complex than that found on their Flemish or Italian counterparts. These regional differences in barring practices are not inconsequential: the fabled singing tone of Ruckers harpsichords was due in large part to the barring style of cutoff bar and ribs. Conversely, the ictus and tonal clarity for which Italian harpsichords were prized was in some measure the result of their practice of cross-barring. It should not come as a surprise that International-style harpsichords (antiques and modern copies) are described as achieving a sound that had both clarity and sustaining power.

Soundboards were normally decorated. Roses, when present, were almost always geometric, often enhanced with color and gold leaf. Some upside-down wedding-cake roses were quite elaborate. As in Italian harpsichords, moldings were applied to strengthen the case sides and give them a more substantial appearance; but unlike Italians (where they were glued to the outside of the top, and often to the inside as well, then topped with a cap molding), here an upside-down molding was glued to the inside of the case, extending into the instrument's interior, with the flat, top portion flush with the top edge of the case. Although International-style harpsichords are integral-case instruments, one often finds reference to their earlier inner-outer heritage, particularly in the keywell. Case exteriors were commonly finished in natural wood, although painted specimens are not infrequent. Keywells in all three regions were often more elaborate than the rest of the instrument. Finally, tonal concepts in all three areas showed a greater concern for variety and contrast than the single sound of the 2×8′ Italian, and the slightly more versatile 1×8′, 1×4′ of the Flemish.

REGIONAL DISTINCTIONS

French instruments achieved variety of sound by placing a 4′ row of jacks between their two 8′ sets, separating the plucking points of the latter. Most of the extant harpsichords have two manuals, giving them the ability to contrast the more nasal sound of the closer-plucking 8′ with the more neutral tone of the back 8′.[3] A set of jacks plucking close to the nut, producing a markedly nasal sound, is seen on many of the surviving seventeenth-century German and English harpsichords. In the latter, these jacks operate in a gap running through the wrestplank itself — a lute stop — but in German instruments this stop is usually part of so-called "spread" or "expanding registers," where three separate sets of jacks pluck close to the nut, in the "normal" position, and far from the nut. Brass plectra are found in some German examples and possibly in an English as well. The French used upper and lower guides, and these are also found in Germany and England; but the Germans also used box guides, and the English put them in their bentside spinets. Register extensions came through the cheek in Germany, whereas the French favored stop levers on the wrestplank, most often protruding through the nameboard. Both schemes were found in England.

While all regions used hardwood for their case walls, the French were partial to walnut, whereas the English at first favored oak, then later, walnut. A variety of hardwoods is found on the German instruments. External moldings divide the cases into panels on both German and English examples.

Seventeenth-century French soundboard painting was not unlike Flemish practice, with the board crowded with flowers, fruit, leaves, birds, and insects. German soundboard decoration was sparser. Painted boards in English harpsichords were common, but only in the early part of the century. French bentside spinets had decorated soundboards, but with few exceptions, English spinets left the boards plain, without even a rose. English virginals had painted soundboards, multiple geometric roses, papered cases, and lid paintings, while the harpsichords had papers in the soundwells and keywells. French harpsichords also used papers. Keywells were visual focal points in all three traditions, but in German instruments they tended to be ornate, with moldings, inlays, and other materials, including the traditional Germanic contrasts of ebony, ivory, mother-of-pearl, and tortoise shell. English keywells were less extravagant, and French, the least.

SUMMING UP

This chapter derives some general characteristics of harpsichord building in three different areas on the basis of relatively few instruments. There is a danger in this approach. If some characteristics appear to be obvious, others are less so, and as more instruments come to light, our ideas about International harpsichords may change. In the long run, it may be self-defeating to attempt to trace these influences too closely — there are too few artifacts with which to do so, and we are too far removed from the times. Nevertheless, it is clear that International-style harpsichords were closer to the older models, such as the 1537 Müller, than to the newer thin-case Italian and heavier Flemish instruments. In this sense the style could be characterized as old-fashioned, since it represented the continuation of what was by then a two-hundred-year-old tradition of mainstream practice. The next three chapters will explore the ways in which this older International style was realized in three great centers of harpsichord building.

[8]

FRANCE

*I*N FRANCE, as elsewhere in the seventeenth century, the production of virginals far outstripped that of grand harpsichords. Notwithstanding, only a single example has endured from this period, an anonymous octave instrument (Paris, Musée de la Musique), although ten or so spinets are extant, two at the octave. From pictures and descriptions it is clear that virginals were very much in International style: oblong, integral-case instruments with slender sides, and heavier spines to take lids. There are a few references to harpsichords early in the century: a clavecin is mentioned as early as 1600, in the de la Barre inventory,[1] and Mersenne includes an illustration of one in 1635;[2] he also notes that it was only in this century that the French started making grand harpsichords. It is not until 1648 that we have the first extant instrument, and from then to the end of the century we are fortunate to have more than thirty survivors, thus providing us with an excellent sample from which to draw information about French harpsichord making between ca. 1650 and 1700.

These instruments look quite different from contemporaneous Italian and Flemish instruments. Attempting neither the architectural refinement of the former nor the naive charm of the latter, the extant exemplars nevertheless often attain an elegance that raises them above the commonplace. Harpsichord building mainly took place in Paris, with a provincial southern school centered around Lyons and the Rhône Valley. *Boalch III* lists the names of thirty-four builders active in Paris and six in Lyons.[3] Other cites, like Strasbourg and Toulouse, list only one each, although the Toulouse craftsman Vincent Tibaut is important for the survival of three of his instruments.[4] Nothing is known of the virginals of these southern builders, but we do have enough grand harpsichords to suggest that they saw the instrument somewhat differently from the Parisians, at least as far as its decoration is concerned.

VIRGINALS AND SPINETS

Even pictorial references to seventeenth-century French virginals are scarce. The drawing in the Cellier manuscript (Illustration 2-9), dating from the 1580s, shows an oblong, thin-case virginal of integral-case construction, with a coffered lid and (presumably) a heavier spine. A painting from the 1630s, *Le Concert,* by Nicolas Tournier (Paris, the Louvre), although coming fifty years after the Cellier drawing, also shows an oblong, thin-case, integral-case instrument with coffered lid. Contemporaneous English virginals had coffered lids too, and even though of a different sort, that feature may have been something of an International characteristic. The shallow case and long jackrail shown in the Cellier drawing are found here as well; in fact, these two virginals look so much alike they could almost be the same instrument. There is no sign of a rose or a soundboard painting in the Tournier virginal, but given the angle of the perspective, either or both could have been present. The case exterior appears to be natural wood, but a border of some sort, either paint, gold, inlay banding, or something else, can clearly be seen. Case-top moldings overlap into the soundwell.

Virginal, octave virginal, and harpsichord were described in some detail in 1635 by Marin Mersenne in his *Harmonie universelle.* Although his words tend to confuse more than to enlighten,[5] his pictures show instruments much like the ones we have been describing. His octave virginal is thin cased, but with a lid (leading us to assume a heavier spine). The GG/BB–f² keyboard is inset, and the jacks operate in slots cut into a leather strip, two to a slot (although Mersenne noted that brass wires divided each opening, separating the pairs of jacks). He does not mention a lower guide, but clearly one must be present. In an earlier discussion of "spinets," which we are calling virginals, he noted that soundboards could be made of cypress, cedar, or fir. Strings were iron, with brass in the lower octaves.[6] Mersenne's lid is not coffered; that refinement may have come to an end by then.

It is thought that Girolamo Zenti introduced the bentside

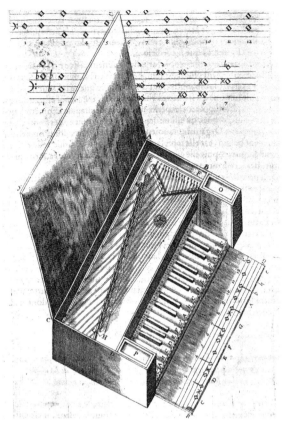

8-1. Mersenne's octave virginal. A triangular right bridge was common on octave instruments.

spinet to France during his first sojourn there, as sometime after his arrival in Paris in 1660, the production of virginals (with the possible exception of octave virginals) seems to have given way to spinets, although both shapes, as well as the grand harpsichord, continue to be subsumed under the name of espinette. French bentside spinets retained many Italian characteristics, including projecting keyboards and box guides. A 1690 spinet assumed to be by Michel Richard (Paris, Musée de la Musique) is an example of the genre. With its plain walnut case and thin scroll-sawn pieces glued to the insides of the projecting cheeks, its Italian ancestry is unmistakable. But the utilitarian bottom molding is too large and plain to be taken for anything made south of the Alps, and the ebony naturals and solid ivory or bone sharps convincingly argue against anything but an International origin; and in fact, even the scroll-sawn cheek pieces, with their false inner-outer reference, are as seventeenth-century French as they are Italian. The area above the soundwell is papered, and the soundboard is decorated. The stand, six turned legs mounted on a low frame, is of a type seen under instruments of this vintage.

Contrasting with the plainness of the Richard is a 1681 spinet by Louis Denis (Bologna, private collection). It has the same 1×8′, GG/BB–c³ tonal resources as the Richard, and its keyboard also consists of ebony-covered naturals with solid ivory sharps; but it is decorated in the high manner. Its soundboard, with a sunken geometric parchment rose, is beautifully painted with a profusion of flowers. Even the top of the jackrail is flowered. The soundwell, keywell, and lid interior are done in Chinese red, and the case is supported by cabriole legs.[9] The "cut-down" nameboard is gracefully scroll sawn at its ends. The exterior of the spinet is decorated in an attractive brown and gold chinoiserie. Musically, these two spinets may not be far apart, but the decor of the Denis suggests that it was intended for someone of high station, while it is likely that the Richard was never meant to be anything more than a workaday spinet.

The 1632 Jacquet inventory, in addition to a clavichord and seven virginals of various sizes, lists three *clavessins;* but grand harpsichords do not seem to have appeared with any regularity before the second third of the century,[14] about the same time that *clavecinistes* such as Jacques Champion de Chambonnières (1602–72), Louis Couperin (1626–61), Jean-Henri d'Anglebert (1635–91), and Elisabeth-Claude Jacquet de la Guerre (ca. 1666–1729) began writing in a lute-derived manner known today as *style brisé*.[15] The earliest extant French instrument, a 1648 by Jean Denis II (Issoudun, Musée de l'Hospice Saint-Roch), is not only the first surviving grand, but also the first known two-manual instrument with aligned keyboards. Jean II (1600–1672) was a member of a large and prominent family of builders. His grandfather Robert (1520–89) made both organs and espinettes, and his father Jean I (1549–after 1634) and his uncles Claude (1544–87) and Robert II (d. 1589) were also makers. Thomas (1585–before 1634) and Pierre (ca. 1600–after 1664), Jean II's two brothers, were both builders of espinettes, as were Jean's three sons, Jean III (ca. 1630–85), Louis (1635–1710), and Philippe (d. 1705). The last known member of this remarkable dynasty was Jean's grandson Pierre II (fl. 1705).[16]

Aside from Jean II's 1648 harpsichord, there are six other instruments extant by members of the dynasty: 1658 (France, private collection) and 1677 (Paris, Musée de la Musique) doubles, and a 1681 bentside spinet (Bologna, private

THE HARPSICHORD AND THE LUTE

The lute was popular in France early in the century —hardly surprising, since both Louis XIII and his prime minister Cardinal Richelieu were devotees of the instrument—and most harpsichord builders also made lutes, guitars, and violins. Consequently, makers were well acquainted with instruments requiring a delicate balance between lightness of construction and richness of sound.

In his discussion of virginals Mersenne provides some clues to the underlying principles of seventeenth-century French building. He says that case sides could be made of linden (basswood), but notes that any wood could be used, as long as the thickness of the sides was proportional to the strength.[7] This concern for weight and lightness of construction is seen in his comparison of the spinet and the lute, where he notes that there are contrary demands on the wood used in both these instruments. The "harmony or resonance of the instrument" requires "delicateness," which leads to "fragility"; but those parts that give it solidity must "be thick and heavy; and what is thick is dull." He goes on to say that instruments can be built with "a great deal of tone," but these are necessarily fragile and not likely to survive. On the other hand, instruments built too heavily, while perhaps more durable, are rendered "dull and inconvenient."[8] Builders did seem to follow these principles, making their slender cases out of hardwood, with each part no weightier than it had to be. Often braced less heavily than the typical Italian instrument, and with none of the sturdy cases and upper and lower braces of Flemish construction, many surviving seventeenth-century French harpsichords could be described as lute-like in the lightness of their construction. Such instruments would not take a great deal of stress, which may explain the intermediate scales of 12–13″.

8-2. It is likely that this beautifully appointed 1681 bentside spinet by Louis Denis was intended for an equally sumptuous room. Undoubtedly the decoration at least doubled the price of the instrument. The "cut-down" nameboard is a characteristic feature of seventeenth-century French harpsichords. Bologna, Tagliavini Collection. Photo by Jean Müllhauser.

collection, mentioned above) by his middle son Louis; a 1667 bentside spinet, by his oldest son Jean III (Varzy, Nièvre, Musée Municipal); and a 1672 polygonal octave spinet (Paris, Musée de la Musique) and a 1674 single by his youngest son Philippe (Nancy, Musée Historique Lorrain).[17] This is a meager legacy from a dynasty of eleven distinguished builders.

Mersenne describes a harpsichord that, like his octave virginal, is thin cased, with square cheeks and an inset C–c^3 keyboard. There is no indication of a lid, but these are present, nevertheless, on all the extant examples. The tail of the case is mitered, as is the bass portion of the bridge. The instrument is disposed 1×8′, 1×4′, indicating that at least for a while, early in the seventeenth century, France was in step with Flanders and Italy (although by this time most Italians were 2×8′). Since the two sets of wrestpins are between the back of the nameboard and the 8′ nut, the 4′ strings must have passed through holes in the 8′ bridge, as they did in Italy. Mersenne does not say whether upper and lower or box guides are used, but since he describes the guides in the same terms that he uses for the octave virginal, it is likely they were separate, leathered registers. Mersenne also mentions harpsichords with two or three keyboards and multiple stops that "vary and are joined, mixing together like those of the organ," but there is no other evidence that instruments so elaborate really existed, particularly with three manuals.[24]

Most of the remaining French harpsichords date from the last third of the century, and most were made in Paris, manifestations of Louis XIV's glittering *grand siècle*. Louis was a capable performer on the lute and harpsichord, although during the seventeenth century the lute declined in popularity as jack-action instruments became more plentiful. Louis undoubtedly supported some builders—Zenti died there while in his service—and it is not unlikely that his lavish court at Versailles prompted his nobles to purchase their own *clavessins*. What the king enjoyed the nobility coveted, and what the nobility owned the haute bourgeoisie fancied. Indeed, references to the harpsichord grew in the last third of the century, particularly in connection with the well born,[25] and some of the extant instruments are quite ornate.

Clearly, these harpsichords differ considerably from the instrument pictured by Mersenne. A letter from de la Barre to Constantijn Huyghens, written in 1648, the same year that Jean Denis's aligned double appeared, mentions that builder as a master whose instruments have two manuals "not in the style of Flanders which play only the same strings, but different in that these make different string sounds from each keyboard."[26] De la Barre might have meant that an 8′ sound was available from one manual and a 4′ from the other; that could certainly be described as "different string sounds from each keyboard," and in fact many seventeenth-century French doubles now have their 4′ jacks placed in front of the two 8′s, thus sounding the higher pitch from the upper manual and the 8′ pitches from the lower (looking down on the jacks one would

THE GUILDS OF FRANCE[10]

In the sixteenth century, instrument makers belonged to guilds organized according to the materials from which their instruments were made. Thus, makers of brass trumpets and brass pots belonged to the same guild, and harpsichord builders undoubtedly rubbed shoulders with cabinetmakers and plucked- and bowed-string *luthiers*. In 1599 Henry IV established an instrument maker's guild in Paris, and from then until 1791, when the guilds were abolished, harpsichord makers in that city were regulated by its statutes. The guilds were protective of their constituents, and no one other than members could make or sell a harpsichord.

There were the usual requirements for admission—a six-year apprenticeship and the production of a masterpiece—but children of members were admitted under much more relaxed standards, and widows of masters could continue to operate their deceased husbands' shops. A great effort was made to see to it that competition was minimized. A builder who discovered a new and superior material was bound to offer it to all members of the guild, so that no one could profit unduly from ambition and initiative. A maker could not take on a second apprentice until the first had completed at least four of his six years, so those with better reputations could train no more workers than their mediocre colleagues, and no one could have a larger shop. An inventory of the tools and instruments taken at the death of the wife of Parisian builder Jean Jacquet (ca. 1575–1658) in 1632 lists three jointing planes and three benches. Frank Hubbard notes that one bench would likely have been used by an apprentice, the second by a journeyman, and the third by Jacquet himself.[11] This three-man shop was probably the norm in France for quite some time.[12]

These regulations tended to stifle initiative and protect the less talented. Hubbard thought that most builders probably ended their careers making the same instruments they had built when they were apprentices.[13] At the same time, members of the royal family were free to import builders from elsewhere and bestow upon them the credentials to build harpsichords in France. It was under those conditions, for example, that Zenti could, on two occasions, spend time building in Paris.

THE DENIS FAMILY AT A GLANCE			
Builder	*Dates*	*Relation to Jean II*	*Extant Instruments*
Robert	1520–89	Grandfather	
Jean I	1549–after 1634	Father	
Claude	1544–87	Uncle	
Robert II	d. 1589	Uncle	
Thomas	1585–before 1634	Brother	
Jean II	1600–1672		1648 harpsichord
Pierre	ca. 1600–after 1664	Brother	
Jean III	ca. 1630–85	Son	1667 bentside spinet
Louis	1635–1710	Son	1658 harpsichord
			1677 harpsichord
			1681 bentside spinet
Philippe	d. 1705	Son	1672 octave spinet
			1674 harpsichord
Pierre II	fl. 1705	Grandson	

see 4′, 8′, 8′). It will be remembered that some two-manual Italian harpsichords with the 4′ on the upper manual are still extant, so it is possible that this sort of arrangement was found in France as well, particularly in the earlier years of the century.[27]

But given their sensitivity to variety of tone color — a concern that did not appear to be part of the Italian aesthetic sensibility — there would seem to be little reason for the French to limit the harpsichord's tonal palette in this manner. It is more likely that de la Barre was referring to the presence of an 8′ sound on each manual, each making a "different string sound" because their jacks were separated by the 4′ jacks (looking down on the jacks one would see 8′, 4′, 8′). With a distance of some 1½″ between the plectra, the choir of 8′ strings plucked by the jacks on the upper manual would produce a more nasal sound — not as intense as the sharp timbre that could be made by German and English harpsichords, but different enough to contrast with the rounder, plainer sound of the strings plucked farther from the nut by the lower-manual jacks.[28] In addition, just after the middle of the century Louis Couperin was already writing in a style known as *pièce croisée*, in which each manual is played by a different hand (presumably with the 4′ stop disengaged), recognizing the manuals' independence, exploiting the tonal distinction between them, and permitting simultaneous doubling of notes. Even earlier, in the first (1643) edition of his *Traité*, Jean Denis writes, "there are harpsichords with two keyboards for passing all the unisons, a thing the lute cannot do."[29] Without two manuals and an 8′, 4′, 8′ placement of the jacks, *pièces croisées* would not have been possible. It is likely that all the extant doubles were made that way, with or without shove couplers.[30]

The cases of Paris harpsichords are of walnut, usually intermediate in thickness,[32] with heavier spines. Sides either sit on or overlap bottoms.[33] The wood was usually finished natural, but marquetry with colored woods was sometimes used with breathtaking effect. The cases could also be painted, but that does not appear to have been the usual treatment. Moldings were applied to the top of the case and overhung into the soundwell. Some instruments have rounded tails, rather than the mitered ones common to both Italian and Flemish traditions, and in some the bass portion of the bridge is mitered, rather than curved. Interior bracing could consist of bottom braces, knees, and sometimes diagonal struts or "post and beam," but most commonly seen is the U-brace.

The normal compass on both spinets and grand harpsichords for the second half of the century was GG/BB–c³. As in Italy, split-sharp short octaves were often found, with either one or both of the lowest two sharps divided. Naturals were covered with ebony touch plates, and the sharps were made of solid pieces of ivory or bone. Rather than arcades glued to them, key fronts were carved in a trefoil pattern. Soundboard barring of grand harpsichords was complex, often with a light cutoff bar and/or a light 4′ hitchpin rail, and with ribs crossing under the bridges (cross-barring), usually with cutouts at those points. Bridges and nuts were lighter than in Flemish style and were either molded or triangular. A painting graced the soundboard, similar to earlier Flemish style in the crowding of motifs, although generally more sophisticated and realistic. Roses were geometric, ornate, and sometimes gilded. The front of the nameboard was "cut down" to the level of the wrestplank, more easily exposing the tuning pins to the seated player. It could be removed by pulling it straight up. The keywell referred to an inner-outer tradition in subtle

---

JURÉS OF THE INSTRUMENT MAKERS' GUILD

An indication of the respect commanded by the members of the Denis clan is seen in those who were nominated and elected as *jurés* of the instrument makers' guild. *Jurés* were the organization's most respected members, the examiners to whom every apprentice submitted himself when it was time to be elevated to membership. But the *jurés* not only passed on the qualifications of apprentices, they also handled the guild's financial affairs, appraised the inventories of deceased members, and guided the association's destiny. Members elected as *jurés* must have been prepared to give up some of their shop time to guild business, since a separate office and a clerk were supplied for their pursuits.[18]

Jean II's father, Jean I, was elected *juré* in 1601, and Jean II followed in 1647. Both his brothers were also elected, as was his nephew Philippe. His other nephew, Jean III, was nominated but was not elected. Even a century later the Denis name was esteemed. The writer of the article on the harpsichord in the 1785 *Encyclopédie méthodique: Arts et métiers* noted that "the best makers of ordinary spinets [by which he undoubtedly meant harpsichords] have been the Ruckers, at Antwerp, . . . and Jean Denis of Paris."[19]

ways, often with ornate scroll-sawn cheek blocks, and its decor often made reference to that legacy as well. Colorful printed papers were frequently found in the soundwell and keywell.

Two-manual instruments all have aligned keyboards, are disposed $2\times8'$, $1\times4'$ and may have had couplers allowing all choirs to be played from the lower manual. In fact, the French seem to have invented the idea of aligned keyboards and the shove coupler, resulting in an important new sound concept. Buff stops are rare. Not yet mentioned is the narrowness of the French octave span—narrower than in any other tradition, and narrower than the French span would be in the next century—as well as the shortness of the key heads, particularly on the upper manual. This daintiness and small-scale elegance contrasts markedly with the large, wide keys of the Flemish and Italian schools. Judged neither as powerful nor as complex in tone as eighteenth-century French harpsichords,[34] these instruments nevertheless have a sweetness, a clarity, and a gravity that well suits the music of Louis Couperin and Jean Henri d'Anglebert.

One of the most stunning instruments to have survived the *grand siècle* is a two-manual harpsichord built in 1681 by a maker named Vaudry (London, Victoria and Albert Museum). Unfortunately, all we know of him is that he was a member of an illustrious family of Parisian builders;[35] but we do know something of the instrument's provenance. It is thought to have belonged to the Duchesse du Maine, a patroness of music and daughter-in-law of Louis XIV. As a result of an involvement in a conspiracy, the story goes, the Duchesse was banished to a château in Burgundy. She brought her Vaudry harpsichord with her, where it remained in a red and gold room until purchased by the museum in 1974. Like almost every early harpsichord, the Vaudry has been rebuilt several times; nevertheless, it was possible to restore it to something approaching its original state.[36]

The Vaudry's case sides are made of walnut, of various thicknesses: the bentside is a little less than ⅜″, and the cheek and tail are slightly more than that. Its cheek is noticeably longer than those in the Flemish and Italian traditions, mainly because Vaudry and his compatriots kept a fairly consistent distance between bridge and bentside.[37] The heavier, softwood spine supports a ½″-thick lid. The bottom and the internal braces are also made of softwood. The bracing is light, consisting of a series of U-braces.[38] A cap molding glued to the top of the case overhangs into the soundwell, strengthening the thin sides and providing an illusion of thickness. The nameboard is gracefully scroll sawn on its ends, with most of its top "cut down" almost to the level of the wrestplank. Stop levers, projecting from slots in the nameboard, are finished with refined metal turnings. The keywell has both endblocks and scroll-sawn cheek pieces, providing a faint echo of a past inner-outer practice. The disposition is 2×8′, 1×4′, and the compass, GG/BB–c³. The keyboards are coupled by pulling out the lower manual for a short distance. Naturals are covered with ebony touch plates, and the sharps, like two rows of grinning teeth, are solid ivory. Trefoils are carved into the fronts of the keys. The case has a mitered tail, but the bass portion of the bridge is rounded. Bridges and nuts are molded. The soundboard was given a complex barring: it has a light 4′ hitchpin rail and no cutoff bar, but it has eleven light ribs distributed over the board, crossing under both the 8′ and 4′ bridges. The analogy of this ribbing to lute barring is strong.

The soundboard is decorated with a fairly crowded painting of flowers, with blue *rinceau* borders, and it has a complex, gilded, geometric parchment rose. The case decoration is done in exquisite

8-3. Mersenne shows a single-manual *clavessin,* but most surviving seventeenth-century French harpsichords have two keyboards.

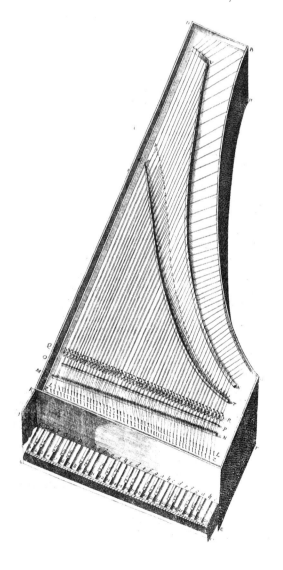

chinoiserie, with figures in copper, gold, and silver on a black ground.[39] An elegant walnut table stand, with seven graceful twist-turned legs[40] and a low frame on ball feet, supports the instrument. Its apron is also japanned in chinoiserie, en suite with the harpsichord. The inside of the case and the lid were later decorated in red and gold (supposedly to match the red and gold of the room in which it resided), although it is generally conceded that the work is somewhat crude compared to the rest of the instrument.[41]

As can be seen from Plate 11, the Vaudry is an impressive piece of Louis XIV furniture; but it is also a magnificent musical instrument. Derek Adlam, its restorer, talks about its "singing treble," its "reedy" tenor and bass, and the way the "unison registers complement . . . the somber majesty of so much 17th-century French keyboard music."[42] "To judge from this harpsi-

---

THE SHOVE COUPLER

The shove coupler seems to have been invented by French builders.[31] The two manuals can operate independently, with the more nasal 8′ on the upper, and the plainer 8′ and the 4′ both available on the lower, either separately or together. By pulling out the lower manual (or on some instruments, pushing in the upper), coupler dogs on the ends of its key levers engage the bottoms of the upper manual keys, moving them when the lower manual keys are pressed, like the jacks of a Flemish mother pushing up the backs of the keys of the child. When coupled, the sound of the two 8′s together, or the full 2×8′, 1×4′, can be called on from the lower manual, and the single, more colorful 8′ is still available on the upper manual.

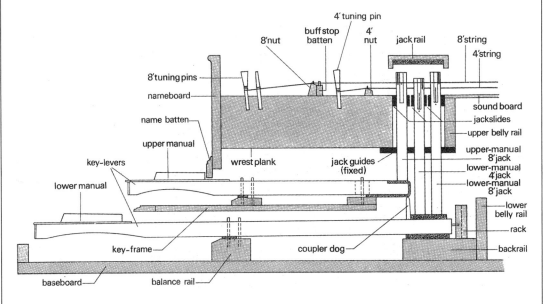

8-4. The French coupler allows the manuals to be used independently. By means of the coupler dogs, the upper keyboard can be operated from the lower. © Macmillan Publishers Ltd., *The New Grove Musical Instruments Series: Early Keyboard Instruments*, 1989.

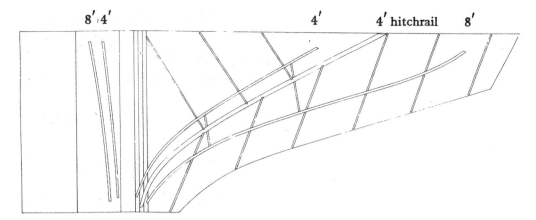

8' 4'　　　　　　　　　　4'　　4' hitchrail　8'

8-5. The soundboard of the 1681 Vaudry harpsichord is barred in a complex but typically International manner. London, Victoria and Albert Museum.

chord alone," says Adlam, "Vaudry is assured of his place in the section of Parnassus reserved for the great instrument makers of the past."[43]

LYONS AND ELSEWHERE

As noted earlier, seventeenth-century French harpsichord building also took place around Lyons and the Rhône Valley, although instruments were also made in other places in the south, such as Toulouse. An ornate double from 1678 or 1679,[44] built by Gilbert Desruisseaux (Paris, Musée de la Musique), comes from Lyons.[45] Desruisseaux (1652–1703) was born in Moulins, apprenticed with Michel Richard in Paris, then went to Lyons to set up his shop. Like the Vaudry, Desruisseaux's harpsichord is of walnut, with a heavy spine, a long cheek, and a cap molding overhanging into the soundwell. Its compass is GG/BB–c³, its naturals are covered with ebony touch plates, and its stop levers project through its cut-down nameboard. The soundboard is decorated, and it has a lovely gilded upside-down wedding-cake rose.

There are differences between this and the Vaudry, however. The Desruisseaux's tail is curved, rather than mitered. Its sharps, instead of solid ivory, are ebony covered with ivory slips. The case exterior is painted with large, colorful flowers and garlic bulbs[46] on a black ground, and a fine "Orpheus charming the beasts" graces its lid.[47] The interior case walls in the soundwell, the front of the nameboard, and the top of the jackrail are covered with colorful floral papers. Finally, the instrument sits on a table stand with a low frame on ball feet, an apron, and five twist-turned legs.

This brief comparison does not sufficiently distinguish be-

8-6. The gilded rose of the 1678 or 1679 Gilbert Desruisseaux is one of the finest examples to be found on a seventeenth-century French harpsichord. Paris, Musée de la Musique.

tween this instrument and the Vaudry as pieces of furniture. The Vaudry has real elegance, while the Desruisseaux (see Plate 12), despite its rather nice lid painting and beautiful rose, makes its effect mainly through color and appears to be provincial by comparison. The stand's music drawer seems out of place, adding an element of heaviness to the ensemble (although it may be a later addition). En suite with the harpsichord, the stand is rather pedestrian compared to the refinement of the design and the delicacy and complexity of the turnings of the Vaudry.

Vincent Tibaut,[48] a builder from Toulouse in southern France, is survived by three double-manual harpsichords, a 1679 (Brussels, Musée Instrumental), a 1681 (Paris, private collection),[49] and a 1691 (Paris, Musée de la Musique).[50] Where the Vaudry was finished in chinoiserie and the Desruisseaux with painted floral designs, the Tibauts have a natural walnut finish, with the earlier two enlivened by marquetry. The three instruments are remarkably similar, differing in appearance only in the degree of embellishment to their cases and table stands.[51] Structurally, they are also consistent with other seventeenth-century French harpsichords, although their spines are only slightly heavier than their other case members; nevertheless, made of walnut, they are thick enough to support lids.

Great care was lavished on the decoration of the 1679 Tibaut. In addition to marquetry borders on the case exterior and the interior case walls over the soundwell, the jackrail and both sides of the lid are marquetried with birds, flowers, and acanthus leaves. An unidentified coat of arms (in marquetry) graces the interior of the flap, suggesting that it was built for an important personage.[55] The apron of the stand and even the low frame member are marquetried. The eight twist-turned legs of the stand are beautifully done, with the pediments and capitals ringed in ivory. Four fierce, carved walnut lions serve as end-blocks to the keyboards. The 1679 is a symphony in marquetry; yet, like the Desruisseaux, despite some of its more sophisticated features it seems to be somewhat provincial. Naive birds and flowers, and Tibaut's rather large, cursive signature on the nameboard, in marquetry, *Fait Par moy Vincent Tibaut A Toulouse,* (plus the date), could scarcely be called elegant.

All this talk of provincialism is, of course, really an expression of taste; still it serves to make the point that seventeenth-

HERMAPHRODITES ON
THE SOUNDBOARD

The earlier two Tibauts also have unusual ornate, carved-wood, oval-shaped roses,[52] depicting a lutenist surrounded by acanthus leaves and shells, and on the bottom, one on either side, two winged hermaphrodite torsos.

The torsos appear to have both beards and breasts. Hermaphrodites often signified human-kind before the division into man and woman, and the presence of the lutenist may be symbolic of the power of music to unify the sexes.[53] Curiously, the 1648 Jean Denis II, made thirty years earlier in Paris, also has a carved-wood, oval-shaped rose with a lutenist, acanthus leaves, shells, and winged, hermaphrodite torsos.[54] The Tibaut device may have been copied from the Richard, but why a maker from Toulouse would copy a rose from a thirty-year-old Paris instrument, and why either should use something other than the usual circular, parchment, geometric rose, is impossible to say.

8-7. The rose of the 1679 Vincent Tibaut harpsichord. The oval, wooden, lute-player rose is an exception to the usual circular, parchment, geometric rose found in seventeenth-century French harpsichords. © IRPA-KIK, Brussels.

century harpsichord building south of Paris—at least in decoration—reflected somewhat different traditions. As more instruments from these southern regions reveal themselves, the patterns of those traditions may become clearer. What can be gleaned at this point is that the French variety of the International school seems to have been practiced throughout the country from before the middle of the seventeenth century and into the first years of the eighteenth,[56] creating a product particularly well suited to the contemporary French repertoire. It is

therefore somewhat amazing that the construction of these majestic instruments practically ceased toward the end of the century and the beginning of the next, as builders took on a new task, the rebuilding (*ravalement*) of Ruckers harpsichords and of making new instruments in the Ruckers mold.

SUMMING UP

The French version of International style, although it shared many of the building practices of German and English instruments, differed in tonal concept from other seventeenth-century harpsichords. Italian instruments were almost universally disposed 2×8′, and Flemish, for most of the century, 1×8′, 1×4′. German and English harpsichords (particularly the former) favored a highly colored organlike variety of sounds. But by separating the two sets of 8′ jacks with the 4′, the French established a different sort of harpsichord sound, one with a subtle, but noticeable, difference between the slight nasality of the closer-plucking 8′ and the rounder, sweeter character of the far 8′. Hence, the player had two 8′ sounds available; yet, because the distinction was moderate, the two 8′s could blend easily when coupled. To this ensemble the 4′ could be added for brilliance. It could also be added to each 8′ alone and might have been used as a solo stop as well. Yet, the front 8′ sound was still available from the upper manual, to contrast with the 1×8′; 2×8′; 1×8′, 1×4′; or 2×8′, 1×4′ ensemble on the lower manual. The French also extended the stop levers through the nameboard, allowing the player easy access to them. The result was an extremely flexible arrangement, and one that had a strong influence on other builders in the next century.

Nevertheless, although a maker from Germany might have been puzzled at the French proclivity for two manuals with coupler and the 2×8′, 1×4′ disposition, he would have had no trouble recognizing his Gallic colleague's constructional practices. With the integral case of walnut, walls of intermediate thicknesses, a heavier softwood spine with a lid, the use of U-braces, fancy geometric roses, and intermediate 12–13″ scales of iron or brass, he would have felt right at home.

[9]

GERMANY AND AUSTRIA

$\mathcal{O}$THER GRAND harpsichords did not appear in Germany until almost a century after the 1537 Müller harpsichord was made. Despite this gap in time, most of these later instruments demonstrate remarkable resemblances to the Müller, particularly in disposition, since they also separate the registers into deep- and close-plucking sets of jacks. As noted earlier, an inclination toward highly colored sounds was part of the German aesthetic for a long time.

A majority of the survivors were built in an opulent style — probably court instruments — and most were built before 1650, thus giving us a skewed picture of an entire century of harpsichord building. Furthermore, there is no strong evidence that harpsichord building was a particularly important activity in Germany; on the contrary, its keyboard instrument makers tended to be organ builders who also made harpsichords and clavichords. *Boalch III* indicates that there were no centers of harpsichord building in this century; instead, the activity took place all over, and those dozen or so towns that did have known builders had only one or two.[1] Certainly, the Germans continued to import instruments from England, Italy, and the Low Countries, just as they had in the previous century.[2] Nevertheless, the few instruments that survived the century indicate that, although seventeenth-century German harpsichord building may have been sporadic, the results were often extraordinary.

The earliest source to give concrete information about plucked keyboard instruments in Germany is Michael Praetorius's 1619 *Syntagma musicum*.[3] His book includes a valuable appendix, the *Theatrum instrumentorum*, consisting of forty-two woodcut illustrations of instruments, including virginal, spinet, ottavino, grand harpsichord, and clavicytherium. A scale is provided on each woodcut, making it possible to determine the sizes of most of the instruments.

Praetorius's virginal, a thin-case oblong instrument with a centrally placed inset keyboard, is fairly sizeable — nearly 5′6″ in length and 19″ in width. Its compass is $C/E–d^3$, a normal range for an early-seventeenth-century keyboard instrument, although Praetorius shows two split sharps in the bass (split-sharp short octave) and split sharps for all the E♭s. Like all his keyboard instruments, the virginal is shown without a lid; however, hooks for two hinges can be seen on the spine, and a hinged fallboard is in place. It seems clear that Praetorius simply omitted the lid to save room on his crowded page, and although no other examples have signs of hinges, the general absence of lids can be explained in the same way. Hence, Praetorius's jack-action instruments likely had cases with sides of intermediate case thickness and with spines heavy enough to support a lid (although the possibility of inner-outer construction cannot be completely dismissed).

An anonymous South German oblong virginal from ca. 1600 (Berlin, Staatliches Institut für Musikforschung), although smaller and at quint pitch, is nevertheless quite similar in appearance to the instrument portrayed by Praetorius. Its inset keyboard is centrally located, and both left and right bridges are similar in shape to those on the woodcut (however, the details of the jackrail holder are different from the Praetorius instrument, and exceptionally, the Berlin virginal does not have a box on the left side of the keywell). The compass of the Berlin virginal is the same $C/E–a^2$ found on some sixteenth-century Flemish examples, and a close cousin to the $C,D–g^2,a^2$ of the 1537 Müller. Thin sides with a heavier spine with lid, a geometric parchment rose, a soundboard painting, molded bridges, marquetry on the outside of the case, and the use of moldings to frame portions of the exterior of the case and the nameboard are indications of its International roots. Other than a soundboard rose, no decoration is visible on Praetorius's virginal.

His spinet is a thin-case six-sided virginal with a $C/E–f^3$ compass and projecting keyboard. Hubbard believed it to be Ital-

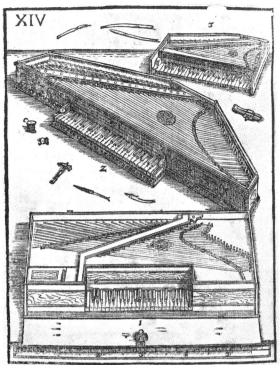

9-1. Octave virginal, polygonal virginal, and oblong virginal from Praetorius's *Syntagma musicum.* Praetorius called them ottavino, spinet, and virginal.

ian,[4] but another anonymous virginal of German origin dating from the early part of the seventeenth century (Salzburg, Museum Carolino Augusteum)—about the same time as *Syntagma musicum*—is also thin cased and six-sided, and like Praetorius's oblong virginal, its jackrail is supported on the left by an arm extending from the front of the case. To be sure, with its inset keyboard and narrower C/E–c³ compass, it differs from the instrument in Praetorius's illustration; nevertheless, it demonstrates that thin-walled polygonal virginals were by no means necessarily Italian. Evidently, German builders made polygonal virginals for quite some time. An anonymous South German instrument of ca. 1700 (Berlin, Staatliches Institut für Musikforschung) is also six-sided, with case walls of intermediate thickness (less than ½″), a lid, the usual box on the left side of the keywell, and the jackrail arm extending from the left side of the case. The keyboard was placed to the extreme left of the case, ensuring that the jacks pluck the strings quite close to the bridge.

The ottavino pictured by Praetorius is a small 4′ virginal. The shape is basically oblong, although (since most of the spine follows the line of the jackrail at a shallow angle) it is technically pentagonal in form. The compass is the same C/E–g²,a² found on the Berlin quint virginal. A 1598 octave virginal by the Nuremberg builder Lorenz Hauslaib (New York, Metropolitan Museum of Art), a removeable part of a small claviorganum, is virtually identical to the one depicted in *Syntagma musicum,* even to the same rounded bridge shape (the bridges on many ottavini simply consist of two angled members) and slanted spine.[5] Even the jackrail holders are similar.

From Praetorius's woodcuts and from the surviving examples, it seems clear that German virginals were either oblong or polygonal (Praetorius calls the latter spinets), with octave versions. It is likely that German builders had no firm commitment to either projecting or inset keyboards. Spinets, in the sense in which we have defined them, with the bass strings in the rear of the case, seem to have been limited to octave instruments. But the known sample is pitifully small, and it would be a mistake to regard these conclusions as anything but tentative.

HARPSICHORDS

Praetorius depicts a harpsichord in grand shape, with a compass of C/E–c³,d³. Once again, Hubbard was convinced it was Italian,[8] but there are clues that point generally to an International, and specifically to a German, origin. First, its bentside is not as Pythagorean as a typical Italian would be; second, it is obviously strung 2×8′, 1×4′, an uncommon disposition in Italy; and third, the jackrail, which is a prominent feature of the instrument, is fairly wide and noticeably wider in the bass than in the treble.[9] This "expanding jackrail," a characteristic of many seventeenth-century German harpsichords, covers registers that angle away from each other. The reason for the shape of the jackrail can be readily envisioned by referring back to the 1537 Müller, where, it will be recalled, the two registers that are angled and deep-plucking share a jackrail, while the third, which plucks close to the nut, has its own. If these two jackrails had been connected at both ends—merely joined together at the treble, where they practically touch, but with a connecting crosspiece at the bass, where they are inches apart—or if they had been combined into one large, wedge-shaped piece of wood, the resulting structure would be described as an expanding jackrail.

Exactly that sort of cover is found on a small (under 6′), anonymous, early-seventeenth-century South German harpsichord (Budapest, Magyar Nemzeti Múzeum). Similar to the Müller, it has a 2×8′ plus buff disposition, but with two, not three, registers; nevertheless, one of them is angled out from the wrestplank, allowing its jacks to pluck deep into the strings. The other register is a nasal one, set close to the nut, and there is strong evidence that it was originally quilled in brass. Both registers are covered by a single contrivance, shaped precisely as described hypothetically above: one portion of the jackrail covers each of the registers, and both portions are joined together at the treble, with a connecting crosspiece at the bass end. The whole forms a shallow, open triangle.

9-2. This anonymous six-sided seventeenth-century German virginal is similar to the polygonal virginal (spinet) pictured in Praetorius's *Syntagma musicum,* although its keyboard is inset. Salzburg, Museum Carolino Augusteum.

A more complex example of an expanding jackrail is found on a somewhat larger (about 6′6″) 1619 harpsichord (Salzburg, Museum Carolino Augusteum) by the Stuttgart court builder Johann Mayer

THE OCTAVE SPINETS OF AUGSBURG

In the early part of the seventeenth century, Samuel Biderman (1540–1622) of Augsburg and his sons Samuel the Younger (1600–after 1653) and Daniel (1603–63) built little jewel-like octave spinets capable of playing six different tunes by propelling a pinned barrel with a key-wound, spring-driven clockwork. Thus, like a music box, these spinets could provide automatic music, although they could also be played in the normal way, with the fingers on the keys. Eight or so of these little gems survive, all from the seventeenth century. Those I have seen have all been highly decorated, most of them looking like chests or sewing boxes when closed up. A particularly fine example dates from ca. 1640 (Nuremberg, Germanisches Nationalmuseum). Lacquered in black, with rippled moldings, lovely hinges, a delicately painted soundboard, a tiny geometric rose, and a lid with a silvered plaque flanked by two fine miniature paintings, the spinet has a limited $C/E-e^2$ compass. It is so tiny it could be considered to be at 2' pitch.[6] Although it is unlikely to have been regarded as a serious musical instrument, it is a quintessential objet d'art.

9-3a. This tiny ca. 1640 automatic spinet by Samuel Biderman contains a pinned barrel operated by a clockwork. It is capable of playing six tunes. Nuremberg, Germanisches Nationalmuseum.

Such instruments must have been known beyond Germany, since Mersenne wrote about them with great amazement: "One can further relate to our time the invention of the . . . barrel which is used to perform many pieces of music on the spinet without using the hand, for the Germans are so ingenious that they have more than fifty pieces played by means of many springs . . . without there being any need to touch the instrument after having wound its springs."[7]

(continued on next page)

(continued from previous page)

Like the Bidermans, Anton Meidting (fl. 1587), another maker from Augsburg, might have specialized in gemlike instruments. Only one of his creations has survived, a 1587 combined virginal and regal (reed organ), both at 4′ pitch (Vienna, Kunsthistorisches Museum). Meidting's combination instrument is ornate, as would be expected, and when closed up forms chess and backgammon boards. The virginal portion has a compass of F,G,A–a² and, except for the V-shaped bridge, is similar to Praetorius's octave virginal. Along with Biderman instruments, this example suggests that Augsburg builders may have made a specialty of small, exotic keyboard instruments.

9-3b. The keyboard, pinned barrel, and clockwork of the ca. 1640 Biderman automatic spinet. Nuremberg, Germanisches Nationalmuseum.

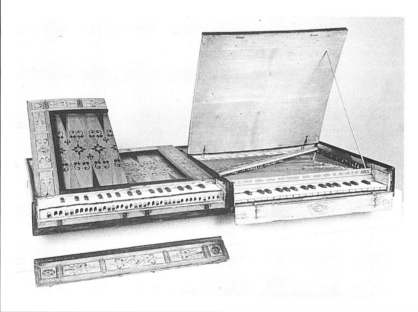

9-4. When closed, this 1587 combined octave virginal-regal by Anton Meidting becomes chess and backgammon boards. Vienna, Kunsthistorisches Museum.

(1576–1626).[10] Also similar to the Müller, there are three rows of jacks with a 2×8′ disposition; but these registers are placed in three, not two, different positions—front, middle, and back. The front, nasal row is close to and parallel to the nut, the middle row is placed where one might find a "normal" harpsichord register, and the back row plucks deep into the strings. Rather than separate but connected jackrails, the cover is made from a single piece of wood. This large, wedge-shaped rail, measuring about 3″ in the treble, and expanding to twice that width in the bass, is, to say the least, a prominent feature of the Mayer. It was quite possibly this version of the expanding jackrail that Praetorius was hinting at in his woodcut.

An even more complex example of expanding registers is found on a ca. 1630 German anonyme (Munich, Bayerisches Nationalmuseum).[11] Once again, the instrument is disposed 2×8′; but here, five registers pluck two sets of strings—two in front, two in the middle, and one deep in the back. The registers in this instrument, spread extremely wide, call for a three-piece jackrail of Brobdingnagian proportions.

These three intriguing examples of seventeenth-century German harpsichord building deserve closer examination. The Budapest instrument, though anonymous, has a history. According to the museum, it was originally owned by the Viennese court, then given to an Ursuline convent by the Hapsburg Emperor Joseph II, and later acquired by an antique dealer who donated it to the museum in 1875. It is thin cased, with a deeply curved bentside, a heavy spine,[12] a short scale, and brass stringing. Moldings applied to the tops of the sides overlap into the soundwell. The tail is a rare double miter, similar to one to be discussed shortly on a ca. 1620 clavicytherium in Nuremberg. Box guides enclose the jacks, and they and the buff rail are

9-5. German harpsichord from Praetorius's *Syntagma musicum*. The jackrail appears to widen in the bass.

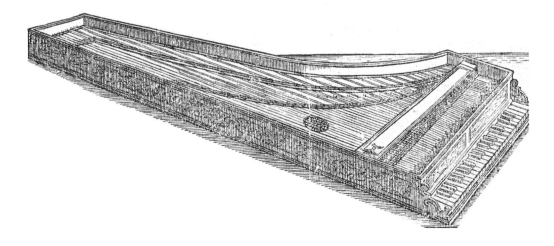

controlled by turned brass knobs projecting from the cheek. The soundboard is cross-barred, with a partial cutoff bar and seven ribs. There appears to be no internal framing at all. A striking-looking harpsichord in the opulent tradition, it is not difficult to believe that it was intended to be a court instrument.

There is little in the way of decoration on the outside of the plain natural-wood case, although it is possible that at one time the exterior had a more ornate finish. In typical Teutonic fashion, the keywell is the center of visual interest. The nameboard is veneered in tortoise shell and inlaid with five ivory tiles depicting women singing and playing organ, gamba, lute, lyre, flute, trombone, and cornetto, all in colorful sgraffito.[13] Small squares of mother-of-pearl bracket the ivory tiles. Six-pointed stars of mother-of-pearl, set off in frames of ivory, enliven the side panels of the cheeks. The natural touch plates of the C/E–f^3 keyboard are each made of three segments of mother-of-pearl, with the heads and both parts of the tails all of equal length. The tops of the ebony sharps are animated by finely cut ivory inlays. The key fronts are ivory under fret-sawn ebony. These contrasts of black and white, dark and light, are typically German and particularly South German, especially when expressed in ebony, ivory, tortoise shell, and mother-of-pearl.[14] The soundboard is sparsely flowered, but that element of the decoration is overshadowed by a spectacular double upside-down geometric wedding-cake rose. Large, layered, intricate, and gilded, this is undoubtedly the most extravagant rose to appear on any harpsichord, anywhere, at any time.

Graceful, refined, ornate, and finished in natural woods, Johann Mayer's harpsichord, seen in Plate 13, makes a statement of elegance and luxury. The keywell is dazzling: the mahogany-veneered nameboard is embellished by three sunken, framed, walnut panels, each containing an ivory sgraffito consisting of a central cartouche of musical motifs surrounded by leaf, vine, and wrought-iron patterns. More ivory sgraffito, various winged figures, and groupings of fruit and vegetables float outside the frames. The prominent expanding jackrail is similarly decorated. The cheeks are scroll-sawn, the natural keys are covered with mother-of-pearl touch plates, and the sharps are made of ebony. The compass of the keyboard is an apparent BB♭–c^3, but the BB♭, shorter than the other accidentals, may have been an added note, with the original compass starting on GG/BB.[15]

The Mayer's sparsely painted soundboard has an elaborate, gilded, geometric rose, which, although not comparable to the one on the Budapest anonyme, is still of unusually delicate beauty. Narrow panels of light wood against dark, each panel framed with a lighter stringing, decorate the soundwell. The

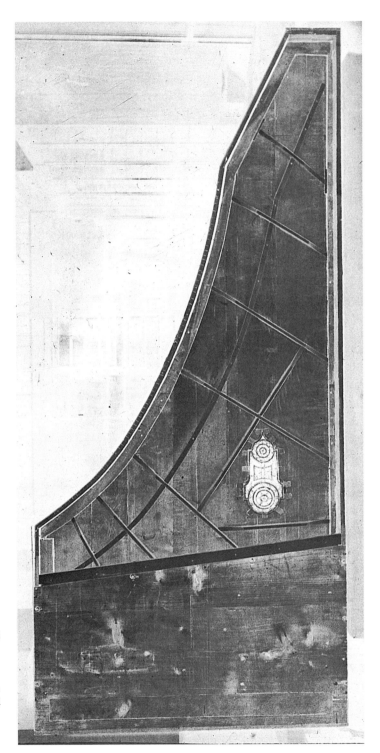

9-6a. The soundboard barring of the Budapest anonyme, with an abbreviated cutoff bar and seven ribs. An eighth rib helps protect the soundboard around the rose. Budapest, Magyar Nemzeti Múzeum.

mahogany veneer of the exterior is set off by carefully arranged panels of burl-wood, over which are placed ebony fret-sawn leaf and vine patterns reminiscent of the sgraffito patterns on the nameboard. These panels—one each on the cheek and tail and five on the deeply curved bentside—are framed by ebony moldings. Three nicely turned brass knobs projecting from the cheek control the three box registers. The thin sides are enhanced by ebony cap moldings, wide enough to overhang both the outside of the case as well as the soundwell. Ebony moldings surround the bottom of the case as well. The instrument sits on a table stand with five classically inspired turned legs on a low platform.

The colorful appearance of the 1619 Mayer is mirrored in its sonic qualities. With a short scale, it is strung in brass, and one of the 8′ sets of strings can be buffed. Reportedly, all three sets of jacks were originally quilled in brass. Like the Budapest anonyme, it is disposed 2×8′; but its three rows of jacks, producing nasal, normal, and deep-plucking timbres, separate the instrument into three basic sounds.

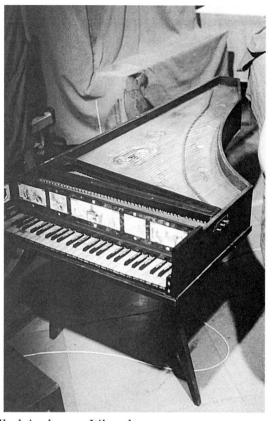

9-6b. The Budapest anonyme, with its wedge-shaped jackrail. Budapest, Magyar Nemzeti Múzeum.

The Munich anonyme is another ornate instrument, although its exterior is now painted black and its lid papered, which is unlikely to have been its original state. Its soundboard is also sparsely painted, and its rose is missing, leaving only an octagonal hole in the soundboard. Typically, its nameboard is highly decorated, with delicate light-wood arabesques set into five framed panels on black-stained walnut. Similar ornamentation is found on the soundwell walls. The keyboard of boxwood naturals and black-stained walnut sharps is not as fancy as the mother-of-pearl and ebony we have temporarily become accustomed to, but the sharps are embellished with gold arabesques. Although the forty-five-note C/E–c^3 keyboard does not project from the case, the cheeks are slanted in a manner foreshadowing those of the Viennese instruments of the next century. Many of the moldings are rippled.

Made of softwood, the sides and spine are just under ⅜″. This is a minimal thickness for a spine designed to take the stress of a lid; International-style instruments invariably have a heavier member there. Accordingly, it may originally have been an inner-outer.[16] The framing consists of several half-U braces, with the kneelike rise going to the bentside liner, and the other end straight to the spine.[17] Van der Meer reports that there are no visible indications revealing its internal bracing, but notes that the soundboard is barred with several ribs crossing under the bridge.[18] Like the Müller, the Munich anonyme has a "hollow wrestplank," a rail of some 2½"—just wide enough to take two rows of wrestpins—placed against the nameboard. The spruce soundboard extends across the gap to the back of the nameboard, with five sets of oversized slots cut into it: two close to the nut, two angling out (as if in a normal angled gap), and one angling far out for a deep-plucked sound. Moveable registers, operated by six wooden stop levers projecting through the nameboard, sit on top of the soundboard slots, while the lower guides are fixed. The scale is about 11½", and it is strung in brass. There is also a buff stop, and evidence suggests that one of the lute registers was originally quilled in brass. This instrument is capable of an organlike variety of sounds: the flutey quality of the deep-plucking register; the normal harpsichord sound, plucking either one or two 8′ choirs for dynamic variety; the two close-plucking nasal registers, which again can be played one or two at a time; the pizzicato of the buffed 8′ plucked in any of its three positions; and the bold sound of the brass plectra.

The instrument's exotic sonic qualities aside, the visual feature that overwhelms all others and that absolutely dominates this harpsichord is its enormous expanding jackrail. Its three separate sections cover five sets of jacks, and expand from just a few inches in the treble to a spectacular foot or so in the bass. The three rails are joined at the treble and connected at the bass end by a crosspiece. Open fretwork carving fills the elongated triangles between the rails. This is the Colossus of jackrails, and the keyboard, with its elongated bass keys reaching well under the soundboard, is equally impressive.

9-6c. The double rose of the Budapest harpsichord. No other extant instrument has a rose this flamboyant. Budapest, Magyar Nemzeti Múzeum.

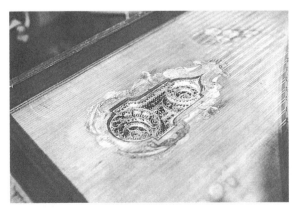

Hollow wrestplanks may well have been an occasional feature of International-style harpsichords. Although no seventeenth-century French instruments have been discovered with one,[19] at least two more extant Germans were constructed in this way, and three surviving English instruments. Both the Germans are 2×8′ undated anonymes (Basel, Historisches Museum;[20] Hamburg, private ownership), the first with two sets of jacks, the second with three.[21] The Hamburg harpsichord has seen better days. Almost all of its soundboard is gone, but what little remains demonstrates that it extended over the gap to the nameboard, with a narrow wrestplank underneath, and was slotted for the jacks. Portions of the slender, ladderlike lower guides remain, and one assumes moveable upper guides. The internal structure consists of a bottom brace and four rather large knees supporting the thin bentside. Like the Munich instrument, its spine is also thin, and it too supports a lid, which has a rather nice painting. Its exterior is now painted green, but this may not have been its original decor. Finally, also like the Munich instrument,

9-7. This anonymous harpsichord in Munich takes the concept of expanding registers to the ultimate. Munich, Bayerisches Nationalmuseum.

its cheeks are slanted. It is likely that neither this nor the Munich anonyme were court harpsichords, leaving us free to infer that the separation of registers was not linked to opulent embellishment, but was a typically Germanic trait found on humbler instruments as well.

That conclusion is reinforced by an anonymous clavicytherium of ca. 1620 (Nuremberg, Germanisches Nationalmuseum), which, while much plainer than the Munich harpsichord, it is also well equipped in its sonic abilities. Like the Budapest instrument, the compass is C/E–f^3 with a 2×8′, 1×4′ plus buff disposition, and four fanned-out registers. It is a variation on a now familiar theme, but with a twist: like German organs of the time, the registers are divided, making it possible to play the bass or treble of each independently. Thus, for example, one could play off the sweetness of the deep-plucking register in the treble with the snarling sounds of the close-plucked strings in the bass. The registers are controlled by eight small, vertical levers, four on either side of the jack guides.

As would be expected, the case walls are fairly thin, but with a heavier spine and a lid (which, more appropriately for a clavicytherium, should be called a door). A narrow molding runs around the rim, extending into the soundwell. Like the Budapest instrument, the tail has a double miter. Even though this is a workaday instrument (in fact, it has handles on spine and cheek, to aid in its transport) with little in the way of decoration, the keywell is enlivened by naturals with ivory touch plates, and sharps nicely inlaid with a small lozenge in the centers and edged with thin ivory stringing. Scroll-sawn ebony cheeks brace the keywell. The jackrail is large, of course, growing to something like 9″ in the bass; but it is relatively plain—a walnut plank, framed by a heavy molding. At one time the soundboard had three roses, but now only the holes remain, each surrounded by a filigreed square done in black ink. These inked areas, with the inclusion of smaller squiggles at either end of the 4′ bridge, constitute the only decoration on the soundboard.

Praetorius shows a clavicytherium quite similar to the Nuremberg anonyme in general appearance, even down to the three roses on the soundboard, the shape of the cheek brackets, and the handles on the sides for transporting. The large panel above the keys, nicely divided into two decorative segments, may combine the functions of nameboard and jackrail. The woodcut shows a single-strung instrument, and in his text Praetorius distinguishes the sound of the clavicytherium from that of the harpsichord, saying that the former "produces a sound almost the same as that of cithers and harps."[22] It is possible, then, that at least some seventeenth-century German clavicytheria were, like harps, strung in gut.[23] Gut-strung harpsichords—*Lautenwerk*—were not unknown in Germany, and in the next century J. S. Bach would own two. But no matter what the stringing material, Praetorius's instrument could have had two spread registers hidden beneath that large jackrail.

There is no question that the fascinating German instruments

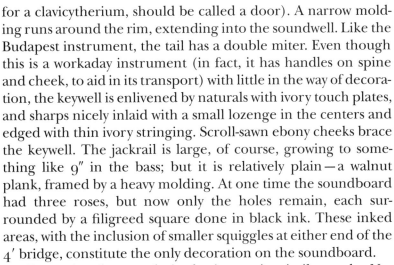

304 *Klavicytherium,*
Deutschland um 1620
(GNM, Slg. Rück).

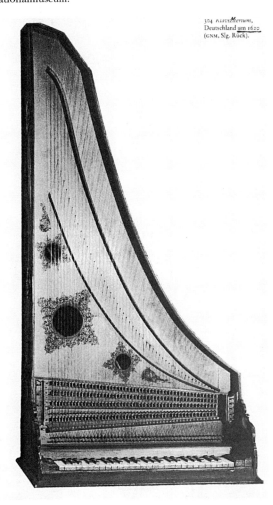

9-8. An anonymous ca. 1620 clavicytherium. Plain but dignified in appearance, its sonic capabilities are extraordinarily wide. Nuremberg, Germanisches Nationalmuseum.

described here were uniquely equipped to play certain portions of the seventeenth-century German repertoire. Secular pieces by Johann Pachelbel (1653–1706) and Georg Muffat (1653–1704) would be comfortably at home on both German organs and these harpsichords. The many works in variation form by composers such as Hans Leo Hassler (1564–1612), Samuel Scheidt (1587–1654), and Johann Jacob Froberger (1616–67) would particularly benefit from the variegated colors of spread registers. Pieces like Alessandro Pogletti's (d. 1683) suite *Rossignolo* (Nightingale) and *Sopra la Ribellione di Ungheria* (The Hungarian Rebellion), full of variation and descriptive writing, practically beg for an instrument with the resources of the Munich anonyme or the Nuremberg clavicytherium.

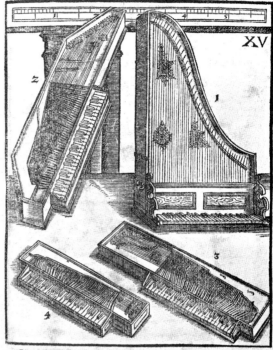

1. Clavicytherium.   2. Clavichordium , Italianischer Mensur.
2. Gemein Clavichord.   4. Octav Clavichordium.

9-9. The clavicytherium from Praetorius's *Syntagma musicum*. The large panel over the keys may be hiding spread registers.

Nevertheless, it could be a mistake to assume that all, or even most, seventeenth-century German harpsichords were built with spread registers. For one thing, we know that it is the unusual, the expensive, the opulent, and the bizarre that tend to be preserved, whereas workaday instruments get used up and discarded. For another, there are some seventeenth-century German harpsichords whose registers line up in the perfectly ordinary manner. One is the Basel anonyme with hollow wrestplank, mentioned earlier; another is the ornate 1675 clavicytherium by Martin Kaiser (fl. 1675–98) (Vienna, Kunsthistorisches Museum) that once belonged to Holy Roman Emperor Leopold I. This instrument was made in the form of a double-bentside pyramid, with two bridges arranged symmetrically on the soundboard. The longest strings run up the middle of the instrument, and the remainder alternate left and right, until the two highest-sounding courses are found on the right and left sides of the case. A roller board links the jacks with their proper strings.[29] As a court instrument, the Kaiser is elaborately decorated with tortoise shell, ivory, mother-of-pearl, and bronze mounts; still, it has a standard 2x8′ disposition, with the registers in the usual position.

MORE ON PRAETORIUS AND OTHERS

Like many of the theorists we have been quoting, Praetorius mentions a variety of practices that stretch our imagination. One is the convention of placing a virginal at quint pitch on top of a larger, 8′ instrument.[24] Did Praetorius mean that they were to be played together, in the manner of a Flemish mother and child, or that they were to supply different pitches, like a Flemish two-manual harpsichord with unaligned keyboards? The second seems more logical, but in organ-dominated Germany it could be that combining 8′ and quint sounds in a jack-action instrument was considered desirable, and perhaps was looked on as another tonal resource of a large sonic palette.

Praetorius also indicates that harpsichords could have two, three, or even four sets of strings, and he claims to have seen one strung entirely in gut that had two 8′ strings, one set at quint pitch, and one at the octave.[25] Such references crop up all the time, but if such instruments existed, none have survived. Aside from a 1723 3×8′, 1×4′ instrument by Hieronymus Hass (Copenhagen, Musikhistorisk Museum), the only quadruple-strung instruments extant are a handful disposed 1×16′, 2×8′, 1×4′, and these are almost exclusively North German and eighteenth century. Praetorius also describes the elusive arpichordum, a harpsichord with metal brays.

Praetorius is not alone in tossing off such allusions. Mersenne mentions harpsichords with seven or eight stops and two or three keyboards, in which the jacks pluck one, two, or many sets of strings.[26] There are a few extant harpsichords with three keyboards, but only one is judged to be authentic, a 1740 also by Hieronymus Hass (Paris, private ownership). On the other hand, these theorists may have been referring to instruments like the 1619 Ioannes Ruckers two-manual harpsichord-quint virginal combination, which does, after all, have three keyboards.[27] One wonders if these complex multistrung and triple-keyboard instruments really existed in the seventeenth century, or if those who wrote about them were simply passing along received wisdom, claiming to have seen them themselves so as not to appear provincial and uninformed. Still, a 1566 inventory taken of the instruments of Raymund Fugger, Jr. (1528–69) of Augsburg mentions both a harpsichord from the Netherlands with four manuals, made so that four people could play on it at once, and another, from Cologne, with two manuals, but made "so two could play together on each one."[28] It is impossible to know what these putative multiplayer instruments could have looked like.

AUSTRIA[30]

Only two Austrian instruments have survived the seventeenth century, both claviorgana, and both by the Linz maker Valentin Zeiss (dates unknown), who became court builder to the Holy Roman Emperor Ferdinand III in 1639. Little is known of the 1646 instrument (Austria, private collection), which *Boalch III* reports only as a 1×8′ with lute. Like the Kaiser clavicytherium, the earlier 1639 claviorganum (Salzburg, Museum Carolino Augusteum) has a 2×8′ disposition, also with both registers parallel to the wrestplank. It is another ornate court instrument, shaped like a large, nearly square, Prussian-blue box, with gilded carvings inside ripple-molded frames. The box rests on a walnut platform, which supports a walnut column at each corner. These, in turn, support the lid. The entire soundwell is covered with soundboard wood, although only the portion involved in the harpsichord is active. The board is decorated in the same sort of sparse, colorless manner seen on the German examples and has a lacy, gilded, upside-down wedding-cake rose. With the large lid off, the visual center of the instrument is the keywell, with its rippled-molding frames and carved gilded patterns (the latter also found on the jackrail). The C/E–c^3 keyboard has boxwood-covered naturals and ivory- or bone-topped sharps.

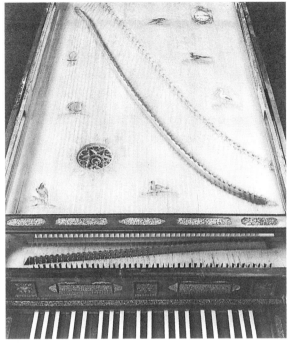

9-10. The small but imposing 1639 claviorganum by Valentin Zeiss, with lid removed. The sparse soundboard painting is typical. Salzburg, Museum Carolino Augusteum.

We would be hard put to draw any conclusions about Austrian harpsichord building from this one example. Nevertheless, it is possible to note that it shares some characteristics with the German instruments just discussed — most, if not all of them, from nearby South Germany. It is disposed 2×8′, with an intermediate scale calling for brass stringing. It has a gilded geometric rose, sparse soundboard decoration, box guides with the stop knobs projecting from the right side of the case, and an eye-catching keywell decoration. It does not have the varied and colorful stops of most of the German examples, but it is difficult to know how typical those instruments really were. By the beginning of the next century those color machines no longer seemed to be in fashion in southern Germany (at least, on the evidence of the survivors), and the Austrian instruments we will see bespeak of a different tradition altogether. Finally, the Zeiss is a claviorganum, and while it is possible to make comparisons between it and harpsichords, it is a little like comparing grapes and grapefruit.

SUMMING UP

Seventeenth-century German instruments were not built in a manner markedly different from the French. Both continued the tradition of thin case sides, but with thicker spines to carry a lid. German harpsichords may not have been built in quite as lutelike a manner as some of the Gallic examples; nevertheless, they were made according to the same principles, and lightness of construction, cross-barred soundboards, and intermediate scales are obvious characteristics of both. Differences in decor were clearly culturally inspired but would have had little effect on their sounds. The major distinction between them, obviously, was in their concepts of harpsichord tone. The French preferred a bit of separation in plucking points, just enough to achieve a distinction between the front and back 8′ jacks, but not so much that the registers would not easily blend (and in single-manual 2×8′ instruments that distinction would be even more subtle), while the 4′ strings could be used as a solo stop and to provide brilliance to the 2×8′ ensemble. Judging from the survivors, the German tonal aesthetic could not have been more different. The plucking points of the registers were isolated from each other, producing a palette of sounds ranging from intense nasality to simple sweetness. Metal plectra and buff stops added to the complexity of the tonal resources. Clearly, the blending of registers did not seem to be an important part of the German aesthetic. The Budapest anonyme, for example, though simply disposed, was obviously designed to make two very different sounds—one, the round, muselar-like tone of deep-plucking jacks; the other, the nasal, astringent sound of close-plucking jacks quilled in brass. A unison of these two registers, if intended at all, would be quite distinct from the tonally similar unisons of the typical seventeenth-century 2×8′ Italian or French harpsichord.

This desire for tonal diversity is also found in the 1619 Johann Mayer and the Munich anonyme, both disposed 2×8′, but each wringing a variety of sounds from its two sets of strings. The Nuremberg clavicytherium, with its 4′ strings and split registers, is even more complex. It is often said that these instruments were influenced by the organ—a logical assumption, since the Germans were such great organ builders; but it is more likely that both the variegated sounds of the German harpsichord and the prismatic tones of their organs sprang from the same proclivity toward colorful timbres. This was, after all, a sound world in which krummhorns, rauschpfeifen, ranketts, and zinken were still heard. Furthermore, although seventeenth-century French builders adhered to a certain tonal design, they were likely constrained to do so by guild regulations. German builders, on the other hand, were free to pursue more esoteric timbres if they so wished. In some of the instruments we have examined, not only is it obvious that this was desired, but it was part of the harpsichord-building culture. Nevertheless, our small sample of extant instruments, consisting mainly of examples from the early part of the century, does not constitute proof that those variegated sounds were typical of all or even most German harpsichords before 1700. And aside from the 1675 Kaiser clavicytherium, which, with its strange arrangement of strings, may well be an anomaly, and the Basel anonyme (which may even date from the 1700s),[31] we really have no knowledge of instruments in the latter half of the century.

[10]

ENGLAND

$\mathscr{Q}$UITE A FEW jack-action instruments survived from
the forty-five seventeenth-century English (mainly London)
builders identified by *Boalch III*,[1] but these are virginals and
bentside spinets, rather than grands. We have twenty virginals,
and approximately twice that number of bentside spinets, but
only three harpsichords—one undated, and the others from
1622 and 1683.[2] Aside from the usual reasons, two other events
could explain the dearth of grands. First, the Fire of London in
1666 devastated the city, and almost anything made of wood
went up in flames. Second, there was an abrupt change in harpsichord style after 1725, and seventeenth-century English harpsichords did not lend themselves to the sort of rebuilding and
modernizing possible with Flemish and French instruments.
Hence, it is likely that many were discarded as useless when the
large, heavy-case, Ruckers-inspired models became the standard
in the eighteenth century. However, a group of seven harpsichords built between 1700 and 1725 still survive, and they have
a far greater kinship with the Internationally inspired seventeenth-century English instruments than they do with the ones
that followed. Although they will be discussed in Chapter 16,
they represent the last vestige of the Internationally based indigenous English harpsichord.

If there was a dynasty at work in England during this time, it
would have been the Haward family. Little is known of its members, but Charles (fl. ca. 1660–87) is survived by a 1683 harpsichord and nine spinets, a record unequaled by any other En-

glish builder before the eighteenth century. He sold a spinet in 1668 to the famed diarist Samuel Pepys, and Queen Anne is supposed to have owned one of his virginals.[3] Other members of the family include a few Johns, another Charles, and some Thomases, but their dates and the relationships between them are unknown; in fact, it is not even certain that they were all members of the same family.

Gabriel Townsend (ca. 1604–ca. 1662) seems to have been another well-respected builder, although he is survived only by a 1641 virginal (Brussels, Musée Instrumental). However, that instrument was made for Elizabeth, Queen of Bohemia and sister of King Charles I, who was the reigning monarch when it was made. A painting of Orpheus charming the beasts graces the lid, and *Boalch III* notes that the Orpheus "bears a striking resemblance to Charles I."[4] Since Charles was then at odds with Parliament, the mocking humor of the painting could not have been lost on Elizabeth.

Townsend's master was Thomas White, whose son (d. 1660) and grandson (fl. 1669) were both named Thomas. Thomas II also had a son, James (fl. 1656–70), and between the four of them they left seven virginals, dating from 1638 to 1684, spanning the entire known history of that instrument in England. Townsend, in turn, was master to John Player (ca. 1634–ca. 1705–8), who is survived by one virginal and ten bentside spinets. Stephen Keene (ca. 1640–ca. 1719), another of Townsend's apprentices, left behind two virginals and twenty-six spinets, two more spinets with Edward Blunt (ca. 1678–1718), a former apprentice, and yet another with Charles Brackley (ca. 1688– after 1719), an apprentice he took in partnership. A legacy of thirty-one instruments is rare among builders at any time and must indicate that Keene's work was highly prized.

VIRGINALS

Given that so few French and German seventeenth-century virginals have survived, it is somewhat surprising to find that there are some twenty extant from England, all signed and all but the earliest two appearing in a forty-six-year period beginning in 1638. (Frank Hubbard, noting this clustering phenomenon with some amusement, likened the string of instruments to a "platoon of marching soldiers.")[5] The relationship between these instruments and the virginals of the previous century must remain speculative; nevertheless, that they are so similar to each other may indicate that they come at the end of a long tradition of English virginal making.

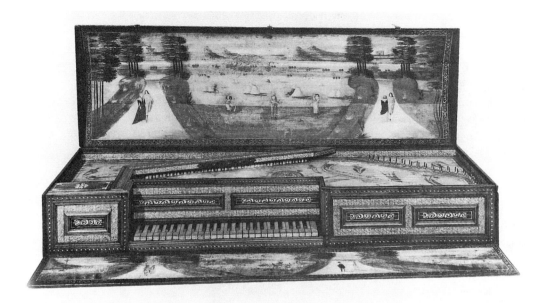

Because of these similarities one can easily generate a description that encompasses all of these instruments. With lengths varying from 5'6" to 6' (depending on the compass), and widths shy of 2', they are similar in size to their Flemish cousins. Sides are of oak, intermediate in thickness, with a heavier softwood spine supporting a coffered oak lid attached with wrought-iron strap hinges. The lid is divided into three longitudinal sections, with the main panel raised by two narrower angled pieces.[6] The interior bracing is that found on all virginals: an extension of the cheek walls back to the spine. The soundboard was normally reinforced with a cutoff bar and a few ribs in front of the jacks. Scales were short, generally somewhere around 10"–12", suggesting that brass stringing was the norm.[7] With the keyboard placed to the left of the case, plucking points are close to the left bridge, producing a pleasantly nasal, almost buzzy sound. The left end of the jackrail is captured by an arm extending between the outer portion of the left cheek and the tool box that fills the front left corner. The natural keys were normally covered with boxwood, and the sharps made of stained fruitwood or oak; or naturals could have ebony or snakewood touch plates, with sharps of solid bone. Key fronts were adorned with gilt embossed paper.

A strip of leather, slotted for the jacks, two to a slot (but with a separating strip between them), was glued to the spruce or fir soundboard, and a slotted lower guide with sides to stiffen it was glued to the case bracing. The compasses of these virginals vary, generally increasing from C to c³ (1642 Thomas White, London, Victoria and Albert Museum) to GG/BB–f³ (1684 Thomas Bolton, Cheshire, Warrington Museum).[8] (The GG/BB short octave may seem to violate the English predilection for chromatic basses, but such is not the case; rather, it represents the addition of bass notes below the chromatic C–c octave.) Interestingly, many English virginals have an additional string and slot in the bass, but no extra key. To sound the extra string the player removed the jack of the lowest note of the keyboard, dropped it into the added slot, tuned the string to the desired pitch, and played it from the lowest key. This arrangement was provided in order to furnish a note normally not available to the keyboard — say, a low AA in a compass beginning on C.[9] Of course, the C is no longer obtainable when the auxiliary second slot is in use; and even if an additional jack was available, as in the case of the 1641 virginal by Gabriel Townsend (Brussels, Musée Instrumental), where it is stored in the tool box, having both in position would play both strings simultaneously only when the C key was pressed. The same benefit could have been gained by simply retuning the C string, but evidently this system of an additional string and slot was considered superior, perhaps because a heavier string, more suitable for a lower note, was used.

Although not as lightly built as Italian inners, these virginals certainly do not have the heft associated with heavy-case Flemish instruments. Both cut-in and applied moldings were used profusely, giving them a somewhat deceptive appearance of robustness. Applied moldings are also found on the case front, framing panels of patterned papers or white scrolling on a black ground. Often the case moldings were decorated with some simple, repetitive design painted on the natural wood, something reminiscent of early Flemish practice, although not as complex. On a few virginals ivory studs on the case molding outline the instrument, in sixteenth-century Italian style. Otherwise, the soundwell, keywell, and case front were covered with embossed, gilded paper. Soundboards were painted, with blue borders and scallops as in Flemish virginals. Unlike the variety on Flemish boards, the motifs on English virginals are almost exclusively birds and flowers. Complex roses vary from one to four per soundboard, almost all geometric in pattern, made of wood and/or parchment,

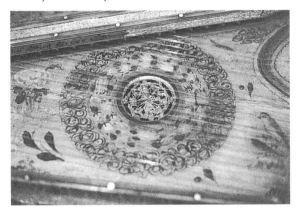

10-2. One of the elaborate roses and wreaths of the 1668 Stephen Keene virginal. Edinburgh, Russell Collection of Early Keyboard Instruments, University of Edinburgh.

ORIGINS OF THE ENGLISH VIRGINAL

Until recently, conventional wisdom had held that the English virginal was copied or taken over from the Flemish spinett.[12] Raymond Russell believed "that they derive from the virginals made in the Ruckers workshop, which they resemble closely."[13] Frank Hubbard was of the same opinion, noting correspondences in the basic layout, the placement of the keyboard, the bridge sections, the use of upper and lower guides, and the slotted leather strip on the upper guide.[14] Germann, dealing with decorative aspects, notes that English virginals were so Flemish derived that they "could almost be considered a Flemish Provincial style."[15] But with increasing awareness of the existence of the International style, opinion has now shifted. The authors of *Early Keyboard Instruments* suggest that the virginals "derive from the same non-Flemish tradition represented by Praetorius' illustration and the surviving 17-century harpsichords and virginals from Germany and France."[16] In his capsule history of plucked string instruments, John Henry van der Meer ascribes a German origin to the English virginal.[17] In her current writings on the subject, Sheridan Germann now recognizes an International connection.[18]

There now seems to be little question that with characteristics like intermediate case thicknesses, gilded geometric roses, applied molding, molded frames on the case exterior, the use of decorative papers, and intermediate scales, these virginals appear to be International in derivation. But their oak cases and chromatic keyboards indicate some specifically English traits as well.[19]

and gilded. Floral wreaths and arabesque patterns around each rose tend to be large and elaborate, and it is these, rather than the more casual flowers and birds, that are the most eye-catching feature of the board. The maker's name and the date, and sometimes the city, were painted on the side of the jackrail facing the player.

The coffered lids always hold a painting of an outdoor scene, often one that has been described as "St. James Park," a genre perhaps descended from the courtly pastoral (one such example can be seen in Plate 14).[10] Paintings on the fallboards usually continue the motif of the lid scene. These paintings can be as rigidly formal and balanced as those found decades earlier on Flemish virginals, although the appearance differs considerably. The English examples look emptier and far more casual than the highly detailed Renaissance lid-painting style. The subject matter of these lids differs—Orpheus serenading the beasts, peasants farming, or gentry walking or hunting—but the style of execution is remarkably similar from one to the other, leading Sheridan Germann to conclude that many of these lids, and the soundboards as well, were done by the same hand.[11]

If a closed Flemish virginal was "supposed" to resemble a block of green porphyry marble, there is little doubt that an English virginal was "supposed" to represent a common chest of some sort, although open: a blaze of color revealed a garden of delights on the soundboard, a stylized lid painting, moldings galore, the contrast of natural and painted wood, and colored and gilded papers. The resemblance between these virginals and those of the Ruckers family may be superficial, but the appeal of both to seventeenth-century bourgeois taste was not.

BENTSIDE SPINETS

Bentside spinets began to appear in England soon after Zenti's 1664 stay at the court.[22] They were also made in Italy, Germany, France, and elsewhere during the late seventeenth and eighteenth centuries, but nowhere in the numbers found in England, which produced them in vast quantities for well over a hundred years. There is no question that the English version of the instrument owed much to its Italian origins: scales were short, calling for brass stringing, jacks were supported in box guides, keyboards were projecting (although the cheeks were slanted rather than scroll carved), and cases were unpainted. But rather than thin-case inner-outers, they were made in Internationally inspired English style, with walls of intermediate thickness, a heavier spine supporting a lid, and tails either rounded or mitered. Although some cases were made of oak, most were constructed from walnut, or a softer wood veneered with walnut. As on virginals, the only bracing was an extension of the cheeks back to the spine, with perhaps a knee or two at the bentside. Stringing with lighter woods, contrasting woods in the soundwell, and the use of other veneers on the exterior are all found in these instruments, although it is the later, eighteenth-century examples that tended to be more elaborate. Like the late virginals, compasses generally started with GG/BB, sometimes with one or two split sharps in the short octave, and ascended to c^3, d^3, or even f^3. Compasses eventually were extended to g^3, and sometimes the basses were chromatic down to GG. Stands were light and gracefully turned trestles, made from the same wood as the case, and generally followed prevailing furniture styles.[23]

There were many shops in which both virginals and bentside spinets were produced side by side, and the two instruments shared many common traits, including compasses, scale, brass stringing, close plucking points, and keyboards with ebony naturals and solid bone or skunk-tail sharps.[24] But in decoration they were worlds apart: virginals were painted, with decorated soundboards and elaborate roses, while spinets were unpainted, with natural wood finishes and veneers, and with no soundboard decoration and no roses. Moldings and framing were an integral part of the decor of virginals, but moldings were used sparingly and inconspicuously in the spinets and never utilized to form framed panels. Although virginals were covered with gilded embossed papers, about the only decorative devices found in spinets was an oval marquetry inlay of flowers and birds on the nameboard over the keys, ornamental brass hinges

THE ENGLISH VIRGINALISTS

England experienced a great musical flowering in the late sixteenth and early seventeenth centuries, particularly in the genres of the madrigal, the accompanied solo song, and solo music for the lute and harpsichord. A group of composers, variously known as the madrigalists, the lutenists, or the virginalists (depending on the medium for which they were writing), produced vast quantities of attractive music, mostly for amateur consumption. Since the English called all jack-action instruments virginals at that time, it is clear that any harpsichord or virginal would have been appropriate for the performance of this music. Sadly, we have no working extant instruments that would have been available in the early 1600s, when most of this repertoire was composed. The 1579 Theewes, the earlier two of the three extant harpsichords, and the two early, undated, anonymous virginals (Edinburgh, Russell Collection; National Museum of Scotland) mentioned in Chapter 2 (see note 1) are all that remain of what must have been a thriving building tradition.

Other than these, by the time of the first dated extant virginal, the 1638 motherless child, most of the virginalists had died, which means that few if any of the other surviving virginals would have been built when the music was written. Bentside spinets would seem to be even less appropriate vehicles for this repertory, since they do not begin to appear before 1660. Finally, we have only one extant English grand harpsichord that would have been available to the virginalists, the 1579 Theewes (to be discussed shortly). We really know very little about the instruments for which this marvelous body of harpsichord music was composed.

Nevertheless, it is clear from Henry VIII's 1547 inventory, and from other sources as well,[20] that Italian and Flemish instruments were plentiful in England during those years, so there was no lack of instruments on which to play. Furthermore, the virginalist repertory, in repositories such as *My Ladye Nevells Booke, Parthenia or the Maydenhead of the First Musicke that ever was printed for the Virginnals,* and the *Fitzwilliam Virginal Book,* continued in popularity for decades after it was written. *Elizabeth Rogers' Virginal Book,* for example, was compiled ca. 1656, well after the death of most of the virginalists. Hence, modern performance on later seventeenth-century English instruments, including bentside spinets, would not be inappropriate, nor would hearing them on clavichord or chamber organ.

Queen Elizabeth (1533–1603; r. 1558–1603), known to have been a skilled keyboardist as well as a lutenist, is particularly associated with the virginal because of her reputed ownership of an ornate Italian instrument (London, Victoria and Albert Museum). But Elizabeth must have owned other virginals, English ones among them, and undoubtedly played them all. In his memoirs Sir James Melville, ambassador of Mary Queen of Scots to the Elizabethan court, described how he blundered into Elizabeth's chamber one evening, drawn there by her excellent playing. After chastising him for his impertinence, Elizabeth asked Melville if she was a better player than his queen. Melville responded with a diplomatic, but probably truthful, affirmative.[21]

Major composers of the virginalist school	Major sources of virginalist music
William Byrd (1543–1623)	*The Mulliner Book* (ca. 1550–75)
Thomas Morley (ca. 1557–1602)	*The Dublin Virginal Book* (1583)
Peter Phillips (ca. 1561–1628)	*My Ladye Nevells Book* (1591)
Giles Farnaby (ca. 1563–1640)	*Parthenia or the Maydenhead of the First Musicke*
John Bull ((1562–1628)	*that ever was printed for the Virginnals* (1613)
Thomas Weelkes (1576–1623)	*Fitzwilliam Virginal Book* (1609–19)
Thomas Tompkins (1572–1656)	*Benjamin Cosyn's Virginal Book* (ca. 1610–27)
Orlando Gibbons (1583–1625)	*Will Forster's Virginal Book* (1624)
	Elizabeth Rogers' Virginal Book (ca. 1656)

10-3. Typical of the seventeenth-century English bentside spinet, this 1700 instrument by Keene is simple and restrained in appearance. The compass is GG/BB–d³, with split sharps for the two lowest accidentals. The soundboard and bridge are not original. Museum of Fine Arts, Boston. Reproduced with permission. © 2000 Museum of Fine Arts, Boston. All rights reserved.

on the lid, and in a few, embossed paper key fronts. Even later in the eighteenth century, when they were at their most elaborate, the decoration of bentside spinets was restrained.

Some questions need to be asked about these spinets. Why did they become so popular? Why did they supersede the virginals so quickly? Why did they eschew the typical International decorative schemes of the seventeenth century, including the use of papers, moldings, geometric roses, and decorated soundboards? The answers are intertwined. There was a change in furniture style in England around the time the spinet was introduced, right after a terrible outbreak of plague in 1665 and the Fire of London in the following year. English oak, with its open grain, had been the furniture wood of choice since the Middle Ages; but taste now turned to walnut, a wood with a closer grain that lent itself to a fine polish and lighter, more graceful shapes. Domestic instruments were as much furniture as music-making devices, and the refined bentside spinet — probably thanks to Zenti, who serendipitously wandered into the picture at this time — fit this aesthetic. On the other hand, the stolid, chestlike exterior of the old oak virginal, as well as its flamboyant interior, must have rather quickly come to be regarded as hopelessly outmoded. Probably of equal importance in the ascendance of the bentside spinet, however, was its efficient shape. These spinets were about a foot shorter than virginals, and this would have appealed to anyone trying to fit an instrument into an already crowded chamber.[25] It is probably largely for this reason that bentside spinets began to replace virginals all over Europe around this time.[26]

HARPSICHORDS

Forty-three years after the Theewes, another English harpsichord survived, and it is in even worse condition than its predecessor. Built by John Hasard[27] in 1622 (Knole, National Trust), it is missing most of its soundboard as well as its keyboard, action parts, lid, and almost all of its internal structure. Nevertheless, it confirms some of our suppositions about the nature of English harpsichord building. It is quite long, more than 8′, with a narrow tail. The case sides are oak, about ⁵⁄₁₆″ thick, and it is evident that the heavier spine originally carried a lid. Only one bottom brace remains, but originally there were four, with five diagonal struts running from the bentside liner to the spine and lower bellyrail. The gap angles away from the nameboard in the bass, like some Italian and German harpsichords we have seen. Applied moldings at the top and bottom of the sides add the illusion of breadth to the case, and vertical moldings divide the bentside, cheek, and tail into four discrete framed areas. A Latin motto exhorting the viewer to praise God with "well-sounding instruments and music from heaven" is painted in the soundwell, on the interior of the case sides.[28] It sits on a handsome and elaborately carved and fluted nine-legged oak stand, with arcades at the top and stretchers at the bottom.

There are some conjectural elements about the Hasard, and several scholars have attempted to divine them.[29] Koster scrutinized the instrument at great length and has come to some conclusions, however tentative, that seem to have eluded earlier investigators. It has three rows of tuning pins, indicating three sets of strings: one back near the nameboard, and the other two together, closer to the gap. The lower guide, still in place, has slots for three sets of jacks. Koster postulates that there were three nuts and two bridges, with one register approximately a fourth below normal pitch, and two an octave above that. One of the octave nuts is close to its jacks, suggesting a nasal register. Further, there is evidence to suggest that one of the nuts had a buff or arpichordum rail behind it. The Hasard also has a partially hollow wrestplank, with one of the nuts on a free soundboard. Finally, Koster estimates the compass to have been C–e³, a range also found on some of the virginals.

At low pitch, with three nuts, and with 1×8′, 2×4′ on two bridges and all on one manual, it is obvious that the Hasard is a different sort of instrument; but that disposition may be put into a little clearer perspective if it is remembered that the 2×8′, 1×4′ registration of the Theewes harpsichord may also have been revolutionary for its time. The sound world of the Theewes and the Hasard, with metal plectra (or at least an indication that these were used), arpichordum stops (or at least the possibility of them), and close-plucking nasal registers, are, of course, squarely in the International tradition. What is unusual about these instruments, then, is not so much their idiosyncrasies, but that only two of them are still here. The two other survivors of seventeenth-century England are much more conventional.

An undated instrument bearing the name Jesses Cassus[30] (Encinitas, Calif., private ownership) has cautiously been accepted into the corpus of seventeenth-century English harpsichords,[31] mainly on the basis of decorative aspects such as the gilt-embossed paper on the nameboard and the presence of a royal English coat of arms; but its physical characteristics are certainly English, or at least, International. The 2×8′ Cassus is a small instrument, less than 5′6″ long, and it has an extremely short scale, only 8⅞″. Because of this, and also because its bentside has the deep curve characteristic of higher-pitched instruments, it is likely that it was intended to sound at something higher than the norm—perhaps at the fourth or fifth. It has a heavy softwood spine, and its ¼″-thick oak sides and nameboard are divided into panels by applied moldings. Embossed, gilt papers decorate the nameboard and the interior of the soundwell. The natural touch plates are made of boxwood, and the sharps are elaborately inlaid. The current compass, AA–f³, may not be original.[32] There are two roses on the soundboard.

Like the Hasard, the gap slants away from the nameboard and the instrument has a hollow wrestplank. One of the registers is always on, and the other is controlled by a projection through the cheek. The Cassus also has a genuine lute stop—a set of jacks riding in a second gap, between the main gap and the nut. What is really different about the Cassus, however, is that its case and lid are painted, and according to McGeary, with a level of sophistication far in excess of the primitive style found on virginals.[33] In this sense the Cassus is unique, although it is not the only painted English harpsichord.

The last known English harpsichord to have survived the seventeenth century is a 1683 single by Charles Haward (England, private ownership), and it, too, has its idiosyncrasies. It has a rounded tail—the first to be seen on an English grand—with the bass section of the bridge mitered.[39] The soundboard contains four geometric roses, outdoing both Praetorius's clavicytherium and the ca. 1620 anonyme in the Germanisches Nationalmuseum by one, but reminding us of the four roses on the

THE PEDALS OF JOHN HAWARD

The oldest of the John Haward builders (d. ca. 1667) is known as the inventor of a pedal mechanism for changing registration. A harpsichord fitted with this device, which he called a *Pedal* to distinguish it from an ordinary *Harpsicon*, was described by Thomas Mace (ca. 1612–ca. 1706) in his 1676 treatise *Musick's Monument*. Mace's description is readily available elsewhere,[34] but a short excerpt will serve to illustrate his breathless, italicized admiration for the device:

> *This Instrument* is in *Shape and Bulk* just like a *Harpsicon; only it differs in the *Order* of *It*, Thus, *viz.* There is made right underneath the *Keys*, near the *Ground*, a kind of *Cubbord*, or *Box*, which opens with a little *Pair* of *Doors*, in which *Box* the *Performer* sets *both his Feet.* . . . There being right underneath his *Toes* 4 *little Pummels of Wood*, under *each foot* 2, any one of *Those* 4 he may *Tread* upon at his *Pleasure;* which by the *Weight of his Foot drives a Spring*, and so *Causeth the whole Instrument to Sound*, either *Soft* or *Loud*, *according as he shall chuse to Tread any of them down.* . . . And by *This Pritty Device*, is *This Instrument made Wonderfully Rare, and Excellent:* So that doubtless it *Excels* all *Harpsicons*, or *Organs* in the World.[35]

Although Mace's words have been quoted often, no one has asked why he, and evidently many others, including Henry Purcell,[36] played an instrument with an "automatic" mechanism for changing stops.[37] Certainly, the modern study of performance practice tells us that sudden and dramatic changes of registration were not part of the aesthetic of seventeenth-century music;[38] but perhaps the innovation was considered desirable for the same reason so many virginals were fitted with the "automatic" ability to play an extra-low bass note. In both instances the desired change could have been made almost as easily—moving a harpsichord's hand stop, or retuning the last string in a virginal—by slightly more labor-intensive means. This is hardly a convincing explanation for either phenomenon, but neither was found in any of the other traditions; nor did they survive in England. Bentside spinets, which had superseded virginals as the home instrument of choice before the end of the seventeenth century, did not have the additional slot and string, although the musical requirements had not changed; and Haward's pedal harpsichord died out after enjoying a life of about twenty years. Pedals did not reappear in England until after the middle of the next century and operated in a manner quite different from Haward's invention.

1668 Stephen Keene virginal. Its case walls are of ⁵⁄₁₆″ walnut, with a heavier softwood spine supporting a lid. Its internal support consists of six modified U-braces.[40] The gap slants, and the stop knobs originally projected through the cheek. The instrument is disposed 2×8′, with a short 10¼″ scale, and originally had a lute stop (signs of it remain, although the wrestplank has been replaced). The compass is wide—FF,GG–d³. The naturals are ebony and the sharps bone. The nameboard and jackrail are decorated with marquetry.[41]

Like the bentside spinets, the Haward seems to answer to the new lighter, more graceful post-1660s furniture aesthetic. Molding is used sparingly, and external decoration is limited to the beauty of the close walnut grain. Nevertheless, with its thin sides, U-braces, slanted gap, lute stop, and marquetry-enhanced keywell and jackrail, it is still squarely in what we could dare to call the mainstream of seventeenth-century English harpsichord building.

SUMMING UP

Four harpsichords in the space of 104 years scarcely constitute a trend; still, with the concomitant picture of the French and German versions of International style to call upon, with the additional clues furnished us by the virginals and spinets, and with the cluster of extant English grands built between 1700 and 1725 available for comparison, it is possible to conjecture what English harpsichord building was like then. Most were long instruments, with narrow tails. Before the 1666 Fire of London their sides were of oak, intermediate in thickness, with a heavier spine of softwood and with a lid; later, walnut replaced oak as the case material. Internal bracing consisted of U-shaped bottom braces and perhaps diagonal struts. Hollow wrestplanks, slanted gaps, and mutation stops—particularly the nasal or lute stop—are all found. Stop knobs projected either through the nameboard or through the cheek. Scales were short to intermediate. Compasses were chromatic down to C, and later, lower than that. Although we have no witnesses, the example of the virginals and spinets would suggest that at least some keyboards would have started with a GG/BB short octave. Until the advent of the walnut case, applied moldings were utilized to divide the cases into panels, and the use of embossed and gilded papers in the keywell and soundwell were common. After that, the emphasis changed to a plainer, less decorated look.

1. The ca. 1480 Royal College of Music clavicytherium. The instrument is shown here in its outer case. London, Royal College of Music, Museum of Instruments. Clavicytherium, (?) South German, ca. 1480, RCM 1.

2. *Apollo Crowning the Singer Marc Antonio Pasqualini* by Andrea Sacchi, ca. 1640. This painting is full of classical symbolism. The tortured figure in the background is the satyr Marsyas, who had the temerity to challenge Apollo to a music contest. The figure on the "bentside" of the instrument is the nymph Daphne, caught in the act of turning into a laurel tree, while Apollo crowns Pasqualini with a laurel wreath. New York, Metropolitan Museum of Art.

3. An anonymous sixteenth-century octave spinet. Strumming his lute (a "modern" replacement for the lyre), Arion is borne triumphantly to shore on the back of a dolphin. In this version of the legend the dolphins evidently capsized the ship, sending the larcenous sailors into the sea. London, Victoria and Albert Museum.

4. This anonymous instrument, built for the Duke of Cleves in 1568, is unique among Flemish virginals in its sarcophagus shape, carved case, little feet, and wealth of mottoes. London, Victoria and Albert Museum.

5a. The 1580 Martin van der Biest mother and child spinett virginal. The child's keyboard can be seen in the compartment in the right side of the case and can be partially withdrawn or even removed for playing. Nuremberg, Germanisches Nationalmuseum.

5b. The child of the 1580 van der Biest has been removed from its case and placed on top of the mother, with the latter's jackrail removed. The mother's jacks push up the backs of the child's keys, enabling the player to activate both sets of strings from the mother's keyboard. Nuremberg, Germanisches Nationalmuseum.

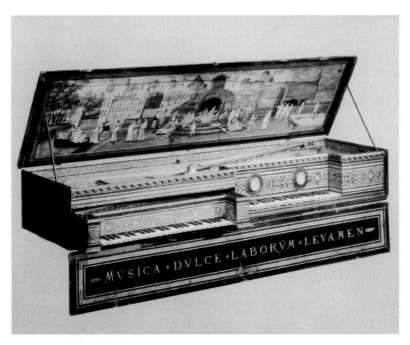

6. The 1581 Hans Ruckers mother and child muselar virginal. The child, on the left, has been partially withdrawn from its compartment. This is a particularly rich and striking instrument. New York, Metropolitan Museum of Art.

7. When new and fresh, the colors on the exterior of this 1560 inner by Guido Trasuntino must have been dazzling. It may never have had an outer case. © Bildarchiv Preussischer Kulturbesitz, Berlin, Musikinstrumenten Museum.

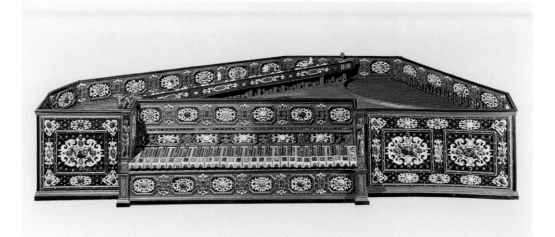

8. In both materials and workmanship, this 1577 instrument by Annibale dei Rossi is probably the most spectacular-looking virginal ever made. London, Victoria and Albert Museum.

9. This large 1666 2×8' inner-outer by Girolamo Zenti is typical of his precise but unassuming work. The outer case has been redecorated. New York, Metropolitan Museum of Art.

10. Michele Todini's eye-popping golden harpsichord and its attendant statues are full of classical allusions. New York, Metropolitan Museum of Art, The Crosby Brown Collection of Musical Instruments, 1889. Accession no. 89.4.2929.

11. The 1681 Vaudry harpsichord. This beautiful court instrument is one of the finest extant examples of seventeenth-century French harpsichord making and decorating. London, Victoria and Albert Museum.

12. This striking 1678 or 1679 harpsichord by Gilbert Desruisseaux is an outstanding example of a provincial style of decoration. The large white plants painted on the exterior are bulbs of garlic. Paris, Musée de la Musique.

13. The 1619 harpsichord by Johann Mayer. Disposed 2×8', it has three rows of jacks and produces three distinct kinds of timbres. Salzburg, Museum Carolino Augusteum.

14. The lid painting on this 1666 virginal by Adam Leversidge was once thought to be of London's St. James Park. New Haven, Yale University Collection of Musical Instruments.

15. The 1697 harpsichord by Carlo Grimaldi. The gold-on-black decoration of the outer case was probably originally all gold. The Baroque stand visually overwhelms the harpsichord itself. Nuremberg, Germanisches Nationalmuseum.

16. The 1785 Joachim José Antunes harpsichord is a large, powerful instrument, seemingly typical of the late-eighteenth-century style of Portuguese harpsichord building. Goudhurst, Finchcocks, The Richard Burnett Collection of Historical Keyboard Instruments.

17. The famous 1770 harpsichord by Pascal Taskin demonstrates the powerful appearance of the late French double. The external decoration is nineteenth century. New Haven, Yale University Collection of Musical Instruments.

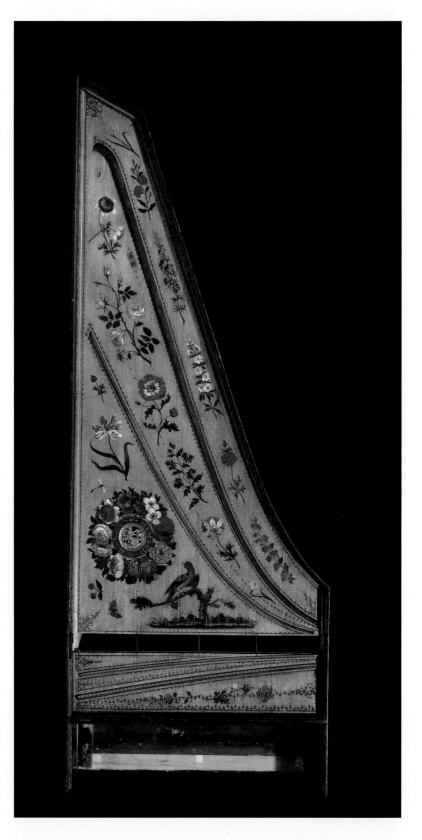

18. The soundboard painting of the ca. 1736 harpsichord by the Parisian builder Henri Hemsch. Museum of Fine Arts, Boston. Reproduced with permission. © 2000 Museum of Fine Arts, Boston. All rights reserved.

19. Among the world's most beautifully decorated harpsichords, François-Etienne Blanchet's 1733 instrument left its home only once, to return to Paris for the addition of an f³. Château de Thoiry-en-Yvelines, France.

20. The rose and wreath of the 1769 Pascal Taskin harpsichord, by the "Earlier Taskin Painter." Edinburgh, Russell Collection of Early Keyboard Instruments, University of Edinburgh.

21. Done in the nineteenth century, the decoration on the case of this ca. 1736
Henri Hemsch harpsichord is extraordinarily beautiful. Museum of Fine Arts,
Boston. Reproduced with permission. © 2000 Museum of Fine Arts, Boston.
All rights reserved.

22. This ornate 1716 harpsichord by Pierre Donzelague of Lyons has some advanced
features not yet seen in Paris; nevertheless, it sits on a lovely but old-fashioned
stand. Le Musée Lyonnais des Arts Decoratifs.

23. This beautiful 1702–04 single by Michael Mietke, known as "the white harpsichord" because of the porcelain-like appearance of its white ground, was finished by the famous japanner Gerard Dagly, decorator to the Berlin court of Frederick I. Berlin, Stiftung Preussische Schlösser und Gärten Berlin-Brandenburg/ Fotograf.

PART IV

The Eighteenth Century

[*11*]

THE DECLINE OF
THE ITALIAN HARPSICHORD

*I*TALIAN HARPSICHORD building changed little in the eighteenth century. While French, English, and German builders would be making instruments with two manuals, the 2×8′, 1×4′ disposition, buff stops, and lute stops, Italian craftsmen almost never departed from their basic 2×8′ single-keyboard models. Both true and false inner-outers continued to be built, but many instruments were made with relatively plain cases, often with neither moldings nor much reference to the inner-outer tradition. Some instruments had expanded compasses of up to five octaves, but others were built with old-fashioned C/E–c³ keyboards. Internal bracing still consisted of combinations of bottom braces, knees, and diagonal struts, even on heavy-case instruments. Some extant harpsichords have beautifully embellished cases, but for the most part the decoration is external to the instrument, rather than an integral part of its aesthetic. Furthermore, Italian harpsichord building seemed to decline in activity after 1700, with far fewer craftsmen working then compared to the previous century. For example, *Boalch III* lists almost eighty makers active in Rome and Florence between 1600 and 1700 but counts only thirty or so in the hundred years after.[1]

The instruments themselves are scarcer yet. All the extant eighteenth-century Italian harpsichords, virginals, spinets, and ottavini, including both signed and anonymous instruments, number little more than one hundred.[2] True, nothing like that number of eighteenth-century German harpsichords are extant, and the count of surviving French instruments would not be that much greater; but evidence suggests that the Germans were not prolific harpsichord builders, and we know that many French instruments were destroyed during and after the Revolution (neither circumstance was a factor in England, where many of the thousands of harpsichords made still exist). Accordingly, it seems strange that after two hundred years the region of Europe that formerly produced such large numbers of instruments should have slacked off so sharply in its production. The disparity may have been exacerbated by the fact that the earlier instruments could have been valued more than the later, and thus were more likely to survive into and past the nineteenth century. And certainly, like builders everywhere, a certain amount of makers' efforts went into modernizing and restoring older instruments. Nevertheless, some of the most ingenious harpsichords were built during this time, by the Florentines Bartolomeo Cristofori, Giovanni Ferrini, and Vincenzo Sodi.

FLORENCE

Florence became the adopted home of one of the most famous of all harpsichord makers, Bartolomeo Cristofori (1655–1732). Although now known and revered as the inventor of the piano (the *gravicembalo col piano e forte*), he was primarily a maker of jack-action instruments.[3] Cristofori was born in Padua, and although nothing is known of his training or his work there, he must have established himself as a master builder. He and Grand Duke Ferdinand de' Medici are supposed to have met in 1688, when the latter, traveling from Venice to Florence, stopped off in Padua. The duke was much taken with Cristofori's work (the story goes) and offered him employment at the Florentine court.[4] Cristofori accepted, and the following year he moved to Florence, where he took up his duties as head of the instrument-making workshop. Whatever the circumstances of his hiring, it is likely that Cristofori was attracted to the position for a number of reasons. The duke, reportedly fascinated by mechanical gadgets, may have assured him of the opportunity to pursue his inventive nature in a manner not possible for him in Padua. The managerial aspects of the job may also have appealed to him, and as a son of the poor Christofani (as the family was called in Padua) family,[5] the recognition, and the opportunity to work at the most glittering court in Italy, alongside the finest artisans to be found anywhere, must have played a strong role in his decision.[6] He remained in Florence for the rest of his life, although he noted in his will that he had always intended to return to Padua.[7]

Once in his new location, Cristofori was busily engaged in building harpsichords for his patron (and eventually for others), as well as restoring older instruments belonging to the court. His own accounts of the years 1690–98 note that he undertook sixteen restorations and built six harpsichords, two spinets, and one organ. They also show that he spent a great deal of time tuning and moving harpsichords between his house in Florence (near the Uffizi Palace), the duke's abode in Poggio a Caiano, the Medici villa in Pratolino, and the Palazzo Pitti (the Medici palace, the second largest in Italy).[8] There is archival evidence documenting Cristofori's activities; as a consequence, far more is known about him than about most Italian builders. For example, an inventory of 1700 notes that by this date Ferdinand owned seven instruments built by Cristofori: two grand harpsichords, two spinets (which could have been bentside spinets or polygonal virginals), a *spinettone* (an instrument of his own invention, to be described shortly), a clavicytherium, and an *arpicembalo*—a piano.[9] When Ferdinand died in 1713 his father, the Grand Duke Cosimo, elevated the builder to the position of keeper of all the musical instruments, an occasion that prompted yet another inventory, in 1716.[10] Other accounts from 1704–13 give details and costs of Cristofori's repairing, maintaining, and tuning of Ferdinand's instruments.

Cristofori must have spent considerable time in what today we would call research and development, because in addition to conventional harpsichords, he also made a new variety of 2×8′ virginal (the "oval" virginal), a new type of spinet (the *spinettone de teatro,* or *spinetta traversa*), and a new kind of harpsichord action, in which the strings are struck by hammers, rather than plucked by quills. This last, of course, was the piano, which at that time he called the *arpicembalo.* From the accounts and surviving exemplars it is obvious that Cristofori made at least seven kinds of stringed keyboards: clavichords, clavicytheria, spinets (which may have been conventional virginals or bentside spinets), "oval" virginals, *spinettoni de teatro,* grand harpsichords, and pianos.[11] Henkel estimates that he probably built something like two hundred instruments over his lifetime, of which 170 or so were jack action and the remainder pianos.[12] Given his other duties in Florence, which also included performance (Cristofori was one of Ferdinand's *virtuosi da camera*), that figure seems exceedingly high; but the fact remains that only eight of his works have survived.[13] None of his clavicytheria remain, although it is obvious from the accounts that he built them.[14] The same is true of his conventional spinets, whether true *spinetti* or *virginali.*

Only one of Cristofori's "oval" virginals is extant, a 1693

2×8′ inner-outer with C–c³ compass (Leipzig, Musikinstrumenten-Museum der Universität Leipzig). It is one of the two he made for Ferdinand — the other was dated 1690 — and it is likely that he never built any more.[15] The design of this 2×8′ virginal was obviously well thought out, both in its mechanics and in its appearance. Although often described as oval in shape,[16] it is actually oblong, with an extension resembling a gothic arch at either end.[17] This instrument is, in fact, the result of the "joining" of two normal virginals, one the mirror image of the other, and the protruding arches are the result of "cutting away" the four unneeded corners. Both the thin case sides and the soundboard are made of cypress, as are the V-shaped jackrail and the centered geometric rose. The bridges are of ebony. The projecting keyboard is to the left, and the rest of the area in front of the oblong case is decorated with ebony and boxwood inlays. The keyboard is also of ebony and box, with the lighter wood used for naturals and the darker for sharps. The natural heads each have an oval inlay of ebony, and the tails are bordered with ebony stringing. The sharps are also detailed, with boxwood stringing. The entire case is artfully inlaid with squares, lozenges, and diamonds of ebony, and ebony moldings surround the case, top, and bottom. A similarly decorated music desk of cypress contains the Medici coat of arms. The decor is dark on light on the exterior of the case but the opposite for the interior. The effect of the embellishment is one of restrained and aristocratic beauty and, while not outside the Italian tradition, is certainly not of the sort often seen on musical instruments.

The inventiveness of the shape and decoration of the "oval" virginal is mirrored in the originality of its action. The two longest strings, for C, run through the middle of the case, from end to end, with a jack slot on either side of the pair. The C♯ strings are above them, also with jack slots on either side. The D strings are below the C's, again with slots on either side. Accordingly, adjacent pairs become farther apart as the compass ascends, culminating with the highest b³ couplet near the spine of the case and the two c³ strings near the keyboard. This means that the even-numbered key levers become successively longer as they ascend the compass, with the b³ the longest, whereas the odd-numbered levers get shorter, with c³ the shortest. The differences in the lengths of the key levers may have created something of a touch problem for the player, particularly in the treble; but one can assume that the master anticipated that and made every effort to smooth out the inequalities. The virginal was also capable of playing on either one or both sets of strings, by moving the keyboard in or out. This is a daring solution to the problem of the 2×8′ virginal; as far as we know, only one of this type was ever

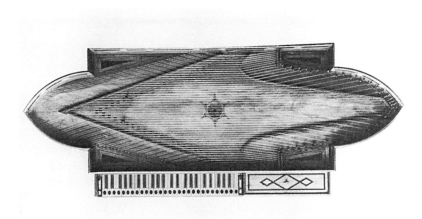

11-1a. This beautiful and ingenious 2×8′ double virginal was made by Bartolomeo Cristofori in 1693 for his Medici patron. Its outer case, now lost, was made of spruce and covered with red leather, green taffeta, and gold and red ribbons. Leipzig, Musikinstrumenten-Museum der Universität Leipzig. Photo by Volkmar Herre.

made again, in 1726 by the Bolognese builder Giuseppe Maria Goccini (Copenhagen, Musikhistorisk Museum).

The ca. 1720 *spinettone de teatro* is another example of Cristofori's inventiveness. A large 1×8′, 1×4′ instrument, nearly eight feet long, with a FF,GG,AA–c^3 compass (enlarged to f^3 in 1795), it resembles a bentside spinet, but with the right side severely angled, rather than curved. It has a heavy integral case of poplar or a similar wood, veneered with cypress on the inside, but with no other reference to an inner-outer tradition. The soundboard is also made of cypress, the wood Cristofori used for that purpose on all his extant instruments, with a geometric rose. The 1×8′, 1×4′ disposition is extremely rare for a spinet, although this instrument's size is well beyond the realm of the normal domestic instrument. Furthermore, through an ingenious system activated by moving the keyboard in or out, either the 8′ or the 4′ choir could be used as a solo stop, or both could be played together.[18] But that is not this instrument's only point of interest. It has two cypress bridges and two nuts—normal for a 1×8′, 1×4′—but they do not continue to the top of the compass. Instead, separate bridges are provided for the top octave and a half, to accommodate a change from brass to iron stringing at that point.[19] A glance at the soundboard geometry in the treble shows why: with the jacks arranged in rows of fours, and with the shortness of brass strings in that register, there would have been no room in the treble for the bridges and nuts; or, if accommodation was made for the short strings, there would have been no room for the jacks. To make room for both, Cristofori had to go to a longer scale at that point, with iron stringing. Cristofori did not use a normal miter joint for the bass section of his 8′ bridge; instead, he provided three small independent sections parallel to the main bridge for the bottom five strings. This became his usual practice. From the Medici accounts it seems clear that Cristofori made at least four of these spinettoni, but this is the only one to have survived.[20]

This instrument raises questions. Why did Cristofori construct this strange shape, rather than simply build a normal grand harpsichord? Well over a century after the 4′ became obsolete in Italy, why did he find it necessary to build a 1×8′, 1×4′ instrument, and why did he go to the trouble of ensuring that the 4′ could be used as a solo stop? Why did he give this instrument such a wide range, wider than all but one (the 1720 piano) of his surviving stringed keyboards? And why did he designate this spinettone (the suffix -*one* indicating that it is a large spinetta) as a theater instrument? The answers seem fairly clear. The instrument was specially designed for use in the opera pit, and the narrow configuration, with the player facing the stage, would be advantageous in a theatrical context. A solo 4′ would have been useful for special effects, such as furnishing music for an ottavino stage prop. Combined with the 8′, it would have lent an incisiveness to the attack appropriate for an orchestral continuo. The extended range would have been useful in opera, adding its low notes to those of the theorbo and arch lute (we have already noted other large Italian instruments with expanded basses). All in all, the *spinettone de teatro* appears to be an extraordinarily useful, if entirely unconventional solution to the needs of the opera pit, and it was undoubtedly that idiosyncrasy that kept it from being adopted elsewhere.[21]

Of the six remaining extant Cristofori instruments three are harpsichords and three pianos.[22] None exceeds c[3] in range, as would be expected from brass-strung instruments with scales between 10½″ and 11″. An undated 2×8′ known as the "ebony"

11-1b. The keyboard to the 1693 virginal. The even-numbered key levers become successively longer, while the odd-numbered levers get shorter. Leipzig, Musikinstrumenten-Museum der Universität Leipzig. Photo by Volkmar Herre.

harpsichord (Florence, Museo del Conservatorio) begins on GG,AA, and the 1720 piano (New York, Metropolitan Museum of Art) originally commenced with FF,GG,AA; but the other two harpsichords, a 1722 2×8′ (Leipzig, Musikinstrumenten-Museum der Universität Leipzig) and a 1726 1×8′, 1×4′, 1×2′ (also Leipzig, Musikinstrumenten-Museum der Universität Leipzig), and the other two pianos (1722, Rome, Museo Nazionale degli Strumenti Musicali; 1726, Leipzig, Musikinstrumenten-Museum der Universität Leipzig) both start on C. In addition, there is a Cristofori action of ca. 1725 (Vancouver, private ownership) no longer attached to a case, and its compass is also C–c³. It seems strange that the builder would restrict the bottom end of the compass in this manner, particularly since instruments of the Northern traditions routinely descended to GG or lower at the time; but one has to assume that they were built for specific purposes for which that range was deemed appropriate.

The general appearance of both the harpsichords and the pianos is unusual. With the exception of the "ebony" harpsichord these are heavy-case instruments, and except for scroll-cut cheek pieces, the inner-outer conceit is almost entirely ignored. The workmanship is precise, but the outer appearance of the instruments is utilitarian, with plain, flat, bottom moldings and plain vertical battens lending the already heavy case the sort of strength one would expect from a packing crate. Both case walls and soundboards are of cypress, and there are no roses. The exteriors are unpainted and have no decoration of any sort.[23]

The undated "ebony" harpsichord, an inner-outer instrument (although the outer case is gone), is mentioned in the inventory of 1700. With its ebonized case walls and ivory and ebony keyboard, it is closer to the "oval" virginal in its elaborateness and richness of detail than it is to the other extant examples of Cristofori's oeuvre.[24] The 1722 harpsichord is a "conventional" (insofar as that term has meaning with anything we know of built by Cristofori) 2×8′, but with a wooden gap spacer between every third note. The 1726, with a 1×8′, 1×4′, 1×2′ disposition, again raises questions. The 4′ register, as pointed out earlier, had been obsolete for more than a century, and aside from some diminutive spinettini, no Italian

11-2. The 1720 1×8′, 1×4′ *spinettone de teatro* is almost 8′ long, but not as wide as a normal grand harpsichord. Note its unusual shape and the multiplicity of bridges and nuts. Leipzig, Musikinstrumenten-Museum der Universität Leipzig. Photo by Volkmar Herre.

harpsichords—indeed, with the exception of two extant mid-century German instruments, no harpsichords of any tradition—used a 2' stop.[25] By means of extensions projecting from both cheek and spine, as well as stop levers mounted on the wrestplank, any of the registers could be used as a solo stop or combined with any of the others.[26] Furthermore, the 8' register is split between c and c♯, so that the bottom octave of the 8' could be used independently of the rest of that choir. This is not the same sort of register splitting we saw with the buff and arpichordum stops on Flemish harpsichords and muselars, where the compasses are more or less evenly divided into two different sounds; here, the only conceivable use of the split would be to add the weight of the lowest octave of the 8' to the 1×4', 1×2' combination, or to the solo 1×4' or 1×2'.[27]

In all three of his extant harpsichords Cristofori employed gap spacers, thus necessitating the use of upper and lower guides rather than the ubiquitous Italian box guides. Further, in a practice going back to the 1533 Dominicus Pisaurensis, the 1537 Müller, and other instruments in Italy, Germany, and England, the soundboard of the 1726 extends over the gap and covers the wrestplank, with oversized slots for the jacks cut into the board at the gap. The upper guide, running under the soundboard wood, is moveable. The lower guide is a piece of wood of soundboard thickness connecting wrestplank and belly-rail, and slotted for the jacks. The narrow wrestplank measures less than 2½", so the nuts are on freely vibrating soundboard wood. As with all three harpsichords, the gap slants, carrying the bass jacks well away from their nuts. In the "ebony" harpsichord the soundboard barring is more or less conventionally Italian, with three ribs crossing the bridge;[28] but in the 1722 harpsichord and the 1722 and 1726 pianos, ribs (eight in the harpsichord, ten in the pianos) radiate from a cutoff bar (curved, to follow the bridge) to the spine. Barring in the 1726 harpsichord is unusual, with 4' and 2' hitchpin rails, a 2' cutoff bar, and nothing else. It is possible the maker thought that the three bridges on top of the board and the two rails and cutoff bar underneath constituted sufficient reinforcement.[29] As with all his harpsichords in the 1720s, Cristofori used a redesigned jack that had its brass leaf spring in front, rather than in back. The nuts and bridges themselves are pure Cristofori: once again we see separate portions for iron strings, in the f¹–f² octave of the 2' choir, and for their final one-and-a-half octaves the iron 2' strings share the 4' bridge and nut. According to his usual practice, the bass portion of the 8' bridge is set parallel to the main bridge.[30]

Despite the singularities of Goccini's 2×8' virginal and the spinettoni by Solfanelli and Ferrini, the designs of neither the "oval" virginal nor the *spinettone de teatro* had a future, and perhaps none was intended. But the same cannot be said for Cristofori's greatest invention, the arpicembalo, or *gravecembalo col piano e forte* (grand harpsichord with soft and loud), also known as the *gravecembalo a martelli* (grand harpsichord with hammers), or the *pianoforte, fortepiano,* or simply the piano. The history of this instrument, is, of course, outside the province of this book, but it cannot be ignored entirely. It was a cembalo that could vary both dynamics and tone quality by touch, and in this sense quite different from the harpsichord. Nevertheless, its tone quality must have been similar; it certainly bore little resemblance to the sound of the modern piano, or even to the Viennese fortepiano. In fact, until the last quarter of the eighteenth century the piano was still regarded as a particular sort of harpsichord, and it was only one of several instruments that fit that description. Interestingly, by that time harpsichords themselves had developed the ability to make convincing crescendos and diminuendos by means of machines and swells, so that particular proficiency was no longer the exclusive province of the piano. This will all be explored in greater depth in later chapters, but for now it will be sufficient simply to describe Cristofori's new hammer harpsichord.

In an amazing stroke of coincidence, a description of the new instrument, a diagram of its action, Cristofori's thoughts about it, and his building practices were committed to paper in 1709 by an extraordinary personage named Scipione Maffei (1675–1755). At one time or another Maffei was a soldier, a dramatist, a critic of Italian dramatic arts, a scholar, and an archaeologist; but in this instance he was acting as a journalist. With the librettist Apostolo Zeno (1668–1750), Maffei had just established a literary journal, the *Giornale de' letterati d'Italia,* and undoubtedly was on the lookout for suitable articles. He engaged Cristofori in a wide-ranging interview (almost certainly the only harpsichord builder to be interviewed before the twentieth century) in which the master not only described his gravecembalo col piano e forte, but also explained the need for temperament, the effects of humidity on a harpsichord, the salary paid to him by the Grand Duke, and his unhappiness at being forced to work in a large room full of other

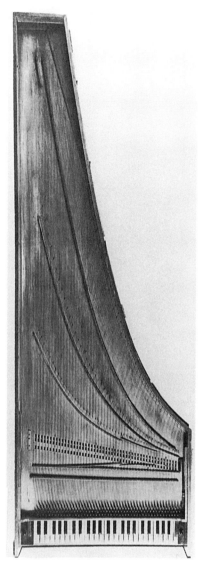

11-3. This 1726 instrument is one of Cristofori's most elaborate harpsichords. The independent section of bass bridge is one of his trademarks. The separate portions of the 2′ nut and bridge were intended for iron stringing. Leipzig, Musikinstrumenten-Museum der Universität Leipzig. Photo by Volkmar Herre.

artisans when he first arrived in Florence. Cristofori also told Maffei his theories about openings in the case of a harpsichord or piano, and the deleterious effects on an instrument of wood under stress. He even offered several reasons to explain the "squeaking" that Maffei complained of in his own harpsichord.[31] The article itself, which finally appeared in 1711,[32] went into a great deal of detail about the action and included the diagram mentioned above. Maffei noted that while some thought Cristofori's invention a wonderful new instrument, others criticized it for its dull sound and weak tone. The author found these criticisms unfair and thought that the piano should be accepted on its own terms.

Aside from that source and the occasional mention of pianos in the Medici accounts, our knowledge of Cristofori's new invention comes from the slender database of three instruments and an orphaned action. He completed his first arpicembalo by 1700 (it was inventoried in that year), and between that time and his death in 1732 he produced approximately twenty-five more; but only the three mentioned earlier, from 1720, 1722, and 1726, plus the ca. 1725 action survive.

Until this time, Italian harpsichords had been fabricated with an internal structure of bottom braces, knees, diagonal struts, or some combination of the three; but Cristofori invented a new sort of bracing which, while inspired by past practice, departed from it considerably. In his instruments of the 1720s he used a fairly heavy case construction which is — in essence, although not in appearance — an inner instrument glued into an outer case. There are a series of shaped internal frame members, looking like large, modified U-braces. The bottom surfaces were

11-4. The plain appearance of this 1720 piano by Cristofori, with its square tail and vertical battens, is typical of all his extant keyboard instruments of the 1720s. New York, Metropolitan Museum of Art.

glued to the bottom of the case, but rather than fastened directly to the bentside case walls, the ends of these braces were scooped out and the remaining protuberances rounded in a dowel-like fashion and fitted into holes in the liners. Running through these members, or from one to another, from tail or bentside to bellyrail, are a series of longitudinal struts. Combined with the heavy case, the gap spacers, and a well-braced soundboard with barring across the bridge, this construction gave Cristofori's harpsichords enormous solidity.

The pianos and the 1726 harp-

CRISTOFORI THE MECHANICAL GENIUS

There are problems inherent in hitting a string with a hammer that do not exist when it is plucked by a quill. Mechanical genius that he was, Cristofori not only recognized these problems, but he solved them brilliantly. He realized that since hammer heads must rebound as quickly as possible, so as not to damp the vibrations they have just set into motion, heavier stringing under greater tension was required. Cristofori also understood that the last part of the accelerated flight of the movement of the hammer toward the strings had to be free — that is, not controlled by the mechanism that propelled it there — to prevent the hammer from remaining in contact with the strings and, again, effectively damping them. To give the player the greatest amount of control this distance had to be as small as possible; but this meant that there was a danger of the hammer "blocking" — that is, jamming against the strings. To avoid this, Cristofori invented an escapement, so that the hammer could fall from the strings even though the key still remained depressed. Since part of the raison d'être of the piano was its ability to play loud, the hammer had to be able to travel at high speed; so he used a double-lever system, which accelerated the hammer at eight times the speed with which the key was depressed. This also increased the weight of the touch by a factor of eight, but Cristofori compensated for that by making the action as light as possible. However, a light, fast-moving hammer could rebound from its resting point and restrike the string, so he provided a check (back check) to arrest the hammer after its strike. Harpsichord-like damper jacks ran in a guide, allowing the strings to be stilled when the keys were released. There was no way to disengage all (or even half) the dampers at once, but two of the three extant pianos have a provision for an *una corda* — a way to shift the keyboard so that the hammers strike one string of a pair, rather than both. Finally, Cristofori provided his pianos with gap spacers, to counteract the greater tension of the heavier strings and prevent them from pulling the wrestplank into the gap.

Cristofori's hammer head was perhaps the most sophisticated element in the action. It is deceptively simple in appearance, merely a section of a glued-up roll of paper or parchment with a cap of leather on top. When striking the string, the hammer — following Newton's law of inertia — wants to continue in the same direction in which it was propelled; but the springiness of the hollow parchment head acts as a restoring force, helping the hammer rebound from the string. Subdued playing only slightly compresses the leather, so the hammer appears to be relatively yielding to the string. Exciting a string in this manner tends to suppress higher frequencies and produces a tone that is quiet and less vibrant in tone color. But with an increase in hammer velocity, and a concomitant increase in the force with which it strikes the string, the leather is compressed more and more, bringing the harder underlying parchment into play. The greater the velocity of the hammer, the harder its mass appears to the string. Now higher frequency components are generated as well, so that at a *forte* level the tone fairly crackles with acoustical energy.[33] Cristofori must have realized right from the beginning that his gravecembalo col piano e forte could allow for gradations of tone quality as well as dynamics, and it is likely that it was this quality more than any other that eventually established it as an instrument in its own right.

11-5. A hammer from Cristofori's 1726 piano. His hammer heads were sections of rolled-up parchment or paper, with a piece of leather glued to the top. Leipzig, Musikinstrumenten-Museum der Universität Leipzig.

sichord were similarly constructed, but because of the greater strength required, with some further refinements. The soundboard was attached not to the bentside liner, but to a thin inner bentside independent of the heavier outer wall. The shaped braces are massive, reaching across the width of the instrument, but attaching at only two points at the spine and two at the bentside. At the bentside, the upper of the two dowel-like protuberances travels through openings in the inner bentside and fits into holes in the heavy liner. The wide hitchpin rail, sandwiched between the heavy bentside liner and the inner case veneer, cantilevers out over the soundboard. Thus, the strings exert a pull on the heavily braced case, but not on the soundboard. Whether piano or harpsichord cases, this sort of tanklike construction was well outside Italian building practices.

The key to understanding Cristofori's concept of harpsichord and piano building seems to be in his desire, both stated and implied, to avoid any strain on the instrument. In his *Giornale de' letterati d'Italia* article, Maffei notes that Cristofori "asserts that the lack of resonance in new [instruments] arises principally from the property of elasticity, which is retained by the bentside and the bridge; for when these apply force upon the soundboard to restore their shape, the sound remains imperfect, and if this elasticity were to be entirely taken from them before putting them into operation, this defect would immediately be removed."[34] This explains perfectly what Cristofori was attempting to do with his independent inner bentside and his cantilevered hitchpin rail. Of course, he was going counter to all normal concepts of harpsichord building, in which the "elasticity" of the various parts of the instrument are—or are supposed to be—in dynamic balance. That Cristofori's instruments succeeded so well only proves that there is more than one way to build a harpsichord; but in fact, his concept of separating the tug of the strings from the soundboard has found vindication in the modern piano, where the strings are hitched to the iron frame and the soundboard is independent of their pull.

Another way in which Cristofori attempted to avoid strain in his wood was his practice of laminating or kerfing any piece that needed to be curved, including bentsides, liners, hitchpin rails, bridges, nuts, and moldings. Laminating—bending thin strips of wood around a form and gluing them together so that they retain the curve—was a procedure used by builders from time to time to make bent parts; but kerfing—cutting the wood partially through with a thin saw blade at close, regular intervals—though often applied to bentside liners, was a technique used by no other builder with the frequency of this master, who evidently thought that the strain or "elasticity" imparted to a piece

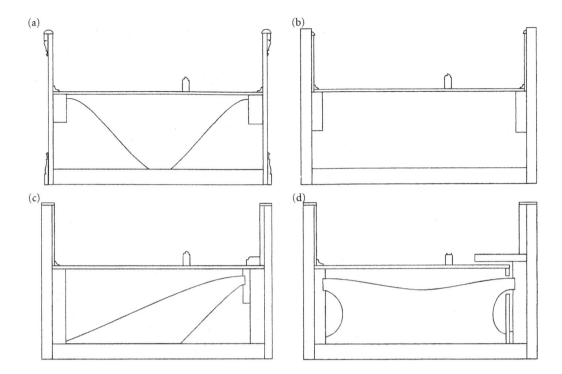

11-6. Schematic cross sections of Cristofori's harpsichords (left) and pianos (right). These case-bracing schemes are extremely strong. Courtesy of David Jensen.

of wood through bending would be deleterious to its function. His internal bracing was also designed to remove that strain from the bentside, and in his pianos he actually continued the straight part of the internal bentside right up to the bellyrail, creating what has come to be known as an "A-frame" (another concept that found its way into piano building). His use of separate bass bridges parallel to the main bridge may have been another of Cristofori's attempts to avoid the "strain" on the soundboard caused by a mitered joint.

Cristofori's ideas about the harpsichord's rose hole, though not directly concerned with strain and elasticity, nevertheless serve as one more demonstration of the builder's individuality. In that same 1711 *Giornale* article, Maffei noted that Cristofori differed from other (Italian) makers, who by this time rarely put roses in their soundboards. Cristofori told Maffei that a harpsichord had to have an aperture, since without it "the air within cannot yield and escape, but remains harsh and fixed, and the soundboard does not move, and hence the sound emerges somewhat dull and short, and not resonant." But, continues Maffei's account, if a hole is made, the soundboard will be more flexible, and the resulting tone will be stronger. He goes on to say that Cristofori claimed to have studied the work of natural philosophers who investigated the "inclinations and effects of air and of motion." Since Cristofori did not want to put a hole in the soundboard, which would allow dust to fall into the instrument, he would put a few holes into the bellyrail instead.[35]

Contrary to the master's statements, and despite his appeal to the authority of natural philosophers, there are many fine Italian harpsichords that have neither roses nor other apertures. Cristofori, it would seem, fell prey to the commonly held notion that a harpsichord's sound is produced within and needs to be allowed to escape. Although it is true that the vibrations of the volume of air in the body of the instrument contribute to its overall sound, it is not through any aperture, but by a coupling mechanism with the soundboard. Furthermore, although an aperture could affect an instrument's sound (and, indeed, this is true in the guitar and violin families), to do so to a cembalo, it needed to be much larger than a rose hole or some small holes in the bellyrail.[36]

Cristofori's science may have been flawed, but that should not affect the awe with which we regard this great genius. He seems to have set out to change almost every aspect of harpsichord building, and certainly did not stop after his brilliant invention of the gravecembalo col piano e forte. Furthermore, many of his radical departures from normal building practice can be found in the modern piano, even if piano builders had to reinvent most of them. His genius was recognized during his lifetime, not only in Florence but elsewhere as well. An anonymous eighteenth-century dictionary of music noted that "Christofori Bartolomeo [*sic*] . . . was the famous harpsichord maker, a distinguished restorer rendering even better good instruments made by other past masters and he was also the inventor of harpsichords with hammers, which produce a different quality of sound on account of both the hammer striking the chord and the completely different internal structure of the body of the instrument, not visible from the outside."[37]

Cristofori's innovations in case construction, while not affecting harpsichord making elsewhere,[38] influenced other Florentine builders. He worked with two men, variously described as apprentices, students, or assistants, Domenico Del Mela (from Gagliano, fl. 1739) and Giovanni Ferrini (from Florence, fl. 1699–1758). Little is known of Del Mela, except that he was another harpsichord-building priest and is survived by an upright piano (Florence, Museo degli Strumenti Musicali). Its construction, action, and strange, sinuous shape show no sign of the master's hand. In fact, Del Mela's connection with Cristofori is somewhat tenuous, resting on the latter's bequeath of his worldly goods to the Del Mela sisters, who evidently took care of him during some illness; but it is not really known if the builder Del Mela was related to the sisters Del Mela.[39] On the other hand, two of Ferrini's instruments are extant, and they both show that he took his lessons seriously. The earlier, dated 1731 (Pistoia, Museo Clemente Rospigliosi), is a 1×8', 1×4' *spinettone de teatro*, cast in the same mold as Cristofori's ca. 1720 instrument. Like its model it is capable of 8' and 4' solo stops as well as an 1×8', 1×4' ensemble, it has a cypress soundboard with a rose, and its bridges and nuts are divided for iron stringing in the top octave. Ferrini even made his jacks like Cristofori's, with the brass leaf spring in front.

Ferrini's second survivor is a 1746 GG,AA–e³ two-manual combination 2×8' harpsichord-piano (Bologna, private ownership). It is a technical tour de force of which his teacher would have been proud.[40] With its moldings and well-defined false inner-outer appearance it looks more conventionally Italian than Cristofori's instruments do, but its structure shows striking similarities to the latter's innovations. Among these are the heavy case walls resulting from the gluing together of a case within a case, the independent inner bentside, the shelflike hitchpin rail cantilevered over the soundboard, the shaped internal braces, the kerfing and laminating of bent and curved elements, jacks with frontal leaf springs, the use of gap spacers (although his were of iron), a cypress soundboard without a rose, and holes in the bellyrail. Other than the changes engendered by a two-manual dual-purpose instrument, his piano action (available from the upper manual), including the damper jacks and the hollow parchment hammer heads, is modeled directly on Cristofori's work. But like his master, Ferrini was also an innovator. The unison strings are closely paired, for the convenience of the piano portion of the instrument; thus, the harpsichord jacks, riding between the wide pairs, must pluck their respective strings from the outsides of the close-spaced unisons. Ferrini solved that problem by resorting to a ploy first seen almost two centuries earlier, in harpsichords by Bortolus and Celestini: he made the ends of his lower-manual keys S-shaped, so that the closer jack plucked the right unison, while the jack on the S section plucked the left.

Ferrini's composite instrument had another innovation, one that Cristofori almost certainly would have used had he thought of it first. One of the problems in hitting a string with a hammer is that the blow tends to drive the string up the nut pin, thereby decreasing the string-to-nut coupling. On two of his pianos Cristofori solved that problem by using a so-called "inverted" wrestplank; that is, a plank in which the nut is mounted on the under surface and the strings pass under, rather than over, its top (the wrestpins go completely through, so they can be turned and tuned from above). Thus, when the string is struck the blow tends to drive it onto, rather than off, the nut. Ferrini went at the problem a different way. He mounted short wooden posts on the wrestplank, one for each pair of strings. He pierced the posts horizontally with metal pins, making a miniature cross, and ran each pair of strings under the pins of a post, then at an upward angle to a nut, and then downward to the tuning pins. Hence, rather than depend on down and side bearing to ensure proper contact of string to nut, he achieved it by providing an up bearing. This is the same principle utilized by the *capo tasto* and the *agraffe,* invented by piano makers during the first quarter of the nineteenth century to solve the problem to which both Cristofori and Ferrini had already provided answers.

Vincenzo Sodi (fl. 1778–99) was another Florentine builder influenced by Cristofori. A 1789 piano of his (Vermillion, private ownership),[41] although its action owes more to Stein than it does to Cristofori, nevertheless shows Florentine influences in its interior structure.[42] Its curved surfaces are kerfed, and its internal braces are similar to those seen in Cristofori's 1722 and 1726 pianos, as well as his 1726 harpsichord. His soundboard barring is also similar to Cristofori's.[43] At least five Sodi harpsichords are extant, a 1778 (or 1799)[44] (Hamburg, private ownership), a 1779 (New York, private ownership), a 1782 (Vermillion, Shrine to Music Museum), a 1782 (Exeter, Royal Albert Memorial Museum), and a 1791–92 (Bologna, private ownership).[45] These are large, powerful instruments, beginning on FF, GG, or C and usually ascending to c^3 or f^3 (some or perhaps most of the compasses have been enlarged by one or more notes).[46] Those we have seen are highly decorated on the outside — several are done in chinoiserie. The cheeks are slanted, like Viennese fortepianos, and the tail is most often rounded, rather than mitered. A relatively plain molding runs around the bottom of the case. Generally speaking, these instruments show little reference to an inner-outer tradition.

The 1782 Vermillion harpsichord, a $2\times8'$ strung in brass with a five-octave FF–f^3 compass, seems typical both of Sodi's work and of his adherence to the Florentine tradition originated by Cristofori. Its curved parts are kerfed, and a strut between bentside and bellyrail reflects the principle of the A-frame. Four shaped braces, sloping in Ferrini's style, have the dowel-like terminations that insert into holes in the bentside liner. The soundboard (likely spruce) has no rose, but there are four holes in the bellyrail, and the cypress bridge has the same sort of molded cross section that both Cristofori and Ferrini used. Sodi also continued the inventiveness that seemed to be the hallmark of eighteenth-century Florentine style. For example, on this and

OTHER FLORENTINE INSTRUMENTS?

As the characteristics of the eighteenth-century Florentine style have become more apparent, some hitherto anonymous or misattributed instruments have been ascribed to Cristofori or his circle. A large 2×8′ harpsichord (Toronto, private ownership), though anonymous, is known through its extensive use in recordings. It has a painted exterior, a lid painting, and a Rococo-style cabriole table stand; but David Jensen, who examined the instrument thoroughly, notes that these decorative elements were added later in the eighteenth century and are not original.[48] Jensen observes that it has the typical Florentine case-within-a-case construction, with the sound-well veneered in cypress. It also has a cypress soundboard with no rose, a bellyrail with three holes, nine internal case braces with dowel-like terminations, kerf-bent curved elements,[49] typical Florentine soundboard barring, and other structural and decorative elements that point straight to Cristofori. Jensen goes on to postulate that Cristofori not only developed a new structural design for harpsichords, but a new way of building them. He convincingly demonstrates that Cristofori — and any other maker building in this style — would first have to build the heavy inner case, whose sides would come no higher than the soundboard liners. He would then install the soundboard, and only then glue on the outer skin, to which would be applied the interior cypress veneer. This, comments Jensen, is the method of construction subsequently used by nineteenth-century piano makers.

A 2×8′ harpsichord purchased from Franciolini around 1900 (Ann Arbor, Stearns Collection of Musical Instruments) and dated 1693 bore an attribution to Giusti. For years this was unchallenged, but when David Sutherland restored it in 1975 he found that the nameboard came from some other instrument, and that the harpsichord showed many of the signs common to Cristofori's circle. Subsequent investigation by Sutherland, particularly in comparing it with Ferrini's 1746 combined harpsichord-piano, led him to conclude that the instrument was built by Ferrini around 1750. He reports similarities in soundboard layout, interior bracing, bridge layout, and other, smaller details such as moldings and key arcades, but he also notes that Ferrini continued Cristofori's experimental bent, which also seemed to have been part of Florentine style. The Stearns harpsichord has a spruce soundboard, with the grain angled twenty-five degrees to the spine; and instead of kerfing and laminating, the curved portions were heat bent.[50]

An anonymous late Italian harpsichord (Prague, National Museum) with an FF–f[3] compass, slanted cheeks, rounded tail, plain lower molding, and finished in chinoiserie bears all the external earmarks of Sodi's work. If not by him, it would be by some otherwise unknown builder working in his tradition.

Cristofori and his followers also left their mark on instruments by other builders that went through Florence for repair or restoration. One example is an anonymous seventeenth-century inner-outer (New Haven, Yale Collection of Musical Instruments), whose soundboard was supplied with a new bridge and new barring. The case also got a new bellyrail and new internal bracing. Traces of Florentine work include the cypress bridge with its characteristic cross section and kerf-bending, soundboard barring across the bridge, the addition of gap spacers, the three holes in the bellyrail, the shaped internal bracing, and an A-frame brace. Sutherland believes that the repair work was carried out by Sodi.[51]

Other instruments touched by Florentines include an anonymous 2×8′ inner-outer restored by Cristofori (Edinburgh, Russell Collection), and the 1666 Zenti harpsichord refurbished by Ferrini in 1755 (New York, Metropolitan Museum of Art). Both have independent bass-bridge sections parallel to the main bridge.[52] With the growing knowledge of the work of Cristofori and his followers it is possible that additional instruments from that circle will appear, as well as others that give evidence of having passed through their hands.

the 1778 or 1799 instruments he used upper and lower guides, but joined them together so that they moved and acted like box guides. Both were also supplied with wide, double-tongued jacks, quilled in leather, that plucked both left and right. The tongues were undoubtedly fitted with both hard and soft leather plectra, so that when in one position they plucked one of the unisons with the hard leather, but when moved to the other side by the stop lever the strings would be plucked by the softer leather, producing a softer, rounder sound. This contrivance, known as the *cembalo angelico,* will be seen again, on two instruments of 1778 and 1779 by the Antwerp builder Johann Peter Bull and on a 1745 by Johann Daniel Dulcken that Bull modernized around that time. Even the French builder Pascal Taskin used it, on a 1770 harpsichord. [47]

Despite their striking originality, with the elegance of their long cases, the deep bentsides showing faithfulness to Pythagorean scaling, and the adherence to a single keyboard and a $2\times8'$ disposition, Sodi's instruments could not be mistaken for anything but Italian in origin. They come at the end of that tradition—either his 1792 or 1778 (or 1799) is the last known grand produced in Italy—but despite the slanted cheeks, the Northern-inspired double bentside, and the lack of an inner-outer allusion, they are still faithful to the fundamental qualities of the Italian harpsichord, most of which were established nearly three hundred years earlier.

ROME AND ELSEWHERE

Judging by the number of makers, the bulk of the harpsichord-building activity in eighteenth-century Italy still took place in Rome, although at a pace far removed from its former activity. The instruments were produced by competent craftsmen, but names with the luster of Boni, Zenti, Giusti, and Ridolfi are conspicuously absent. The Cremisi family, for example, consisted of Giovanni (b. ca. 1652), his son Pietro (b. ca. 1682), Pietro's sons Simone (ca. 1707–ca. 1789) and Giovanni II (b. ca. 1722), and Simone's son Filippo (ca. 1739–92). Invoking the Koster formula once again, and assuming that on the average a builder could produce instruments for twenty years, and with the help of his apprentices and journeymen could turn out five instruments a year, one would have expected the five Cremisis to have produced at least five hundred instruments over the course of more than a century. Yet, not a single one is extant. Another family, Pietro Paolo Palazzi (ca. 1700–after 1752), his son Nicola (ca. 1731–1810), and his grandson Vincenzo (ca. 1783–after 1842) have no existing harpsichords, although Nicola is survived by a 1776 inner-outer clavichord (location unknown).[53] The usual reasons could be responsible for this dearth of Roman instruments—ravages of time, used up and thrown out, etc.; but it could also be that harpsichord builders were applying more and more of their energies to rebuilding, refurbishing, and updating earlier instruments. This may explain why one of the few facts we have about the Cremisi dynasty is that Giovanni II was paid some money for restoring a harpsichord.[54] Whatever the reasons, eighteenth-century Roman harpsichords themselves are so scarce that *Boalch III* is able to record only two, one of which may be a forgery.[55]

As before, Italian harpsichord building remained a decentralized activity, and instruments are extant from smaller towns like Genoa, Modena, Lucca, Pisa, Monte Carotto, and Viterbo, as well as the larger centers like Milan and Florence. Unlike in other countries, where they were considered obsolete, virginals continued to be made. Two survive from the Milanese workshop of Giovanni Domenico Birger (fl. 1746), a 1746 (Toulouse, Musée Paul-Dupuy), and a 1759 at quint pitch with a C/D–d³ compass (Rome, Palazzo Venezia). A 1710 inner-outer triangular octave spinet with C/E–c³ compass (Edinburgh, Russell Collection) made by Petrus Michael Orlandus (fl. 1702–10) is a plain instrument with little to distinguish it from ottavini built a century earlier, except that its moldings and scroll-sawn cheek pieces lack the character and delicacy of the earlier examples. Inscribed on its nameboard is the motto-riddle mentioned in Chapter 5, DUM VIXI TACVI MORTVA DVLCE CANO (While alive I was silent; now dead, I sweetly sing). Orlandus also made a 1702 inner-outer polygonal virginal (London, Horniman Museum).

Carlo Grimaldi (fl. 1697–1703), who worked in Messina, where he made organs and lutes as well as harpsichords, is survived by three instruments. The earliest (Nuremberg, Germanisches Nationalmuseum), a 1697 2×8′ with a GG,AA–d³ compass, is a true inner-outer. With its simplified moldings, slender waist, and long length, it is a picture of restraint and dig-

11-7. An octave spinet from 1710 by Petrus Orlandus. Even in the eighteenth century, Italian builders were still making octave spinets. The answer to the motto-riddle is a tree, which makes no sound when alive, but when "killed," turned into lumber, and made into an instrument, is now capable of making beautiful music. Edinburgh, Russell Collection of Early Keyboard Instruments, University of Edinburgh.

11-8a. Folding harpsichord by Carlo Grimaldi. The instrument could be collapsed into a portable box with a carrying handle. Rome, Museo Nazionale degli Strumenti Musicali.

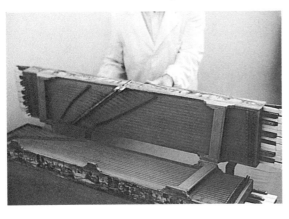

11-8b. Grimaldi's folding harpsichord. The treble portion swings up to join the middle section, which folds over onto the bass segment. Rome, Museo Nazionale degli Strumenti Musicali.

nity. Its outer case, however, tells a different story. As seen in Plate 15, it appears to have had gilt flowers and arabesques applied to an indented black ground, the whole surrounded by gilt moldings; but Sheridan Germann discovered that the original finish was all gilt, with the indentations outlining the designs. Later (perhaps as early as 1725–35), she suggests, the finish was considered old-fashioned, too heavy-handedly "Baroque," and the black patterns were applied over the gold.[56] The stand supporting the instrument is a sinuous, carved and gilded phantasmagoria, one of the most ornate known. The second Grimaldi (Paris, Musée de la Musique), dated 1703, with a GG–c³ compass is quite similar, with the same sorts of moldings and dignified mien, and a keyboard with mother-of-pearl touch plates. It lacks an outer case. Interestingly, its soundboard was laid in with the grain at about a forty-five-degree angle to the spine, approximately perpendicular to the bridge. A few Italian harpsichords were made with such soundboards, and the grain conformation is simply another way of controlling the stiffness of the board. At some recent date, probably in the twentieth century, the 1703 was converted to a tangent-action instrument. Grimaldi's third instrument is a folding harpsichord of uncertain date.

The Bolognese builder Giuseppe Maria Goccini (1675–after 1733) left four, or possibly five, instruments, a not inconsiderable number for an eighteenth-century Italian builder. His authorship of the earliest one, a 1707 inner-outer octave spinet (Munich, Deutsches Museum), is questionable.[57] The second and third survivors are both single-manual 2×8′ grand harpsichords, and both have curious features. The first of these, an inner-outer, with a cypress case, a wood and parchment rose, and a GG,AA–d³,e³ compass, dates from 1721 (Bologna, private ownership). Its novelty is that it seems to have been built for an Englishwoman, Elizabeth Parker, perhaps as a present on the occasion of her wedding to Sir William Heathcote of Macclesfield. The outer case, of polished mahogany, is thought to be of English origin, and the legs of the

slender mahogany trestle stand combine balustrade and cabriole legs in the English manner.[58]

The other grand harpsichord, a 1725 false inner-outer with a GG–AA–c³ compass, has a strange feature. Beneath the keyboard is a sliding keyframe with eleven *controtasti* ("under keys") located under the eleven normal keys from G to f♯ (there is a space between the G and F controtasti, since the lowest octave lacks the GG♯). And there are twelve controtasti found under the twelve c♯¹ to c² keys. The lower set of controtasti crank to the left so that their ends are under the corresponding keys an octave lower, while the upper set crank over to the right, with their ends under the treble keys an octave higher. The under keys are inoperative in their most forward position, but when pushed back a bit by a knob protruding from the front molding, raised bosses on the fronts of the controtasti contact the bottoms of the fronts of the regular keys. In turn, the tails of the under keys raise the bottoms of the corresponding keys an octave lower in the bass and an octave higher in the treble. In other words, with the controtasti in operation, playing anywhere in the range of G to f♯ would produce a deep 2×16′, 2×8′ sonority, while playing in the c♯¹ to c² range would result in a rather brilliant 2×8′, 2×4′ sound.[59] Such a device would have been impractical for most solo and continuo playing, but it would have been useful in orchestral situations, where fullness of sound and attack would have been more important than the disconcerting appearance and disappearance of octave doublings. In any event, full chords played in the appropriate octaves would have produced a stentorian 2×16', 2×8', 2×4' effect.

Goccini's next surviving instrument, an elaborate 1726 false inner-outer virginal (Copenhagen, Musikhistorisk Museum), is also unusual. It is, in effect, two rectangular virginals, one normal, the other a mirror image, joined at the center, very much like Cristofori's "oval" virginal; but instead of two arches protruding from the ends, the four corners of this instrument have been "cut off" to make it octagonal in shape. Like Cristofori's version, one of the 8' choirs can be coupled to the other. With its enclosed keyboard, deep case, and painted decoration, it bears no resemblance to the Florentine instrument; nevertheless, although there is no evidence that Goccini ever saw one, and while he could have invented such an instrument independently, it may represent an homage to the master. His final extant harpsichord is an octave instrument in grand shape, a false inner-outer with a C/E–c³ compass from 1730–33 (Bologna, private ownership). These are the only surviving eighteenth-century harpsichords from Bologna known at this time.

A few other instruments may be of passing interest. The Milanese builder Antonio Scotti is known for his one extant harpsichord, a 1753 2×8' with a C–f³ compass with no trace of an inner-outer conceit (Milan, Museo degli Strumenti Musicali). It has a dizzying herringbone parquetry of contrasting walnut and maple covering the exterior and soundwell, all banded with ebony inlays and an ebonized bottom molding. A ring of ivory and ebony surrounds a geometric rose, and the bridge and nut are made of ebony or ebonized wood. The nameboard is embedded with mother-of-pearl (including dancing angels) and contrasting woods. Ivory patterns cover the dark natural key covers, and the sharps and the end blocks are also inlaid with ivory filigrees. Ivory note names are prominently set into the backs of the naturals, a practice long abandoned by other Italian builders. The instrument sits on three square tapered legs (not original). The fame of this harpsichord does not rest on its decoration; it was said to have been given to Mozart in 1770, when he was in Milan to produce his opera seria *Mitridate, rè di Ponto*.[60]

11-10. This elaborate 1753 harpsichord by the otherwise unknown Antonio Scotti was supposedly given to Mozart when he was in Milan in 1770. Milan, Museo degli Strumenti Musicale, Castello Sforzesco.

Aelpidio Gregori, a builder whose dates are unknown, but who probably came from Sant' Elpidio, is survived by two conservative inner-outer harpsichords, both 2×8′, and both with four-octave C/E–c³ ranges. The 1726 (Edinburgh, private collection) makes only perfunctory reference to the inner-outer tradition and, except in the area of the keywell, has no prominent "inner" moldings. The 1797 or 1779 (Goudhurst, Finchcocks Collection)[61] is a dressier harpsichord, but its minimal "inner" moldings would scarcely have been dignified with that word by earlier builders like Boni or Zenti. Its nicely decorated exterior, with paneled scenes painted on the case and a table stand with cabriole legs, is thought to date from the late nineteenth century. It should be emphasized that the conservative nature of these instruments does not reflect on their ability to make music: both are excellent harpsichords.

SUMMING UP

For the most part, eighteenth-century Italian harpsichords differed little from their predecessors of the preceding century. Both true and false inner-outers continued to be made, although the latter began to look more and more like plain, workaday heavy-case instruments, solid looking and impressive in sound, but lacking the grace and delicacy of earlier instruments. But no matter what the appearance, builders continued to brace their cases with various combinations of bottom braces, knees, and diagonal struts. Even though compasses of up to five octaves can be found — and were seen even earlier, of course — the conservative C/E–c³ keyboard never went out of style. The same can be said of the 2×8′ disposition, brass stringing, the single manual, and the almost complete lack of interest in tone-altering devices, even one as simple as the buff stop. But the most interesting part of eighteenth-century Italian harpsichord building is not told by reciting these traditional building practices: for that we need to look at the exceptional work of the Florentine builders Bartolomeo Cristofori, Giovanni Ferrini, and Vincenzo Sodi. Here we find innovation in case construction, soundboard barring, and tone production, as well as an atypical appreciation for individuality and invention. The Florentines took harpsichord building in a different direction, down a road that soon branched off to a new thoroughfare called the piano.

$\begin{bmatrix} 12 \end{bmatrix}$

THE IBERIAN PENINSULA

$\mathscr{E}$XTANT IBERIAN harpsichords from any time are scarce, and none appear to have survived before the eighteenth century.[1] The destructiveness of war must have been a major factor, exacerbated in 1755, when Lisbon was leveled by one of the most destructive earthquakes ever to hit Europe. Furthermore, the harpsichord did not seem to be particularly popular on the Peninsula, where many of its functions were replaced by the harp and clavichord. Most of the known builders were primarily organ or string-instrument makers, only secondarily involved in harpsichords and clavichords. Beryl Kenyon de Pascual notes that the majority of Spanish instrument makers were members of the carpenter's guild.[2] In the late fifteenth century the wind-instrument makers belonged to the *torners* (turner's) branch of that guild, and the string-instrument makers were *violers;* while the makers of keyboard instruments came from the ranks of *mestres de orgues e de simbol e clavicímbol e manacort* (masters of organs, stringed instruments, harpsichords, and clavichords). But by the sixteenth century the carpenter's guild in Seville stated that keyboard instruments were made by *violeros,* or makers of stringed instruments. Beryl Kenyon de Pascual opines that few Spanish builders would have been able to make a living solely by building harpsichords.[3]

"Spanish harpsichords have for long been a mystery," wrote Kenyon de Pascual in 1991,[4] and nothing has happened since to change that assessment. One part of the enigma is the question of terminology. Until modern times, the generic Spanish term for any jack-action instrument was *clavicordio.* A clavichord was known as a *manicordio,* and a small *clavicordio* or octave instrument was an *espineta.* Occasionally, the word *clavicimbalo* was also used to mean harpsichord, usually an instrument in grand shape, and in that context clavicordio could mean virginal. By the last third of the eighteenth century these terms had begun to fall into disuse, and the common word for harpsichord became *clave.*[5] The modern terms for harpsichord are the more pan-European ones of *clavicímbalo, clave,* or *clavecin.*[6]

Beyond that, plucked keyboards do not seem to have been common in Spain. In his 1549 *Declaración de Instrumentos Musicales,* the theorist Juan Bermudo (ca. 1510–after 1555) mentions the organ, clavichord, vihuela, harp, and guitar, but not the harpsichord.[7] Until the first half of the eighteenth century the harp, vihuela, and organ were considered to be the important polyphonic instruments, the ones appropriate for continuo, accompaniments, and obbligatos.[8] Furthermore, Domenico Pietro Cerone, an Italian singer and theorist who spent many years in Spain, remarked in 1613 that Spanish gentlemen thought the enjoyment of music was beneath them, and that the practice of an instrument on an amateur level was inappropriate to their station. Music, they felt, was useful only to priests and monks.[9] Hence, a distaste for music and the instruments on which it was made seemed to be part of the culture, at least for some levels of the populace, although certainly not among royalty. But given that attitude, it seems clear that the demand for harpsichords normally found elsewhere simply did not exist in Spain.

Nevertheless, harpsichords were built in Spain as early as the fifteenth century.[10] A small one is depicted in a ca. 1480 Spanish manuscript (although there is no way of knowing if it originated in Spain).[11] Contemporary archives note that a maker from Seville named Maestre Enrique (fl. 1470) was a "master of the construction of harpsichords."[12] A Pedro Bayle, who lived in Saragossa, was described in a 1505 document as "a master builder of organs and clavicembalos."[13] Mohama Mofferriz (fl. 1483–1545), known as the "Moor of Saragossa," was another builder of harpsichords and organs.[14] Records indicate that in 1483 he repaired a harpsichord for Prince John[15] (son of the Catholic sovereigns Ferdinand and Isabella), who was supposed to have owned and played the organ, clavicimbalo, clavicordio, and monocordio.[16] Another seemingly common Spanish instrument was the *claviórgano,* or claviorganum.[17] John played one. The archives of Sancho de Paredes, who was chamberlain to Queen Isabella, record that around 1480 he owned two claviorgana.[18] Mofferriz made these hybrids, and references to them crop up in connection with nobility, royalty, and the church.[19] An inventory taken at the death of Philip II in 1598 lists two claviórganos in addition to nine clavicordios.[20] Harpsichords are also mentioned in major treatises by Juan Bermudo, Louis Venegas de Henestrosa (dates unknown), Tomás de Santa Maria (ca. 1510–70), and Hernando de Cabezón (1510–66), four of the great organists of sixteenth-century Spain.

Seventeenth-century references to harpsichords are not plentiful. An inventory of instruments taken at the Royal Palace in Madrid in 1602 lists eleven jack-action instruments, three of which were claviorgana. Most of the others were small triangular instruments, perhaps octave spinets.[21] The Italian harpist Bartolomeo Jobernardi, who was in Madrid in the service of Philip IV around 1635, wrote about his own invention, a *cimbalo perfetto* — the perfect harpsichord;[22] but that hardly tells us anything about Spanish building practices. There are a few other references, such as the inventory taken at the death of the builder Domingo Carballeda in 1684, listing five harpsichords and seven spinets.[23] But the cleric Pablo Nassarre, writing at the end of the seventeenth century, noted that because of the dearth of builders, claviorgana and large harpsichords (by which he likely meant those disposed 2×8′, 1×4′) were rare. Nevertheless, Nassarre goes on to describe the sorts of harpsichords then built in Spain. The grands had one, two, or three sets of strings, and there were also 8′ spinets (although it is not clear if they were triangular or bentside), as well as 4′ spinets.[24]

MARÍA BÁRBARA'S INVENTORY

Despite this somewhat dreary picture of Spanish clavicordios, some of the instrument's most glorious music came out of that country, and no discussion of Spanish music would be complete without mentioning one of the harpsichord's greatest composers, Domenico Scarlatti (1685–1757).[25] The son of the famous Neapolitan opera composer Alessandro Scarlatti (1660–1725), the Italian-born Domenico came to Lisbon to direct the chapel choir and to teach harpsichord to King John V's (1689–1750) daughter María Bárbara (1712–58) and his younger brother Don Antonio. When his royal pupil married Prince Ferdinand

RAYMUNDO TRUCHADO'S GEIGENWERK

Early in the sixteenth century Leonardo da Vinci designed a fretted stringed keyboard instrument on which sounds could be sustained. To the best of our knowledge he never made the device, but in 1575 an amateur builder from Nuremberg named Hans Haiden (ca. 1540–1613) built the first successful *Geigenwerk,* or keyboard instrument with bowed strings. Rather than use plectra, hammers, or tangents to excite its strings, it had five or six rosined wheels that protruded

12-1. This bowed string keyboard instrument, made by the Spanish monk Raymundo Truchado in 1625, is an obvious, though crude, copy of the *Geigenwerk* invented by the German Hans Haiden. © IRPA-KIK, Brussels.

through the gap, set into motion by a foot treadle or hand crank. A simple mechanism pulled a string down onto its turning wheel when its key was pressed, setting it into vibration as if it were bowed. The string would continue to sound as long as the wheel turned, or until contact was broken. Haiden claimed that his instrument could make crescendos and diminuendos and could also produce a vibrato, all through finger pressure.

Many imitations of Haiden's Geigenwerk were made, and one of the earliest to survive (Brussels, Musée Instrumental) is a rather crude version of Haiden's design, with a slant side instead of a bent side, and four wheels, rather than five or six, made in 1625 by a Spanish monk named Raymundo Truchado. Haiden provided both a pedal with which to turn the main wheel and a crank at the tail end, but Truchado's instrument has only a crank. Perhaps the most curious feature of Truchado's Geigenwerk, however, is its four stubby legs. One either placed the instrument on a low table in order to play it or sat on the floor in front of it.

It seems coincidental that Truchado, like Haiden, was an amateur builder; even stranger, however, would be the events that exposed the monk to a Geigenwerk, allowing him to copy its mechanism. One can only assume that a Haiden instrument was imported to Spain, along with the many other harpsichords of German origin. But how did the monk gain access to it, what possessed him to attempt a copy, and what happened to the instrument from which he copied?

of Spain (1713–59) in 1729 and moved to Madrid, Scarlatti accompanied her and remained at the Spanish court for the rest of his life. It was for his patroness that he composed most of his *Essercizi per gravicembalo,* the works commonly known as the sonatas. Scarlatti was a brilliant composer for the harpsichord and understood its capabilities as well as anyone who ever wrote for it. Obviously, some knowledge of the harpsichords available to him would be extremely useful and could give us some insight into Spanish building practices.[26]

A list of such instruments does exist, in an inventory of María Bárbara's instruments taken at her death.[27] Occupying prominent positions in the inventory are five pianos, four of which were Florentine and probably made by Cristofori or Ferrini (the fifth may also have come from Florence, but the list does not say so). This is a remarkably large number of *clavicordios de martillos* (hammer harpsichords) to have in one place, indicating that the Spanish—or at least the queen—had an unusual liking for Cristofori's instrument. In view of this, it is, to say the least, surprising to learn that two of them were converted into harpsichords.[28] More to the point, however, it is clear that the court, María Bárbara, and Scarlatti had access to pianos. Undoubtedly, his music was played on them, although as stated earlier, the sound of the Florentine piano was probably much more harpsichord-like than the more familiar Viennese instrument of the 1790s.

The inventory lists three harpsichords with walnut cases, one of which had five registers, four sets of strings, and fifty-six keys.[29] Evidence indicates that it was made by Diego Fernández (1703–75), María Bárbara's court builder.[30] Giovenali Sacchi, the biographer of the famed castrato Farinelli, reported that according to the singer, the queen was dissatisfied with the harpsichords available to her and expressed a desire for something more complex.[31] Farinelli, then at the Spanish court, claimed that he and Fernández designed the instrument together. Sacchi goes on to relate that the finished product was secretly brought into the queen's chambers so she could discover it by accident. Presumably she was delighted by the gift. Kenyon de Pascual and others are of the opinion that it is this large walnut instrument that María Bárbara bequeathed to the castrato.[32]

The use of walnut for the case material of a Spanish instrument might seem strange, since we have not seen this wood used for cases in the South of Europe. Nevertheless, the inventory taken at Philip II's death lists a clavicordo of walnut by Mohama Mofferriz,[33] and we will see references to other walnut instruments of Spanish origin as well. Furthermore, there is evidence that both Italian-style instruments and Northern-style walnut-cased instruments were produced in Spain, even by the same builder.[34] A bill from 1761 for a harpsichord made by Diego Fernández for Prince Gabriel, son of Charles III, noted that it was made of cedar and cypress with an exterior of white poplar—

the same sort of instrument that Charles Burney would describe as Italian in style and "put into a second case."[35] Fourteen years later Fernández built another harpsichord for Gabriel, this one with a walnut case and a soundboard of cypress.[36] Another walnut harpsichord by Fernández was reported in 1784, and another was advertised for sale in 1799.[37] Accordingly, there is little reason to doubt that all three of the walnut instruments in the inventory were native products, probably by Fernández.[38]

Aside from a Flemish instrument, whose place of origin is clearly stated, the three other harpsichords listed on the inventory are described as having interiors of cedar and cypress, exteriors of poplar, ebony naturals, mother-of-pearl sharps, and sixty-one-note compasses. Thus, María Bárbara's collection consisted of both imported and domestic stringed keyboards. In the former group were the three Florentine pianos, the two pianos converted to harpsichords, and the Flemish harpsichord.[40] The native instruments, probably all by Fernández, were the three of walnut and the three of poplar. It is likely that each of the Queen's three main residences was provided with a piano, a four-and-a-half-octave walnut harpsichord, and a five-octave poplar harpsichord. The rest of the instruments would have been found at her main residence in Madrid, the Palacio Real.[41]

THE COMPASSES OF SCARLATTI'S HARPSICHORDS

A minor mystery surrounds the ranges of the instruments for which Scarlatti's sonatas were intended. Thirty of these works require a top g^3, and four more go to $f\sharp^3$, this note without question implying the existence of an (unused) g^3. The three poplar harpsichords are the only ones in the inventory that have sixty-one-note, five-octave compasses, so they were undoubtedly GG–g^3. However, one sonata calls for a range of FF–g^3, and this presents something of a puzzle, since none of the instruments in the inventory had a sixty-three-note compass, or even a sixty-two-note FF,GG–g^3. But a compass of FF,GG,AA–g^3 was not unheard of and would have filled the bill, since Scarlatti never called for FF$\sharp$.[42] He never called for a GG$\sharp$ either, so that note could have been tuned down to FF.

LATER SPANISH INSTRUMENTS

There seems to be little question that Diego Fernández was a central figure in Spanish harpsichord building in the eighteenth century. After María Bárbara's death he continued to maintain the king's instruments and built new harpsichords for Prince Gabriel. Diego also built other large walnut instruments and may even have made them his specialty; but it is also clear that he continued to build more modest ones with poplar, cedar, and cypress. Archives and sales advertisements in newspapers attest to the regard in which Diego's instruments were held. Even after the turn of the nineteenth century his harpsichords, converted into pianos, continued to hold value. Diego's nephew, Julián Fernández, succeeded him in his courtly duties, although without his uncle's official title. There is reference to only one of Julián's instruments, in 1788: a sale notice of a large walnut harpsichord, similar to those made by his uncle.[43] Unfortunately, none of these instruments are extant, nor are those of well-known builders such as Juan de Mármol (1737–after 1800) or Francisco Flórez (before 1784–1824).

There are a number of surviving harpsichords suspected of being of Spanish origin, although proof is lacking. An anonymous eighteenth-century instrument (Barcelona, Museu de la Música), with a 2×8′ disposition and a GG/BB–c³ compass, is generally Southern in mien. It has the deeply curved bentside of an Italian harpsichord, and the case is fairly shallow. The naturals have boxwood touch plates, and the sharps are black-stained fruitwood. It has an Italianate parchment rose, and jacks with double dampers. It also has a rounded tail and a cut-down nameboard. A stop lever on each side projects into the keywell. It has thin sides with a heavy spine, the sides and nameboard are framed with external moldings, and applied top moldings project into the soundwell. There is a buff stop. The grain of the soundboard is angled, something seen on only a few Italian and

12-2. This anonymous harpsichord with rounded tail is thought to be of Spanish origin. Barcelona, Museu de la Música.

English instruments. The bridge and nut are Northern in section. The wrestplank is extremely wide. The nameboard is crenelated to receive the long sharps. The soundwell and keywell are decorated with papers in a sort of reverse of chinoiserie, since the figures on the papers are eighteenth-century Europeans performing everyday tasks. Many of these features are, of course, found on seventeenth-century French and other International instruments. Other characteristics are more difficult to assess. Nevertheless, the harpsichord is thought to be Spanish.

Another eighteenth-century anonyme (Barcelona, Museu de la Música) is quite different in appearance. Its walnut case and sides are heavier, but it also has a rounded tail. The disposition and compass are both old-fashioned: 1×8′, 1×4′ with buff stop, and C/E–c³. The registers project from the cheeks. The naturals are covered with bone or ivory, and the sharps are of black-stained fruitwood topped with tortoise shell. Note names are written on the naturals, an archaic practice still seen, though rarely, in the eighteenth century. There are applied moldings on all surfaces, and the top molding overlaps into the keywell. There is no rose, but a hole in the soundboard is surrounded by a guitarlike inlay. There are no moldings surrounding the soundboard. The cheeks are slanted. The exterior of the harpsichord is covered with large gold acanthus leaves on a blue ground, and there is a lid painting. This seems to be an anomalous instrument, partaking of several traditions, but ultimately relating to none.

The one characteristic these two harpsichords apparently have in common with later Spanish instruments is the rounded tail, and further confirmation of this trait can be found in several other examples.[44] Both a 1745 piano by the Seville builder Francisco Pérez Mirabal (known only through its picture in a 1922 book on furniture)[45] and a Mirabal harpsichord dated 1754 (also known solely through a photograph, taken around the turn of the century)[46] have rounded tails, although unfor-

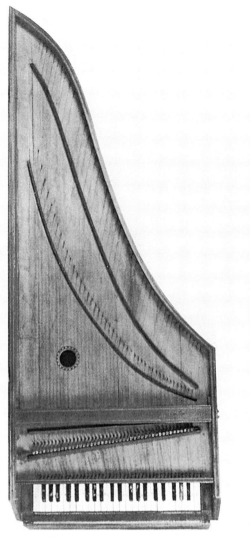

12-3. Also with a rounded tail, the case of this anonymous harpsichord is made of walnut. Its rose hole is surrounded by a guitarlike inlay. Barcelona, Museu de la Música.

tunately both have disappeared.[47] Kenyon de Pascual mentions six other instruments—four privately owned harpsichords and two pianos—with this attribute.[48] But if the rounded tail is a characteristic of Spanish instruments, it is not an exclusive one. A 1728 C/E–c^3 single by Andrès Fernández Santos of Valladolid (fl. 1728–54) (Milan, private collection) and another eighteenth-century anonyme (Scotland, private collection) have mitered tails.[49]

We cannot draw firm conclusions based on some written accounts and on these few instruments—some of which, it could turn out, may not even have been made in Spain. Nevertheless, if one attempts to pierce the veil that shrouds Spanish harpsichord building, it might be possible to suggest that two or three influences can be discerned: an Italian, an International, and possibly a Flemish. The first may be inferred from the reports of thin-case cedar and cypress inner-outer or false inner-outer instruments with shallow cases, the molded nuts and bridges, the mitered bass bridges, the Italianate roses, and the use of box-wood for naturals. The second is seen in the walnut cases, the rounded tails, the case exteriors framed with moldings, the cut-down nameboards, the use of papers, and the many-choired dispositions. Bone or ivory naturals, the $1 \times 8'$, $1 \times 4'$ disposition, and the buff stop might have been Flemish influences. Furthermore, these characteristics do not seem to have been used with any purity, since one sees instruments like the $2 \times 8'$, GG/BB–c^3 anonyme in Barcelona, which appears to partake of all these influences. A tentative conclusion would be that Spanish harpsichord building never developed a strong character of its own[50] and borrowed from the many instruments imported into that country,[51] but this is speculation. Other Spanish instruments may surface and may either confirm or contradict this hypothesis. As Beryl Kenyon de Pasqual perceptively observed, "perhaps it is the very lack of a coherent pattern that typifies harpsichord-making in Spain."[52]

PORTUGAL

Since harpsichords (*cravos* in Portuguese) were built at least as far back as the sixteenth century in the areas we have examined so far, one would expect the same to be true of Portugal; but there are no records to indicate that this was so. *Boalch III* lists only seven known builders for the country.[53] In the eighteenth century the principal names in Portuguese harpsichord building are those of Joachim José Antunes (fl. 1785) and his probable relative, Manuel Antunes (fl. 1789).[54] Each is survived by two instruments. Both of Joachim José's are dated 1785 (Lisbon, Museu de Música;[55] Goudhurst, Finchcocks Collection), and both are singles, disposed $2 \times 8'$. These are large, heavy-cased, and heavily built harpsichords. Plainly decorated, with few moldings, they are painted a dark green on the outside, with natural tulipwood[56] in the keywell and soundwell. These are not fancy instruments, although the one in Finchcocks has exterior bands and a classical lid painting. The bridges and nuts are Northern in section, and the bentsides show the deep curve of Pythagorean scaling and brass stringing. Both have boxwood naturals and ebony sharps. The first has a conservative C–e^3 compass, but the second is a five-octave GG–g^3. Both sit on bench stands with inverted-heart cutouts, a decorative gesture that has come to be associated with Iberian, and especially Portuguese, stands. An unusual feature of these harpsichords, to be found also on the two surviving instruments of Manuel Antunes, is a wide hitchpin rail reminiscent of the cantilevered hitchplates on Cristofori's pianos; but the cases do not reflect the latter's unique double-sided construction. Instead, the hitchplates are merely hollowed out underneath, and not independent of the soundboards.

The Finchcocks Antunes, seen in Plate 16, is playable and makes a full, rich, and somewhat mellow sound.[57] Since it has been restored in modern times, the details of its interior structure are known. It has bottom braces in the Italian manner, with diagonal struts taking the thrust of the bentside. The soundboard is extraordinarily thin but is braced by two cutoff bars and a plethora of smaller secondary braces.[58]

Manuel Antunes's 1789 harpsichord (Lisbon, Museu de Música) is similar in appearance to the instruments of Joachim José. Again one sees a large, heavy, deeply curved case with little molding, a tulipwood (or some other light wood) interior, and with Northern-style bridge and nut. A single manual $2\times8'$ scaled for iron stringing, its FF–a^3 compass is exceeded in width only by the EE–a^3 of the 1786 Jacques Joachim Swanen double (Paris, Musée des Arts et Métiers). Interestingly, the soundboard is decorated, although the bridge goes right over the painted flowers. This means, of course, that the soundboard was painted before the bridge was glued in place, strongly implying that it was recycled from an older harpsichord. Manuel's other instrument is a 1767 piano (in Portuguese, a *cravo de martelos*) with a C–d^3 compass (Vermillion, Shrine to Music Museum),[59] but visually both instruments are quite similar.[60]

A 1780 harpsichord by Jozé Calisto (Vermillion, Shrine to Music Museum), with its $2\times8'$ disposition, brass-strung GG–g^3 compass, Northern-style bridge and nut, plain heavy case, green exterior and tulipwood interior, on two bench stands with inverted-heart cutouts, fits the emerging pattern of the late Portuguese instrument. The same is true of an anonymous late-eighteenth-century harpsichord (Lisbon, Museu de Música) which is very much in the same style. The only other known Portuguese harpsichord (Berlin, Staatliches Institut für Musikforschung) is somewhat problematic. Tentatively dated 1700, it is by Manuel Anjos of Beja, a town in southern Portugal. An octave harpsichord disposed $2\times4'$, with a compass of C–d^3, it is a false inner-outer with cypress veneer on the interior. The heavy case sides sit on the bottom. Although it does not fit well with either the earlier Bocaro or the later Antunes-style instruments, there simply is not enough information on which to draw firm conclusions.

Manuel Antunes's 1767 piano deserves some comment. For one thing, it has a beautifully made Florentine-style action; and for another, it has survived in a relatively pristine and playable condition, possibly giving us some insight into the sounds of the pianos of Cristofori himself. Its hammers, covered with a soft, thick leather, produce a full, yet rather quiet, mellow, refined sound, with a sweet treble, a prominent tenor, and a direct, nicely aggressive bass. Played forte, its percussive sound is not unlike a good Italian harpsichord, and at low volume its tone is positively seductive. It is much more harpsichord-like in sound than the later and more familiar Viennese fortepianos. Its dark green exterior and tulipwood interior are similar to the other Portuguese instruments described, except that some additional decoration was later applied to the case and interior of the lid. Like the other Portuguese stringed keyboards discussed, this one copies Cristofori's cantilevered hitchpin rail, but not his unique double-sided construction; hence, the rail is not independent of the soundboard, although it is hollowed out underneath. In fact, all the known Iberian pianos but one have this wide, cantilevered hitchpin rail.

All in all, four eighteenth-century Portuguese pianos have survived, plus another three harpsichord-piano conversions, and like the 1767 Antunes, their actions all derive from Cristofori. The second, dated 1763 and signed by Henri-Joseph van Casteel (1722–90) (Lisbon, Museu de Música), has the plain heavy-case construction, C–d³ compass, green exterior, and tulipwood interior that link it squarely to the late-eighteenth-century Portuguese tradition. Van Casteel himself, however, was born in Tournai. For some reason he moved to Lisbon, where he was active as a builder of harpsichords and pianos between 1757 and 1767. After that he moved to Brussels, where he continued to build. The third piano (London, private ownership), from about the same time as the van Casteel, also has a C–d³ compass and is similar to it in many ways. Both are decorated

12-4. Looking very much like a Portuguese harpsichord, this 1767 piano by Manuel Antunes has an action derived directly from the instruments of Cristofori. Vermillion, America's Shrine to Music Museum.

with green paint and tulipwood, and both have boxwood naturals and ebony sharps; but the similarities extend farther than that. Both use internal bottom braces scooped out in a shallow U shape, and both have typical Iberian bench stands with inverted-heart cutouts.[61] Whether this points to van Casteel as the builder of both instruments, or to two representatives of a common Lisbon piano-building tradition, is difficult to say; but Christopher Nobbs, who examined both instruments closely, believes that the anonymous piano is the earliest known example of Portuguese piano building, perhaps even predating the 1755 earthquake.[62]

SUMMING UP

Once more, it must be said that whatever we know about Iberian harpsichord making is but a pale palimpsest of what must have been a vigorous, if spotty, sideline by craftsmen who were primarily organ builders. Only in the eighteenth century do we have any instruments on which to draw, and even with these our conclusions must be tentative. It seems clear, however, that the twentieth-century view that Iberian harpsichords were identical to Italian models is not completely accurate. In Spain influences of two or possibly three practices appear to have existed side by side. Characteristics such as heavy, shallow, poplar cases with deeply curved bentsides, cedar interiors with little decoration, soundboards of cypress, molded nuts and bridges, mitered bass bridge sections, and keyboards of boxwood naturals were likely derived from the eighteenth-century Italian false-inner outer tradition. On the other hand, attributes such as round-tail walnut cases framed with applied moldings, ebony naturals, mother-of-pearl sharps, papers, lowered nameboards, and more complex dispositions were probably influenced by International style via Germany. A Flemish influence is also possible (and not surprising, since many Flemish instruments were imported to Spain) in features like bone or ivory naturals, buff stops, and the 1×8′, 1×4′ disposition. But as far as we know from the extant examples, Spanish harpsichords were all short-scaled, with deeply curved bentsides, and were likely to have been strung in brass.

With their plain, heavy, painted cases and 2×8′ dispositions, Portuguese harpsichords probably relate to the Spanish instruments with poplar cases and soundwells veneered in cedar; or more likely, both might have been derived from Italian models, but modified locally. Again, the scales are short, the bentside curves are deep, and the stringing was probably mostly in brass.

The bridges and nuts are Northern in section. Brazilian tulip-wood seems to have been the veneer of choice for the sound-well, but other exotic New World woods are found here and there as well. The most astonishing characteristic, though, is the presence of the wide Cristofori-like hitchpin rails.

The thriving Florentine-related piano tradition is one of the more interesting aspects of eighteenth-century Iberian building. Although we are well aware of the dissemination of Cristofori's ideas to Germany via Gottfried Silbermann, it is likely that Iberian builders were successfully using Florentine action principles in their cravos de martelos even earlier than Silbermann, and it is clear that they continued doing so until late in the century. But it is equally clear that their harpsichord building seems to have been more derivative than that found in most other areas.

$$\left\lceil 13 \right\rceil$$

HARPSICHORD BUILDING IN FRANCE UP TO THE REVOLUTION

HE CLASSIC eighteenth-century French double-manual harpsichord, with its 2×8′, 1×4′ disposition, shove coupler, gold bands, gilded moldings, and Louis XV or XVI stand is the end product of a century and a half of building by a variety of masters, most of them working in Paris. In many ways that harpsichord evolved from its seventeenth-century predecessor, where the 2×8′, 1×4′ disposition and the shove coupler are first found; but in matters of case construction, soundboard barring, scale, plucking points, stringing material, and tonal quality, it was strongly influenced by the work of the Ruckerses and Couchets. At first, the popularity of Flemish harpsichords *à petit ravalement*—that is, with French actions, narrow keyboards, and slightly wider compasses, but without enlargement of the case—supplanted the Internationally based seventeenth-century native style.[1] It was, in fact, this rebuilding of Flemish instruments that occupied much of the time of French builders from the end of the seventeenth century to the eve of the Revolution. And the Ruckers sound was so admired that even new instruments were made in the style of rebuilt Flemish harpsichords. As late as 1771 a writer named Anton Bemetzrieder, in a treatise on harpsichord playing and harmony, characterized a five-octave FF–f[3] harpsichord as a *clavecin à grand ravalement*, meaning that it was the newly built equivalent of a Flemish harpsichord that had undergone the fullest sort of rebuilding, with an expansion of all its resources, and redecorated to suit current taste.[2]

Building practices in the earlier years of the century show a changing admixture of International and Flemish characteristics, and the fully evolved classic French double does not appear on the scene much before 1730. By 1770 it begins to transmute into something that, with its *peaux de buffle* (soft quills of buffalo leather) and machine stops with *genouillères* (knee levers to change registration), goes beyond the traditional character of the harpsichord and the music written for it. Accordingly, the history of the harpsichord in eighteenth-century France nicely divides itself into four parts: the *ravalement* of Flemish instruments, the development of the classic instrument, the Ruckers-inspired French double, and the final years of the French harpsichord. By that time the winds of change were in the air and would affect all of Europe's institutions. When the Bastille was stormed in 1789 the glittering world of the French monarchy and its attendant nobility began its precipitous descent, taking with it all the trappings of the court of Versailles, including the aristocratic harpsichord. But even before that date the harpsichord was threatened by a revolution from within: by then Pascal Taskin and many of his contemporaries were already making pianos.

RAVALEMENT[3]

The process of rebuilding and enlarging seventeenth-century Flemish harpsichords, particularly those by the Ruckerses and the Couchets, has been alluded to many times. Already acclaimed while their builders were alive, by the end of the seventeenth century these instruments took on a hallowed patina of superiority matched only by that which later accrued to the violins of Antonio Stradivarius. The thought of discarding an obsolete 1×8′, 1×4′ C/E–c³ single or a nonaligned double would never have occurred to an eighteenth-century owner; instead, the instruments were modernized, sometimes with a thoroughness that left little of the original except some soundboard wood and the all-important Ruckers or Couchet rose. In many cases they were modernized not once, but two or three times, and could command prices anywhere from two to fifteen times that of a new harpsichord *mis à grand ravalement*.[4] With the ability of the Ruckers or Couchet name to bring in this sort of return, it is no wonder that a brisk business of counterfeiting sprung up.

At first, the updating was done by crowding a few more notes into the case without making any structural changes: a *petit ravalement*. A more thorough renovation, which included enlarging the case as well as the compass, was the *grand ravalement*. Looking at the process in a different way, William Dowd proposes five classifications of the corpus of extant Ruckers and Couchet doubles.[5] In the first go the very few instruments that have remained musically unaltered. The second includes double-manual harpsichords whose keyboards have been aligned — the *petit ravalement*. In the third class are those doubles that have been extended to five octaves or close to it — the *grand ravalement*. The fourth class includes singles that have been converted to doubles, or were mostly new instruments with old Flemish soundboards or even soundboards pieced together from virginals. The final class encompasses the many instruments attributed to members of the Ruckers or Couchet families, but that are actually fakes, counterfeits, and outright phonies.

Petit ravalement of singles usually involved changing the disposition from 1×8′, 1×4′ to 2×8′, 1×4′, filling out the short octave in the bass, and possibly adding a note or two in the treble, all without widening the case. Sometimes the original keyboard was kept and enlarged, with space for the additional notes in the bass found by removing the endblocks. This provided room for the two extra Cs and Ds as well as their sharps, although the keyboard had to be shifted upward in pitch. The strings for the additional notes were provided for by adding pieces to the nuts and bridges, along with the appropriate pins. The gap would need to be widened, usually by taking wood off the wrestplank, and three new upper guides provided, narrower than the originals, along with a new lower guide. Such a rebuilding now provided a harpsichord updated to a 2×8′, 1×4′ disposition and a full four octaves, although the original scale was destroyed.

Most of the time, however, the *ravalement* was carried out by replacing the Flemish keyboard, with its wide octave span, with a new keyboard of the narrower French span. With such a keyboard a d^3, along with a $c\sharp^3$, could be added on top. Of course, this shifted the pitch back down, making the scale quite long. To compensate, the 8′ nut would be removed and reglued in a position closer to the gap (since the 4′ was not affected as much its nut was generally left alone). Again, the scaling would be nothing like the original, but that probably mattered not one whit to the builders and even less to the owners. An obsolete instrument had been resurrected and had once again become a useful music-making tool. Besides, the soul of a Ruckers or Couchet harpsichord was thought to reside in its soundboard, and as long as that remained relatively intact, and as long as strings were not so long that they were breaking regularly, or so short that they sounded false, the violence done to the scale was probably not thought to be of any consequence.

The process of *petit ravalement* in doubles was more complex

THE VAN BLANKENBURG PROBLEM

Grant O'Brien has ascertained that even before the Ruckers and Couchet singles underwent *petit ravalement*, many of then were changed from 1×8′, 1×4′ instruments to 2×8′s. This was done by removing the 4′ strings, affixing new bridge and nut pins to the left of the existing 8′ strings, adding a second set of strings, and either extending the bottoms of the old 4′ jacks (so that they would pluck in the higher plane of the 8′ strings) or providing a new set of jacks. If the instrument retained its original compass,[6] it created a problem first articulated by Quirinus van Blankenburg in 1739.[7] (Van Blankenburg, it will be remembered, was the Dutch organist who thought muselars grunted like piglets in the bass. He was also critical of the keyboard players of the previous century for their presumed inability to transpose, thereby supposedly forcing the Ruckerses and Couchets to make unaligned doubles.)

The problem can be stated as follows: since the original 8′ string is plucked by the jack whose plectrum is facing right, the new string must be placed to the left of the original, in the position of the old 4′ string (although now on a plane with the original 8′ string), so that its jack can face left. Unisons, of course, are wide pairs, so the new leftmost strings of the pairs will be considerably longer than the originals, and quite close to, if not actually at, their breaking points. If tuned up to its original pitch, the harpsichord now has to endure the strain of a considerable increase in string tension caused by the long lengths of the new strings. While the situation is being pondered, the added tension is depressing the soundboard and destroying the case.

Van Blankenburg proposed one solution: to put the new string on the right side, add another note's worth of jacks (which would require another set of slots in the upper guides), and displace the keyboard up a half step but tune the strings down a half step, thus simultaneously reducing the tension and restoring the instrument to its original pitch. It also gave the instrument an extra note in the bass. The van Blankenburg problem reared its head any time an instrument underwent *ravalement*, and it was dealt with in a number of ways. Sometimes the nut was moved closer to the bridge, or the strings were respaced, or the instrument was strung at its normal tension and played at a pitch level different from its original; or sometimes, certainly, it is likely that the problem was simply ignored and the constant breaking of strings was endured.

and involved the filling in of the "missing" bass notes of the upper manual, adding an additional set of 8′ strings along with nut, bridge, and wrestpins, and aligning the two keyboards. Of course, the C/E–f³ lower manual had to have its keys rearranged, but without any further alterations both keyboards could now stand at GG/BB–c³. Provision was made for coupling the keyboards by providing a standard French shove coupler.[8] The wide, four-register gap presented something of a problem, since only three registers were now needed. Either a thin piece of wood was put in place of the rearmost guide, or three new, wider ones were made. Room could be made for a c♯³ and d³ in the treble by trimming the endblocks and making a new set of keyboards with the narrower French octave span.[9]

A *grand ravalement* of a single required some widening of the case, usually by adding material to the bentside and moving the cheek to the right. A replacement wrestplank had to be made, since the old one could no longer span the greater distance between spine and cheek; but the old wrestplank veneer would normally be preserved and glued to the new plank, with additional wood added where needed. New soundboard wood would also be needed at the cheek, and all the bridges and nuts would be given extensions. The new wood would be painted by French artisans familiar with Flemish-style decoration, with the new blended into the old as much as possible.[10] The nameboard would need to be pieced out with additional wood, and a new namebatten, registers, and jackrail were required. With a new, narrower French keyboard the compass was now normally $C–f^3$. Eventually, musical requirements dictated that these instruments be given even wider compasses — at first $GG–e^3$, then $FF–e^3$, and finally $FF–f^3$.

For doubles, a *grand ravalement* required some enlargement to the case, usually done on the treble side but sometimes at the spine as well. For the latter, the old spine was planed down to

13-1. The compass of this 1627 Ioannes Ruckers single was enlarged from $C/E–c^3$ to $C–e^3$, and the disposition was changed from a $1 \times 8'$, $1 \times 4'$ to a $2 \times 8'$. Neither the soundboard, bridges, nuts, nor wrestplank are original. © Bildarchiv Preussischer Kulturbesitz, Berlin, Musikinstrumenten Museum.

the level of the liners, a new spine was glued to it, and new soundboard wood filled the gap between the edge of the old soundboard and the new spine. A new set of keyboards of the narrower span would be supplied, and the strings would be respaced. A new wrestplank, jackrail, nameboard, and namebatten would be required, along with new jacks and registers. Often the case bracing would be reinforced to take the strain of the additional strings. As in any *ravalement,* the builder needed to take the van Blankenburg problem into account, and some succeeded better than others.

By the middle of the century, when the mania for Flemish instruments seemed to be at its height, builders started to convert singles (most of which had already undergone *petit ravalement*) into doubles. As would be expected, the task of transforming a small C/E–c^3 1×8′, 1×4′ Ruckers single into a double-manual French harpsichord with a compass close to five octaves was a formidable one. Case sides had to be extended outward, and the front of the instrument had to be lengthened. Some of the nameboard had to be removed in order to get a second keyboard into the case. And, of course, there would be the usual new wrestplank, soundboard wood, registers, jacks, strings, pins, and so on. On the small instruments it was not possible to descend lower than GG,[11] but the larger singles with chromatic basses were sometimes taken down to FF. It would then be redecorated and probably given a new table stand in one of the Louis styles.

The instruments in Dowd's class five — the counterfeit Ruckerses and Couchets — constitute one of the more interesting episodes in the history of the French harpsichord, although they really have nothing directly to do with *ravalement.* With the almost unbelievable value placed on a rebuilt Flemish product, it was only a matter of time before builders began to find ways to attach the Ruckers or Couchet cachet to a non-Ruckers or non-Couchet instrument. Perhaps the easiest way was to take an old harpsichord, either Flemish or French, and give it a Ruckers or Couchet rose. These roses were available from old instruments —

13-2. Originally a nonaligned double, this 1646 Ioannes Couchet was modernized by widening the case at the cheek, aligning the keyboards, adding a second set of 8′ strings, and extending the compass from GG/BB– c^3 to GG/BB–f^3. The *ravalement* was probably done in Flanders, rather than France. © IRPA-KIK, Brussels.

13-3. This single-manual 1680 Ioseph Ioannes Couchet had its case enlarged and was converted to a double by Blanchet in 1750. Further alterations were carried out by Taskin in 1781. Museum of Fine Arts, Boston. Reproduced with permission. © 2000 Museum of Fine Arts, Boston. All rights reserved.

particularly from virginals, which by this time were considered obsolete. But if one of these was not obtainable, counterfeit roses were; all that was required was a plaster cast of a genuine device, and lead copies could be poured to heart's content. Also, a rose of a different maker could be changed to look like a genuine Ruckers or Couchet. For example, the IC "Ioannes Couchet" rose on an instrument rebuilt by Taskin in 1783–84 (Edinburgh, Russell Collection) was discovered to have originally been a Jean or Jacques Goermans IG rose from which the horizontal bar of the "G" was deliberately and skillfully removed. Rather than the Couchet harpsichord (rebuilt by Taskin) it appears to be, it is now clear that the instrument had been built by one of the Goermans in 1764.[12] Twenty years later Taskin altered the rose and stained the soundboard to make it look older. He made other changes as well, to update it musically, and undoubtedly sold it for many times its original worth.[13]

Because of their age, the instruments of Hans Ruckers were even more valued than those of the succeeding members of the dynasty; consequently, there are several instances of AR roses that were turned into HR's by simply cutting open the top of the "A," and straightening the angled legs to make an "H." As clever as these conversions were, a knowledge of the characteristics of the roses of Flemish builders made it next to impossible to fake an instrument convincingly on that basis alone. Ioannes Ruckers, for example, used different styles of roses for his virgin-

13-4. Anonymous harpsichord signed "1573 Hans Ruckers." Aside from the rose, which is almost certainly a genuine AR rose altered to an HR, there is nothing Ruckers or Flemish about this instrument. The lid painting is on canvas glued to the wood. Munich, Deutsches Museum.

als, his singles, and his doubles.[14] Thus, the presence of a virginal rose in a Ioannes harpsichord would immediately alert a knowledgeable observer. But for the most part, the people buying the faux Ruckers and Couchet instruments were not that discriminating, and in fact, the detailed study of these roses is a modern phenomenon. In the eighteenth century, the presence of any rose bearing HR, IR, or AR initials was probably sufficient to establish the instrument's value.

Another way of faking a harpsichord by one of the revered Antwerp masters was to make a new instrument and score it with markings that suggested that it was a Flemish harpsichord *mis à grand ravalement*. The score marks, of course, did not represent the joining of new wood to old, but were simply indented lines intended to deceive. A beautifully decorated instrument (Paris, Musée de la Musique) bears a Hans Ruckers inscription on the nameboard, an HR rose, and the date of 1590 on the soundboard. At a casual glance, one would believe it to have been a genuine Ruckers harpsichord that had undergone a full five-octave *ravalement*. Clinching the deception, a more careful examination would reveal traces of the joints where the rebuilder would have been expected to add new wood. For years it was considered to be a genuine Ruckers, but when it was opened up for repair, the signature of Jean-Claude Goujon (fl. 1743–58) was found on the inside of the soundboard. Further inspection revealed the date of 1749 on some of the jacks.[15] Clearly Goujon, a skilled and respected Parisian builder, had made a phoney Ruckers with a GG–d³ compass, decorated it in a stunning gold chinoiserie on a black ground, put it on an elaborately carved and gilded stand, and undoubtedly sold it for many times the amount it would have fetched had his name been on the nameboard.

It is shocking to think that the members of the great Blanchet and Taskin families, respected artisans who held the title of *facteur des clavessins du Roi* (harpsichord builder to the King) and who are acknowledged as among the greatest builders of all time, would stoop so low as to deliberately counterfeit old instruments for pecuniary gain; but they and many others did it

13-5. This famous instrument is signed "Hans Ruckers 1590," but was built by Jean-Claude Goujon ca. 1749 with all the visible signs of a *grand ravalement*. A deliberate counterfeit, it is nevertheless a fine instrument, decorated in gold chinoiserie on a black ground, and set on an ornately carved and completely gilded Louis XV cabriole stand. No. 923, clavecin, Jean-Claude Goujon, Paris, 1749, ravelé par Joachim Swanen, 1784, E. 233. Paris, Cliché Musée de la Musique.

RAVALEMENT OF VIRGINALS

Virginals themselves sometimes underwent the *ravalement* process, usually by moving the cheeks out and inserting a few notes in the bass, to fill out the C/E short octave, and a few in the treble, to extend the range to e^3 or f^3. Since the cheeks are part of a virginal's interior bracing, that would also have to be moved. New slots for the extra jacks would be cut into the soundboard, the bridges added to it, and the additional strings and pins supplied. The keyframe would be rebuilt, and the new keys would be added. Alternately, a new keyboard with the narrow octave span could be supplied, but this meant that the slotted piece of leather covering the mortises in the soundboard would have to be removed and discarded, and the portion of the soundboard with the existing mortises excised. A new segment of soundboard with the appropriately positioned mortises would be glued in its place and covered by a fresh piece of slotted leather. The lower guide would be replaced in the same way. Of course, these changes would destroy the instrument's original scale, so on occasion the bridges were removed and repositioned, or new bridges were made, in an attempt to restore the appropriate string lengths, even though that changed the relationship between the bridges and the barring. Nevertheless, it is likely that many Ruckers and Couchet virginals had an extended life because of these expediencies and were played long after the virginals of other builders had been discarded as old-fashioned.[19]

13-6. A 1610 Ioannes Ruckers muselar mother and child. The compass of the mother was altered from the original C/E–c^3 to C–f^3 by moving both cheeks outward. This decreased the size of the child's compartment, and it can no longer be stored there. The exterior has been redecorated at least six times. © IRPA-KIK, Brussels.

with little sign of conscience or remorse.[16] It was the way the world worked in France in the eighteenth century, and in other parts of Europe as well. Furthermore, these instruments should not be denigrated simply because they were intended to defraud. No matter who the builder, the ca. 1749 Goujon is still a fine instrument, and as Dowd observed, harpsichords of this ilk would not have been so highly thought of and so elaborately decorated had they not been.[17]

When it became difficult to acquire Flemish harpsichords, builders began to take old virginal soundboards and, by judiciously plugging the jack mortises and adding new wood, fashion them into harpsichord soundboards that they could put into new French cases. Of course, the thinning of the board would have been all wrong, but the aura surrounding a Ruckers or Couchet soundboard was so powerful that this did not seem to be a matter for concern. A "1632 Ioannes Ruckers" (France, private ownership) is a large GG–e³ double made by our friend Jean-Claude Goujon in 1757.[18] The soundboard was constructed by piecing together parts of a virginal board as well as other old soundboard wood and carries an IR rose. This instrument was also enlarged later, into an FF–f³ harpsichord *mis à grand ravalement*. The rebuilding process went on right to the very end.

THE DEVELOPMENT OF THE CLASSIC FRENCH HARPSICHORD

French craftsmen began to modify their Internationally based building practices at the end of the seventeenth century, and this constituted a new development in the harpsichord's history. Prior to this time neither Italian, Flemish, English, German, nor French builders had ever shown interest in incorporating elements of a foreign practice into their own. As we have noted, harpsichord building was a conservative, local activity that changed slowly, generally with little attention paid to what was going on across borders. Now, however, the Ruckers style had become hot — so hot that to many of Western Europe's builders it finally became a case of adapt or sink. Faced with that choice, French builders gave up their old ways and adapted. It took a third of a century for Ruckers-style building practices to displace International ones, but by the 1730s elements of the indigenous style had almost completely disappeared. The French retained their large double-manual 2×8′, 1×4′ harpsichords with shove couplers, stop levers protruding through the nameboard, leather-covered registers, beautifully built keyboards, and all the other elements that made these instruments

MARIUS AND HIS *CLAVECIN BRISÉ*

Jean Marius (fl. 1700–1716) was a Parisian harpsichord maker with an innovative turn of mind, although everything he thought of, including the *clavecin à maillets,* or hammer harpsichord,

seemed to have been invented before. In 1700 he went before the Académie des Sciences with a folding harpsichord, an instrument whose utility was no doubt balanced by its dubious musical value; nevertheless, the Académie granted him a twenty-year patent to produce and sell them. Consisting of three hinged sections that folded up into a (large!) suitcase-sized package, the contrivance had several antecedents in seventeenth-century Italy, which was probably its true home, with Giuseppe Mondini the likely inventor.[20] Marius's total production of *clavecins brisés* is unknown, but five survive: two from 1700 (both in Paris, Musée de la Musique), a 1700–1704 (Berlin, Staatliches Institut für Musikforschung), a 1709 (Brussels, Musée Instru-

13-7. Frederick the Great's grandmother lent him this 1700–1704 Jean Marius *clavecin brisé* so he would have a keyboard instrument available when he went to war. © Bildarchiv Preussischer Kulturbesitz, Berlin, Musikinstrumenten Museum.

mental), and a 1713 (Leipzig, Musikinstrumenten-Museum der Universität Leipzig).

The 1700–1704 was owned by Sophia Charlotte, queen of Prussia, who loaned it to her grandson Frederick the Great to take on his military campaigns. It is fairly complex for a traveling instrument, with a 2×8′, 1×4′ disposition and a GG/BB–c³ compass. It even includes a device to give a tuning note. The atypical soundboard painting consists of not only flowers and insects, but also wrought-iron patterns and figures from the commedia dell'arte, one of whom is doing something fairly naughty to another.[21]

so elegant and playable; but they embraced Flemish-style softwood heavy cases with upper and lower braces, cut-in moldings, cutoff bar and rib soundboard bracing, a gently curved bentside sitting on the bottom, and gilded cast-metal roses. Most importantly, they adopted what they believed to be the essence of the Ruckers-Couchet sound.

This course of events is clearly illustrated by the practices of Nicolas Blanchet, one of the luminaries of Parisian harpsichord making early in the century. The founder of the Blanchet-Taskin dynasty, Nicolas is important both as a rebuilder of Flemish instruments and as a creator of new models in the Franco-Flemish style. His first extant harpsichord,[22] made in 1693 (France, private ownership), has sides of intermediate thickness, slightly over ½″. The bentside is parabolic in shape and overlaps the bottom, and the top molding is set into a rabbet and overlaps into the soundwell. Insofar as it has been seen, the soundboard barring seems to be International in style—at least there is no cutoff bar—and the 4′ bridge has a molded cross section. The compass is GG/BB–c³ with one split sharp in the bass (the treble was later enlarged to d³). On the other hand, it has a long, 14¼″ scale—even longer than the usual Ruckers scale.[23] The case is built of poplar or lime, rather than a hardwood, and the 8′ bridge is Flemish in appearance. William Dowd, whose examination of the instrument forms the basis for this description, convincingly characterizes it as more seventeenth century than eighteenth.[24] Still, the use of a softwood case and a long scale indicates just as convincingly that Blanchet was making a break with the past.

Blanchet's next survivor, a 1696 trapezoidal octave spinet (France, private ownership), need not detain us long. It is, in every way, a typical product of a seventeenth-century French workshop, and other than its wider GG/BB–c³ compass (later rebuilt to GG,AA–d³), differs little from the spinet described by Mersenne sixty years earlier. The case is of thin walnut with a heavier softwood spine for the lid. Sides overlap the bottom, and the top molding fits in a rabbet and overhangs into the soundwell. Octave spinets of this sort continued to be built throughout the eighteenth century.

Two bentside spinets, from 1709 (London, Horniman Museum) and 1710 (Angers, Musée des Arts), are Blanchet's next extant instruments. Both are made of pine, with sides slightly more than ⅜″ thick overlapping the bottom. The spines are heavier. Both have compasses of GG/BB–c³, with one split sharp in the bass, and both have Flemish-style bridges with seventeenth-century-style molded nuts. But even in the space of one year there are subtle changes from old to new. For one thing, the top molding of the 1709 is set into a rabbet and overhangs inside; but the molding in the 1710 is cut into the top, as the Flemish did. And for another, while the 1709's sides overlap the bottom, the 1710's sides are set into a mortise cut into the bottom—a technique sort of halfway between Flemish and International practices.

Blanchet's second surviving harpsichord (Paris, private ownership) is undated, but has been assigned to ca. 1715 on the basis of the decoration.[25] The bentside is still somewhat parabolic and has not yet taken on the characteristic half-bent, half-straight conformation shortly to prevail, and the sides still overlap the bottom; but compared to the 1693, it is obvious that Blanchet was attempting to make his instruments conform more to a Flemish mold. The case is of softwood, with ⅝″-thick sides. Both bridges and nuts are Flemish in cross section, and the compass is GG–e³ (later enlarged to FF–f³), a range to be used by the Blanchet shop for some time to come. The scale is 14″. Clearly, Blanchet is building heavier cases (although he still overlaps the bottom), he has adopted the more business-like triangular shape of the Flemish bridges and nuts, and most importantly, he has abandoned the lutelike lightness so characteristic of the instruments he first learned to make.

For purposes of illustrating the transition from the indigenous style to the Franco-Flemish, this recital of the Blanchet harpsichords comes to an end with the next extant example, dated 1730 (Framingham, Mass., private ownership). By this time Nicolas had taken his son into the business, and the instrument is signed "N. et François Blanchet." The poplar case has sides about ⅝–1¹⁄₁₆″ wide, with cut-in moldings. The sides sit on the bottom, and the bentside conforms to the mature French half-bent, half-straight shape. The hefty internal bracing consists of three lower braces and seven upper. The bentside liner is kerf-bent, and the soundboard is braced with a cutoff bar and ribs plus a few additional small ribs. The scale is long. The original compass was FF–e³, with f³ added later. And, of course, the keyboards could be joined with a shove coupler. There is no buff stop; despite its universal presence on Flemish examples, this device was still rare on French instruments at this time. In short, we have finally arrived at the classic French harpsichord. But typical as this instrument may be, there are some curious things about it: the cheek shows signs of having been mortised for protruding register extensions, such as were found on the Flemish harpsichords of the previous century (and which were still being used there in the eighteenth), and the instrument has a removeable nameboard. These are unexplainable anomalies, but as we have seen before, the closer we examine individual harpsichords, the less meaning there is in the concept of "typical."[26]

THE RUCKERS-INSPIRED FRENCH DOUBLE

The classic French double is a large instrument, although not much longer than the normal Ruckers double; the latter is usually about 7′4″, and the former may vary from a little more than that to 7′10″ or so. The differences are accounted for not so much by the scale, which remains much the same, and many times a bit shorter,[27] but by the absence of the short octave and the extension of the low register down to FF. These two factors simply add more bass notes, and good bass tone demands longer strings, requiring that the case be lengthened proportionally. French harpsichords are wider than Flemish for the same reasons—there are no short octaves and the compass was extended downward. However, they are not a great deal wider, because the French octave span was narrower than the Flemish. Thus, the fifty keys of a 1615 Andreas Ruckers double (Antwerp, Vleeshuis Museum) produced a case width of about 31″, while the case of the five-octave 1769 Taskin, with a range of sixty-one keys, is only 5⅝″ wider.[28] Furthermore, the expansion of the range to f³ generates a sharper curve in the treble part of the bentside. This, along with the eighteenth-century French bentside conformation of half-curved, half-straight, produced a characteristic shape quite distinct from the Flemish parabolic bentside.

The size of the case parts of French instruments varies considerably, but generally speaking, they are either similar to Flemish dimensions or larger. Using the measurements of the 1615 Ruckers and 1769 Taskin once again, the Ruckers sides measure about ½″ with the spine slightly heavier, while the Taskin sides are about ¾″, with a ⅞″ spine.[29] The French braced their harpsichords in the same manner as the Flemish, but the bracing members were heavier and sometimes more numerous; the 1615 Ruckers has three upper braces, while the Taskin has four. Upper and lower offset bellyrails were used, as in Flemish practice, although the later builders strengthened the upper bellyrail by gluing a narrow piece on the inside to make a "T" section. The case parts are of poplar or lime, the walnut case and light construction of the previous century having long been abandoned. Moldings similar in section to that of the Ruckers were cut into the case sides, and applied moldings are nowhere to be found. Clearly, the addition of a second 8′ choir and another ten or so triplets of strings increased the stresses on the case, requiring heavier parts and bracing; but the French went farther than they really needed to, and produced extremely strong instruments.

French builders were also quite subtle in the thickness of their case parts. They were fairly heavy at the keyboard end, where heft was needed; but they often tapered from there to the tail. They sometimes tapered in height, too, from the keyboard to the tail, so that if measured, the soundboard would seem to be rising in the case; but because of the illusion of the perspective, from the player's point of view the soundboard did not appear to be sloping downward. For example, the spine of the 1770 Taskin (New Haven, Yale Collection), seen in Plate 17, is close to 1″ thick at the front and tapers to about ¾″ at the tail;

the cheek is also close to 1″ in front, tapering to ⅞″. The bent-side averages about ¾″, and the tail is ⅞″. The case diminishes in depth a subtle ⅛″ from front to rear.[30]

Soundboard barring and the profiles of bridges and nuts were also copied from Flemish practice. The barring consisted of a relatively heavy 4′ hitchpin rail, a cutoff bar, and four or five ribs running from the cutoff bar to the spine.[31] Triangular bridges and nuts were typically Flemish in cross section, although somewhat more massive. Many builders mimicked the pattern of the cast-metal Ruckers rose, with its harp-playing angel, but with their own initials. The keyboard end of the instruments, however, abandoned Flemish conventions. Although not as short and dainty, and without the solid ivory or bone sharps, eighteenth-century French keyboards derived directly from those of the previous century. Natural touch plates were made of ebony, with ebony or black-stained sharps topped with bone or ivory. Rather than the trefoils cut into the fronts of the keys, these were now covered with arcades similar in pattern to those found on Italian harpsichords. An even greater distinction from Flemish practice is found in the way in which the keys are balanced. The Ruckerses and Couchets set the balance points for their keys somewhat forward, making for a heavier touch; but such a balance point has the advantage of relaying to the player a strong sensation of the moment of pluck. The French provided their keyboards with a more favorable balance point, although at the expense of that immediacy of sensation; nevertheless, they managed to compensate with very precise work and by removing as much weight as feasible from the key levers.

To keep the action as silent as possible the upper and lower guides were given oversized mortises and covered with thin leather slotted for the jacks. Damping on French harpsichords was similar to that found on Flemish. The French did not use mouse-ear dampers, but employed side or crush dampers: cloth that (like mouse ears) contacted the string from the side, rather than like little flags sitting on the top. Hence, with the 4′ in the off position and its strings free of their dampers, that choir would ring sympathetically when either or both 8′ choirs were played, allowing them to achieve the same effect of sympathetic resonance possible on a Flemish harpsichord. In addition, some instruments provided stop levers for the front 8′ jacks. At first thought such an enhancement would appear to be unnecessary, since that 8′ choir is exclusive to the upper manual and consequently is always "on," although not sounding unless played. But by disengaging the upper 8′ dampers from their strings, that choir was free to vibrate sympathetically with the back 8′.

Considering the ease with which a buff stop can be supplied, and considering that Flemish harpsichords all had them, it is curious that these were rare on French harpsichords before the middle of the century. The reason could have something to do with the prevailing style of French music. A buff stop might have been marvelously effective in a seventeenth-century variation set, where figuration in the treble could be accompanied by buffed chords in the bass, or to buff both bass and treble in imitation of the sound of a lute; but in the prevailing *style brisé* texture of so much eighteenth-century French music, it is likely that the buffed harpsichord sound would have been out of place.

DECORATION[32]

French harpsichords received a variety of decoration, some of it depending on the taste and purse of the purchaser.[33] All instruments received a soundboard painting consisting mostly of flowers, sometimes with fruit. Except for an insect now and then, the monkeys, people, angels, birds, and edibles that adorned Flemish boards were generally avoided. Like the Flemish, French borders were also blue; but either they consisted of wide scallops with a few arabesques in the corners, or more often, they were of a more complex nature—baroque *rinceau* scrolls or rope patterns. A blue ring—the same blue used to make the borders—usually encircled the gilded rose, and the maker's name was normally painted there in a dull yellow or pale mustard color. A large wreath of flowers surrounded the ring. Typically, a miniature scene consisting of a small island with a bird or two in a tree was painted on the soundboard, between the gap and the rose, facing the player. The tree is obviously dead, but live branches nevertheless issue forth from it, and sometimes a dull red glow can be seen in the end of the stump. The scene is a manifestation of the resurrection theme noted so often before; but here the motif of a dead tree bringing forth a live, singing harpsichord is given visual form. Often the bird was a goldfinch, the same resurrection symbol found on Flemish soundboards.[34]

Eighteenth-century French soundboards seem to have been much more carefully planned than the happy but dense profusion of motifs found on seventeenth-century French and Flemish boards. As seen in Plate 18, a ca. 1736 instrument by Henri Hemsch, the flowers are fewer, larger, riper, and more carefully spaced, with five or so in the area between the bentside and the 8' bridge, another five between the 8' and 4' bridges, three or four in the triangle of the 4' bridge, gap, and spine (also occupied by the rose and the bird scene), and three or four on the wrestplank. The painters were also careful to control the sweep of the eye by the direction in which the flowers pointed.[35] The style of these French artisans was more painterly that the crewel-like work of the Flemish decorators, and it is certain that they were better trained. Still, French soundboard-style painting was far from the sort of sophisticated brushwork of some contemporary easel painters. Instead, these decorators worked in a quick, almost impressionistic style, with a layering, rather than blending, of colors. Unlike the practice in the Ruckers and Couchet shops, the French builders did not have painters who worked for them; instead, harpsichords were hauled to a decorator's atelier for the soundboard painting.[36] Nevertheless, as was the practice of the Flemish decorators, their French counterparts cooperated with the builders by painting flower stems, bugs, and moths over scarf joints and flaws in the wood.

At this point in its construction the harpsichord case itself was finished but unpainted—in the white, in the parlance of the instrument builder—except for its soundboard painting, and what happened next was up to the customer. If he was content with one color, or the more usual two colors with the lighter on the inside, the builder normally supplied that service. In response to a query from a customer, Pascal Taskin, who was at that time working in the Blanchet shop, offered the choice of black, white, gray, blue, green, or red for the exterior;[37] but it is likely that builders were more accommodating than that, since a dark, almost black green, commonly and somewhat coarsely known as *merde d'oie,* and a light Chinese red or vermilion interior was a common combination. Gold bands, applied over the paint, would outline the bentside, cheek, tail, and interior of the lid, and the moldings would also be gilded. Usually this

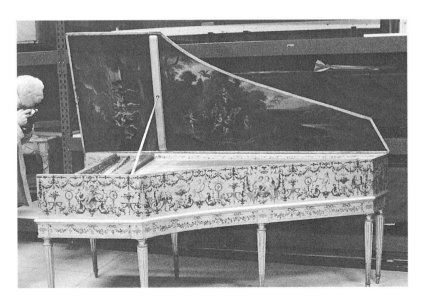

13-8a. The 1646 Andreas Ruckers/1756 Blanchet (?)/1780 Taskin in its final incarnation as a French harpsichord *mis à grand ravalement.* Paris, Musée de la Musique.

was real gold leaf, but sometimes cheaper bronzing powders were used instead. All that was required now was a table stand, which could be made in the builder's shop, but was probably furnished by a *menuisier*, a furniture maker who specialized in chairs and tables — a leg expert, in other words. The stand would be painted in the exterior color of the harpsichord, and parts

of it might also be gilded. The finishing was now complete and constituted the normal and usual decoration.

13-8b. A detail of the *vernis martin* decoraton. Perched on a comfortable cushion, an angelic putto plays his violin among the grotesques. Paris, Musée de la Musique.

Other customers required a more highly decorated instrument, and after the soundboard was attended to, floral garlands would be painted in the keywell, on the jackrail, and usually in the soundwell as well. The exterior of the case could then be finished in a variety of ways, including chinoiserie, painted grotesques, easel-style paintings, and *vernis martin,* where the entire case is gold leafed, and overpainted with colorful grotesques, garlands, putti, and *singeries* (scenes with monkeys imitating human behavior). Often a lid painting, sometimes by a well-known or fashionable painter such as Charles Natoire (1700–1777), would be provided. Similar finishes would also be supplied for precious Flemish instruments that had been rebuilt. A 1646 Andreas Ruckers, for example, started life as a nonaligned double-manual harpsichord with a chromatic bass. Its keyboards were aligned sometime during the first quarter of the century, and it was redecorated in *vernis martin* at that time. In 1756 the case was widened, and new keyboards, jacks, and registers were provided. Taskin strengthened the case and added *genouillères* and a fourth set of jacks quilled with *peau de buffle* in 1780. He also supplied a new Louis XVI stand. It is a strikingly beautiful harpsichord, and the expensive decoration pays homage to its Ruckers ancestry.

13-8c. A detail of the lid painting. Seated on the top of the rock, Apollo with his lyre joins in a concert with the nine muses. The locale is Mount Helicon, where Pegasus is seen on high. The spear-carrying figure on the left may be Bellerophon, the only mortal who rode the winged horse. Paris, Musée de la Musique.

Stands for such instruments could also be ornate. Aprons and cabriole legs lent themselves to elaborate carving, and sometimes the entire stand would be gilded (see the ca. 1749 Goujon, Illustration 13-5). The stands themselves were in one of the Louis styles, with the turned and fluted legs of the neoclassical Louis XVI stand coming after 1760 or so. The fancier stands

followed the trends of court furniture, but lagged behind by as much as a generation—an indication of the intense conservatism of harpsichord building. Eighteenth-century French furniture is famous—one might almost say notorious—for its curved surfaces; but excluding the bentside, the only part of the French harpsichord on which curves can be found is the stand. In the same way, marquetry and ormolu mounts, so characteristic of the ornate chests, desks, and tables fashionable among the rich and noble in mid-eighteenth-century Paris, are conspicuously absent from harpsichords.

THE BLANCHET-TASKIN DYNASTY[38]

After the Ruckerses and the Couchets, the Blanchets and the Taskins are probably the next best known of all harpsichord makers. The dynasty originated with Nicolas Blanchet, who was born in or near Rheims in 1660, and whose surviving harpsichords were discussed earlier in this chapter. By the age of twenty-six he was in Paris and married and three years later was admitted to the guild as a master. His first son, Nicolas Pierre, became a priest, but his second son, François-Etienne (ca. 1695–1761), followed him into the business, becoming a full partner in 1722. The Blanchet shop prospered more than just a little; evidently, Nicolas had a head for finance. In 1701 he had amassed enough discretionary cash to buy a sizeable annuity. In 1717, when he became treasurer of the guild, that organization showed a positive balance, perhaps for the first and last time. When he died in 1731 his business was worth a great deal of money.

François-Etienne married in 1722, the same year he became his father's partner. He seems to have inherited his father's Midas touch—his bride came with a sizeable dowry and a court connection. Two children were born to that marriage, but both appear to have died prematurely. His wife died in 1726, soon after the birth of the second child; but early in 1727, only three months later, François-Etienne married again, gaining another dowry almost as large as the first. This union also came with the opportunity to move the Blanchet shop to a large house with four floors and at least twenty rooms. François-Etienne and his second wife produced two children: Elizabeth Antoinette (b. 1729), and the son François-Etienne II (1730–66), who eventually followed his father and grandfather into harpsichord building. François-Etienne's second wife also died prematurely, in 1737. Although unlucky in wives, his fortunes as a builder continued to improve. In 1739 he was elected a *juré* of the

CHARACTERISTICS OF SEVENTEENTH- AND EIGHTEENTH-CENTURY FRENCH HARPSICHORDS COMPARED

	Seventeenth Century	Eighteenth Century
Case sides	Mostly intermediate	Mostly heavy
Case material	Usually hardwood — walnut	Usually softer wood — poplar, lime
Internal bracing	U-bracing, post-and-beam	Upper and lower braces
Building philosophy	Light	Heavy
Side-to-bottom joint	Sides around bottom	Sides on bottom
Bentside configuration	Roughly parabolic	Half bent, half straight
Soundboard barring	Usually across the bridge	Cutoff bar and ribs
Rose	Parchment, geometric	Metal, representational
Soundboard decoration	Many tight flowers	Fewer looser flowers
Moldings	Usually applied	Cut in
Compass	GG/BB–c^3 common	GG–e^3, expanding to FF–f^3
Scale	12–$13''$	$14''$
Number of keyboards	One or two	Two
Coupler	Yes	Yes
Exterior finish	Painted or natural wood	Painted, gold bands
Stand	Twist-leg with stretchers	Louis XV or XVI, no stretchers

guild, a sign of the esteem in which he and his instruments were held.[39] In 1752 he was appointed *facteur des clavessins du Roi.* Already occupied with *ravalements,* shop time now became consumed by the maintenance of the many harpsichords at Versailles, and the production of new instruments must have slowed down considerably.

There are only four extant harpsichords bearing François-Etienne's name. The first is a 1733 with an FF–e^3 compass (France, private ownership). This instrument is similar to the 1730 mentioned above, but its interest lies in its decoration, a symphony of *singeries,* birds, and grotesques on a gold-bordered grayish-white ground, supposedly painted by the artist Christophe Huet (1700–1759), who also decorated the room in which the harpsichord still resides.[40] The instrument was returned to the Blanchet shop in 1745 for the addition of an f^3, but other than that, it has never left its home. The 1733 François-Etienne, seen in Plate 19, is generally regarded as one of the most beautifully decorated harpsichords in existence.[41]

The next extant instrument by François-Etienne is a 1736 (unknown ownership), one of two known eighteenth-century French harpsichords with only one keyboard. Dowd, who examined the instrument closely, reports with a builder's insight what he calls "a frightening example of an eighteenth-century craftsman's miserly use of wood." Evidently in possession of two pieces of oak, neither one of which was long enough to use for a wrestplank, François-Etienne joined them in the middle.[42] A 1746 (Versailles) is the first of the extant Blanchets to point the way toward the heavier instruments that Taskin would learn to build. Dowd characterizes its tone as "very full and rich," more complex than the sound of the earlier Blanchets and similar to the Taskin instruments to follow.[43] Its decoration is standard eighteenth-century French: a *merde d'oie* exterior with a vermilion interior, and the usual gold bands, on a Louis XV stand painted and gilded en suite. Little is known of the last surviving François-Etienne, which is in private ownership in Paris.

François-Etienne II began working for his father as a journeyman before he was twenty years old. He became a guild member in 1751 but did not marry until four years later. He inherited the shop in 1761, at his father's death, and soon after took on a Belgian journeyman already in his thirties named Pascal-Joseph Taskin (1723–93), instructing him in the ways of building harpsichords in the Blanchet tradition. A 1765 double by François-Etienne II (Japan, City of Hamamatsu) is the last extant harpsichord to bear the Blanchet name. Dowd notes that it is even closer to the coming Taskin models than the 1746.[44] Although the soundboard is beautifully painted, a joint in one of the planks is disguised by a flower stem painted at right angles to the spine. This last surviving Blanchet is also the first to have a buff stop.[45] In 1765, like his father, François-Etienne II was elected a *juré* of the guild; but he died the following year, at age thirty-six, leaving behind his wife, two daughters, and a young son, Armand-François-Nicolas (1763–1818).

Six months later Pascal Taskin became a master, and a month after that he married François-Etienne II's widow, thereby acquiring not only a wife but also a booming harpsichord business, a large house with shop, and the position of *facteur des clavessins du Roi*.[46] He took three-year-old Armand-François-Nicolas under his wing, and after his apprenticeship his stepson went on to work in the family business that could now be traced back to his great-grandfather.[47] Taskin was also assisted by three of his nephews, Pascal-Joseph Taskin II (1750–1829),[48] Henri-Joseph Taskin (1779–1832), and Lambert Taskin (dates unknown). Taskin and his associates took the shop to ever greater heights, making new instruments that in reputation outshone even those of his illustrious master. The *ravalements* that had occupied the shop since the beginning of the century continued,[49] with not only Flemish but also French instruments undergoing updating and refurbishing.[50] In 1774 Taskin assumed the position of *Garde des instruments de musique de Chambre du Roi* (Keeper of the King's Instruments), a post evidently distinct from *facteur des clavessins du Roi*. Since at least part of that work had to be done at the

13-9. This rich and powerful 1746 instrument by François-Etienne Blanchet is a harbinger of the sort of complex sound preferred by the French in the latter part of the century. Versailles, Musée National du Château de Versailles.

château at Versailles,[51] Taskin arranged for it to be performed by Pascal-Joseph II, and in 1777, to avoid the time-consuming carriage rides between Versailles and Paris, had him move there. Like so many of his illustrious predecessors, Taskin served as a *juré* in 1775–76, but he was the last harpsichord builder to do so. The instrument-maker's guild was abolished in February 1776.[52]

Taskin is survived by nine or possibly ten instruments (a 1767 in Bucharest, National Museum of Art, has not been fully accepted as a genuine Taskin), all doubles except for a single and two octave spinets. Without a doubt the most famous of these is the second of two survivors from 1769 (Edinburgh, Russell Collection), a superb example of a late FF–f^3 plus buff French double. It was the harpsichord consulted by the piano firm of Érard when it decided to revive the instrument at the end of the nineteenth century, and it has been the harpsichord most copied by modern builders. Its sound is smooth and seductive, and, as Dowd describes the 1765 Blanchet, also powerful and complex. Its case decoration, though not original, is an example of the basic French finish: a light green exterior with a salmon interior and the usual gold bands and moldings, on a Louis XV stand finished en suite. The soundboard painting, executed by the decorator that Sheridan Germann identifies as the "Earlier Taskin Painter," is particularly beautiful.[53] The rose and wreath can be seen in Plate 20.

Taskin's next survivor, from 1770 (New Haven, Yale Collection), is equally beautiful, both in sound and in decoration, although the exterior painting is late nineteenth or early twentieth century (see Plate 17). Following the example of the late Blanchet instruments, it is both deeper and heavier than his earlier work. For some reason Taskin decided not to use a rose; instead, in its place, he carved a shallow hemisphere into the soundboard and had his decorator put the initials "PT" in that area in script. Around this, however, is the expected *Pascal Taskin élève de Blanchet* and the floral wreath. This harpsichord is similar to the 1769, but the gap is wide enough to take four registers. Evidently, Taskin had started putting a fourth register quilled with *peau de buffle* into some of his instruments around this time and simply decided to make a four-register gap standard. Even three-register harpsichords were sometimes fitted with *peau de buffle* instead of bird quill on the back 8', and it must have been such an instrument that Charles Burney saw in France, at the home of the organist and composer Claude Balbastre, when he remarked that one of the unisons of Balbastre's rebuilt Ruckers was of buff.[54] If only three registers were required, as in the 1770, the guides would simply be made a little wider.[55] Taskin's almost fanatical attention to detail can also be seen in his jacks. Although of normal construction, he cut slots in all the jacks to lighten them, increasing the size of the slot, and therefore the lightness of the jack, as they ascend into the treble. That the lower-manual was fitted with a set of double-tongued *cembalo angelico* jacks has already been noted.[56] One set of tongues was quilled in *peau de buffle*. The 1770 also has a double buff stop: the pads are arranged so that they can mute either 8' string.

Two trapezoidal octave spinets (New Haven, Yale Collection; Paris, private collection) date from the year 1778. It is strange to think that little octave instruments were still being made at this late date, and even stranger that Taskin built two of them in the same year. Both are lavishly decorated, and both were given an EE–f³ compass.[57] The low EE is problematical; it could have been intended to be tuned down to CC, or its purpose could have been to improve the tone of the FF. It has also been suggested that it was done for visual balance, giving each end of the keyboard two naturals after a cluster of three sharps. Taskin's next survivor, dated 1782 (Portugal, private ownership), has a Ruckers rose and is "signed" by Ruckers on the namebatten, although "Fait par Pascal Taskin a Paris, 1782" appears on the wrestplank. The 1786 (London, Victoria and Albert Museum) is a *rara avis,* a miniature harpsichord (although to call it a miniature may be misleading, since it does have a normal scale and string lengths), likely made for a child's hand — and one with money, since it is beautifully decorated in chinoiserie and sits on a richly carved and gilded Louis XVI stand. With only one manual and a 2×8′ plus buff disposition, its keys are 2½″ narrower per octave than Taskin's normal span. It was given a full compass, however, EE–f³.

13-10. Pascal Taskin's 1769 double is probably the best-known harpsichord in the world. Edinburgh, Russell Collection of Early Keyboard Instruments, University of Edinburgh.

The last extant Taskin is another double, dated 1788 (Milan, Museo degli Strumenti Musicali), also with an EE–f³ compass. Though obviously late French and made by the master, it was given an Andreas Ruckers rose (carved in wood, of all things, and gilded) and a "vaguely 'Flemish' soundboard painting."[58] Thus, with this last survivor, the illustrious Blanchet/Taskin dynasty ends with the counterfeiting of a Ruckers harpsichord. This may say more about the staying power of the Ruckers name in eighteenth-century France than it does about the chicanery involved.

Taskin was not only one of the great builders of the harpsichord, but one of its most distinguished innovators as well. He is credited with establishing the use of buffalo hide as a plectrum material, and the development of *genouillères* and machines as a means of changing registration. He also built pianos — his earliest seems to have been made in 1780 — but by that time many of his Parisian colleagues were doing the same thing. Taskin was an exceptional self-promoter of his instruments and services, and it was his practice to glue his business card to any instrument that went through his shop, whether for a *grand ravalement* or for a requilling. He shamelessly traded on the illustrious Blanchet name, indicating on his card that he was *élève de Blanchet* (a student of Blanchet), and went so far as to sign his earlier instruments *Pascal Taskin élève de Blanchet*. Of an experimental bent, he focused his analytical eye on many of the elements of harpsichord building. He rounded the edges of the structural members of his instruments, probably in an effort to reduce unnecessary weight; in fact, he was so fond of this stratagem that he even used it on his *ravalements*. He increased the mass of his liners, but by rounding them avoided unnecessarily stiffening his soundboards at their boundaries. He rounded the edges of his 4′ hitchpin rails too and undercut them to increase the compliance of the soundboard in those areas. He curved his cutoff bar to match the curve of the 8′ bridge, undoubtedly in an attempt to refine the vibrating area of the treble section of the soundboard. In his 1770 harpsichord he also changed the shape of his bridges and nuts, from the serviceable but pedestrian triangular shape inherited from Flemish models, to a more free-flowing form, concave on one side and convex on the other.[59]

OTHER PARIS BUILDERS

With well over one hundred builders known to have worked in Paris in the eighteenth century, one might expect that city to have produced an enormous number of harpsichords. But Koster's formula (a builder and his workers could be expected to manufacture five instruments a year for twenty years) does not apply here. The *ravalement* of Flemish harpsichords and the upgrading of even relatively new French instruments took such a toll in time that the production of new instruments might have been only a quarter of what could otherwise have been expected. Also, one senses a growing reliance by everyone, not just royalty and nobility, on the skills of the professional builders to maintain and tune instruments. Consequently, despite the relative dearth of new French harpsichords, there must have been enough business to keep all those craftsmen going. Still, as the Ruckerses and Couchets did in Antwerp a century earlier, the Blanchets and the Taskins dominated the harpsichord business in Paris, and that appears to be reflected in the numbers of surviving instruments. Only the Hemsches, with eight extant, and the Goermanses, with eleven, left anything like the numbers of their more famous colleagues.

The brothers Henri (1700–1769) and Guillaume (1709–66) Hemsch were born in Germany, near Cologne, and made their way to Paris when Henri was about twenty years old. Henri is survived by five doubles, but he must have been a prolific maker: there were fourteen harpsichords under way in his shop at the time of his death, an unusually large number.[60] In 1746 he was elected a guild *juré*, an indication of the respect in which he was held. Henri's best-known instrument is a ca. 1736[61] with an FF–e^3 compass (Boston, Museum of Fine Arts), seen in Plate 21 (see Plate 18 for the soundboard). Its fame rests not so much on its worth as a musical instrument (although it is a fine harpsichord), or its soundboard painting (by the "later Blanchet painter"),[62] or its charming Italianate lid painting of Apollo and the muses. But, in fact, both that decoration and the lid painting were done in the nineteenth century, probably in the same atelier that redecorated the 1770 Taskin.[63] The ornate carved and gilded stand is original. Henri's other four instruments are standard French doubles, and there is no need to rehearse their details. Their dates and locations are 1751, 1754, and 1756 (private ownership in France), and 1761 (Paris, Musée de la Musique). Guillaume's extant instruments, 1763, 1766, and a third of unknown date, are also in private collections.

Jean Goermans (1703–77) was also born in Germany, and like so many of his countrymen went elsewhere to seek fame and fortune. He was in Paris by 1730, the date at which he was admitted to the guild as a master, and following long established custom, he married in that year. His colleagues and customers knew him as Jacques Germain, the name he adopted in France.[64] Of his seven children, one, Jacques (1740–89), became a builder. Jean is survived by eight instruments. The 1748 (Philadelphia, private ownership), 1750 (Oxford, Bate Collection), 1765 (private ownership), and 1768 (location unknown) are all standard French doubles needing no further description. The 1754 (New York, Metropolitan Museum of Art) was converted into a piano sometime in the nineteenth century, and its upper manual was simply covered with a board. The 1764 (Edinburgh, Russell Collection) is one of the many instruments worked over by Taskin. It was discussed earlier and is the harpsichord whose rose Taskin changed from an IG to an IC in 1783–84. An instrument of Jean's dated 1738 (Stockholm, Musikmuseet) is perhaps the only known octave harpsichord made by a French builder.[65] It is a delightful little miniature of four and a half octaves, done in chinoiserie on a pale vermilion ground.

Jacques Germain, Jr., was admitted as master in 1766 and set up his own shop. Three of his instruments are extant, two of which, 1771 and 1774, are standard doubles in private collections.[66] The third, 1785 (Vermillion, Shrine to Music Museum), is also a standard double with four registers, and has achieved some renown in the United States as the only antique French double west of the East Coast. It is an outstanding example of the full, rich, powerful, and complex tone of the late French product and has been recorded many times. Its case decoration is not original, but was done early in the twentieth century. The lid painting is nineteenth century. Although a complete recitation of its modern history would be out of place here, it is worth noting that instruments such as this magnificent example were so little thought of in the early twentieth century that the American builder John Challis was able to purchase it in 1950 for a reported $150.[67]

13-11. This 1785 harpsichord by Jacques Germain is considered one of the finest examples of the late French instrument. Vermillion, America's Shrine to Music Museum.

There were, of course, many other builders in Paris. Some of the better-known names are Benoit Stehlin (before 1732–74), Sebastian Érard (1752–1831), Jean Marie Dedeban (dates unknown), Pierre Bellot (ca. 1675–1732–47) and his two sons Pierre II (dates unknown) and Louis (dates unknown), Antoine Vater (1689–after 1759), Jacques Joachim Swanen (fl. 1783–1816),[69] and the earlier-mentioned Jean-Claude Goujon. But it would be beyond the scope of this book to attempt to enumerate and describe their instruments, which, all in all, were not very different from those coming from the Blanchet, Taskin, Hemsch, and Germain shops.

LYONS AND ELSEWHERE

After Paris, the only other city that seemed to support a harpsichord-building center was Lyons, which, it will be remembered, was also an active area in the previous century. *Boalch III* counts eighteen makers doing business in Lyons in the 1700s — a far cry from the well over one hundred then in Paris, but with something of the same ratio in both places from one century to another. To put it another way, harpsichord building thrived in Paris and, to a lesser extent, in Lyons as well.

The principal builders in Lyons were Pierre Donzelague (1668–1747), the brothers Collesse *l'aîné* (the elder, fl. 1763–70) and Joseph (died 1776), and another German maker, Christian Kroll (dates unknown). Pierre was the son of a François Donzelague, who was born in Bruges, Belgium, but who moved to Aix-en-Provence, where he built harpsichords and where Pierre was born. He must have been trained by his father, since he arrived in Lyons when he was twenty, to take up a triple career as builder, singer in the newly formed opera company, and bass gambist and continuo player.[70] Pierre may be survived by as many as seven instruments, but only two can be definitely attributed to him. One, a 1711, is in private hands; but the other, a 1716 (Lyons, Musée Lyonnais des Arts Décoratifs), is fairly well known and can be seen in Plate 22. The original decoration of both these instruments is ornate, suggestive of seventeenth-century French practices; but they both have original FF–f³ compasses and buff stops (although the one on the

> ### HARD TIMES FOR THE GERMAINES
>
> The Germaines did not fare well in the final years of their lives. Pierre Hardouin[68] relates that starting around 1770, Jacques fell victim to a gradual paralysis and had to turn over his business to his foreman, Jean Hermès, who soon after married Jacques's youngest daughter. Relations between Jacques, now sixty-seven years old, and his new son-in-law turned sour, and Jacques's wife Lucie became so disturbed by the dysfunctional relationship that she began to lose her mind. Lucie's screams and Jacques's doddering so alarmed their children that they attempted to have their parents declared incompetent. Jacques died before this could be accomplished, but Lucie was held to be unable to handle her own affairs, and her assets were used to place her in a house where she was cared for until her death in 1783. At that time the remainder of her estate was distributed to her children.
>
> In the meantime, Jacques's builder-son, also named Jacques, was living out of wedlock with a young woman named Marguerite André and her son. They had a daughter together in 1787, at which time Jacques married Marguerite; but except for telling one of his brothers, he kept the union secret. Two years later he died, suddenly, at the age of forty-nine. His brother-in-law, Jean Hermès, who was still running the deceased father's shop, not knowing of the marriage, thought the considerable estate of his brother-in-law would come to him; but the details of the marriage were revealed, the widow Marguerite and her children got the money, and Hermès was thwarted.

1716 may not be original). The 1716 also has the half-curved, half-straight bentside typical of the mature Parisian style. That these provincial instruments should have these features, particularly the five-octave compass, before they are found in Parisian harpsichords is difficult to explain. Donzelague may have been something of an innovator.

Like Pierre Donzelague, the Collesse brothers, as well as their father Jacques, were both builders and performers.[71] Joseph is survived by a 1768 instrument (France, private collection) and a 1775 (Paris, Musée de la Musique). Despite the fact that this last instrument is dated a year before Joseph's death, he died before it could be completed, and that task was undertaken in 1777 by the builder Jean Franky. Looking very much like a Paris harpsichord finished a step beyond two basic colors (black and light green, in this case) and gold bands, the soundwell, keywell, and jackrail are also decorated, with swags of flowers on a light gray ground. But there are some anomalies. The stop levers, on the wrestplank, do not project through the nameboard,[72] and the soundboard painting has neither a bird scene nor a rose. In place of the former is an attractive boating vignette, and for the latter is substituted a painting of a bouquet of mixed flowers (including roses) in a vase. There is another instrument, dated 1760, possibly by Joseph, in a private collection in Canada. Only one extant harpsichord is ascribed to Collesse *l'aîné*, a 1768 (France, private ownership).

Christian Kroll is another shadowy builder. His dates and his training are unknown; in fact, about all that is known about him is that he worked in Lyons between 1770 and 1774.[73] Four surviving instruments are attributed to him, all with the late EE–f³ compass. Three, two from 1770 and one from 1774, are in private collections, and a 1779 is in Paris, Musée Grévin. Little is known of these instruments, but both the 1774 and the 1779 have the old-fashioned trefoil-carved key fronts.

Outside Paris and Lyons there was little other harpsichord-building activity in France. Strasbourg had a few builders, the best known of whom is Johann Heinrich Silbermann, the nephew of the more famous Gottfried Silbermann of Freiburg, Germany.[74] Johann Heinrich made clavichords and pianos, but in plucked keyboards he is survived by fourteen bentside spinets, all five-octave instruments in

13-12. The soundboard of a 1775 harpsichord from Lyons by Joseph Collesse. The size and tightness of the flowers are suggestive of an earlier style. The vase of flowers substitutes for a rose. Paris, Musée de la Musique.

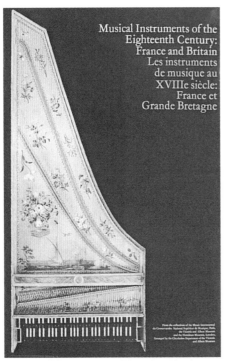

Musical Instruments of the Eighteenth Century: France and Britain Les instruments de musique au XVIIIe siècle: France et Grande Bretagne

From the collections of the Musée Instrumental du Conservatoire National Supérieur de Musique, Paris, the Victoria and Albert Museum, and the Horniman Museum, London. Arranged by the Circulation Department of the Victoria and Albert Museum

13-13. This ca. 1770 bentside spinet by Johann Heinrich Silbermann of Strasbourg looks quite different from the high-style instruments with Parisian decoration. Basel, Historisches Museum.

natural wood. A spinet from ca. 1770 (Basel, Historisches Museum), with book-matched veneers, a floating-panel lid, gracefully carved cabriole legs, and a variant of the Silbermann rose is fairly typical of his work. The instrument has an excellent sound with an overwhelmingly wondrous bass.[75]

Three makers worked in Marseilles, on the Mediterranean Sea: Jean and Louis Bas (dates unknown for both), who together are survived by three harpsichords (1737, 1781, and 1778–86) and two spinets (1783, 1786), and someone named Basse[76] (dates unknown), who left a bentside spinet of 1791.[77] Louis Bas is perhaps better known for a piano of 1781 (Vermillion, Shrine to Music Museum). With a Cristofori action, including an inverted wrestplank, it is the earliest known French grand piano.

THE LATE FRENCH HARPSICHORD

Sometime early in the second half of the eighteenth century a few builders began to experiment with knee- and foot-controlled contrivances intended to shift stops quickly and to make dynamic changes. The earliest record of one of these devices was in 1758, when an instrument with a *genouillère*-operated machine by a builder named Weltman (or Wittman; dates unknown) was advertised for sale. A year later Weltman presented a harpsichord equipped with such a machine stop to the French Académie des Sciences.[78] Other makers also produced machine stops, but the only sort commonly found on surviving instruments is the one invented by Pascal Taskin in 1768.[79] Taskin devised a system of rods, levers, cranks, springs, and rockers, with the external portions of the mechanism mounted on the exterior of the instrument's left cheek. Five (or rarely, six) knee pommels attached to the stand, positioned in back of the front apron (under the keyboard), articulated with the machinery through holes in the instrument's bottom.

It is likely that the French machine stop was always found in conjunction with a fourth register quilled in *peau de buffle*. This somewhat soft and woolly material, quite different from the hard cow leather sometimes now used in the Low Countries, England, and elsewhere as an alternate to bird quill, was adapted for the harpsichord by Pascal Taskin in the 1760s,[80] perhaps as a means of utilizing the fourth register in a *grand ravalement* Flemish nonaligned double. Taskin quilled the register in this soft leather and set it behind the normal 8′, 4′, 8′. It plucked the same string as the back 8′, but not, of course, at the same time, and its position and properties produced special qualities. First, because the leather plucked deep into the string, its tone was less colored than the other stops. Second, because the plectra were wider and softer than the usual bird quill, they produced a sound with fewer higher partials. And finally, the plectra were adjusted more to brush the strings than to pluck them, thus opening up the possibility of small dynamic changes through finger velocity. At any rate, the *peau de buffle* was the quietest stop on the instrument.

Each of the three normal lower-manual registers (the back 8′, the 4′, and the *peau de buffle*) was under the control of a notched pommel, which, when raised by the player's knee, turned that stop off and allowed it to be locked into that position by shifting it to the side. A fourth pommel, on the extreme

---

ANOTHER LOOK AT THE *PEAU DE BUFFLE*

Twentieth-century scholars and players have made much of the supposed inability of *peau de buffle* to make the dynamic nuances claimed for it, and the need for extremely good adjustment for it to work at all. Yet the *Encyclopédie méthodique* of 1782 described the stop in glowing terms, stating that one could "swell at will by pressing more or less strongly on the keys." It also remarked that rather than pluck the strings, it caressed them, producing "passionate, tender, or expiring sounds."[81] In fact, the authors go on for several pages, extolling the beauty, reliability, and effectiveness of plectra of *peau de buffle*, stating that a harpsichord so equipped was far superior to a piano. In a moment of unintended prophesy, they recognized that "while in the establishment of the vendor they [pianos] are able to please and seduce, but if one casts an attentive glance into the interior, their complication will alarm one in an instant."[82]

Even allowing for the hyperbole of the *encyclopédists*, it seems obvious that the *peau de buffle* was considered a worthwhile addition to the harpsichord. There was no sign anywhere of any discontent with it, nor was there any suggestion that it needed constant attention. On the contrary, it was claimed that quills of *peau de buffle* lasted far longer than bird quills—a figure of five years (and counting) is mentioned—and it was suggested that this made them ideal for instruments going to the provinces, where little or no maintenance could be provided. Clearly, the efficacy of this soft leather seems to have been misunderstood.

---

right, raised the *peau de buffle* jacks off the backs of the key levers, to remove unnecessary weight (which would make the touch a little weightier) from the keys. Hence, when not in use, the *peau de buffle* pommel would be in the locked position with the keys free of their jacks. The fifth pommel, found on the extreme left, was the machine stop, which, when raised quickly, took off everything already in the on position and substituted the *peau de buffle,* thus allowing sudden dynamic changes from forte to piano and back; but when raised slowly it removed the registers one at a time and produced a diminuendo. The reverse, of course, would provide a crescendo.[83] Accordingly, the player could diminuendo from the full 2×8′, 1×4′ harpsichord to the soft, pianolike sound of the *peau de buffle,* which itself was subject to further dynamic control through the

fingers. The machine stop also retracted the front 8′ jacks, which, equipped with side dampers, would have allowed its strings to vibrate sympathetically with the *peau de buffle,* lending a shimmer to the already ethereal sound of the soft leather. Finally, since each register was under "knee control," dynamic nuance could be supplied by advancing or retreating the quill from the string just a bit, providing the player with the opportunity to shade cadences as a clavichordist or pianist might. A sixth pommel, present in only a few survivors, was used to couple the manuals; normally they were linked by hand.[84]

Accordingly, the late-eighteenth-century French harpsichord was capable of exquisite dynamic control as well as its usual variety of tone colors. Frank Hubbard thought that these dynamic accoutrements served the instrument and its music poorly, and his words have had a profound influence on our appreciation of the effectiveness of those devices. He said, "More than any other style the baroque depends on the conflict of substance and medium . . . upon hearing its music we sense the endless tension between the implied nuance of the line and the meticulous but rigid statement. To express every implication is to deflate the music utterly. Yet this is exactly what the French set out to do."[85] In the same vein, Edwin Ripin remarked that

13-14. The *genouillères* of this 1646 Andreas Ruckers / 1756 Blanchet (?) / 1780 Taskin can clearly be seen behind the apron of the stand. From left to right: machine, 4′, 8′, coupler, *peau de buffle,* and lifters for *peau de buffle* jacks. This is one of the few survivors to have a sixth, coupler pommel. Paris, Musée de la Musique.

"nothing could be farther from the true spirit of the music of Couperin, Bach, Handel, Rameau, or Scarlatti than the addition of extrinsic crescendos and decrescendos."[86]

But Hubbard and Ripin may have missed the point. When the editors of the *Encyclopédie méthodique* discussed the harpsichord in 1785, they mentioned Scarlatti and Rameau, but they also named Alberti, Mütel, Wagenseil, and Schobert as its premier composers and praised the "grace and lightness" they had brought to harpsichord music. The older style, they stated, was more like organ music.[87] The fresh breath of a new style was in the air after the 1760s, one in which crescendo and diminuendo were part and parcel of the expressive design. Players, and hence builders, were far more interested in contemporary music than they were in the fusty, rigid concoctions of the past, and the late French harpsichord was an excellent instrument on which that music could be expressed.[88] In fact, despite the change in musical style and the piano's built-in ability to make those dynamic nuances with fingers alone, it took hammer-action instruments much longer to achieve popularity in France than they did in England and Germany. The French believed that they had brought the harpsichord to perfection and did not easily give it up.

SUMMING UP

The production of new harpsichords was not the only activity of French builders and, in some cases, may have been distinctly secondary. The Blanchets and Taskins spent a considerable amount of their time tuning, maintaining, voicing, and quilling the many instruments at the château de Versailles, and all builders seemed to do a lot more tuning and maintaining than was previously the case. But mostly, it was *ravalement* that took the time away from new construction. Ruckers and Couchet instruments were rebuilt everywhere in Europe, but nowhere with the consistency and amount of effort as in France. In fact, it was those century-old Flemish products that defined the French harpsichord of the 1700s. Within thirty years, the noble clavecin of Louis Couperin, Jean-Henri d'Anglebert, and Jacques Champion de Chambonnières, with its light, lutelike construction, thin walnut case with U-shaped bracing, cross-braced soundboard, intermediate scale, and marquetry decoration, was transformed. The French harpsichord was now heavily built and heavily reinforced, with Flemish soundboard bracing, a long scale, and a painted and gilded decoration; but it still retained the aligned keyboards, shove coupler, leathered registers, and beautifully crafted keyboards of the native French product. In the process, the true tone of the Flemish harpsichord was inevitably compromised, and what resulted was a quality half-Flemish and half–something new; but it was a powerful amalgam, creating a lush, complex, highly colored, even romantic timbre.

Not only Flemish, but old French harpsichords were rebuilt as well. With the export of Flemish instruments in the first half of the seventeenth century and the production of Internationally inspired native French clavecins in the second half, the eighteenth century opened with a large stock of old instruments that were obsolete in their compasses and in the alignment of their keyboards. The choice of building new instruments or rebuilding old ones probably seemed fairly clear to Nicolas Blanchet and his colleagues, and with their skills in *ravalement,* they succeeded in turning once cherished but now outmoded harpsichords into up-to-date instruments whose worth almost went beyond value. As a 1767 encyclopedia noted, "A harpsichord by Ruckers or Couchet, carefully altered and enlarged, with jacks, slides, and keyboards by Blanchet, is today considered a very precious thing."[89]

Was it really that precious — that is to say, was there some ineffable quality of "Ruckers-ness" or "Couchet-ness" that survived the process of enlarging and strengthening the case, adding soundboard wood, changing the scale, widening the compass, respacing the strings, moving the nuts, and replacing the action? Or were they — the players, the listeners, and particularly the buyers — simply taken in by the hype that surrounded those two godlike names? Undoubtedly, it was more than just a little of the first, but perhaps mostly the second. Had it not been, would the builders have been able to succeed with all the forgeries and counterfeits they produced? Like the buying public at any time, people were not all that knowledgeable. Told it was a genuine Ruckers by a seemingly reputable source, it is quite likely they were willing to believe it. Bragging rights were probably more important than a "genuine" Ruckers sound, although for the most part the builders attempted to conserve as much of the original quality as possible. And like Goujon, as good builders, they were perfectly capable of turning out excellent instruments, whether under their own names or with a purloined or counterfeited Ruckers rose in the soundboard.

Ravalement continued to occupy French builders right up to the Revolution. The Ruckers and Couchet instruments influenced builders in England and Germany too, but their harpsichords were not called *mis à grand ravalement,* which is to say they made no attempt to connect their instruments with those of the Flemish masters. Nor, for the most part, did they attempt to palm their work off as anyone else's. Clearly, the effect of the Flemish instrument in France was profound and, just as clearly, unprecedented. But it also marked the swan song of the indigenous French harpsichord.

The inclusion of the *peau de buffle* and the machine stop with *genouillères* into the French harpsichord has been denigrated in modern times, often viewed as decadent encrustations that somehow compromised the inherent nobility of the instrument. But French builders, perhaps more than those of other countries, have always been sensitive to the needs of the music, and it is still a truism that nothing suits French music like a French instrument. These craftsmen did not change the basic character of the harpsichord; instead, they gave it greater capabilities and the means to express contemporary music properly. In this they were no different from the Italians who transformed the sixteenth-century harpsichord with its $1{\times}8'$, $1{\times}4'$ iron-strung disposition into the classic $2{\times}8'$ brass-strung form in the seventeenth, or the seventeenth-century German makers who equipped their instruments with a variety of tone-altering registers, or the earlier French makers who developed the flexibility of the two-manual harpsichord with shove coupler. In providing their harpsichords with these appurtenances, the eighteenth-century builders were not attempting to compete with the piano, in vain or otherwise; they were simply trying to give their customers instruments that could play the music they wanted to hear.

[*14*]

THE LOW COUNTRIES IN
THE POST-RUCKERS ERA

*T*HE SLAUGHTER of the Thirty Years' War finally came
to an end in 1648, with the signing of the Peace of Westphalia.
One of the conditions of this treaty, however, was that Amsterdam's economic growth be stimulated at the expense of Antwerp's. Accordingly, the Scheldt River was closed to Antwerp,
denying that city access to the North Sea and severely crippling
its ability to export its goods. Traveling through Antwerp in the
1770s, Charles Burney described it as a virtual ghost town and
noted that the Scheldt, which formerly harbored ships from all
over the world, was now bereft of even a fishing boat.[1] Less than
ten years after the signing of the treaty, both Andreas Ruckers II
and Ioannes Couchet would pass away, effectively bringing that
great dynasty to an end. With its major builders gone, and with
no ability to export its once famous product by sea, harpsichord
making in Antwerp slowed down considerably, a victim of both
changing tastes and geopolitics. Undoubtedly, many Antwerp
craftsmen immigrated to the now favored Amsterdam, in the
north Netherlands (the modern country of the Netherlands),
which, while it could boast of only eleven harpsichord makers in
the seventeenth century, now counted twenty-five.[2] In contrast,
Antwerp, Brussels, The Hague, Leiden, Middelburg, Utrecht,
and other cities in the Low Countries could support no more
than a few builders each.[3] Obviously, the construction of harpsichords was no longer a major activity in this part of Europe.
Nevertheless, for whatever reason — perhaps chief among them

the almost complete lack of competition — a few well-respected builders were active there.

ANTWERP

Chief among these builders was Johann Daniel Dulcken, the patriarch and best-known member of the Dulcken dynasty.[4] There is little information about the Dulckens, other than that they moved around a great deal and they liked to name their male children Johann or some variation thereof. Johann (or Johan or Joannes) Daniel Dulcken (1706–57) was born in Germany, but by 1738, at the age of thirty-two, he had set up shop in Antwerp. At some point prior to that he was in Maastricht (in the southern tip of the Netherlands), where his eldest son Johann Lodewijk (or Jan Louis, or Louis) the elder (1733/34– after 1793) was born. Both Johann Lodewijk the elder and Johann Daniel's other son, Johannes (or Joannes) (1742–75), became builders. Johann Daniel died fairly young, at the age of fifty-one; nevertheless, he is survived by ten instruments, all built in Antwerp. Burney mentioned him, calling him the greatest Antwerp builder after the Ruckerses.[5]

Johann Daniel's son Johann Lodewijk the elder moved about. In 1755 he was in Amsterdam, and a year later he married. Between 1761 and 1765 he moved to Middelburg, and he may have gone to Antwerp in 1774. He also may have gone to France, since there was a Louis Dulcken working in Paris from 1783 to 1793. After Johann Daniel's death in 1757 his younger son Johannes, then twenty-one, moved to Brussels with his mother, where the two of them attempted rather unsuccessfully to carry on his father's business. Nine years later, in 1771, Johannes was in the The Hague's North Sea port of Scheveningen, where he married. He died at the age of thirty-six, but one of his instruments is extant. Johann Lodewijk the elder's son, Johan [*sic*] Lodewijk the younger (1761–after 1835), was born in Amsterdam, just before his father moved to Middelburg. Also trained as a maker, he was called to Munich, perhaps as early as 1781, as a builder to the Bavarian court, where he spent the rest of his life.[6] Johan Lodewijk the younger had a son who followed him into the business, which by that time consisted entirely of piano making.

Johann Daniel's extant harpsichords consist of five singles: a ca. 1740 (Edinburgh, private collection), a 1745 (Newton Centre, Mass.), a 1747 (Antwerp, Vleeshuis Museum), a 1755 (Hamburg, private collection), and another 1755 (Rouen, private collection); and five doubles: a 1745 (Washington, D.C., Smithsonian Institution), another 1745 (Vienna, Kunsthistorisches

Baptized	Other Names	Dates	Where He Lived
Johann Daniel	Johan, Joannes	1706–57	Germany, Maastricht, Antwerp
Johann Lodewijk the elder	Johan, Jan Louis, Louis	1733/34–after 1793	Maastricht, Amsterdam, Middelburg, Antwerp? Paris?
Johannes	Joannes	1742–75	Brussels, Scheveningen
Johan Lodewijk the younger	Louis?	1761–after 1835	Munich, Paris?

Museum), a ca. 1745 and a 1755 (both in Brussels, Musée Instrumental), and another 1755 (Brussels, private collection). The doubles are big instruments in every way. Superficially, they resemble eighteenth-century French harpsichords, but they are longer by as much as a foot and have narrower tails. They are all disposed 2×8′, 1×4′, with a five-octave FF–f³ compass, and they all have lute stops, a device which, while not used by the Ruckerses or their seventeenth-century Flemish colleagues, nevertheless had a long International tradition behind it.

Like contemporary English builders, Dulcken used the dogleg rather than the French coupler. He also placed the 4′ jacks last, farthest from the keyboard, putting the two sets of 8′ jacks adjacent to each other for maximum blend. Looking down at the jacks, one would first see the 8′ jacks for the "cut-through" lute register, then (in the gap) the 8′ dogleg jacks, the back 8′ jacks, and finally the 4′ jacks. Hence, the available resources on the lower manual were the back 8′ alone; the dogleg 8′ alone; the 4′ alone; back 8′ plus the dogleg 8′; one of the 8′s with the 4′; and 2×8′, 1×4′. The dogleg 8′ was always available on the upper manual, and the bright combination of lute plus 8′ dogleg could also be used; but the lute register could be played only if the back 8′ was disengaged, since both those sets of jacks plucked the same choir of 8′ strings. Thus, while this colorful registration had the unique ability to contrast two combinations of 2×8′ sounds—the more neutral back 8′ and 8′ dogleg, and the brighter 8′ dogleg and lute—what it could not provide was the ability to dialogue one 8′ choir against another. If the player attempted it, both 8′s would sound from the lower manual. Lute and back 8′ were also impossible, since both plucked the same strings; and lute and dogleg 8′ would both sound from the upper manual. On some of his doubles, Dulcken overcame this minor defect by allowing the upper manual to slide in and out, so that it could be withdrawn from the dogleg. It would then be possible to dialogue the lute against the dogleg 8′. Dulcken's registers were controlled by hand stops that ran under the wrest-plank and protruded through the nameboard, the same sort of scheme first seen in 1579, on the Theewes claviorganum.

At least one of Dulcken's survivors, the 1745 single, has one of its 8′ registers furnished with wide jacks with two tongues. One tongue is fitted with bird quills, in the normal manner; but the other, which swivels in the opposite direction, has plectra of hard leather (not *peau de buffle*). Hence, in its normal position, these jacks pluck the leftmost set of 8′ strings; but when moved to the right by a knee lever, they pluck the other choir of 8′ strings with the leather plectra. This instrument was modernized by Dulcken's student, Johann Peter Bull, in the 1770s or 1780s, and it is likely that the double jacks were supplied at that time. These dual-tongued jacks have been seen before, on the 1778 and 1780 harpsichords of Vincenzo Sodi and on the 1770 Taskin, so the idea of the *cembalo angelico* must have been in the air; but by operating Dulcken's with a *genouillère*, the performer could change colors and dynamic levels instantaneously. The back 8′ jacks are equipped with leather plectra, rather than the usual bird plectra, and although that might have been done by Bull as well, they could be original.

Dulcken's cases were constructed of poplar,[7] the traditional case material used by his illustrious Antwerp predecessors, but he added an internal feature of his own, an inner bentside — a frame inside the case, not touching the exterior bentside. The purpose of this additional framing is not clear. It is possible that Dulcken, like Cristofori, was attempting to relieve some of the strain on the soundboard; nevertheless, he later abandoned this

14-1. Section through Johann Daniel Dulcken's dogleg action. By using a dogleg configuration, the 8′ jack nearest the wrestplank could be played from either the upper or lower manual. © Macmillan Publishers Ltd., *The New Grove Musical Instruments Series: Early Keyboard Instruments*, 1989.

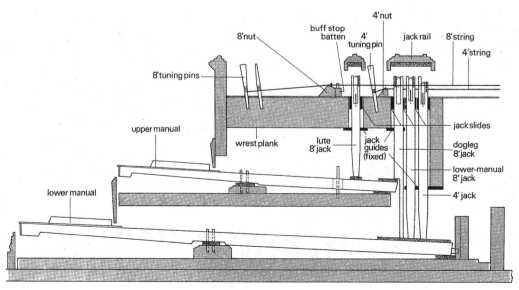

inner bentside.[8] His soundboards were barred in typical Flemish style, with a cutoff bar and ribs. His rose was a gilded metallic device, but not based on the harp-playing angel used by the Ruck-erses and so many of their fol-lowers. The soundboards were painted with flowers, and although these were executed in a more sophisticated manner than those found on the Ruckers and Couchet instruments,[9] the motifs are rather flat and mundane and not as painterly as contemporary

14-2. This long, dignified-looking 1745 Dulcken is a fine example of eighteenth-century Antwerp harpsichord making. Draw knobs protrude through the nameboard, just over the keys. Washington, D.C., Smithsonian Institution.

French boards. Without resurrection scenes or other subtexts, the purpose of the painting was purely one of floral decoration. Dulcken's keyboards did not seem to follow any particular tradition: he used both ebony naturals and ivory- or bone-topped sharps, and the reverse.[10] Regardless of the covering, the body of his sharps was made of a light fruitwood. His key fronts were normally covered with paper.

The five singles are not as unified as the doubles. Three of them originally had compasses of GG/BB–d³ (one has been enlarged to AA–e³, one GG/BB–e³, and the third still has the original range). The earliest single, the ca. 1740, is FF–e³, and the 1747 is FF–f³. Not surprisingly, these last two instruments are about 8′ long (about the length the doubles would be without the second keyboard), while those with the short octave are about 9″ shorter. It seems strange, and almost benighted, to find keyboards in the middle of the eighteenth century still constructed with short octaves, but once again we are reminded of the conservatism of players and builders, even those like Dulcken, who experimented with long cases and a special interior framing. But it is also clear that Dulcken was building for a clientele that either welcomed the short octave, was neutral about it, or was willing to put up with it.

Probably the best known of the Dulcken harpsichords in the United States is the 1745 double in the Smithsonian Institution.[11] Coincidentally, it is the only extant Dulcken still retaining its original black case painting and gold bands. Its bottom and wrestplank have been replaced, and its internal bentside was removed in restoration. The balustrade stand is not original. Like all the Dulckens, it is a rich and powerful-sounding harpsichord, with a pungent, singing tone. It has been copied extensively and successfully by many twentieth-century builders.

Johann Daniel's son Johannes, who, with his mother, carried on his father's business in Brussels, signed his one surviving instrument Johann Daniel Dulcken (Brussels, Musée Instrumental). But its date, 1769, makes it clear that it could not have been made by the older builder, and the namebatten gives the place of origin as Brussels, rather than Antwerp. Otherwise, the double seems to be like those of his father in every way.

As far as we know, Jacob van den Elsche (ca. 1689–1772) is the only builder who spans the gap between the Ruckers-Couchet and the Dulcken dynasties. Like so many other builders we have discussed, little is known of his life, other than his dates and his entrance into the St. Luke's guild in 1717. From the evidence of his one extant instrument, a double of 1763 (Antwerp, Vleeshuis Museum), and from a comment by Burney, who remarked that his work had "a considerable share of merit,"[12] he must have been a fine builder. In many ways the 1763 is similar to the Dulcken instruments contemporary to it. It is large (nearly 9′ long) with the characteristic Antwerp narrow tail, a compass of FF–f³, and it is disposed 2×8′, 1×4′ plus lute. The stops are controlled by three hand levers projecting through the nameboard, and by two knee levers operating the lute and the dogleg 8′.[13] The natural touch plates are ivory or bone, and the sharps either ebony or a black-dyed wood. There is no soundboard painting, although it does have a gilded rose, and the soundwell and keywell are in natural wood. The case exterior is painted, with applied half-round gilded moldings. The heavy stand, with twist-turned legs, is decorated en suite.

It is obvious that more than merely time has passed since the last instruments of the Ruckerses and the Couchets. The ab-

14-3. The large, powerful 1763 harpsichord by Jacob van den Elsche. Antwerp, Vleeshuis Museum.

sence of a soundboard painting alone suggests a radical departure from the instruments of the past century, and the impressive length would no doubt have astonished any of the seventeenth-century Flemish builders except Ioseph Ioannes Couchet, whose last extant instrument, a ca. 1680 1×8′, 1×4′ single (Stockholm, Stiftelsen Musikkulturens främjande), was almost as long as van den Elsche's (and in its rebuilt state, altered into an even longer double). The natural wood interior is another departure from earlier Flemish practice, but with a false cap molding projecting into the soundwell, and the external moldings, an International influence and the intention of a false inner-outer allusion are clearly indicated.

14-4. This 1779 single by Johann Peter Bull has wide front 8′ jacks with two tongues pointing in opposite directions, one with bird quill, the other with *peau de buffle*. Antwerp, Vleeshuis Museum.

Considering the depressed economic conditions of Antwerp, it is difficult to understand why a German craftsman would want to go there to seek his livelihood, but Johann Peter Bull (1723–1804) did so in 1745, to apprentice with Johann Daniel Dulcken, probably because of that master's considerable reputation. Bull is survived by two singles, a 1776 (Brussels, Musée Instrumental) and a 1779 (Antwerp, Vleeshuis Museum), and two doubles, a 1778 (Watertown, Mass., private ownership) and a 1789 (Brussels, Musée Instrumental). Bull emulated his master in almost all respects. The instruments are large: the singles are about 8′ in length, and the doubles 6″ longer than that. The tails are narrow (the one on the 1776 single is rounded), a seventeenth-century International characteristic to be seen in many eighteenth-century German harpsichords. His key fronts are covered with stamped paper. Like the 1745 Dulcken single, Bull's 1778 double and 1779 single have a front 8′ register of double-tongued *cembalo angelico* jacks, fitted with bird quill and *peau de buffle,* and operated by a knee lever. In the double, these are the dogleg jacks, so the *peau de buffle,* as well as a 2×8′ quilled combination, would be available from either manual.

One innovation that Bull seems to have introduced is an interior gusset designed to strengthen the cheek-to-bentside joint. This is a "shelf" whose edges are glued to the case walls and whose top is glued to the bottoms of the soundboard liners. He may have done this because he saw English instruments failing at that joint, even though "English cheek disease" rarely struck the instruments of other countries. Otherwise, his framing, like that of his contemporaries in Antwerp and other cities in the Low Countries, is Northern, with the typical upper and lower bracing derived from Ruckers.

TOURNAI

As far as we know, Albert Delin (1712–71) was the only builder of any stature in the eighteenth century who was active in Tournai (like Antwerp, also in the south Netherlands, now modern Belgium). He was born in the town of Ath, near Tournai; but there is no hard information about where and with whom he apprenticed, when he came to Tournai, and where he spent his professional life (although he was there by 1728, when he married).[14] One wonders what brought him to that city (then part of the Netherlands), which was not only far from other harpsichord-building centers but was also undergoing difficult economic times. But if there were reasons for a craftsman to migrate to an area like Paris, which was filled with harpsichord makers, there were also reasons for him to seek out places with less competition.

Delin is survived by ten instruments, all built within the period from 1750 to 1770.[15] Only two of these are grand harpsichords: a 1750 (Berlin, Staatliches Institut für Musikforschung) and a 1768 (France, private ownership); a third is a polygonal virginal (Brussels, Musée Instrumental); and four are bentside spinets: a 1763 (Antwerp, Antwerp Conservatoire), a 1765 (Berlin, Staatliches Institut für Musikforschung), a 1766 (private ownership), and a 1770 (Brussels, Musée Instrumental). The remaining three are clavicytheria: a 1751 (Brussels, Musée Instrumental), a 1752 (Berlin, Staatliches Institut für Musikforschung), and a ca. 1760 (The Hague, Gemeentemuseum). The harpsichords and the clavicytheria are all singles, disposed 2×8' with buff. None of them have a 4' choir, nor are there any wide *cembalo angelico* jacks with bird quill and *peau de buffle* in tongues going in both directions. There are no lute stops, and no knee levers. The registers are changed by extensions of the slides through the cheek, just as the Ruckerses had done it a century and a half earlier. Even the buff rail extends through the cheek.

Obviously, these are not advanced harpsichords, and Delin represents a different sort of maker from this part of Europe,

one far more wed to the principles
practiced by the Ruckerses and the
Couchets than by Dulcken, van den
Elsche, and Bull. His instruments
are more lightly built than those of
his contemporaries, and the poplar
case sides are not nearly so thick.
The internal construction is not as
sturdy, nor does it need to be.
Soundboards are braced in typical
Northern style, with a cutoff bar
and ribs. Both his grand harpsichords and his clavicytheria are

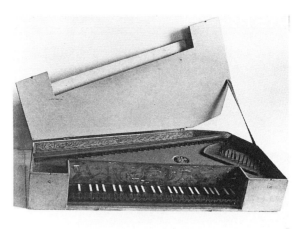

about 7′ in length, a far cry from the long, narrow-tailed instruments of his Antwerp colleagues. Judging from the survivors, his
instruments are both modest and consistent in their compasses.
The virginal and the bentside spinets are all C–e³,[16] and the
grand harpsichords and clavicytheria GG,AA–e³.[17]

14-5. Albert Delin's
1750 hexagonal octave
virginal appears to be a
throwback to earlier
times. It is possible that
this instrument was a
special commission, and
outside his normal
output. © IRPA-KIK,
Brussels.

The 1750 virginal, Delin's first survivor, is a strange instrument, with some unexpected features. First, few Northern builders were producing virginals at this late date. Second, it is at 4′
pitch, although that in itself is no great surprise, since it will be
remembered that Taskin and others were making octave instruments at a fairly late date (although those were spinets, not
virginals). Third, it is six-sided, like the ones seen in sixteenth-
century paintings, the 1548 and 1550 examples of Karest, and
the 1591 spinett virginal of Hans Ruckers. Hence, it is the first,
and as far as we know, the only, polygonal virginal to survive from
the Low Countries in almost two hundred years. Fourth, the case
material is willow, a fairly soft wood not normally used for string
keyboard instruments.[18] With its unpainted exterior and soundboard and hexagonal shape, the instrument looks faintly Italianate; but the keyboard is inset, the bridges are Flemish-looking,
there is a nondescript decoration in the soundwell and keywell,
and a lower guide is used, rather than a box guide. The soundboard has Delin's usual gilded metal rose, with the harp-playing,
left-facing angel used by the Ruckerses and the Couchets, but
with the initials "AD."

Delin's four surviving bentside spinets seem to be fairly similar to one another. Their string scales are virtually identical.[19]
Their cases are made of poplar, with sides about ½″ thick, and
only the bentside is curved, not the small sections at the left and
right that meet the spine. The interior bracing is simple, with
two lower braces running from front board to spine, as extensions of the cheeks. Another bottom brace runs from spine to
bentside. The soundboards are barred with three ribs.[20] In con-

trast to most of the traditions that adopted the Italian bent-side spinet, Delin's models do not use box guides; instead, in the fashion of the old Flemish virginals, the jacks operate in a slotted leather strip mounted on the soundboard, with two jacks per slot, and with a separate, unleathered lower guide. Evidently, Delin preferred to control his plucking points by using a straight nut and a slanting line of jacks, rather than a gap perpendicular to the keys and a slanting or curved nut. Soundboards are flowered, with the usual Delin gilded metal rose, and exteriors are simply decorated, with paint. As with all his instruments, the natural touch plates are ebony and the sharps bone or ivory slips on fruitwood. Old-fashioned trefoils are carved into the key fronts.

The two extant grand harpsichords and three clavicytheria of Delin owe a great deal to Ruckers. Grant O'Brien notes that in matters of soundboard layout, barring, and scale, Delin was following his earlier Flemish masters.[21] Certainly, he seemed to emulate the same minimalist philosophy of his illustrious predecessors, although instead of the $1 \times 8'$, $1 \times 4'$ disposition he chose the $2 \times 8'$. He even used a divided buff, something not seen since the days of the Ruckerses. Still, he was not a slavish follower, and his case bracing differed a bit from the Ruckerses'. His full-height lower braces were placed so that they were perpendicular to the bentside, rather than the spine, and he added a small bottom brace between bellyrail and bentside at the cheek, to strengthen that vulnerable joint. He sometimes used one or two

14-6. One of his four surviving bentside spinets, this 1765 instrument is typical of Delin's unassuming but fine workmanship. © Bildarchiv Preussischer Kulturbesitz, Berlin, Musikinstrumenten Museum.

THE EIGHTEENTH CENTURY

14-7. Delin harpsichord of 1750. The ends of the registers and the buff rail extend through the cheek. Neither the stand nor the "improvisational" case painting is original. © Bildarchiv Preussischer Kulturbesitz, Berlin, Musikinstrumenten Museum.

upper braces, one of which went from the bentside to the upper bellyrail.[22] His soundboard bracing also deviated somewhat in that the cutoff bar is curved and graduated in width like a 4′ hitchpin rail, a refinement also seen in the instruments of Pascal Taskin. As mentioned earlier, the ends of the registers and of the buff rail projected from the cheek; evidently this "primitive" system of changing registers was still viable. Delin was a conservative builder, but that was probably what his customers wanted.

Few of these late Low Country harpsichords retain their original case decoration, and Delin's instruments are no exception. The 1759 grand harpsichord has been painted a bluish green, with improvisatory streaks of yellowish-mustard. The 1768 grand is now finished in a lovely *vernis martin*. The case of the ca. 1760 clavicytherium is now painted a luscious cream color and has been supplied with a cream and gilt Rococo-style fret-sawn door. Even its mitered tail was given a rounded facade.[23] Flowers on soundboards in all traditions are usually placed without regard to gravity; but hanging swags around the rose of this clavicytherium leave no question as to which way is up. Otherwise, Delin's soundboards are nicely decorated with flowers done in a somewhat flat style. Motifs are often outlined, as the Ruckers painters used to do, and little detail is provided in the leaf and stem work, all of which seem to be a single shade of green. The three clavicytheria and the 1768 harpsichord have attractive and unique endblocks, made of a slice of ebony sandwiched between two pieces of ivory or bone. This seems to have been a Delin trademark.[24]

Because of the relationship of keys to jacks, clavicytherium actions seem to differ with every builder who made one. Delin's solution was simple, yet elegant. As in a normal grand harpsichord, a jacklike slip of wood running in upper and lower guides rests on the back ends of each key. When the key is depressed, the slip is raised and in turn raises the end of a separate L-shaped device. The real jack, hinged to the top of the L, is pushed forward, toward the player, and the string is plucked. The mechanism is balanced so that the return of the jacks is effected by gravity, rather than by the spring-loaded return used by some other builders. Great care must have gone into the concept, because the action feels quite good to the fingers, which is not a statement one can always make about a clavicytherium. As with all clavicytheria, close proximity to the soundboard provides the player with an overwhelming sense of sonic immersion.

Compared to contemporary Antwerp harpsichords, Delin's appear to be downright reactionary. The instruments of Dulcken and his circle were concerned with variety of colors and

14-8. Delin's clavicytherium action is so well balanced that the jacks are returned without the use of springs.

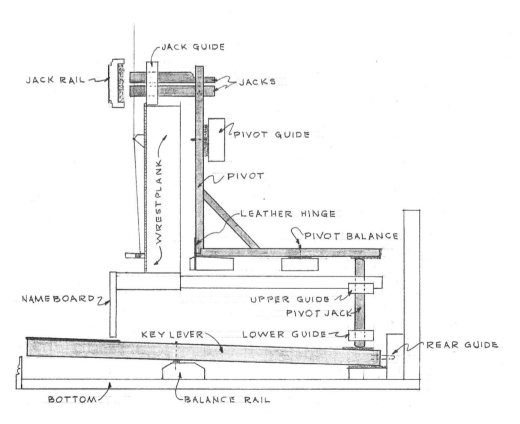

dynamics, and the ability to shift these instantaneously, while Delin's offered nothing more than a basic 1×8′ or 2×8′ sound (although the two 8′s are slightly differentiated), and the dryness of a buffed 8′ is the only real distinction in timbre. The handy draw knobs, stop levers, and *genouillères* of his Antwerp contemporaries obviously did not interest Delin, and one assumes that they did not concern his customers either. Actually, aside from a few French examples, this is the first time outside of Italy that we have come across a simple, basic eighteenth-century harpsichord. The large, powerful instruments represented by Dulcken and Taskin, and in England and Germany by Shudi, Kirkman, and Hass, are interesting harpsichords, and the various mechanical devices imposed upon them offered exciting new possibilities. But there was another side to that coin. Italian builders, it will be remembered, rarely succumbed to the siren song of varied colors and dynamic changes, and it will be shown that the same pertains to Austria as well, where the single-manual 2×8′ harpsichord was built until the end of the century (by which time harpsichords of any sort were no longer made). Even the English turned out a substantial number of single-manual 2×8′ instruments.

14-9. The striking beauty of the case work, though not original, is amply matched by the beauty of sound of Delin's ca. 1760 clavicytherium. The Hague, Gemeentemuseum.

The relatively narrow compasses of Delin's bentside spinets, descending only to C, also deserve comment. FF or GG seemed to be the necessary lower limits for "serious" instruments, those intended for professionals or well-to-do amateurs; nevertheless, even in the late eighteenth century, ranges of C–d^3, C–e^3, or C–f^3 were quite common on smaller or more modestly endowed plucked instruments. The same held true for clavichords and organs, although on the latter there were sound technical and economic reasons to start the keyboard at C. Nevertheless, many pianos of the time also started on C, and although it would be simplistic to consider it "the amateur's lowest note," in practice the statement has some validity. Written notes descending below that limit would have been taken up an octave by the player. Thus, it seems clear that Delin was filling a need for simple instruments simply disposed, and in this sense he was neither a throwback nor a reactionary builder. Despite the modesty of his work, he was known as a fine maker and still has that reputation.

ELSEWHERE

Johann J. Heinemann, a builder from Brussels, is survived by one instrument, a 1793 2×8′ single (Brussels, Musée Instrumental). This is almost certainly the last extant harpsichord from the Low Countries, and with a C/E–d³ compass, one of the most conservative of the late instruments to come from that region. Clearly, on the eve of their disappearance from the keyboard scene, harpsichords were still being built with C/E short octaves. A 1710 harpsichord by van den Elsche, destroyed during World War II, reputedly bore the legend that it had been rebuilt by Heinemann, and that he was blind.[25] If true, Heinemann would have been the sole known sightless harpsichord builder.

With only one extant harpsichord, whose whereabouts are unknown and whose details are obscure,[26] Jérôme Mahieu (died 1737) nevertheless seems to have been an important figure in Brussels keyboard building in the early part of the century. He made both singles and doubles, but he also dealt in Ruckers instruments. It is possible that he made and sold counterfeit harpsichords, since an example dated 1617 and signed "Andreas Ruckers" on the nameboard, but bearing an "HR" rose (Nuremberg, Germanisches Nationalmuseum), is believed to have been by him.[27] Interestingly, Mahieu is reported to have made old-fashioned 1×8′, 1×4′ singles.[28]

Earlier it was noted that *Boalch III* listed twenty-five builders in Amsterdam in the eighteenth century. Despite this appearance of activity, neither this nor any of the other cities of the north Netherlands seem to have had makers of the stature of Dulcken or Delin. It is likely that most of them were probably organ builders who may have made a stringed keyboard from time to time. One of the very few Amsterdam harpsichords to survive is a 1768 (New Jersey, private ownership) by Carl Friedrich Laescke (1732–81), a German who came to Amsterdam around 1755.[29] Other than the one instrument, the fact that he died of tuberculosis, and that, like almost everyone else, he was engaged in rebuilding Ruckers and Couchet harpsichords, little is known of him.[30] The 1768 instrument is a single-manual 2×8′, 1×4′ with the conservative but common C–f³ compass.[31] Registers are changed by extensions through the cheek. The case is braced with three lower members, and no uppers, and the bentside shows the parabolic curve common to Ruckers instruments, rather than the more modern half-straight and half-bent. The soundboard has a 4′ hitchpin rail and cutoff bar with ribs, but there are some additional ribs as well, with cutouts where they pass under a bridge. The instrument is well made, and both it and the matching Louis XV stand are lavishly decorated in *vernis martin*.[32]

Another harpsichord with stops projecting through the cheeks is a 1787 instrument (The Hague, Gemeentemuseum) by Abraham Leenhouwer (1752–98). This builder worked in Leyden, about twenty miles to the southwest of Amsterdam, so it is not surprising to see the same sort of conservatism at work, even though the compass of the two-manual instrument is FF–f³.

The 1735 harpsichord/virginal combination by the organist and amateur builder Johannes Josephus Coenen from Roermond was discussed briefly in Chapter 5, where it was speculated that he was attempting to make a historical copy of a Ruckers instrument. That may have been so; but when the conservatism of the Netherlandish builders is taken into account, Coenen's motivation for making this instrument might appear to be a little clearer, and a little less reactionary. Its GG/BB–c³ compass is only two notes less than the short-octave single-

ROGER PLENIUS

Rutger Pleunis (1696–1774), an inventive Amsterdam craftsman of considerable notoriety, was born in Orsoy, Germany, but at a young age moved to Amsterdam to live with an uncle who also bore his name. Nothing is known of his training, but in 1735 he advertised a two-manual harpsichord with 1×16′, 2×8′, 1×4′ disposition. Pleunis's instrument may have had a separate 16′ division, or it is possible that it descended into the 16′ register, perhaps to CC; but since he also claimed that it had two soundboards, it is likely that it was indeed a harpsichord with 16′ built in the manner of Hieronymus Hass, who mounted the 16′ bridge on a separate section of soundboard between the 8′ and 16′ hitchpin rails, and whose first extant instrument with suboctave is dated only a year earlier.[33] Sometime before 1741 Pleunis left Amsterdam for London, where he took the name under which he is best known, Roger Plenius. He developed a cornucopia of devices that could be applied to harpsichords, including weights to keep the strings in tune, plectra of ivory and tortoise shell, regulating screws for jack tongues, key levers hollowed out to prevent their warping, and a pedal-operated buff stop. Perhaps his best-known invention is the *lyrichord,* a complex gut-strung mechanically bowed keyboard instrument, something like Hans Heiden's Geigenwerk,[34] except that it was powered by a clockwork. This instrument, claimed Plenius, imitated bowed string instruments and the organ in its ability to sustain tones and make crescendos and diminuendos. It even had a lid with a swell cover. At least one was built and was described in a 1755 periodical, *The General Magazine of Arts and Sciences.*[35]

Two further bits of information are known about Roger Plenius. He went bankrupt in 1756, apparently unable to generate sufficient interest in his instruments and his inventions. Nevertheless, he must have had something of a reputation, because in 1761 George Washington, while still a farmer at Mount Vernon, sent a letter to a London agent ordering a spinet from Plenius. Washington suggested that the London shipper tell the builder that the instrument was for himself, rather than for someone who would be regarded as a hick farmer in far-off America.

manual harpsichords of Johann Daniel Dulcken, and Coenen could have seen registers projecting through the cheeks of many of the instruments of his north Netherlands contemporaries. His 2×8′, 1×4′ disposition is modern (the Ruckerses never made anything other than 1×8′, 1×4′), as is the use of the dogleg. The only really retrospective aspect of this instrument is its built-in virginal.

SUMMING UP

Despite the examples of French instruments, and the advanced doubles of Johann Daniel Dulcken, Jacob van den Elsche, and Johann Peter Bull, many of the harpsichords built in the Low Countries in the eighteenth century were singles with short octaves and abbreviated compasses. From our limited sample of survivors, it seems clear that the larger, more powerful, more experimental harpsichords, with wider ranges and fuller dispositions, and with knee levers and plectra of *peau de buffle,* were built in Antwerp, whereas the simpler, smaller, more restricted, more traditional instruments, with narrow compasses, short octaves, and registers projecting from the cheeks, were made in the cities of the north Netherlands. This could be seen as a reaction to the growing complexity of the eighteenth-century harpsichord, but it was likely nothing more than filling a need for simple, serviceable instruments which, while not able to deliver powerful bursts of sound and make instantaneous changes of timbre and dynamics, made fewer demands on the players. There had always been a market for such harpsichords, and we will encounter them again.

[15]

GERMANY, SCANDINAVIA, AUSTRIA, AND SWITZERLAND

*A*S IN THE preceding century, German keyboard craftsmen were mainly organ builders, and their production of harpsichords (or *Clavicembali, Cembali, Claviers,* or *Flügel,* as the Germans commonly called them) was still a sideline.[1] Furthermore, later in the century it was clavichords (which were most often meant by the word *Clavier*), rather than harpsichords, that took the fancy of the German keyboard-buying public, and builders were more likely to have reasons to make these, rather than plucked instruments. Hieronymus Albrecht Hass, for example, is survived by six harpsichords but eleven clavichords, and his son Johann Adolph by only two of the former but eighteen of the latter. The Erlangen-born builder Johann Christoph Georg Schiedmayer is survived by a dozen or so clavichords, but as far as we know, he never made jack-action instruments. With the explosive popularity of the *empfindsamer Stil* (expressive style) in the second half of the century and its close connection to the intimate qualities of the clavichord, and with the encroaching piano, the harpsichord was less interesting to the musical public. But whatever the popularity of the clavichord and the piano, the harpsichord was still needed in the teaching studio, the

---

The title of this chapter might suggest that Austria was a separate political entity during the eighteenth century, but along with many German states and Bohemia, Moravia, and Silesia, it was part of the Habsburg empire. *Boalch III* lists some builders from that large area of Bohemia, Moravia, and Silesia, but only one harpsichord is known to be extant, a 1671 1×8′, 1×4′ single (private ownership) by Johannes Miklis of Prague.

opera pit, the theater, and the orchestra. Furthermore, the first part of the century saw some of the greatest music ever written for the harpsichord come from the pen of Johann Sebastian Bach (1685–1750), so the instrument's light was hardly buried under a bushel.

No one city in Germany could boast of anything like the one hundred or so builders to be found in eighteenth-century Paris or London. *Boalch III* lists only eighteen craftsmen building harpsichords in Dresden, fifteen in Hamburg, and thirteen in Berlin. Other cities had far fewer. In all of Germany there were only 250 or so builders,[2] but even that is a misleading number. For the most part, the Paris and London craftsmen were exclusively harpsichord makers, although admittedly the French seemed to devote an inordinate amount of their time to *ravalement;* but as noted earlier, the Germans were primarily organ builders who made harpsichords and clavichords on an occasional basis, and many apparently specialized in the latter instrument to the exclusion of the former. Furthermore, rather than having makers concentrated into large metropolitan areas, German harpsichord building remained a provincial cottage industry. A 1684 history, for example, noted that "violins, basses, viola da gamba, harpsichords, spinets, and citterns" were made in the villages of Thuringia.[3] And in addition to organs, harpsichords, and clavichords, during the course of the century German builders became increasingly engaged in making square and grand pianos, *Pantalons, Tangentenflügel,* and a few more exotic instruments with keyboards, some of which will be discussed later. Nevertheless, harpsichord building was apparently as much an ongoing activity in Germany in this century as in the last.

In France and England the Ruckers paradigm superseded the native proclivity for sharp sounds and vivid tonal contrasts, and Internationally based forms of the older harpsichords disappeared in favor of the new model, or to be more precise, in favor of the Ruckers model as rebuilt and brought up to date in compass and disposition. In some ways Hamburg instruments were also Ruckers-inspired. While their rounded tails, tall, narrow bridges and nuts, and eclectic, colorful decoration may have given some of their harpsichords a different look, their soundboard barring, layout, and scaling were similar to those used in England and France.[4] Nevertheless, the Ruckers-style soundboard and layout were put into an Internationally inspired German case. Furthermore, while the sonic ideal of Hieronymus Hass and his son Johann Adolph still seemed to be concerned with strong timbral contrasts and a variety of dispositions, the same could not be said of most other German builders. The unique spread registers, metal plectra, and highly colored sounds that characterized the few extant seventeenth-century German harpsichords are no longer to be found among the eighteenth-century Northern survivors.

Notwithstanding, Central German harpsichords seemed to flow in large part from the older models, although they tended more toward relatively plain workaday instruments, eschewing a tendency toward tonal and decorative overabundance. The few surviving examples from this region are usually finished in natural wood, or simply painted or stained, with plain, undecorated soundboards and some International-style moldings on the case. The tails are mitered rather than rounded, and some of these instruments faintly remind one of their contemporaneous French and English cousins; but the Ruckers influence is slight here, if it can be found at all.[5] Central Germany is perhaps more important as the birthplace of the German piano, which first came to life in the Freiberg workshop of Gottfried Silbermann, who replicated the Cristofori action in a German case.[6]

Of South German practice we know little, except that it seems to have been similar to harpsichord building in Vienna, which apparently marched to a different tune. The internal case-building practices, reinforced slanted cheeks, and adherence to $2\times8'$ dispositions bespeak of a unique tradition. The instruments look very much like the fortepianos which were to follow them later in the century. The name of Johann Andreas Stein is closely connected with that piano, as the inventor of the Viennese action; but with that instrument it becomes difficult to ignore that tonally and musically we have left the Baroque and the sound of the harpsichord and entered the world of Viennese classicism, where the piano becomes an instrument in its own right, distinct from its plucked cousin.

RIVALS OF THE HARPSICHORD

Eighteenth-century Germany was particularly rich in plucked, struck, touched, and bowed keyboard instruments, all of which went by the generic name of *Clavier,* or *Cembalo,* or *Clavicembalo.* Falling into none of these categories, because it did not have a keyboard, was the *Pantalon* (or *Pantaleon*), a large dulcimer invented by and named after the Saxon musician Pantaleon Hebenstreit (1667–1750) just before the turn of the century. The instrument itself, more than 9′ long and oblong in shape, was a prodigious marvel, with a wealth of strings both in gut and in metal. It was played by handheld hammers, and one of the enticements of Hebenstreit's performances was his leaping around as he negotiated the instrument's EE–e^3 fifty-five-note compass (diatonic in the bass up to G) and switched from metal to gut strings. Another element of its charm seemed to be the undamped ringing characteristic of all dulcimers. August II, the Elector of Saxony, was so taken with Hebenstreit and his new instrument that he gave him a privileged position at court, along with a commensurate salary (including an allowance for strings!). Gottfried Silbermann, who came to the Dresden court in 1722, made and sold reproductions of the Pantalon until 1727, when Hebenstreit, angered at the builder for some reason, obtained a court order forbidding him to make them any more.[7] In Dresden the Pantalon died as quick a death as its eponymous maker, but it was kept alive elsewhere by Georg Noëlli, one of Hebenstreit's students, who toured Europe with it until the 1780s (Noëlli's instrument was advertised as 11' long, with 276 strings). Thus, the reverberant ring of the Pantalon remained part of Germany's sound world for almost the entire century.[8]

As early as 1731 a Leipzig newspaper ran an advertisement for a keyed Pantalon by the Saxon builder Wahl Friedrich Ficker. Its characteristics included bare-faced wood hammers, undamped strings, a down-striking action, a cloth strip between the hammers and the strings meant to emulate the sound of leather-covered hammers, quadruple stringing, and an extended bass.[9] The keyed version is described by Adlung in 1758, who said that most of them were made by Ficker, who seemed to have found a niche for himself in the German instrument-building world. Adlung noted that the cloth strip, which acted as a moderator, was controlled by a pedal, so as to simplify the playing of forte and piano; in fact, he was quite taken with the instrument's ability to express dynamics.[10]

The tangent piano, or *Tangentenflügel,* was another piano-like keyboard instrument that competed with the harpsichord. Probably invented by Franz Jacob Späth (1714–86) of Regensburg, perhaps as early as 1751, it was developed jointly by him and his son-in-law and partner Christoph Friedrich Schmahl (1739–1814) and became popular in the 1770s.[11] Looking very much like a Viennese fortepiano, its action consisted of wooden jacks or tangents that rested on the ends of the keys, exactly like the jacks of a harpsichord, but which were thrown up against the strings when the keys were depressed (an intermediate lever was involved). The tops of the jacks were uncovered, so bare wood struck the strings and the sound was not unlike that of a plucked instrument. Dynamics could be achieved through finger velocity.[12] Moderators (strips of cloth between hammer and strings), buff stops, *una cordas,* and damper lifters, operated by hand stops and knee levers, were standard and provided a range of color possibilities. Without the complexity of a piano action, and provided with mutation stops as well as the ability to make dynamic nuances, it would seem that this instrument should have had a great deal of appeal. Evidently, for a while it did; Michael Cole notes that there are as many extant Späth and Schmahl *Tangentenflügel* as there are pianos by Stein.[13] But by the end of the first decade of the nineteenth century the instrument was obsolete, no doubt for the same reason as the harpsichord: it was incapable of the piano's infinite variety of tone colors obtainable with the fingers alone. In other words, it lacked the ineffable soul of the piano.

Square pianos abounded in Germany in the latter part of the eighteenth century. Many of these were the "normal" square, with leathered hammers and dampers. Often they had no escapement or back checks; thus their expressive and dynamic abilities were limited, and they were not much louder than clavichords. Another type was the *Clavecin Royal,* an adaptation of the Pantalon, with bare wooden hammers, no dampers, and an assortment of mutation stops. These instruments, collectively known in Germany as *Tafelklaviers*—or table pianos, since they were small enough to be placed on a table when played—were poor substitutes for grand harpsichords and pianos, but such a statement misses the point. Grands were expensive instruments, owned by the moneyed classes. It was the simple clavichords and Tafelklaviers that enabled a middle-class merchant to connect with the powers of music. To own one was to enter the special class of those able to commune with the muses.

Two other types of keyboards were the *Lautenwerk,* or gutstrung harpsichord, and the *Geigenwerk,* or bowed keyboard. The first seemed to have had some currency—there are numerous references to such instruments throughout the first half of the eighteenth century. Adlung dedicates half a chapter to a description of the Lautenwerk, stating that after the organ it was the most beautiful of keyboard instruments. He thought it so lutelike that even a lutenist would mistake it for the real thing.[14] In addition to the normal Flügel form these instruments came in a variety of shapes, including rectangular, oval, and hemispherical with a lutelike bowl, and some had a 4′ set of metal strings. J. S. Bach owned two Lautenwerken, one of which was made for him by Zacharias Hildebrand (1688–1757), a well-known Berlin builder, and the master's E minor Suite (BWV 996) was probably written for that instrument.[15]

The idea of a bowed-string keyboard instrument remained alive well after its invention at the end of the sixteenth century. *NGEKI* reports that at least two of Hans Haiden's Geigenwerken were still extant early in the eighteenth century,[16] so examples were there to stimulate builders' imaginations. A number of such instruments were built in Germany as well as in France and England. Emanuel Bach wrote a sonata for a bowed keyboard instrument, the *Bogenklavier*, made in 1754 by the Berlin builder Johann Hohlfeld (1711–71). Reputedly, this sonata was used in that same year to demonstrate the Bogenklavier to Frederick the Great.

When the organ, the harpsichord, the clavichord, and the grand piano are added to this formidable list, it is clear that eighteenth-century Germany enjoyed a variety of keyboard instruments unlike anything before or since.[17] What may not be so obvious, however, is that the distinctions among them were not at all clear-cut. With the exception of the organ and bowed keyboards, their tonal qualities were not as different from one another as our present-day experience would lead us to believe. Grand pianos sounded much more harpsichord-like than they do today, and square pianos, leathered hammers or not, were close to the clavichords from which they descended. The Germans were not so much interested in the distinctions of tone color between one or the other (although they were interested in mutation stops), or in how the string was set in motion, as they were in how the instrument executed dynamic nuance.

HAMBURG

Harpsichord building in the great seaport of Hamburg appears to have been dominated by the Fleischers, the Hasses, and Christian Zell. Instruments from this region are often referred to as products of the Hamburg school, but one could hardly ascribe the sort of unity implied by that word to a group of makers whose only common element was the general use of pine for case parts, a loose adherence to International principles of case building, the incorporation of a buff stop, fairly wide keys, rounded tails, and table stands with turned legs and low stretchers (similar to the French and German stands of the previous century). In matters of disposition, compass, number of keyboards, key coverings, and the thicknesses of case parts, they differed widely, even among the same maker. Nevertheless, their scales were around 14″, and it is likely that they all adhered to iron stringing.[18]

The earliest known Fleischer, Hans Christoph (1638–before 1694), was primarily a lute maker who also made harpsichords and bowed strings.[19] Of Hans's nine children, the first and fourth became builders. The eldest son, Johann Christoph

(1676–ca. 1728), like his father before him, made lutes, bowed strings, and keyboard instruments.[20] This last activity evoked objections from the joiners guild, which evidently considered casework building its exclusive domain.[21] Whether this meant it was joiners who normally built harpsichords (joiners often became harpsichord makers), or that the activity of harpsichord building was so rare in Hamburg at that time that craftsmen fought over its jurisdiction, is impossible to say. Aside from the Fleischer brothers, Johann Middelburg (dates unknown), an organ and clavichord maker, seemed to be the only other turn-of-the-century builder of any renown, although he is not survived by any harpsichords. Coincidently, it was Middelburg who married Hans Christoph's widow after the latter's death, and therefore may have been his apprentice.

Johann Christoph Fleischer is survived by six stringed keyboards, but five of them are clavichords. The only harpsichord, a 1710 GG–c³ single (Berlin, Staatliches Institut für Musikforschung), is disposed 2×8′, 1×4′ with buff; but in a manner reminiscent of the practice of some seventeenth-century German instruments, it is strung 1×8′, 1×4′, and the two sets of 8′ jacks both pluck the same 8′ choir. The registers are now set up with the 8′ jacks in the front and middle registers, but that allows little differentiation in tone color.[22] In typical German fashion, the stop levers are mounted on the wrestplank. The round-tailed case is reminiscent of German-flavored International construction, and it is surprisingly light. The pine sides and spine are of intermediate thickness with cut-in moldings, but the interior structure consists only of two U-braces and two diagonal struts. This is not much reinforcement, and it is possible that Johann Christoph was trying to make a particularly lightweight case and used only one set of 8′ strings to keep the tension as low as possible. The soundboard is braced in Northern style, with a cutoff bar and ribs, and a light 4′ hitchpin rail. The nuts and bridges are tall and molded.

The soundboard is nicely decorated, with a charming bucolic vignette between the rose and the gap, facing the player, where the French normally put a bird scene. Like the soundboard treatments of Dulcken and Delin, the effect is rather flat, less painterly, and more purely decorative than French soundboard painting.[23] Nevertheless, the beautiful, delicate, gilded upside-down wedding-cake rose is surrounded by a wreath of blue flowers and hanging swags, a rare example of the acknowledgment of gravity on a soundboard painting.[24] The naturals are covered with ebony and the sharps with ivory slips, with embossed, gilded papers glued to the key fronts. The case is decorated in chinoiserie, with gold and bronzing powders on a

15-1. This elegant-looking 1710 harpsichord by Johann Christoph Fleischer has three sets of jacks but only two sets of strings. Its light internal construction seems to look back to the seventeenth century. © Bildarchiv Preussischer Kulturbesitz, Berlin, Musikinstrumenten Museum.

red ground. Despite the ogee curve that was cut into its cheeks at some time in the past, and its present lack of a lid,[25] it is a lovely looking Flügel; but as a Hamburg harpsichord, in construction and disposition it is perhaps more typical of the instruments of the previous century.

Johann Christoph Fleischer's younger brother Carl Conrad (1680–1737) is survived by three harpsichords. The 1716 (Hamburg, Museum für Hamburgisches Geschichte) and 1720 (Barcelona, Museu de la Música) are both singles, disposed 2×8′, 1×4′ with buff. The first has pine case walls of intermediate thickness, a conservative four-octave C–c³ compass, and a soundboard with a Ruckers-style layout. Interestingly, the upper surface of the 4′ hitchpin rail is chamfered so that only a small area (reminding one of the slender hitchpin rails of International style) is glued to the soundboard.[26] It is a colorful instrument, decorated on all surfaces including the spine. The exterior of the case is painted with action scenes — a boating motif is on the cheek, and scantily clad dancers grace the bentside. Flowers cover the outside of the lid, with the addition (probably later) of a violin and some music. The inside of the lid has a musical scene said to have been inspired by Handel's *Messiah,* and an elongated tableau of Orpheus serenading the beasts is on the nameboard. The cut-in moldings are gilded. The lid painting and external decoration are not original and not particularly well done, but the effect is immediate and dramatic. On the soundboard, a complex upside-down wedding-cake rose of parchment, stained or lightly painted in red, white, and blue, is surrounded by a tight wreath of flowers. The soundboard painting seems more Flemish than French in style, but there are no borders, blue or otherwise, and once again the motifs are rendered in a rather direct and flat manner. One obvious feature of this board is a large, pale-red bird with outstretched wings, perhaps a scarlet macaw, placed near the spine, to the left of the rose. The naturals have bone or ivory touch plates, and their fronts are covered with gilded embossed papers over a red ground. The sharps are covered with tortoise shell. The keys are quite wide, more so than most other European traditions. Carl Conrad's 1716 is a lovely sounding harpsichord — not particularly powerful, but with a clear and refined voice that seems to respond readily to any sort of music. Like many North German harpsichords, the individual elements of the decoration appear to have been overdone; yet taken as a whole, the eclectic ensemble seems to transcend these apparent excesses.

The 1720 Carl Conrad single has the same 2×8′, 1×4′ with buff disposition and pine case with sides of intermediate thickness as its 1716 brother, but the similarities stop there. The GG–c^3 compass is larger, but more importantly, the wrestplank is very wide, with the bass of the gap slanting away from the keyboard,[27] thus allowing the bass of the 8′ nut to angle dramatically back toward the nameboard. The effect is to provide an ever-deepening plucking point as the compass descends into the bass. Thus, although the soundboard layout, barring, and scale appear to be Ruckers-inspired, the desire for a hollow, deep-plucked sound, particularly in the bass, was probably influenced by—or more likely, was a continuation of—seventeenth-century tonal concepts. Like the 1716, the natural keys are wide, a Hamburgian trait. The exterior of the painted case is in a bland false marble, perhaps not original; but the soundboard painting, possibly done by the same decorator as the 1716, is attractive. Once again, a tight wreath of flowers surrounds the same red, white, and blue–colored upside-down wedding-cake parchment rose.

Little is known of either Hieronymus Albrecht Hass (1689–after 1744) or his son Johann Adolph (fl. 1740–75), although they are the most famous of the Hamburg builders. The father left a legacy of six extant harpsichords, and his son is survived by two. But those eight instruments are more than sufficient to establish them as extremely creative builders. Like the surviving Fleischer instruments, the soundboard layout, scale, and barring (at least, of those in which it is known) are Ruckers derived; but they differ from the Fleischers and from each other in number of manuals, compasses, dispositions, and complexity.[28] All the Hass instruments have the rounded tail typical of Hamburg instruments, with sides of intermediate thickness and with cut-in moldings. The internal bracing is inventive but based on International principles. All also have the wide octave span

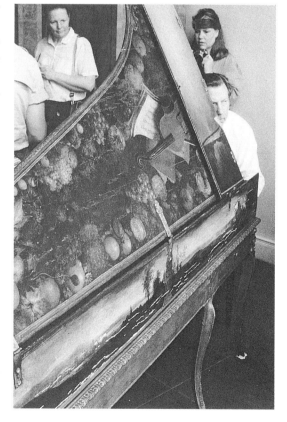

15-2. It appears that every inch of this fine 1716 single by Carl Conrad Fleischer is decorated with paint. Hamburg, Museum für Kunst und Gewerbe.

typical of Hamburg instruments, although strangely, the spans on the extant Hass harpsichords differ from one another.[29] Like the German instruments of the preceding century, the keywells are the visual focal points. The soundboards are decorated with flowers and sometimes a vignette but have no roses. The instruments are diverse enough to deserve some description.

1. A 3×8', 2×4' double of 1721, compass FF–d³ (Göteborg, Göteborgs Museum). This large (8½') instrument had been converted to a piano and the upper keyboard discarded; notwithstanding, Lance Whitehead was able to ascertain its original and unique disposition.[30] A 3×8', 2×4' stringing is unusual but has certain undeniable advantages. One set of 8' strings can be plucked by the upper manual, close to the nut, producing a sound almost as nasal as a lute stop. Plucking directly behind that register, and still on the upper manual, a 4' set of jacks intensifies the already penetrating 8' sound. The lower manual would then have a 2×8', 1×4' disposition, with the ability to use any or all of those registers, all plucking farther back (particularly if, as Whitehead suggests, the lower manual 4' is in front of the two 8's, closest to the player).[31] Such a disposition offers a great tonal contrast between the two keyboards, with the ability to dialogue without doglegs or coupler. One cannot help thinking how useful such a setup would be for a work such as J. S. Bach's *Italian Concerto,* where it would offer greater tonal variety and a better balance between manuals than the conventional 2×8', 1×4' disposition on which it is now universally performed.[32]

2. A 3×8', 1×4' double of 1723, compass FF–c³ (Copenhagen, Musikhistorisk Museum). This is another 3×8' disposition, but with one set of 4' jacks. However, these jacks are doglegged and activated by a coupler,[33] so the same sort of tonal contrasts offered by the 1721 are possible here. Nevertheless, because only one set of 4' jacks separates the nasal 1×8' available on the upper register from the deeper plucking 8's on the lower, the distinctions would not be as great. This instrument has a single stepped 8' nut, with one set of 8' strings going over the lower portion and reaching the wrestpins through holes in the upper part.[34] John Koster opines that this is the disposition called for by Carl Philipp Emanuel Bach (1714–88) in his sonata W. 69

15-3. Although scale, soundboard barring, and bridge layout on the 1720 harpsichord by Carl Conrad Fleischer are derived from Ruckers models, the wide wrestplank, steep angle of the nut, and slanting gap result in much deeper plucking points. Barcelona, Museu de la Música.

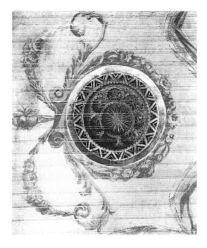 
(H53; Berlin, 1747), one of the very few examples of harpsichord music with registration indicated.[35] He further speculates — and not without good reason — that such "playful and colorful" registrations would have been particularly appropriate for a work also written in the 1740s, by C. P. E. Bach's father, the *Goldberg Variations*.[36]

The 1723 is a beautiful harpsichord, decorated on the exterior with a bronze and polychrome chinoiserie and a green false tortoise shell border. A lid painting, surrounded by a wide border of gold on red, depicts an outdoor concert in a formal garden. The keywell and fallboard have more colorful chinoiserie on an ivory ground. The naturals are covered with tortoise shell, the light-colored sharps are topped with ivory slips, and key fronts are embellished by paper patterns glued over a red ground. One of the finest examples of eclectic Hamburg decoration, its visual effect is extraordinary.

3. A 1×8', 1×4' single of 1726, compass FF–d³, later extended to f³ (Leufsta, Leufsta Bruk Manor). With two sets of jacks, this is the simplest extant harpsichord by either of the Hasses. The soundboard is decorated, and the exterior of the case is painted vermilion. Naturals are ivory covered, and sharps are blackened wood topped with ebony slips. This harpsichord, perhaps intended for continuo use, contrasts with the complex machines usually associated with the Hass name; but these were craftsmen who built on commission, and there is no reason why they would not do simple instruments as well. More than likely the Hasses made other basic harpsichords, but as we know, it is the large, complex, highly decorated exemplars that tend to be preserved.[37]

4. A 2×8', 1×4' single from 1732, compass C–d³ (Oslo, Kunstindustriemuseet). This is the only Hieronymus Albrecht

15-5. This colorful 1723 harpsichord by Hieronymus Albrecht Hass has a 3×8', 1×4' disposition, making possible vivid tonal contrasts between the two manuals. Copenhagen, Musikhistorisk Museum og Carl Claudius' Samling.

harpsichord with the 2×8′, 1×4′ disposition. Like the Antwerp instruments contemporary to it, the two 8′ sets of jacks are in front of the 4′, indicating that the unity of sound of the unison ensemble was considered more important than the distinction in tone quality to be gained by separating the two 8′s. The soundwell and keywell are decorated with veneers, while the exterior and the lid painting are done in a colorful and wonderfully naive chinoiserie.[38] The natural keys have ivory touch plates.

5. A 1×16′, 2×8′, 1×4′ plus lute double of 1734, compass GG–d³ (Brussels, Musée Instrumental). Hass instruments with 16′ are physically imposing, because the choir of suboctave strings is given its own soundboard, bridge, and hitchpin rail, adding length to the case not only at the tail, but also at the cheek. The 1734 is nearly 9′, with a cheek almost 3′ long. With 4′, 8′, and 16′ bridges and the 8′ hitchpin rail visible on the soundboard, the instrument looks quite complex. The 8′ hitchpin rail is a separate interior partial bentside, and that member also serves to support one edge of the slightly raised 16′ soundboard. The case is made of oak, a departure from the pine seen so far in Hamburg instruments.[39] Including the close-plucking lute, the instrument has five registers. All four choirs of strings are available from the lower manual, while the doglegged front 8′ jacks can be played from either keyboard. The lute stop, of course, is also on the upper. This arrangement can pit anything from a single 8′ on the lower manual against a single 8′ or a lute 8′ on the upper, and was doubtlessly designed to present registral possibilities somewhat different from those seen so far. Since the two 8′ sets of jacks are separated by the 4′, three 8′ sounds—back, middle, and close-plucking (the lute)—are possible. The exterior of the instrument is painted a plain creamy gray, but its lid has a complex scene telling the story of the fall of Troy[40] and a vignette of a goddess—probably Minerva—on the soundboard, just above the gap. The keywell is especially handsome and vibrates with geometric patterns in tortoise shell, ebony, and ivory. The ivory naturals and ebony arcades are complemented by ebony sharps topped with dazzling ebony and ivory chevrons.

6. A 1×16′, 2×8′, 1×4′, 1×2′ plus lute, plus buff, triple manual of 1740, compass FF,GG–f³ (France, private collection). This is almost certainly the most elaborate harpsichord built in historical times. It is big—more than 9′ long. With a 2′ bridge, the soundboard is divided into five discrete strips and a triangle (at the left-hand front), even more of a thicket than the 1734's board. Five sets of jacks fill the gap, with the lute stop carrying a sixth. From the bellyrail to the wrestplank, the 16′ and the 2′

(it seems generally agreed that the purpose of the 2′ was to brighten the 16′) are available from the third, lowest manual, which pulls out like a drawer when required. The middle manual is arranged as an 8′, 4′, 8′ dogleg, giving the two 8′ choirs some distinction from one another and making the dogleg 8′ also available on the upper manual. The upper has that dogleg 8′ and also the lute. Hence, with the lowest manual pushed in, the instrument functions like a normal 2×8′, 1×4′ with dogleg and lute; but with the lowest manual pulled all the way out, the middle manual is coupled to it and the full resources of the instrument are available. And if the lowest manual is pulled out to within ½″ of its full extension, it can be used independently.

The complexity of this harpsichord's disposition is matched by its decorative beauty. The exterior is done in chinoiserie superimposed over faux tortoise shell. The lid painting is a scene showing the builder — presumably, none other than Hass himself — presenting this very harpsichord to an unidentified woman, presumably the new owner.[41] The jackrails (the normal one and the one for the lute stop) as well as the walls of the soundwell are painted a glowing Chinese red. Case moldings are gilded. A complex vignette is in the usual position on the soundboard. The keywell is a symphony of tortoise-shell patterns on an ivory ground. The naturals are covered with tortoise shell, with ivory arcades, and the ivory-topped sharps are inlaid with tortoise shell. The stand, with seven turned legs and low stretcher, is decorated en suite with the case. Hass's 1740 masterpiece is one of the most magnificent harpsichords known, and with its emphasis on complex dispositions and a decorative tradition both exotic and eclectic, it could not have come from anywhere but Hamburg.

7. A 1×16′, 2×8′, 1×4′, 1×2′ plus buff double of 1760, compass FF–f³ (New Haven, Yale Collection).[42] Johann Adolph's harpsichord has the same disposition as his father's 1740 (although without a third keyboard), with the same five strips and a triangle dividing the soundboard; but its resources are somewhat different. There is no lute register, although the gap accommodates six sets of jacks. From the bellyrail back to the wrestplank the 2′ (but only up to c²), the 16′, and the 8′, 4′, and dogleg 8′ are accessible on the lower manual. The upper manual plays the dogleg 8′, and another set of jacks pluck the same 2′ strings (but this time only up to b). Like his father's 1740, the lower manual has the basic 2×8′, 1×4′ resource, with the 2′ available to brighten the 16′ when the suboctave is used. The upper manual, on the other hand, uses the 2′ strings to sharpen the 8′ sound, but when used this way the 2′ cannot also be used in conjunction with the 16′; hence, it is likely that the 8′, 2′

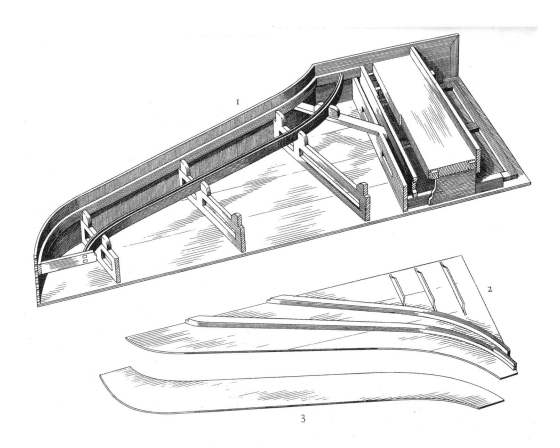

combination on the upper manual was intended to balance the 2×8′, 1×4′ on the lower. Again, there are implications for a work like the *Italian Concerto*. Hass's case bracing shows that he combined upper and lower braces along with U-braces and knees into one member; or, it could just as easily be said that his braces were one-piece post-and-beam constructions. Beneath the soundboard are found both 2′ and 4′ hitchpin rails. The 8′ hitchpin rail is the partial internal bentside.[43]

The 1760 is decorated externally with faux tortoise shell over a red ground, with eight square-tapered legs painted en suite, and with a lid painting of polychrome chinoiserie on a red ground. The keywell is veneered in natural wood. Once again, naturals have tortoise-shell touch plates and ivory arcades, while the light-wood sharps are topped with ivory slips.

8. A 2×8′, 1×4′ single of 1764, compass FF–f[3] (Edinburgh, Russell Collection). Like his father's 1732 single, this Johann Adolph instrument is disposed 2×8′, 1×4′; nevertheless, the 4′ is between the two 8′s here, whereas on the 1732 it is behind them. The exterior finish, a herringbone veneer of rosewood, dates from a 1935 restoration; originally the case was painted.

15-6. The internal case structure and bottom of the soundboard of the 1760 Johann Adolph Hass. Reprinted from *Hubbard 1965*, with permission.

15-7. This imposing 1760–61 harpsichord by Johann Adolph Hass is disposed 1×16′, 2×8′, 1×4′, 1×2′. The case is finished in a red false tortoise shell. New Haven, Yale University Collection of Musical Instruments.

The bentside is of oak, and with the evidence of two uses of that wood—this and Hieronymus Albrecht's 1734 instrument—it seems that oak was used at least occasionally in Hamburg for case parts.

These eight harpsichords vary as much in decoration as they do in disposition. Although most of them have painted sound-boards and table stands with turned legs and low stretchers, their external decor varies dramatically, from a single color to chinoiserie over false tortoise shell. Sheridan Germann's penetrating comment that the decoration of the 1702–4 Mietke (to be discussed shortly) "is living proof that 'eclecticism' should not be a word of denigration"[52] could well apply to these instruments. The Hasses were the opposite of production builders like the Ruckerses, or even their later colleagues in Paris, and it is likely that they made harpsichords in response to specific commissions. The same could be said of the other Hamburg builders as well, although none of them went to the decorative extremes of the Hasses; and perhaps more importantly, none of them explored a variety of dispositions like the Hasses. It has been said that this was the result of their experience as organ builders, but virtually all eighteenth-century German makers were organ builders, and the more mundane dispositions of their harpsichords would indicate that they knew the difference between the two instruments.

We can make good guesses about the disposition, compass, number of keyboards, size of keys, and decoration of a typical

THE 16′ STOP

The few surviving German instruments with 16′ choirs are of great interest. They have been described as experimental in nature, attempts to introduce something of an organ quality with a choir of strings at the suboctave. Frank Hubbard held this belief, even though his knowledge of instruments with 16′ was scanty.[44] But there is evidence that the 16′ choir was far more widespread than he realized. For example, Jacob Adlung mentioned that it was possible to remove one of the 8′ sets of strings from a harpsichord and replace it with a set of wound 16′ strings.[45] In fact, that is what has been claimed for the so-called "Bach" harpsichord, a ca. 1700 instrument from Thuringia, thought to be anonymous, but now attributed to the workshop of Johann Heinrich Harrass (Berlin, Staatliches Institut für Musikforschung). Although its original disposition may never be known, it is supposed that it was originally disposed 3×8′, 1×4′, with one of the 8′s replaced with a set of wound 16′ strings. This instrument will be discussed in more detail later on.[46]

A news source from 1783 observed that Johann Heinrich Silbermann had built a harpsichord at 16′ pitch.[47] Notice of a harpsichord by Michael Mietke with 16′ appeared in 1778, along with the information that this was one of the two with 16′ made by that builder.[48] An extant 1777 *vis-à-vis* harpsichord-piano combination by Johann Andreas Stein has a choir of 16′ strings, and Stein built other combination instruments with 16′ that no longer exist. The widow of organist Johann Caspar Vogler (1696–1763), who was one of J. S. Bach's students, advertised for sale in a Leipzig newspaper in 1776 an extremely large and complex harpsichord belonging to her late husband.[49] According to the ad, it had a pedal division with 1×32′, 1×16′, 2×8′, and two manuals disposed 2×8′, 1×4′ plus lute, but with a six-octave compass of CC–c⁴.[50] Another ad, in the same Leipzig newspaper, but from 1775, attempted to sell a 1×16′, 2×8′, 1×4′ FF–f³ harpsichord with five registers by Zacharias Hildebrand.[51] Even England was not immune to the 16′ stop, and it is seen in a large, complex 1780 harpsichord-piano combination with recording device by John Joseph Merlin.

Judging from the relative frequency of references such as these, the 16′ suboctave stop, while uncommon, was not at all rare. Nevertheless, it did not become a regular feature of German harpsichords, and its greatest influence seems to have been on early-twentieth-century harpsichord building.

eighteenth-century French harpsichord, but exactly the opposite must be said about the Hass instruments. Each survivor seems to represent a solution to a particular problem. We can only speculate on the number of harpsichords the Hasses may have produced, and the marvelous instruments that may have been lost to us. If there was some reason that these flamboyant exemplars were made by the Hasses rather than by any of the other Hamburg builders, it is likely buried deep beneath the sands of time.

Christian Zell (dates unknown) was the third of the well-known names of Hamburg harpsichord building. He does not seem to have been an apprentice of Carl Conrad Fleischer, although he married Fleischer's widow Florentina in 1722. Godparents to one of their children was Gabriel Tielcke, the son of the lute maker Joachim Tielcke, and Catherina Fleischer,

Frank Hubbard thought that the German organ and the French harpsichord were the two major influences on eighteenth-century German harpsichords. The organ impact was manifested by the presence of 16′ and 2′ choirs (mimicking the practice of combining pipes of different octaves), and the French influence by the 2×8′, 1×4′ disposition which Hubbard thought so common on German instruments.[53] As to the former, only a tiny percentage of the extant eighteenth-century German harpsichords have anything other than 8′ and 4′ choirs; but the 16′ loomed large in Hubbard's mind because it was so common in the instruments built in the early part of the twentieth century. As to the 2×8′, 1×4′ disposition, John Koster observed that Hubbard, who along with William Dowd introduced the modern harpsichord world to the standard classic French disposition, was predisposed by that experience to think it a uniquely French characteristic.[54] Hubbard's words were: "sight must not be lost of the extremely important fact that most German harpsichords show the same disposition as the French: 2×8′, 1×4′, on two manuals with coupler."[55] But Koster notes that Hubbard wrote this before many of the extant German instruments were known, and that he was so predisposed to seeing a French influence that he misunderstood his own data. Of the fifteen German harpsichords he knew, reports Koster, only seven had the French 2×8′, 1×4′ disposition on two manuals — certainly not "most."[56] In the long run, however, Hubbard was probably right, even if for the wrong reasons: except for the Hass examples, many extant German instruments *are* disposed 2×8′, 1×4′. Nevertheless, the French arrived at that disposition by adding another 8′ to the basic 1×8′, 1×4′ of the Flemish, while the Germans added the 4′ to their basic 2×8′.

Hubbard did not have a high opinion of the Hass harpsichords. Although he called them "superb technological achievements," he thought that the "imposition of tonal concepts appropriate to the organ" was "barbarous" and the result "grotesque."[57] But it is doubtful that he ever heard one of the Hasses with 16′, and if he had, it certainly would not have been under optimal conditions of stringing and quilling. Frank Hubbard, like all of us, was a product of his time.

Carl Conrad's aunt. Zell is survived by three harpsichords: 1728 (Hamburg, Museum für Kunst und Gewerbe), 1737 (Barcelona, Museu de la Música), and 1741 (Aurich, Ostfriesische Landschaft). If only the 1728 double were extant Zell would still be remembered as a great builder. With an FF–d³ compass disposed 2×8′, 1×4′ plus buff and with coupler, it has many International features, including sides of intermediate thickness with heavier spine, an internal construction consisting of knees and some upper braces, and case sides of pine that overlap the bottom. Box guides are used, with stop levers on the wrestplank. A veneer lining the soundwell, and a cap molding make the bentside look heavier than it is. Both the veneered and crossbanded walnut removeable nameboard and the coupler rail are crenelated.[58] The soundboard is Ruckers derived, with a 4′ hitchpin rail, cutoff bar, and four ribs, but no rose. The instrument is scaled at about a = 415 Hz. The bridges are taller than would be found on a Northern instrument, but thinner, so the mass of either is about the same.

The 1728 Zell is one of the most eye-catching harpsichords

of eighteenth-century Germany and a worthy foil for any of the extant Hasses. The case is painted in a dense, raised polychrome chinoiserie on a dark-green ground, with many birds flying about. Raising the lid reveals a rubicund vermilion soundwell with gilded moldings, and a lovely soundboard painting of flowers and more birds. In place of a rose there is a vignette of the Roman goddess Minerva accompanied by a marching band of two companions playing lute and violin. The lid is in three parts, each with its own painting, done some time after the instrument was completed. The paintings deal with mythological subjects, and "gods, goddesses, nymphs, angels, mortals, and putti engage in a whirl of activity in forests and gardens."[59] Almost all the favorite Germanic contrasts are present here. Each panel of the lid is bordered with red false tortoise shell. The walnut keywell is also colorful, with four-point ebony and ivory stars inlaid into the nameboard and cheeks. Naturals are covered with ivory and faced with ebony arcades, and sharps are topped with tortoise shell. The case sits on a table stand with eight elaborately carved and painted legs and a low serpentine stretcher.

The ensemble hits the eye with a riot of color, an effect which must have been breathtaking when the paint and gilding were fresh and new. Beyond that, though, the numerous

15-8. The 1728 2×8', 1×4' double by Christian Zell is one of the finest extant harpsichords, both in sound and in appearance. Hamburg, Museum für Kunst und Gewerbe.

birds, nymphs, angels, and putti flying around in the case and lid paintings give the instrument a unique sense of motion. An objet d'art, which this certainly is, could scarcely be more densely adorned than the 1728 Zell, and, in fact, by modern standards, it seems over-elaborately decorated; yet, the effect seems to work. Decoration aside, the 1728 Zell is a fine-sounding harpsichord. It makes a sonorous, authoritative sound, with a distinctive, but not overpowering attack. The individual registers are slightly dry, but clear and clean-sounding. The bass is distinctive and highly colored, the tenor is prominent, and the treble is hard and bright. It is one of those rare instruments that seems to lend itself to any sort of music, and a higher compliment could not be paid to any harpsichord. Restored in the 1970s, it has been played and recorded regularly.[60]

The 1737 is a C–d³, 2×8′, 1×4′ single with pine case, decorated with chinoiserie, with soundwell and keywell veneered with natural wood. Surprisingly for a Hamburg instrument, the natural touch plates are made of boxwood. The harpsichord lacks a soundboard painting but may originally have had one; all the other known Hamburg instruments do. The 1741 is another 2×8′, 1×4′ single, also with a C–d³ compass.

SCANDINAVIA

Almost all the harpsichord building in Scandinavia took place in Stockholm. In the victorious aftermath of the Thirty Years' War and the Peace of Westphalia in 1648, Sweden entered into a period of intense artistic activity, with some of Europe's best artisans, painters, musicians, and craftsmen invited to its thriving cities (Zenti, it will be remembered, was an early arrival in Stockholm, in 1653). It is likely that the Swedes were introduced to North German harpsichords at this time — particularly those from Hamburg — because it was from those instruments that their own were derived. In 1756 the Swedish government imposed a ban on foreign imports, forcing native craftsmen to build their own wares; nevertheless, with their rounded tails and colorful decoration, the extant Swedish instruments often seem indistinguishable from North German products.

The father of Stockholm harpsichord building seems to have been Johan Petter Roos (d. ca. 1732), an autodidact who claimed to have taught himself instrument making while still a child. He apprenticed to the organ builder Niclas Cahman and by 1727 was licensed by his guild to make "Clave Symbaler, Symbaler, Spinetter, Claver, etc."[61] Roos is survived by a few clavichords, but no harpsichords. Lars Kinström (1710–63), the son of an iron worker, was another autodidact. Although he made his living as an organist, in 1742 he was granted a license to produce instruments without having served an apprenticeship, claiming that he had learned to build by fraternizing with instrument makers. Kinström is survived by two or possibly three harpsichords. A 1753 single (Boras, Boras Museum), now with an unusual C–c^4 compass, was made into a piano. Another, of unknown date, is in service at the Royal Theater at Drottningholm Palace, outside Stockholm, where until recently it was used for continuo playing. Externally, aside from the Swedish-style case decoration, it would be impossible to distinguish it from a Hamburg instrument. Kinström had something of a reputation for making unusual keyboard instruments. He advertised keyboards for sale from time to time, including a lute-*Cymbal,* a harp-*Cymbal,* and a harpsichord with pedals. His widow continued his business after his death.

Philip Jacob Specken (1680/90–1762) seems to have been the first important Swedish builder. He studied with Gottlieb Silbermann, a Dresden maker who does not appear to have been related to the members of the better-known Silbermanns of Freiberg and Strasbourg.[62] After his apprenticeship Specken went to Stockholm and by 1730 was working for another builder, Gustaf Berg; but three years later he was in the employ of Roos's widow, and it is likely that Specken took over that shop and perhaps even married the widow Roos. There seem to be two extant Specken harpsichords, a single of ca. 1740 (Lulea, Norrbotten Museum),[63] and a 1748 double (Stockholm, Musikmuseet). The last, probably a fair representation of his work, is a graceful-looking instrument in the Hamburg style, with a heavy spine, a relatively thin bentside, a rounded tail, and an internal structure of U-bracing made up of knee and bottom braces. The case sides overlap the bottom. The bridges and nuts are slightly molded, and as seems to be the case with Swedish harpsichords, there is no soundboard painting. It is disposed 2×8′, 1×4′, with a compass of FF–f^3.

After Specken's death his shop was run by his journeyman, Gottlieb Rosenau (ca. 1720–ca. 1790), an expatriate German who was born in Königsberg and who moved to Sweden when he was in his late teens or early twenties. His work must have been fairly well respected,[64] because he did a considerable amount of exporting and even sent ten instruments to St. Petersburg in Russia. Only one of Rosenau's harpsichords has survived, a lovely 1786 double (Copenhagen, Musikhistorisk Museum), with an FF–f^3 compass and a 2×8′, 1×4′ plus lute disposition with coupler.[65] Once again, we see all the usual Hamburg characteristics—the heavy spine with thin round-tailed case, and even the contrast of a red-painted exterior with a veneered key-well of herringbone patterns and burls. Gold chinoiserie on a blue ground graces the interior of the lid. Despite the colorful decoration of red, blue, gold, and natural wood, the 1786 lacks the flamboyance found in some of the Hass instruments; but it is likely that this sort of uninhibited display simply was not part of the Swedish decorative milieu. The stand is a modest table with eight sedate cabriole legs.

Johan Broman (ca. 1717–72), a Stockholm contemporary of Rosenau, was one of the first builders to accept the theories of Brelin and Faggot. He applied them in one of his two surviving harpsichords, an FF–f^3 double of 1756 (Stockholm, Musikmuseet). Following Faggot's ideas, Broman succeeded in doubling the lengths of the descending strings for almost the entire compass of the instrument, although this resulted in a harpsichord nearly 12' long, probably an all-time record length for a historical instrument. It has been assumed that the purpose of this exercise was to produce a loud harpsichord,[68] but that assumption could be unwarranted: Broman may merely have been attempting to produce an instrument in which all elements were in balance. At any rate, according to reports it makes no more sound than the average instrument.

Other than length, there are many interesting features about this harpsichord, including a Hass-like disposition of 3×8', 1×4' plus buff.[69] These registers line up from the nameboard back to the bellyrail as 8', 8', 4', 8'. The frontmost 8', on the upper manual, would be fairly nasal, the second 8' was dog-legged and therefore available on either manual, and the usual combinations of 2×8', 1×4' were on the lower manual. The stop levers are not found in their usual location on the wrestplank; instead, they run under it and project through the nameboard, Dulcken style. Furthermore, the upper manual is split, and either half can be coupled independently to the lower keyboard. The spine is heavy, but the bentside is only ⅝" thick. Bjarne Dahl, who took some measurements of this strange instrument, notes that the internal bracing consists of four 2"-high bottom members, with an unspecified number of 4"-high beams running from end to end, parallel to the spine — an unusual sort of case reinforcement.[70]

In accordance with Brelin's theories, the soundboard grain runs at an angle to the spine, and more or less at right angles to the 8' and 4' bridges, which are parallel to each other. The 8' bridge is carefully carved to make way for the strings, and narrow strips of ivory are laid on the bridge as close to right angles with the strings as possible. The strings are pinned in front of the ivory strips and back-pinned behind them (these features are

NILS BRELIN AND JACOB FAGGOT

Between 1740 and 1760, under the aegis of Sweden's newly organized Royal Academy of Science, two investigators, Nils Brelin (1690–1753) and Jacob Faggot (dates unknown), developed theories designed to optimize the balance of string tension and scale in clavichords and harpsichords. Their work had its effect on Swedish clavichords, particularly the bridges and soundboards; but with one prominent exception, to be discussed below, as far as we know it had little impact on harpsichords.

Born the son of a poor tenant farmer, Nils Brelin was twenty-two before he could begin his education. After studying law and theology he held a series of university positions at Uppsala and Lund. Between 1719–21 and 1735–38 he traveled extensively and developed a flair for understanding and building mechanical devices of all sorts, including windmills, ploughs, and ovens, as well as harpsichords and clavichords. In 1739 he was elected to the Royal Academy of Science and published his ground-breaking paper "Reflections on the Great Improvement of the Quality of Clavichords and Harpsichords."[66] The study concerned itself primarily with two elements of stringed-keyboard making: one, the effects of the direction of grain on the stiffness of the soundboard; and the other, a method of shaping and pinning the bridge in order to equalize the tension on both strings of a course. Brelin's work had a strong impact on Swedish clavichord builders, and one can instantly spot a late Swedish instrument by its deference to his precepts. Other contributions by Brelin, such as a polygonal clavichord (also 1739) and a clavicytherium, probably with hammer action (1741), were not quite so momentous. In 1743 Brelin was appointed vicar of Bolstad, a position he held until his death ten years later. He continued his instrument work, however, and in 1751 developed a new design for harpsichord jacks.

Little is known of Faggot's life, at least before he became a member of the Royal Academy of Science. His contribution was to balance string tension by stressing the Pythagorean purity of strings that double in length every octave as they descend. Undoubtedly, Brelin's and Faggot's work on behalf of the academy represent the only time in the history of the harpsichord that a government agency took such close notice of stringed keyboard instruments.[67]

found on the bridges of Broman's clavichords as well). Hence, the strings cross the bridge almost perpendicularly and are therefore quite close to being equal in length and tension. The 4′ strings are not hitched to the normal under-the-soundboard hitchpin rail, but run through holes in the 8′ bridge to the 8′ hitchpin rail.

The Broman harpsichord does not have a painted soundboard. The case is now all in natural wood, but that probably was not its original condition, since in 1969 Dahl reported that the exterior was painted a dark blue and the lid interior was white.[71] Whether that was the original finish or not is unclear, but the keywell is beautifully finished in veneers and marquetry. The keyboard has ivory naturals with embossed-paper key fronts, and the sharps are tortoise shell. The instrument sits on a table stand with eight cabriole legs. Judging from the Musikmuseet's negative report on its sound, it was not a completely successful experiment, although it is hardly fair to pass judgment on Brelin and Faggot's ideas on the basis of a single instrument.

15-9. The 12′-long 1756 Johan Broman harpsichord is the largest ever made in historical times. Stockholm, Stockholm Musikhistorisca Museet, harpsichord signed by Johannes Broman, inventory # NM 83118.

Nevertheless, Broman had greater success applying those concepts to the clavichord, and, in fact, through Broman and others, Brelin and Faggot did succeed in changing the look and sound of the Swedish version.[72]

Broman's other surviving harpsichord (Stockholm, Musikmuseet), a 2×8′, 1×4′ double with a C–e³ compass, is undated. It is 9′ long, even though it goes down only to C. Had it descended to FF, it likely would have been as long as Broman's 1756 Goliath. Its exterior and lid interior are nicely finished in chinoiserie, and it sits on a rather delicate cabriole-legged stand.[73]

Danish harpsichords can be discussed briefly, since there were few builders, and the extant handful resemble North German instruments. *Boalch III* lists a dozen builders in Denmark,[74] and while they all made clavichords, it is likely that there was some production of harpsichords as well. Moritz Georg Moshak (1730–ca. 1772), born in Copenhagen, is survived by a single 1770 one-manual 2×8′ instrument (Nykøbing Falster, Falsters Minder Museum), and there is a 1762 virginal by Christian Ferdinand Speer (dates unknown), an immigrant from Silesia (Rosenborg, Rosenborg Castle Museum). *Boalch III* lists only two makers from Norway, both clavichord builders, and only one from Finland.[75]

BERLIN

Thirteen Berlin builders are listed by *Boalch III,* but only two are survived by harpsichords.[76] Nevertheless, we know of others through chance remarks. Charles Burney, for example, casually observed that the otherwise unknown builder Johann Christian Schramm (fl. 1768–73) made very good harpsichords, and that "Hildebrand" (he probably meant Christian Friedrich Hildebrandt) was the best harpsichord maker in Berlin. Such references give us pause, since almost nothing is known of these builders and their instruments. As with all the cities of Germany, the true extent of harpsichord building in Berlin will likely never be understood.

The best-known Berlin maker was Michael Mietke (before 1665–1726 or 1729). He was little more than a name before 1985, when Sheridan Germann, through a series of clever deductions, linked him with two exquisite unsigned instruments in Schloss Charlottenburg in Berlin. Considered a fine craftsman during his lifetime, Mietke was appointed instrument builder to the Berlin court of Frederick I and Sophie Charlotte around the turn of the eighteenth century and later held the title of keyboard tuner and organ builder. Eighteenth-century lexicographers Johann Gottfried Walther (1684–1748) and Ernst Ludwig Gerber (1746–1819) both spoke highly of his instruments.[77] Sales notices in newspapers indicate that used Mietke instruments were still changing hands late in the eighteenth century.[78] But aside from a few mundane details of his life, little else is known of this great builder.[79]

Nevertheless, there are two intriguing bits of information that have made Mietke the object of some intense investigation. The first is that in 1719, while J. S. Bach was employed as Kapellmeister at the court of Prince Leopold in Cöthen, he traveled to Berlin at the behest of his prince to purchase a two-manual Mietke harpsichord described as large and unusually expensive.[80] This instrument has not survived, and we know nothing of it — unfortunately, for if we did we might gain considerable insight into Bach's ideas about harpsichords. The second piece of information has already been mentioned: many years after his death in 1719 it was reported that Mietke had made two harpsichords with a 16'. There is at present no way to verify this information; but if true, it would mean that Mietke may have been an early builder to use the 16', since the first of the known Hass harpsichords so disposed was not completed until 1734. There has been some speculation surrounding the description of the Mietke that Bach purchased as "large and unusually expensive." The extra expense might be explained if it had been extensively decorated, but that would have cost far more than the 130 Thaler Bach paid on Prince Leopold's behalf. On the other hand, it might have been unusually expensive — and large — because it was one of the Mietkes with a 16'.

An inventory of the keyboard instruments owned by J. S. Bach, drawn up a few months after his death in 1750, lists five harpsichords, a spinet of some sort, and two Lautenwerken, one of which was the instrument made for him by Zacharias Hildebrand.[81] One of the harpsichords was veneered and valued at 80 Thaler, as opposed to the 50 Thaler appraisal placed on three of the others (the last of the harpsichords was a *kleiner*—a small instrument, perhaps at 4′ pitch). There has been some conjecture as to why the veneered harpsichord was worth more than the others. Stauffer, for example, is of the opinion that it was a double-manual instrument with GG–d³ compass (the range Bach first calls for in his *Clavierübung*, written between 1726 and 1731), and that the 50 Thaler instruments were also doubles, but with the narrower compass of C–d³.[82] In truth, such speculation leads nowhere. In Germany as elsewhere, harpsichords were as much visual objects as they were musical, and their value probably reflected the degree of their decoration. It is logical to assume that a large but plain Central German harpsichord might have cost considerably less than a smaller but more ornate Hamburg instrument.

The question of Bach's harpsichords has been complicated by the recently mentioned instrument ascribed to the workshop of Johann Heinrich Harrass. This large double, uncritically accepted in the first half of the twentieth century as having belonged to Bach, had a 16′ choir of strings, and with an organlike disposition of 1×16′, 1×8′ on the lower manual and 1×8′, 1×4′ on the upper is now considered to have given a false picture of the sort of harpsichords the master had available to him.

The possibility that Bach might have had an instrument with a 16′ choir of strings at his disposal is intriguing.

Three of Mietke's harpsichords survive, a 1702–4 2×8′ single, a 1703–13 2×8′, 1×4′ double (both in Berlin, Schloss Charlottenburg), and a 1710 2×8′ single (Hudiksvall, Sweden, Halsinglands Museum).[83] The 1702–4 (see Plate 23), which goes by the name of "the white Mietke," is better known for its decor—an exquisite gold and polychrome chinoiserie on a white ground—than as a musical instrument. Done in a rare, porcelain-like style, the decoration is accepted with virtually no reservation as the work of Gerard Dagly, court decorator during the time of Mietke's tenure as court harpsichord builder. His title for several years was *Kunstkammermeister*, which translates as "Master of the Curio Cabinet" (a huge room in which masses of imported Chinese porcelain were displayed), and undoubtedly he was one of Frederick I and Sophie's cultural adornments. Dagly specialized in chinoiserie, and famed as the finest japanner[84] in Europe, he was the master of the difficult porcelain style found on the white harpsichord.

The 1703–13 double, christened "the black harpsichord" for its chinoiserie on a black ground, was also probably decorated by Dagly, and although not as spectacular as its white sister, it is still a masterfully finished object. The 1710 is more simply done, with a greenish-blue exterior and lid interior, with a gilded decoration on the latter. The soundwell is veneered, likely in sycamore, but the keywell is painted the same color as the exterior. This is not typical of the decor normally used by Dagly, nor of anything we have seen so far in northern Germany. Since the soundwell is veneered while the keywell is painted—the opposite of what one would expect in a German harpsichord—it is possible that this is not the original decoration.[85]

The three surviving Mietkes originally had two different compasses. The 1710, which has never been enlarged, is GG, AA–c³, and that seems to have been the range of the white harpsichord as well; but by the end of the eighteenth century it had been expanded to FF,GG–e³. Originally, the black harpsichord had one more note that the white, FF,GG,AA–c³, but it was later increased to FF,GG–e³. In all three, the naturals are covered with ebony and the stained hardwood sharps with ivory. The case walls are of basswood, about ⅜″ thick, and overlap the bottoms. Applied moldings on the rims of the cases project into the soundwells. The internal framing combines bottom braces and knees. Soundboards are braced with cutoff bars and ribs, but also with a series of short ribs under each of the bridges. The high, narrow bridges and nuts are molded. Scales are short. Box guides are used, with stop levers on the wrestplanks. The gaps angle away from the nut, allowing deeper plucking points in the bass. The octave spans are all narrow, reminiscent of seventeenth-century French practice.[86] Surprisingly for such elegant instruments, the soundboards are without decoration—not even a rose. The keywells are veneered with natural wood (except for the 1710, which now has a painted keywell but which may have originally been veneered), and with prominent fret-sawn cheek pieces. The 1702–4 white single measures a little over 7′ in length, and the 1703–13 black double is about 6″ longer than that. Under the Mietke harpsichords are typical eighteenth-century German table stands with low stretchers on ball feet, and seven or eight square-tapered or turned legs, decorated en suite with the instrument.[87]

Christoph and Johann Christoph Oesterlein were father and son builders in Berlin. The father (end of seventeenth century–middle of eighteenth) has left no instruments, but Johann Christoph (ca. 1728–after 1792) is survived by a 1792 double (Berlin, Staatliches Institut für Musikforschung). This large and powerful-looking harpsichord—more than 8′ long, with a compass of FF–f³ and a disposition of 2×8′, 1×4′ with coupler—is one of the last produced in Germany. Nevertheless, its inner construction reveals the same International roots as the Mietkes built in the first part of the century. Its birch case sides are of intermediate thickness with a heavier spine, and the case bracing consists of low bottom members and knees. The soundboard is braced with a 4′ hitchpin rail and a series of ribs crossing under the bridges. Bridges and nuts are characteristically tall and molded, with parallel sides. A slanting gap and a wide wrestplank ensure that the bass strings are plucked far

J. S. BACH AND EQUAL TEMPERAMENT

Equal temperament, with the comma distributed equally within the octave, grew in popularity alongside the piano in the nineteenth century. It had triumphed almost universally by the beginning of the twentieth, which viewed it as an evolutionary end product. It was seen as the final resolution to the problem of the comma, the "perfect" solution that superseded the "imperfect" meantone and revolving (or circulating) temperaments of earlier times. With the reawakening of interest in the music of J. S. Bach, the legend developed that the *Well-Tempered Clavier* was written for the purpose of persuading recalcitrant keyboard players to tune their instruments in equal temperament. To a rationalist, post-Darwinian world, this evolutionary conclusion seemed not only obvious but inevitable.

This assumption was challenged around the middle of the twentieth century, as more information about revolving temperaments came to light.[88] It was now believed that the purpose of the *Well-Tempered Clavier* was to demonstrate the superiority of revolving temperaments over meantone. With "Werckmeister III," or "Kirnberger," or "Vallotti," or one of the many other revolving schemes, one could play in all keys; and since the sizes of the semitones differed, these temperaments had the added advantage that keys had their own distinctive sounds, with the simpler ones less dissonant than the more complex ones. This view made sense, since meantone temperament, conceived well before the advent of key theory and practice, was useful only in signatures up to three flats and two sharps (or the reverse, depending on which thirds were tuned pure); and even then, if the music modulated some distance from the home key, meantone could produce some impossibly harsh dissonances. But with a suitable revolving temperament, acoustical dissonance became a matter of degree. "Simple" keys, like C, G, and F, had a large proportion of the more consonant-sounding triads, while keys like D♭ and F♯, although usually usable, were less consonant sounding. Thus, each key could be said to have a "character."

Toward the end of the twentieth century a revisionist view became popular, based on sources not formerly considered as well as a rereading of the earlier materials.[89] Once again, but for entirely different reasons, the view gained currency that Bach intended equal temperament for the *Well-Tempered Clavier,* and by extension, his keyboard works in general. The argument will undoubtedly continue to simmer for decades to come.[90]

from the nut. The scale is a longish intermediate 13½″. Even at this late date, a hint of inner-outer tradition is seen in the elaborate fret-sawn cheek pieces in the keywell. The unpainted Oesterlein is severely plain, with little decoration other than the cheek pieces and a prominent molding around the bottom of the case. Ebony-covered naturals and ivory-slipped sharps provide the only contrast to the neutral color of the case and soundboard. It sits on a stand with a narrow apron and four large square-tapered legs, quite unlike the ornate baroque constructions of the past.

HANNOVER AND BRUNSWICK

The Hamburg organ builder Martin Vater (fl. 1670–95) was the father of two makers: Antoine, who emigrated to France and who was mentioned briefly in chapter 13, and his older brother Christian (1679–1756). The latter practiced his trade in Hannover, to the west of Berlin, and early in his career worked for the great organ builder Arp Schnitger (1648–1719). He is survived by a 1738 single (Nuremberg, Germanisches Nationalmuseum) with a 2×8′ disposition and a GG/BB–e³ compass. The round-tailed bentside and cheek are made of fairly thin birch, and the heavier spine of pine. The scale is short, 10½″. Decorative elements include the keyboard with black-topped naturals and bone or ivory slips on the sharps, a gilded geometric rose, scroll-sawn cheek pieces, a black-painted case with some large gold interlaced designs on the cheek and bentside, and a stand with a low stretcher and six twist-turned legs. In common with a number of other instruments, the inside of the lid was never finished — a painting may have been planned but never executed. This is a conservative instrument, restrained in its decoration, with its International characteristics reminding us of the German and particularly the French products of the previous century; but it is an excellent harpsichord, with a tone quality full of variety.[91]

As usual, there are tantalizing traces of builders not represented by surviving harpsichords. Braunschweig (Brunswick), also west of Berlin, was the home of Barthold Fritz (1697–1766), an inventive builder who made not only organs, harpsichords, and clavichords, but also mechanical devices of all sorts including clocks, looms, and horizontal windmills. Only some of his clavichords are extant, and none of his harpsichords. Karl Tölleke (dates unknown) was said to be the only instrument maker in Brunswick, which obviously is not true, but nothing at all is known of him, other than it was reported that he had apprenticed with Reinecke, an even more obscure builder.[92] Perhaps the best-known Brunswick maker was Karl Friedrich Wilhelm Lemme (1747–1808), whose instruments were said by the music historian Johann Nikolaus Forkel (1749–1818) to rank among the best, as good as Silbermann's and Stein's;[93] but Lemme is survived

15-10. This 1738 2×8′ single by the Hannover builder Christian Vater, though relatively plain, is a fine example of a more restrained style of North German harpsichord building. Nuremberg, Germanisches Nationalmuseum.

only by a few clavichords, a grand piano, and a maintenance manual for clavichords and pianos.[94]

It is clear that harpsichord building in northern Germany revolved around several axes. Hamburg and Berlin were major centers, but Hannover and Brunswick may have been another, and undoubtedly there were yet others whose instruments are lost to us. From the little we can tell, they all seemed to have Internationally inspired internal bracing, with rounded tails and case walls of intermediate thickness often overlapping the bottom. Nuts and bridges were slender, high, and molded, with parallel sides. Roses, when present, were geometric and of paper or parchment. Aside from the variety found in Hamburg, key coverings generally consisted of ebony or black-stained naturals and ivory- or bone-topped sharps, with papered fronts. Both box guides and upper and lower guides were used in Hamburg and Berlin. Slide-in nameboards were common, as were buff stops and stop levers mounted on the wrestplank. With the exception of the 1792 Oesterlein, which in any case may be too late to be representative of the traditions discussed here, cases were painted. Any other characteristics they have in common are likely to be negative: for example, they did not normally use hardwoods like oak or walnut for case sides (although there are two extant Hass instruments with oak cases), and they did not use Ruckers-derived bridges and nuts.

Otherwise, the traditions of these areas appear to have been somewhat dissimilar. The concept of the harpsichord as a color machine with varied dispositions was particularly strong with the Hasses; but other instruments from Hamburg, and from other areas of the North, had more conventional dispositions of 2×8', 1×4' or 2×8'. Hamburg instruments used the Ruckers soundboard and bridge layout, but elsewhere in the North, Ruckers barring was combined with cross-barring. Scales were long in Hamburg, but mainly short in Berlin. The Hamburg instruments were probably strung in iron and the Berlin in brass. Octave spans were wide in Hamburg, wider than anywhere else; but they were narrow in Berlin, as narrow as the French spans of the previous century. Fret-sawn cheek pieces were used in Berlin and Hannover, but not in Hamburg. The Hamburg instruments had cut-in gilded case moldings, whereas the others had cap moldings. The Hamburg instruments had painted soundboards, but the Berlin examples did not.

In view of the disparity of traditions, we are forced to conclude that it is not possible to speak of a monolithic northern German tradition. Clearly, each region had its own concept of harpsichord building, although they shared some general International characteristics. Nevertheless, we come to this position through the examination of the very few known extant instruments. If more reveal themselves, our view of North German harpsichord building may have to change. One thing we do know, however: the few playing instruments we have are impressive sounding.

GROSS BREITENBACH

Gross Breitenbach, a small Central German town in the province of Thuringia, was home to the Harrass family, all four of whom had the same first name: Johann Heinrich (1665–1714), Johann Mathias (1671–1746), Johann Heinrich, Jr. (1707–78), and Johann Nicol (dates unknown). Other than the father-son connection between the two Johann Heinrichs, the relationships between the other members of the family are unknown. The earliest Harrass survivor is the double attributed to the workshop of Johann Heinrich dated ca. 1700 (Berlin, Staatliches Institut für Musikforschung). This instrument, the so-called "Bach" harpsichord, has been mentioned before. A large FF–f³ double more than 8′ long, with a round-tailed bentside and an intermediate scale of 13″, it is now in natural beech wood, although originally painted a light gray with gilded moldings.[95] Its inner construction consists of a complex combination of bottom braces, diagonal struts, a U-brace, and narrow upper braces, some of which must date from a nineteenth-century restoration. The soundboard has a light 4′ hitchpin rail and a cut-off bar and ribs, with additional ribs crossing the bridges. The bridges and nuts are high and narrow. With two bridges, three nuts, and four registers, originally it could have been disposed 3×8′, 1×4′ with coupler, like the 1723 Hass. The nameboard is nicely veneered in geometric patterns, and the keywell is further enlivened by large scroll-sawn cheek blocks of ebony. The keyboard scheme is ebony naturals and ivory-topped sharps.[96]

When it first came to the attention of collectors in the late nineteenth century, it was disposed 1×16′, 1×8′ on the lower manual, with 1×8′, 1×4′ on the upper. This "Bach" disposition was thoroughly discredited after the middle of the twentieth century, and the instrument was then thought to have originally been 3×8′, 1×4′. At this writing it is once again believed to have had a 16′, but that it replaced one of the 8′ choirs, and that the disposition was 16′, 4′ on the lower manual and 2×8′ on the upper.[97] Adlung not only described the practice of replacing a choir of 8′ strings with wound 16′s; he states that such harpsichords with 16′ were to be found in Gross Breitenbach.[98] Another Johann Heinrich double exists (Sonderhausen, Staat-

15-11. The disposition of this large ca. 1700 harpsichord attributed to Johann Heinrich Harrass has been in dispute for more than a hundred years. © Bildarchiv Preussischer Kulturbesitz, Berlin, Musikinstrumenten Museum.

lichen Heimat-und-Schlossmuseum), a 1710 with 2×8', 1×4' disposition, and an FF–f³ compass. The 1710 is signed, and it is because of the similarities between it and the ca. 1700 that the earlier instrument has been assigned to Harrass.

An anonymous ca. 1715 2×8' single (Eisenach, Bach-Haus) is considered to be a Thuringian harpsichord, but it looks nothing at all like the instruments of Harrass. It has several archaic elements, including a conservative four-octave C–c³ compass and a 2×8' disposition, with the registers extending through the cheeks. Its most unusual feature, however, is its hollow wrestplank, a narrow batten at the nameboard, with the nut sitting on active soundboard wood. This sort of construction was found in Germany in the previous century, but this is the only extant example of it from the eighteenth. Nevertheless, there is evidence that the hollow wrestplank might have been used in other harpsichords. When Adlung described German building in the first half of the eighteenth century, he stated that the jacks pass through the soundboard.[99] This can only happen when the soundboard crosses the gap, and it does that only when there is a hollow wrestplank. If Adlung was writing about the instruments he knew, which was almost certainly the case, then harpsichords with hollow wrestplanks, a tradition going back to the 1537 Müller, may not have been as rare in eighteenth-century Germany as is now assumed.[100]

The implications of this instrument are far-reaching. If the hollow wrestplank survived into the eighteenth century, then why not spread registers, metal plectra, and other elements of the earlier German harpsichord? That such instruments have never been found is no evidence that they never existed. Adlung talked about the *Harfenzug,* or harp stop;[101] Sprengel mentioned the *Schnarrwerk,* the German for a snarling sound similar to the arpichordum;[102] and there were other mentions of mutation stops that would seem to indicate that these were common on German instruments. Harpsichords with these devices no longer exist, but it may simply have been that at some point they were seen as old-fashioned and discarded, or that those special devices were suppressed. Once again, we are forced to conclude that the mere handful of exemplars that have survived are probably giving us a dim and perhaps not very accurate picture of the true state of German building.

DRESDEN

Dresden, the capital of Saxony, was an important port city on the Elbe River as well as one of the great cultural centers of Germany. Rich in architectural beauty and known for its fine china[103] and its opera, it had something of a harpsichord-producing tradition as well: *Boalch III* lists eighteen or so builders active there in the eighteenth century, more than in Hamburg.[104] Most of those makers are no more than names today; nevertheless, four Flügel have survived bearing the name of Gräbner, a family that evidently dominated Dresden building for most of the century.

The Gräbners were a dynasty of nine builders and organists (six of whom were given the first name of Johann) comprising four generations. The seventeenth-century patriarch was Johann Christoph Gräbner (dates unknown), who is not survived by any instruments, but who had two sons. The oldest, Johann Christian (fl. 1678–1704), left no harpsichords. His brother, Johann Heinrich the elder (1665–1739), also had two sons, one of whom, Johann Heinrich the younger (ca. 1700–ca. 1777), was appointed to the Dresden court as organ and harpsichord builder.[105] Johann Heinrich the younger had four sons of his own—three by his first wife and one by his second—who became builders. The first, Ernst Gottlob (1734–59), died at the age of twenty-five. The next, Johann Gottfried (1736–1808), replaced his father as court builder. Practically nothing is known of Johann Wilhelm (1737–98), other than that he went into the piano business with his older brother Johann Gottfried in 1786. The fourth son, Karl August (1749–1827), the product of Johann Heinrich's second marriage, became a partner of his half-brother Johann Gottfried for a short while after

Johann Wilhelm's death.[106] Like most German builders, by the end of the century the Gräbners were making pianos.

Johann Heinrich the elder is survived by three harpsichords and Karl August by one; of these four, two are early, two are late. A 1722 double (Prague, Villa Bertramka) is the earliest Johann Heinrich. Disposed 2×8′, 1×4′ with buff stop and shove coupler, its original compass was FF–d³ but was changed in an early rebuilding to EE–e³.[107] It is noteworthy that this instrument, like all the extant Gräbners, has a mitered tail, rather than the rounded versions more often found in Germany. Elaborate fretsawn cheek pieces enliven the keywell, which is painted, while the soundwell is veneered in natural wood — a reverse of the more usual German tradition of painted soundwell and veneered keywell. The exterior of the instrument is now in white, with gilded moldings, and the lid is painted red, but the original color seems to have been a dark green. The cheeks have been cut on a slant, but none of the other extant Gräbner harpsichords have this feature, and it is unlikely that it is original. Its ornate carved and gilded cabriole-legged stand is also not original.[108] Whatever the merits of this instrument, its fame now rests on its connection with Mozart, who is claimed to have played it in the Villa Bertramka when he was in Prague in 1787 to produce *Don Giovanni*.[109]

Many of the characteristics of the 1722 are found in the three other surviving Gräbners. These include pine sides of ⅜″ or less that overlap the bottom, and that are faced in the soundwell with about ¼″ of veneer (light-colored wood in the 1722 and 1739, walnut in the 1774[110] and 1782). All have applied cap moldings, inserted into a slot in the earlier two, as in Italian inner-outers, and fastened to the top of the sides, in International style, in the later two. A wide molding runs around the bottoms of the cases. Internal construction is based on diagonal struts (the 1722) and knees with posts and beams (the other three). Soundboards are cross-barred and, except for paper or parchment roses, undecorated. Bridges have parallel sides and are nearly square in section. The keyboards have black naturals and bone-topped sharps. The scales on all four instruments are intermediate, in the range of 13″ to 13½″. Interestingly, they are completely non-Pythagorean; instead, they are shorter in the tenor and longer in the treble.[111]

The four instruments are disposed 2×8′, 1×4′ with buff. They all have jack guides connected by vertical posts, making them, in effect, lightweight box guides. Both the 1722 and the 1739 have spacer bars of about ⅜″ between the front and middle guides, thus increasing the distance from the nut of the plucking points of the 4′ and the back 8′. The reason for this can only be attributed to a continuing Teutonic desire for sharp distinctions of tone quality, since the back 8′ jacks are separated from the front by the width of almost two registers, rather than the usual one. This feature is not found in the later two instruments, which, ascending to f³, require narrower gaps. The 4′ appears to separate the two 8′s on all the instruments. Like the keyboards of Mietke, the four Gräbner harpsichords have rather narrow keys and short heads. The nameboards are crenelated, with the long sharps of the upper manual disappearing into the cutouts. The same arrangement is found on the coupler rail, to accommodate the lower manual sharps. This feature will be seen on other Central German instruments.

15-12. Karl August Gräbner's 1782 harpsichord is a quiet visual contrast to the colorful instruments of northern Germany. Nuremberg, Germanisches Nationalmuseum.

The 1739 harpsichord (Dresden, Museum für Kunstgewerbe)[112] is signed simply Johann Heinrich Gräbner, but is probably by the younger builder.[113] Like all the Gräbner examples, it is a two-manual instrument disposed 2×8′, 1×4′ plus buff, although it has an unusually low and apparently original DD–d³ compass. There are elaborate fret-sawn cheek pieces in the keywell, and the exterior of the case is painted a black-green, with the lid and keywell in vermilion. Johann Heinrich the younger's other surviving harpsichord is the 1774 double (Leipzig, Musikinstrumenten-Museum der Universität Leipzig), and although it was built thirty-five years after the 1739, and its FF–f³ compass is a third higher, and it has no fret-sawn cheek pieces, it is otherwise quite similar in style.[114] Sometime before 1892, in an effort to give it a "Bach"-like disposition, a set of 16′ strings was substituted for one of the 8′ choirs, placing the 16′ and 8′ on the lower manual and the 4′ on the upper. It was returned to its original disposition around 1955.[115]

Karl August Gräbner is the only other member of the family survived by a harpsichord.[116] His FF–f³ double dated 1782 (Nuremberg, Germanisches Nationalmuseum) seems to be typical of what we can now identify as the Gräbner tradition. It is disposed 2×8′, 1×4′ with buff, its case wood is stained pine or a similar wood, the tail is mitered, the keyboard is black naturals and white-topped sharps, the soundboard is unpainted, the

THE GRÄBNERS AT A GLANCE			
Name	*Dates*	*Relation to Johann Heinrich the Younger*	*Extant Harpsichords*
Johann Christoph	Unknown	Grandfather	
Johann Christian	Active 1678–1704	Uncle	
Johann Heinrich the elder	1665–1739	Father	1722
Johann Heinrich the younger	ca. 1700–ca. 1777		1739, 1774
Christian Heinrich	1704–69	Brother (but not a builder)	
Ernst Gottlob	1734–59	Son by first wife	
Johann Gottfried	1736–1808	Son by first wife	
Johann Wilhelm	1737–95	Son by first wife	
Karl August	ca. 1749–ca. 1796	Son by second wife	1782

molded bridges are almost square, with parallel sides, and there are few moldings.

Except for the one under the 1722, Gräbner table stands are relatively simple looking, with square-cut cabriole legs, no carvings, and few frills. The general appearance of the ensemble is one of plain gentility. Like much furniture, these instruments are quiet in countenance, with neither the flamboyance of the Hass and Mietke harpsichords, the architectural dignity of the Italians, nor the beautiful veneer work of the English.[117]

FREIBERG

Andreas Silbermann (1678–1734) and his younger brother Gottfried (1683–1753) were born in the little Saxon town of Kleinbobritzsch. Andreas received his training as an organ, harpsichord, and clavichord builder somewhere in Germany, and at age twenty-five he emigrated to Strasbourg, in France.[118] He became a successful builder, with thirty organs to his credit; unfortunately, we know nothing of his stringed keyboards. Gottfried began an apprenticeship in Germany as a bookbinder, but broke his contract and ran away to Strasbourg to study instrument building with his brother. In 1710 Gottfried returned to Germany, settled in the Saxon city of Freiberg, and became a famous organ builder. He is, of course, equally well known for his role in bringing the piano to Germany. Silbermann copied Cristofori's action but not his revolutionary case design; instead, he put the piano actions into what was essentially a Central German harpsichord case, although he did use Cristofori's "inverted" wrestplank. Gottfried was also the inventor of the *Cembal d'amour*, a long clavichord whose tangents contact the middle of the strings, thus activating both sides.[119]

Gottfried amassed a great deal of money as a builder and

died a wealthy man, a feat achieved by few instrument makers. A bachelor with no heirs, he left his business to his nephew, Johann Daniel Silbermann (1717–66), Andreas's second son; but Daniel seems to have built only organs and pianos.[120] Johann Heinrich Silbermann (1727–99), the youngest son of Andreas, apprenticed with his uncle Gottfried in Freiberg for two years, but then returned to Strasbourg. Some of his bentside spinets are extant (see Chapter 13).

A few of Gottfried's pianos have survived,[125] but of his jack-action instruments, only an unsigned FF–f^3 two-manual harpsichord with shove coupler dated ca. 1740[126] (Berlin, Staatliches Institut für Musikforschung) has been cautiously ascribed to him. More than 8½' long, and with an intermediate scale of 13″, it is strung 2×8', 1×4', with the 4' behind the two 8's. The jacks run in upper and lower guides. It does not look very different from other Central German harpsichords we have seen: the plainly finished natural-wood oak case has little decoration, other than a simple cap molding on top of the sides and a wide molding around the bottom. The internal construction consists of U-braces, and the sides overlap the bottom. The soundboard has a cutoff bar and 4' hitchpin rail, but is also cross-barred with a series of eight ribs under the 8' bridge, five under the 4', and two more between the cutoff bar and the spine. Bridges and nuts are molded and almost square in section. The soundboard is undecorated, but has the characteristic Silbermann family rose—a geometric device of paper, with a circle in a triangle containing the initial "S." The keys have ebony naturals, and the ends of the ivory-slipped sharps disappear into crenelations in the nameboard and coupler rail. With a floating-panel lid, the case sits on four square-tapered legs.

GOTTFRIED SILBERMANN, J. S. BACH, AND THE PIANO

Sometime between 1732 and 1736 Gottfried Silbermann made two pianos, with the actions apparently derived either from the drawing in Scipione Maffei's 1711 article "Nuova invenzione d'un gravicembalo col piano e forte . . ." in the *Giornale de' letterati d'Italia*,[121] or from one of the models constructed by Christoph Gottlieb Schröter (1699–1782), who insisted that his invention of the hammer harpsichord preceded Cristofori's.[122] It is clear that these pianos were not as successful as they could have been. Adlung relates that Silbermann's friend and colleague, J. S. Bach, tried one of them out and noted that although the new instrument had a good sound, the treble was weak and the touch too heavy.[123] According to Adlung, Bach's words angered Silbermann, who, after all, was by this time considered a great master; but he recognized the validity of the criticism and for a while stopped making pianos.

Somehow, Silbermann must have gained access to a Cristofori instrument, because when he started building pianos again, sometime before 1746, their actions were almost identical to those found in the Italian master's surviving work. Frederick the Great seemed to have liked them, since he purchased some from Silbermann. J. S. Bach played them on his famous visit to Potsdam, where his son Carl Philipp Emanuel was then employed; in fact, it was on these pianos that Bach improvised for the king. His opinion of the later version of Silbermann's piano was quite different from his earlier judgment, and he was impressed enough to act as Silbermann's agent in the sale of a piano to a Polish count in 1749.[124]

15-13. This large 1740 harpsichord, likely by Gottfried Silbermann, demonstrates the Central German concept of the *Flügel* as a piece of nice but ordinary furniture. © Bildarchiv Preussischer Kulturbesitz, Berlin, Musikinstrumenten Museum.

15-14. Like other families of builders we have seen, the Silbermann brothers shared a rose design. The devices of Johann Heinrich in Strasbourg are more complex, but are still based on the idea of an S inside a circle inside a triangle inside a circle. © Bildarchiv Preussischer Kulturbesitz, Berlin, Musikinstrumenten Museum.

Aside from an obvious adherence to a common style of case building based on sides of intermediate thickness, and bottom, U-, and knee bracing, the few harpsichords we have from Thuringia and Saxony in Central Germany bespeak of a tradition quite different from that seen in the North. The instruments tend to a sobriety of appearance, with simply painted, stained, and natural-wood finishes, few moldings, unpainted soundboards, mitered tails, and quiet stands. Cross-barred soundboards seem to have been the norm. The earlier examples had fret-sawn cheek pieces. The common disposition was 2×8′, 1×4′, with the 4′ either behind or between the 8′s, and with a shove coupler. From the extant examples, the keyboard tradition was exclusively black naturals with ivory- or bone-slipped sharps. The Ruckers influence that swept France and England in the eighteenth century seemed to have made little impression on these builders, and the case construction, soundboard barring, and scale owed far more to the Germanic International milieu from which these instruments emerged, and to which they were still strongly connected. These are straightforward harpsichords, but it would be a mistake to consider them second-rate. Those that are still playing are

ANOTHER MYSTERY HARPSICHORD

An anonymous double (Barcelona, Museu de la Música) bears a superficial resemblance to the 1740 instrument described above and ascribed to Silbermann. The case is plain, of natural wood, with cap and bottom moldings, supported by four turned legs. The lid is of floating-panel construction. The disposition is 2×8′, 1×4′, and the compass FF–f³. The keyboard has ebony naturals and ivory-slipped sharps. It also has a rose similar to those used on the bentside spinets of Johann

15-15. Superficially, this "mystery" harpsichord reminds one of Central German instruments, particularly with the Silbermann-like rose; but to our knowledge, soundboard painting and rose gilding are not found anywhere else in that area. Barcelona, Museu de la Música.

Heinrich Silbermann, although the central section of the rose, with the initial, is missing. Although it is 6″ shorter than the 1740, the two instruments share a resemblance of bridge and nut layout. But there are differences. The rose is gilded, an adornment found neither on the 1740 nor, with one exception,[127] on the extant bentside spinets of Johann Heinrich. The soundboard is decorated in a style reminiscent of North German instruments, with both a rose and a vignette. Furthermore, the instrument has some apparent crudities, such as large, thin, square cheek blocks and a lid with a single, large floating panel.

Museums and collections are full of mystery instruments such as this one, often indicating that our neat little stylistic classifications frequently break down, and that harpsichord building may not have always been as tightly compartmentalized as we would like to think. Nevertheless, a 1700 double with 2×8′, 1×4′ disposition and FF–d³ compass, by the Strasbourg builder Friderich Ring (1666–1701) (Stuttgart, private collection), with whom Andreas Silbermann worked when he first came to Strasbourg, bears some resemblances to this mystery instrument. Like Silbermann's bentside spinets, the Ring instrument is squarely Germanic, with an oak case veneered in birch, an inlaid keywell, and ebony naturals and ivory-topped sharps. Perhaps most importantly, it has a decorated soundboard, something not seen in Germany except in the North.[128] By no means does this suggest that our enigmatic harpsichord had a Strasbourg origin; but it does point up once again the imperfect picture we have of German harpsichord building.

NORTHERN AND CENTRAL GERMAN HARPSICHORDS AT A GLANCE			
	Hamburg	*Berlin*	*Thuringia/Saxony*
Case side thickness	Intermediate	Intermediate	Intermediate
Case side material	Pine, oak	Linden, birch	Pine, oak, beech
Shape of tail	Rounded	Rounded	Mitered, rounded
Case top molding	Cut into sides	Applied	Applied
Case decoration	Complex, colorful	Complex	Simple
Soundboard decoration	Yes	No	No
Internal bracing	International	International	International
Disposition	Hass varies, others 2×8′, 1×4′	2×8′; 2×8′, 1×4′	2×8′, 1×4′
Lute stop	Yes	No	No
Registers	Upper, lower, and box guides	Upper, lower, and box guides	Upper, lower, and box guides
Soundboard barring	Northern	Combined Northern and cross-barred	Cross-barred and combined
Nuts and bridges	High, narrow	High, narrow	High, narrow; square like
Scale	Long	Intermediate, short	Intermediate
Octave span	Wide	Very narrow	Narrow
Key coverings	Black-white, and white-black	Black naturals, white sharps	Black naturals, white sharps
Stands	Turned legs, low stretchers	Turned legs, low stretchers	Square-cut cabriole legs

impressive sounding and represent mainstream European tonal values in a utilitarian case.

AUGSBURG

Only one major builder, Johann Andreas Stein (1728–92), can be identified in the south of Germany, but he is a figure of immense importance to the history of stringed keyboard instrument building. Stein was born in the state of Baden, in southeast Germany, just over the border from France. His apprenticeship must have been somewhere in Germany, but at age twenty-one he spent a year in France, in Strasbourg, with Johann Heinrich Silbermann, Gottfried's nephew, presumably working on organs, harpsichords, clavichords, and Cristofori-action pianos. From there he went to Augsburg, where he established his own shop. Soon after that he built an organ for one of the local churches, and in 1757, at age twenty-nine, he also became that church's organist. The following year found him in Paris, and when he returned to Augsburg in 1759 his interest in organs seemed to have waned in favor of pianos. His earliest efforts are no longer extant, but it is likely that they contained the Cristofori actions with hollow hammer heads he worked on in the shop of his Strasbourg mentor. He was also interested in clavichords and produced many of these, including the small traveling instrument he made for the Mozart family in 1763 (Budapest, Magyar Nemzeti Múzeum).[129]

Stein's harpsichord building remains something of an unknown quantity, although there is no question that he was regarded as one of the best builders of his time. For example, the composer and poet Daniel Schubart (1739–91) noted that Stein's "organs, harpsichords, fortepianos and clavichords are the best one knows of."[130] Stein built twenty-one harpsichords between 1750 and 1777;[131] nevertheless, the only jack-action instruments that have survived are two combined harpsichord-pianos. This was a synthesis that seems to have intrigued him. He realized it first in a contrivance he called the *polytoni-clavichordium*, which consisted of a three-manual instrument combining a two-manual harpsichord disposed 3×8′, 1×16′ and a piano, all in the same case.[132] None are extant. The *vis-à-vis*, a large oblong with a piano at one end and a harpsichord at the other, was another attempt at uniting the two instruments, and two of these complex machines have survived.

The earlier is a large instrument of 1777 (Verona, Museo Civico), 9½′ long, with four manuals: three at the harpsichord end, the lowest of which plays the piano by means of trackers passing underneath the instrument, and one for piano alone at the other end. Both ends have a five-octave FF–f³ compass. The harpsichord is disposed 1×16′, 2×8′, 1×4′, but to state it this way is misleading, since the 4′ bridge takes only the bottom sixteen notes, and after that the stringing breaks back to 3×8′. The 16′ bridge does not go down to FF, but lacks the lowest seven notes. These peculiarities are due to the restricted soundboard area, which is only slightly larger than usual, although the intermediate scale of 12¾″ allows the 8′ bridge to be more centrally located on the board, thus providing more room for the 16′. The front set of 8′ jacks is doglegged and available from either manual, and all four sets of strings are played from the middle keyboard. The harpsichord is provided with hand stops on the wrestplank, two of which control the piano dampers (bass and treble damper stops are provided at the piano end as well). The two instruments share a hitchpin rail.

Quite unexpectedly, the harpsichord is provided with an arpichordum stop, a row of metal hooks, in the place normally occupied by a buff stop.[133] This mutation device has not been seen on surviving instruments since the seventeenth-century Flemish muselar, and perhaps in the 1579 and 1622 English harpsichords by Theewes and Hasard; nevertheless, something quite similar to it was used by Gottfried Silbermann, in pianos of 1746 (Potsdam, Sans Souci) and 1749 (Nuremberg, Germanisches Nationalmuseum).[134] Stein could have seen such devices in the instruments of his teacher, but it is also reasonable to assume that these sharp, jarring mutation stops remained in the memory of German builders for a long time, and it is possible that they were used on other instruments no longer extant.

The piano end is equally interesting. Although there are some Stein pianos that appear to be earlier, it has been pointed out that these instruments have one date on their nameboards and later ones written underneath their soundboards; accordingly, this may be the earliest extant piano by the master.[135] The action is transitional, something between the Cristofori type Stein learned to build in Silbermann's shop — even to the extent of having an "inverted" wrestplank — and the later German (or Viennese) action. Interestingly, its solid pearwood hammers are bare, with no leather covers.[136] As suggested above, the bass and treble dampers were operated independently, by hand stop. Other stops controlled a moderator and a bassoon.

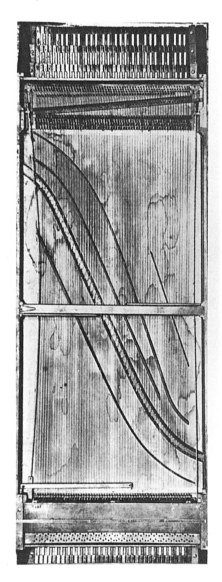

15-16. This imposing 1777 *vis-à-vis* combination harpsichord-piano by Johann Andreas Stein combines a two-manual harpsichord with a piano. The harpsichord's third keyboard allows the performer to play the piano from the harpsichord end. Verona, Museo Civico.

The second extant *vis-à-vis* is dated 1783 (Naples, Naples Conservatoire). Both ends have an FF–f³ compass, and the harpsichord is disposed 2×8′, 1×4′, with the stops controlled by three knee levers. One set of jacks is quilled in leather, perhaps originally *peau de buffle*.[137] The harpsichord end has two manuals, but the upper plays only the piano, while the lower is dedicated to the harpsichord. The other end, of course, has a single piano keyboard. Thus, the piano could be played from either end (and piano and harpsichord together from the harpsichord end), but not the reverse. The piano action is typical of Stein's later German action, and the hollow wood hammers are covered with leather. With a length of slightly more than 9′, the 1783 instrument is almost as imposing as the 1777.

Earlier, in 1753, Stein invented an instrument he called the *Saitenharmonika,* a normal double-strung piano with a third set of strings activated by a "very elastic material."[138] It has

15-17. The second of the two surviving Stein *vis-à-vis* combinations, dated 1783. The reinforced slanted cheeks, plain case, turned legs, and floating-panel lid are also typical of contemporary Viennese harpsichords. Berlin, Bildarchiv Preussischer Kulturbesitz.

generally been assumed that this referred to a jack action with an unusual plucking material.[139] If so, then this is yet another of Stein's combination instruments, and the plectra might have been made from a soft leather such as that used in the *peau de buffle*. In any event, the attachment seems to have been successful in its intended effect, which was to fill the dynamic range between the piano's softest sound and nothingness — "between *pianissimo* and silence," as Koster would put it.[140] The composer Johann Friedrich Reichardt (1752–1814) heard the instrument played by Stein's daughter, Nannette (1769–1833), in 1790. He reported that Stein excitedly pointed out that "You think that you still hear something at the end; but you hear nothing, absolutely nothing, absolutely nothing at all."[141] Stein completed and delivered at least two *Saitenharmonikas*, and a much-rebuilt triple-strung instrument of 1783 (Boston, Museum of Fine Arts) is assumed to have been one of these.[142]

Stein's importance to the history of stringed keyboards lies not so much in these strange combination instruments, but in his invention of the German, or so-called "Viennese," piano action, in which the hammer, mounted on the end of the key, is activated by an escapement mechanism. Stein ignored the case structures of Silbermann and other German piano builders who came before him. Instead, he built his cases of much heavier members, with an outer "skin" of thin case walls glued to a heavy inner shell, and with slanted, reinforced cheeks. This is, in fact, the sort of case building we will see in Vienna. It is possible that Stein borrowed his case concept from his neighbors to the South, but it is more likely that both southern Germany and Vienna shared a similar style of case building, one outside both Northern and International practices. Unfortunately, the only evidence for this is the general appearance of the two *vis-à-vis* pianos; but both of these have plain cases, reinforced slanted cheeks, ebony naturals and ivory sharps, and intermediate scales. These are characteristics we will see in Vienna.

Stein's innovations influenced German and Austrian piano building for the next forty years.[143] Nevertheless, as we have noted previously, with Stein's mature work we are no longer dealing with the hammer harpsichord, but with an entirely new instrument, with its own sound, technique, and literature, and as such, one that is outside the scope of this book. Still, it is important to remember that people did not easily abandon their harpsichords as pianos grew in popularity, and that harpsichords were still being made in Germany in the last decade of the eighteenth century.[144]

AUSTRIA

Vienna was the keyboard-instrument-making center of Austria in the eighteenth century. About one hundred organ builders worked there between 1700 and 1800, and almost all of them made stringed keyboards; but there really is no way of knowing how many of them made harpsichords. In fact, the major portion of their nonorgan output was undoubtedly clavichords and, later, pianos.[145] Furthermore, builders born later in the century, such as Johann Halbig (ca. 1761–93), Johann Jakesch (ca. 1763–1840), and Anton Moser (ca. 1773–1823), probably never built any harpsichords at all, since by the time they reached their majority the production of jack-action instruments had slowed to a trickle, or stopped entirely, in favor of pianos.

Viennese harpsichord builders seemed to be as conservative as their trans-Alpine neighbors to the south. Richard Maunder points out that the *Orgelmacher*'s guild played an important role in maintaining a traditional building practice that lasted almost through the century, and he is undoubtedly correct;[146] nevertheless, cultural forces also seemed to be at work here, since with few exceptions, during all the harpsichord's history the most conservative instruments were made in Italy, in the South of Europe. Aside from Cristofori and a very few others, Italian builders were content to follow in the paths their fathers had made. Yet, builders seemed to become more adventurous farther north. The visual flamboyancy and tonal variety of the Hass instruments is one example, and the application of scientific principles to late-eighteenth-century Swedish clavichords is another. It might be too simplistic to create a "conservative to innovative" continuum from Southern to Northern Europe, but the tendency was there, nevertheless.

Eleven Viennese instruments with jack actions — eight grand harpsichords and three spinets (one of the latter at the octave) — have survived from the eighteenth century, and they show an extraordinary unanimity of constructional techniques. The earliest signed harpsichord, built in 1703 by Franz Walter (ca. 1656–1733) (Vienna, Kunsthistorisches Museum), almost defines the genre.[150] It is a single-manual 2×8′ instrument, a little more than 7′ in length, with a mitered tail and a deeply curved bentside. The compass of FF/C–f³,g³ is uncommonly wide for so early in the century, although certainly not unheard-of. The case construction is unusual. An inner shell of softwood, almost ⅝″ thick, with a bellyrail around 1″ in thickness, is reinforced by upper and lower rails that surround the interior of the framework at the bottom and at the soundboard level. The rails are connected by a series of vertical posts. There are also five diagonal struts, but they were added at a later date, perhaps when the instrument was converted to a piano. The whole forms a massive "inner" case to which an outside skin of thin hardwood sides of about ⅜″ is glued. The sides sit on the bottom, and the joint is hidden with a molding. The soundwell is veneered in maple, with a walnut cap molding on top of the case. The scale is a short 10½″, indicating that brass stringing was probably intended. Like some South German examples from the previous century, the cheeks are cut on a slant; but more wood is glued to their inside surfaces, in front of the removeable nameboard, reinforcing them and making them almost 1″ thick.[151] In keeping with long-standing Germanic tradition, the keywell is inlaid with walnut, ivory, and ebony in geometric patterns, and aside from a geometric soundboard rose, this is the only decoration on the case. The jacks run in box guides, operated by extensions through the cheek. Ivory-topped naturals contrast with ebony-topped stained fruitwood sharps. Key fronts are embossed paper with green silk showing through.

The FF/C "multiple-broken" short octave[152] needs some explanation, particularly since it appears to have been a frequent feature of Viennese harpsichords, clavichords, and pianos during the eighteenth century.[153] In essence, it is a downward extension of the C/E short octave (which itself is a downward extension from F). The keyboard appears to descend from F diatonically to C—in other words, the conventional C/E short octave extended by a D and a C. The apparent C sounds FF. The apparent D is divided front, middle, and rear into three different keys, sounding (from front to rear) GG, AA, and BB♭. The apparent E is divided twice, with the front portion sounding C and the rear BB.[154] From here on up the diatonic notes sound as they appear; but the F♯ and G♯ are both split front and rear, as in a conventional split-sharp short octave. Accordingly, the front of the F♯ sounds D and the rear F♯, and the front of the G♯ sounds E while the rear gives the G♯. All together the scheme gives a bottom octave of FF, GG, AA, BB, C, D, E, and F. From there on the scale is chromatic. Of course, those keyboards could have been made with the actual diatonic keys, but that would have made the instrument wider, and a slim case always seems to have been desirable.

The 1703 Walter is not the first Viennese harpsichord to survive the eighteenth century. Two earlier exemplars, both anonymes, one tentatively dated 1680–1700 (Prague, National Museum) and the other ca. 1700 (Nuremberg, Germanisches Nationalmuseum), share many of the characteristics of the Walter described above. The

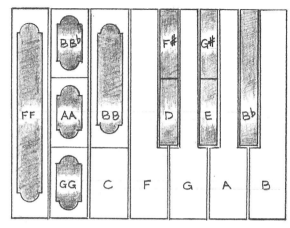

thin exterior walls of the Prague instrument are veneered in walnut, with the typical reinforced slanted cheeks and marquetried keywell. It is disposed 2×8′, with one 8′ fixed and the other moveable from inside the case. Its original compass was FF/C–c³, later enlarged to d³. The multiple-broken short octave is identical to the one seen on the Walter and includes the decorative elements on the three bottom keys. Unlike the Walter, the bentside has a rounded tail. Its walnut bridge is also rounded in the bass and is molded (comparison with the Walter bridge is not possible since it was replaced in one of the rebuildings). The naturals and sharps are covered in two Germanic favorites, mother-of-pearl and tortoise shell. Otherwise, there are some unusual elements to this instrument. First, it is only 5′ long and has an extremely short scale of 8″, indicating that it was probably tuned significantly higher than normal pitch. Second, its stand is a piece of utilitarian furniture: a harpsichord-shaped chest of drawers with a cupboard in front of the player's legs. And third, it has a lid painting, something unexpected in the natural-wood Viennese style, and perhaps not original.

The Nuremberg harpsichord was only slightly longer than the Prague example, but was converted to a piano around 1780 and at that time, or possibly earlier, lost half a foot of its length. Thus, although its tail is now mitered, it might originally have been rounded. But it shows the same thin sides (probably walnut, although now covered with paint and varnish) with reinforced slanted cheeks, and its other characteristics also seem typical: a 2×8′ disposition, a molded walnut bridge, a keywell veneered in walnut with inlaid contrasting woods, "white" naturals with "black" sharps, and the multiple-broken short octave. It also has a lid painting, although that probably is not original. The 11½″ scale could have been for either brass or iron stringing.

Three instruments from the middle of the century show

15-18. Viennese instruments having this "multiple-broken" short octave also have a peculiar decorative scheme on the bottom two or three notes. The apparent C is either a contrasting solid color or has a contrasting oblong inlaid into the touch plate. The apparent D, split into three, has a similar sort of design on each part. The back portion of the apparent E may have another inlay of contrasting color.

that the traditional Viennese Flügel was still in vogue. The first was made in 1747 by Johann Christoph Pantzner (dates unknown) (Vienna, Kunsthistorisches Museum); the next in 1755 by Johann Leydecker (dates unknown) (Graz, Steiermärkisches Landesmuseum); and the third, dated 1750–60, is anonymous (Halle, Händel-Haus). They are (or were—the third was converted to a piano) all disposed 2×8′ with box guides, thin walnut sides, reinforced slanting cheeks, inlay-decorated keywells, and multiple-broken short octaves starting with FF/C and ascending to f³ in the first two and e³ in the Händel-Haus anonyme. All have short scales of 10″, 10½″, and 12″, respectively. The appearance of the keyboards of all three is also similar, with "black" naturals and "white" sharps.[155] There are some minor differences; the first two have mitered tails, the third a rounded tail. Like the Prague harpsichord, the Pantzner sits on a chest-of-drawers stand.[156] The last two eighteenth-century Viennese survivors are a 1778 2×8′ single with rounded tail by Mathias Blum (dates unknown) (Austria, private collection), and a similar instrument of the same date by Gottfried Mallek (1733–98) (Bratislava, Mestske Museum).[157] Despite their late dates, the Blum and Mallek instruments fit squarely in the now almost century-old tradition of the Viennese harpsichord, differing only in their fully chromatic keyboards.

The three spinets have many of the same characteristics as the harpsichords. The thin case sides and bridges are of walnut,

15-19. The 1747 harpsichord by Johann Christoph Pantzner. The unusual stand, looking like a harpsichord-shaped chest of drawers, was not uncommon in Vienna. Vienna, Kunsthistorisches Museum.

the keywells are decorated with fancier woods, and the scales are short. The earliest, an anonymous triangular octave spinet with a bentside (but not a bentside spinet), has a GG/D–c³ compass with a black-on-white keyboard. Dating from the late seventeenth century, its multiple-broken short octave descends only to GG; but the apparent D shows the characteristic decorative pattern found throughout much of the next century. The other two instruments, a 1799 by Engelbert Klinger (ca. 1751–99) (Prague, National Museum) and an 1804 by Christoph Bock (dates unknown) (Vienna, Kunsthistorisches Museum), are both bentside spinets. Though they date a century later than the octave spinet, they also exhibit the now familiar thin-case walnut construction, but with chromatic white-on-black keyboards.

15-20. The walnut case, reinforced slanted cheeks, inlaid keywell, and multiple-broken short octave of this 1755 harpsichord by Johann Leydecker are typical characteristics of the eighteenth-century Viennese harpsichord. Graz, Steiermärkisches Landesmuseum.

A sample of eight grand harpsichords over the course of a century hardly constitutes overwhelming evidence of a school; nevertheless, all eight are so faithful to an archetype that it seems justified to cautiously conclude that such a Viennese school did indeed exist, that it included many fine builders,[158]

15-21. This little anonymous late-seventeenth-century Viennese octave spinet with a charming "Orpheus serenading the beasts" lid painting displays an early example of the multiple-broken short octave. Salzburg, Museum Carolino Augusteum.

that many of its characteristics were unique, that it may also have been the style of South German harpsichord building, and that it does not seem to have been emulated elsewhere in Europe. Its basic construction, a heavy, softwood inner portion to which an outer skin of thin hardwood was applied, is of course found in the Viennese piano, whose case obviously sprang from the harpsichords; but there are no known antecedents.[159] With the exception of the 1703 Franz Walter, all the cases are of thin walnut, ranging from ¼″ to ⅜″. They all have reinforced slanted cheeks, and all are disposed 2×8′, with box guides and without stop levers. Bridges are molded on those instruments that still have their original soundboard fixtures. Their scales are short, probably indicating brass stringing (with the exception of the 1778 Mathias Blum and the Händel-Haus anonyme).[160] Their keywells are decorated with geometric veneer patterns. Strangely, with such uniformity, both mitered and rounded tails are found; but this minor incongruity only serves to heighten the enigma of the Viennese harpsichord.

SWITZERLAND

Only a dozen or so eighteenth-century Swiss builders can be identified,[161] most of them also organ and/or string-instrument makers, and most of them either German immigrants or of recent German ancestry.[162] Only a half dozen instruments have survived, three from Basel, one from Berne, and two from Zurich. The greatest activity seems to have been in Berne, where five builders worked: Johann Ludwig Hellen (ca. 1716–81), Emanuel Bossart (b. 1729), Abraham Baumgartner (dates unknown), Hans Howard (1730–1800) and his son Johann Howard (b. 1757), and Theophile Gottlieb Gleiniger (1766–1823), who was born in Saxony.

The only surviving instrument from this cohort is a ca. 1775 combination harpsichord-piano by Hellen (Berlin, Staatliches Institut für Musikforschung). This one-manual FF–f³ instrument is double strung, but only one choir of strings is plucked by the harpsichord jacks. We cannot possibly extrapolate information about Swiss harpsichord building from this one late example; however, it seems to have many International characteristics. The interior construction is a curious mélange of bracing, including knees and upper braces, a combined upper and lower brace, and a combined post and beam with upper brace of the type last seen in Hass harpsichords. The soundboard has a thin cutoff bar and ribs but is also cross-barred. The scale is an intermediate 12″. The bridge and nut are molded. The soft linden case walls are thick, with cut-in moldings, and covered with a paneled and cross-banded walnut veneer. The tail is mitered. A budding flower grows out of an elaborate sunken rose surrounded by a stylized ring of three-dimensional acanthus leaves and some painted flowers. These last, as well as the rest of the soundboard painting, are done in a somewhat naive style, tending toward the use of solid colors. Flowers were also painted in the soundwell, but these appear to have been done in a little more sophisticated manner, although the result does smack of folk art. The interior of the lid and flap is also bordered by floral designs, similar to those in the keywell. There is a lid painting of a bagpiper and four dancing monkeys, and a flap painting of a knight, obviously done by a different hand. Bookmatched veneers in the keywell and blackened fret-sawn endblocks complete the decor. An aproned stand with sedate cabriole legs is finished en suite.

Three bentside spinets come from Basel. Peter Friedrich Brosi (1700–64), a Bavarian who trained with Johann Andreas Silbermann at Strasbourg, emigrated to Basel about 1745 and became a citizen. Although primarily an organ maker, he produced some jack-action instruments as well. His two extant spinets are both of plain wood, one dated 1755 (Zurich, Schweizerisches Landesmuseum), the other undated and unsigned (Basel, Historisches Museum) but attributed to Brosi because of its similarity to the 1755 and because of its Saxon-style rose. The compass of the 1755 is only four octaves, C–c³. The other spinet originally had a wider range, AA–e³, but it was converted to a piano by inserting a Viennese action in place of the jacks and given a C–e³ keyboard. Brosi's son Johann Jacob, who spelled his last name Brosy, is survived by a 1775 FF–f³ spinet (Basel, Historisches Museum).[163] Other Basel harpsichord makers include Christian Schlegel (fl. 1730), who made wind instruments and harps as well, and Jeremias Schlegel (fl. 1730–92), probably his son.

Leonhardt Schmuz (1681–1769) was a harpsichord maker and Kappelmeister in Zurich. A four-octave 1733 ottavino of his survives (location unknown). A 1761 2×8′ harpsichord (Prestegg, Altsätten, Historisches Museum) is extant by his son Conrad (1721–71), who was a goldsmith as well as a harpsichord maker.

Few conclusions about Swiss building can be drawn from this handful of instruments,[164] other than that there does not seem to have been any strong indigenous tradition, and the prevailing influence seems to have been German—which, considering the origins of the builders, is not surprising.

Our pitifully small sample of harpsichords from eighteenth-century Germany, Austria, and Scandinavia indicates that there were a variety of traditions involved in those parts of Europe. With the exception of Austria (and possibly South Germany), which had an entirely different manner of building, they all seemed to be loosely based on the International principles of case construction inherited from the previous century, including sides of intermediate thickness, and the use of U-, bottom, and knee bracing. Only a few other characteristics can be identified as pan-Germanic: the tendency to make the keywell the visual center of attention, the removeable nameboard, the use of geometric roses (when present), and the employment of contrasting materials such as ebony and ivory, mother-of pearl and tortoise shell, and paint and natural wood. Otherwise, individual instruments and practices varied widely. For example, the Hasses used a modified but strong post-and-beam system, while Mietke used knees and diagonal struts; but aside from these elements, the instruments differ in soundboard barring, use of upper and lower or box guides, shape of the tail, shape of the bridges and nuts, octave span, scale, stringing materials, key coverings, use of applied moldings, case and soundboard decoration, disposition, and shape of stands. Furthermore, only in Hamburg did the string scale and soundboard barring scheme of the Ruckerses take hold; elsewhere, builders simply seemed to ignore the sort of construction derived from seventeenth-century Antwerp that we now identify as Northern, and which by then dominated French, English, and Low Country building.

Written evidence shows that harpsichord building was practiced all over Germany, Austria, and Scandinavia, not just in Stockholm, Hamburg, Berlin, Hannover, Gross Breitenbach, Dresden, Freiberg, Augsburg, and Vienna; but only in Hamburg with the instruments of the Fleischers, the Hasses, and Zell, Dresden with the Gräbners, and Vienna with a corpus of eight harpsichords in the course of the century, do we have enough samples from which to draw semimeaningful conclusions. This makes it difficult for us to grasp the essence of German harpsichord building at this time. For example, we have mentioned the name of Zacharias Hildebrand, who built in Leipzig; but other than an account of his having made a *Lautenclavier* for J. S. Bach, we know little about his work or of the sort of harpsichords made in that historic city in the course of the century. Or to take another example, of harpsichord building in Munich we know only that a maker named Joseph Glonner (fl. 1753–72) was employed by the Bavarian court, to which he supplied at least six harpsichords sometime after the middle of the century.[165] It is almost impossible for us to make any statements about South German harpsichords, except that we know they were made, and that we suspect they may have shared a tradition with Vienna. Viennese harpsichords constituted an independent school that combined a unique case construction and appearance, one upon which the Viennese piano was to be based.

With our present state of knowledge we cannot say why eighteenth-century German harpsichord building was so fragmented. It has been noted that this state of affairs was only reasonable, given that Germany at that time was a collection of independent cities and states, and not a unified country like France. But Italy was also a collection of independent states, and although there were differences between the harpsichords built in one region or another, the Italians nevertheless seemed to be able to agree on what a harpsichord should look like and what sort of sounds it should make. The same cannot be said of Germany.

Finally, almost all eighteenth-century German builders were primarily organ, clavichord, and (later) piano makers, and only secondarily concerned with harpsichords. For most of them, whatever they did make in the way of harpsichords is lost, leaving only the memory of their names. For example, the Friedericis were an eighteenth- and nineteenth-century dynasty centered in Gera, a Central German city roughly sixty-five miles west of Dresden. Their fame was established with their organs, clavichords, and pianos, but there is evidence that they made Flügel as well. Christian Ernst Friederici (1709–80), a student of Gottfried Silbermann, was the best known and evidently the most inventive of the clan — according to Gerber, in 1770 he advertised that he had made a harpsichord capable of producing vibrato.[166] Adlung noted that he had also made a *Lautenwerk*.[167] The Mozart family owned Friederici instruments, and when Wolfgang went to Augsburg to visit Johann Andreas Stein, his father cautioned him not to mention the Gera builder, believing Stein to be jealous of Friederici.[168] The great poet Johann Wolfgang von Goethe (1749–1832), in his memoirs *Dichtung und Wahrheit,* mentioned that his parents owned a harpsichord by Friederici and noted that his instruments were famous.[169] But unless new evidence arises, or some of his harpsichords are discovered to be extant, the contributions of Christian Ernst Friederici, not to mention the tradition of harpsichord building in Gera, will remain unknown.

It could be said that while eighteenth-century French and English harpsichords differed from one another, ultimately they were speaking dialects of the same Northern sound — individual sounds, of course, but cut from the same modernized Flemish cloth. While that statement certainly applies to some German harpsichords, it cannot be applied to all of them.

[16]

GREAT BRITAIN AND AMERICA

$\mathcal{W}$E HAVE noted that fewer instruments came from Italy between 1700 and 1800 than in the previous two centuries, that relatively few makers were practicing in the Low Countries, that evidence suggests only sporadic building in Iberia, that in Germany the production of harpsichords was a sideline (albeit an important one) to organs and clavichords, and that even though builders were quite active in France, a good portion of their effort went into restoring and refurbishing older instruments. Clearly, harpsichord making seemed to have slowed down, perhaps because a well-built harpsichord, properly maintained and modernized when necessary, can go on making music for centuries. By the end of the 1700s there was a sizeable inventory of such instruments available throughout much of Europe, and builders spent more and more of their time repairing, rebuilding, and updating them to contemporary requirements.

Eighteenth-century England presents a different picture. The production of harpsichords was prodigious: over a period of fifty years the Shudi family produced an average of twenty harpsichords a year, and the Kirkman family's output was probably twice that. We are no longer dealing with instruments built by a master with a journeyman and an apprentice or two — it was factory production, on a scale not seen since the Ruckerses early in the previous century. Furthermore, spinet making was a full-time activity for a large number of builders — as many as 150 in all of Great Britain. Nearly two hundred grand harpsichords have survived and an equal number of bentside spinets. In addition, we know quite a bit about the major builders — their dates, where they came from, with whom they apprenticed, who their apprentices were, whom they married, where they lived, when they moved, their production records, what they charged for their harpsichords, who bought them, what people thought of them, and even who tuned them and how much they charged. With all these instruments and this abundant documentation, it is possible to build a fairly complete picture of the history of plucked instruments in the island kingdom.

Both in sound and in appearance, eighteenth-century English harpsichords were impressive and powerful instruments. Charles Burney thought the harpsichords produced in his country to be vastly superior to all others. While in Italy, he observed that "To all persons accustomed to English harpsichords, all the keyed instruments on the continent appear to great disadvantage," and he remarked that the three English harpsichords he found in Italy were "regarded by the Italians as so many phenomena."[1] Burney's opinion was probably shared by many knowledgeable people, although perhaps not in so harsh a form. Even Frank Hubbard, who championed the French harpsichord, sang the praises of English instruments, remarking that "For sheer magnificence of tone, reedy trebles and sonorous basses, no other harpsichord ever matched them."[2] These were not only splendid harpsichords, they were also magnificent examples of furniture. With veneers of walnut, mahogany, satinwood, and other cabinet and show woods, their decorative tradition was unlike anything on the Continent.

HARPSICHORD BUILDING
FROM 1700 TO 1725

It was not until after the first quarter of the century that the instrument described above would appear. Prior to that, and even for some time after, harpsichord construction followed the same International principles that guided building practices in the previous century. A corpus of seven pre–ca. 1725 grand instruments has survived, and it is worth examining them briefly, since they are the last vestiges of the earlier indigenous English tradition.[3]

1. A 1700 double by Joseph Tisseran[4] (dates unknown) (Oxford, Bate Collection). This is the earliest surviving two-manual instrument in the English tradition. With a GG/BB–d^3 (with split low E♭) compass, and disposed 2×8', 1×4' with shove coupler (now a dogleg), its thin sides surround the bottom, and it has an applied top molding, a mitered tail, an intermediate

scale of 12½", and a deeply curved bentside. Little more than its date separates it from the harpsichords directly preceding it. Additionally, though, it is a beautifully decorated instrument, with a densely painted soundboard, a veneered exterior, and a keywell with inlays and painted cartouches. The shaped endblocks are of the type normally found on bentside spinets, and the keyboards have ebony naturals with solid ivory sharps. Old-fashioned embossed gilt papers grace the key fronts. Turned brass stop knobs protrude through the removeable nameboard. Elaborate strap hinges, graduated in size, are similar to those already seen on bentside spinets and will remain characteristic of English instruments for the rest of the century.

16-1. The 1700 harpsichord by Joseph Tisseran, the first extant double-manual instrument from England, is an excellent example of Internationally inspired English building as well as a beautifully decorated harpsichord. Oxford, © The Bate Collection of Musical Instruments.

2. A 1709 single by Thomas Barton (1685–ca. 1735) (London, private ownership). Barton, who apprenticed with Stephen Keene, was primarily a maker of bentside spinets, of which fourteen or fifteen still survive. His one extant harpsichord is a 2×8', with a GG/BB–d^3 compass, box guides, and a short scale. The soundboard is cross-barred, the bentside is deeply curved, and the tail is mitered. Like the Tisseran, it has sides of intermediate thickness that surround the bottom, an applied top molding, fancy hinges, and turned brass stop knobs projecting through the removeable nameboard. Its endblocks are similar to those on the Tisseran, and it also pays homage to a long-forgotten inner-outer tradition with scroll-sawn cheek pieces.[5] Unlike the Tisseran, however, its case is of unpainted walnut, and there is no soundboard painting.

3. An undated single by Benjamin Slade (b. ca. 1669) (London, private ownership). Slade was a spinet and harpsichord builder who apprenticed with the otherwise unknown James Aland. In turn, Thomas Hitchcock and William Smith both apprenticed with Slade. Tisseran and Slade must have worked together, since a bentside spinet bearing both their names still survives, with strap hinges identical to those on the Tisseran harpsichord. In addition to his one grand, Slade is survived by eight spinets. His 2×8' harpsichord with intermediate scale has

a GG–g³ compass, the first five-octave English grand we know of (although an Asten and Barton spinet of 1709 was probably the first English instrument with a full five octaves, and a 1684 GG/BB–f³ Thomas White virginal has nearly that compass). Its case is of walnut, with sides of intermediate thickness, a deeply curved bentside, and a rounded tail. It also has the shaped endblocks characteristic of all these instruments, and ebony naturals with skunk-tail sharps. Its nameboard is fixed, but the expected brass stop knobs protrude from it.

4. A 1720 single by Thomas Hancock (dates unknown) (Edinburgh, Russell Collection). A 2×8′ harpsichord with GG–e³ compass, intermediate scale, walnut sides of intermediate thickness, a mitered tail, a deeply curved bentside, a cap molding overlapping the soundwell, and a removeable nameboard, this is the only instrument of the group in which the gap slants. The keyboard has ebony naturals and skunk-tail sharps and is flanked by the usual shaped endblocks.

5. A ca. 1720 single by William Smith (dates unknown) (Oxford, Bate Collection). With a 2×8′ disposition, GG–g³ compass, walnut case of intermediate thickness, an intermediate scale, overlapping cap moldings, a mitered tail, shaped endblocks, ivory naturals, skunk-tail sharps, and brass stop knobs, the characteristics of the 1720 Smith seem to be consistent with the other instruments in this cohort. However, there are three things about it that are particularly noteworthy. First, it seems to have little internal structure other than a single bottom brace and two soundboard bars parallel to the bridge.[6] Second, the grain of the soundboard runs approximately at a forty-five-degree angle to the spine. This is usually explained by observing that Smith was primarily a spinet maker, since in the domestic instrument the grain direction is usually laid in parallel to the gap, putting it at an angle to the spine;[7] but this argument assumes that Smith did not know the difference between a grand harpsichord and a spinet. It also ignores the fact that other builders were also spinet makers, and they

16-2. It has been claimed that this ca. 1720 harpsichord by William Smith, a rather plain example of early-eighteenth-century English harpsichord building, might possibly have belonged to George Frideric Handel. Oxford, © The Bate Collection of Musical Instruments.

chose not to place their harpsichord soundboards at an angle. Finally, it disregards the fact that until 1750 or so, the soundboard grain of spinets usually ran parallel to the spine. It is more likely that Smith had some reason to choose that particular method of controlling the stiffness of his soundboard, as Grimaldi did in his 1703 harpsichord, and Farrini in his ca. 1750.[8]

6. A ca. 1725 double by Francis Coston (Edinburgh, Russell Collection).[9] This is another early two-manual instrument, with a GG,AA–d^3,e^3 compass, a 2×8′, 1×4′ disposition with dogleg, and a 12½″ scale. The case is of oak, with walnut veneer, Northern-style upper and lower braces, a mitered tail, and a removeable nameboard. Like the Smith, the soundboard is not cross-barred, but has a cutoff bar with two smaller parallel bars. Like the Tisseran, the soundboard is painted.[10] The keyboard has ivory naturals and skunk-tail sharps, with embossed gilt paper on the key fronts. The usual English case hinges and turned brass knobs are present.[11]

7. A ca. 1725 double by Thomas Hitchcock the younger (ca. 1685–after 1733) (London, Victoria and Albert Museum). Hitchcock was one of a family of builders, the son of the Thomas Hitchcock mentioned in Chapter 10 as the builder of the earliest known English bentside spinet. Together, the two Thomases left thirty-five extant spinets. John Hitchcock (d. 1774), the son of Thomas the younger, is survived by at least thirteen spinets and a late double-manual harpsichord of unknown date (Lyme Park, Cheshire). However, the ca. 1725 harpsichord, by Thomas the younger, is the only early grand ascribed to the family. It has a GG–g^3 compass, a 2×8′, 1×4′ disposition, and an intermediate 13″ scale. It now has fixed manuals and a dogleg, but may originally have been built with a shove coupler. It also has a lute stop, the only one in this cohort, but that also may not have been original.[12] Once again we see a walnut case of intermediate thickness, but with a rounded tail. Like the ca. 1720 Smith, the grain of the soundboard is at an angle to the spine. The keyboard has ivory naturals and skunk-tail sharps and is flanked by scroll-sawn endblocks. The case hinges are long and elegant.

In Chapter 10 we observed that the sum total of our knowledge of English grands in the sixteenth and seventeenth centuries comes from four instruments, by Theewes, Hasard, Cassus, and Haward. The seven early-eighteenth-century instruments just described continue that indigenous building style, particularly in elements such as intermediate scales, the use of both brass and iron stringing, relatively plain walnut cases with bentsides of intermediate thickness, heavy spines, removeable nameboards, applied moldings, shaped or scroll-sawn endblocks,

16-3. With its plain walnut case of intermediate thickness, the 1725 Thomas Hitchcock double reflects the International paradigm of early English harpsichord building. Its angled soundboard is unusual, but the straight bentside with a sharp hook at the treble end adumbrates later English practice. London, Victoria and Albert Museum.

and even, on some, key fronts of embossed and gilded papers, rounded tails, and soundboard paintings. The fondness for colored sounds, seen in the early use of the lute stop, is no longer found, and neither are hollow wrestplanks nor, with one exception, slanted gaps. The instruments from the first quarter of the century demonstrate a trend toward simplicity of sound, but they represent the last vestiges of the Internationally based indigenous English harpsichord.

HERMANN TABEL

Around the turn of the century a journeyman builder named Hermann Tabel (d. 1738) emigrated from somewhere in the Low Countries to London, where, by 1716, he had established himself as a master. According to James Shudi Broadwood, the son of John Broadwood[13] (who was apprenticed to Burkat Shudi in 1761, who in turn had been taught by Tabel), the master himself was trained in Antwerp, in the shop of one of the Couchets, and was thus a direct descendent of the Ruckers tradition.[14] Throughout this book it has been suggested that no matter where they were trained, when they moved to another area harpsichord builders made instruments in the local manner; but on the evidence of his one surviving instrument, a 1721 double (Warwick, County Museum), this seems to have been only partially true of Tabel.

Externally, the walnut case looks to be in the indigenous English tradition. The cheek, bentside, and tail are cross-banded, and the soundwell and keywell are veneered with sycamore, with walnut stringing. English strap hinges identical to those found on the ca. 1725 Hitchcock grace the lid. Naturals are covered with ebony, and the sharps are topped with ivory slips. The instrument also has a bentside with a long straight section ending in a sharp hook at the treble, a typical English configuration already seen in the Hitchcock. But Tabel's harpsichord also has case walls ¾″ thick, sides that sit on the bottom, a long scale, a metal rose, and a Ruckers-derived soundboard barring and case bracing. It also has a 2×8′, 1×4′ with dogleg disposition and an FF,GG–f^3 compass, both of which become standard on English doubles for decades to come. A lute stop is present, and that device could have been found in England as well as Flanders; but considered as part of the two-manual 2×8′, 1×4′ with dogleg setup, it is difficult not to conclude that Tabel carried these Low Country characteristics to England. Tabel's harpsichord is, in other words, a Flemish instrument — or at least a greatly enlarged and strengthened eighteenth-century Low Country version — in an English-style case.[15]

For one who became so famed a builder, there is little we know about Tabel other than a few anecdotes. In 1723 he advertised in the *Evening Post* that he was going out of business and wanted to sell his remaining stock;[16] in 1733 he placed a notice in the *St. James Evening Post* saying that, despite reports of his death, he was still very much alive.[17] Tabel married twice and had two daughters, both probably by his second wife, Susanna Virgoe. Although the evidence is sketchy, it appears that he died poor, which is strange, since builders with the sort of reputation he was supposed to have had usually did fairly well.[18] But if our knowledge of Tabel is sketchy, we have volumes of information about his two most famous apprentices, Burkat Shudi and Jacob Kirkman.[19]

SHUDI, KIRKMAN, AND THEIR COMPETITORS

Shudi (1702–73) was born Burckhardt Tschudi in Schwanden, canton of Glarus, Switzerland, and apprenticed as a joiner under his uncle; but with hard times in the region's timber trade, the sixteen-year-old came to London in 1718. He learned harpsichord making with Tabel and, it seems, before long became his right-hand man (Charles Burney referred to him as "Tabel's foreman").[20] By 1729, the date of Shudi's earliest extant harpsichord (Tokyo, Ueno Gakuen College), he had left Tabel, anglicized his name, married, and set up on his own, probably with the help of his prosperous father-in-law, Hans Jacob Wild. Not surprisingly, his 1729 instrument is similar to Tabel's 1721. The heavy case is of cross-banded walnut, the keyboards have ebony naturals and ivory-slipped sharps, and the similarities continue in scale, compass, disposition, and hardware. Shudi's instruments changed little over the course of his lifetime.

The 1729 harpsichord bears an inscription (in Italian) on the back of the nameboard, noting that it was given to Anna Strada del Pò in 1731.[21] It has been widely accepted that George Frideric Handel was the purchaser of this instrument, and that he presented it to Strada, who was one of his Italian protégées, personally selected by him and brought to London in 1729 to sing in his opera company at the King's Theatre. Unlike many of Handel's singers, Strada—a soprano with an extraordinary voice but with an appearance so ungainly she was nicknamed "the pig"[22]—did not desert him for a rival company when Handel's venture folded, and the composer must have been particularly grateful. When she left London in 1738 she took her harpsichord with her. Handel was well acquainted with Shudi, and the latter's grandson reports that the composer was a frequent dinner guest at the builder's home, no doubt as hungry for German conversation as he was for beer and schnitzel.[23] He may even have enjoyed the welcome sight of Burkat's young wife, Catherine. Shudi's friendship with an artist of Handel's stature probably had a more than favorable effect on his business, particularly since the composer owned one of his instruments.

It was also Shudi's good fortune to become acquainted with the Zurich-born impresario John Jacob Heidegger, as well as John Christopher Smith, Handel's business manager. These men were able to open doors for him, and the builder was quick to take advantage of these opportunities. He thrived financially and had a reputation as the finest builder in London, with many well-to-do and famous patrons on his order list, both in England and on the Continent. One of his most distinguished customers was William Prince of Wales, whose important patronage entitled Shudi to hang the prince's crest, the Plume of Feathers, in front of his house.[24] Other illustrious clients included Empress Maria Theresa, Franz Joseph Haydn, Thomas Gainsborough, and the Americans Charles Carroll and Francis Hopkinson, both signers of the Declaration of Independence.

Shudi made five harpsichords for Frederick the Great, the first of which was a gift to the king in 1765, in thanks for his victory the previous year at the Battle of Prague.[25] Before this harpsichord was shipped off to its royal destination, it was played by the nine-year-old Mozart and his sister Nannerl (then fourteen), who visited Shudi's shop while in London with their father. The completion of this instrument was also the occasion for Shudi to commission a painting of himself, Catherine, his sons Joshua and Burkat the younger, and the family cat, all gathered around the royal harpsichord as the master tuned it.[26] The other four instruments were ordered by Frederick after the Seven Years' War, as furnishings for his great new palace in Potsdam. The king, pleased with Shudi's work, not only paid for his harpsichords, but also presented the builder with the gift of a valuable ring. These four harpsichords may have been among the first that Shudi fitted with a machine stop, a device for dynamic expression (to be described in detail shortly) similar to the French machine stop, but operated by a pedal rather than *genouillères*.

Shudi had seven children with Catherine. Three girls and a boy did not survive childhood, but they were followed by Joshua (1736–54), Burkat the younger (ca. 1738–1803), and daughter Barbara (1748–76). Joshua died at age eighteen, but Burkat the younger followed his father into harpsichord building. Catherine passed away sometime before 1759, and in that year Burkat married again, to Elizabeth Meier. Shudi's nephew, also named Joshua (1739–74), was taken into the business shortly thereafter, in 1761;[27] but Joshua's work was reported to be unsatisfactory, and relations between master and nephew became strained. In 1766 Joshua left his uncle and set up on his own, claiming to have been the guiding spirit behind the construction of the four extraordinary harpsichords made for Frederick the Great. An acrimonious exchange of advertisements took place in the pages of the local *Gazetteer* in 1767, with Burkat denigrating his nephew's work, calling him a mere joiner, and Joshua replying in appropriately wounded tones that harpsichord builders must be joiners, and that his uncle himself had begun his professional career as one. He went on to invite the gentry to visit his shop for "convincing proof" of his skills as a builder.[28] At the same time, three of Shudi's journeymen swore in an affidavit that Joshua Shudi never finished a single harpsichord while in his uncle's employ.[29] After Joshua's death his widow Mary placed an advertisement informing the public that she had for sale "a great variety of exceedingly fine toned single and double harpsichords,"[30] presumably made by her late husband. Joshua Shudi is survived by a few instruments.

In 1761, the same year that Joshua went to work in Shudi's shop, the twenty-nine-year-old John Broadwood (1732–1812), a journeyman cabinetmaker from Scotland, was taken on, and in 1769, in time-honored fashion, Broadwood married Shudi's daughter Barbara. A year later he and his father-in-law became partners, and the firm's name was changed to Shudi and Broadwood. One would have expected Shudi to take his son Burkat the younger as a partner rather than someone from outside the family; but it seems clear that the young man lacked the requisite skills needed to build instruments and run a business, whereas John Broadwood had them in abundance.

Burkat Shudi retired a year later, in 1771, when he was sixtynine years old. He was able to look back on a life of hard work, but one filled with many accolades. He was respected not only as a great builder — as famed in London as Taskin was in Paris — but also as an inventive one. For example, he made a large number of harpsichords (including those in the group of four sent to Frederick the Great) with a five-and-a-half-octave range, descending chromatically to CC. The Venetian swell was another of his important contributions. Since the middle of the century English harpsichords had often been fitted with nag's head swells, in which a section of the lid is opened and closed by a pedal. In the year of his daughter's marriage to Broadwood, Shudi patented the Venetian swell, a second underlid, consisting of a frame that fitted neatly into the perimeter of the soundwell, supporting a series of narrow rotatable slats — like Venetian blinds — running from jackrail to tail. Like an ordinary lid, it could be raised and supported by the prop stick; but when lowered, the slats were controlled by a pedal found on the right side of the instrument. With the pedal up the slats were in a closed position, and the muffled harpsichord sounded as if it was being played with the lid closed, which indeed it was; but when the pedal was depressed the slats opened, effectively doing away with the closed-lid effect.[31] A softer-to-louder result was achieved, although the impression was not so much one of crescendo (or, when reversed, diminuendo), as of a muffled to an open sound.[32] Thus, the swell served both as a tone-altering device and as a means of dynamic expression, and proved to be a popular addition to the harpsichord's expressive capabilities. Shudi not only used it on his own instruments, but licensed it to others as well.

Shudi died only two years after he retired, but the firm of Shudi and Broadwood continued, with Burkat the younger taking his father's place. However, sometime before 1792, probably because he lacked both skill and interest in harpsichord building, Burkat the younger dissolved the partnership. One of the conditions of Shudi's will gave Broadwood the rights to the Venetian swell, with the proviso that the younger Burkat be paid forty pounds a year from the licensing fees. With that annuity in hand, Burkat Shudi the younger disappeared, leaving John Broadwood in full command of the business. The dissolution could not have been more fortunate. Broadwood, as fine a craftsman as his mentor, took the firm to new heights. His harpsichord business was in full swing, building not only for the English trade, but also for a thriving business abroad. He supplied harpsichord parts to other builders, and for a fee, licensed others to use the Venetian swell. Following a long-established practice of Shudi's, he rented out harpsichords for concerts and events of various sorts (the painter Joshua Reynolds, who did not own an instrument, was one of his steady customers) and had a stable of rental instruments that included two Ruckerses.[33] He also did a great deal of harpsichord and piano tuning and maintenance, often entering into contracts for monthly visits. Finally, he was also a dealer in guitars and other musical instruments.

John and Barbara had a daughter and two sons, James Shudi (1772–1851) and Thomas (1786–1861). Barbara died in 1776 at the age of twenty-seven, probably during the birth of their third son, John Jr.; but Broadwood married again, in 1781, to Mary Kitson, a union that produced six more children. But only James and Thomas came into the business. By the time James joined his father as partner in 1795 the firm had begun to produce pianos, an instrument in which Shudi had seemed completely uninterested, but which intrigued Broadwood. Nevertheless, for a time the production of harpsichords continued at an even greater pace. Citing Broadwood's journals, Wainwright reports that it was not until 1783 that the sale of pianos began to outstrip those of harpsichords;[34] yet harpsichord sales continued to grow as well. In 1784 Broadwood sold thirty-eight harpsichords, a number probably representing twice the business that Shudi could manage to do in his best year; but in that same period he also sold 133 pianos, indicating that in the twelve years in which he had run the business he had increased production by well over a factor of ten.[35] Nevertheless, by the time Broadwood shipped Charles Carroll's harpsichord to America in 1789, sales had begun to fall. The last extant Broadwood harpsichord is dated 1793 (Edinburgh, Russell Collection), and it is doubtful that the firm made any others after that.

Sometime in the 1730s the Alsatian-born cabinetmaker Jacob Kirchmann (1710–92) left his native town of Bischwiller, near Strasbourg, and came to London. Like Shudi a decade earlier, he found work in the shop of Hermann Tabel; and again like Shudi (who by this time was out on his own), he quickly worked himself into a position of responsibility.[36] By the time of Tabel's death in 1738 he had anglicized his name to Kirckman, then somewhat later to Kirkman (although he continued to sign his harpsichords Kirckman).[37] One month after Tabel died,

Kirkman — like Taskin — married his master's widow, Susanna, and acquired Tabel's house, business, tools, stock of wood, and order book. Within two years Susanna died, and Kirkman, with no heirs, never married again. A few years later, in 1772, he brought his nephew Abraham (1737–94) in as a partner, and the firm became Jacob and Abraham Kirckman. Jacob retired in 1790, when he was eighty years old, after a fine career as a builder. He died only two years later, and his nephew Abraham two years after that. The firm continued, however, as Abraham's second son Joseph (d. 1830) succeeded him in 1789. It was Joseph who presided over the last harpsichord produced in the Kirkman shop and perhaps the whole of England, in 1800.[38] Joseph's son, also named Joseph, took over from him, but by that time they were no longer making harpsichords.

Kirkman seems to have been a shrewd businessman and was involved in more than just harpsichord making. He was known to be a moneylender, and he also dabbled in real estate, buying, selling, and leasing houses all over London. He installed machine stops on his instruments when requested and used Shudi's Venetian swell as well, figuring it was more advantageous to pay the licensing fee than to send customers into the arms of his competitor. Around 1770, when a craze for the English guitar threatened to replace harpsichords as the domestic instrument of choice for ladies of culture, Kirkman was said to have purchased some guitars and given them to poor working women, thus ensuring that gentle ladies would recoil from having anything to do with an instrument now connected with the lower classes.[40] It was also around this time that the Kirkman shop began to make pianos, and jack- and hammer-action instruments were made side by side for the next thirty years. By the time the builder died, not only had he gained a reputation as one of the greatest makers of his time, but he had also amassed a considerable estate.

Kirkman built other instruments as well, including some bentside spinets. He also made an enharmonic harpsichord around 1757 for Robert Smith, a professor of astronomy at Trinity College, Cambridge, who had an interest in temperament.[41] Smith's single-strung instrument was able to obtain more than one temperament by means of hand stops, undoubtedly employing a combination of strings and registers to sound different flavors of the chromatic tones. Kirkman also made some claviorgana in collaboration with the London organ builder John Snetzler (1710–55).[42] One of these combinations, built in 1745 (Scotland, private ownership), has survived.[43]

Burney preferred Shudi harpsichords, thinking them more durable, even though Kirkman's harpsichords were more expensive; but each had its champions. When Thomas Jefferson (1743–1826) was in the market for a harpsichord he chose a Kirkman.[44] Kirkman was patronized by kings George II and George III, the father and son of William Prince of Wales, who was Shudi's royal celebrity of choice. Undoubtedly, some chose one builder over the other on the basis of their political leanings.[45] Overall, however, Kirkman was the more prolific builder. It has been estimated that the Shudi firm produced something over one thousand harpsichords, but Kirkman's output seems to have been two to three times that. By happenstance, about fifty Shudis have survived, and a little more than three times that number of Kirkmans. Thus, about 5 percent of the output of these two makers is still with us, a remarkably high number when compared to other builders, and a tribute to the value their owners placed on the instruments. Of course, the fact that there were no major floods, earthquakes, fires, invasions, or revolutions also helped preserve them.

KIRKMAN'S MARRIAGE

Charles Burney, writing in Rees's *The Cyclopedia*, tells the story of Kirkman's courtship of Tabel's widow Susanna:

> Kirchmann [*sic*] worked with the celebrated Tabel as his foreman and finisher till the time of his death. Soon after which, by a curious kind of courtship, Kirchmann married his master's widow, by which prudent measure he became possessed of all of Tabel's seasoned wood, tools, and stock-in-trade. Kirchmann himself used to relate the singular manner in which he gained the widow, which was not by a regular siege but by storm. He told her one fine morning at breakfast that he was determined to be married that day before twelve o'clock. Mrs. Tabel, in great surprise, asked him to whom he was going to be married, and why so soon? The finisher told her that he had not yet determined whom he should marry, and that if she would have him he would gladly give her the preference. The lady wondered at his precipitancy, hesitated a full half an hour, but he, continuing to swear that the business must be done before twelve o'clock that day, at length she surrendered; and this abridged courtship preceded the marriage act, and the nuptials could be performed at the Fleet or May Fair without loss of time or hindrance to the business, the canonical hour was saved, and two fond hearts were in one united in the most summary way possible just one month after the decease of Tabel.[39]

One suspects that Kirkman told this story many times, no doubt embellishing it with each repetition. Whatever the personal relationship between Jacob and Susanna, the marriage was profitable for both. Jacob got his master's business, and Susanna kept the security laboriously built up by her and her deceased spouse.

ROBERT FALKENER AND HIS KIRKMAN HARPSICHORDS

At least one builder attempted to pass off his own harpsichords as the work of Kirkman. A 1770 double (Glasgow, Glasgow University) has a nameboard with Kirkman's name on it (and the date of 1748), and that part seems to be genuine; but it was likely taken from another instrument, because the underside of the soundboard bears the signature of one Robert Falkener. (Of German origin, Falkener settled in London around 1750. Not only a builder, in 1762 he wrote an instruction book on harpsichord playing that went to a second edition in 1774.) The quality of the materials and the workmanship of Falkener's instrument were not up to the Kirkman standard, and as might be imagined, Kirkman was not happy with this deception and took him to court. The outcome of the legal action is unknown, but Charles Mould suggests that with his usual business acumen Kirkman might have found it more advantageous to allow Falkener to continue his deceptive practices in exchange for a royalty on every instrument sold.[47] The proposal is not unreasonable, because another Falkener/Kirkman exists, this one from 1773 (Edinburgh, Russell Collection), again with the counterfeiter's signature and date on the underside of the soundboard. Interestingly, Falkener did not attempt to copy Kirkman's instruments closely (the soundboard barring is completely different, for example, with the ribs parallel to the cutoff bar),[48] and anyone familiar with the latter's style would have discovered the forgery immediately; but eighteenth-century English harpsichords were so generic looking that the deception must have been fairly easy to bring off.

Falkener must have sold instruments under his own name as well. The *Boston Gazette* of June 27, 1763, noted that a "double key'd" (two-manual) harpsichord by "the Famous Falconer" [*sic*] had just arrived from London.[49] But he succumbed to the temptation to cash in on a name greater than his own, an enticement not unknown to many of his fellow builders in Paris. That may well be where he got the idea.

Shudi and Kirkman were certainly not the only harpsichord builders making grands after the first quarter of the eighteenth century, nor were they the only apprentices or journeymen that Tabel ever had. On the bottom of the soundboard of his 1730 harpsichord (London, private ownership), the otherwise unknown John Wilbrook (dates unknown) wrote, "Johannes Wilbrook Londini fecit Tabel's man." Wilbrook is survived only by one other instrument, a bentside spinet of unknown date (Sussex, Parham Park). Another maker of grand harpsichords was Joseph Mahoon (d. 1773), whose 1738 double (Bethersdon, Kent, Colt Clavier Collection) and 1742 single (whereabouts unknown) still exist. Mahoon is also survived by thirteen spinets, but Thomas Blasser (dates unknown) is known only by a 1744 double (Goudhurst, Finchcocks Collection), an early example of the use of mahogany veneers. John Crang (d. 1792) was an organ builder who also made harpsichords and spinets, and a double of his, originally part of a claviorganum (London, private ownership), still makes magnificent sounds. There are others—John Joseph Merlin, for instance, who will be discussed shortly—but almost all of them are known as spinet, rather than grand, harpsichord makers. Shudi and Kirkman dominated the English market so thoroughly that few others could gain a toehold, although many of them did quite well supplying English households with spinets.

The only other real competitor to these two builders was the firm of Longman and Broderip. It was founded by James Longman (dates unknown) around 1767 as a publishing house that also dealt in keyboard and wind instruments. Longman was joined by Lukey (dates unknown) in 1769, and in 1775 by Francis Fane Broderip (ca. 1750–before 1807). A year later Lukey left, and Longman and Broderip remained in business until they went bankrupt in 1798. Neither partner was a builder, and they purchased all their harpsichords for resale from a variety of makers. Thomas Culliford (fl. 1750–1800), for example, who worked for several builders, moonlighted by making harpsichords for Longman and Broderip.[46] The dealers' names were on the instruments, but Culliford usually managed to sign his name somewhere — on the back of the nameboard, or under the soundboard; and in fact, of the surviving Longman and Broderip instruments that are signed by the actual builders, almost all are by him. Longman and Broderip left thirty-six instruments (two by Longman and Lukey): four doubles, seventeen singles, and fifteen bentside spinets.

Outside London, Thomas Haxby (1729–96) of York was probably the most important as well as the most prolific builder. He seems to have been extremely ambitious and talented; in addition to making harpsichords, spinets, organs, and pianos, he also built citterns and violins, and he invented and patented a machine stop different from the one used in London. One of his two surviving harpsichords, a 1777 single (York, Castle Museum), is fitted with that device. Only seven of his spinets still exist, but twenty or so square pianos are still extant, all built in his last twenty years. Haxby must have had a large staff, since in that space of time his workshop produced 375 instruments, or an average of eighteen or nineteen a year. Despite his inventiveness, his harpsichords closely resemble those of Kirkman and Shudi, as did the harpsichords of all British builders after ca. 1730.

THE RUCKERS-INSPIRED ENGLISH HARPSICHORD

The instruments of Kirkman and Shudi are often compared, and not without reason, since both trained with the same master. Shudi's instruments were said to be better constructed than Kirkman's although they both used the same sort of Ruckers-derived case, soundboard bracing, long scale, and iron stringing. The sides of their harpsichords were heavy, about ¾″ thick, and they were strongly built. The undated Kirkman whose internal structure can be seen in *Hubbard 1965*, plate XXI, with its upper and lower braces, a short cheek-to-upper-bellyrail brace, and diagonal struts from the upper bellyrail to the first lower brace, is typical. But despite the heavy framing and thick oak case walls, the cheek-to-bentside juncture frequently failed (perhaps more in Kirkmans than in Shudis). This is all too obvious a condition in the surviving instruments. Charles Mould, who made a study of English harpsichords,[50] suggests that their bracing was ill-conceived, relying on trapezoids rather than triangles.[51] Be this as it may, this tendency to "cock the cheek" (also known as "English cheek disease") was the curse of eighteenth-century English harpsichords. It affected pianos as well, until the 1820s, when iron bracing was successfully introduced.[52]

Soundboards, of spruce, were barred in the Ruckers manner, with a heavy 4′ hitchpin rail, a cutoff bar, and ribs. Kirkman put a metal rose in his soundboards, but Shudi used none. Otherwise, soundboards were undecorated. Instead, the visual focus of these instruments was the beautiful veneers that covered their oak sides. Tabel's surviving harpsichord was veneered in walnut, the wood of choice in the first quarter of the century. After that there was a growing use of mahogany veneer, as it was found that walnut was subject to attack by woodworms, and the heavy tariff on importation of mahogany was removed. Nevertheless, walnut continued to be used, alongside mahogany, although more sparingly than before, until finally, by the last quarter of the century, it disappeared.[53] Typically, bentsides on single-manual instruments were divided into two veneered panels, while doubles were given three. Cheek and tail were treated as separate areas. Cross-banding surrounded a field of attractively grained veneer, usually mahogany, sometimes in burl, with the two separated by lighter stringing of maple, holly, or boxwood, or some complex built-up inlay banding. Other cabinet veneers could also be used. Lids were often decorated in a similar manner and also had a molding applied to the edges. Except for a few examples, spines were nearly always left undecorated, since it was expected that the instrument would stand next to a wall.

Lighter-colored woods, such as satinwood, tulip, and sycamore, were sometimes used in the soundwell and keywell, particularly in the late instruments. Marquetry, ranging from trophies of instruments to intricate intarsia, could be seen in the keywells of some of the more elaborate examples, and sometimes in the soundwells as well. The builder's name is usually found in a florid Gothic lettering, inked on a light-wood cartouche inlaid into the namebatten. The endblocks and the batten in front of the keyboard (and also, in doubles, the batten between the manuals) were also decorated in the style of the nameboard. Keyboards were uniformly made with ivory touch plates on the naturals and ebony sharps. A piece of molding covered the front of each key.

Contrasted against all this natural wood (although there is nothing "natural" about veneering, cross-banding, and stringing) were the three large, fancy, strap hinges connecting lid to case, descending in size from front to tail, and the three smaller but equally ornate hinges between lid and flap. Also frequently of brass were the casters on the legs of the stand, the stop knobs protruding through the nameboard, and the hooks and rings — one on the cheek, two on the bentside — employed to ensure that the lid closed down tightly to protect the interior of the instrument from the notorious vicissitudes of the English climate. Until the late 1760s or so, music racks were not part of the harpsichord's furniture; after that date, however, both Shudi and Kirkman began increasing the height of their instruments by ½″ (creating the illusion of lowering the tops of their nameboards and jackrails), thus allowing a music desk to be slipped into the front of the case.

English builders never abandoned the trestle stand for the more ornate forms of support such as those found under eighteenth-century French instruments. Instead, they continued to make simple bases, often from the same wood as the instruments and sometimes finished en suite with veneers. For the most part the stands — mainly the legs — showed only a passing relationship with contemporary furniture forms. Old-fashioned turned legs were common on the earlier instruments,[54] to be followed by square, then tapered square legs. Occasionally, in some late examples, Queen Anne cabriole legs were grafted to the trestle legs, below the bottom stretcher, combining two disparate furniture styles in an uneasy alliance.

From their first instruments Shudi and Kirkman used a five-octave FF,GG–f³ compass; it was not until the 1770s that Shudi began to supply the low F♯, and Kirkman did the same shortly thereafter. As noted earlier, Shudi built a series of instruments that descended to CC, and twelve of these impressive doubles, dating from 1765 to 1782, have survived.[55] As far as we know, Kirkman did not use that extended compass, although on one occasion he did build an instrument whose treble extended to c⁴. The reason for these extended basses is unknown. Although there was no written keyboard music that descended to CC, the extra notes could have doubled bass lines at the octave, in the way a 16′ stop would. They certainly would have been used in improvisation and accompanying. And it is possible that Shudi built these large harpsichords because it was something that set his instruments apart from those of his rivals. Few were built, and they would have been quite expensive.

Shudi and Kirkman normally made five different models of grand harpsichords: a single-manual 2×8′; a single-manual 2×8′, 1×4′; the same with lute stop; a double with 2×8′, 1×4′ with dogleg; and the same with a lute stop. The buff stop, known in England as the harp stop, was commonly found on any of the instruments made after 1760 or so, and occasionally before that date. The manuals were fixed; that is, there was no coupler. As was the practice almost everywhere but in France, both 8′s were in front of the 4′, and on doubles the first 8′ was doglegged and available from either manual. Thus, on the larger instruments 1×8′; 1×8′ with buff; 2×8′; 1×8′, 1×4′; and 2×8′, 1×4′ were all available on the lower manual. The middle 8′, the 2×8′, or the 2×8′, 1×4′ could all be contrasted with the front 8′ on the upper manual, or if the instrument was so equipped (as it usually was), with the lute. Obviously, the sort of subtle contrast between the closer-plucking front 8′ on the upper manual and the more distant-plucking back 8′ on the lower, and the ability to dialogue between the two, so characteristic of contemporary French harpsichords, was not possible on the English double. But *pièce croisée* was never part of the vocabulary of eighteenth-century English composers, so this could not have been

16-5. In a passing reference to contemporary furniture styles, the stand on this 1772 Shudi and Broadwood double combines old-fashioned balustrade legs above the stretcher, and cabriole legs below. The instrument's "cheek disease" is readily apparent. Museum of Fine Arts, Boston. Reproduced with permission. © 2000 Museum of Fine Arts, Boston. All rights reserved.

seen as a deficiency.[56] Furthermore, by having the two 8′s next to each other, English harpsichords had a better-blended unison than their French counterparts. In any case, the true contrast of the English instruments was between the 8′s and the lute.

DEVELOPMENTS AFTER 1760

The desire for tonal contrast and dynamic flexibility strongly affected English harpsichord building after ca. 1760, with the growing popularity of the melodically expressive Gallant style. Both Shudi and Kirkman began using leather plectra on their second (back) 8′ ranks, in order to create some contrast between the two unison sets of strings, and to provide a rounder, less brilliant sound.[57] Shudi's instruments were redesigned to give deeper plucking points, again yielding a more rounded tone. They also used softer leather, like the French *peau de buffle,* in an attempt to produce some dynamic change through touch. However, perhaps the most successful means of providing crescendos and diminuendos was the machine stop,[58] a device that offered both a mechanical means of changing registration and the ability to make gradual dynamic changes.[59] It was a collection of trap work, levers, rockers, and springs connected to the

ENGLISH WRESTPINS

The English adopted a unique manner of placing their 4′ wrestpins on the wrestplank. The pins were lined up in straight rows, in Flemish or Italian style, rather than staggered, to mirror the pattern of naturals and accidentals, as the French did. The bottom two octaves of pins were placed between the 4′ and 8′ nuts, where one would expect them; but the pins for the upper three octaves were found in a row behind the 8′ nut, with the strings passing through holes in that nut to get there (the Italians, it will be remembered, did that sort of thing for the entire line of 4′ pins). This scheme was probably adopted because the presence of a lute stop did not allow enough room to place the upper octaves of pins between the two nuts. Nevertheless, wrestpins were arranged in this fashion even on instruments without lute stops, and even on rebuilt Flemish harpsichords. It was simply the way the English did it.

16-7. A 1761 Jacob Kirkman harpsichord. The 4′ wrestpins are located between the 4′ and 8′ bridges for the lowest two octaves, but for the upper three they are found behind the 8′ bridge. For these pins, the strings pass through slots in the 8′ bridge. © Bildarchiv Preussischer Kulturbesitz, Berlin, Musikinstrumenten Museum.

registers, and operated by a large, wood, paddle-shaped pedal attached to a board hung vertically from the left of the stand's front stretcher. The external part of the mechanism was found on the outside of the left cheek, covered by a box made of the same wood as the case. A knob on the interior of the left cheek was used to operate a latch that engaged the machine. With the knob pulled back toward the player, the mechanism was disengaged, and the normal resources of the instruments were available through the hand stops. When the knob was pushed forward, the machine stop was engaged.

With the machine on, but without depressing the pedal, the instrument had the dogleg 8′ and the 4′ locked into the lower manual, and the dogleg 8′ on the upper. The second 8′ could be added, by using the hand stop for that register. If the player now depressed the pedal, the machine turned off the 4′ and the dogleg 8′ (which meant it could not be accessed from either manual), and brought the 8′ lute into play on the upper manual. The second 8′ was available on the lower, provided the player had turned that register on with the hand stop (although on some instruments it was possible to access both 8′s by means of the machine). Thus, four registrations were available by means of the machine: a 1×8′, 1×4′ (or 2×8′, 1×4′) on the lower manual; the dogleg 8′ on the upper; the second 8′ on the lower; and the lute on the upper.[60] The player was by no means limited to the contrasts afforded by pedal up or pedal down, but could easily contrast full harpsichord against lute, or the second 8′ against the dogleg 8′.[61] And, of course, the buff stop (which usually muted the second 8′) could also be brought into play; in fact, on some instruments the buff was operated by a separate pedal.

The machine could also be used to make gradual dynamic changes, since depressing the pedal slowly took the stops off one at a time. Thus, when playing with full harpsichord on the lower manual, a diminuendo would be effected by first removing the 4′ and then the dogleg 8′, leaving only the second 8′, which well might have been quilled in either hard sole leather or the softer *peau de buffle*. The upper manual would go from dogleg 8′ to the quieter nasal lute. If the player was at all skillful with the left foot, the diminuendo would be even more convincing as the plectra of the 4′ and the dogleg 8′ were gradually withdrawn, with less and less of the plectra attacking the strings. A crescendo was available just as easily, by gradually letting up on the pedal. Thus, equipped with a machine stop, the mature English double was an extremely flexible instrument.

Of course, when the machine was not engaged by the latch, the player had the normal disposition of the harpsichord at his or her disposal and changed registration by means of the stop knobs protruding through the nameboard. These usually numbered five, for the two 8′s, the 4′, the lute, and the buff. Despite its seeming complexity the machine stop worked efficiently and became a regular feature of late English instruments. It was easily retrofitted to older harpsichords as well, and it becomes difficult to determine whether a given device was original to an instrument or not.

Single-manual 2×8′, 1×4′ harpsichords were also provided with machine stops, usually removing the 4′ and an 8′ and leaving the second 8′ (which may have been quilled in leather or *peau de buffle*). On some instruments the buff stop would also be engaged, providing a sudden dynamic change or a diminuendo from full harpsichord to buffed 8′. Of course, the player could stop the foot before the buff was brought into play, but as with doubles, a second pedal was sometimes furnished for the buff stop alone. Singles were also often fitted with lute stops, making the operation of the machine somewhat more complex. Kenneth Mobbs and Alexander MacKenzie of Ord have suggested that in such instruments machine stops were never "off," but worked differently in the forward and back positions.[62] With the machine knob pushed forward (the "on" position in a double), the full 2×8′, 1×4′ resources were invoked. Pressing the pedal removed first the 4′, then the front 8′, then the second 8′, and ended up with the lute stop on. Thus, if the pedal was depressed quickly, the instrument went from full harpsichord to lute; but depressed slowly, a convincing diminuendo could be produced. Reversing the process, of course, provided a crescendo. With the machine knob pulled back (corresponding to "off" on a double), the second 8′ was on, and the front 8′ and the 4′ could be set either on or off with the hand stops. When the pedal was depressed, the second 8′ was withdrawn. Accordingly, a sudden or gradual change from full harpsichord to single 8′ (or 1×8′,

16-8. The mechanism of the machine stop of a 1785 Longman and Broderip single. Bristol, Mobbs Collection.

1×4′) was effected, with the reverse possible by letting up the pedal. Thus, even on a single-manual harpsichord, the machine allowed a great deal of tonal and dynamic flexibility.

Perhaps the eighteenth-century English harpsichord's most interesting accretion was the swell. The early version was the nag's head—a section of the lid that rose or fell through operation of a

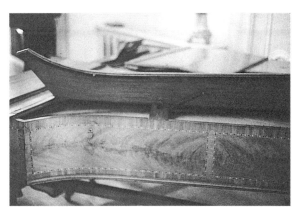

pedal. These first appeared on Kirkman's instruments as early as 1754 and were still employed after the introduction of the Venetian swell. The purpose of either swell may not have been as obvious as it seems. It did create the impression of dynamic changes, and when used in conjunction with the machine stop it would certainly add to the effectiveness of the crescendos and diminuendos. But the swell was probably more convincing as a mutation stop, shifting, with a movement of the foot, between the open harpsichord sound and the softer, muffled, lid-down tone. One of its purposes—perhaps its primary purpose—was likely to have been simply to reduce the amount of sound coming from the instrument. These were powerful harpsichords, capable of a great volume of sound, and even a single 8′ might have been overwhelming to an amateur flutist, violinist, or singer.[63]

16-9a. The nag's-head swell of this 1780 Jacob and Abraham Kirkman double is operated by a pedal. A portion of the lid is hinged to swing up and down. Hamburg, Museum für Kunst und Gewerbe, Sammlung Beurmann.

The concept of a harpsichord with sustainable sounds—a keyboard instrument whose strings were caressed by rosined bows or wheels, first invented by Leonardo da Vinci and developed by Hans Haiden late in the sixteenth century—never lost its allure. In 1741 Roger Plenius (1696–1774), the inventive transplanted Dutchman, patented a *lyrichord,* a sophisticated version of Haiden's instrument in which the rosined wheels turned at different speeds, and the strings were tuned with suspended weights.[65] Evidently at least one was built, because an auction announcement of 1772 mentions "a *Lyrichord,* a capital melodious instrument made by the famous Rutgerus Plenius."[66]

16-9b. The slats of the Venetian swell of an 1800 Jacob and Abraham Kirkman double in the open position. When closed, the slats completely enclose the soundwell and act as an inner lid. Bethersden, Colt Clavier Collection.

With the encroachment of the piano late in the century, several English makers tried their hands at the combined harpsichord-piano. A 1777 five-octave 2×8′ instrument (Washington, D.C., Smithsonian Institution), with the piano on the upper manual and the harpsichord on the lower, is attributed to

Robert Stodart (fl. 1775–99), a student of Broadwood's. A similar instrument was patented by James Davies (dates unknown) in 1792. But the most famous of these combinations was the one built by the French-born John Joseph Merlin (1735–1803), who came to England in 1760 as part of the retinue of the Spanish ambassador. Among other things, Merlin built harpsichords and pianos — Burney owned one of his instruments, a piano with an extended six-octave compass intended for four-hand playing. His only extant harpsichord-piano, which he called a "compound harpsichord," is dated 1780 (Munich, Deutsches Museum).[69] It is a phenomenon, although in external appearance it varies little from a conventional large, late English harpsichord, paneled and cross-banded in mahogany and sitting on a stand with square-tapered legs veneered en suite.[70]

A single with a five-octave FF,GG–f³ compass, it is disposed 1×16′ (this stop is quilled in leather and is the only occurrence of the 16′ we know of in England), 1×8′, 1×4′, buff (here called "Welsh harp"), "celestial harp" (not a celestine stop, but a device that raises the 8′ jacks off the strings, allowing them to vibrate sympathetically), and a down-striking piano action. A second set of 8′ strings is present, joining with the first when the piano is brought into play. It has three pedals, for 16′, piano on, and piano off. Merlin's instrument also has a recording device, designed to preserve improvisations for posterity. This consists of a 9″-wide frame mounted over the soundboard, containing a roller at each end with a continuous sheet of paper between them. Pencils were attached to trackers, and these, in turn, were attached to the jacks. The apparatus was operated by a clockwork, and when the paper was in motion, the pencils marked the exact temporal durations played by their jacks.[71] It was an extremely clever contrivance, to say the least, but Merlin's recording device was never heard of again, perhaps because of the difficulty of keeping pencils (one for every jack!) sharp and properly adjusted. And, of course, the resultant data had to be translated to conventional notation, although Merlin seemed to have worked this out too.

BENTSIDE SPINETS

The spinet was the middle-class harpsichord of both choice and necessity. Not nearly as expensive as a grand, but still an attractive instrument with a five-octave compass, it could play almost anything that could be done on a large double with machine stop and swell. Of course, with its single-strung disposition, and without even a buff stop, it could not compete with the grand for flexibility and variety; nevertheless, it served the harpsichord literature. Most eighteenth-century English builders contented themselves with building and selling this instrument, since it seemed almost impossible for them to compete with the giants Shudi and Kirkman. Turning again to *Boalch III,* we find that in London alone there were about a hundred builders turning out spinets, with something like forty-five builders active in all the other cities in England. Bristol could boast of six spinet makers during the course of the century and Cambridge, four; but most other cities seemed to have just one or two builders, who no doubt satisfied local demand.[77]

English spinets changed gradually over the course of the eighteenth century. The normal five-octave GG–g^3 compass was established fairly early, with some instruments later adopting the FF,GG–f^3 more common on grands (with the FF$\sharp$ added after 1770, as in the grands); but the short scale, brass stringing, and Italianate box guide that had been characteristic of the English spinet since Zenti introduced it in the 1660s prevailed until spinets were no longer made. Interior construction was fairly simple, with lower braces to the back wall on either side of the keyboard, and often with a brace perpendicular to them behind the keyboard. There were a few upper braces fastened under the liners, Ruckers fashion, and perhaps a knee or two. Around the middle of the century some builders adopted a more Northern style of case work, using heavy sides of oak rather than thin sides of pine. In these cases the sides sat on the bottom, rather than surrounding it. External decor followed the grands, with the same use of veneers, paneling, crossbanding, and stringing. Bentsides were usually, but not necessarily, curved at the tail, and the left side of the case often curved to the spine as well. Lids had a molding applied to the edge, and a brass hook and ring to keep them down tight. Stands were trestles, and followed the same styles as the grands.

The biggest name in spinet making was probably that of Hitchcock. It will be remembered that Thomas Hitchcock the younger, whom we met earlier in this chapter in connection with his ca. 1725 double, was the son of Thomas the elder, who

In the 1770s the builder Adam Walker (dates unknown) invented and patented the *celestine* stop, a device that produced a sustained tone and could be attached to an existing harpsichord. The mechanism consisted of a revolving band of silk that passed under the strings and was set into motion by a treadle. The strings were first sounded by a down-striking hammer, which impacted them at the point of the rotating band. Presumably, the bowlike passage of the silk band convinced the strings to continue to vibrate, just as a violin bow does to its strings. The Walker device was yet another application of Haiden's bowed-keyboard principle and probably would have been relegated to the dustbin of history, were it not for the fact that Thomas Jefferson, who was in Paris at the time, was in the process of purchasing his Kirkman harpsichord. Jefferson, first through an intermediary and then directly, asked Charles Burney to oversee the purchase of the instrument for him and to have it fitted with a celestine stop.[67]

Burney replied that Kirkman was opposed to Walker's invention, because the rosin on the silk band fouled the strings. The builder would not install it himself, so the instrument would have to go to Walker's shop after it was completed. Jefferson wrote back that he imagined that simply cleaning the strings from time to time should keep things in proper working order, and that in any case, he would use the device sparingly, only in movements in which he thought it appropriate. He further asked Burney to see if it were not possible to cause the silk to rotate by means of springs or weights, rather than by treadle (or as Jefferson put it, "the constant motion of the foot on a treadle diverts the attention and dissipates the delirium both of the player and hearer").[68] Burney's final letter noted that Walker had consented to try this new wrinkle, and that the stop on Jefferson's harpsichord was operated by a clockwork. Furthermore, said Burney, the new version of the celestine stop was far superior to the older. Finally, he told Jefferson that his new Kirkman harpsichord was the best he had ever heard. Unfortunately, Jefferson's instrument has not survived.

was building bentside spinets as early as 1660. John (d. 1774) was probably the son of Thomas the younger, and the line of builders ended with him. Curiously, all three Hitchcocks were members of the Haberdasher's Company, the hatmakers' guild, and they all left it to pursue careers as spinet makers. The family is survived by about fifty spinets in the eighteenth century, all of them of the softwood variety, with case walls of intermediate thickness surrounding the bottom. It is difficult to assign instruments to one or the other of the Hitchcocks, since they never dated their work; but they did mark them with numbers that help place them in some sort of chronological order. The numbers go up past two thousand, which would represent a lot of spinets; but we noted that Kirkman probably made at least the same number of grand harpsichords, and spinets certainly took less time to produce, so the numbers may not be out of line.

There were at least four Harrises building spinets in the eighteenth century: Joseph, John, Baker, and William, although only the first two seem to be related. Joseph (fl. 1737–65) is survived by ten instruments, but little else is known of him. He must have taken some pride in his work, because on the back of the nameboard of a 1757 instrument (private ownership) he wrote, "This is not one of my Comon instruments But the Best Ton'd I ever made."[78] His son John (fl. 1730–72) has a bit more history. Early in his career, in 1730, he "invented" a new sort of harpsichord, a 2×8′ that could also play at 16′ and 4′ pitches (perhaps using a set of couplers under the keyboard; such an arrangement was employed by Giuseppi Maria Goccini in 1725). None have survived, and, indeed, none may have been built. In 1768 John immigrated to the New World and set up shop in Boston. Eight of his spinets are extant, perhaps half of which were made while he was still in London. William (fl. 1765–93) is another unknown figure and left ten spinets. Baker Harris (fl. 1740–80) left twenty-two spinets and perhaps a few harpsichords.[79] Other names could be mentioned, but like harpsichords, spinets were all fairly much alike in compass and decor, although some used fancier veneering and marquetry on the nameboard. Spinets built outside London were generally indistinguishable from their big-city siblings.

MERLIN THE VERY INGENIOUS MECHANIC

John Joseph Merlin was a craftsman of considerable talents (Fanny Burney, Charles Burney's daughter, called him "the very ingenious mechanic"),[72] and some of his inventions proved to have lasting value. In addition to his harpsichord and piano building, he was a prolific developer of labor-saving devices. One was his tea table — a table with a central samovar that, when properly charged with the correct beverage and rotated by the hostess's hand, would automatically pour the appropriate amount of tea into the twelve cups set on its perimeter. His gold scale, which weighed gold coins to be sure that none of the precious metal had been shaved off, was a more practical contrivance. Another of his gadgets was a music-desk table for eight performers, which could be raised or lowered, depending on whether the players were seated or standing (Burney owned one of these "Merlin tables"). He also invented the Dutch oven and the wheelchair, contrivances that — particularly the latter — are still useful today.[73]

Although not English-born, Merlin was not above allowing his name to be associated with that of the legendary King Arthur's famous sorcerer. To this end, he opened a museum, which he called "Merlin's Cave," that contained all sorts of mechanical, musical, and phantasmagoric devices, including "an automatic organ, imitating the performance of a full band."[74] Merlin has often been cited as the inventor of roller skates, although that method of personal propulsion was already in existence since at least ca. 1700. The mistaken ascription was made by Thomas Busby, who, in a never-to-be-forgotten description of Merlin at his most outrageous, described the mechanic's antics at a party:

> One of his [Merlin's] ingenious novelties was a *pair of skates,* contrived to run on wheels. Supplied with a pair of these and a violin [he was skating and playing at the same time], he mixed in the motley group of one of the celebrated Mrs. Corneily's masquerades at Carlisle House, Soho Square; when, not having provided the means of retarding his velocity, or commanding its direction, he impelled himself against a mirror of more than Five hundred pounds value, dashed it to atoms, broke his instrument to pieces and wounded himself most severely.[75]

Despite this unseemly breach of manners, Merlin was a charmer, much in demand at parties and social events of all sorts. His witty, French-accented English appeared to have delighted the ladies, and his propensity for outrageous but essentially harmless behavior only seemed to make him more endearing to London society. Indeed, he was an amazing fellow.[76]

Nine eighteenth-century Scottish builders are listed in *Boalch III,* with eight of them from Edinburgh.[80] No grand harpsichords have survived from these builders, and only a handful of spinets. By the second part of the century, four builders, Richard Livingstone (fl. 1782–1804), John Johnstone (dates unknown), James Logan (fl. 1774–90), and Christian Shean (ca. 1711–94) seem to have been the dominant spinet makers in Edinburgh, and no doubt they also made the occasional grand or two.[81] Johnstone and Logan are each survived by a spinet, but there are five Sheans extant. Shean was born in London, but came to Edinburgh around 1760, no doubt hoping to escape the fierce competition of the big city. Interestingly, in his London spinets Shean used the common GG–g^3 compass, but when in Edinburgh he seems to have switched to the FF–f^3 keyboard more common on harpsichords. Another builder, Andrew Rochead (dates unknown), is represented by a 1795 spinet (also FF–f^3), which may well have been the last of these instruments produced in the British Isles. Like most builders at that time, Rochead ended his career making pianos. Neil Stewart (dates unknown), a dealer like Longman and Broderip, purchased instruments from Logan, and perhaps from Rochead as well, and certainly others, and put his name on them for resale.

As far as we know, the only eighteenth-century harpsichord builders in Ireland worked in Dublin, and *Boalch III* lists seven-

16-10. This ordinary bentside spinet by Thomas Haxby, made in 1764, is typical of the domestic instrument of eighteenth-century England. Haxby was a well-known spinet maker in York. Museum of Fine Arts, Boston. Reproduced with permission. © 2000 Museum of Fine Arts, Boston. All rights reserved.

teen of them.[82] Most of them are names only, but three makers are survived by instruments: Ferdinand Weber (1715–84), Henry Rother (fl. 1762–74), and Robert Woffington (d. 1823). There seems to have been a Dublin school that favored the production of clavicytheria, since of the nine surviving instruments by these craftsmen, four are upright harpsichords.

Weber was born in Germany, trained there as an organ builder, and immigrated to Dublin in 1739. Like Shudi, he became a friend of Handel, who came to that city in 1741 to present performances of his oratorios *Messiah* and *Saul* and undoubtedly was grateful for some German food and conversation. Weber is survived by seven plucked instruments: four grands, a bentside spinet, and two clavicytheria. The grands, all singles, are similar to the London products, but with some differences. His 1746 (England, private ownership) is disposed 2×8′ plus lute,[83] and the 1751 (Brussels, Musée Instrumental) is also 2×8′; but the 1768 (Dublin, National Museum) is disposed 2×8′, 1×4′, lute, Venetian swell, and machine and is equipped with knee levers instead of the standard English pedals. His Venetian swell, although similar to Shudi's, differs in some details and is possibly a year older than Shudi's patent. The 1775 (London, Royal College of Music) has the same disposition, swell, and machine as the 1768 and also has knee levers, but it lacks a 4′.[84] This instrument was given an FF,GG–g^3 compass, which seems to have been something of a Dublin specialty.

Weber's 1764 clavicytherium (Dublin, private ownership) is a rare example of a pyramid upright. It differs from the one built in 1675 by Martin Kaiser (and from the anonymous clavicytherium in Rome as well), which has a bow-shaped nut and two bridges, with the longest strings going up the center of the instrument. Here there is the one conventional bridge on the soundboard, and the strings go across the case at an angle, from lower left to upper right, in order to miss the incurving of the bentside on the left. Surprisingly, the instrument is disposed 3×8′.[85] The third string passes over its own nut, close to the gap, giving the sort of nasal stop found on some German harpsichords (like the 1723 Hass, although that instrument combines the two nuts into one of two levels). Weber may have gotten the idea of a third 8′ choir from his master, Johann Ernst Hähnel (fl. first half of the eighteenth century), who was a builder at the Saxon court. At any rate, as far as we know, there was no English tradition of a 3×8′ disposition. The compass is GG–g^3. There are lower and upper sets of doors, with applied moldings on the former, and fret-sawn open-work filigree backed with cloth material on the latter. The heavy case is impressive looking, although except for the keywell and the conventional use of cabi-

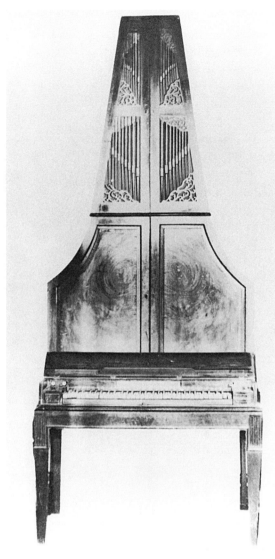

16-11. The 1774 clavicytherium by Henry Rother. Dublin instruments seem to have had a tradition somewhat different from the rest of Great Britain. Almost half of the surviving Dublin harpsichords are clavicytheria. Dublin, National Museum of Ireland.

net woods, visual connections between it and the harpsichords made in London are hard to find. Weber's second clavicytherium (Ireland, private ownership) is of unknown date, again pyramidal, and supposedly with a 2×8′, 1×4′ disposition.

Henry Rother's 1774 clavicytherium (Dublin, National Museum), disposed 2×8′, 1×4′, with an FF,GG–g³ compass, is another pyramid. Its lower doors have floating panels of burl mahogany, and a set of façade pipes peer through the open framework of the upper doors. With the shape and the pipes one could easily be convinced that the imposing case housed an organ; but when the doors are open, a clavicytherium is revealed, of the same type as the Weber, but with the more conventional disposition.

Woffington's one surviving harpsichord, of unknown date (Japan, private collection), is a single with the full disposition of 2×8′, 1×4′, machine, and swell. Like the other Irish harpsichords discussed here, the machine and swell are operated by knee levers rather than pedals. His clavicytherium is also a claviorganum—a harpsichord-organ. The large, imposing, oblong case with open fretwork and large ovals filled with gold façade pipes is designed to sit on a table or platform. Even more than the 1774 Rother, the external effect is one of a chamber organ, not a harpsichord; but it is both. Opening the doors reveals an upright harpsichord of conventional shape (not a pyramid) set into the surrounding case, disposed 2×8′, 1×4′, with an FF,GG–g³ compass.[86] The organ portion of the ensemble is behind the harpsichord and not ordinarily visible.

These Dublin instruments present us with something of a minor mystery. The grand harpsichords have knee levers, rather than pedals. The survivors are all singles, although that could be due to accident of survival. The clavicytheria are the only ones known to have been made in the British Isles,[87] and they favored the complex pyramidal shape. The FF,GG–g^3 compass is seen only in Dublin. Obviously, some tradition other than the one that came from London was at work. Perhaps someday other Irish harpsichords will be unearthed, enabling us to shed a little more light on these interesting instruments.

AMERICA

The thirteen American colonies were part of the British Empire until 1783, when they gained independence at the Treaty of Paris; but both before and after the Revolution, eighteenth-century American builders enjoyed a freedom not found in the mother country or on the Continent. There were no guilds to restrict trade and no laws prohibiting the construction of musical instruments by those who had not gone through a traditional apprenticeship (although London did not have any such restrictions). Consequently, harpsichords—mostly spinets—were built by a variety of craftsmen, ranging from trained masters, to those who made many sorts of instruments, to carpenters or cabinetmakers who built an instrument or two. Furthermore, while the original colonists were British citizens, they were later joined by Germans and craftsmen of other nationalities, some of whom were also instrument builders. Perhaps the most versatile and peripatetic of these immigrants was the Swiss-born James Juhan (1736–97), who, in addition to harpsichords and organs, made pianos, guitars, violins, gambas, cases, and bows in Halifax, Haiti, Boston, Charleston, Philadelphia, Portsmouth, Williamsburg, Richmond, and Petersburg. At one point in his busy life he was also teaching dancing and performing in ballad operas. None of his instruments of any sort have survived.

American spinets were practically indistinguishable from the English versions.[88] Nevertheless, the earliest example was made not by an Englishman, but by Johann Gottlob Clemm (1690–1762), a German born near Dresden who immigrated to the New World in 1733 and settled in Philadelphia, where he made organs and harpsichords. His 1739 spinet (New York, Metropolitan Museum of Art) was built there; but he later moved to New York, and then to Bethlehem, Pennsylvania. The spinet is a much-altered piece, but except for its floating-panel lid, a distinctly German touch (although it will be recalled that Rother's 1774 clavicytherium also had floating panels), it seems English enough. The case is of plain walnut, but not any plainer than other spinets built in London that early in the century. Its original compass was probably GG–d^3.

John Harris, whom we met while he was still living in London, immigrated to Boston and is survived by a handful of spinets. His ca. 1769 (New York, Metropolitan Museum of Art), with its cross-banded mahogany veneers, is beautifully made, as fine an example of the cabinetmaker's art as anything produced in London.

Only two American grand harpsichords are known to be extant. One is by David Tannenberg (1725–1804), who was born in Saxony but trained in Bethlehem with Clemm.[89] He moved to Lititz (also in Pennsylvania) in 1765, where he set up shop. Although primarily an organ builder, he did make some harpsichords and pianos. Little is known of his surviving grand (Salem, N.C., private ownership). A 1794 double by Charles Trute (d. 1807) and Trute Wiedberg (dates unknown) is the other extant American grand. Trute, who first built instruments in London, immigrated to America around 1790 and a few years later entered into a partnership with Wiedberg in Philadelphia. They advertised themselves as prepared to "make Harpsichords, Grand Piano-Fortes, the size and shape of an Harpsichord, and portable and square ditto."[90] They also claimed that the workmanship and tone of their instruments were superior to those hitherto made in Philadelphia and put their wares up against anything from Europe. Their 1794 five-octave double, probably disposed 2×8′, 1×4′, with lute, buff, and machine, could just as easily have been built in London except for one quirk: the case is made of mahogany, rather than oak. But the wood is plain and is veneered with a more highly figured veneer — an interesting but not so clever ploy, since mahogany is

16-12. This 1739 bentside spinet by Johann Gottlob Clemm is believed to be the earliest surviving harpsichord built in America. New York, Metropolitan Museum of Art.

not a good bending wood, and the bentside had cracked from the strain imposed upon it.[91] Just before the turn of the century the partners moved to Wilmington, where Wiedberg died and Trute became an innkeeper.

The place of these American builders and others like them in the second half of the eighteenth century is somewhat blurry. Most of them undoubtedly earned the major portion of their living making organs, with bentside spinets and perhaps a few grand harpsichords no more than a sideline. Their customers were probably found among the more provincial members of the colonies (after 1783, citizens of the new country), although no doubt the average London gentleman would have considered anyone living in America to be provincial. Those who had the knowledge and the wealth probably would have ordered their instruments from London. The Boston-born Benjamin Franklin, while in London in 1757–62 pleading the affairs of Pennsylvania, wrote his wife that he wanted to find a good harpsichord to bring back home. Around that same time George Washington requested that his London agent procure a spinet by Roger Plenius; but by that time Plenius was out of business, and it was not until 1793 that Washington finally got an instrument, a grand from Longman and Broderip. That harpsichord still exists (Mount Vernon, Mount Vernon Ladies' Association of the Union). Thomas Jefferson, as noted earlier, also bought a London instrument, a Kirkman. The Philadelphia lawyer Francis Hopkinson (1737–91) purchased a Shudi and Broadwood in 1783, and the account books of that firm still list the order which, in addition to the "Double Key'd Harpsichord," included three extra sets of jacks with leather plectra, feathers for replacing quills, a leather cover for the instrument, a set of chromatic tuning forks, and even a pair of pliers.

For the first twenty-five years of the eighteenth century, England continued to build Internationally inspired harpsichords. The examples that have survived display common elements such as intermediate scales, the use of both brass and iron stringing, walnut cases with bentsides of intermediate dimensions, heavy spines, applied top moldings, and shaped end-

blocks. It is impossible to know what course English harpsichord making would have taken had Hermann Tabel not appeared on the scene, but it might very well have continued along in the indigenous style seen in the instruments of Tisseran, Barton, Slade, and Coston. From all appearances, it would seem that by introducing the Ruckers paradigm, Tabel, almost single-handedly, transformed English building.

This was an extraordinary accomplishment, not easily understood. We can see why French makers would want to abandon their International roots: their experience with the commercial worth of rebuilt Ruckers harpsichords was easily sufficient to convince them to switch to a product made in the updated image of such revered models. But such was not the case in England. Ruckers harpsichords were rebuilt here, too (although usually without any enlargements to the case), but not nearly on the same scale, and apparently without any suggestion that the old Flemish style was in any way more accepted than that of the indigenous builders. The evidence of the extant instruments would suggest that the indigenous style came to an abrupt end almost as soon as Tabel began building; but it is likely that the transformation was more

---

HOPKINSON AND HARPSICHORD QUILLING

Francis Hopkinson, author, politician, signatory to the Declaration of Independence, and one of the drafters of the Constitution of the United States, was also a harpsichordist. Dissatisfied with the necessary task of replacing broken quills, he invented an "improved" method of quilling a harpsichord, involving the addition of a metal staple to enhance the springiness of the plectrum, and described the process in 1783 in a communication to the Philosophical Society of Philadelphia. Another letter to the society, with further refinements, was sent in the following year, and a completely different scheme using leather plectra was communicated to that body in 1786. Hopkinson also noted that he had supplied himself with a complete chromatic set of tuning forks, thus liberating him from the task of setting a temperament. "There will be found not one in a hundred," he observed, "that can tune a harpsichord."[92]

The significance of Hopkinson's fixation on "improving" the harpsichord lies not so much in the technical aspects of his inventions as much as in the growing dissatisfaction with the instrument's idiosyncrasies. The piano, while by no means free of its own regulation problems, at least did not require the replacement of quills. It also indicates that harpsichord owners either were no longer expected, or were no longer able, to tune and maintain their instruments as they had in the past; and, in fact, it is around this time that the services of a technician seem to have become required to keep one's instrument in regulation and in tune. This phenomenon was not limited to America, but was also true in England and on the Continent, as witnessed by the growing tuning business of builders like Taskin, Shudi, Broadwood, and Kirkman.

---

gradual. Nevertheless, the Tabel model and those of his students Shudi and Kirkman became the standard English harpsichord. On the other hand, while the interior of the instrument may have been Ruckers-derived, on the outside it appeared to differ little from English cases made earlier in the century.

It is also difficult to understand why the Shudi and Kirkman shops so completely dominated London harpsichord building. One is reminded that the Ruckers family did the same in Antwerp more than a century earlier, and in London, as in Antwerp, the reasons why probably had less to do with the inherent superiority of the instruments of these makers as much as with their exceptional business acumen and sense of what we now call public relations and marketing. It was no accident that these three families were able to establish factories employing perhaps dozens of workmen engaged in finding, seasoning, and preparing woods of various kinds, cutting them into planks, making cases and decorating them with veneers or papers and paint, producing stands, keyboards, jacks, and registers, as well as assembling, stringing, voicing, and adjusting the final products.

The late English harpsichord's ability to make crescendos and diminuendos needs to be seen in the context of a European-wide obsession with dynamic flexibility. It has often been said that the French and English machine stops, the *peau de buffle,* and the lid and Venetian swells were the response of harpsichord makers to the encroaching piano and its touch-sensitive dynamic capability. This does not seem to be a reasonable conclusion. Harpsichord makers were quick enough to build pianos if that is what their customers wanted, and it probably mattered little to them if their cases contained jacks or hammers. It is more likely that the metamorphosis of the late harpsichord into a dynamically expressive machine and the growth of the piano were both the result of the popularity of the new style of music that we now call Rococo or pre-Classical. Gone were the comparatively rigid dynamic boundaries of Baroque style that served so well for Henry Purcell, François Couperin, J. S. Bach, George Frideric Handel, Domenico Scarlatti, Jean-Phillipe Rameau, and their lesser contemporaries. In the new style, dynamic change became part of the fabric of melody, part of the *affect.* Any Londoner playing contemporary music in 1770 on a bentside spinet would have been very much aware that there was an element of the music he was not able to realize on his single-strung instrument, which was dynamically inadequate and without even a buff stop. Only a grand harpsichord, with lute, a rank of jacks quilled in leather, and with a machine stop and a swell, would be capable of a full expression of the music's inner soul. Either that or, of course, a piano. Clearly, it was the newer instrument that best suited that music, and the spirit of the times is captured perfectly by the words of the Reverend Thomas Twining, who owned both harpsichord and piano, and who wrote the following to Charles Burney in 1774:

> If it [a newly acquired fortepiano] has deficits which a good harpsichord has not, it has beauties and delicacies which amply compensate, and which make the harpsichord wonderfully flashy and insipid when played after it. . . . There are times when one's ear calls only for harmony and a pleasant jingle . . . but as soon as ever my spirit wakes, as soon as my heartstrings catch the gentlest vibration, I swivel me round incontinently to the pianoforte.[93]

There seems to be no doubt that the first pianos in Britain were considered little more than novelties. True, they had that dynamic capability, but they lacked the English harpsichord's brilliance and power. Nevertheless, as piano builders gained experience, they found ways to increase its power, and they also capitalized on things the harpsichord could not do, like damper effects and the ability to play the two hands at different dynamic levels. Eventually, composers came to consider the piano the more versatile instrument and began writing more idiomatic music for it. That was the true end of the harpsichord. The dynamics in the late sonatas of Haydn can be realized to perfection on an English harpsichord with machine and swell, or on a French instrument with machine and *peau de buffle,* but Haydn's sonatas are piano music and achieve their full potential only on that instrument. His piano music, as well as that of Mozart and Beethoven, continued to be played by harpsichord owners, often well into the nineteenth century. But by that time, after a glorious four-hundred-year existence, the harpsichord was obsolete.[94]

PART V

The Nineteenth and Twentieth Centuries

[*17*]

THE HARPSICHORD HIBERNATES

*F*EW FORCES have changed the Western world as violently as the Industrial Revolution. Even before the nineteenth century, our civilization had begun an inexorable transition from an agrarian economy in which most people lived out their lives in villages or on farms, to a manufacturing society in which large populations lived in cities, working in factories or providing goods and services. The production of commodities was transformed by coal, steel, steam power, and mass-production techniques. Whereas the Kirkman family maintained an average output of twenty instruments a year—then a stupendous production rate—Conrad Graf (1782–1851), who converted a ballroom into a factory to get the room he needed, generated something like one hundred pianos per annum. Later makers far exceeded those numbers: between 1826 and 1861 the Broadwood firm produced 75,700 pianos, an average of two thousand a year.[1] This staggering output of instruments would have been impossible without the steel, coal, and steam that enabled a rail transportation system to bring in massive quantities of lumber and other materials and move out the finished products.[2]

The violence of these societal shifts produced many fascinating conflicts in the Romantic mind, most of which are not germane to this discussion; but the one small contradiction that does concern us was the view of musicians, critics, music lovers, and connoisseurs toward the harpsichord. With the explosive growth of a large, cash-laden middle class, the piano, whether an insignificant square or a magnificent grand, became the icon of the bourgeoisie, the symbol of a solid, successful life — values that Germany and Austria would immortalize as *Biedermeier.* In this environment the harpsichord — if it was thought of at all — was considered an outworn, outmoded relic of a distasteful past, overly delicate in nature, needing constant attention and adjustment, with an inadequate, unattractive, puling sound. Even its music was sometimes denigrated. The acerbic Parisian critic León Escudier (1821–81), reviewing a recital of the pianist Marie Mongin in 1862, wrote in *L'Art musicale* that her performance of some (unspecified) Baroque work in fugal style, while well done, nevertheless turned the piano "into a dried-up instrument like a harpsichord."[3] A year earlier Escudier's brother Marie (1819–80), also a critic, had reviewed a performance of Mozart's D-minor Concerto by Louise Mattmann in *La France musicale* with the words, "God forbid that we should have any more to do with this feeble and poverty-stricken instrument of old, for which the harpsichordists scribbled."[4] Of course, given the musical climate of the time, this attitude was not unjustified. Professional pianists may have heeded Schumann's dictum to "let Bach be your daily bread" as they began their practice routines; but audiences wanted to hear contemporary music. Bach, Handel, Mozart, and the harpsichord were remnants of a bygone day.

Another example of the negative attitude toward the harpsichord can be seen in the 1885 International Inventions Exhibition in London, where more than a hundred early keyboard instruments from all over Europe were exhibited. Were such an assemblage of antiques to occur today, it would be considered a stunning display of priceless treasures from which we could expect to learn important lessons about the past. But those artifacts were not put there to be admired (although no doubt many of the exhibition-goers enjoyed their decor); rather, they were foils against which the progress of the nineteenth century could be judged. The vision of the complex machinery of the modern piano juxtaposed against the "crudeness" and utter simplicity of the antiques was intended as concrete evidence of the triumph of contemporary technology. That this complexity was not needed in a harpsichord was a subtlety probably lost on the viewers.

Nevertheless, there were countercurrents that tended to keep the harpsichord's traditions and sound alive. Primary among them was the nineteenth century's romanticized view of a past that became more attractive as society became more urbanized. While the attitude was by no means universal, artists, writers, poets, musicians, philosophers, and other members of the intelligentsia somehow viewed the country life of old as an Eden from which they had been expelled by the Industrial Revolution. To cite only one example, Beethoven, city dweller though he was, liked nothing better than a tramp through the fields, and his *Pastoral* Symphony is ample testimony to his love of a bucolic life he never really experienced.[5]

Antiquarianism was part of this Romantic Zeitgeist. Prior to the nineteenth century a musical instrument, no matter how beautifully decorated, was primarily considered a practical tool rather than a work of art (necessarily excluding those relatively few with decoration so lavish it overwhelmed their function as music-making machines). When it became worn or no longer useful it was rebuilt, or, at best, like Ruckers harpsichords, it became the basis for a new tool. If it was beyond such salvage it was discarded. But the antiquarian spirit of the nineteenth century suggested that old things be cherished. Furniture, pottery, silver and china services, books, works of art, musical instruments, even ruins — these had relevance because they were old and inspired images of times now far removed. With their quaint, long, narrow, colorful cases, gilded surfaces, lid paintings, decorated soundboards, and fancy stands, harpsichords could be viewed as works of art, and their practicality was not an issue. Accordingly, the antique harpsichord came to be seen as a thing of value, a worthy artifact because of its age.

The rise of historicism, from which developed today's early music movement, was another of these countercurrents. One of its landmarks was Mendelssohn's performance of J. S. Bach's *St. Matthew Passion* in 1829, the first time that great work had been heard in almost a century. Another was the formation in 1850 of the Bach Gesellschaft, dedicated to publishing Bach's complete works. Interest also began to focus on earlier composers, and editions of the music of other Baroque masters were undertaken. Johannes Brahms was one of the editors of the harpsichord works of François Couperin, and Camille Saint-Saëns supervised the edition of the complete works of Rameau. Established in 1825 and named after the patron saint of music, the Cecilian movement was concerned with reviving interest in the a cappella performance of sixteenth-century polyphony, particularly that of the Roman composer Palestrina. Schumann collected a library of instrumental and vocal works going back to the sixteenth century. Brahms inherited that library, and his music often shows how familiar he was with forms and compositional techniques of earlier times.

Historical performances of earlier music on harpsichords and the formation of retrospective ensembles both added to the growing inroads that plucked keyboards made into the consciousness of nineteenth-century musicians and music lovers. These currents grew stronger during the course of the century, until finally, in the last decade, the musical world found that it could no longer do without harpsichords. The firms of Érard and Pleyel each built instruments to display at the Paris Exhibition of 1889, the event that marked the beginning of the harpsichord revival.

SOME BUILDERS

Why the Viennese maker Christoph Bock (dates unknown) should have chosen to make a spinet at this late date is unknown, but he is survived by an 1804 C–f^3 bentside spinet (Vienna, Kunsthistorisches Museum), and he was not the only one to construct jack-action instruments during the nineteenth century. In Italy, Brescia and Bergamo were the sites of what could have been either a resurgence or a continuation of harpsichord making. Nine instruments have survived, all virginals, and all made like square pianos. Two are by anonymous builders: an undated example from Venice (Copenhagen, Musikhistorisk Museum og Carl Claudius' Samlung), with a painted case and a cabriole stand; and a ca. 1820 (Bologna, private collection), with a GG/BB–f^4 compass and a walnut case. The earliest of the others is an 1818 virginal (location unknown) by Zaccaria Respini of Brescia (dates unknown), with a walnut case. Alessandro Riva (1803–68) of Bergamo is represented by three, all with C/E–a^3 compasses: an 1836 (Milan, Museo degli Strumenti Musicali), another from ca. 1839 (Paris, private ownership), and a third dated 1839 (Leipzig, Musikinstrumenten-Museum der Universität Leipzig). G. Borghetti (dates unknown), who worked in Brescia, is also survived by three examples. Little is known of two of them (Brescia, private ownership, and Brescia, Museo Musicale Chitarristico); but the third, dated 1844 (Milan, Museo Teatrale alla Scala), is the last known jack-action instrument made in Italy before the revival at the end of the century. All three are similar, with compasses of GG/BB–c^4, intermediate scales of 12½″, and jacks quilled in leather. Other than these three instruments, nothing is known of this builder, not even his first name.

It is possible that these virginals were made as practice instruments for provincial organists, since many, if not most of them, use a short octave[6] and have signs of pull downs, indicating that they had been given pedal boards. Although a seeming anachronism, this makes sense when it is realized that

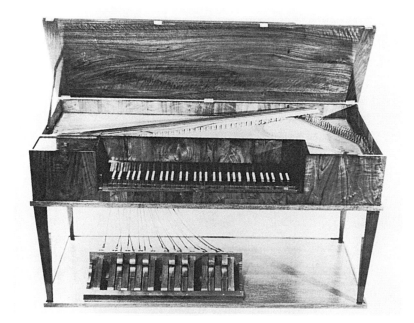

many organs in the poorer parts of Italy were never replaced, still had short octaves and pull-down pedal boards, and, in fact, were still tuned in meantone temperament.[7] Still, why were all but one of these instruments made in Brescia and Bergamo? And if practice instruments for organists were required, why were not clavichords or square pianos utilized? True, the Italians seemed to have little to do with the clavichord in the eighteenth century, but if these unconventional virginals were accepted, there should have been little resistance to other oblong keyboard instruments.

Some building went on even after the 1850s, when in most places the harpsichord as a viable instrument was nothing more than the dimmest of memories. An instrument by Ignatz Lutz (Prague, National Museum), made in the last third of the century, is one of the very few from that late date, although in London an otherwise unknown gentleman named Dove is reported to have built accurate copies of Baker Harris bentside spinets.[8] Other instruments were built as well, undoubtedly by people who were attempting to reproduce in some more or less superficial way an instrument of the past that had somehow taken their fancy. The work of Louis Tomasini was of a different nature, however, and more important. An Italian piano technician working in France, Tomasini made some harpsichords, including one exhibited at the 1889 Paris Exhibition. His work will be discussed more extensively in Chapter 18.

The harpsichord would linger on as a continuo instrument in opera, particularly in Italy, no doubt because old habits died hard in that tradition-bound medium. By and large, however, by the turn of the nineteenth century the piano seemed to have replaced it completely. Still, the sound of the plucked instrument had not entirely disappeared. People who owned them did not always discard them simply because others had declared them outmoded. According to his student Eduard Devrient (1801–77), the noted Lieder composer and arch Romantic Carl Friedrich Zelter (1758–1832) retained and continued to play his two-manual Oesterlein harpsichord.[9] Gioacchino Rossini (1792–1868) learned his keyboard skills on a harpsichord owned by his teacher, Giuseppe Malerbi, in 1802,[10] and in the 1820s young Giuseppe Verdi (1813–1901) did his practicing on a polygonal virginal, probably an ancient instrument owned by someone in his small village of Le Roncole. Well before the end of the century, Prince Edmond de Polignac (1834–1901), who along with his wife Winnaretta Singer was a fan of Baroque music before it became popular again, greeted visitors to his Paris salon by playing his harpsichord. The Rev. Francis Kilvert (1840–79), an otherwise unknown English curate, tells in his diary of a visit to a mill where, while the miller's wife baked bread, the daughter entertained them at a "jingling old harpsichord."[11]

Even if they were no longer played, people were not always eager to dispose of family heirlooms that had once possessed considerable value. Some stored their harpsichords in back rooms, barns, sheds, and attics, often finally selling them to dealers who, in turn, marketed them to antiquarian collectors. Others had their harpsichords converted into pianos. But sometimes the instruments were restored, redecorated in what was considered the archaic style, and retained as pieces of antique furniture. This may have been a minor idiosyncrasy among some owners in Paris during the late 1830s or 1840s: the lavish redecoration of a number of otherwise "useless" French harpsichords, including the ca. 1736 Hemsch double seen in Plate 18, can be traced to an unknown atelier operating there at that time. It is likely that other studios were engaged in this activity as well.[12]

Little by little the sound of the harpsichord began to reappear. The diminutive 1786 Taskin single (London, Victoria and Albert Museum) was restored in 1856 by the Parisian piano maker and technician Charles Fleury, who added a note in the treble and shifted the keyboard upward by a semitone, thus shortening the scale and allowing the instrument to be tuned to a nineteenth-century pitch of just below a = 440 Hz.[13] Apparently that harpsichord was intended to be played. Fleury restored other instruments as well, including, in 1858, the 1734 Hieronymus Albrecht Hass (Brussels, Musée Instrumental). Louis Tomasini, mentioned earlier, refurbished many harpsichords, such as the 1786 Joachem Swanen pedal instrument (Paris, Musée des Arts et Métier).[14] Records remain with a 1787 Longman and Broderip instrument (Bloomington, Ill., private collection), indicating that not only was it cleaned in 1799, 1816, 1818, and 1826, but in 1872 it was also repaired and tuned, and in 1874 tuned again.[15] This is a spotty maintenance schedule, to be sure; but it suggests that the harpsichord was first cared for as an heirloom, then finally, once more, used as a musical instrument.

HISTORICISM AND ANTIQUARIANISM

An important part of the nineteenth century's growing consciousness of the heritage of the past was its increasing sense of historicism, manifested in music by an awareness and respect for composers long gone. With few exceptions, music making before the 1750s was concerned with contemporary efforts, and the concert as we know it, made up of the masterpieces of the last two or three centuries, did not exist. Musicians learned their craft from the previous generation and evinced little regard for music earlier than that of their teachers. But this changed in the generation of Mozart, Haydn, and Beethoven. For the first time composers showed an interest in the music of figures from the dim mists of the past, such as J. S. Bach and George Frideric Handel, people whose styles must have appeared to be not only dated but positively antiquated. These men were now viewed as musical giants whose work was deserving not only of study but of imitation. One can easily see, for example, the growing sophistication in Mozart's contrapuntal writing after 1782, when he became familiar with the fugues of Bach by arranging them for string quartet. And in 1827, when presented with a set of the works of Handel, Beethoven described him as The Master, worthy of emulation by all living composers.

In the nineteenth century the concern for older instruments — harpsichord, viola da gamba, lute, recorder — was intertwined with this concern for older music. Ensembles were formed — the precursors of our modern-day early music groups — and concerts were given that were, in effect, antiquarianism expressed in sound. The musical values of the pieces and the instruments on which they were played were of secondary importance; instead, typically audiences were delighted with the quaint sounds that evoked visions of times gone by. For the harpsichord, this involvement with the old tended to take two forms. On the one hand, the instrument was occasionally played in recitals by pianists, particularly in England, as a sort of practical demonstration of antiquarianism. On the other, a few people started collecting harpsichords because their patina of age and their connection to a now romanticized past conferred an aura of preciousness on them.

One of the first, and certainly one of the best-known, pianists to include harpsichords in their concerts was Ignaz Moscheles (1794–1870). A brilliant musician, he was born in Prague, trained in Vienna, and between 1821 and 1846 lived in London. He was a teacher of Mendelssohn, and at the latter's invitation left England to take a teaching post at the newly formed Leipzig conservatory; but it is his stay in London that is of interest to us. From all accounts Moscheles was the archetypical nineteenth-century virtuoso, famed for his exploitation of piano color and tone; yet, he was struck by the spirit of antiquarianism and, unlike many of his colleagues, did not reject the keyboard music of the past or its intended instrument. Beginning in 1837, while still in England, he gave a series of harpsichord recitals on a 1771 Shudi still owned by the Broadwood piano company. That the special qualities of the harpsichord had already been forgotten can be surmised from the words of Moscheles's wife, who marveled at the Venetian swell and the two keyboards — the latter, she thought, supplied in order to avoid Scarlatti's hand crossings.[16]

Whether Moscheles set a chain of events into motion, or whether he was merely the first to succumb to what must have been considered an exotic aural antiquarianism, a string of other pianists followed in his footsteps. One was the native Londoner Charles Salaman (1814–1901), who inaugurated a series of harpsichord concerts in 1855, some of which were performed for the Royal Family. Interestingly, he played on his own instrument, a 1768 Kirkman with machine and swell that had been in his family since the date of its manufacture. It had been purchased by his great-grandparents for the musical education of his grandmother and had been personally selected for the family by Charles Burney. Salaman was followed by Ernst Pauer (1826–1905), an Austrian who immigrated to London in 1851 and who taught piano at the Royal Academy of Music from 1859 to 1864. Between 1861 and 1867 Pauer played a series of concerts dealing with the history of harpsichord and piano music, employing the same 1771 Shudi harpsichord that Moscheles had used twenty-five years earlier.

Carl Engel (1818–82), a pianist and musical historian from Hannover, settled in London in 1850. One of the great antiquarians of his century, he wrote a monumental series of books on music and musical instruments, including *The Music of the most Ancient Nations, particularly of the Assyrians, Egyptians and Hebrews* (1864) and *Musical Instruments of all Countries* (1869). Engel was also one of the first to collect early keyboard instruments and regularly gave lecture demonstrations with them. He gave his collection to the Victoria and Albert Museum (then the South Kensington Museum) in 1875.

Alfred J. Hipkins (1826–1903) was a remarkable and influential figure in the London keyboard world. Hired by Broadwood in 1840 at the age of fourteen as an apprentice tuner, he achieved the status of "senior workman" only nine years later. He was a revered figure around the factory, although something of a reactionary; it is claimed that it was Hipkins who was primarily responsible for Broadwood's long resistance to using overstringing and the cast iron frame on their pianos.[17] Although he lacked a gentleman's education, Hipkins turned himself into a first-class historian. He contributed articles to the first edition of Sir George Grove's *Dictionary of Music and Musicians* in 1878 and produced several books, including *A Description and History of the Pianoforte, and of the Older Keyboard Stringed Instruments* in 1896. In the 1860s he wrote program notes for Pauer's historical concerts and soon after began giving lecture-demonstrations of his own, often using the 1771 Shudi still owned by Broadwood. In 1886 he presented an elaborate historical recital, using five different instruments, a feat that remains in memory less for its uniqueness than for the fame of his page turner, pianist-composer Anton Rubinstein. Also in 1886, the German musician Johann Heinrich Bonawitz (1839–1917), who at various times lived in Dürkheim-on-Rhine (where he was born), Liège, London, New York, and Vienna, gave recitals in London on a Shudi harpsichord.

The New World was not immune to this antiquarian spirit. One of the most unusual collectors in the United States was Morris Steinert (1831–1912), who was born in Bavaria (where his first music lessons were on an old clavichord) and immigrated to New Haven, Connecticut, where he became an extraordinarily successful piano dealer. His financial future secured, Steinert returned to Bavaria and other parts of Germany, buying up instruments and shipping them back to America. He studied these specimens carefully and became quite adept at their restoration. Assembling a group of working harpsichords, he embarked upon a remarkable lecture tour of the Eastern seaboard with his two sons, Henry and Albert, who played violin and viola, and with Henry Krehbiel (1854–1923), the influential music critic of the *New York Tribune*. Steinert and his sons played the instruments, and Krehbiel lectured on their history. Remarkably, Steinert also persuaded the noted Russian-born pianist Arthur Friedheim (1859–1932) to accompany his band, to play the modern piano and serve as a foil to the historical approach of Krehbiel's lectures. Many of Steinert's instruments were shown at the Exhibition of Music and Drama, held in Vienna in 1892, and at the Chicago Columbian Exposition of 1893, further extending the public's knowledge of the harpsichord. In 1900 he gave the bulk of his holdings to Yale University, thus forming the nucleus of the keyboard holdings of that institution.[18]

Antiquarianism was seen in Paris toward the end of the century, mainly due to the efforts of the pianist Louis Diémer (1843–1919), a distinguished professor at the Paris Conservatoire. During the 1860s Diémer began to interject a piece or two on the harpsichord during his piano recitals, using the century-old 1769 Taskin, now owned by the baritone Émile-Alexandre Taskin (1853–97), the great-grandson of the builder.[19] Later Diémer formed an ensemble, the Société des Instruments Anciens, consisting of harpsichord, viola da gamba, and flute. They specialized in lighter Baroque fare, and Diémer would often interject solo pieces such as Louis-Claude Daquin's *Le Coucou* or Jean-Philippe Rameau's *La Poule*.[20] For these concerts he again was able to use the 1769 Taskin, which had been newly restored in 1882 by Tomasini. He also played in Brussels, using harpsichords from the conservatoire's collection, one of the rare venues where a few instruments were kept in playing condition. Diémer was an influential figure for the harpsichord in the French antiquarian movement. For one thing, his performances introduced the sound of the harpsichord to some composers, particularly Francis Thomé (1850–1909), the composer of *Simple Aveu*, who in 1892 wrote a *Rigodon*, the first piece for harpsichord in modern times; and for another, it was through his antiquarian activities that Pleyel and Érard became interested in making modern re-creations of the harpsichord.

COLLECTORS AND COLLECTIONS

The practice of acquiring paintings, antiques, and other objets d'art can be traced back to the sixteenth century, but almost all the great accumulations of early keyboard instruments in modern museums were formed in the late nineteenth or early twentieth centuries, around the gifts and bequests of individual collectors. Many of them started by purchasing an instrument or two, but as any collector knows, the activity can become habit forming. Some seemed to become obsessed and progressed to buying instruments by the roomful, or even the museumful. Wilhelm Heyer (1849–1913) of Cologne, for example, already owned a vast inventory when he purchased the Florence-based Kraus collection right after the turn of the century. The American Helen Crosby Brown started with just a few instruments, but her hobby became so all-consuming that she continued to buy even after donating her holdings to New York's Metropolitan Museum of Art. These early collectors bought all sorts of musical instruments, and only a few, like Engel and Hipkins in England and Steinert in the United States, specialized in keyboards.

These acquisitions were sometimes dispersed on the death of the owner, but many times arrangements were made for their disposition. As noted earlier, in 1875 the instruments of Engel formed the core of the collection of the Victoria and Albert Museum in London. Hipkins's heirs donated his instruments to the Royal College of Music collection, augmenting the holdings that had come there from George Donaldson (1845–1925) in 1894. Steinert's instruments went to Yale University. The collection of François-Joseph Fétis (1784–1871), director of the Brussels Conservatoire, was bought by that institution after his death, expanding a collection already started in 1846. Brussels also acquired the holdings of the Venetian nobleman Giovanni Correr, who specialized in sixteenth- and seventeenth-century instruments.

Collectors were active in France, too, and, like their colleagues in other areas of Europe, acquired harpsichords only as a part of larger holdings.[21] The earliest of these seems to have been Alexandre-Louis Sauvageot (1781–1860), a violinist at the Paris Opera. In 1856 he gave his collection, which included the 1681 harpsichord of Pietro Faby, to the Louvre.[22] Others were Louis Clappisson (1808–66), Achille Jubinal (1834–75), Jules Audéoud (1838–85), Nathaniel de Rothschild (1812–70), and Charles Davillier (1823–83), all of whom gifted their acquisitions to various French museums. Although none of these collections were as heavy in jack-action instruments as those of some of the people mentioned above, Paris's Musée de la Musique (then a collection attached to the Paris Conservatoire) received an outstanding group of keyboards, many of which had formerly belonged to members of the aristocracy. A collection of instruments at the Paris Conservatoire was envisioned by

COLLECTING IN THE
TWENTIETH CENTURY

Collecting instruments was an activity that continued well into the twentieth century (and still goes on). Carl Claudius gave his keyboard holdings to the Musikhistorisk Museum in Copenhagen around the turn of the century. After having absorbed both the Kraus collection as well as a collection from the Netherlander Paul de Witt, William Heyer gave it all to the University of Leipzig in 1927. The Museum of Fine Arts in Boston houses the Leslie Lindsey Mason collection, given to the museum by William Lindsey in memory of his daughter, who went down with the *Lusitania* in 1915. It was later augmented by the instruments of Edwin M. Ripin.

The bulk of the keyboards in Washington's Smithsonian Institution was a gift from another successful keyboard-amassing piano dealer, Hugo Worch (1855–1938), who seemed to have been a classic example of the obsessed collector. He started by gathering together an assortment of keyboard instruments in the 1880s, thinking to demonstrate the development of the American piano; but then he began to purchase old European pianos, clavichords, and harpsichords. By the time he finished he had amassed almost two hundred stringed keyboards, three thousand books dealing with the construction of the instruments, and a photo collection of more than two thousand items.[26] With holdings of this size Worch faced the two problems common to many of his fellow antiquarians: he needed space to store and display his collection, and he was concerned with its eventual disposition. Worch solved both these dilemmas in 1914, when he gave his collection to the Smithsonian Institution in Washington, D.C. The Smithsonian granted him the title of "Honorary Custodian of Musical Instruments" in 1921, and he spent his retirement years working with his collection.

These are only a few examples of the great instrument agglomerations formed in the 1900s, which was indeed the century of the collector. There are still large numbers of harpsichords in private hands, but at this writing their owners either are making plans for the eventual disposition of their holdings or have already done so. In truth, collecting can become a heavy burden.

the French government as early as 1793, with a call for an Institut National de Musique. Instruments confiscated during the Revolution were stored in preparation for such a museum,[23] but there was little action until 1861, when Louis Clappisson was finally put in place as curator. By that time, however, many of the harpsichords had been destroyed, sold, and even hauled down from the conservatoire attic and burned for firewood during the extraordinarily cold winter of 1816. Although it is appalling to hear of such acts, it must be realized that those instruments appeared to be worthless vestiges of a bygone and unsavory past, doing nothing more than taking up needed room.[24] Despite the dreadful losses of the destroyed harpsichords, the collection, now housed in the Musée de la Musique, has ten French doubles. Had the conservatoire's museum not been established, even those ten might no longer exist.[25]

For the most part, the interests of these earlier collectors were strictly antiquarian: to own and cherish beautiful and delicate treasures of the past; and although they might have been curious about their sounds, few considered restoring instruments to playing condition. It was just as well. The model of the contemporary piano was so persuasive that any wholesale efforts at restoration would have resulted in impractical attempts to strengthen cases, rebar soundboards, string with modern steel wire at high tension, and make the instruments feel as much as possible like pianos. In fact, some harpsichords suffered irremediable damage in just this way. Nevertheless, the instrument began to make its way back into the consciousness of the knowledgeable public during the course of the century, with enough of them finally heard and seen, and with enough historical and antiquarian interest generated, to form a critical mass. The prelude to the harpsichord's defining moment in the nineteenth century, and the moment of its rebirth, came in 1882, when Érard borrowed the newly restored 1769 Taskin, planning to study it and to undertake limited production of new harpsichords. Pleyel was not far behind, and they also borrowed the Taskin for study purposes. Both firms displayed samples of their newly designed harpsichords at the Paris Exhibition of 1889. And *that* was the defining moment.

LEOPOLDO FRANCIOLINI AND THE COLLECTORS

Selling harpsichords to rich and insatiable buyers — indeed, selling instruments of any type, as long as they were old — became a rewarding fin de siècle enterprise for antique dealers. The honest ones acquired their stock from estate sales, from gentry or nobility who needed cash, and through contacts they established in their favorite hunting grounds. One hoped they would charge fair prices, make a reasonable profit, and not misrepresent their merchandise; but there were unscrupulous dealers as well, who discovered it was easier and cheaper to "create" antique instruments and palm them off to unsuspecting collectors as the real thing. The most famous, and certainly the most outrageous, of these fakers was the Florentine Leopoldo Franciolini (1844–1920), who, with a staff of skilled workmen, was in a position to produce forgeries of many types.

Franciolini found it profitable to take harpsichords apart and create new instruments from the pieces. A rose, a keyboard, a nameboard, a soundboard, a case — any of these, even an old piece of furniture, could serve as the basis for an "antique," with new parts often fashioned from plywood (one of the technological innovations of the late nineteenth century). He even redecorated genuine antiques so that they would look like his fakes.[27] In a practice that by today's standards can only be considered brazen, Franciolini frequently "improved" an instrument in one way or another in order to command a higher price. Most of the extant two-manual Italian harpsichords gained their second keyboards in his shop, and the same is true of the half dozen or so three-manual Italian instruments found in collections in Europe, Great Britain, and the United

States. Just about every large instrument collection contains examples of his handiwork.

Franciolini specialized in Italian harpsichords and put the names of many great builders on his instruments — Dominicus Pisurensis, Giovanni Battista Giusti, Johannes de Perticis, Girolamo Zenti, Giovanni Baffo, Nicolaus Dequoco, and Bartolomeo Cristofori, to name a few; and of course, he also sold genuine instruments made by these builders. But he also made up names such as Ioannes Gilius, Petrus de Paulus, Simone Remoti, and Ioseph Mae de Coccinis Bononiensis. He may have taken double delight in these sales: he scalped the European and American antiquarians by selling them forgeries, and tweaked them by putting names, legends, and mottoes on the instruments that, although sounding properly antique, were at best improbable. Or, as has been suggested, Franciolini simply may not have known any better himself.

He gave his creations early-sixteenth- and seventeenth-century dates, since older instruments were intrinsically more valuable, and he was not above changing the numbers on existing harpsichords. Builders' names were frequently misspelled, as were many of the mottoes he painted on his creations. In the light of our hard-won twentieth-century knowledge of early keyboards, some of his instruments now appear ludicrous. The 4′ bridge on the 1627 Bolcioni harpsichord (Edinburgh, Russell Collection), for example, is much larger than the 8′ and is so crude as to defy imagination. The decoration, keyboards, and 4′ bridge on that instrument (although it is by Bolcioni) cry "fake," but evidently not loudly enough to have discouraged Raymond Russell from buying it.[28] A number of instruments that passed through Franciolini's shop emerged as "valuable" rarities with the addition of second keyboards, spurious 16′ choirs, and manuals whose sharps had impossible groupings.

How did Franciolini and others get away with it? For one thing, information about antiques of any sort was not as firmly based as it is today, and even respected art dealers were often hoodwinked by unscrupulous dealers;[29] for another, knowledge about old instruments of any sort was scant; and for a third, most of the collectors were buying these instruments as salon pieces rather than from a concern for their intrinsic worth as harpsichords and were scarcely bothered by the implausibility of some of the old faker's concoctions. Finally, in his book *Instrument Catalogs of Leopoldo Franciolini,* Edwin Ripin notes that Franciolini often reworked the genuine antiques that passed through his hands, making them look more like the forgeries.[30] Thus, in an era in which relatively little information about antique harpsichords was available, genuine and fake instruments often exhibited similar decorative characteristics, mottoes, stands, and levels of workmanship.

Franciolini finally made one shady transaction too many and in 1910 was sentenced to a prison term (which was, however, later commuted to a fine). We may be inclined to view him charitably, as we do those otherwise upstanding French craftsmen who created fake Ruckers harpsichords in the eighteenth century; but the damage he did to many fine instruments is matched only by the obfuscation he created in our understanding of their history.

SUMMING UP

The last historical harpsichord was built by the Kirkmans in 1800 (or 1809, if one is to believe Carl Engel's account); the first commercial instrument of the harpsichord revival was built in 1889; hence, for some ninety (or eighty) years, with the exception of the few curious examples noted, the craft of harpsichord building lay dormant. The century belonged to the piano, whose brilliant advances in design and technology made it inevitable that harpsichords would be universally regarded as primitive, flawed music-making machines, hopelessly delicate, needing constant adjustment, producing little sound, and impossible to keep in tune. Hand-built one at a time by a craftsman, an apprentice, and a worker or two, the harpsichord was a relic of an unmourned past. The piano, on the other hand, was a mass-produced item, generated by coal, steam, and iron, and a mighty symbol of man's progress. In the Darwinian sense, there was no question that the fittest had survived.

Nevertheless, along with the rush to progress there was a mass of confused currents and countercurrents. While neither historicism nor antiquarianism was specifically directed at the harpsichord, its growing strength and influence was seen by the activities of restorers like Fleury, Tomasini, and Steinert, who made the instrument's sounds available to an ever-expanding group of curious performers, by pianists like Moscheles, Salaman, Engel, Hipkins, and Steinert, who actually played them in historical recitals, and by the increasing efforts of collectors and museums to enshrine them as valuable relics of the past. It seems nothing short of amazing: the century would begin with an instrument dismissed, denigrated, almost completely wiped from the collective memory of the musical establishment and viewed as the detritus of a glorious new progress; it would continue with a mounting number of musicians, cognoscenti, and collectors attempting to preserve the harpsichord and its sound as a charming but valuable relic of the old days; and it would end with the harpsichord's triumphant rebirth. With the resumption of the production of harpsichords by Pleyel and Érard for the Paris Exhibition of 1889 the harpsichord, like the phoenix, rose from its own ashes.

[18]

THE HARPSICHORD REVIVAL FROM THE
PARIS EXPOSITION TO WORLD WAR II

*T*HE HARPSICHORD was able to survive its ninety-year dormancy because it was an ingredient of the romantic reverence for the past, but toward the end of the century there was an important change in the way in which it was viewed. To composers looking for new means of expression and new sonic experiences, it offered an attractive option: a fresh sound, but one with links to the past. To the few performers who were seeking to recreate earlier music, it represented a means of performing that literature more authentically. Suddenly the harpsichord had once again become a viable musical tool.[1] Consequently, after the 1769 Taskin was restored by Tomasini in 1882, the piano firm of Érard borrowed it for study purposes, thinking to make a limited number of new plucked keyboards. Shortly thereafter, for the same reason, it was borrowed by the Pleyel company. It is important to realize that these two French piano manufacturers had no intention of reviving the classical harpsichord; but they did want to create a contemporary version of the instrument, one they thought would be useful to the modern musician. In other terms, they wanted to explore a marketing possibility that they thought might turn out to be profitable. To that end, each made a special harpsichord for the Paris Exposition of 1889.[2]

German builders began to produce harpsichords slightly later, at the turn of the century. Like the French, they were piano makers; but whereas Pleyel and Érard took the historical harpsichord as their point of departure (at least at first), in Germany the reference soon became the piano and factory-oriented mass-production techniques. German instruments were also strongly influenced by the so-called "Bach" harpsichord, the large 1×16′, 2×8′, 1×4′ harpsichord with the 4′ on the upper manual mentioned often in these pages.

The young Arnold Dolmetsch made his first harpsichord in 1896, and production got under way in England, though for a while it was to be slow and sporadic. Influenced by the antique harpsichords he had restored, his instruments were closer to the historical models than those of his competitors; still, they were strongly influenced by the revival's perceived view of the harpsichord as a frail, imperfect music-making machine. The American John Challis learned his craft at the Dolmetsch shops in the 1920s and returned to the United States in 1930 to start his own operation. Other English to have an impact on the development of the instrument were Thomas Goff and those in his circle, particularly the harpsichordist Violet Gordon Woodhouse. But the performer who did the most to popularize the harpsichord in the first half of the century, and who was one of the most important influences on its development, was the indomitable Wanda Landowska. The instrument that Pleyel developed for her would become the standard by which early-twentieth-century harpsichords were to be judged.

Almost as soon as harpsichord building resumed, the merits of iron versus wooden frames, heavy construction versus light, 16′ stops, and the "Bach" disposition were argued and fought out in the marketplace, such as it was. But builders and players were almost unanimous about one thing: based on the available examples (few of which were even barely playable), they held that antique harpsichords were fragile, unstable, and underpowered. They thought the case construction was too weak, allowed too much movement, and led to tuning instability. They believed that jacks were imperfectly mated to their guides and assumed that with modern industrial methods they could fit one to the other with tolerances of a mere few thousandths of an inch. They found the keyboards unsatisfactory, lacking the felt bushings they thought necessary to ensure silent operation, and without sufficient weight at the key tails to ensure their return. Jacks were considered too light, without the mass needed to overcome "hangers" (jacks whose quills did not return under the strings after the pluck) as well as gravity. Bird-quill plectra were considered too delicate and short-lived. Soundboards were too thin for proper stability and needed more ribbing to ensure their flatness. Furthermore, they were convinced that a proper harpsichord should have all the resources of which the instrument was capable, including the 16′ stop. Finally, it was almost beyond the understanding of the revivalists that the old builders should have used clumsy hand stops, and that they made no attempt to capitalize on the variety afforded by rapid changes of tone color and registers. That the French and English had attempted exactly this in the late eighteenth century only reinforced their notions. It was an unquestioned article of faith, and would remain so for decades to come, that antique harpsichords suffered from these ills and lacunae. It was the struggle to correct these perceived "flaws" that informed the history of the harpsichord from its revival to the years following World War II.

THE PARIS EXPOSITION OF 1889 AND FRENCH BUILDERS

The Exposition Universelle Internationale, as the 1889 Paris Exposition was called, was only one of a number of world's fairs held in the second half of the nineteenth century,[3] but in many ways it was the most famous. The site was dominated by the newly constructed Eiffel Tower, a triumphant tribute to the industrial use of steel and the tallest structure in the world, awesome in its height and complexity during the day, and breathtakingly illuminated at night by the beauty of newly invented electric lighting. The event was something of an unintended landmark in art and music as well. African art was on display, for example, although certainly not for the first time in a European exposition; but while previously regarded as an ethnographic curiosity, Western artists now saw it as a vital, explosive, and energetic human force, something to be emulated and learned from, rather than ignored or sneered at. Cubism and other genres of twentieth-century art owe their beginnings to that epiphany. In a similar way, the non-Western scales and unfamiliar sounds of the metallophones of the gamelan orchestra, brought back from Java by Dutch coffee growers, captivated and energized composers like Debussy and Ravel. All in all, the exotic features of the exposition impacted violently on rapidly changing late-nineteenth-century ideas of art and music. In this milieu the newly created harpsichords of Tomasini, Érard, and Pleyel probably seemed equally fascinating. Relics of the past in contemporary guise, they emitted a pleasant tinkle that was old in spirit but excitingly new in sound. And sitting on the cusp of the promise of a new century of progress, with the futuristic Eiffel Tower dominating the landscape, newness and excitement were what the exposition was all about.

Tomasini's 1889 instrument (Berlin, Staatliches Institut für Musikforschung) does not appear to be much different from a

18-1. Aside from the Watteau-derived case paintings, this 1889 harpsichord by Louis Tomasini is a fairly faithful emulation of an eighteenth-century French harpsichord. © Bildarchiv Preussischer Kulturbesitz, Berlin, Musikinstrumenten Museum.

late-eighteenth-century Parisian harpsichord. True, the case is covered with landscapes painted in the style of Watteau and is more an example of eighteenth-century decoration seen through nineteenth-century eyes; but the cabriole-legged table stand is convincingly Louis XV in appearance, and the soundboard is decorated in a fair imitation of French soundboard painting. The case sides are of classical dimensions.[4] The disposition is the normal French 2×8', 1×4' with coupler, with hand stops projecting through the nameboard. The keyboards are more or less traditional in length, octave span, coverings, and arcades. The metal rose is an exact copy of the device used by Henri Hemsch, but with the initials "LT" (Louis Tomasini) rather than "HH." In fact, Tomasini had restored a Hemsch, and that instrument had obviously served as a model.[5] But few builders were interested in making instruments such as Tomasini's, which was too similar to the classical examples to be of any use as a "modern" harpsichord.

The instrument that Érard built for the exposition retained many classical features. The case was painted—although again, in the quasi-eighteenth-century manner—and supported by six turned and fluted legs, which, combined with a wide, flat, lower case molding, gave it the appearance of a strangely decorated early Viennese fortepiano. Soundboard painting was limited to a chaste garland of flowers around the metal rose in which the initials "EP" (Érard Paris) are supported by angels. The case sides are more than 1″ thick, and the bentside shows a sharp English hook at the cheek. The case framing is heavy: five brawny lower braces and five upper, without bottom. The soundboard is just under $\frac{3}{16}$″ at the rose, almost half again as thick as classical boards. The slender cutoff bar and 4′ hitchpin rail are crossed by nine bars. The harpsichord is disposed 2×8′, 1×4′, with both coupler and dogleg, and with one of the 8′s in leather and the other in bird quill. The registers are controlled by hand stops clustered in the center of the nameboard, rather than the ends. The dimensions of the keyboards are classical, and like the Tomasini, the naturals are covered with ebony and the sharps with ivory. But the key fronts are also covered with ivory, piano style, contributing to the jarring visual effect of this instrument. There are moldings in the usual places, but their profiles are nontraditional.[6] Érard built only a few harpsichords, then lost interest in the exercise.

Superficially similar to the Tomasini and Érard instruments, the Pleyel is nevertheless somewhat different, even though it comes with a Watteau-inspired case painting, applied rococo moldings, and an ornately carved cabriole-legged stand. The case has a gentle *bombé* profile, a shape common in eighteenth-century French furniture (at least in

18-2. Érard's 1889 harpsichord is less faithful to the classical models than Tomasini's. © Bildarchiv Preussischer Kulturbesitz, Berlin, Musikinstrumenten Museum.

18-3. Louis Diémer is
seated at the 1889
Pleyel harpsichord for
this 1897 concert by La
Société des Instruments
Anciens.

Paris) but virtually nonexistent in plucked instruments.[7] Although the sides appear to be fairly thin — about ⅝″ — they are glued to heavy liners that essentially form an inner case. The inner framing consists of one lower brace and two large beams that run the length of the case, and there is no bottom. Again, the bentside is hooked in the English manner. The soundboard is the same thickness as the Érard's, just under 3⁄16″, and considerably stiffened by the twelve bars that cross both bridges. There is a slender 4′ hitchpin rail, but no cutoff bar. The instrument is disposed 2×8′, 1×4′, but it also has a lute register cut through the wrestplank. The plectra are all of leather. The keyboards are of piano style in dimensions and coverings. The registers and the coupler are controlled by six pedals radiating from a piano-style lyre. Other than a small bottom molding on the case and another on the lid, traditional moldings are absent.[8]

Although the Tomasini, Érard, and Pleyel instruments were built at about the same time, ostensibly after the same model (the 1769 Taskin), and made for the same purpose (for exhibition at the 1889 exposition), when viewed in this admittedly artificial manner they demonstrate the progression of the ingenuity and innovation that would soon lead to the twentieth-century revival harpsichord. All three look vaguely "traditional," with painted cases, some soundboard decoration, wooden jacks and registers, and square cheeks. Two of the three have cabriole-leg stands, while the Érard sits on classical-looking turned legs. But there are jarring features. The Érard has uncharacteristically thick sides, and a dogleg as well as a manual coupler, and its stop levers protrude through the middle, rather than the ends, of the nameboard. The Pleyel has the non-French lute stop, pedals to change stops, and a pianolike keyboard. Its sides are also thick, although that feature is hidden. The bottomless case structures of the Érard and Pleyel are much heavier than found on the classical models, and the soundboards are half again as thick. The barring on these two is in piano style. Clearly the trend was to heavy, bottomless cases, heavy bracing, heavy soundboards, heavy barring, leather plectra, piano-style keyboards, and the use of pedals to achieve rapid dynamic and color changes. Heavier-gauge steel piano strings were also used.[9] Nevertheless, at least superficially, all three resembled the harpsichords the collectors would have known.

If these instruments suggest some hesitation as to how the newly revived harpsichord was to be built, that doubt was removed before the century came to a close. The search was on for an efficient harpsichord built according to modern—that is, piano—principles, a harpsichord in which all the supposed ills of the classical instrument were recognized and remedied. The piano had increased tremendously in strength during the nineteenth century, a stratagem necessitated by the use of heavier and heavier strings and hammers. It seemed obvious, if not inevitable, that the harpsichord should do the same. That such construction was inimical to the physics of a plucked instrument seemed not to have been considered. It simply was not

18-4. This 1896 Érard harpsichord was made for the International Exposition held in Brussels in 1897. Note that the hand stops of the 1889 model have given way to a lyre with pedals. © Bildarchiv Preussischer Kulturbesitz, Berlin, Musikinstrumenten Museum.

recognized that when plucked with a thin quill, a heavy string was incapable of achieving the vibratory amplitudes needed for reasonable amounts of sound, particularly when the instrument had thick, heavily barred soundboards set into immovable cases.

As a new sound, the harpsichord made its mark on French composers. Jules Massenet (1842–1912) wrote an offstage harpsichord part (played by Louis Diémer) for his opera *Thérèse* (1907). Gabriel Pierné used one in his 1919 ballet *Cydalise*. Spanish composer Manuel de Falla (1876–1946) used a harpsichord (played by Landowska in the first performance) in 1923, in his puppet opera *El retablo de Maese Pedro*, and in 1926 he wrote a *Concerto for Harpsichord, Flute, Oboe, Clarinet, Violin, and Cello* for Landowska.[10] Landowska commissioned Francis Poulenc (1899–1963) to write a *Concert champêtre* for her in 1929. Nevertheless, the interest in harpsichords shown by composers did not transfer to their production. Gaveau, with whom Dolmetsch was associated for a short time, manufactured harpsichords only from 1911 into the 1930s. Pleyel continued its building operations until after World War II and thanks to its connection with Wanda Landowska became the most famous maker of harpsichords between the wars.[11] But after World War II France, historically the home of some of the greatest triumphs of the harpsichord maker's art, simply lost interest in building for most of the century.

THE "BACH" HARPSICHORD AND GERMAN BUILDERS

Modern German harpsichord building began in 1899, when piano maker Wilhelm Hirl made a copy of the "Bach" harpsichord. This instrument, described elsewhere in this book, had been acquired in 1890 by the Dutch collector Paul de Witt (1852–1925), who, without any apparent justification, claimed it had belonged to Johann Sebastian Bach.[12] That assertion was enough to convince Philipp Spitta (1841–94), the great Bach scholar, that the Berlin Hochschule für Musik should own it, and he urged its purchase. That transaction took place shortly thereafter, and in the Berlin institution's 1892 catalog its director, Oskar Fleischer, stated not only that the instrument had belonged to J. S. Bach, but that it had been a present from his son Wilhelm Friedemann, and that it had been built by Gottfried Silbermann.[13] Curt Sachs (1881–1959), the eminent musicologist and organologist who had studied with Fleischer and who became curator of the Berlin collection in 1919, added the weight of his authority to the legend in the museum's 1922 catalog (although he cast doubt on the attribution to Silbermann).

One of the reasons the story seemed so inevitably true to Spitta, Fleischer, Sachs, and others was the universal acceptance of the early-twentieth-century view of the harpsichord as a sonically weak and mechanically imperfect instrument, poorly suited for the works of the master ("had Bach only known of the modern piano . . . ," the argument began). But like a harpsichord on steroids, the "Bach" instrument had the appealing disposition of 1×16', 2×8', 1×4' plus buff, with 16', 8' available on the lower manual and 8', 4' on the upper. Relegating the 4' to the upper manual seems rather bizarre to us today, but that organlike registration seemed to be far more appropriate for the lofty creations of Bach—certainly more so than what appeared to be the woefully underpowered 2×8', 1×4' harpsichords of Érard and Pleyel. The instrument's 16' strings shared a bridge with the 8' choirs, dulling the tone of the latter; and the too-short overwound lengths of the former did not lead to the sonorous and majestic 16' sounds achieved by the Hasses.[14] But these flaws were accepted with little question. Fleischer wrote a persuasive article in 1899, "Das Bach'sche Clavicymbal und seine Neukonstruktion," in which he compared the 1889 Érard he saw at the Paris Exposition to Hirl's 1899 copy of the *Bach-flügel*. Not surprisingly, he denigrated the Érard, claiming that its tone was hard and dry and that it was limited in its tonal palette (meaning it had no 16' choir). But the Hirl instrument, he maintained, was just like its original and even better, since it was built more solidly and was therefore more stable, and had pedals, rather than mere hand stops, to effect register changes. Fleischer concluded that Hirl's was the proper instrument on which to realize the works of Bach, Handel, and their contemporaries, and, further, suggested that pianists should henceforth keep their hands off that literature.[15]

Other piano makers began to build replicas of the "Bach" harpsichord, adding their own complexities. The version made by Karl Pfeiffer in 1909 (Washington, D.C., Smithsonian Institution) has overhead dampers, a piano "refinement" later adopted by Pleyel. The copy by Seyffarth, another piano maker building harpsichords, has three manuals, with 1×16', 1×8' on the lower, 1×8' on the middle, and 1×8', 1×4' on the upper, with couplers and half hitches (stops in which the plectra are withdrawn slightly, plucking just at their tips and producing a quieter tone). Georg Steingraeber (1858–1932), Ibach & Sons, and Karl Maendler (1872–1958) also began production of harpsichords in the first decade of the twentieth century, and almost all of them adapted the Bach disposition in addition to heavy cases, beefy framing, thick and heavily barred sound-boards, open bottoms, leather plectra, pedals, and half hitches. When the piano maker Hanns Neupert (1902–80) started making harpsichords he claimed that he was following historic models, and in his eyes, he probably thought he was, since his father, Johann Christian Neupert (1842–1921), was a collector of antique keyboards. But Neupert was unable to see through the prevailing notion that the antiques were primitive instruments. He summed up this view in his *Harpsichord Manual:*

> Early instruments in their original form suffer on account of being unable to stay in tune long enough, or being unable to maintain concert pitch, or from cracked soundboards, improper voicing in the jacks, uneven action of the keys, difficult or improper operation of the register stops and the considerable noise caused by the action. While some of these result from the age of the instruments, others are due to the fact that many technological methods used now were simply not at the avail of the original instrument builders and in consequence many aspects in the construction are quite rudimentary, even awkward, and — this becomes clear when one examines the instruments themselves — are not at all worked out. This must be stated in spite of all respect for the instrument builders of old.[16]

Neupert's was the first of the factories to manufacture *Serien* (mass-produced) instruments, as they were called; but others followed after World War I. The Ammer brothers began production in 1929, and Kurt Wittmayer, who had worked at Neupert, opened his establishment around the same time. Between the wars these three firms turned out tens of thousands of harpsichords of all sorts, ranging from large concert doubles with 16′ and the "Bach" disposition, to less ambitious doubles and singles with 2×8′, 1×4′, to smaller models (including tiny apartment-sized instruments under 5′ in length, disposed 1×8′, 1×4′, and often called *Kleinods,* or precious little things), to spinets and octave spinets. It was the largest outpouring of harpsichords since the days of Shudi and Kirkman, and probably the largest ever!

The *Serien* instruments all shared the characteristics already mentioned. The 16′ choir of the largest instruments usually had its bridge piggybacked on the 8′ bridge, necessitating the use of overwound strings. The bottomless cases were heavily made and braced with large wooden beams, a building style termed *Rasten-konstruktion* (rigid case construction). Even the *Kleinods* were built with this tanklike framing. In an attempt to overcome the perceived instability of the actions of the antiques, makers usually used metal jack guides, closely fitted jacks, and leather

18-5. This impressive-looking harpsichord by Karl Maendler, with 1×16', 2×8', 1×4', has an external metal frame, a piggybacked 16' bridge, and an open bottom. It does not, however, have the Bach disposition. Like a few other builders, Maendler worked in association with a piano factory—in this case, M. J. Schramm. © Bildarchiv Preussischer Kulturbesitz, Berlin, Musikinstrumenten Museum.

plectra. Their piano-style keyboards were heavy, with a key dip of piano proportions. The various models were given the names of famous builders of yore such as Cristofori, Delin, Ruckers, and Silbermann, or of long-dead composers such as Frescobaldi, Scarlatti, Schütz, and Telemann. And, of course, reserved for the largest, with 16' and with the 4' on the upper manual, was the name of Bach. Nevertheless, these instruments made their sounds by plucking strings with jacks activated by a keyboard, and as such helped refamiliarize the music world with the voice of the harpsichord. If they can now be criticized as heavy in action, weak in sound, muddy in the bass, and deficient in the lively, crisp tone characteristic of the historical instrument, one needs to ask if pianists would have played them otherwise; and if not pianists, then who? Had the harpsichord become strictly an amateur's instrument, its revival might have taken place much more slowly, or perhaps not at all.[17]

After the turn of the century German concert life began to include the harpsichord. In 1904 Landowska played in Berlin's Hochschule für Musik on an early Pleyel—one with pedals, but without a 16'. Around the same time a Louis Diémer–like ensemble, the Deutsche Vereinigung für alte Musik, was formed in Munich by Ernst Bodenstein and included harpsichord, violone, gamba, and viola d'amore. Ferruccio Busoni (1866–1924), the Italian-born German composer, used the harpsichord in his 1912 opera *Die Brautwahl* (Busoni also owned a harpsichord, a Dolmetsch-Chickering). Richard Strauss (1864–

1949) used it in an opera, *Die schweigsame Frau*, in 1935. Wanda Landowska was hired at the Berlin Hochschule für Musik in 1913, as the first professor of harpsichord in modern times, and remained there during World War I. During those years she produced a group of students who began teaching and concertizing throughout Germany. Without question, in production and performance, there was more harpsichord activity in Germany between the wars than anywhere else.

ARNOLD DOLMETSCH AND THE ENGLISH HARPSICHORD

Acclaimed builder of harpsichords, clavichords, lutes, gambas, and recorders, equally acclaimed as an accomplished player of all of them, outstanding scholar, consummate teacher, and revered pioneer of the early music movement, Arnold Dolmetsch (1858–1940) was one of the most influential musical figures of the early twentieth century.[18] He was born in France, where he studied piano and violin, learned tuning from his grandfather, and acquired piano-making skills in his father's factory. He married Marie Morel when he was only twenty years old, and with their newly arrived daughter Hélène crossed the Atlantic to Louisville, Kentucky, where for a short time he made his livelihood as a piano technician. But he quickly returned to Europe, and by 1879 he was in Brussels, studying violin with the famous violinist and composer Henri Vieuxtemps (1820–81). He enrolled as a student at the conservatory in 1881, where he was exposed to concerts of Baroque music using the institution's large collection of antique instruments, some of which had been restored to playing condition. Dolmetsch also heard the concerts of early music given by Louis Diémer and his Societé des Instruments Anciens. He was further influenced by François Gevaert (1828–1908), the Belgian musicologist who was then the director of the conservatory, and whose interests were early instruments, early music, and the subject of ornamentation.

Dolmetsch finished his work at Brussels in 1883 and went to London to study at the Royal College of Music. He never finished that program, but at the instigation of Sir George Grove, then director of the college, he took a part-time job as violin teacher at Dulwich College. It was at this time that he began to establish his own collection of old music and antique instruments and undertook the study of the field we now call performance practice.[19] With his wife and daughter (then all of seven years old) he formed his own Diémer-like ensemble, lecturing while he, Marie, and Hélène played the musical examples. At

THE PRE-RAPHAELITES, THE ARTS AND CRAFTS MOVEMENT, AND DOLMETSCH

The antiquarianism and historicism that resulted in the nineteenth century's preoccupation with the music and instruments of the past had its counterpart in the art world. In 1848 the painter Dante Gabriel Rossetti (1828–82) founded the Pre-Raphaelite Brotherhood, a group of British artists who looked to the past for inspiration. They aimed to take painting back to the "purity" of late Gothic and early Renaissance art—that is, painting before Raphael (1483–1520). The Pre-Raphaelites became an influential force in English art, even though the formal brotherhood lasted only until 1854. One of the important Pre-Raphaelite painters was Sir Edward Burne-Jones (1833–98). While still in Exeter College he and fellow student William Morris (1834–96) met Rossetti, and both decided to follow careers as artists. For a while Burne-Jones and Morris roomed together in London, supporting themselves by designing and decorating furniture.

In large part a revolt against the mass production of shoddy and featureless homes, furniture, and household goods, around mid-century Morris extended the Pre-Raphaelites' desire to return to the past to include wood crafts. Called the Arts and Crafts movement (although that title was not used officially until later on), it decried the loss of the skilled craftsmanship of trained journeymen, who had been replaced by interchangeable human cogs staffing assembly lines. The movement aimed both to rediscover the joys of honest craftsmanship and to produce pieces of high quality. It gained momentum in the 1880s, with the formation of the Arts and Crafts Exhibition Society in London, and it also spread to Europe and the United States: Frank Lloyd Wright, Gustav Stickley, and the Greene brothers were all products of that movement. By this time Burne-Jones and Morris had made the acquaintance of Dolmetsch, who not surprisingly shared their views on the worth of the rediscovery of the past and the dignity of handwork. It was at their urging that he built the "green harpsichord," for a show given by the Arts and Crafts Exhibition Society in 1896. Dolmetsch went on to build many more instruments, but they always had a handmade look and a closer visual resonance with the antiques than the factory-made pianolike products of the French and German builders.

first his keyboard instrument was an old square piano, but he replaced that with a spinet he found in a junk shop. He asked Alfred Hipkins to restore it for him, but Hipkins, not having the time, suggested he do the work himself. This successful experience led to further restoration work and more familiarization with antiques, and in 1894 Dolmetsch built his first instrument, a copy of a Hass clavichord in his personal collection.[20] William Morris, the leader of the Arts and Crafts movement, urged Dolmetsch to make a harpsichord for a forthcoming show, and in 1896 the builder created the instrument that, because of its exterior paint color, came to be known as the "green harpsichord" (London, Victoria and Albert Museum).[21]

Dolmetsch's first jack-action instrument could not have been simpler. Apparently modeled after Italian prototypes, it had a fairly light case and was disposed 1×8′, with a compass of GG–f^3.[22] The soundboard, lid, and keywell were decorated with paintings which, while far from traditional in character, at least retained some of the flavor of the antiques. Dolmetsch supplied it with a half hitch and a buff, both operated by pedals. The instrument proved to be a success and was used the following year in Covent Garden, for a production of Mozart's *Don Giovanni*, and in Birmingham, for a revival of Purcell's *Fairy Queen*. Although the "green harpsichord" was one of Dolmetsch's most successful undertakings, he never used that model again, but based his subsequent efforts on Flemish prototypes (from which, however, he soon departed).[23]

In 1899 Dolmetsch and his first wife divorced. He married again, almost immediately, to Elodie Dolmetsch, his younger brother's divorced wife, thereby acquiring not only a new spouse, but — since Elodie was an excellent keyboardist — a new performer for his ensemble. In 1902 Dolmetsch, Elodie, and Mabel Johnson, one of his violin students, came to the United States for a fruitful two-month tour. He returned to America in 1904, not with Elodie, whom he had divorced only months earlier, but with Mabel, now his third wife, and with yet another harpsichordist. That visit was so successful in spreading the gospel of early instruments that the Boston piano firm of Chickering and Sons decided to start building them, and Dolmetsch was hired to make gambas and lutes as well as keyboards. It was during these Boston years that Dolmetsch introduced the 16′ stop, with its bridge piggybacked onto the 8′ bridge. He rejected the Bach disposition, however, disposing his instruments with 16′, 8′, 4′ on the lower manual and lute and 8′ on the upper. Plectra were all of leather. All registers were controlled by pedals, one of which coupled the keyboards, and half hitches were also supplied. The Boston instruments were a long way from the faithfulness to the antique prototypes seen in the "green harpsichord," but the three virginals, three spinets, nineteen octave spinets, and thirteen double-manual Dolmetsch-Chickering jack-action instruments made between 1905 and 1910 avoided many of the excesses of Pleyel and the contemporary German builders.[24] Howard Schott characterized the sound of the Dolmetsch-Chickering harpsichords as follows: "The plectra are of leather, the material to which all harpsichord makers of the revival were now firmly committed. The quality of tone is accordingly mellow, somewhat soft around the edges, so to speak, but very sweet, even noble, without any of the harshness for which so many contemporary concert harpsichords, including the Pleyel, were severely criticized."[25]

Dolmetsch led an almost idyllic existence in Boston, living in a house he had designed himself, supervising the construction of his instruments, and giving wildly successful concerts with his ensemble. But when a widespread depression struck in 1910, Chickering was forced to shut down its early instrument division, and Dolmetsch was faced with the choice of either accepting a piano-building position or finding other employment. He chose the latter. In 1911 he accepted an offer from the French piano maker Gaveau to head an early keyboard department, just as he had at Chickering's, and for four years he produced instruments similar to the ones he had made in Boston.[26] He returned to England in 1914, started his own workshop in Haslemere, Surry, in 1918, and began producing instruments similar to those he had made for Chickering and Gaveau. Many of the English builders who followed him, and some Americans as well, were trained in the Haslemere shops.

18-6. This 1923 Gaveau harpsichord was designed by Arnold Dolmetsch. Disposed 1×16', 2×8', 1×4', it is nevertheless about 2' shorter than comparable instruments by Hass. Much use is made of overwound strings, and the 16' bridge is piggybacked onto the 8'. © Bildarchiv Preussischer Kulturbesitz, Berlin, Musikinstrumenten Museum.

His success as a builder, scholar, teacher, and performer did not prevent Dolmetsch from seeking to "improve" his harpsichords. He was particularly concerned about the slight noise made by the plectrum brushing the string as the jack descended, a sound as much part of the harpsichord's release of a note as the percussiveness of the hammers is part of the piano's attack. For years he devoted himself to a solution to this "problem." Finally, in 1925 he succeeded in equipping a harpsichord with an escapement device, along with a damper-lifting pedal. The "new action" was reputed to be extremely difficult to regulate and never gained any popularity.[27] Another of his innovations was a vibrato device, a series of dowels that sat on the keys and went through holes in the wrestplank up to the strings. Rocking the key up and down, as if producing a *Bebung* on a clavichord, would result in a raising and lowering of the pitch. Like the escapement, this contrivance did not last long. In 1930 he began to incorporate a welded steel frame into his large instruments, hoping to improve their stability. The desire for stability is something any player can appreciate, and there is ample historical justification for the use of pedals to change registers; but the "new action," damper pedals, and the vibrato device seem too far removed from the classical harpsichord to be considered improvements. Had they succeeded they would have changed the basic character of the instrument, something even swells, machines, pedals, and *genouillères* did not do.

Familiar with the classical instrument through his restorations,[28] Dolmetsch was almost alone in understanding that the case structure had to be kept light and the soundboard thin. Thus, his case framing, although still heavy and unlike that of the antiques, was nevertheless lighter than that of other builders, with the concomitant reward of a truer harpsichord sound. The harpsichords he built while at Chickering had neither the form nor the sound of the antiques, but they were closer to the classical instruments than the French and German models with which they competed. Respected in their day, Dolmetsch harpsichords now seem to have been a special and valuable offshoot of the revival harpsichord. Nevertheless, like everyone else, Dolmetsch succumbed to the all-pervasive theory that the harpsichord needed to be improved, made more complete, more stable, and more expressive.

It was not until about 1930 that Dolmetsch began to have the company of other makers in England. The first of these seems to have been the somewhat shadowy Alec Hodsdon,[30] but his most important colleague was Thomas Goff (1898–1975), who started building clavichords in 1933 and who became an influential figure on the London early keyboard scene. An eccentric character, it was said that he went off to war (he served in both world wars) carrying a clavichord among his belongings.[31] Distantly related to royalty, he was a gentleman of independent means who sold very few of his harpsichords; instead, he scattered them about the rooms of his large London home, occasionally renting some out. He had a cabinetmaker, Joseph Cobby, who lived with him and had several workrooms in the attic, and he had a butler, who resided in the basement. Goff learned his building skills from Herbert Lambert, a well-known photographer[32] who was also an amateur harpsichord maker and part of the literary and musical circle that included Goff and the brilliant harpsichordist Violet Gordon Woodhouse. Goff was particu-

---

DOLMETSCH THE RESTORER

Arnold Dolmetsch was active as a restorer in London, Boston, Paris, and Haslemere, where many antique harpsichords passed through his hands. He learned a great deal from this activity, and his work was fairly skillful; still, his restorations did not meet the standards practiced today. He was unable to shake the belief of his generation that the antiques were poorly engineered, and he persisted in reinforcing their framing and adding bars to their soundboards, usually to the detriment of the instrument in question. In the more informed climate of the latter part of the twentieth century, Dolmetsch's soundboard supplements became known as "stifle bars" for their deleterious effects, and many of the harpsichords he "improved" have been opened up and re-restored by removing the Dolmetsch accretions. He was not doing anything differently from other restorers of his time; still, this part of his work has inevitably tarnished his reputation, as may be surmised from this limerick:

> There was an old man with a beard
> Who, as into the Ruckers he peered
> Said, "A fine piece of lechery
> This bit of Dolmetschery
> More stifle-bars, just as I feared!"[29]

larly known for his clavichords (Woodhouse owned five), and these are still held in some esteem today; but he also built fourteen beautifully veneered, modern versions of the eighteenth-century English harpsichord. Superficially resembling the instruments of Shudi and Kirkman, they were disposed 1×16′, 2×8′, 1×4′ plus lute, with pedals, half hitches, and an internal aluminum frame. The impeccable cabinet work was done by Cobby, while Goff made the actions, and strung, voiced, and adjusted the instruments. Not unexpectedly, these harpsichords did not produce a great deal of sound; nevertheless, their tone was generally considered to be attractive. Goff was quite admired by his colleagues, although his reputation as a builder suffered in his declining years.

Goff's house was open to players, builders, students, and music lovers. Only a middling performer himself, he liked nothing better than listening to talented harpsichordists play his instruments, and he encouraged students to practice at his home. Young artists such as harpsichordist George Malcolm, guitarist Julian Bream, and conductor Raymond Leppard first became interested in early music at Goff's house.[33] Builder John Rawson tells how he made several clavichords under Goff's supervision when he was a youngster, and he considers Goff responsible for his career as a builder.[34] Such kindnesses were typical of Goff. Through his instruments, his drawing-room concerts, and his missionary zeal, he was one of the few who helped bring the harpsichord to the notice of the English public, and he was an important presence in the history of the harpsichord in England early in the twentieth century. With the keener insight afforded by the passage of time, his contributions are only now beginning to be appreciated.[35]

Robert Goble was another builder strongly influenced by Dolmetsch. In fact, Goble worked for Dolmetsch at Haslemere for twelve years (although most of his work there was turning recorders) before setting up his own firm of Robert Goble and Sons, also at Haslemere, in 1937. For many years the company consisted of Robert, his wife Elizabeth (a gambist and harpsichordist who had studied both instruments with Dolmetsch), their son Andrea,[40] and a cadre of workmen and apprentices. Goble produced a number of different models, with the heavy cases, iron frames, pedals, piggybacked 16′ bridges, overwound strings, and the slanted cheeks that seemed to define the aesthetic of the harpsichord until World War II and beyond. Nevertheless, Goble's instruments were carefully and beautifully built, and as sought after as Dolmetsch's.

The very few English builders working between the wars seemed to fall into two groups: those like Goff, who worked alone or with a small staff, and those like Dolmetsch and Goble, who ran small factories (or large workshops, depending on one's point of view). They were all influenced by Dolmetsch, both in their Arts and Crafts approach to building and in their use of metal frames. But aside from

VIOLET GORDON WOODHOUSE

A harpsichordist, clavichordist, and pianist of diminutive stature, extraordinary beauty, and smoldering sexuality, with a reputation for artistry and virtuosity that approached if not equaled that of Landowska, Violet Gordon Woodhouse's (1872–1948) work was almost entirely confined to England. She was a good friend of Dolmetsch's, having studied with him in her early years, and she owned several of his instruments.[36] She performed regularly in London and environs, to unbridled critical acclaim, until just before 1930, when her husband came into money and purchased a large estate in Gloustershire. She then turned her attention to broadcasting and recording,[37] and to holding musicales in her drawing room. She gathered around herself a circle of artists, writers, musicians, and intellectuals that included composer Ethel Smyth, conductor Thomas Beecham,[38] poets T. S. Eliot and Edith Sitwell, and adventurer T. E. Lawrence (Lawrence of Arabia). The critics uniformly raved about Woodhouse, and she was proclaimed the equal of artists like Casals and Segovia. Only Landowska was considered her peer as a harpsichordist and interpreter of early music.

Woodhouse's great-niece and biographer, Jessica Douglas-Home, reports that the artist's marriage was unconsummated, and that she chose three men to live with her and her husband, creating possibly the only *ménage á cinq* known to the Western world. Although it created quite a scandal, the group remained together until death claimed first one (in World War I), then another (in World War II), then, finally, Woodhouse. According to Douglas-Home, they all managed to live in complete harmony, perhaps in no small part due to the assuaging powers of Violet's clavichord playing.[39] But her personal idiosyncracies aside, she was a powerfully influential figure on the early music scene in England in the years preceding World War II.

these few, there was little other harpsichord-building activity in England. Still, the early music scene was extremely active, particularly in London. Performers like Woodhouse spread the gospel of Renaissance and Baroque music far and wide, although more through salon performances such as those also mounted by Dolmetsch and Goff than through the sort of public concerts and tours undertaken by Landowska.

WANDA LANDOWSKA AND HER PLEYEL

One theory of history holds that the course of human events is changed by great figures, and a case could certainly be made for such political leaders as Alexander the Great, Napoleon, and

18-8. A large, handsome, double-manual harpsichord by Robert Goble and Sons. Robert Goble is seen inserting a jack. The piggybacked 16' bridge can be seen clearly. Reprinted from *Zuckermann 1969a*, with permission.

George Washington. In music, Beethoven is certainly a candidate for such approbation, and Arnold Dolmetsch would be another. And so would Wanda Landowska (1877–1959), whose combination of talent, skill, iron will, scholarship, and star quality—not to mention her ability to rise above the sexual stereotypes of her time — has rarely been equaled. Few performers have had quite such an electrifying impact on their chosen instrument.

Polish born and a child prodigy on the piano, she attended the Warsaw Conservatory and, while still in her early twenties, continued her studies in Berlin. Then, as the new century dawned, she went to Paris to begin her career. There seems to be no doubt that this young woman was an exceptional performer, and her recitals in Paris and elsewhere in Europe were received with extraordinary enthusiasm by audiences and critics alike. Landowska had always been drawn to the music of J. S. Bach, and as early as 1903 she began to program one or two of his works on the harpsichord during her piano recitals. No less a presence than Albert Schweitzer praised her playing of Bach on the harpsichord. Against the advice of her friends and colleagues, who thought she was bringing a promising career to an inauspicious and untimely end, she decided to devote her life to the harpsichord and its repertoire, particularly the music of Bach. For anyone else it probably would have been an exceedingly foolish career choice, but incredibly, Landowska was able to bring it off. The history of the harpsichord in the twentieth century would almost certainly have been different had it not been for her magnetic presence, riveting playing, and unflagging sense of dedication.

At that time Landowska was using a Pleyel harpsichord similar to the 1889 model the firm had first displayed at the Paris Exposition, and she even toured Russia with it in 1908–9; but she was not satisfied with its capabilities. Landowska and Pleyel's chief design engineer looked at some museum instruments and decided on the features they wanted to see on an all-encompassing, eclectic modern concert harpsichord. The result, which first appeared in 1912, Pleyel's *Grand Modèle de Concert,* was an imposing machine of some 7½′ in length. Gone were the vestiges of reference to the classical harpsichord seen in the 1889-style instruments, and if not for the mitered tail, the two manuals, and the five-octave compass, it could easily have been mistaken for a piano. Like everyone else, Landowska was under the impression that the classical harpsichord was so delicate that moving it—or even simply picking it up—would put it out of tune, so the heavy bottomless case of the Pleyel was braced with large wooden beams. The ¼″-thick soundboard—twice that of the antiques, but thought necessary for stability—was given pianolike barring. A separate bridge was provided for the 16′ strings, but it was placed so close to the 8′ bridge that it needed heavy overwound strings. The instrument was disposed 1×16′, 2×8′, 1×4′ plus lute, all controlled by a set of seven pedals housed in a large box, supported by two fluted columns, at floor level. Like Dolmetsch, Landowska and Pleyel did not succumb to the lure of the Bach registration, and the resources of the instrument were distributed in the traditional manner.

Landowska had found that many of the museum instruments she saw had "hangers," caused by worn-out quills and poor regulation. Hangers are by no means inevitable; in fact, a well-constructed harpsichord with well-designed jacks, kept in proper adjustment, almost never has them. Nevertheless, this was something that concerned Landowska, so to avoid the "problem," the Pleyel's jacks were weighted to ensure the plectrum's return, although the added weight further encumbered the already heavy pianolike touch.[41] That the jacks of the antiques lacked adjustability was also a concern, and Pleyel (and others) supplied theirs with screws to regulate height and the projection of the plectra. Bird quill was deemed too ephemeral a product for use in a modern instrument, so the heavy strings were plucked by thick leather plectra, which, it was claimed, would last for years. Normal harpsichord dampers would have been insufficient to stop the vibrations of the heavy strings, so Pleyel supplied their instruments with overhead dampers, thus adding yet more mass to be moved by the already heavy keys. Flanked by long, ogee-shaped cheeks, the keys of the two piano-like manuals were bushed with felt at the balance and guide pins, then weighted at the key tails to overcome that built-in friction and ensure their return. Rather than normal piano tuning pins, Pleyel devised a double-pin arrangement for coarse and fine adjustments, which they called the *micrometrique* tuning system.[42]

All in all, the Pleyel Grand Modèle de Concert was considered a marvel of modern instrument design. It was the harpsichord brought up to date, enjoying the benefits of the latest in piano technology, and with all the features a proper instrument should have. Nevertheless, it did not live up to its publicity. The Pleyel harpsichord was far more complex than it needed to be. Its touch related more to the piano than to the classical instrument; in fact, Landowska was forced to invent an entirely new technique to handle the unwieldy action. The heavy cast-metal plate, which it was given in 1923, did not prevent it from going out of tune, since the rest of the case was made of wood. Because of its complexity it was in constant need of regulation,[43] and the leather plectra did not stand up to heavy use. And finally, although it was supposed to be more powerful than the classical harpsichord, even when working at peak efficiency the sound level and presence of a Pleyel was far from that of a well-restored antique.

What is surprising is not how badly it failed, but how difficult it was for people to see its problems. The Pleyel seems to have been a perfect example of a modern-day version of "the emperor's new clothes." It was highly regarded because Landowska and her students held it in such lofty esteem — she never played anything else — and Landowska herself was so admired that her choice of instrument could not possibly have been considered inappropriate. Also, it recorded well, and Landowska's disks spread the perception of the Pleyel as a powerful and colorful instrument. In concert, however, the sound was disappointing; yet, somehow people convinced themselves that they were hearing something special.[44] Nevertheless, while it is easy to denigrate the technical complexity of this behemoth, it was no worse than most other harpsichords of the time. If nothing else, it served to introduce countless numbers of music lovers to the instrument and helped pave the way for the second stage of the harpsichord revival, after World War II. A few Pleyels were built

MORE ON LANDOWSKA

Wanda Landowska's life was filled with triumph and happiness as well as displacement and loss. In 1913 she was in Germany, on the faculty of the Berlin Hochschule für Musik, where she established a flourishing legacy of harpsichord playing and teaching. When World War I broke out she was interned as a foreign national but was able to continue teaching. Just after the war her husband, ethnomusicologist Henry Lew, whom she had married in 1900, was killed in a tragic automobile accident.[46] Landowska returned to Paris and set up a studio there — actually, a school dedicated to the study of early music — and also taught at the Fontainebleau Conservatoire. She attracted an international class of harpsichord students, many of whom returned to their homes, ordered their Pleyel harpsichords, and spread the gospel of Landowska's ideas and her love for the instrument and its literature. Landowska also carried on an active life as a recitalist on both harpsichord and piano. Although a diminutive figure, her presence was nevertheless larger than life, a perception enhanced by exploits such as bringing four Pleyel Grand Modèles de Concert along with her on her first American tour. She made her American debut in 1923, taking the music capitals of Boston, Philadelphia, New York, and Chicago by storm. Adoring audiences on both sides of the Atlantic flocked to her recitals, applauding wildly and demanding encore after encore. Pieces were written for her, including the concertos by Manuel de Falla and Francis Poulenc mentioned earlier.

Landowska, who was of Jewish ancestry, remained in France when World War II broke out, believing herself safe. But in 1940 she and her assistant Denise Restout were forced to leave their home in St.-Lieu-la Forêt, only twenty-four hours before invading German soldiers arrived, leaving behind her priceless collection of music, instruments, and a thousand memories of concerts and students. Their escape was hair-raising. As Restout tells it,

> It took us several months before we could find passage on a ship which would take us to America. Finally, in November, 1941, we left from Lisbon. We had to go through Spain from France which was very difficult at that time since Spain was filled with Nazis. We could only get a transit visa. But we did make it to Lisbon safely, sailed for America and arrived in New York City on Pearl Harbor Day, December 7, 1941, which wasn't the best day to arrive with a harpsichord.[47]

Now sixty-four years old, homeless and penniless, Landowska was forced to create a new life for herself in America. She decided to give a recital, and against all advice (since it was thought to be far too heavy a musical fare) programmed Bach's *Goldberg Variations*. But that concert, given the following year to a sold-out audience in New York's Town Hall, was a musical and emotional triumph. More appearances followed, students began to seek her out, recording contracts came her way, and Landowska and Restout finally came to thrive in the New World. In 1946 they moved to a home in Lakeville, Connecticut, and established a new studio. There the grande dame of the harpsichord spent her declining years, teaching, writing, and recording.

following the war, but the firm was then taken over by another manufacturer, and their harpsichord building came to an end.[45]

Neither Landowska nor the Pleyel were without critics. Although she played with great technical mastery, personal flair, and absolute conviction, her interpretations of Bach and her use of ornaments were idiosyncratic.[48] Here and there a critic would dare to question "the emperor's new clothes" and would remark that while Landowska's playing was masterful, the harpsichord was almost inaudible, especially when it was used with other instruments. When she played a Bach concerto with the Philadelphia Orchestra (with the strings reduced by two-thirds) to a sold-out Carnegie Hall audience, one critic complained about the Pleyel's "weak and non-carrying quality."[49] Nevertheless, she was, and still is, a revered figure, and not without reason. Almost single-handedly, she was responsible for the widespread public acceptance of the harpsichord in Europe and (along with Dolmetsch) the United States, and was one of the first artists to demonstrate the feasibility of sustaining a livelihood with the instrument. Toward the end of her life she became aware of the new winds blowing through the harpsichord world, but declared herself too old to change from the Pleyel she had used almost her entire life. For better or worse that instrument, with all its modern accretions, remained firmly associated with her name, and in much of the public eye it was only on a Pleyel that one could even hope to achieve a Landowska-like perfection. Composer and critic Virgil Thomson probably best summed up the way in which Landowska was perceived in his telling review of one of her concerts in 1942, when he said, "She plays the harpsichord better than anybody else ever plays anything."[50]

AMERICA AND JOHN CHALLIS

One of Dolmetsch's most famous students was the American harpsichord maker John Challis (1907–74). At the age of sixteen Challis, who grew up in Ypsilanti, Michigan, became fascinated by a Dolmetsch clavichord owned by his organ teacher. Challis promptly built one himself, although he described the results as "pretty crude."[51] A little later Landowska played a concert in Ypsilanti, and Challis heard a harpsichord for the first time. Learning that his organ teacher was going to England and intended to visit the Dolmetsch shop, Challis, now nineteen, asked him to see if Dolmetsch would agree to take him on as a student. The teacher returned with a "yes" from Dolmetsch, and two weeks later Challis, the first recipient of a Dolmetsch Foundation Scholarship, was bound for England.

Challis spent four years with Dolmetsch in Haslemere, studying recorder, gamba, harpsichord, and clavichord, as well as working on the "new action." He returned to America in 1930 and opened a shop above his father's clock store, often giving recitals on his own instruments. World War II came to America in 1941, but Challis had health problems that exempted him from military service,[52] and he was able to continue building and spreading the word about the harpsichord to his fellow Americans. His instruments reflected the influence of Dolmetsch, from their natural-wood Arts and Crafts appearance to their metal frames, open bottoms, and 16′ choirs. In addition, like so many of his contemporaries, he used a long, 16″ scale and modern steel strings (it would have been impossible for the iron strings used in the antiques to survive that long a scale at modern pitch). Even more than others, he was convinced that the classical harpsichord had irremediable flaws and became obsessed with creating instruments of the utmost stability and reliability. As a youth he had worked for his watch-making father and necessarily learned a great deal about precision work. His harpsichord building reflected this meticulousness and helped him create a sought-after product whose stability went well beyond that of other builders. His story will be continued in the next chapter.

Very few others were making harpsichords in America. One was the German-born Julius Wahl (1878–1955), who came to the United States in 1891 and worked in the Chickering shop during Dolmetsch's tenure, a proximity that doubtless had some influence on him. After leaving Chickering he became the curator of the Belle Skinner collection; but then, in the 1930s, he moved to California and by 1940 had started building harpsichords. In the next ten years he produced an average of four instruments a year, most of them resembling the heavy German *Serien* instruments. Another maker, a professional performer whose limited output was more of an amateur endeavor, was Claude Jean Chiasson (1914–85), a student of the Landowska-trained Putnam Aldrich. He started building in 1938, and with so few makers in America during those years, his work helped fill a void. Although not well known now, he was an important prewar presence for both players and builders. Chiasson grew into harpsichord building by stages, first maintaining and repairing a few instruments, then restoring a Kirkman at Boston's Museum of Fine Arts. His first harpsichord, which he dubbed "the monster,"[53] was based on the Kirkman and Aldrich's Pleyel.

If there was not much harpsichord building taking place in America between the wars, there was, nevertheless, an appreciable amount of harpsichord playing going on.[54] Arthur Whiting (1861–1936), Frances Pelton-Jones (1863–1946), Lotta van Buren (1877–1960), Lewis Richards (1881–1940), Philip Manuel (1893–1959), and Gavin Williamson (1897–1989) are names that have vanished from our collective memories, but they were busy putting the harpsichord on the map in the New World before and after World War I. Whiting was a Dolmetsch student who was playing recitals as early as 1907, on a

Dolmetsch-Chickering instrument. Whiting had the same sort of pioneering spirit as Hipkins and Dolmetsch and gave educational concerts and recitals of early music with other instrumentalists.[55] Pelton-Jones began playing public concerts, also on a Dolmetsch, before World War I, and in 1923 he initiated a series of recitals, called "Salons Intimes," at New York City's Plaza Hotel.[56] Lewis Richards led a fascinating life as a pianist, teacher, and federal administrator[57] before embarking on a career as a recitalist on his Pleyel harpsichord in 1923. He not only was the first harpsichordist to play a concerto with an American orchestra — the Haydn D major with the Minneapolis Symphony, in 1923 — he was also the first to play a harpsichord at the White House, for President Calvin Coolidge, in 1927. Manuel and Williamson were duo-harpsichordists as well as duo-pianists, and between the wars they toured the United States with two Pleyel harpsichords (they owned four altogether) and two Steinway pianos, occasionally competing with Landowska for concert dates.[58]

Other American harpsichordists active before World War II included Landowska students Putnam Aldrich (1904–75) and Ralph Kirkpatrick (1911–84), both of whom went on to distinguished careers as scholars and teachers. In 1939 Kirkpatrick played a ground-breaking recital of harpsichord music by twentieth-century composers. There were yet others, including such luminaries as Yella Pessl and Sylvia Marlowe. But not to be forgotten is Alice Ehlers, who played the harpsichord for the first time in a motion picture, William Wyler's 1939 *Wuthering Heights*. With the words "Madame Ehlers is going to play the harpsichord," movie-goers saw Ehlers seated at her Pleyel and heard her streak through a few seconds of Mozart's *Rondo alla Turca*. The harpsichord had indeed arrived in America.

SUMMING UP

The harpsichord revival began with the creation of new instruments by Tomasini, Érard, and Pleyel for the 1889 Paris Exposition. But although these attempts marked the start of the movement, they were not the models followed by subsequent builders. Early German builders took their cues from the modern piano, reasoning that the harpsichord had undergone continuous improvement over the centuries, and now that building had resumed, advantage should be taken of the advancements made by the piano. It did not seem to occur to these pioneers that pianos and harpsichords were different in nature, and that massive cases, open bottoms, heavy strings, and thick soundboards, while they might add stability to the instrument, were not likely to allow for the production of a lively sound. Instead, they created complex, beautifully engineered plucking machines, claiming for them the mantle of the historical instrument. A complicating factor in Germany was the Bach disposition, along with the 16', both of which found their way to the larger versions of the *Serien* instruments as well as to those made by the smaller makers.

The harpsichords built by Pleyel for Landowska, while different from the German products, nevertheless followed the same reasoning. Her Grand Modèle de Concert was a tribute to Pleyel's ability to transfer piano technology to the harpsichord. Although Pleyel never produced anywhere near the vast numbers of large instruments manufactured by the German builders, they helped establish the presumption that large, heavy, pianolike instruments with 16' were necessary for concert work. That Landowska and her students and followers enthusiastically endorsed the Pleyel made it almost certain that it, or something like it, would be the instrument of choice for a concertizing artist.

Arnold Dolmetsch took a different approach, one that reflected the aesthetic of the Arts and Crafts movement. His early instruments were based on historical precedents; still, like all the revivalists, Dolmetsch was concerned with tuning stability, action reliability, and coloristic possibilities, and succumbing to the prevailing wisdom, his instruments had open bottoms, 16' choirs, leather plectra, pedals, and internal metal frames. Nevertheless, he did not attempt to draw on piano technology as the German builders did, and if his instruments did not look like the historical prototypes, neither did they look like pianos. His framing was heavier than that found on the antiques, but not as armor-plated as those of his competitors in Europe. Dolmetsch's contribution went far beyond his instruments. He not only showed that there was another way to build harpsichords — an approach adopted by other English builders such as Goff and, later, Goble — he also drew acolytes to his cause, spreading the gospel of the harpsichord through the United States and England by means of his many concerts and drawing-room recitals. Nevertheless, his work for Chickering and Gaveau, while important for the influential instruments he made there, did not produce any followers in those countries.

Thanks mainly to the prodigious production rates of the harpsichord factories of Neupert, Ammer, and Wittmayer, by the late 1930s tens of thousands of instruments were available, owned not only by concertizing professionals, but also by many amateurs, as well as schools and other institutions. For a while

A HARPSICHORD TIME LINE, 1889–1940

1889: Tomasini, Pleyel, and Érard exhibit harpsichords at the Paris Exposition.

1892: Oskar Fleischer states that the "Bach" harpsichord belonged to J. S. Bach, was a present from his son Wilhelm Friedemann, and had been built by Gottfried Silbermann.

1896: Arnold Dolmetsch builds the "green harpsichord."

1897: Dolmetsch plays the "green harpsichord" for Covent Garden's *Don Giovanni*.

1899: Wilhelm Hirl builds a copy of the "Bach" harpsichord.

1902: Dolmetsch makes his first American tour.

1903: Wanda Landowska begins to program harpsichord pieces on her piano recitals.

1904: Landowska plays a harpsichord concert in the Hochschule für Musik, Berlin.

1904: Ernst Bodenstein's Deutsche Vereinigung für alte Musik is formed in Munich.

1905: Dolmetsch establishes a department of early instruments at Chickering and Sons in Boston.

1906: Hanns Neupert begins production of *Serien* harpsichords in Bamberg; Maendler-Schramm begins building harpsichords in Munich.

1907: Arthur Whiting plays his first recital in America.

1908: Dolmetsch introduces the 16′ in his Chickering harpsichords.

1908–9: Landowska tours Russia with an early Pleyel (without 16′).

1909: Karl Pfeiffer makes a copy of the "Bach" harpsichord with overhead dampers.

1911: Dometsch begins building harpsichords at Gaveau in Paris.

1912: Pleyel creates the Grand Modèle de Concert.

1913: Landowska is hired as harpsichord professor at Berlin's Hochschule für Musik.

1914–18: World War I

1918: Dolmetsch establishes his shop in Haslemere.

1920: Violet Gordon Woodhouse makes the first commercial harpsichord recording.

1923: Pleyel adds an iron frame to the Grand Modèle de Concert.

1923: Landowska makes her first American tour.

1923: Frances Pelton-Jones begins her "Salons Intimes," which would continue for twenty years.

1925: Dolmetsch invents the jack escapement, damper-lifting pedal, and vibrato device.

1926: John Challis makes his first clavichord in Ypsilanti, Michigan, then goes to England to apprentice with Dolmetsch.

1927: Pleyel introduces a smaller version of its concert harpsichord, with iron frame but without 16′.

1927: Lewis Richards plays a harpsichord at the White House.

1929: The Ammer brothers in Eisenberg and Kurt Wittmayer in Wolfrathausen begin production of *Serien* harpsichords around this time.

1930: Dolmetsch starts to use a welded steel frame.

1930: Alec Hodsdon begins building harpsichords.

1930: Challis opens his shop in Ypsilanti.

1933: Thomas Goff begins building clavichords in London.

1937: Robert Goble and Sons open their shop at Haslemere.

1938: Claude Jean Chiasson starts to build harpsichords.

1939: Ralph Kirkpatrick plays a concert of music for the harpsichord by twentieth-century composers.

1939: Alice Ehlers plays the harpsichord for the first time in a motion picture, William Wyler's *Wuthering Heights.*

1939: World War II begins.

1940: Julius Wahl begins building harpsichords.

the Germans had a near monopoly on harpsichord building, since only Dolmetsch, Goff, Goble, and a few others were working in England. Gaveau was out of business, and harpsichord making in France was carried on only by Pleyel. But by the time hostilities broke out in Europe in 1939, the harpsichord had completed a triumphant comeback. No longer an exotic, unknown instrument of the distant past, it was recognized as a thankfully modernized, up-to-date version of an instrument whose presence was now accepted as nothing less than a historical imperative.

[19]

THE MODERN HARPSICHORD[1]

THE AFTERMATH of World War II saw the manufacturing capability of the Western world turn to satisfying a pent-up demand for automobiles, washing machines, refrigerators, and other consumer goods. Harpsichords were not excepted. After wartime service, the Dolmetsch shop was still active in England, as were Goble (who moved to Oxford in 1947) and Goff. Challis and one or two others were building in the United States. Pleyel was still making a few instruments, and Maendler resumed harpsichord making at the Schramm factory. But the output of all of these shops was minuscule compared to the flood of instruments that would soon pour from the factories of the *Serien* makers. As soon as possible, Ammer, Neupert, and Wittmayer resumed manufacturing their instruments, quickly joined by one of the first new postwar builders, Kurt Sperrhake (b. 1907), a former piano maker who began production in 1948. Twenty years later, with sixty employees, Sperrhake would be the world's largest builder of harpsichords.

At first, neither Sperrhake nor the other makers had much of a market in Germany, or for that matter, in the rest of Europe, which was slowly recovering from the devastation of the war. But there were countless customers for harpsichords in the United States, Canada, Central and South America, and the Middle East, and the unprecedented postwar prosperity soon spread to Western Europe as well. The passion for harpsichords was also fanned by the invention of the long-playing record and a concomitant growing interest in Baroque music. Having committed the standard repertory to disk, the record companies now began to look at Handel, Rameau, Telemann, Scarlatti, and other early-eighteenth-century masters, spurring the sales of harpsichord recordings, particularly those of Landowska.[2] The demand for the instrument grew rapidly, and in the 1950s and 1960s, probably for the only time in its history, it could be said that there was a shortage of harpsichord makers.

Still, the harpsichord was perceived no differently than before the war. Its sound was still described in exotic terms. It was quaint and delicate; it was metallic; it was jangling, tinkling, twangy, twangling, and pluck-a-pluck; it was guitar, banjo, or mandolin-like; or, as *Time* magazine once put it, the harpsichord "jangles like a regiment of mice scurrying through a pile of coins."[3] The antiques were still thought to be deficient in their structural engineering, limited in their tonal resources, mechanically unreliable, lacking in tuning stability, and without appropriate means of changing stops; but this view did not go unchallenged for long. Within the first five years after the war a new breed of builders arrived on the scene, among them Hugh Gough in England, Frank Hubbard and William Dowd in America, and Martin Skowroneck in Germany. For the first time in the history of the revival, now fifty years old, makers began to go back to the antiques (although some with more enthusiasm than others, to be sure), examine them carefully, and attempt to emulate them. The results were startling. The instruments these people made produced more volume, their tone was more attractive and more useful, their form was more graceful, their tuning and maintenance were easier, and their traditional dispositions were found to serve the music better than the entrenched heavily built models. The second stage of the harpsichord revival was under way.

It is difficult to account for this change of attitude. Gough, Hubbard, Dowd, and Skowroneck did not really have access to anything not already known to their predecessors; nevertheless, accumulated scholarship, the growing sophistication of knowledge of the old instruments, the maturation of the early music movement, and the presence of some better-restored and hence better-sounding antiques — all conspired to tip some sort of balance. Undoubtedly, the fact that harpsichord building was starting anew after the war called for a reexamination and a fresh beginning to some, and the loss of a blind faith in modern progress, resulting from two devastating world conflicts, probably was also a contributing factor. This second stage had a limited genesis, at first convincing only a few; but within a decade of the war's end it was possible to see six sorts of building styles competing with each other.

The first of these included builders such as Gough, Hubbard, Dowd, and Skowroneck, who attempted to follow the examples of the antiques. Those in the second group, builders like Herz, and Rutkowski and Robinette, were also concerned with authenticity but tried to blend it with twentieth-century building techniques and materials. In the third group were builders like de Blaise, Morley, and Sabathil, who were not much impressed by the philosophy of returning to the past, and who continued to build with the familiar heavy soundboards, heavy ribbing, heavy bottomless cases, and complex registrations. In the fourth group were the German *Serien* builders, who were selling instruments as fast as they could turn them out. The fifth group was comprised of builders like John Challis and John Paul, who took the harpsichord in new directions; and in the last group were those who used electronic means to produce or amplify harpsichord sound.[4]

Eventually, of course, it was the historically aware instruments that prevailed, and many of the other builders mentioned here — Neupert, Herz, Goble, and Rutkowski and Robinette, to mention only a few — were won over and began making instruments patterned after the antiques. One of the events responsible for this change was the harpsichord festival held every three years in Bruges, Belgium, where players, owners, builders, and listeners had the opportunity to hear these instruments side by side. Another contributing factor was the astonishing popularity of the kit harpsichord, a phenomenon that enabled thousands of people to build instruments demonstrably better than most of those commercially available.

HISTORICALLY INFORMED BUILDERS: GOUGH, HUBBARD, AND DOWD

A seminal figure in the revival's second stage, Hugh Gough (1916–89) took clavichord lessons with Dolmetsch and made a few instruments on his own while still in his teens. He studied economics in college, graduating just in time to serve in the war. Afterward, he decided to become a professional builder, but unlike most of his colleagues — and undoubtedly under some influence from Dolmetsch — he first undertook a study of the specimens in the museums. Then, armed with drawings and measurements from a large number of old harpsichords, he began to build instruments that, for the first time since the beginning of the revival, were cast in the mold of the antiques. His efforts made a huge impact on those who saw and heard them, and Gough quickly developed a reputation for his "authentic" harpsichords, as well as for his clavichords and fortepianos.

Gough was an inspiring and influential figure, both in England and in America (when the young Frank Hubbard left Dolmetsch he was taken on by Gough, who instilled in him the gospel of the historical harpsichord). Gough came to the United States in 1958 and for six months worked at the Hubbard and Dowd shop, providing further direction to these two pioneers. He went back to England, but returned to America the following year, where he remained for the rest of his life, building harpsichords, clavichords, and lutes, running early music concerts, and undertaking restorations. Wolfgang Zuckermann reported that he gave Gough space in his shop in the early 1960s and, in return, was helped to produce a more classically oriented harpsichord than he would otherwise have done.[5] John Koster, the expert on early keyboard instruments whose authority has been brought to bear many times in these pages, was strongly influenced by Gough as a youth and was led by his mentor to a career as a builder, restorer, scholar, and museum curator. While it would not be entirely accurate to say that the second stage of the harpsichord revival sprang from the work of Hugh Gough, it would be as difficult to overstate his influence at the century's midpoint as it would to overstate Dolmetsch's at its beginning.

If Gough was influential in spreading the gospel of building in the style of the antiques, it was Frank Hubbard (1920–76) and William Dowd (b. 1922) who brought his ideas to fruition. More than anyone else, these men were able to change the course of the instrument in America, and it was this country that was soon leading the rest of the world in what came to be considered as enlightened harpsichord building. Hubbard and Dowd were childhood friends. They both went to Harvard to study English literature (Hubbard was two years ahead of Dowd), and both served in the military during World War II. Afterward Hubbard returned to Harvard to begin work on a master's degree, and Dowd went back to finish his undergraduate studies. Dowd had long been fascinated with the harpsichord, to the point of attempting to build one before he left for the service. When he returned to school after the war he tried again, this time with a large double, which also remained unfinished. At the same time, Hubbard started a violin and then a clavichord.

By this time both men had become increasingly dissatisfied with their chosen career tracks. Dowd's youthful passion for the harpsichord, meshing with the beginning of the postwar early music movement, began to suffuse them both with a sense of purpose they were not finding otherwise. They agreed that academic life would probably be too confining and decided to attempt careers as builders. That they burned their potential academic bridges behind them and set out to become harpsichord makers now seems like a step of the greatest perspicacity, but to their friends and relatives it must then have appeared downright foolhardy; but their scheme worked.[6] Dowd went to Detroit to study with Challis, gaining considerable experience working on cases and actions, voicing leather plectra, and repairing. He also absorbed his mentor's high level of professionalism. With funds available to him through the GI Bill,[7] Hubbard crossed the ocean to Haslemere, to the keyboard division of the Dolmetsch shop. But Hubbard was somewhat frustrated at Dolmetsch's, where he was an unpaid apprentice. In his words,

> At Dolmetsch's I was permitted to drill identical holes in thousands of small objects, make tea at eleven each morning, and sweep. Occasionally, but not always, my questions were answered. Still by watching, if not by doing, I learned something of woodworking and the sort of compulsiveness that makes a craftsman. Of the history of the harpsichord or the glorious examples still extant I learned nothing.[8]

After that year Hubbard went to London and became associated with Hugh Gough, devouring the older man's notebooks, which were full of measurements and details of antique instruments. Hubbard also met Donald Boalch, who at that time was compiling his dictionary of harpsichord and clavichord makers, and who shared with him his extensive bibliography of works on early keyboard instruments. He was also able to visit many of the important European collections and make measurements of his own. In 1949 Hubbard returned from England, Dowd from Detroit, and the two opened a shop in Boston. In his typical amusing, erudite, and self-deprecating manner, Hubbard described that historic event:

> In November of 1949 Dowd and I rented an unheated loft in a ramshackle building on Tremont Street in Boston's South End. We managed to scrape together enough money to buy a circular saw, band saw, drill press, two benches, and a surplus army coal stove which devoured endless quantities of fuel without producing any noticeable heat. Cold winter mornings we huddled around that stove until eleven before we could find the courage to venture into corners of the room. Even so, we did manage to lay down four harpsichords.[9]

Those four instruments, based on a Ruckers single of 1637,[10] were sold before they were finished,[11] and were followed by some clavichords, Italians singles, and English doubles. The

In a 1971 interview with Harold Haney, Frank Hubbard clearly enunciated his view of the historical harpsichord:

> In order to bring most music to life, there are really three efforts involved. First is that of an editor who sorts the music out and gets down what really was on paper. Second is that of a performer who examines the performance practices of the period and attempts to bring it to life in those terms and, third, that of a maker who attempts to supply instruments suitable to the music. . . . We are dealing with the best composers of all times, and the arrogance which is involved in saying "well I can cook up something in my back kitchen that will improve his music" is ridiculous. This man, this composer from the past, had a talent greater than anything I will ever have. He used the means at his disposal in an imaginative way that staggers my imagination. Therefore, the only word I can apply is arrogance to the people who feel they can devise a harpsichord more suitable to his music than the instrument he had, because he wrote his music for that harpsichord.[12]

Haney had earlier interviewed William Dowd, who covered some of the same issues:

> You see, one of the things that happened to us was that we went to museums. When it was possible, we heard these instruments and found them beautiful. We felt that the whole German school, Neupert, Wittmayer, and Pleyel, who is sort of the chief anti-Christ of them all, must all have plugs in their ears. They were not making anything that was remotely like an antique harpsichord. . . . We discovered a resonant, flowering sound which we liked. . . . We, with the enthusiasm and rash brashness of the young, believed we knew how to bring back the authentic instrument upon which early harpsichord music was all based.[13]

duo were also asked to undertake many restorations, increasing their knowledge of the antiques even more.

These ground-breaking instruments adhered to the constructional practices of the antiques, but only up to a point, as Hubbard himself noted.[14] The nervous, almost paranoid concern for tuning stability that still plagued the harpsichord dictated the use of plywood for case construction, since it was thought that this material, immune to the expansion and contraction across the grain that characterizes all plank wood, would solve the problem of case instability. Plywood, however, expands and contracts in all directions; thus cases made of that material not only varied dimensionally with changes in temperature and humidity, but did so in uncontrollable ways.[15] What was not yet realized was that Ruckers, Taskin, and their colleagues knew all about wood movement, and that their designs and constructional practices allowed for it.

Modern jacks were a particular problem. Not tapered the way antique jacks were, they needed to fit tightly in their slots. To avoid jamming when the upper and lower guides expanded with increased humidity, the historically informed builders often used aluminum, brass, Plexiglas, or some similar material for upper and particularly, lower guides, in an effort to provide stability. These materials frequently created new problems, since they were more stable than the case itself, and when the case wood moved, the guides did not. Jacks were given end pins to adjust their height and screws to regulate plectrum projection, since these were still considered useful modern additions. But the end pins added weight to the jacks, tended to get caught in the strings when the jacks were removed, and could scuff the felt on which they rested.[16] Furthermore, their presence was an open invitation to their owners to turn them, whether the adjustment was needed or not — and usually it was not, since once the height of a jack is adjusted properly it rarely needs to be changed.[17] Top screws to adjust voicing were undeniably handy, but subject to the same invitation to the often unknowing owner to destroy the regulation of a carefully voiced register.

The keys were often still pianolike in weight, width, and depth of touch, since it was assumed that pianists were the primary consumers of harpsichords and needed to feel comfortable at the keyboard. Case framing, though based on historical principles, was heavier than it needed to be, because it was still believed that the historical models were underbuilt, and the criticism of once again building fragile, unstable cases was to be avoided. Pedals, still thought to be a worthwhile and necessary improvement over hand stops, were used to change registers. These practices were not necessarily all found in the Hubbard and Dowd instruments, but were characteristic of almost all harpsichords at that time made after historical principles.[18]

In 1955 Hubbard went back to Europe to continue his research on antiques. In 1958, shortly after his return to America, he and Dowd ended their brief but historic partnership and pursued their individual paths. The result of Hubbard's European research, in 1965, was his landmark *Three Centuries of Harpsichord Making*, the book cited many times in the present work. It represented an extraordinary scholarly effort to synthesize the knowledge of harpsichords hidden in records, old tomes, encyclopedias, inventories, archives, chance remarks, and the evidence of the instruments themselves, and has remained an invaluable resource for builders and historians. In the finest of scholarly traditions, Hubbard accepted no preconceived notions, but formed his conclusions from the data. That he erred now and then is due in part not only to the incompleteness of his pool of samples — we

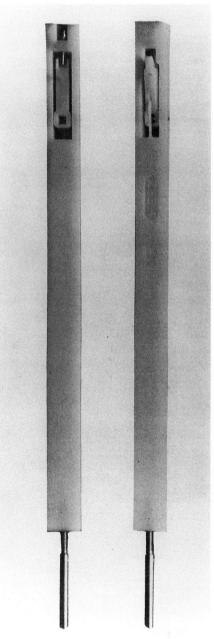

19-1. A well thought-out and well-made Delrin jack by builder Eric Herz, with top and bottom adjustment screws. Reprinted from *Zuckermann 1969a*, with permission.

The revivalist view of the harpsichord as a flawed instrument persisted well past the end of World War II. In a 1956 talk to the Royal College of Music entitled "The Harpsichord since 1800," Raymond Russell expressed the prevailing view that leather was a more reliable plectrum material than bird quill, was less noisy, and at any rate the resulting sound was practically indistinguishable from bird quill. He dismissed the overhead dampers found on the instruments of Pleyel and a few other makers, but thought that some of the resonance of the antiques resulted from strings that were too lightly damped. He held that pedals were useful for controlling registers, although he felt that their presence encouraged constant changing of colors by unenlightened players. In common with almost all his contemporaries, he believed that any instrument suitable for concert work should be an all-purpose harpsichord, and the question of the special qualities of Flemish, French, German, Italian, or English instruments was not addressed at all. In the discussion period after his talk, a Mr. Basil Lam expressed the fear that a lightly built harpsichord — meaning one built on historical principles — would go out of tune too readily. Thurston Dart, a scholar and performer of some reputation, thought that the harpsichord needed to be electronically amplified in order to make itself heard. The American Ralph Kirkpatrick (for some reason in London at that time) made it clear that a harpsichord with 2×8', 1×4' was all he needed, but that half hitches were useful.[19]

Even so astute an observer as Wolfgang Zuckermann, writing in 1969, managed to carry the vestiges of these revivalist views. Reliability was still an issue, and Zuckermann thought it unreasonable to expect *all* the 250 jacks in a large harpsichord with 16' to work *all* the time. He dismissed bird feather as an appropriate quilling material, and dismissed leather as well, since it was affected by humidity. He accepted the newly developed Delrin, but grudgingly and with reservations. He expressed the universally held belief that the thin soundboard and resonant case of a good harpsichord must have inevitably resulted in tuning and action instability. He believed that the ideal modern harpsichord should have plastic jacks with top adjustment screws and end pins, Delrin plectra (but carefully voiced — he still had his reservations), and a Plexiglas lower guide. Curiously, Zuckermann voiced some misgivings about the historical instrument that had not been heard before. He thought the spacing between strings was too narrow, and that it was extremely difficult to provide enough space in the gap for the jacks to operate freely. He also felt that the 4' hitchpin rail was a troublesome member — that if it was too heavy it would adversely affect the tone, and if too light would lead to the distortion of the soundboard. In other words, even to Zuckermann, an apologist for modern harpsichords built in the manner of the antiques, the instrument was basically and naturally flawed. His views were shared by nearly everyone.[20]

know of many more instruments than he did — and the generally poor condition of the antiques he saw and heard, but also to his own strongly held views. Nevertheless, it is those views that illuminate the material, saving the book from what could have been a dry-as-dust fate.

As the shops of both men thrived in the 1960s, the anachronisms earlier thought so necessary for tuning and action stability were gradually dropped from their instruments. Dowd, for example, redesigned his keyboards in 1965, to better reflect the narrower keys, balance points, and lightness of the historic models. In the following year he stopped using plywood in his cases. By the end of the decade he would build instruments with pedals only if the customer insisted on them and shortly thereafter, ceased that practice altogether. Top adjustment screws on jacks also fell by the wayside, as well as brass or Plexiglas upper and lower guides. In his early work Dowd made a few instruments with 16′, but after 1970 refused to do so any longer. Hubbard's instruments followed a similar path.

It is one of the delightful accidents of the history of our instrument that these two men, intelligent, erudite, insightful scholars as well as excellent and visionary craftsmen, should both have appeared on the early keyboard scene at the same time. Without Hubbard's book it would have been much more difficult for the second stage of the revival to have continued its progress. Dowd was no mean scholar himself, and he too did important work that has contributed to the advancement of our knowledge of the instrument.[23] And neither really abandoned

---

THE DELRIN STORY

Shortly before Hubbard and Dowd dissolved their partnership they developed a new design based on the 1769 Taskin, the very same instrument upon which Pleyel and Érard had based their 1889 harpsichords. One of these harpsichords was the first to be quilled with the new Delrin plastic plectra.

In their early years together Hubbard and Dowd attempted to find a suitable modern substitute for crow quill. A friend introduced them to Alfred C. Weber, who was then a research associate at DuPont's Experimental Station. Delrin plastic had just been invented, but at that time (about 1958 or shortly thereafter) DuPont was not sure what the material could do—they needed to test it for such things as resiliency and resistance to fatigue. Weber supplied the two builders with some of the material, asking in return for a "full test report," no doubt envisioning a document full of quantifiable information. What he got back was, " 'Delrin' works even better than crow quill. . . . We've calculated that a harpsichordist could practice Bach's 'Chromatic Fantasy' for four hours a day, every day for two years without 'Delrin' breaking or showing more than the slightest signs of wear."[21]

Delrin did indeed prove itself to be a superior quilling material, even though it tends to work-harden and initially needs periodic revoicing. Nevertheless, there was a strong bias against its use at first, despite its promise of bird-quill-like properties and long wear, and even though leather, particularly when voiced by the typical amateur, wore out rather quickly. But it was thought that leather was a "natural" plectrum material, since it had been used for that purpose from the beginning of the harpsichord revival (and, of course, in the eighteenth century as well), and that it produced a rich, full, round sound. Plastic, on the other hand, was a new and synthetic material, and the Delrin pluck was characterized as thin, artificial, and somewhat weak. Eventually Delrin was acknowledged as a material close to bird quill, and its acceptance was near universal. About 1985 Celcon, a new plastic material closely related to Delrin, was adopted as a plectrum material by many builders, but by this time quite a few makers and players were once again using bird quill. As Hubbard wryly put it in a 1974 talk, "Delrin quill replaced leather plectra because it sounds more like crow quill. Now in subtle insight several builders have discovered that crow quill sounds even more like crow quill than Delrin does."[22]

teaching, but rather than hold forth on English literature, they created a new generation of builders. Of no less importance, the excellent harpsichords built by both men set standards of craftsmanship and faithfulness to an ideal that strongly influenced the generation of builders who followed.

One of the first Europeans cast in the Gough-Hubbard-Dowd mold was the German Martin Skowroneck (b. 1926). Born in Berlin and trained in the Musikschule in Bremen as a flute and recorder teacher, he built a harpsichord or two in 1953, patterning his work after the ubiquitous *Serien* instruments. But he became dissatisfied with this model and, independent of the work of Hubbard and Dowd, undertook a study of the museum specimens. The series of instruments that followed were built uncompromisingly in the mode of the antiques, with practically no concessions to modernity. His cases were made of plank wood, with classical case framing; he used wood, rather than brass or plastic for his upper and lower guides, and like the antiques, his jacks had no adjustment screws; his keyboards were light and of harpsichord proportions, and he rejected the use of pedals. Skowroneck, in other words, immersed himself in the building practices of the antiques and did his best to emulate them. He succeeded brilliantly. His work became known more rapidly than it might have otherwise through the efforts of Gustav Leonhardt, a historically oriented postwar harpsichordist who used Skowroneck's instruments in his concerts and on his recordings.[24] Skowroneck's instruments were in such demand that by 1969 he had a twelve-year backlog of orders.

William Hyman (1933–74), born in Brooklyn, N.Y., was one of the first Americans to go to the same lengths as Skowroneck in the authenticity of his instruments. He started building in 1953, while still working as a commercial artist in an animated cartoon studio, and made a number of *Serien*-inspired harpsichords. Soon after he went into the army and served in Europe, where he took the opportunity to examine the instruments in the great museums. Returning to America, he set up his shop in Hoboken, N.J., and in 1963 came to fame with a French harpsichord based on the Blanchet school. Hyman was as single-minded in his search for authenticity as Skowroneck, and his instruments, with their compelling, robust sound, were extremely influential on a series of American builders and players. At the time of his premature death he had a backlog of orders amounting to more than thirty instruments.[25]

At first hampered by the still current revivalist view of the inherent fallibility of the historical instrument, it finally became clear that the closer the maker came to the building practices of the antiques, the better the ensuing sound. By the beginning of the 1970s, the instruments of Hubbard, Dowd, Hyman, Skowroneck, and an increasingly large cohort of builders like them[26] had had an opportunity to prove themselves. It was found that properly cared for, the models based on the antiques were as stable as they needed to be. With the growing incorporation of air conditioning and humidity control into modern life, the need for the supposed stability-providing characteristics of metal frames, beamlike construction, plastic registers, and the like began to fade, and the case thicknesses and framing the old builders used proved perfectly adequate for structural stability. Furthermore, mainly through the rediscovery of historical temperaments, it was realized that harpsichord tuning was not that difficult and could easily be done by owners, even on a 2×8', 1×4' French double with 183 strings. Players found that the frequent changes of registration afforded by pedals, no matter how convenient, simply were not needed with the variety provided by the lively toned classical timbre. Finally, with the growing availability of good harpsichords, artists found it less necessary to travel with their own all-weather behemoths. Most of all, though, it was realized that the best of these instruments shared the same sort of robust, responsive, and indescribably beautiful sounds that emanated from the best of the restored antiques, and that light, unbushed, properly balanced keyboards gave performers the freedom to phrase, articulate, and even produce limited dynamic changes that harpsichords made earlier in the century could never achieve. If an important lesson had been learned, it was that Ruckers, Taskin, and the rest knew what they were doing, and that the task now set before harpsichord builders was to attempt to recapture that knowledge.

AUTHENTICITY WITH STABILITY: HERZ, SCHÜTZE, AND RUTKOWSKI AND ROBINETTE

Stability! Stability! Stability! Nothing haunted the harpsichord more than that word over the course of much of the twentieth century. Another group of builders who started working after World War II also advocated returning to classical principles, but believed that following them too closely would lead to deficient instruments. As Hubbard and Dowd did at first, these builders constructed their cases of plywood, braced them heavily, and used Plexiglas or brass registers, complex jacks with adjusting screws, and pianolike keyboards. Additionally, however, they felt that a twentieth-century harpsichord had special demands placed on it, and they endeavored to build instruments that could meet them. Consequently they often used special sound-board materials including laminated woods, they used more metal, longer scales, and heavier stringing, and their jacks were often more complicated. Today we would have to admit that their instruments suffered a concomitant loss of sound when compared to the products of those in the first group.

The earliest of these makers was Eric Herz (b. 1919), who was born in Cologne, Germany, and who was a flutist in the Israel Philharmonic during World War II. After the conflict he came to America and for two years apprenticed with Hubbard and Dowd. He began building in 1953, in Harvard, Massachusetts, then moved his shop to Cambridge. Herz adopted a scale of about 14½″, somewhat longer than the classical iron scale, putting more tension on his cases, which were heavily braced. He glued the 4′ hitchpin rail to his case framing, ensuring a rigidity of the soundboard not present in the antiques. He used brass and Plexiglas for his upper and lower guides. For a while he employed a soundboard composed of a sheet of fiberglass sandwiched between two thin sheets of spruce. The plywood for his cases was also made up of thin sheets of wood with fiberglass in between. Herz's use of fiberglass was a determined attempt to increase the stability of his harpsichords, and they did indeed have that reputation. They were also spoken of highly as reliable and good-sounding instruments.

Rainer Schütze (1927–89) was active in Germany at the same time as Skowroneck. After World War II (a large part of which he spent in a Russian prison camp) he pursued architectural studies in Karlsruhe and earned an engineering degree. He then studied harpsichord building with Walter Merzdorf, an old-time builder who had been making *Serien* harpsichords since 1920. Somehow Schütze avoided falling into the mold of his mentor, and in 1959 he began making instruments in the style of the antiques. For a long time he and Skowroneck were the only German makers working in that style, and both of them spent time writing articles defending the theoretical bases of their work.[27] Schütze's instruments fell somewhere between those of Skowroneck's purity and Herz's modern modifications. His scale, case framing, soundboard thickness, bracing, and keyboards were in the classic mode, but subtly rearranged to suit his many theories. He used plywood liberally, and his keyboards and jacks were complex. His background as an industrial engineer led him to attempt to improve — and sometimes complicate — many aspects of harpsichord construction, from the coupler to the stand. Still, his instruments were eagerly sought after in the postwar years, when any sort of historically oriented instrument was certain to find a buyer.

Frank Rutkowski and Robert Robinette have been in business since 1957, but as Zuckermann noted in 1969, "Rutkowski and Robinette do not welcome publicity, shop visitors, or curiosity seekers; they want to be left alone to do their work."[28] That remark is as true at this writing as it was then. Rutkowski was trained in the Challis shop, and the partners' earlier instruments had many of the characteristics of his mentor, including aluminum frames and wrestplanks. Nevertheless, their notion of harpsichord tone was closer to the antiques than Challis's, and they attained useful and admired sounds in their instruments. This observation raises an issue that Zuckermann discussed many times in *The Modern Harpsichord:* that a builder's concept of harpsichord tone seems to be more important than the materials he uses to achieve it. A good builder, in other words, knows how to wring the sound he wants out of his materials, no matter what they are. This was certainly true of the old makers. We have observed, for example, that there was an agreement about the tone of Italian harpsichords that lasted for centuries, regardless of whether a given instrument had a thin- or thick-walled case, or had a spruce or cypress soundboard. Rutkowski and Robinette probably were as familiar with the museum instruments as any other builder in the 1950s and 1960s, and they knew the sound they wanted.[29] Further, they were perfectly capable of building close copies of antiques, and did so when called upon; but like so many others at that time, their designs were driven by a concern for stability.

Other makers also built in this modified classical mode. Christopher Bannister (1937–96) apprenticed in the Hubbard and Dowd shop for three years, simultaneously obtaining a degree in harpsichord performance from Oberlin College (he was Oberlin's first graduate with this new degree). He opened his shop in Hopewell, New Jersey, in 1961, loosely modeling his instruments on the antiques, but building with that paranoid concern for stability that by this time had infected the harpsichord world for nearly seventy years. His case framing was heavy, and he used a plate made of plywood under the soundboard as extra reinforcement. His upper guides were made of brass and his lower of Bakelite. Bannister used pedals as a matter of course. His instruments were beautifully and carefully constructed and were extremely stable; but their sound and general lack of volume were not up to the levels reached by the best of the historically informed makers. Nevertheless, stability was still considered such a paramount issue that both the builders and their customers were willing to accept those strictures in return for the promise of less tuning and maintenance.

Los Angeles–based Richard Jones began building in 1952.

He used plywood for his cases, his framing was heavy, and his upper and lower guides were aluminum; but by 1969 he had produced close to four hundred instruments. This is a large output, and although Jones was relatively unknown, by that time he may have made more harpsichords than any other builder in the United States. He produced so many instruments that he was able to obtain a special-order three-ply spruce for his soundboards. Interestingly, he thought that instruments of his type were the wave of the future, and that the "historical preciousness" of builders like Skowroneck would experience a declining market.[30]

BUILT TO LAST: DE BLAISE, MORLEY, AND SABATHIL

The revolution sweeping through America—and creeping through Germany—had little effect in England at first. When the Goble firm resumed harpsichord building after the war, they made the same sort of instruments they had previously. Heavy soundboards and ribbing, thick, bottomless cases, beam-like framing, 16′ stops, overwound strings, complex registrations, half hitches, and pedals were part and parcel of the Goble philosophy of building, and they saw no need to change. Why should they? Their many customers admired their products and thought them superior to almost anything else available. Indeed, they were fine instruments when considered by their own lights, exhibiting the same sort of Arts and Crafts workmanship found in Dolmetsch's work.

Joining the Gobles in the production of these semifactory instruments was John Morley (b. 1932), a piano and harp maker who started in 1955. Heading a small factory of twenty-five workers, by 1969 Morley was producing 240 instruments a year.[31] As with Goble, the central issue with Morley seems to have been stability. His heavy, bottomless cases were braced with thick beams, and his soundboards were made of birch plywood with a veneer of pine on top. To further ensure the immobility of his structural elements, the insides of Morley harpsichords were sprayed with waterproof paint. Morley's harpsichords were as well made as Goble's and had the same slanted cheek that the *Serien* builders first popularized. Morley did use a different pedal system than his competitors, however: he simply went back to the eighteenth-century English system, securing his pedals to two boards attached to the stretcher between the front legs, allowing him to avoid the complex trap work necessary with the usual lyre-and-pedal system. Morley also avoided using the 16′, and in this and his pedals he was a bit more attuned to the past than some of his fellow builders.

William de Blaise (b. 1907) was a native of Latvia and lived in many countries (he was a flutist in the Israel Philharmonic while Eric Herz played there) before settling in London in 1952. He struck up an alliance with the Welmar piano company, whose employees constructed his cases, while de Blaise worked on the stringing, the action work, and the voicing. In this way, with just a few helpers he was able to produce an average of sixty instruments a year.[32] De Blaise harpsichords were handsome looking, and with their lovely veneer work vaguely resembled eighteenth-century English instruments; but they were heavy cased with open bottoms, beamlike framing, thick, heavily ribbed sound-boards, brass upper guides, piano-sized keyboards, leather plec-tra, pedals, and the "Bach" disposition. De Blaise invented a new shape he called the "cembalo traverso," in which the normal bentside is a straight-line continuation of the cheek, and the spine has a slantside-like lurch to it. His largest harpsichord, with 16′, three keyboards, and seven pedals, weighed 440 pounds,[33] probably more than twice that of an eighteenth-century Hass with a similar disposition.

Claude Jean Chiasson continued making heavy harpsi-chords after the war, although they did get lighter after a while. He remained an influential figure, still one of the very few American builders in the United States other than Challis. Canada had Sabathil & Son, a firm that had its start in Munich early in the century but that moved to Vancouver after the war. Once again we see open bottoms, aluminum frames, thick, heavily ribbed soundboards, long scales, piano keyboards, and the "Bach" disposition. Zuckermann was particularly harsh on Sabathil ("Sabathil seems to have chosen to bring this tradition [the German production harpsichord] to its highest pinnacle of non-achievement"),[34] and described the tone of his big Bach III model as issuing forth "not with a bang but a whimper."[35] However, a different story was told by Canadian harpsichordist Joyce Rawlings, who commissioned from Sabathil an enormous *vis-à-vis* harpsichord, with two keyboards at either end. She described its sound in glowing, if not exactly meaningful, terms: "You see, the overtones on this instrument are quite extraordinary. When you are playing you can hear these overtones and it seems that you throw it back from one end to another."[36] The truth probably lies somewhere in the middle, and these harp-sichords were no better or worse than the other heavy-cased instruments. Nevertheless, Sabathil's product did have some

19-2. This unique *vis-à-vis* harpsichord was built by Sabathil & Son in 1972. Photo courtesy of Harold Haney.

strange quirks, like key levers 1½″ thick, a 16′ bridge 2″ in height, and 4′ strings running through slots in both the 8′ and 16′ bridges in order to hitch at the bentside.

THE *SERIEN* BUILDERS: AMMER, NEUPERT, WITTMAYER, AND SPERRHAKE

Ammer,[37] Neupert, and Wittmayer resumed building as soon as possible after the war, and within a few years were back in full swing. They were joined by Sperrhake in 1948, and together these four companies produced thousands of well-made instruments, all of which were snatched up by harpsichord-hungry schools, orchestras, amateur and professional performers, and aficionados. While not exactly as alike as peas in a pod, they were similar in appearance, construction, disposition, and tone. To a generation of music lovers brought up on these instruments, they and the Pleyel represented the timbre of the harpsichord, and the fact that this was only distantly related to a historical sound meant little, since only a small coterie of specialists had ever heard an antique. Even when the historically aware harpsichord began to make real inroads on the consciousness of the early keyboard world the *Serien* builders expressed little concern, since the rate at which their instruments were selling continued unabated, reinforcing their honest belief that they were on the right track. As Hanns Neupert observed in a speech to a European piano congress in 1965, annual sales of 5 million marks for German harpsichord builders would indicate that "one is perhaps not on the wrong path."[38] It might have appeared so in 1965, but the message was quite different only three years later, at the second harpsichord festival at Bruges, where *Rasten-konstruktion* came face to face with historically informed instruments. Derek Adlam briefly described that seminal event:

> In 1965 Bruges became an important forum for all those interested in the harpsichord. At first the exhibitions were dominated by German series builders, but in the three years that elapsed between the first two meetings, a revolution took place. Not only were makers of historically based instruments in the ascendant, but they were actively leading the performers away from styles of playing developed for "modern" harpsichords. Builders were demonstrating the essential economy of means of the instrument, depriving the players of their pedals and forcing them to discover authenticity.[39]

Most of the *Serien* builders either have become makers of historically oriented harpsichords, or have disappeared. Instruments in that style are no longer built, and there is no longer anything that could be considered factory production of harpsichords.

NEW DIRECTIONS: JOHN CHALLIS AND JOHN PAUL

John Challis never ceased searching for ways to make his harpsichords more stable. In addition to an aluminum frame he used a wrestplank of the same material, drilled with oversized holes into which were set phenolic bushings, with the tuning pins inserted into the bushings. His soundboards went through a series of changes, from plank wood to plywood and finally to a thin aluminum plate. Wooden bridges and nuts were superseded by hollow brass channels, with holes drilled to lighten them. By the 1970s the Challis harpsichord was an all-metal machine, with the wood of the case no more than a cosmetic skin. Rather than the extruded plastic almost all other builders were using, his jacks were fabricated from hard rubber. His two-manual instruments were made without coupler or dogleg; instead, an additional set of jacks plucked the 8′ strings from the upper manual. Since neither set of 8′ jacks could have dampers — if they did, one set would be muting while the other was playing — Challis provided a set of damper jacks to do nothing but act on the 8′ strings. Challis used thick leather plectra for most of his career, but in the 1970s he switched to a plastic, which he also cut thick. Among the metal-frame builders, Challis was almost the only one to really achieve the stability the other makers boasted of,[40] even though his frame, soundboard, wrestplank, bridges, nuts, 16″ scale, and thick plectra combined to produce a sound quite different from the historically oriented harpsichords then gaining currency.

But Challis was not interested in a historically oriented tone, and made no bones about it. He told Harold Haney that "there are still some people who have a very deep prejudice against my improvements. They claim that the tone I produce is not an accurate 18th-century tone. I must admit that this is somewhat true. But I have never found an 18th-century instrument that I have played that had a tone I would consider beautiful."[41] In a letter to physician John Brodsky, Challis likened the building of harpsichords to the practice of medicine. "Both of us practice," he wrote, "but neither of us really *know*. . . . Yet I have found very few physicians who are content to practice medicine according to the best knowledge of 1890. Now there are many who would advocate following 1750 methods of harpsichord building — or even earlier!"[42] A gracious gentleman to the end of his life, Challis commended Zuckermann on his 1969 book, even though the views it expressed went contrary to his own. He wrote,

> There has never been a time in the four centuries of harpsichord making when instruments of such wide variety and consummate skill have been made. There has never been a time when so many harpsichord makers have given their art such complete devotion to their individual ideal. I can understand and admire all of them without ever losing my own ideals. . . . Fortunately we live in a country where individualism is allowed and still encouraged. Let us never lose it! Let us never forget that every purchaser of a harpsichord has a right to the kind of instrument he likes and to dislike others.[43]

Challis was an important postwar influence on American builders and players. The excellence of his workmanship set a standard toward which many other makers aspired. The stability of his instruments won him numerous customers among professionals, who were convinced that touring with a lightly built historically informed instrument in the extremes of the American climate — particularly in those days, with little or no indoor humidity control—would be foolhardy in the extreme. And they might well have been right.

Many of the builders discussed in this chapter and the last could be called eccentric: that appellation could certainly fit John Paul (1920–91), who was born in Kent, England. He started building shortly after the war, converting early-nineteenth-century pianos into harpsichords. His first instruments were in the *Rasten-konstruktion* tradition, with heavy sides, open bodies, and metal frames above the soundboard à la Pleyel. When he realized in the early 1970s that the harpsichord world was changing, he abandoned his revival instruments and began designing new models vaguely based on historical principles. He continued doing so for the rest of his life and considered himself an artist and designer, rather than a copyist.

Like Challis, Paul was consumed by the quest for reliability and in his early days even built an instrument with an aluminum soundboard. He developed theories about the behavior of the air enclosed in the body of the harpsichord, and devised methods to improve its resonance and enhance its relationship with the soundboard. When visited by Zuckermann in the late 1960s, he was attempting to use the instrument's structural members to create discrete chambers, and was "tuning" those chambers with holes of various sizes in the bottom of the case.[44] Although Zuckermann was somewhat amused by his theories, Paul may not have been entirely off the track. The air in the harpsichord does interact with the soundboard, and an important feedback mechanism takes place;[45] but his method of controlling this seems suspect. Paul was too restless to settle on any specific building mode and continued to experiment during his life. Unlike Challis, he had some respect for antiques, although he thought they were built "off the cuff,"[46] meaning without much thought to the underlying principles involved. In his own

19-3. This fanciful clavicytherium was built by John Paul some time before 1969. Both the external frame and the soundboard are aluminum. Reprinted from *Zuckermann 1969a*, with permission.

harpsichords he liked to take a bit from English builders, a bit from the Italian tradition, a bit from Taskin, and more than a bit from Paul, hoping to combine these elements into superior instruments. Some of his concoctions, such as his modernistic clavicytheria, were really quite unusual, and he almost never built two harpsichords alike. Paul was a minor force on the English harpsichord scene for some time, and offered help, encouragement, and advice to many of today's best builders.

Other builders also attempted to take the harpsichord in new directions, either like Challis, spurred by the desire to create something of a new instrument and a new sound, or like Paul, with some sort of appreciation for the antiques and a desire to combine their best elements with modern techniques and technology. If their instruments did not meet the demands we now place on them, they nevertheless expanded the knowledge of how the harpsichord works. And even at this writing there are builders who will put holes in the bottoms of their otherwise historically illuminated instruments, with the claim that it increases their resonance.[47] But the all-metal instruments of Challis seem to be a thing of the past.

THE ELECTRONIC HARPSICHORD: WITTMAYER, BALDWIN, AND THE ELECTRONIC KEYBOARD

It was inevitable that the harpsichord should meet the technology of electronic sound amplification. The early revival instruments projected so poorly that a judiciously placed microphone was almost a necessity if the instrument was to be heard in an ensemble. Electronic enhancement did help the sound of the early revival instruments, and it is for this reason that the words "but it records well" were so often appended to descriptions of the harpsichords of Pleyel, Goff, the *Serien* builders, and others. The lack of volume was a genuine problem for these instruments, particularly since it was so often claimed that they had more sound than the antiques. Those who heard the powerful, crashing chords of Landowska's Pleyel on recordings, for example, were inevitably disappointed at the puniness of its real-life sonic projection. Finally, after the war Wittmayer "solved" the volume problem by building an instrument with magnetic pickups mounted above the strings, an on-board amplifier, and two large speakers built into the soundboard. This massive, 9′ long harpsichord was given the "Bach" disposition and the provocative name of *Bach Elektronik*. Zuckermann reported that two such instruments were used in a concert given in Carnegie Hall

by the Berlin Philharmonic, with Herbert von Karajan conducting. As he related the event,

> Herbert von Karajan imported the two amplified Bach models, weighing a total of over 1,500 lbs, to use them as continuo instruments in a Bach clavier concerto — in which the solo part was taken by a piano. Any small but lively single harpsichord would have comfortably replaced these two machines, but von Karajan conducted from one of them (in the baroque style) playing a few chords now and then when his arms were not engaged in beating time; the rest of the time a poor performer, playing second harpsichord to the conductor and completely obscured by the orchestra, picked up the threads dropped by von Karajan. All this time the solo piano contributed a foreign sound which mixed uneasily with the continuo.[48]

The German harpsichordist Isolde Ahlgrimm related an amusing story about the sonic characteristics of one of these instruments:

> And now, with the electronic age, they are adding so many things to harpsichords. I played a very modern harpsichord, with which you can fortify the sound electronically. I had to play one with an ensemble and when I sat down to play, here were red lights and green lights. It looked like the control panel of an airplane. I started to play and the people I was playing with thought it was terrible so I turned it off. And then the manager came and listened for a while and then said, "I

paid 20,000 Deutsch Marks for this electronic instrument and I want to hear it." So I turned it on again.[49]

A later attempt to pick up string sound, amplify it, and play it through speakers was the Baldwin electric, which the company called the "combo." Shaped like a small harpsichord, with sides of aluminum channel and a lid of transparent Lucite, the "combo" had three crude wooden legs bolted to the channel members. The "soundboard" was made of Masonite, but any material—or none at all, for that matter—would have done equally well, since it was the sound of the plucked string, not anything that emanated from the soundboard, that was amplified. There was no bridge and no need for one: the strings were simply hitched to the edge of the soundboard and then to a nut on an aluminum wrestplank. Like Challis, Baldwin drilled oversized holes in the wrestplank and set the wrestpins into plastic bushings. Magnetic pickups were mounted on a wide metal bar running over the tops of the strings. A pedal provided dynamic changes and, if desired, could generate an electric guitar–like "wow-wow-wow." The result bore little resemblance to a genuine harpsichord sound; nevertheless, the "combo" did have a certain currency, providing a "harpsichord" sound in pop and jazz music.

A third type of electronic harpsichord developed after the war was an instrument constructed along the same lines as the electronic organ, with harpsichord-like sounds generated by transistors. The Allen portable harpsichord, looking very much like a square piano, was one such example, and there were others, such as the Roland (still used by many at this writing). The difficulty with such machines was their limited ability to evoke a true harpsichord tone as well as the transient sounds of the characteristic pluck. Still, if they did not come close to the true nature of the instrument, retuning was never required.

With the development of integrated circuits and their ability to perform countless transistor-like operations in nanoseconds, a more true-to-life harpsichord tone was made possible by the use of sampling techniques. Machines endowed with these microchips were no longer designated as electronic harpsichords, but either as electronic pianos with a harpsichord stop, or simply as electronic keyboards capable of producing many different types of sounds, the harp-

19-5. The Baldwin electronic instrument, called the "combo," was used by some jazz and popular groups in the 1960s and 1970s in an effort to reproduce harpsichord sound. Reprinted from *Zuckermann 1969a*, with permission.

THE HARPSICHORD IN POPULAR CULTURE

The sounds of the harpsichord became connected with jazz and popular music before the middle of the twentieth century. While the combination may at first seem unlikely, jazz was as resolute as art music in seeking out new sounds, and the percussive, nonromantic harpsichord certainly met that criterion. Also, the similarity between the harpsichord's historical function as an improvising continuo instrument and the role of the piano in jazz and swing bands did not go unnoticed. Harpsichordist Yella Pessl played some jazz on a radio broadcast in 1939 and may have been the first to do so,[50] but the first big moment in the encounter of the harpsichord with jazz came early in the 1940s, when harpsichordist Sylvia Marlowe made a record — her first — called *From Bach to Boogie-Woogie*. As a result of the notoriety, she was hired as an "act" for the Blue Room, a night club on the sixty-fifth floor of Rockefeller Center in New York. In her words, "I played on a revolving stage with glamorous spotlights and the whole bit. I would play a few classical things then some boogie and other popular numbers."[51] Marlowe also played jazz harpsichord on the air, in radio programs such as "Lavender and New Lace," "New Portraits of Old Masters," and "The Chamber Music Society of Lower Basin Street." Her crossover style did a great deal to familiarize the musical world with the sound of the harpsichord.

Another landmark event in the marriage of jazz and the harpsichord was its use in some 1940 recordings by the Gramercy Five, a group headed by the inventive clarinetist Artie Shaw; but perhaps the first great postwar harpsichord splash in the popular field was Stan Freeman's accompaniment to singer Rosemary Clooney in an improbable song in Armenian dialect titled "Come On-A My House," recorded in 1951. Freeman subsequently made a minicareer out of playing pop harpsichord and recorded many more pieces, including "Come On-A Stan's House." Starting back in the 1960s, Donald Angle, a fine harpsichordist as well as a technician in Dowd's shop, began playing and recording ragtime, jazz, and popular music on the harpsichord. Organist E. Power Biggs recorded two albums of Scott Joplin rags on his large Challis with pedal division in the 1970s, and other harpsichordists also played and recorded rags. For a while it was quite the rage.[52]

The appearance of Alice Ehlers and her Pleyel in the 1939 motion picture *Wuthering Heights* was another landmark in the acceptance of the harpsichord in popular culture. It was heard every so often in other films, but its big moment came in 1963, with the Tony Richardson film *Tom Jones,* an adaptation of Henry Fielding's eighteenth-century picaresque novel, with an Oscar-winning score by John Addison that heavily featured the harpsichord. The television series *The Addams Family* introduced the harpsichord to untold millions, when the instrument was played almost weekly by Lurch, the butler. In fact, that program, which ran from 1964 to 1966, may have done more to popularize the harpsichord than any other postwar event.

All this activity and much more served to bring the harpsichord to the public eye, and, combined with the growing number of harpsichord recitals and recordings, ensured its acceptance — although perhaps for different reasons — by both concert-going audiences and the general public.

sichord among them. Stored in the memories of these machines were digitized "samples" of harpsichord sounds, and these could be electronically manipulated to reproduce any pitch. However, the acoustical behavior of the harpsichord is so complex that unrealistically large amounts of computer memory and extremely fast microchips would be necessary to accurately mimic an "acoustic" instrument, with its tonal distinctions be-

19-6. An Allen electronic harpsichord.

tween registers, its combinations of 8' and 4' stops, lute stops, buff stops, and the complex transients of the pluck and release. There is also the problem of duplicating the unique touch of the harpsichord, not to mention the replication of the sounds of the various Flemish, French, German, English, and other varieties of the instrument. Nevertheless, while an absolutely convincing electronic harpsichord—or piano or organ, for that matter—may never be achieved, it is certain that the advances in electronics and microchip technology will enable manufacturers to get closer to that goal.

The combination of the harpsichord with MIDI (Musical Instrument Digital Interface) technology has had little use as yet, but that is bound to change. It is well ensconced in the piano world, where countless MIDI-controlled instruments are sold daily. With a MIDI interface, performers can "record" their own efforts and store them on a computer disk. By inserting the disk into a drive mechanism the piano "plays" back what was just played into it. A bonus of this technology is that properly equipped owners could purchase disks of the playing of other artists, like the piano rolls of yore, and by simply inserting them into their MIDI drive could not only enjoy, say, harpsichordist Trevor Pinnock playing the *Goldberg Variations,* but enjoy it in their own music rooms, on their own instruments. It is the player piano brought up-to-date, and it is only the economics of instrument sales that has prevented the spread of the MIDI interface to the harpsichord.

KITS

Wolfgang Zuckermann was born into an academic family in Germany and came to the United States in 1938. After a stint in the military and a short career as a child psychologist, he became a piano technician and through that business became interested in harpsichords. In 1954, in his own words, he "built a harpsichord after looking at an old Italian and a modern Dolmetsch."[53] He kept that first instrument, but built another, sold it immediately, and found himself with orders for five more. For the next few years he produced about a dozen instruments annually, until 1958, when a fire destroyed his shop. Although he was put out of business for a while, the publicity from the fire brought in further orders, and by 1960 he was back in full production. By that time he had built seventy or eighty instruments, but the calls for servicing, often asking him to do no more than change a string or replace a plectrum, began to encroach on his building time. In an oft-quoted remark, he noted that "most people approach a harpsichord with caution, the way they do a vicious dog,"[54] and he reasoned that if his customers participated in the building process, they would be able to maintain their instruments themselves. In a move that can only be termed pure genius, he put a set of parts into a box, and the harpsichord kit was born. By 1969, when *The Modern Harpsichord* was published, ten thousand kits had been launched into the world.

Consisting of a carton of wood, wire, pins, felt, jacks, a plywood soundboard, a piano-style keyboard, a drawing, and the now famous *Build your own Harpsichord* construction manual, the kit was to be supplemented by the builder's purchase of a sheet of plywood for the bottom and the framing, and some hardwood for the case exterior and lid (walnut plywood was recommended). The outer case of ½″ cabinet wood was glued to an inner case of ¾″ plywood, making a heavily framed case capable of taking a great deal of punishment, to say the least. The kit was inexpensive,[55] and the construction, though challenging, was not beyond the means of the average amateur craftsman. The result was a single-strung slant-side (rather than bentside) instrument with an AA–f³ compass, a buff stop, a half hitch, and plastic jacks quilled with leather. The 5′-long case was too short for the bass strings, and the bottom three or four notes lacked authority. Nevertheless, the soundboard barring was based on classical principles and helped to contribute to a useful sound at a surprising volume. The instrument had the additional virtue of simplicity: rather than a complex machine designed to provide an instantaneous variety of colors, it was a basic keyboard that plucked the strings.

19-7. The cover of the original do-it-yourself harpsichord kit by Wolfgang Zuckermann. Stonington, Zuckermann Harpsichords International.

Build your own Harpsichord

CONSTRUCTION AND MAINTENANCE MANUAL

ZUCKERMANN HARPSICHORDS, INC.
115 Christopher Street, New York 14, N. Y.

19-8. A Zuckermann 5′ slant-side harpsichord. Thousands of these instruments were constructed during the 1960s and 1970s, and many are still in use today. Reprinted from *Zuckermann 1969a*, with permission.

Hence, despite its considerable flaws, a well-built kit harpsichord could give more musical results than many of the thousands of revival instruments then in service.

Wolfgang Zuckermann never intended to become a phenomenon; he only hoped to satisfy a demand for harpsichords he himself could not accommodate. Nevertheless, his harpsichord kit spawned a unique movement whose heyday lasted for twenty years and helped fuel the instrument's revival. Some of today's finest builders got their start with a Zuckermann slant-side kit, or a "5′ Z-Box," as it is now affectionately called.

Frank Hubbard also produced a kit in the early 1960s, a 2×8′, 1×4′ "eighteenth-century French" harpsichord that could be had in either a single- or double-manual version. This was a more serious instrument than the Zuckermann effort, many times more expensive and complex, and for an amateur builder represented a significant outlay of money, time, and skill; hence, sales came nowhere near matching those of the Zuckermann kit. Actually the instrument was far from a classical French model: the plywood framing was more English than French, and the keyboards were heavy and pianolike; but the soundboard was solid spruce, barred in eighteenth-century French fashion, and the case was meant to be given moldings, paint, and gold bands. Unlike the Z-Box, it had a bentside, and it was long enough to provide for bass strings of appropriate length. Hence, although it was not as "pure" as Hubbard's custom French instrument, there were many things about its appearance and construction that were historically informed. All in all, Hubbard's French kit, if properly built, voiced, and adjusted, was a genuine harpsichord and superior in sound to any but the few instruments from builders like Dowd, Hyman, or Hubbard himself.[56]

Over the years Hubbard's French harpsichord kit was considerably improved and was joined by other excellent and historically appropriate kit designs. When Hubbard died in 1976 his widow, Diane, retained control of the company, and the talented builder Hendrick Broekman was brought in to supervise the shop and continue Hubbard's work with both the kits and the finished instruments. Hubbard Harpsichords is as well thought of today as it was when Zuckermann wrote *The Modern Harpsichord.*

The appearance of Zuckermann's *The Modern Harpsichord* in 1969 was in itself a significant milestone in the development of the twentieth-century harpsichord. A grand guide to the world's makers, it was also a heavily biased shopping primer. Zuckermann made no effort to hide his prejudice, which was in favor of the new trend toward harpsichords built according to the classical principles of the antiques, and he was pitiless in his negative descriptions of the *Serien* builders and all others who were not building instruments with historical awareness. He also reviewed his own 5' harpsichord, and while he made much of its classical elements, he was also able to bring himself to describe its imperfections.[57]

Zuckermann's book was published by October House, a company owned by David Jacques Way, at that time the proud owner of a Zuckermann kit harpsichord. A dedicated pianist, Way had had to give up his piano when he moved to a small city apartment. To assuage him, his wife bought him a harpsichord kit, which he built and greatly enjoyed. He subsequently became acquainted with Zuckermann, and as he began to learn more about harpsichords, it occurred to him that a book dealing with the worldwide production of the instrument would make a timely and interesting publication. Zuckermann agreed to undertake the project, which resulted in *The Modern Harpsichord;* but his travels brought him to the realization that he was a

European at heart, and on returning to New York he declared his intention to move to England. Way agreed to purchase the kit business, and Zuckermann Harpsichords had a new owner (with Zuckermann retained as a consultant).

By this time the production of Zuckermann kits had become a mail-order business. Parts were made and packed in one corner of a large woodworking plant in Philadelphia, and orders for kits were simply transmitted to the factory for shipment. Way probably could have ridden the kit phenomenon to its crest in 1982 with the Z-Box; instead, he immediately designed a 6′ slantside instrument and a new injection-molded plastic jack, both of which were considerable improvements over their predecessors. Other designs followed: a Flemish single in 1971, a French double in 1974, an Italian virginal soon after that, and so on, all more or less based on historical precedents. The venerable slantside models were abandoned. At first it was believed that the case wood and soundboard had to be laminated for the sake of stability, but with each succeeding "run" of five hundred or so instruments made and packed by the Philadelphia plant, Way rid his kits of plywood, extra structural members, jacks with adjustment screws, heavy keyboards, and other accoutrements left over from the revival. In his early days he was much assisted by builders William Post Ross and William Hyman, both of whom aided him with his designs, and he also explored the instruments in museums in the United States and Europe, gradually transforming himself from a dilettante to a knowledgeable harpsichord builder.

The kit business changed substantially in 1982, when a severe economic recession brought the sale of unfinished instruments to a virtual halt. By the time the economy picked up again, inflation had substantially driven up the price of the kits. Furthermore, they were now instruments of far greater sophistication, and that also added a great deal to their price. The Zuckermann firm, which by now had moved to Stonington, Connecticut, was forced to convert from a shop involved in the research and development of kits, with parts manufactured in Philadelphia, to a custom shop, building high-quality harpsichords to order while cutting their own kit parts. Sales never recovered their former vigor, but kits continue to be made and sold today. In addition to Hubbard and Zuckermann in the United Sates, other major kit suppliers are The Paris Workshop in France and The Early Music Shop and D. H. Bolton in England. Others have tried to produce kits, and some, like Herbert Burton of Lincoln, Nebraska, had some success; but as many a builder has discovered to his regret, the kit market has not been an easy one to penetrate.

By the 1970s Europe had caught on to the revolution in harpsichords that had occurred in America. Consequently, many of the kits of both Hubbard and Zuckermann were sold overseas, and Way developed a network of European agents to handle that business (he had American agents as well). One of these was Marc Ducornet, a builder who had apprenticed with the Paris-based Englishman Anthony Sidey. Beginning as an agent in 1973, in ten years Ducornet's business had blossomed to the point where he and Way assumed the role of partners, with Ducornet assisting Way in the design of new instruments and producing kits and parts in his Paris shop. Way was committed to producing the best possible instruments, whether made in his shop or by his kit builders, and he struggled constantly to improve his designs and the quality of his materials. He would have been better off financially had he simply left the designs alone; instead, a large part of the income of the shop went into the constant improvement of his older models as well as the creation of new kits. David Way truly believed that he was helping people achieve the dream of harpsichord ownership, and he dedicated himself to that conviction. Zuckermann may have started the kit movement, but it was Way and the Hubbard shop who brought it to fruition by combining it with historically informed practice.

David Way died in 1994, and his widow, Katherine, asked Richard Auber, a builder who had worked in both the Way and Ducornet shops, to take over the Zuckermann operation. In 1997 Auber purchased the business from Katherine Way and became the owner of Zuckermann Harpsichords. The relationship between Auber and Ducornet ended in 1999, and both shops continue to build high-quality custom instruments as well as sell kits (Ducornet under the rubric of "The Paris Workshop").

The concept of building a harpsichord from a kit seems to be here to stay. The task is far more complex than it was in 1960, but most kit manufacturers offer their instruments in various stages, ranging from a set of unassembled parts to a completed but unfinished case. The customer base also seems to have changed considerably. Today, the average builder is a serious amateur harpsichordist who wants a quality instrument as well as the joy of building it. Such was not often the case in the 1960s. There is little doubt that the 5′ slant-side kit was able to capture the interest of what was then known as the "do-it-yourself" movement that swept through the Western world in the 1960s and 1970s. It was a discovery of the delight in working with one's hands, and it coincided with both the general anti-establishment stance then common among youth, as well as the swelling popularity of Baroque music. The idea of building a harpsichord—a genuine musical instrument—for an affordable few hundred or even few thousand dollars created an entirely new class of harpsichord builders and owners. To many, it was simply an interesting craft project. Some built a single instrument that gave them a lifetime of enjoyment. To others, who built kit after kit, often selling them cheaply and even giving them away, the harpsichord kit was a siren whose song was impossible to ignore. Yet others decided that harpsichord building represented a rewarding lifestyle.[58] Nevertheless, the kit harpsichord transcended what could have been the stigma of the living dead. Like almost all custom-made harpsichords, the kits have been improved in all respects and have provided the means for countless people to create a useful musical instrument.

At the turn of the twenty-first century the harpsichord shows every sign of having survived its revival. Composers have written for it again for over a hundred years now, and it has a vast modern literature.[59] Twenty or thirty years ago no matter what their philosophy, few builders were making really good harpsichords. The opposite is true today. Builders all over the world have returned to the principles that guided the old masters, and fine instruments can be had almost anywhere.[60] Still, there are some anomalies. For the sake of uniformity, the eighteenth-century French octave span has been adopted by most as standard, even though during the harpsichord's historical period there were a variety of octave spans in use, including some just as large as the modern piano's.[61] The 16′ stop, viewed as a misguided, organ-inspired accretion, was banished long ago; but although antique harpsichords with 16′ stops were uncommon, the stop was not as exceptional as once supposed, and properly built, there is no reason why it could not be used in appropriate instruments. The past decade has seen a revision of the earlier view, and some builders, Hubbard among them, have started to make instruments with the 16′ once again, with that string choir properly given its own bridge and section of soundboard.

There is still a stigma attached to the use of pedals and knee levers to shift registers, despite the evidence that they were used in a number of traditions, and not only in the late eighteenth century. But Hubbard's disdainful view of the historical use of pedals still colors our perception that these devices are associated with the harpsichord of the immediate past, and therefore are to be avoided. Nevertheless, a few builders have begun equipping their copies of late French harpsichords with *genouillères,* and it is likely that pedals and knee levers will return, in an appropriate context. There has been a minor resurgence of interest in revival instruments with 16′ and pedals, particularly since they are needed to play the harpsichord literature of the early twentieth century. This all serves to indicate that as always, we are building instruments for our own time, and to suit our concepts of what a harpsichord should be.

SUMMING UP

The fifty-five years between World War II and the writing of this book saw a complete turnabout in the way in which harpsichords were perceived as part of our Western heritage. At first the harpsichord was still considered to be an object of another era, somehow magically brought back to life out of its own time. But that view changed, and today the historically informed harpsichord, found almost everywhere in the civilized world, is accepted as a contemporary instrument and as a part of modern life.

At first, the instrument continued to be regarded with an air of preciousness, with adjectives describing its sound as quaint and plucky, and as something belonging to the past. From what we can tell from early recordings — and even from Alice Ehler's all-too-brief stint in *Wuthering Heights* — the playing was also precious, with constant changes of color, dynamics, and registers achieved via pedals. Registration was considered to be an essential part of the player's arsenal, and the idea that by pressing the same key a plucked keyboard instrument could produce a variety of tone colors, muted sounds, octave shifts, and couplings of all sorts captured the attention of both audiences and critics and made the harpsichord an object of fascination and delight. Composers were quick to focus on this aspect of the instrument, and for almost seventy-five years scores bristled with directions for registral changes to be effected by the omnipresent pedals. While it was recognized that the music of Bach was better served by the harpsichord because of its cleaner, leaner sound and its articulative abilities, it was nevertheless the registral possibilities that were most often mentioned. Instruments with simple dispositions of $2\times8'$, or even $2\times8'$, $1\times4'$, particularly if with hand stops, were looked upon as incomplete harpsichords. Such instruments were built, but as with organs, it was assumed that one owned a smaller instrument because one could not afford a larger one.

Some of the earliest revival builders, like Tomasini, were concerned with re-creating the instrument as an antiquarian exercise; but most simply wanted to afford it the same sort of modernization that the piano had gone through. No right-minded person would have asked that piano makers return to thin wood cases, soft iron strings, light actions, and small, leather-covered hammers;[62] so why would it be asked of the harpsichord? If evolution was a historical imperative, then the harpsichord needed to go through it, just as the piano and all other instruments had. Accordingly, except to a very few, the harpsichords of Pleyel, Dolmetsch, Challis, and the *Serien* builders were unquestioningly accepted as the legitimate heirs to the ancient tradition. Even when this view began to change, the conviction held sway in many quarters that the antiques and the instruments built like them were unsuited to modern life.

It is axiomatic that when an instrument is changed to gain something it previously lacked, it also loses some quality it previously had. To cite only a few examples, when the flute changed from a conical to a cylindrically bored instrument it gained power, but it lost its characteristic sweetness of tone. When the French horn was given valves it gained an evenness of tone quality, but lost its *Waldhorn* character.[63] When the organ gave up its trackers for electrical circuits it gained in its ability to combine ranks, but the player lost the ability to communicate directly with the pipe work. It did not seem to be that different with the harpsichord. If the tone of the revival instrument was not as attractive or beautiful as that of the antiques, sacrifices of one sort or another were always to be expected when changes were made. That was understood. Viewed from a logical point of view, and leaving aside the heavy baggage of our early-twenty-first-century prejudices and preferences, it must be conceded that the Pleyels, Dolmetsches, Challises, and Neuperts had a valid point. From the piccolo to the organ, every instrument these builders knew had been modernized in the nineteenth century.

Nevertheless, a century later, the modern harpsichord as we know it has reached this juncture by returning to the building principles of the seventeenth and eighteenth centuries, a process that seems contrary to the normal course of events. But the harpsichord in the twentieth century evolved according to the needs of those involved with it, and it did not have to take the course it did. With a better understanding of the principles entailed, it would have been perfectly possible for builders to have made instruments with all the accoutrements of the revival, but with more of a historically oriented sound. Certainly, that was the direction of builders like Herz and Rutkowski and Robinette. And the idea of building more stable instruments, while originally founded more on misunderstanding than fact, was assuredly not a bad one.

At the turn of the twenty-first century, conventional wisdom has it that we have fully reclaimed the historical instrument;

but it might be truer to say that the harpsichord has evolved in new ways. Is the contemporary harpsichord better than last century's revival instrument? Perhaps, from the viewpoint of a builder, player, or listener; but from a historian's viewpoint the answer has to be no, it is not better. But it certainly is different.

[20]

INTO THE FUTURE

Predictions are hard to make,
particularly when they're about the future.
— *Yogi Berra, baseball player*

ORE THAN two hundred years ago the harpsichord was declared obsolete and thrown on the junk heap of history; yet almost miraculously, ninety years later, the Queen of Instruments was brought back to life and flourished once again. Given that near brush with death, and in light of the transformations the harpsichord has gone through in the twentieth century, it may not be inappropriate to ask, Where does the harpsichord go from here? To those involved with the instrument the question is an important one; but it is really part of a larger issue: Where does music go from here?

The modern harpsichord is part of the early music movement, and without its attachment to that enterprise it might not exist at all in any viable form. But as noted in a previous chapter, what we call the early music movement is the current manifestation of an activity whose origins can be traced as far back as the beginnings of Viennese Classicism. Prior to Haydn's generation a composer learned his craft through reference to the music of the immediate past; in other words, he learned from the music of his teachers and his teacher's contemporaries. But Haydn, Mozart, Beethoven, and their contemporaries looked back not only to the works of their mentors, but to earlier generations as well. The composer who most attracted their attention, of course, was J. S. Bach, with Handel a close second; but earlier styles were also consulted. Beethoven, for example, in writing his *Missa Solemnis,* examined the music of Palestrina. Bach remained a model for composers throughout the nineteenth century. When Schumann advised pianists to "let Bach be your daily bread," he was referring to the technical benefits pianists would derive from regularly playing his music. But Schumann's own compositions show traces of his familiarity with the Baroque master; for example, Bach's characteristic use of diatonic dissonances employed sequentially became an integral part of Schumann's style. As noted earlier, Schumann's library of Renaissance and Baroque scores went to Brahms, who added to it, absorbed it, and made elements of older music, such as late-sixteenth-century Venetian choral writing, part of his harmonic rhetoric. Mendelssohn also studied music of the past assiduously; his oratorios, for example, were firmly based on the Handelian model. Also mentioned earlier were such seminal events as the establishment of the Cecilian Movement in 1825, Mendelssohn's production of Bach's *St. Matthew Passion* in 1829, and the founding of the Bach Gesellschaft in 1850. Clearly an interest in early music was an integral part of the Western musical tradition throughout the nineteenth century. The harpsichord, as we now know, was part of that interest, as attested to by the activites of Moscheles, Diémer, Hipkins, and others.

Although the twentieth century was laced with cultural countercurrents of various sorts, an interest in music of the past nevertheless continued to manifest itself. Neo-Classicism, Neo-Romanticism, the Collegium Movement, the Baroque orchestra, Historically Informed Performance, and the New Romanticism all are movements or currents that called on earlier music in one way or another. When seen against this backdrop, the revival of "obsolete" instruments is, unmistakably, another facet of this interest. And it has not only been the harpsichord that has undergone a rebirth: the clavichord, fortepiano, lute, recorder, Baroque and Classical brass and woodwinds, and bowed strings have all passed through the same process. First the modern "improved" versions are made, then comes the realization that the antiques were actually better tools for making earlier music, then follow the builders who begin making instruments along more historical lines. Interest in historical organs and even historical dance is all very much a part of this long-lived early music movement. Hence, the existence of the modern historically oriented harpsichord is intertwined with a twentieth-century movement which is in itself only part of a trend that has been functioning now for more than 250 years.

Will there be a continuation of this fascination with music of the past? This brings us back to our original question: Where does music go from here? As Yogi Berra indicated, without the ability to peer into the future there is no way to answer that question. The past, however, can give us a hint. For whatever reason, in the second millennium of the Common Era some element or other of Western musical style has changed about every 150 years. The dawn of the eleventh century saw Western music transformed forever by the development of a viable system of notation. Around 1150 ways were developed to fix not only pitches but rhythms as well, and polyphonic music became possible. The Ars Nova, commencing around 1350, was a period in which great rhythmic flexibility was developed. The 150 years from 1450 to 1600, the Renaissance, saw changes in the relationships of intervals, with thirds and sixths, rather than fifths and octaves, operating as the important building blocks of music. The Baroque was a period of textural change, with melody supported by a harmonic bass. Large formal structures and the technique of development informed the Classic-Romantic era from 1750 to 1900. The twentieth century was one of a drastic redefinition of harmony. There is no guarantee that changes will continue to occur, or that they will occur with this sort of regularity; but it may well be that the arts, indeed, perhaps even Western society in general, are obeying a cultural clock only dimly perceived and scarcely understood.

The concern with early music has now been around through the 1750–1900 cycle — the one we call Classicism and Romanticism. This concern has grown even stronger in the current cycle, which began about 1900 and which as yet has no name beyond the unimaginative "Contemporary Music." If the cultural clock continues to tick as it has in the past, a new cycle may begin around 2050. Accordingly, for at least the first half of the twenty-first century it is likely that the harpsichord will continue to be here, very much in the form in which we now find it. Perhaps a hundred years from now our descendants might wonder why their twentieth-century ancestors chose to revive those quaint acoustic instruments of the past, and why they devoted so much of their lives to playing obsolete music. Or — a more happy thought — in fifty or a hundred years we may have a new aesthetic, one in which the harpsichord may find a part — indeed, it may play a vital part in it, perhaps by that time having become an instrument separated from early music, existing independently, with a viable contemporary literature and enthusiastic contemporary audiences.

Glossary

ARCADE. A thin, ornamental piece of wood, ivory, or other material, incised with semicircles, used to face the front of a key.

ARPICHORDUM STOP. An arrangement whereby small pieces of metal are placed close to a choir of strings. When plucked, the vibration of the strings is sufficient to cause contact with the metal pieces, producing a metallic buzz. The arpichordum stop is found almost exclusively on Flemish muselars, where a batten with metal staples was placed next to the straight, bass portion of the bridge. The stop was activated by moving the batten forward slightly.

BALANCE POINT. The point at which a key is drilled for the balance pin.

BALANCE RAIL. The portion of a key frame that acts as a fulcrum for the keys. A balance pin driven into the rail passes through a hole somewhere near the center of the key lever.

BATTEN. A thin, narrow piece of wood.

BELLYRAIL. The structural element of a harpsichord attached to the spine and the cheekpiece that constitutes one wall of the gap. In some traditions the bellyrail is one piece, extending downward from the soundboard to the bottom board. In other traditions, the bellyrail consists of separate upper and lower members, usually offset.

BOTTOM BRACE. *See* LOWER BRACE.

BOX GUIDE. A one-piece register, thick enough so that no other system of support is needed for the jacks.

BRAYS. Protrusions found on Renaissance harps that contact the strings, causing them to buzz. The arpichordum stop is thought to have been an imitation of this sound.

BROKEN SHORT OCTAVE. *See* SPLIT SHARPS.

BURL WOOD. Wood cut from a portion of a tree where the grain is wild, producing interesting and unpredictable patterns. Burl wood is almost exclusively found in hardwood veneers.

CEMBALO ANGELICO. A reference to a harpsichord with jacks having two tongues working in opposite directions, each carrying a different plectrum material.

CHECK, OR BACK CHECK. A device to prevent the hammers of a piano from rebounding and restriking the strings.

CHEEKS. The inside surface of the cheek piece and of the front portion of the spine. The cheeks enclose the keyboard(s) and form part of the keywell.

CHINOISERIE. A decorative style in imitation of Chinese painting. The lacquering technique used to apply it is called japanning.

COUPLER RAIL. In harpsichords with two keyboards, the wooden rail separating the upper and lower manuals.

CRENELATED. Indented, or notched.

CROSS-BANDING. In veneer work, a wide border of wood whose grain runs at right angles to the main field of veneer.

CUTOFF BAR. A heavy bar glued to the underside of the soundboard, roughly parallel to the bridge but some distance away from it, serving to limit (but only at certain frequencies) the vibrating portion of the soundboard.

DIAGONAL STRUT. In Italian and International traditions, a piece of wood attached at one end to the bentside liner, and at the other to the instrument's bottom.

DOGLEG JACK. A jack used in a two-manual instrument, in which an oblong portion has been sawn out of the front edge. The bottom of the jack rests on the end of the lower-manual key, while the flat portion of the dogleg rests on the end of the upper-manual key. Hence, the jack can be operated from either keyboard.

ENDBLOCKS. The blocks found between the cheeks and the first and last keys.

GAP. The space between the bellyrail and the wrestplank. The jacks operate in registers set in the gap.

GAP SPACER. A thin slip of wood or metal set between bellyrail and wrestplank to prevent the pull of the strings from closing the gap.

GROTESQUE. A style of decoration that had its beginnings in the late fifteenth century, derived from images of masks, mythological creatures, birds, dolphins, garlands, and trophies, intertwined with acanthus leaves, found in Roman grottos.

GUIDES. *See* REGISTER.

HOLLOW WRESTPLANK. A narrow wrestplank set against the nameboard, and covered with a veneer of soundboard wood that extends to or across the gap. The portion of the soundboard veneer to which the nuts are glued is free to vibrate, since there is no wrestplank wood beneath it. Obviously it is the space underneath the veneer, not the wrestplank itself, that is "hollow."

INSET KEYBOARD. A keyboard enclosed by the cheeks of the case sides, as opposed to a projecting keyboard, in which the keys appear to be jutting from the nameboard.

INTARSIA. A decorative style of inlay.

JACKRAIL. A board with cloth tacked to its underside that sits over the jacks, and either stops their upward motion, or prevents them from bouncing on the key ends, or both.

KEYWELL. The area surrounding a recessed keyboard(s), bounded by the interior portions of the spine and cheek piece and the nameboard.

KNEE. A triangular interior structural member, attached to an interior case wall or bellyrail and the bottom.

LEATHERED REGISTERS. Upper and lower guides that are covered with thin leather. The guides are given oversized mortises, and the leathers are mortised to fit the jacks.

LINER. A strip of wood glued to the inside of the spine, tail, and cheek piece, to which the soundboard is glued.

LOWER BRACE. A structural member of some height, usually set on edge, that crosses the grain of the bottom and is fastened to the case walls.

MORESQUES. Ornaments and decoration in Moorish style.

NAMEBATTEN. A removeable strip of wood below the nameboard, often carrying the maker's name.

NAMEBOARD. The board behind the visible portion of the keys. To facilitate the removal of the action the board is either removeable or has a removeable namebatten.

NARROW PAIRS. The unison strings of a harpsichord are spaced widely apart so that jacks may pass between them. A string and its semitone neighbor constitute a narrow pair. In virginals and spinets, which are single strung, both wide and narrow pairs differ in pitch by a semitone.

NONALIGNED DOUBLE. A Flemish double-manual harpsichord in which the keyboards are offset from one another by a fourth or some other interval.

OTTAVINO. The Italian term for an instrument at octave pitch — normally a spinet, but also a virginal or harpsichord.

POST AND BEAM. Light upper and lower braces connected by vertical reinforcing members glued to spine and bentside.

PROJECTING KEYBOARD. *See* INSET KEYBOARD.

REGISTER. 1. The mortised wooden batten through which the jacks operate, and generally of two types: upper and lower, and box. Also called a guide. 2. A set of strings and/or jacks, often qualified by a particular octave or tonal characteristic, such as "4′ register," "lute register," or "back 8′ register." 3. A reference to the distinctive tonal qualities of the various parts of a harpsichord's compass, such as the treble, tenor, and bass.

SGRAFFITO. The decorative technique of incising a line in a solid material and filling the incision with a color or an ink.

SHORT OCTAVE. A space-saving scheme in the bass, where some notes are assigned pitches other than their apparent ones. The two most common schemes are the C/E and GG/BB short octaves. In the first, the apparent E sounds C, and the apparent F♯ and G♯ sound D and E. In the second, the apparent BB is tuned to GG, and the apparent C♯ to AA, and E♭ to either BB or BB♭.

SINGERIES. Scenes with monkeys imitating human behavior.

SOUNDWELL. The open area above the soundboard, bounded by the interior portions of the spine, tail, bentside, and cheek piece.

SPLIT SHARPS. Accidentals in which the fronts and backs are split into two different notes, each with its own key lever, string, and jack. In short octave schemes the lowest two accidentals may be split, thus allowing both the short-octave note and the apparent note to be played. When split sharps appear in other accidentals they allow the production of two tunings, one for the flat version, the other for the sharp. Hence, the accidental between g and a, when split, would allow both a g♯ (in meantone, tuned pure to e) and an a♭ (pure to c).

STRAPWORK. A trompe l'oeil painting of straps on wood.

STRING BAND. The plan view of all the strings of a harpsichord.

STRINGING. 1. The wire strings of a harpsichord, one end attached to the hitchpins, the other end to the tuning pins or wrestpins. 2. In veneering, thin, narrow strips of material, usually of wood, but also of metal, ivory, mother-of-pearl, or some other substance, usually separating a border from the main field of wood.

TOUCH PLATE. The thin pieces of material covering the exposed portion of a key lever. Touch plates are normally in two pieces, heads and tails, and are usually made of wood, bone, or ivory, although other substances, such as mother-of-pearl and tortoise shell, are also found.

U-BRACE. A lower brace that appears to be scooped out in the middle, making an elongated

U shape, and whose ends rise to or near the tops of the liners. U-braces combine the functions of bottom braces and knees.

UPPER BRACE. A flat structural member that runs across the width of the case and whose ends are attached to the liners.

UPPER, LOWER GUIDES. Upper guides are the registers found at soundboard level. Lower guides are similar but are usually immovable and found several inches below the uppers.

VERNIS MARTIN. A generalized term for painting with colorful grotesques, garlands, putti, and singeries over a gold ground.

WIDE PAIRS. *See* NARROW PAIRS.

WRESTPIN. Tuning pin.

WRESTPLANK. The heavy member into which the wrestpins are driven. In modern terms, a pin block.

Notes

INTRODUCTION

1. *Howell 1979–80*, 15. One wonders how seriously Paulirinus's praise can be taken, since he thought that many other instruments, including the *cimbalum*, a metal bell enclosing a stone, also sounded "sweet."

2. *Denis*, 61–64.

3. *Diderot and d'Alembert 1791*, cited in *Hubbard 1965*, 260.

4. The 1956 edition of Boalch's *Makers of the Harpsichord and Clavichord* listed six hundred makers. With more than twelve hundred entries, *Boalch II* doubled that number in 1974, and *Boalch III*, in 1995, listed more than sixteen hundred builders. This does not include anonymous builders and their thousands of instruments.

5. I have resisted mentioning instruments unknown to or not accepted by the scholarly world. I have been told, for example, of the existence of a list of seventy-five extant seventeenth-century French harpsichords; but until those instruments are reported in print, with descriptions and authentications by experts, it seems best to leave them to be treated by the next person to write a history of the harpsichord. I am also aware of a group of instruments purported to have been built in Spain in the seventeenth century; prevailing opinion suspects them of being forgeries, and until the matter is clarified I think it wise simply to make reference to them, but not to include them in the text. As long as evidence remains to be discovered, verified, and interpreted, the definitive history of the harpsichord cannot be written. Even then, like every history, each generation will need to redefine the instrument according to its own lights.

6. There are dangers in this approach, such as a tendency to ignore or minimize builders who span the break between two centuries; and when such builders are cited, it is sometimes difficult to choose the century (and in some cases, the country) in which they should be discussed. I have tried to overcome both problems by taking a rather loose approach and discussing a builder where it seems most appropriate, even if doing so is not the most chronologically correct. Hence, Nicolas Blanchet appears in the chapter on eighteenth-century France, even though he was born in 1660.

7. *O'Brien 1990*, 62. O'Brien's conclusions are cautiously accepted by Nicholas Mitchell in *Mitchell*, an article that helps reveal, if not explain, the complexity of the pitch issue. See also *Segerman*.

8. *Koster Forthcoming*, 65. I am extremely grateful to Professor Koster for sharing the manuscript of this work with me prior to its publication. His scholarship has been an enormous help as well as a source of inspiration, especially in the earlier chapters. Page references to his work refer to the unpublished manuscript.

1. FROM PSALTERY AND MONOCHORD TO HARPSICHORD AND VIRGINAL

1. John was finally released, for a ransom and some hostages. When one of his stand-ins escaped, as a point of honor John voluntarily returned to imprisonment in England, thereby performing perhaps the sole act of distinction in his otherwise lackluster reign.

2. Paris, Bibliothèque Nationale, ms. fr. 11205, f. 91v, cited in *Ripin 1975*, 15.

3. See *Page 1984*, 113. *Pollens 1995*, 268, n. 5, offers a fairly complete bibliography of the *chekker*. Two provocative papers not on his list are *Barry 1985* and *Howell 1990*. *Thomas and Rhodes 1979* point out a truism so obvious it is often ignored: before wire-strung instruments could be invented, the art of drawing malleable metal through a series of holes of ever-decreasing diameter had to have been developed. The authors note that the earliest extant English reference to wire drawing dates from 1369, although wire drawing was practiced long before that: *Goodway and Odell*, 20, date the earliest reference back at least a century earlier, and *Wraight 1997*, 40, refers to an example of drawn gold wire from ca. 400. *Kinsela* presents an excellent summary of the research on the chekker. Kinsela believes that the instrument was a clavichord whose keys and strings ran in the same direction, as in a harpsichord.

4. *La Prise d'Alexandrie*, ed. M. L. de Mas Latrie (Geneva, 1877), 35–36, cited in *Ripin 1975*, 15–16. The entire passage reads: Orgues, vielles, micanons, / Rubebes & psalterions, / Leüs, moraches & guiternes, / Dont on joue par ces tavernes, / Cymbales, citoles, naquairs, / Et de flaios plus de x. paires, / C'est à dire de xx. manieres, / Tantdes fortes com des legieres, / Cors sarrasinois & doussainnes, / Tabours, flaüstes traverseinnes, / Demi doussainnes & flaüstes, / Dont droit joues quant tu flaüstes, / Trompes, buisines & trompettes, / Guiges, rotes, harpes, chevrettes, / Cornemuses & chalemelles, / Muses d'Aussay, riches & belles, / Et la fretiaus, & monocorde, / Qui à tous instrumens s'acorde, / Muse de blé, qu'on on prent en terre, / Trepié, l'eschaquier d'Engletere, / Chifonie, flaios de saus.

5. Cited in *Ripin 1975*, 16–17.

6. "Segons que havem entes, vos havets un ministrer entrels alres que abte de tocar exaquier [e] los petit orguens"; cited in *Ripin 1975*, 17. *NGEKI*, 174, disagrees with Ripin's article, holding that the clavicytherium cannot be identified before the 1460s. Since Ripin was the principal author of the original *Grove* article on the harpsichord, it appears that he is contradicting himself; but he died in 1975, the same year in which *Ripin 1975* appeared. His *Grove* article was enlarged and substantially revised by other scholars for *The New Grove Dictionary of Musical Instruments*, a spin-off of the original *New Grove* (1980), and further revisions were made for the paperback *Early Keyboard Instruments*, a spin-off of the spin-off. The first mention of the clavicytherium under that name appears in *Virdung*. For a discussion of the stringed keyboards in *Virdung*, see *Stradner*.

7. See, e.g., *Kinsela*, 69–70.

8. *Ripin 1975*, 23.

9. See *Segarizzi*, cited in *Strohm*, 63.

10. The letter, from Lodovico Lambertacci to his son-in-law in Pavia, describes his meeting with Poll, whom he presented as the inventor of the *clavicembalum*; see *Esch*, cited in *Koster Forthcoming*, 8; see also *Howell 1990*, 8–10, and *Strohm*. The last two scholars hold that Poll was not only the first-named builder of the harpsichord, but was indeed the instrument's inventor.

11. *Segarizzi*.

12. *Howell 1990*, 4. *Bowles 1966*, 162, suggests that the earliest string keyboard builders were probably makers of clocks—craftsmen who would also have a knowledge of mechanics and the commensurate skills.

13. *Cersne*, 24, cited in *Ripin 1975*, 17–18.

14. Small organ keyboards of three octaves or so, fully chromatic except for the bass, must have been in existence since at least 1320, when such a compass was required by the Robertsbridge Codex. *Kinsela 2001*, 355, notes that "The keyboard has been called the most versatile interface ever devised between man and machine, the 'ergonomic masterpiece' of the second millennium. It can be operated by a two-year-old, yet was indispensable to the rise of Western music."

15. *Pollens 1995* may have been the first to characterize the clavichord's action with the pithy yet descriptive term "touching," as opposed to the harpsichord's "plucking" and the piano's "striking."

16. The strings of a psaltery normally run from side to side, but in some they run the long way. It was this version of the *micanon* that served as the resonance body for the new, mechanized version. An excellent diagram of psaltery types can be seen in *Kaufmann 1980*, 16.

17. *Bowles 1977* identifies thirteen painted, carved, and stained-glass representations of harpsichords, plus a clavicytherium and a keyed psaltery. Three additional instruments are described in *Page and Jones*.

18. Two playing positions seem to be found in the fifteenth-century iconography: the conventional one, where the harpsichord is set on a horizontal surface in front of the player; and another, in which the harpsichord appears to hang downward, presumably supported by a strap around the player's neck or by a belt around the waist. Since both playing positions—horizontal and hanging vertically—were also used with the psaltery, it is entirely possible that they were used on the mechanized version of the instrument as well. Further, the depiction of a harpsichord in the hanging position lends credence to the view that some actually were that small, no larger than the usual psaltery.

19. Four of the harpsichords in *Bowles 1977*, and one in *Page and Jones* are reversed in this way. For some early "backward" organettos, see *Shuman 1971*.

20. See *Bowles 1977*, plates 18, 19.

21. See *Bowles 1977*, plates 22, 23.

22. See *Bowles 1977*, plate 20. The spine of this instrument is cut down to the soundboard level, a meaningless structural or decorative gesture which may have been no more than a figment of the artist's imagination.

23. *Hubbard 1965*, 45, is of this opinion, but *Koster Forthcoming*, 8, rejects the hegemony of a Burgundian style (although he holds that Burgundy, France, and the Netherlands were significant areas). Instead, he suggests that the majority of the early written accounts and iconographical evidence of harpsichords, including the ca. 1470 clavicytherium in the Royal College of Music (to be described shortly), are English, Burgundian, and German, and it would be more accurate to speak of a "Gothic" style. Professor Koster also made available to me a conference report, "Toward a History of the Earliest Harpsichords," for which I am also much obliged.

24. The fief of Burgundy, an area roughly comprising the present region in eastern France, was given to Philip the Bold in 1364. Philip and his successors John the Fearless, Philip the Good, and Charles the Bold expanded the territory until it included most of Belgium, Holland, Luxembourg, and part of France. During Philip the Good's long reign (1419–67) Burgundy became the most powerful political presence in Europe. It was also an artistic force of incomparable richness, employing Europe's greatest musicians, artists, and craftsmen.

25. This is the thrust of *Page 1984*. It is worth noting that the lute was a monophonic instrument in the 1400s, but by the end of the century a change in playing position and the abandonment of the plectrum in favor of plucking with fingers gave it polyphonic capabilities.

26. Now in London's British Library (formerly the British Museum), Add. Ms. 28550.

27. Faenza, Biblioteca Comunale 117.

28. Philadelphia, Curtis Institute of Music. Transcriptions of all this music are found in *Apel*.

29. For the history of early wire drawing see *Goodway and Odell*, 19–22. *Latcham 2000*, while dealing with wire drawing in connection with late-eighteenth- and nineteenth-century pianos, is an excellent study of the subject.

30. In fact, animal glue was used in furniture manufacture up through the beginning of the twentieth century. Many instrument builders still use it today and claim it superior to modern glues.

31. See *Page 1978*.

32. This is true for all strings, no matter what their origin or composition, and has been known for centuries. Renaissance and Baroque tutors for lutes and gambas, for example, often advised the player to tune the top string (the one that takes the most tension) as high as it could go without breaking. Thus *Robinson* instructed the would-be gambist to tighten his first string "so high as you dare venture for breaking."

33. It is not so much the strings that react to these changes as the wood of the case. When the case expands the strings are stretched more tightly, and pitch goes up.

34. See *Goodway and Odell*, 61–65.

35. See *Thomas and Rhodes 1979*.

36. *Wraight 1997*, 20, maintains that in the sixteenth century most harpsichords scales started from the f^1, while in the next century the c^2 prevailed.

37. A just scale is often called a Pythagorean scale, after Pythagoras, the sixth-century B.C. Greek philosopher and mathematician who first discovered the 2:1 relationship between a string's length at one pitch and its length when producing a pitch an octave higher.

38. *O'Brien 1990*, 17–20, presents a detailed discussion of scale that is well worth reading.

39. Paris, Bibliothèque Nationale, Ms lat. 7295. For a modern facsimile edition see *Le Cerf and Lebande*. *Koster Forthcoming*, 91–106, presents a closely reasoned description and analysis of Arnaut's text and diagrams. *Howell 1990*, 6, makes the point that Arnaut was another in the line of medical astrologers who left manuscripts dealing with astronomical tables, scientific instruments, clocks, and musical instruments. Le Cerf and Lebande are responsible for dating the ms at ca. 1450, but *Wraight 1997*, 43–44, disputes this and suggests a dating of 1453–66.

40. An illustrated account of the building of a harpsichord from Arnaut's drawing can be found in *Kaufmann 1980*.

41. *Dulce melos* is Latin for dulcimer, making it clear that the instrument was a mechanized version of that instrument. The plan drawings of the *clavicordium* and *dulce melos* can be found in several modern sources, including *Bowles 1977*, plates 4, 28, 29, and *NGEKI*, 144, 190. The manuscript also includes technical drawings for the lute and organ.

42. *Koster Forthcoming*, 92, notes that Arnaut's plans were likely one-quarter of full size. Many such plans survive, in architectural drawings, organ cases, and clocks, to mention a few. Normally, however, harpsichords, like almost all artifacts, were built by using proportions. See *O'Brien 1999*. For a view somewhat different from O'Brien's see *Birkett and Jurgens*.

43. A translation of Arnaut's text is found in *Pollens 1995*, 9–14, and 17–19.

44. *Koster Forthcoming*, 93, notes that organ keyboards at that time commonly began with that low B.

45. *Koster Forthcoming*, 91, coined this term and points out that the scales of many of the Northern survivors subsequent to a 1581 instrument by Hans Ruckers (see Chapter 3) are rising, Pythagorean only in midcompass.

46. A translation of Arnaut's description of the four actions and a detailed description of their workings is found in *Lester. Pollens 1995*, 8 ff., also translates the text dealing with the actions. *Kaufmann 1980* used the first of the three plucking mechanisms (the one that Arnaut called the best) in his reconstruction and provides pictures of his version of the device (53–54), which seems clumsy compared to the conventional jack mechanism that soon superseded it, or even may have existed as an alternate to it.

47. There is no other evidence that a hamFmer action was in use in Arnaut's day. *Pollens 1995*, 25–26, believes that the *dulce melos* may have existed only in the confines of the Burgundian court.

48. An upright harpsichord is shown in a sculpture in St. Wolfgang's Church in Kefermarkt, Austria, dated ca. 1490; see *Bowles 1977*, plate 31.

This is also an example of a "backward" keyboard, with the longer strings farther away from the player's body. *Van der Meer 1978,* points out that the sculpture was restored in the nineteenth century, and there is no guarantee that the original instrument was this clavicytherium. *Van der Meer 1978* says, "For all we know, the angel may originally have played a portative organ" (249). However, English maker Peter Bavington built a "reconstruction" of the Kefermarkt altar piece (but forward, rather than backward) and reported excellent musical results. See *Bavington.*

49. *Le Cerf and Lebande,* 21.

50. *Koster Forthcoming,* 17, observes that Arnaut is describing the process of making a harpsichord in the shape of a clavichord, not converting one of the latter to one of the former. It is worth reminding ourselves that harpsichord keys and strings run in the same direction, while on clavichords—and virginals—the strings run at approximately right angles to the keys.

51. Arnaut's diagram can be seen in *NGEKI,* 145.

52. See p. vi, plate 2; p. viii, plate 6; p. ix, plate 2; p. x, plate 3; and p. xi, plate 5 of *De Clavicordio 1994.*

53. See *Virdung,* 102.

54. Later virginals seem to fit this description, but their strings are not parallel to the spine.

55. See *Howell 1979–80.* Paulirinus's encyclopedia is part of a manuscript now in Kraków, Uniwersytet Jagielloński, Biblioteka Jagiellońska, Codex 257.

56. See *Howell 1979–80,* 18.

57. See *Howell 1979–80,* 18.

58. *Howell 1990,* 1–17.

59. That *Mersenne,* 168, includes a drawing of an old-fashioned clavichord—thin-case, pentagonal, strung straight across—is an indication that even one hundred years later such instruments were by no means considered obsolete.

60. *Koster Forthcoming,* 17–18, goes into considerable detail on the development of the virginal.

61. It is presumed to be from Ulm because a piece of paper glued to the interior of the instrument refers to a legal action that took place in that city.

62. See *Wells 1978.* A museum drawing of the clavicytherium exists, and several builders have made copies of the instrument. I am indebted to one of them, Ted Robertson of Bloomington, Indiana, who was kind enough to supply me with information not available from other sources.

63. *Koster 2000d,* 121, suggests that the rising scale of the clavicytherium is the result of its having been "conceived as an organ with strings." Koster notes that measuring the strings from bridge to bellyrail (rather than nut), analogous to measuring an organ pipe from top to mouth,

would produce a nearly Pythagorean scale. Something similar, says Koster, is more or less true for the Arnaut harpsichord.

64. The E♯ is a normal-looking accidental key between the E and the F. For a technical report on how this compass was arrived at see *Debenham.*

65. *Van der Meer 1978.*

66. *Mersenne,* 166.

67. *Bonanni,* plate 44.

68. New York, Metropolitan Museum of Art.

69. A detailed discussion of the instrument in this painting is found in *Ford 1984.*

70. The soundboards of surviving Northern harpsichords are ordinarily made of coniferous wood, usually European spruce (*Picea abies*) or fir (*Abies alba*), sometimes collectively and erroneously called "Swiss pine." It is practically impossible to distinguish between them with the naked eye.

71. *Hipkins,* 74, claims that when he examined the instrument in 1885 it had traces of brass plectra. *Wells 1978, 569,* holds that the instrument shows no sign of ever having been quilled in metal; however, she also notes that the present jack tongues are most likely later replacements.

72. The RCM clavicytherium is not playable; but a replica, made by Derek Adlam in 1971, is in the museum and heard frequently.

73. Both *Ripin 1977, 72,* and *Koster Forthcoming,* 8–10, note that German instrument makers were active in the Low Countries in the fifteenth century. Nor were German craftsmen limited to making keyboard instruments: *Hellwig 1974, 35,* notes that German builders, either at home or in Italy, made almost all the lutes in Europe. *Williams 1980, 70,* gives an account of the German organ maker named Berhard Dilmano, who built an instrument in Milan, Italy, in 1464–66. More than three centuries later *Burney 1773,* vol. 2, 145, stated that "the Germans work much better out of their own country, than they do in it."

74. *Ripin 1977, 71,* notes that this change seems to have come to Italy somewhere between 1479 and 1510, just around the time of the RCM clavicytherium.

2. THE EMERGENCE OF THE NORTHERN HARPSICHORD

1. Two anonymous undated English virginals may have been built toward the end of the sixteenth century. These instruments (Edinburgh, Russell Collection; National Museum of Scotland), described in *Martin 2000,* were examined by Darryl Martin, who notes the similarities in construction and materials between them and the Theewes harpsichord (to be described shortly). Martin cautiously attributes both virginals to London, between 1580 and 1600, and although not by

Theewes, to someone from the same workshop tradition.

2. I will continue to use the word "harpsichord" to refer to both the virginal and the grand harpsichord, even though most of the jack-action instruments produced in the North in the sixteenth century seem to have been virginals.

3. Cited in *James*, 33.

4. See *Stellfield*, cited in *Russell 1959/1973*, 41. The earliest name mentioned is a Daniel van der Distelen, in 1505.

5. This is the opinion of *Boalch III*, 79, which also states that Hans van Cuelen was the father of Ioes Karest (101). Both men were important and influential builders, so it is tempting to believe this lineage; but there is no proof that it was so.

6. *Koster Forthcoming*, 15. *Ripin 1970a*, 13–14, believed that van Cuelen "profoundly influenced organ-building both in Antwerp and in the Netherlands." Ripin also speculates on the nature of van Cuelen's *clavicenon*, assuming it to be one of the newer, thin-case instruments, rather than a heavy-case fifteenth-century design. Van Cuelen's instrument was for an important personage, though; Eleanor was the wife of Charles V of Burgundy, who became king of Spain in 1516, and three years later, Holy Roman Emperor.

7. See *Boalch III*, 134.

8. The Guild of St. Luke will be discussed in greater detail in Chapter 3. It is interesting that although Karest made Antwerp his new home at an early age, thirty-one years after attaining citizenship in that city he still identified himself on his instruments as coming from Cologne (*Ioes Karest de Colonia*). Earlier, Hans van Cuelen had followed a similar practice. It may well be that a German origin was considered more prestigious than a local one.

9. See the listing in *Boalch III*, 709.

10. *Boalch III*, 693–94.

11. *Boalch III*, 117–18.

12. Reported in *Koster 1980*, cf. 65.

13. Bristol Archives Office, C.T.04352. See *Goodman*. Because of the imprecise terminology the exact number of masters and apprentices is difficult to pin down, but there appear to have been at least six.

14. This is the opinion of *Barry 1982*.

15. See *Smith 1980*.

16. It is possible that the higher-pitched instruments were considered obsolete when "full-sized" harpsichords at "normal" pitch became more popular. However, it should be borne in mind that smaller ones continued to be built, although most of them were virginals—and later, spinets—rather than grand harpsichords.

17. See *Bowles 1977*, plates 22, 23, 25, and 27a. On the other hand, harpsichords were preserved in Italy from as early as 1515 on; accordingly, the study of these harpsichords in Chapter 4

will depend much less on the more ephemeral sorts of evidence.

18. See *Boalch III*, 695–708.

19. *Koster 1998b* remarks that in this sense all German makers were provincial. He cites a 1684 history of Thuringia which proudly notes that "here in villages they build . . . stringed instruments such as violins, basses, viole da gamba, harpsichords, spinets, and citterns." I thank Professor Koster for this quote, which he in turn got from *Geiringer*, 5.

20. We have already mentioned the description of the *clavicimbalum* by *Virdung*. *Agricola*, based on Virdung, generally copied his less-than-accurate woodcuts.

21. This seminal instrument was first described by *Van der Meer 1966a*. *O'Brien 1990*, 20–23, compares the Müller to contemporary Italian instruments. See also *NGEKI*, 25–26.

22. Already in 1511 Virdung reports F,G–f² keyboards, sometimes with an added f#² and g². Virdung explains it as adding one note to each end of the medieval G–e² gamut. See *Virdung*, 126.

23. I thank John Koster for this information, given in a private communication.

24. *Van der Meer 1998a*, 98–99, discusses this transposing keyboard in some detail.

25. Translation from *O'Brien 1990*, 20–21.

26. This statement is a little misleading, since Arnaut did mention the possibility of installing a second set of strings above the first. The Müller, however, has them side by side.

27. Cypress is often found as a soundboard wood on Southern instruments, but this is one of the few instances we know of its appearance in a Northern board. Although there is no evidence for it, it is possible that the earlier use of cypress was not uncommon in Northern instruments, but that it died out in favor of spruce or fir earlier in the sixteenth century. Nevertheless, cypress is found later, in seventeenth-century England, used for moldings and veneers.

28. There are some other ribs, but it is likely that they are later additions. Some stiffening ribs are also found parallel to the jacks and the nut.

29. I thank Professor Koster for pointing this out to me. It is also the scheme that will be found on a 1579 Theewes (to be discussed shortly).

30. Again, my thanks to Professor Koster for this. A buff stop between registers makes no sense, while there is evidence that arpichordum stops appeared on other sixteenth-century instruments.

31. The moldings on the Müller are "rippled"; that is, flutes have been cut into them in a repetitive, angled, crosswise pattern, giving an impression of undulation. Ripple moldings are particularly characteristic of German instruments, and it is interesting to see that they are found as far back as 1537.

32. Thanks to *O'Brien 1990*, 22–23, for this information. He goes into some detail and relates the use of Hungarian ash (which he says is nothing other than European ash, not at all exclusive to Hungary) to later Flemish decoration.

33. *O'Brien 1990*, 22, among others, is of that opinion. *Koster 1998c*, 83, reports that the bridge was glued in its present position sometime after the 1960s.

34. *O'Brien 1990*, 22, suggests that the alteration was done in Italy in the eighteenth century.

35. *Koster 1998c*, 83–86.

36. The lowest four were possibly tuned C/E, D/E♯, F, E/G♯; see Chapter 1.

37. This is also the view of both Edwin M. Ripin, in *Ripin 1977*, 70, and the authors of *NGEKI*, 45. But *Van der Meer 1966a* was one of the first to express the idea.

38. The case walls taper, so that their bottoms are about twice as thick as their tops, and hence sufficiently hefty to take nails or treenails (thin wooden pegs) driven up through the virginal's bottom board. The case material, maple, was also used in two early clavichords (both in Leipzig, Musikinstrumenten-Museum der Universität Leipzig) and in instruments of the sixteenth-century Neapolitan school (see Chapter 4).

39. *O'Brien 1990*, 24, believes the natural key coverings on both virginals as well as on the Müller to be "briar or maple (sycamore?) root," and he identifies the sharps as bog oak.

40. Large lower guides of this sort are found occasionally on other instruments. They are sometimes referred to as "second" soundboards, or "counter" soundboards, but part of their function may have been to stiffen the thin-walled cases. *O'Brien 1990*, 25, calls them "noise boards," since they tend to amplify the sound of the jacks as they pass through the guides. *Koster Forthcoming*, 139, taking an opposite view, believes that leathering the points of contact in the upper and lower guides actually reduced the action noise.

41. For arguments see *O'Brien 1990*, 25–26, n. 4; *Barry 1991*, 124–28; and *Koster 1998c*, 86–88.

42. Two of the four Flemish pentagonal virginals depicted in *Ripin* (Catharina de Hemmesen, *Girl at a Spinet*, plate 54; and Cornelis de Zeeuw, *Family Portrait*, plate 57) show two roses, with the larger circular and the smaller roughly triangular.

43. Virginal stringing is inherently uneven. Since the jacks must go between pairs of strings, virginals appear to have the same string configuration as a 2×8′ harpsichord; but whereas the wide pairs on the harpsichord are unisons, on a virginal they are a half-step apart. Thus, alternate strings will vary from the ideal scale by either a little more or a little less than on a harpsichord. *O'Brien 1990*, 25, takes this into account when he gives lengths of virginal strings.

44. Koster (private communication) reports that up to about 1849 organs with short-octave keyboards were being made in Bavaria.

45. It is worth reminding ourselves that if exceptional notes were required the pitches of the short octave could easily be retuned on stringed keyboard instruments: the C on a C/E keyboard could be tuned down to GG or AA, for example.

46. I thank Sheridan Germann for this fortuitous insight. Not only is Germann a scholar, painter, and decorator of the first rank, she is also a dedicated amateur harpsichordist.

47. It is worth noting that the C/E short octave was not exploited in England. The works of Peter Philips written in England require a low F♯ and G♯, but he no longer included them after 1582, when he was on the Continent. In fact, as can be seen from the examples, some of those later works cannot be played on an instrument without a short octave.

48. *O'Brien 1990*, 24, says, "the dolphin does not feature in this decoration." O'Brien and I differ here. I clearly see dolphins, as does Sheridan Germann in her forthcoming monograph on harpsichord decoration; even so, O'Brien has a valid point. These designs were based on grotesque decorations, an ornamental style developed in Italy in the fifteenth century. If the pattern on the Karest includes dolphins, it also includes monsters, human heads, animals, birds, fruits, plants, and flowers. Did the viewers of Karest's virginal in 1550 see dolphins, with all their classical connotations, or did they merely see a grotesque decoration in a style that would have embellished many other artifacts?

49. The same sort of painted decoration is seen on the pictures of virginals found in *Ripin 1977*, plates 54–57, and will be seen again on English virginals. One could also draw a parallel between these painted touches and the filigree carvings and ivory buttons on the RCM clavicytherium.

50. *Ripin 1977*, 68–69.

51. "Soundwell" is *O'Brien 1990*'s term. It is less awkward than "the interior case walls above the soundboard," and resonates with "keywell."

52. Black-and-white reproductions of the Floris and de Zeeuw paintings can be seen in *Ripin 1977*, plates 55–57.

53. In addition to the paintings discussed here, a similar virginal, portrayed in El Greco's *The Annunciation*, ca. 1570–77, in Madrid's Prado Museum, was until recently thought by some to be Flemish, in the style of the Karest instruments. However, *Kenyon de Pascual 1992* presents convincing evidence that it is probably Italian, rather than Flemish. The article contains a color reproduction of the El Greco virginal (619).

54. See *Verlet*, cited in *Ledbetter*, 2.

55. See *Boalch III*, 695–98.

56. See *Koster 1980*, 48.

57. See *Lesure*, 14.

58. *Mersenne*, 212.

59. His other instruments were a clavichord and two virginals; cited in *Hubbard 1965*, 88.

60. The drawing by Jacques Cellier is part of a manuscript including renderings of musical instruments used in the late sixteenth century. See *Gétreau and Herlin 1996*, 90–91. See also *Ledbetter*, 3–4.

61. The recognition of International style began to occur soon after Raymond Russell and Frank Hubbard noted that historical harpsichords seemed to divide themselves into Northern and Southern schools. Few sixteenth- or seventeenth-century German, French or English instruments were known then, and these were not easily fitted into the North-South dichotomy. It was reasoned that if only two schools existed, any harpsichord not belonging to one or the other must represent a combination of the two. Consequently, International-style instruments were regarded as hybrids, partaking of both Northern and Southern characteristics. The existence of the International style has been recognized for at least thirty years. Its characteristics were first described in *Ripin 1977*, 72, although he does not use the term; that honor goes to Michael Thomas, in *Thomas 1976*, 196, where he presented a list of fourteen features he defined as international in scope. Perhaps the clearest explanation of the origins of the International style is found in *Koster 1980*.

62. The two early virginals described in *Martin 2000* both have their lids coffered in the later English style.

63. British Library, Harley 1419. The inventory can be found in *Russell 1959/1973*, 155–60, and *Hubbard 1965*, 134–35. *Barry 1982* is an excellent explication of the language of the inventory, as well as a knowledgeable interpretation.

64. There is at least one reference to the instrument in the singular, in a poem written on the wall in an English manor house during Henry's time. The first two lines are: "A slac strynge in a Virgynall soundithe not aright / It dothe abyde no wrastinge it is so louse and light"; cited in *James*, 24.

65. For the etymology of this term see *Barry 1982*, 33.

66. It is still customary in England to refer to the instrument in the plural, as in "she played a recital on the virginals."

67. This may not be exactly true. *Boalch III*, 117–18, relates that in 1530 the King's Privy Purse Expenses notes that William Lewes sold to the court "ii payre of Virginalles in one coffer with iiii stoppes." Although Boalch thinks it unlikely that this is anything other than a double-manual harpsichord, it is also possible that it was a 2×8′ single, with one set of strings served by two sets of jacks and the other having a buff stop. We have

seen such instruments in seventeenth-century Germany. On the other hand, *Barry 1982*, 40, suspects it might have been a claviorganum. More than likely, it was what was described: two instruments in a single case.

68. *Barry 1982*, 37. Darryl Martin, private communication, notes that pitch was still oriented to the medieval gamut, and doubled notes referred to pitches below the gamut — that is, lower than G.

69. *Barry 1982*, 35–36, notes that the inventory has not a single mention of registers or stops in connection with harpsichords in grand shape.

70. *Barry 1982*, 38, imagines them to be harpsichords rather than clavicytheria because of the word "long," suggesting a horizontal orientation.

71. It is, of course, possible that the two early virginals described by Martin in *Martin 2000* may yet turn out to be sixteenth-century instruments.

72. See *Martin 1996*, 87.

73. *Parthenia* is famous not only because it is the first example of printed music in England, but also because it is a repository of the keyboard works of William Byrd, John Bull, and Orlando Gibbons. It was soon followed by another publication, *Parthenia In-Violata*, for keyboard and bass gamba.

74. It is likely, however, that an instrument like this is the one Shakespeare had in mind in *Sonnet 128*, in which a gentleman expresses his envy for the intimate contact between his lady's hands and her virginal.

75. See *Boalch III*, 693–94. We have one tantalizing reference indicating that sixteenth-century English instruments were found overseas, in the 1566 inventory of the Augsburg collector Raymund Fugger, Jr. (1528–68). One of the items refers to a harpsichord "covered with black leather" from England. See *Smith 1980*, 40.

76. *Boalch III*, 191, offers "Theeuwes" as the preferred spelling, but John Koster, private communication, suggests that is a rare spelling of the name. On the instrument it is spelled "Theewes," and in the Antwerp archives the usual form was "Theeus." The spelling "Theewes" seems to have been adopted by early keyboard scholars in the last few years.

77. See *Koster 1980*, 48. Koster believes that the real number may have been several times this.

78. Malcolm Rose (private communication), who has examined the Theewes closely and most recently, is fairly convinced that it met its demise by being flooded. Water probably lay on the soundboard for at least several hours, soaking off the bridges and dissolving the soundboard painting. Rose thus sees the Theewes as a time capsule, halted in its tracks, rather than representing the more usual series of alterations.

79. *Koster 1980* suggests that the lowest C♯ could have been tuned down to AA, since con-

trary to Continental practice, that note, as well as the bass notes F♯ and G♯, were not infrequently called for in English music of the time.

80. *Koster 1980* proposes solutions to many of the questions raised by this instrument. *McGeary 1973* is another article that should be consulted for information about early English building styles. McGeary points out that the Theewes harpsichord was built in the same year that Hans Ruckers was admitted to the Guild of St. Luke; hence, the building practices that Theewes brought with him to London were pre-Ruckers. *Barry 1990*, also required reading for this instrument, describes the organ portion of the combination as well.

81. Malcolm Rose is "90 percent certain" that the harpsichord and organ were not constructed simultaneously; nevertheless, Theewes certainly could have known the projected dimensions of the yet unbuilt organ case.

82. See *Koster 1980*, 53.

83. See *Koster 1980*, 50.

84. *Barry 1990*, 9, is of the opinion that Northern harpsichords with arpichordum registers must have been common before the seventeenth century.

85. *Hubbard 1965*, 133.

86. *Koster 1980*, 65–66.

87. *Koster Forthcoming*, 20–21.

3. ANTWERP HARPSICHORD BUILDING BETWEEN KAREST AND RUCKERS

1. Antwerp, the artistic center of the "Flemish school," was in Brabant, not Flanders, and "Southern Netherlands" would be the correct way to designate that school. Nevertheless, the term "Flemish school" has become deeply entrenched in our thinking and is used here in the traditional, broad, cultural sense, rather than with any historical or geographical accuracy.

2. Bruges had been an important seaport since its founding in the ninth century, but by 1490 its inlet from the North Sea had completely silted up, and the port could no longer be used for major shipping.

3. Many of the Jewish diamond merchants and cutters expelled from Spain and Portugal in the 1490s settled in Antwerp. The diamond industry is still an important part of that city's economy.

4. According to *Hubbard 1965*, 44, who believed there may well have been others.

5. *O'Brien 1990*, 13. Luke was the patron saint of painters.

6. *Lambrechts-Douillez 1977*, 41, notes that in inventories of that time harpsichords were more likely to be identified by the names of the artists who created the lid paintings than by the builders who made the instruments.

7. Translations of the text of the Guild document can be found in *Russell 1959/1973*, 146–48, and in *O'Brien 1990*, 300–301.

8. There was considerable building going on in the Dutch Republic, as shown by *Curtis* and *Gierveld*.

9. *Van Roey* is a short but informative article on the rise and fall of Antwerp. It includes the reproduction of an anonymous painting depicting the Spanish Fury, which is also reproduced in color on p. 136.

10. See *Hubbard 1965*, 44. Goosens was listed in Guild records as an apprentice painter in 1519. Hubbard mistakenly assumed that he was an apprentice harpsichord maker. Actually, he was, but not until 1537, when for some reason he decided to change careers (but not guilds).

11. *O'Brien 1990*, 14–15, describes this somewhat bizarre situation in considerably more detail. A translation of the contract is on pp. 299–300.

12. For more detailed descriptions of this intriguing instrument see *Schott*, 26–28, *O'Brien 1990*, 26, and *Koster Forthcoming*, 83–85.

13. *Koster Forthcoming*, 85, says, "Thus, the 'Duke of Cleves' virginal, containing elements both of the later practice followed by Bos, van der Biest, and, eventually, the Ruckers, and of an earlier practice [the Karest virginals], would serve as a Rosetta stone for interpreting the unknown from the known." He also discusses this instrument in *Koster 1998a*.

14. *O'Brien 1990*, 26, suggests that it probably sounded a tone above normal pitch. *Koster Forthcoming*, 84–85, disagrees and argues that it was likely tuned to normal pitch.

15. See *Koster Forthcoming*, 83–85.

16. The present keyboard has a compass of A–f³, but it is not original.

17. Some seventeenth-century German virginals had centered keyboards. Two examples are an anonymous polygonal virginal from the first half of the seventeenth century (Salzburg, Museum Carolino Augusteum), and an anonymous South German oblong virginal from ca. 1600 (Berlin, Staatliches Institut für Musikforschung). Nevertheless, their left-hand bridges, and hence their plucking points, are fairly close to their jacks.

18. Information about this engraving is taken from *Ripin 1977*, 70, 74 (n. 14), and plate 58.

19. *Ripin 1970a*, 15.

20. The Italians, on the other hand, would not begin to surrender the thin-case polygonal design for another century.

21. *Kenyon de Pascual 1992*, 629, n. 37, observes that this instrument "has been variously dated as 1570, 1572, 1578 and 1579." *Koster Forthcoming*, 74, dates it at 1578. Bos had a son, Hans Bos, Jr., a builder not listed in *Boalch III* but mentioned in *Lambrechts-Douillez and Bosschaerts-Eykens 1987*.

22. Bos must have been fairly well known, since *Praetorius*, 16, calls him an excellent builder.

23. *Ripin 1970a*, 15–16. *Koster Forthcoming*, 74–77, goes into some detail about the longer scaling.

24. In the decorative arts, the word "grotesques" does not refer to things misshapen or ugly, but to a style of design that had its beginnings in the late fifteenth century, derived from motifs found in Roman grottos. The dolphin is one of those motifs.

25. Some of the papers have linear interlacing patterns whose origins are found in Islamic decoration. Another common pattern was interwoven vines, which likely derived from early Renaissance manuscript illumination.

26. I thank Sheridan Germann for this term.

27. Only a handful of virginals are graced with courtly pastoral paintings, and all of them were built in the sixteenth century. In addition to the ones to be discussed in this chapter, there is a 1583 Hans Ruckers spinett (Paris, Musée de la Musique) at quint pitch. Another is a muselar mother whose child is missing (Lisbon, Museu da Música). It has been dated 1620 and attributed to Hans Ruckers, but this is patently impossible since the master died just before the turn of the century. *O'Brien 1990*, 278–79, believes the instrument to be Flemish, but not a Ruckers, and dates it from 1570–90 on the basis of the lid painting. The last is an undated spinett mother and child by Ioannes Ruckers (Milan, Museo degli Strumenti Musicali) — coincidently, aside from the van der Biest, the only extant Flemish mother and child in spinett form. Some of the instrument's decorative features are discussed in *Bonza and O'Brien*.

28. A color photo of the Bos virginal appears in *Kenyon de Pascual 1992*, 618. A black-and-white view of the soundboard can be seen in *Boalch II*, plate 25.

29. *Kenyon de Pascual 1992*, 617.

30. Grouwels's son, also Lodewijck (fl. 1593–1600), was a builder, and a 1600 mother and child spinett virginal of his (New York, Metropolitan Museum of Art) survives. It is another of that handful of virginals with a courtly pastoral painted on the lid. The virginal is described by *Koster 1977*, 84–86, and is pictured in *Rueger*, plate 21. *Pollens 1998*, 165, notes that the child was made by Arnold Dolmetsch in 1896, to replace the lost original.

31. The same is true of the 1600 virginal made by his son Lodewijck.

32. César Snoeck, the Belgian collector from whom the instrument was acquired, attributed the painting to Peter Bruegel the Elder, but that seems unlikely since Bruegel died in 1569. Of course, the lid painting may have been copied from an earlier Bruegel work.

33. *O'Brien 1990*, 29, notes that while the three roses differ from each other, the mother's smaller rose is identical to the one in the Grouwels virginal, indicating that at least some makers bought geometric roses from a common supplier.

34. *O'Brien 1990*, 165, thinks both these paintings were likely done by the same hand. They are indeed similar in style. The van der Biest also has a painting on its front flap, but it was done later.

35. In fact, this instrument has been recorded by the Germanisches Nationalmuseum, and even after four centuries it is capable of making beautiful music.

36. Sheridan Germann, private communication, has suggested that the mother and child combination might literally have been intended to be played by a mother and her child. The child could remove the virginal from its compartment, take it to another room to practice, and return it to the mother when prepared to play the duet.

37. *Praetorius*, 62, suggests that it was the practice to place octave virginals on top of larger instruments. He is undoubtedly describing the simple expedient of putting 4′ and 8′ registers at the disposal of the player by placing a smaller instrument atop a larger. While it could be contended that the idea of combining 8′ and 4′ virginals was not unknown (after all, the model of the harpsichord, which combined both 8′ and 4′ in one instrument, was near to hand), apparently it was the Flemish who thought of creating a compartment in which to park the child, and the clever idea of arranging things so that the jacks of the mother could be used as coupler dogs to push up the ends of the smaller instrument's keys.

38. It is famous not only as the earliest surviving Ruckers virginal, but also because it was supposedly a gift from Philip II of Spain to a Peruvian noblewoman known as "Daughter of the Incas"; see *Libin 1989*, 14–15. The virginal is the subject of an entire article in *Libin 1998a*, and *Pollens 1998*, 136 ff., describes it in detail. Although badly damaged by woodworms, it is otherwise in excellent condition. *Pollens 1995*, 144–45, believes that some of the repairs to the virginal were made while it was in Peru.

39. It was not until 1699 that we see the name *muselar*, used in *Douwes*, 105, a treatise by the Dutch organist, teacher, and amateur builder Klaas Douwes (ca. 1650–ca. 1725). The anonymous, childless, mother and child muselar mentioned earlier (Lisbon, Museu da Música), though signed "Hans Ruckers, 1620," is thought to be Flemish, but not by Ruckers, and because of its decoration, considerably earlier than 1620. It might well date from around the same time as the Ruckers 1581 and could even be a bit earlier.

40. *Koster Forthcoming*, 79, and *Koster 1998c*, 90, view the implications of this dual scaling as another Rosetta stone, "that is, a document in

which the same meaning (in this case, the same pitch level) is embodied in two different languages (in this case, the contrasting practices of using strings that are long and thin or short and thick)."

41. *Koster Forthcoming*, 78.

42. *O'Brien 1990*, 62–66. Nevertheless, based on the same data, O'Brien and Koster reach different values for the pitch level of Ruckers harpsichords and virginals. *O'Brien 1990*, 62, concludes that normal Ruckers pitch was approximately a semitone below our modern standard, a = 440 Hz. *Koster Forthcoming*, 65, arrives at a pitch of two semitones below 440.

43. Moermons had a son, Hans the Younger (fl. 1642), who is survived by a 1642 double (London, private ownership).

44. *O'Brien 1990*, 29–32. *Boalch II*, 134, says it is "probably by Joannes [Hans] Ruckers." Since it is now classified as anonymous, *Boalch III* does not list it at all. *O'Brien 1998*, 49–52, discusses it in detail.

45. A ca. 1618 painting, *Allegory of Hearing*, by Jan Bruegel the Elder (Madrid, Prado Museum), shows a two-manual Flemish harpsichord with three registers. *Ripin 1968* discusses such instruments. The implications of the four-register non-aligned double will be considered in Chapter 5.

46. *Koster 1982*, 49, notes that the keyboards, jacks, bridges, and soundboard have been replaced. *O'Brien 1990*, 32–33, also discusses this instrument.

47. *Hubbard 1965*, 63, mistakenly thought that the 4′ was extremely rare in Italy; on the contrary, it was found there on the earliest surviving instruments, and sixteenth-century Italian harpsichords routinely included it.

4. EARLY ITALIAN STYLE

1. Leonardo was trained as a painter, goldsmith, sculptor, engineer, and musician. He left Florence for Milan and Mantua, returned to it in 1500 as a military engineer and friend of Machiavelli, and found time to paint the *Mona Lisa* before leaving again in 1506.

2. Michelangelo was raised in Florence, carved his *David* there in 1500, and worked on other projects between the times he was in Rome, to which Pope Julius summoned him to paint the ceiling of the Sistine Chapel.

3. See *Wraight 1986*.

4. See *Wraight 1997*, part I, 14 and 154. In *Part II: Catalogue of the Instruments* of this dissertation, Wraight catalogs nearly all the surviving Italian harpsichords, both signed and unsigned. The dissertation has been published by University Microfilms, Ann Arbor, Mich. (UMI no. 9735109). Much of our current information on Italian harpsichords comes from Wraight's research, and his work is much appreciated and highly valued.

5. According to *NGEKI*, 10.

6. *Boalch III*, 704–8.

7. *Boalch III*, 46. The name of Giles de Rouais of Tournai appears in a Burgundian account of 1385, noting that he was paid 12 francs for an *eschequir*.

8. Queen Elizabeth's anonymous, ca. 1570 virginal (London, Victoria and Albert Museum) was made in Italy.

9. The last known sixteenth-century Italian harpsichord with a 1×8′, 1×4′ disposition was built in 1628 by the Roman builder Orazio Albana (Bologna, Museo Civico); cited in *Koster 1994*, 12, n. 21; see also *Wraight 1984a*. Later builders occasionally made harpsichords with a 4′ register, but invariably added it to a 2×8′ disposition.

10. It was *Hubbard 1965*, 20, who named this style of case construction "false inner-outer." The earliest known Italian false inner-outer instrument is a 1587 virginal by Giovanni Celestini (fl. 1587–1610) of Venice (Hamburg, private collection). Celestini's next extant virginal, a 1589 (The Hague, Gemeentemuseum), is also a false inner-outer. These instruments are cited in *Koster 1994*, 12, n. 29.

11. See *Boalch III*, 190. In the "Geographical and Chronological Conspectus of Makers," 691–713, Boalch lists the names of at least thirteen makers who were born before 1500.

12. See *Boalch III*, 190.

13. *NGEKI*, 9. This date is, of course, conjectural; but the intarsia does show a type of instrument that no longer exists.

14. *NGEKI*, 10, interprets the admittedly crude representation of the bentside's cap molding as implying a thick case construction without cap moldings.

15. See *Virdung*, 126. F–a², a common range at the end of the fifteenth century, was subsequently expanded upwards to f³. *Wraight 1986*, 536, reports that an "F" short octave could be found at this time, where the lowest key was divided front and back into F and G. For a detailed discussion of the short octave in early Italian instruments see *Wraight 1990*.

16. The intarsia shows a row of jacks under the jackrail, but there does not appear to be a guide of any sort. Either one existed and the artist overlooked it, or the soundboard projected across the gap with slots for the jacks, as in the Müller harpsichord, or the jacks were the pivoting type described by Arnaut.

17. *NGEKI*, 10.

18. Both the Genoa and Vatican intarsias are depicted and discussed in *Winternitz*, 118–19, plates 30a, 51b.

19. See *Ripin 1977*, plate 57. This instrument was also discussed in Chapter 2.

20. *NGEKI*, 113, is also of this opinion, but limits it to Italian virginals.

21. *Hubbard 1965*, 22. Filippo Brunelleschi (1377–1446) was the renowned Florentine architect who designed and built the dome for the Cathedral of Santa Maria del Fiore, a marvelous engineering feat and one of the great landmarks of Florence.

22. The relatively stiff cypress holds the details of fine molding with great sharpness.

23. For a listing and description of some of these see *Hellwig 1977*, 30. Notice that Hellwig adds another instrument to his list in his first note (36). Hellwig's anonyme in Bristol has since been authenticated by Denzil Wraight as by Giovanni Battista Boni; see *Wraight 1997*, part II, 83. A third 1×8′ Boni is in Miami's Dade County Museum. Another instrument, described in *Libin and Shanks*, adds yet one more single-strung Italian to the list, at the comparatively late date of 1704. The definitive list is in *Wraight 1997*, part I, 158.

24. See *Wraight 1997*, part I, 158.

25. *Koster 1994*, 21, n. 17, identifies some works that utilize the notes above c^3. He also observes that the extended range would surely have been used in improvisation. *Wraight 1997*, part I, 311–16, discusses this compass at length, particularly in reference to improvisation.

26. We cannot always be absolutely sure about this, since the positions of registers and jacks can easily be moved and exchanged.

27. An anonymous ca. 1550 1×8′, 1×4′ Neapolitan harpsichord (Boston, Museum of Fine Arts) has a maple case and soundboard; see *Koster 1994*, 3–15.

28. Two examples are the 1515 Vincentius Livigimeno and the 1521 Hieronymus Bononiensis, both mentioned earlier.

29. Like the 1537 Müller's rose, the 1515–16 Vincentius's is carved into the soundboard. Although not unheard of—lute roses were normally done in this way—it is extremely rare in harpsichords.

30. I believe the wedding-cake simile was first given voice by *Germann 1978a*, cf. 57.

31. *Wraight 1992a*, 82–83.

32. See *Russell 1959/1973*, 127, cited in *Wraight 1992a*, 82, n. 51.

33. For more information on instruments with pulldowns and independent pedal divisions, see *Ford 1997*.

34. *Wraight 1986*, 535.

35. See *Howell 1979–80*. Paulirinus's encyclopedia is now part of a manuscript in Kraków, Uniwersytet Jagielloński, Biblioteka Jagiellońska, Codex 257.

36. *Virdung*, 127.

37. "Clavecin à un clavier . . . avec un clavecin de pedalle"; cited in *Hubbard 1965*, 108–9. *Hubbard 1965*, 110, describes the pedalboard harpsichord as "elusive as the shy unicorn and possessed of the same menacing charm."

38. *Hubbard 1965*, 111, 315, found this information in documents in the *Archives Nationales, Minuitier Central*.

39. *Adlung 1758*, 556, cited in *Hubbard 1965*, 270–71.

40. Germany preferred to apply pedals to the clavichord, and some were made with separate pedal divisions: a 1760 instrument by the Saxon David Gerstenberg (1716–96) consists of two clavichords (the second in a drawer beneath the first) sitting on a long pedal clavichord (Leipzig, Musikinstrumenten-Museum der Universität Leipzig).

41. *Adlung 1768*, vol. 2, 161, cited in *Hubbard 1965*, 272.

42. The modern Italian term is *virginale*.

43. According to *Wraight 1992a*, 80.

44. *Burney 1771*, 288.

45. A 1×8′ could be converted to a 2×8′ with the addition of another set of strings, bridge and nut pins, wrestpins, and jacks. Another box guide would be required, and the gap would have to be widened to make room for it.

46. Most 1×8′ instruments had short scales and are presumed to have been strung in brass to sound at normal pitch. Virginals are presumed to have been strung in iron at normal pitch. These are presumptions.

47. See *O'Brien 1990*, 18–19; and *Wraight 1986*, 537.

48. See *Koster 1994*, 11, n. 17. Although Koster has stated his views in several places, perhaps the most compelling review of the evidence for assuming brass stringing and a concomitant low pitch for sixteenth-century Italians, as well as a summary of the pertinent literature, is found here. Koster cites evidence that at least some early Italians sounded a fourth lower. One example is a document from ca. 1630 describing a harpsichord by Guido Trasuntino as sounding a fourth lower than normal pitch. In another context, *Wraight 1988a* identifies some other long-scaled low-pitched Italian instruments: a 1574 Giovanni Baffo (London, Victoria and Albert Museum), a 1579 Baffo (Paris, Musée de la Musique), and a 1561 Franciscus Patavinus (Munich, Deutsches Museum). *Koster 1981* observes that the wrestpins of the Patavinus had been gilded, and suggests that since the visual aspect of the pins was considered to be so important, only brass strings could appropriately be wound on them. Koster also reports that the present compass of the Patavinus is GG/BB–c^3, but assumes that like almost all sixteenth-century Italian harpsichords, originally it would have been C/E–f^3. If this is the case, and if the instrument were strung in brass, it would have sounded somewhere very close to 16′ pitch. That Italian instruments at this pitch level were

not unprecedented, says Koster, is confirmed by a reference to a "harpsichord at the bass octave" found in a 1598 inventory of the Este family (cited in *Van der Straeten*, vol. 6, 122). Wraight deals with low-pitched instruments again in *Wraight 1997*, part I, 52–76, 235–36, 317–22, and concludes that iron and brass were used in the sixteenth century and brass in the seventeenth.

David Sutherland (private communication) is of the opinion that either iron stringing at higher pitches, or brass string at lower, were both possible and probably both employed in the sixteenth century, depending on the effect desired. He further notes that the wide C/E–f^3 keyboard made it possible to transpose freely up and down an octave. For example, higher notes could be useful in echo pieces.

49. See, for example, a review of a recording of Frescobaldi's music on an Italian harpsichord pitched a fourth lower than normal in *Tyre*, and an essay on Palestrina performance in *Dixon*. On the other hand, *Wraight 1997*, part I, 257, is not convinced.

50. See *Koster 1994*, 19. Koster defends this view by reasoning that the short bass strings of virginals would be too slack if they were forced by an all-brass stringing to sound lower pitches.

51. *Shortridge 1960*.

52. *Barnes 1965*.

53. *Thomas and Rhodes 1967*.

54. *Barnes 1973*.

55. *Koster 1994*, 11, n. 18, reports that sixteenth-century Italian scales ranged from 275 mm. (11″) to 424 mm. (16.7″). He concludes that stringing practice remained standard—that is, strings were calculated to be drawn up to near their breaking points—and pitch standards varied with the scale. This issue is far more complex than stated here; it is summarized at some length in *Wraight 1997*, part I, 14–20. It is also dealt with in *Wraight 2000*, required reading for anyone interested in stringing problems.

56. *Wraight 1997*, part I, 260–94.

57. *Barnes 1977*. It was almost literally when writing this note that I received word of John Barnes's untimely death.

58. *Hubbard 1965*, 3.

59. *Russell 1959/1973*, 31.

60. *Wraight 1992a*, 62, notes that he knows of no unaltered sixteenth-century Italian harpsichords. However, he also reports that most virginals from this period have not been modified.

61. *Hullmandel*, 286b, cited in *Hubbard 1965*, 1.

62. Mottoes are found on Italian instruments, too, but not often.

63. These themes are not limited to Italian instruments, and can be found on lids in all regional styles.

64. See *Victoria and Albert*, 32. Schott reports

that it was Sheridan Germann who discovered that the immediate source for the painting was an engraving by Giorgio Ghisi, whose model was a ca. 1550 painting by the minor artist Luca Penni, who in turn had copied it from Raphael's ca. 1511 "Parnassus."

65. The Battle of Lepanto is immortalized on the lid of at least one string keyboard instrument—a four-octave fretted clavichord, probably Italian in origin (Paris, Musée de la Musique). One would think that a naval battle involving almost five hundred ships would be too much for the lid of a small clavichord. It is indeed a rather busy painting. Cervantes, the author of *Don Quixote,* lost the use of his left arm in that battle.

66. Nevertheless, by this time the seeds of its decline had already been sown. Its trade with Greece, Turkey, Syria, Lebanon, and other countries on the eastern shore of the Mediterranean had been reduced ever since 1453, when Constantinople fell to the Turks. Its position as east-west broker was also dealt a heavy blow in 1488, when the Portuguese discovered that the Far East could be reached by an alternate, all-water route, by sailing around Africa's Cape of Good Hope.

67. See *Karpiak*. One of the few Western scholars to see this instrument in modern times, Karpiak believes it was probably made by Brunetto dalli Organi of Verona. Only one Bernardus harpsichord exists (London, private collection), and it appears to be genuine.

68. *Wraight 1997*, part II, 300, disputes this date, and prefers 1573 or 1574.

69. Some sixteenth-century Italian paintings show harpsichords partially pulled from their outer cases, and there are some instruments in which the external decoration extends only as far as the cheek—in other words, only the part that would show when partially withdrawn. Other paintings show inner instruments on tables, entirely withdrawn from their outer cases. Hence, there is a strong suggestion that these practices were carried on at least on occasion; but whether this was done simply to reveal the decoration, or because of supposed acoustical considerations, is unknown. It is commonly held that freeing an inner from its outer allows its bottom to vibrate more freely. While this may be so, *Kottick 1985*, 64, suggests that it makes little difference either way in terms of radiated sound.

70. *Boalch III*, 663, asserts that the 1560 was originally a 2×8′, later changed to a 1×8′, 1×4′. Actually, the reverse is true: telltale marks of the 4′ can still be seen on the soundboard. Boalch also states that the 1571 has no 4′ bridge, deducing that its original disposition was 1×8′, or 2×8′. But the instrument does have a 4′ bridge (and nut), and the location of the rose makes it clear that it was originally built in this way.

71. The staff at the Germanisches National-

museum in Nuremberg restored this instrument for the Museo Civico in the 1980s and made a copy, which is kept in the museum.

72. Quarter-comma meantone temperament was first described in 1523 by the Italian theorist Pietro Aron, in his treatise *Toscanello*. *Wraight 1997*, part I, 267–72, offers convincing evidence that at least some organs and clavichords were tuned in third-comma meantone, and it is possible that this temperament may have been used on harpsichords as well.

73. It is commonly but incorrectly held that Renaissance music employs *keys*, a term implying tonal and functional relationships not existing in that music. However, a piece can be assigned a *tonality*, and the distinction between being in the *key* of F and in an F *tonality* is not a small one. Hence, the oft-repeated statement that meantone temperament "works" in keys with up to two flats or three sharps, although true, is misleading for Renaissance and early Baroque music. On the other hand, meantone temperament lingered on in the provinces long after it had outlived it usefulness. Many small Italian churches, for example, lacked the resources to convert their organs to one of the new eighteenth-century revolving temperaments.

74. *Wraight and Stembridge*, 155, hypothesize that the earliest Italian split-key harpsichord is an ornate anonyme (Berlin, Kunstgewerbe Musem, Schloss Köpenick), built perhaps as early as 1559 and possibly even earlier.

75. Often, however, the extra notes were omitted in the highest octave, perhaps because rapidly moving treble figuration would tend to mask the tuning discrepancy.

76. I thank David Sutherland for this insight.

77. See *Stembridge 1992* and *Stembridge 1993*. These articles, along with *Wraight and Stembridge*, are compulsory reading for anyone interested in keyboards with split sharps.

78. *Praetorius*, 64–66, reports seeing a harpsichord with nineteen notes per octave in Prague, owned by the court composer Carl Luyton. Evidently the instrument was also transposable through three whole tones, prompting Praetorius to call it an "Instrumentum Perfectum."

79. See *Stembridge 1992*.

80. Evidently, Vicentino was able to have an *arcicembalo* built for him, or perhaps he even built it himself, since one was seen in Ferrara by Scipione Stella, a Neapolitan musician in the service of Gesualdo, who traveled there in 1594 with the prince for the latter's marriage to Eleanor d'Este. Returning to Naples, Stella collaborated with a mathematician, Fabio Colonna, to produce what they called a *sambuca lincea*, a thirty-one-note-per-octave instrument shaped like a harpsichord but with a clavichord-like action. Unfortunately, that instrument no longer exists, but several pieces written for it by Colonna and Mayone are extant. See *Martin 1984* for more information and for transcriptions of some of Mayone's pieces.

81. For an English translation of Vicentino's treatise see *Kaufmann 1966*, 165–72. For an article dealing with the practical aspects of Vicentino's proposed instrument see *Tiella*.

82. See *Kaufmann 1970*.

83. *Deutsches Museum*, 70, notes that the roses themselves are replacements.

84. An anonymous ca. 1620 Italian instrument (Edinburgh, Russell Collection) literally has its wrestplank hollowed out under the nut. Much has been made of the role of the active soundboard veneer in front of the wrestplank, but it is unlikely that this section of the instrument contributes much to the radiated sound. More likely, the nut, which would vibrate more freely than on a normal wrestplank, acts to dissipate the sound of the instrument a little more quickly.

85. *Boalch III*, 227, lists two other extant Baffo harpsichords, a 1574 and a 1578 (both in private hands), and a 1570 virginal (Paris, Hotel de Cluny). But *NGEKI*, 248, states that only the 1574 and 1579 harpsichords and the virginal are authentic. *Wraight 1997*, part I, 55, casts some doubt on the authenticity of the 1579. *Boalch III*, 228–30, notes that an additional eight instruments were falsely attributed to him. Baffo was a popular man.

86. See the discussion in *Boalch III*, 47–48.

87. *NGEKI*, 15, believes that Dominicus Pisaurensis and Dominicus Venetus were one and the same, but *Boalch III*, 48, is not as sure. *Wraight 1997*, part II, 152, says they are not to be confused.

88. *Wraight 1992a*, 99–101. Wraight's monograph examines the moldings on Dominicus's instruments with great care. *Nixon*, 255–60, recites the attribution history of a "1590 Dominicus Pisaurensis" (Dublin, National Museum), first thought to have been built by Dominicus (whose name is on the instrument), then to Franciscus Brixiensis (whose name appears on the back of the nameboard), then to Gian Francesco Antegnati (who may have been the same person as Franciscus), then to Marco Jadra (who may not have been a builder at all, but a dealer handling the work of Franciscus). *Wraight 1997*, part II, 164, ascribes it to Franciscus.

89. See *Zarlino*, 140. The conventional assumption, repeated in *NGEKI*, 23, and elsewhere, is that Dominicus's harpsichord had nineteen notes to the octave. But *Stembridge 1993*, 46–54, citing the introduction to Martino Pesenti, *Correnti, gagliarde, e balletti diatonici, trasportati parte cromatici, e parte henarmonici . . . libro quarto*, op. 15 (Venice, 1645/46), demonstrates conclusively that the instrument almost certainly had twenty-four keys per octave. Pesenti also compared Dominicus's keyboard with a 1601 by Guido Tras-

untino containing twenty-eight divisions of the octave. *Wraight 1997*, part II, 141, believes this instrument was originally strung in brass.

90. It was not until much later, in 1671, that Ioseph Joannes Couchet would build the first Flemish 2×8′ harpsichord. Nevertheless, a 1652 instrument by Ioannes Couchet (his last extant) was originally a 2×8′.

91. *Boalch III*, 296, errs in calling this a polygonal virginal.

92. A mid-sixteenth-century virginal (Berlin, Staatliches Institut für Musikforschung) has an apparently bogus signature of Dominicus on the nameboard. However, by comparing moldings, Wraight ascertained that, although an attempt had been made to deceive by replacing the true nameboard with one on which Dominicus's name had been forged, the virginal actually was by that maker. The mysteries surrounding this maker will probably never be solved; nevertheless, he — or they — must have been among Venice's finest builders in the sixteenth century. See *Wraight 1992a*, 81–82; and *Wraight 1997*, part II, 101–24.

93. See *Wraight 1993*.

94. See *Wraight 1993*, 122.

95. *Wraight 1993*, 123, notes that the two Celestini instruments are not the only Italian harpsichords with S-shaped keys. Others include a ca. 1540 Bortolus (Naples, private ownership); an elaborate anonyme, probably sixteenth century (Berlin, Schloss Köpenick); another anonyme, probably seventeenth century (Budapest, Magyar Nemzeti Múzeum); and a 1695 Francesco Neri (Salzburg, Museum Carolino Augusteum). Another harpsichord, a 1614 Pasquino Querci (Berlin, Staatlisches Institut für Musikforschung), may have had S-shaped keys but was lost in World War II. A ca. 1599 harpsichord (Hamburg, private ownership), attributed to Celestini, also has S-shaped keys, but *Wraight 1997*, part II, 103, has not examined it and is reluctant to confirm that attribution. *Kukelka* was probably the first to notice S-shaped keys, on the Carolino Augusteum's 1695 Neri. Kukelka compared the Neri to the Budapest instrument but was not aware of the others with S-shaped keys. Kukelka opined that the purpose of close pairs might have been to provide alternate tunings of the meantone accidentals, but this argument is effectively countered by *Wraight 1997*, part II, 130 ff.

96. *Wraight 1993*, 133.

97. For further information see *Beurmann and Pilipszuk*. An English summary of this article is in *Das Musikinstrument* 40, no. 10 (October 1991), 66–68. *Beurmann 1990* is less accessible. All three articles repeat much the same information, but their pictures differ.

98. Actually, there is another, built by Bartolomeo Cristofori in 1693; but it is so different from these that it merits a later discussion on its own.

99. *Wraight 1993*, 133.

100. The half-recessed keyboard is considered to have been a specialty of Milanese virginals, but it is occasionally found on instruments built elsewhere.

101. See *Victoria and Albert*, 29–31, for further information. Although the instrument is anonymous, the decoration is so Venetian in style that it seems safe to ascribe its origin to that city.

102. Ebonized wood — pear or some similar wood treated and stained to look like ebony — was often called *ebano bastardo*.

103. Schott, *Victoria and Albert*, reports that in 1965 John Barnes found the name of Franciscus Brixiensis inscribed on the underside of the soundboard. *Boalch III*, 6, suggests that Brixiensis was really Gian Franco Antegnati, a member of a Brescian family of organ and virginal builders active from the fifteenth through the seventeenth centuries, but Schott finds little evidence to support that view, and neither does *Wraight 1997*, part II, 165. Whatever the origin of the instrument, there is no question that it came from the same area as the Floriani, that both may have been made by the same builder, and that both may have been decorated in the same shop. A kindred mystery of a kindred nature involves the 1571 Floriani, an anonymous virginal of ca. 1570 (Berlin, Staatliches Institut für Musikforschung), and a 1565 Marco Jadra (Moscow, Muzei Muzykal'noi Kul'tury imeni M. I. Glinki). On the basis of the similarity of the decoration, Berlin attributes its virginal to Floriani; but Berlin's instrument is even more similar to the 1565 Jadra. On the other hand, Jadra may not have been a builder at all, but a dealer. For more information on the Moscow virginal see *Karpiak*. These little mysteries are another reminder of the gaps in our knowledge of early Italian harpsichord building and decorating.

104. See *Boalch III*, 707–8.

105. One of these, dated 1571, is in private ownership and not generally known; see *Boalch III*, 547.

106. An exception, of course, is the 1568 Duke of Cleves virginal, but *Germann 1978a*, 59–60, notes that this "sculptural sense" is particularly Italian.

107. *Wraight 1992a*, 80, notes that seven-sided virginals were made only in Milan and Brescia. Six-sided virginals were also made there, as well as in Venice, but most virginals were pentagonal in shape.

108. *Nocerino 1998* provides some concentrated information about Naples and its builders. I thank John Koster for bringing this article to my attention.

109. According to *Koster 1994*, 13, n. 46, maple was also used occasionally in Florence and Rome as well.

110. Koster first reported on this tradition

in a paper, "A Distinctive Group of Sixteenth-Century Italian Stringed Keyboard Instruments," at a meeting of the American Musical Instrument Society in 1992 and describes it in print in *Koster 1994*, 9–10.

111. *Karl Marx University Clavichords*, 23–28. These two clavichords are also discussed in *Steiner* and *Wraight 1992a*, 63–76.

112. See *Koster 1995*. This is the earliest example we have of the unique Neapolitan manner of virginal making.

113. Described in *Koster 1994*, 3–15.

114. I thank John Koster for this information; see also *Nocerino 1998*.

115. *Hubbard 1965*, 22.

116. *Germann 1978a*, 105.

5. THE RUCKERS-COUCHET DYNASTY

1. There are about one hundred extant Ruckers and Couchet instruments and some 150 Kirkmans. No other builders even came close to that sort of survival rate.

2. *O'Brien 1990*, 6, estimates that Antwerp supported between fifteen and twenty harpsichord makers at that time.

3. *Praetorius*, 16, mentions Bos in connection with an attempt to describe English pitch, so he must have had some reputation; see *Koster Forthcoming*, 74.

4. Some builders, like Bos and van der Biest, chose to leave Antwerp because their Protestant affiliations made them second-class citizens. *Van der Meer 1998b*, 174, mentions a group of builders who moved out of Antwerp for this reason.

5. *O'Brien 1990*, 62–66, and *Koster 1998c*, 89 ff.; see also *Barry 1991*.

6. It is tempting to assume that less inharmonicity is good and no inharmonicity even better, but studies have shown that we prefer a certain amount of it in harpsichords, pianos, guitars, and other string instruments whose sounds are impulsively generated; see, e.g., *Fletcher, Blackham, and Stratton*.

7. One would think it would be simple for the Ruckers' competitors also to adopt heavier stringing. But *Lambrechts-Douillez 1973*, reporting on a document discovered in the Antwerp archives, notes that Hans allowed one of his workmen to build an instrument that Hans would pass off as his own and sell for a commission; but Hans insisted that the stringing be done according to his usual practice, so that the instrument could sound like one of his own. This may indicate that Hans considered his new stringing practices a competitive advantage.

8. Information on the Ruckers and Couchet families has been taken mainly from *O'Brien*

1990 and *Boalch III* (who in turn acknowledges his debt to *O'Brien 1990*). Both authors pay tribute to Jeannine Lambrechts-Douillez, one of the foremost scholars in Ruckers research. That tribute is offered here as well, particularly for the series of documentary studies, *Mededelingen van het Ruckers-Genootschap*, done with M. J. Bosschaerts-Eykens. *O'Brien 1979*, while containing most of the information that eventually appeared in his book on the Ruckers family, is a lovely article on the brothers.

9. *Van der Meer 1998b*, 175, notes that about a third of the Netherlands makers were of German origin.

10. One of the recorded witnesses at his wedding was Marten van der Biest, and although there is no direct evidence, there is some speculation that Hans apprenticed with that builder. *Ripin 1970a*, 15–16, examined the matter, concluding that "the identity of Hans Ruckers' master remains an open question."

11. One such appearance is in connection with a somewhat bizarre incident. It seems that some money was stolen from the wife of one of Hans Ruckers's workmen. Fearing to tell her husband, the wife borrowed funds from Ruckers's wife, but then would not (or could not) pay it back. Hans took the husband to court. The story is related in *Lambrechts-Douillez 1973*, 12. The workman in question, by the way, is the one mentioned in n. 7, who built an instrument for Hans.

12. Van der Biest is survived by his 1580 mother and child spinett virginal. However, a virginal bearing his name on the jackrail appears in a painting in the Hague, Gemeentemuseum. Bos and Grouwels are also survived by a single virginal each (see Chapter 3).

13. *Lambrechts-Douillez 1973*, reports that in 1585 Hans's shop was in the attic of his home. Not until 1597, the year before his death, did he move to larger quarters. Hence, during his productive career he did not have room for many benches, tools, jigs, and workmen and was probably not able to support a large output.

14. This association with organs was certainly not limited to the Ruckerses. Similar connections have been noted with almost all the harpsichord builders encountered so far, and indicates that the trades of organ and stringed keyboard building were closely related.

15. Because everyone seemed to be named Ioannes, these relationships are confusing. Even more befuddling is the variety of names used by the Ruckerses and those around them. To quote *Boalch III*, 160, "Hans, and his eldest son Ioannes, referred to themselves, and were referred to by others, by the different forms of the names Ioannes, Joannes, Johannes, Jan, Jean, and Hans." The second edition of Boalch referred to the father as Hans the elder and his first son as Hans the younger, but *O'Brien 1990* introduced the practice

of referring to them as Hans and Ioannes, a termi-nology adopted by *Boalch III* and this book.

16. Cited in *Stellfeld*, 32. Huyghens was the proud owner of a Couchet and was quick to point out that Louis XIV's harpsichordist, Jacques Champion de Chambonnières, also owned an in-strument by him.

17. Ioseph's affliction was officially recog-nized in 1694, the year in which he was admitted to a hospice where he spent the rest of his life; see *Lambrechts-Douillez and Bosschaerts-Eykens 1986*, 33–35.

18. *Lambrechts-Douillez 1998b*, 20, suggests that the precipitous decline in Antwerp harpsi-chord building had less to do with economics than that "the leaders died and the children were still too young." An epidemic of plague might also have been a contributing factor.

19. *O'Brien 1990*, 53.

20. Even the great piano builder Conrad Graf (1782–1851), who converted a ballroom into a factory, could claim a lifetime output of only about three thousand instruments.

21. *O'Brien 1990*, 53, based on his examina-tion of the instruments, holds that sharps and jacks were made by outside suppliers. *Schann 1985* goes so far as to suggest that most of the other harpsichord makers in Antwerp were kept busy making parts for the Ruckerses.

22. Other than some early examples, the oc-tave virginals are an exception.

23. *O'Brien 1990*, 73, maintains that the soundboard wood in all Ruckers instruments is *Picea abies*, possibly shipped in from the Alps or the Carpathian Mountains.

24. This is the point made in *Leonhardt*.

25. *Gierveld*, 117–18, tells of the hundreds of collections of popular tunes made by harpsichord teachers for the use of their students.

26. *Leppert*, 131, notes that "harpsichords ap-pear frequently in paintings whose settings are the homes of wealthy persons. . . . A harpsichord was both very expensive to buy and costly to main-tain. . . . Its presence in a scene denoted both wealth and musical taste."

27. There are tantalizing clues indicating that entire instruments, called *arpicordos* or *ar-pichordums*, were constructed with brays. *Virdung*, 103, describes an instrument that was like a vir-ginal and strung in gut, with brays; but he says it is a new instrument, and he has seen only one. *Praetorius*, 67, identifies an instrument he calls the "arpichordum" that had metal brays and pro-duced a harplike sound. The harpsichord made in 1579 by Lodewijk Theeuwes appears to have had an entire brayed register, while the mother of the Hans Ruckers 1581 mother and child has a split arpichordum stop, the only extant example of a muselar with the treble brayed, as well as the bass. Otherwise, there are no extant examples of an *arpicordo,* and such is the belief of *Neven.* On the other hand, *NGEKI,* 176–78, states that the similarity of *arpichordo* and *arpichordum* is only co-incidence, and that the former is simply a specific kind of virginal. Finally, in an inventory of the instruments of Henry VIII taken in 1547, there are references to "longe Virginalles made harpe fasshion." These may have been brayed instru-ments, although *Barry 1982* believes that both "longe Virginalles" and "harpe fasshion" would likely indicate only grand harpsichords. *Koster 1994*, 35, offers the suggestion that the effect of the arpichordum stop may have been more like that of a bagpipe, rather than a harp, and notes that *muselar* was a Flemish term for a bagpipe.

28. This point is eloquently made in *Koster 1977.*

29. *Van Blankenburg,* 142, cited in *O'Brien 1990*, 297. Van Blankenburg was a prominent musical figure in the Hague, where he settled in the 1680s. His inability to reconcile his admira-tion for Ruckers and Couchet harpsichords with what he considered their wrong-headed building practices has been noted many times.

30. *Reynvann,* cited in *O'Brien 1990*, 295–96.

31. *Douwes,* 104–24, writing at the end of the seventeenth century, described the virginals made by the Ruckerses and Couchets and identified only spinett and muselar versions. Also an ama-teur clavichord maker, Douwes is much quoted by historians of the harpsichord, even though he was writing almost a half century after the end of the Ruckers-Couchet dynasty.

32. *O'Brien 1990*, 36, notes that all the extant Ruckers virginals at a step above normal pitch (5-*voet*) are muselars; however 5-*voet* spinetts were made by other Antwerp builders, and he cites a 1636 spinett by Cornelius Hagaerts in the Rockox House Museum in Antwerp. O'Brien attributes this lacuna to the vicissitudes of time and assumes that the Ruckerses made them, too.

33. The *voet* was divided into smaller units called the *duim,* with 11 *duimen* to the *voet.* Inter-estingly, the *duim* is almost the equivalent of the modern inch. Readers interested in more infor-mation about the *duim* should consult appendix I in *O'Brien 1990*, 284–85. However, there is little question that these instruments were conceived by means of proportions, rather than with com-plex fractions of *duimen. Koster 1998d* deals with this subject, describing not only the proportional-ity of Flemish harpsichords, but also the means by which it was achieved. Koster also relates how the builders marked out the major components of the harpsichords on their bottom boards (41 ff.).

34. *Douwes,* 104, notes them as 6, 5, 4, 3, and 2½ *voeten.* For some reason he fails to identify the 4½-*voet* (quart) virginal. Only two of this size sur-

vive, a 1610 Andreas muselar (Boston, Museum of Fine Arts) and a 1629 Ioannes spinett (Brussels, Musée Instrumental), so it might have been one of the rarer types. *Koster 2000b*, 11, notes that the practice of making virginals in integral or half-integral numbers probably stemmed from the cabinetmaker's custom of making chests in such units. In some locations this ratio was a legal requirement.

35. *Douwes*, 104–5.

36. We also find the opposite condition. The 1628 Andreas muselar (Brussels, Musée Instrumental) is a childless mother.

37. Only one of the smaller octave virginals is extant, a 1610 Andreas, although it is of course likely that others were built.

38. See appendix VI in *O'Brien 1990*, 292–93.

39. Commerce between the Low Countries and England was extensive. All sorts of goods and materials were sent from Flanders to England, even illuminated Books of Hours made especially for the English trade.

40. See *Lambrechts-Douillez and Bosschaerts-Eykens 1986*, 24, 28. In 1656 Angela van den Brant, the widow of Ioannes Couchet, and Simon Haegerts, harpsichord builder, signed a contract in which the builder agreed to take Angela's son Petrus as an eight-year apprentice. A condition of the agreement was that Haegerts would have to supply a number of instruments (presumably to Angela), among them two sizes of harpsichords *in the English way* (my emphasis).

41. For a detailed account of this instrument see *Van der Meer 1965*. An octave harpsichord not by a Ruckers, but apparently Flemish, is in Lisbon, Museu da Música; see *Ripin 1970b* and *Pereira 1978*. All three writers think the instrument to be of Flemish origin. I examined it briefly in 1993 and also thought it Flemish: see *Kottick and Lucktenberg*, 180; but *O'Brien 1990*, 43, is not convinced and thinks it may be Italian. As always, O'Brien's opinions, more informed than most, are not to be taken lightly.

42. Almost all the extant Ruckers doubles have been rebuilt and their keyboards aligned. Only one still has its unaligned keyboards, a 1638 Ioannes (Edinburgh, Russell Collection). A 1637 Ioannes (Rome, Museo Nazionale degli Strumenti Musicali), whose keyboards were aligned in a rebuilding, has been restored to its unaligned state by John Barnes. See *Van der Meer 1966b*.

43. *Ripin 1950*, relying on iconographical evidence, assumed that Flemish builders were making doubles with contrasting keyboards, as well as with nonaligned, early in the seventeenth century. *Van der Meer 1977* comes to the same conclusion and surmises that the Ruckerses had been building aligned keyboards since about 1610, if not earlier. *O'Brien 1990*, 181, stating that "it seems likely that no aligned doubles were ever made by any member of the Ruckers family," disagrees with both scholars.

44. See *O'Brien 1990*, 181. Other than the fact of their present location, one might wonder why chromatic singles would go to England but chromatic doubles to France. *Koster 1982* takes exception to the theory, first expounded by O'Brien in his article in the *New Grove* (see *NGEKI*, 33), since most extant seventeenth-century French harpsichords had a GG/BB short octave, and French music written during that time does not require GG♯s or BB♭s. Koster repeats his objections in his review of *O'Brien 1990* in *Koster 1992*.

45. See *O'Brien 1998*, 55–57.

46. Hubbard used the term "transposing double" to characterize these instruments, and called later harpsichords with aligned keyboards "expressive doubles." The terms used in this book, nonaligned and aligned (or contrasting), make no judgments about the way instruments might have been used.

47. *O'Brien 1990*, 228, cites *Clark*, 7 ff. and 23 ff., as an excellent source for information on organ transposition.

48. However, it will be remembered that the anonymous ca. 1580 Flemish double (Brussels, Musée Instrumental, no. 2934) also had only three registers of jacks and was also assumed to have been 4', dogleg 8', 4'; so Ioannes's instrument may not have been unique in that respect.

49. See *O'Brien 1990*, 280, and *Boalch III*, 577. Koster's argument, from which I have drawn the ensuing description, is found in *Koster 2000a*. I thank Professor Koster for making a preprint of this paper available to me.

50. For more on non-Ruckers doubles see *Van der Meer 1998a*. As a result of his examination of this instrument, *Koster 2000a*, 133, proposes the addition of "non-simultaneous contrasting double" to the existing categories of "non-aligned" and "aligned (contrasting)" doubles.

51. This point is explored in *Koster 2000a*, 136–37.

52. The problem existed for only the E♭ and G♯ strings. The other accidentals were all tuned appropriately for both keyboards: C♯/F♯; F♯/B; G♯/C♯; and B♭/E♭.

53. See fig. 6 in *O'Brien 1998*, 57.

54. *Van Blankenburg*, 142, cited in *O'Brien 1990*, 197.

55. *Marcuse.*

56. *Russell 1959/1973*, 44–45.

57. *Hubbard 1965*, 63 ff.

58. *Meeùs 1980;* see also *Meeùs 1986.*

59. *Shann 1984. O'Brien 1990*, 41, is particularly unhappy with Shann's arguments; see also *Shann 1985.*

60. *Shortridge 1985*

61. *O'Brien 1990*, 227–29.

62. *Byers 1997* thoroughly rejects O'Brien's argument. When *O'Brien 1990*, 228, says, "A student or assistant taking these [choir] rehearsals would have found the Ruckers double-manual harpsichord . . . indispensable," Byers replies, "If your assistant director couldn't transpose down a fourth, you'd be more likely to beat him with a stick than to buy him a $20,000 harpsichord" (6).

63. *Meeùs 1998*.

64. *Koster 1998c*, 94.

65. *Van der Meer 1998a*, 100.

66. We know of a number of amateur builders of harpsichords and clavichords in historical times. The German organist and writer Jacob Adlung, a contemporary of Coenen's and one of the most famous amateur builders, was supposed to have made sixteen clavichords. Van Blankenburg, also an amateur builder, rebuilt a Ruckers instrument and wrote about the event in his *Elementa musica* (*Van Blankenburg*). But none of these instruments can be found, and Coenen may be the only one among them represented by a survivor.

67. Originally a 1×8′, 1×4′, the instrument was altered twice, the first time to a 2×8′, 1×4′. In 1768 Pascal Taskin rebuilt it into a double.

68. The standard reference work on harpsichord decoration is *Germann 1978a*. See also her article on decoration in the forthcoming *The Clavichord and Harpsichord,* vol. 2 of *Encyclopedia of Keyboard Instruments,* ed. Igor Kipnis and Robert Palmieri (New York: Garland Publishing), and her forthcoming monograph on harpsichord decoration, a volume of *The Historical Harpsichord,* ed. Howard Schott (New York: Pendragon Press). *O'Brien 1990,* 128–71, has an extensive chapter on the decoration of Ruckers instruments.

69. Papers were also used on seventeenth-century German, French, and English instruments, so their appearance on Flemish harpsichords and virginals can scarcely be considered unique.

70. *Bonza and O'Brien,* 322–23.

71. For an essay on how bog oak is harvested, seasoned, and worked, see *Downing*.

72. According to *Lambrechts-Douillez 1998b,* 15, the marbling on Ruckers harpsichord cases resembled marble from the village of Rochefort—the same marble used on Antwerp's city hall, built in 1561.

73. In an unexpected regard for aesthetic design, the Ruckerses seemed to make their strap-work cases about ½″ higher than the marbled cases; see *O'Brien 1990,* 90.

74. *Germann 1978a,* 70–71, was the first to identify the four painters who worked for the Ruckerses and Couchets. Their styles were suffi-ciently distinct that they can easily be differentiated by someone schooled in the decorative arts. The work of the earlier artists seems to be derived from early Renaissance manuscript illumination, or at least borrow many motifs from it; but with the later decorators the painting becomes somewhat freer and more naturalistic.

75. Some of the early Ruckers roses were made of papier-mâché, but they looked convincingly metallic when gilded.

76. Tulips were introduced into the Netherlands in 1593 and quickly became favored flowers. Rare at first, they were valuable treasures to their owners who sold their bulbs at high prices. From 1634–37, the period known as the "tulip mania" (or "tulipomania"), speculation in tulips got of out of hand, and rare bulbs went for (in today's terms) tens of thousands of dollars. The flower remained popular, even after its market crashed.

77. See *Hamel,* 232–57. *Germann 1978a,* 68, observes that the angels on the 1640 Andreas (New Haven, Yale University) resemble late-fifteenth-century manuscript illuminations in their stylized facial expressions and the draping of their robes.

78. *Germann 1978a,* 69, characterizes this proclivity as *horror vacui.*

79. No grand harpsichord lids prior to that time have survived, except for the Hans Ruckers combined harpsichord/virginal of 1594, and its lid painting is not original.

80. In 1637 no less a personage than England's Charles I ordered a Ruckers harpsichord. The instrument had a lid flap painted by Rubens, which doubled its price. See *Hubbard 1965,* 231, or *O'Brien 1990,* 304. For a more complete account of the transaction see *Woods.*

81. See *O'Brien 1990,* 131–33. Prior to ca. 1600, when they were printed in light brown, the papers more resembled wood grain. After that date they were more greenish, perhaps, as *O'Brien 1990,* 133, indicates, now meant to suggest watered silk.

82. *O'Brien 1990,* 166, identifies sixteen different mottoes found on Ruckers virginals and harpsichords. *McGeary 1981* presents all the mottoes to be found on historical harpsichords, with translations and discussions of their origins. The translations of the mottoes given here, as well as in the rest of this chapter, are McGeary's.

83. See *O'Brien 1990,* 155–56.

84. I am indebted to *McGeary 1980* for many of the ideas expressed in this paragraph.

85. *Moens* notes that in the sixteenth century, keyboard instruments in general and virginals in particular became associated with female virtues, as well as virtuousness, a connection that lasted well into the next century.

86. This was not a mere philosophical con-

cept. The great German astronomer (and astrologer) Johannes Kepler (1571–1630), who discovered the laws governing planetary motion, was convinced that the heavenly bodies were sounding a great celestial chord—the music of the spheres.

87. I thank *Germann 1978a*, 68–69, for these insights.

88. We assume that pre-1600 harpsichords were decorated in the same manner as virginals, but since there are virtually none extant, the statement must remain conjecture.

89. *O'Brien 1990*, 170.

90. *Biedermeier* was the name applied to a style of furniture design—and generally, to a bourgeois life style—in early-nineteenth-century Germany.

91. *Van Blankenburg*, 144, cited in *Gierveld*, 121, notes that most of the "Ruckers" instruments advertised for sale were actually by other builders. However, Koster (private communication) holds that van Blankenburg was really talking about makers who took Ruckers singles, rebuilt them into doubles, and sold them as "originals."

6. LATER ITALIAN STYLE

1. Caccini first defined this style in his collection of monodic solo songs and madrigals called *Le nuove musiche* (The New Music) (Florence, 1602).

2. According to *Wraight 1993*, 124–30.

3. *Wraight 1997*, part I, 154–57, discusses Italian compasses in detail.

4. Chromatic basses were infrequently seen in seventeenth-century Italy, although some keyboards avoided the short octave by beginning GG,AA,BB,C or something similar.

5. *Wraight 1992a*, 62, noted that he had "not yet found a single 16th-century Italian harpsichord which has not had its compass, scale, or disposition altered."

6. Although made in the eighteenth century, the three surviving grand harpsichords of Giuseppe Maria Goccini (one is an octave harpsichord, and all three are in a private collection in Bologna) have no bottom battens. A 1725 instrument in a private collection in London, by Franciscus de Paulinis, has no internal bracing at all. In *Zuckermann 1969b*, Wolfgang Zuckermann described his restoration of a 1689 harpsichord by Baptista Carenonus Salodiensis (location unknown) in which no internal bracing was evident. Finding that the case was not strong enough to take the tension of the strings, Zuckermann solved the problem by adding some knees; but one wonders about the instrument's original pitch.

7. *Boalch III*, 706–7.

8. *Boalch III*, 21 and 212, notes that much of our information on Boni and Zenti comes from *Barbieri* and *Hammond*.

9. *Hammond*, 40. The Barberini nephews are known to students of Italian Baroque art as world-class patrons, but clearly, their largesse was not limited to paintings.

10. A virginal dated 1617 with a chromatic keyboard and bearing Boni's name (Washington, D.C., Smithsonian Institution) had been considered authentic, but on the evidence of the moldings, *Wraight and Stembridge*, 152, assigned it to Francesco Poggio, and it is so reported in *Boalch III*, 251. But in *Wraight 1997*, part II, 75, Denzil Wraight reassigned the instrument, this time to Stefano Bolcioni.

11. The arrangement of the split naturals may also be GG, AA/BB♭, BB/C, or possibly AA, BB♭/BB, C/E♭; see *Wraight 1997*, part II, 83, and *Hellwig 1977*, 31–32.

12. *Ripin 1973* is a foundational study of Zenti, not only for the details of his life, but also for the physical evidence of moldings and fretsawn cheek pieces for purposes of authentication.

13. One of Zenti's perverse claims to fame is connected with an opera, *Il palazzo incantato* (The Enchanted Palace), a day-long extravaganza written for the 1642 Carnival season by Luigi Rossi (ca. 1597–1653) and produced by Cardinal Antonio Barberini. As part of the continuo group the opera called for two harpsichords *ottava bassa* (probably instruments descending to CC); but instead of Zenti getting the commission, it went to the otherwise unknown builder Alessandro Urbani. Zenti was relegated to making the stands.

14. See *Gai*, 6, cited in *Boalch III*, 213.

15. William Dowd ("Dowd's Law") maintained that no matter where a maker was trained, when he built elsewhere he worked in the local tradition. The University of Leipzig collection has a 2×8′ harpsichord bearing Zenti's name and the date 1683. Since it has been established that the builder died around 1666, either the date is incorrect or Zenti did not build it. Hubert Henkel, in *Karl Marx University Harpsichords*, 72, suggests that the date is really 1653 and was built when Zenti was in Stockholm. *Van der Meer 1997* lists Zenti as the builder of a 1668 2×8′, 1×4′ harpsichord (Paris, Musée de la Musique), but *Boalch III*, 688–89, expresses doubts about Zenti's authorship. Boalch calls it a "typical seventeenth-century Parisian double-manual harpsichord," so even if it is by Zenti, it is in the French, rather than the Italian, tradition. Italian 2×8′, 1×4′ harpsichords are extremely rare. *Wraight 1997*, part II, 319–20, is also doubtful.

16. *Wraight 1991* maintains that the harpsichord was originally a single-manual 2×8′ with a compass descending to CC. In *Henkel 1990*,

and again in *Deutsches Museum,* 77–81, Hubert Henkel holds that the instrument had originally been built with two manuals and three registers. Wraight also contends that about 20″ had been cut off the tail; if he is correct, the instrument would have been almost 10′ long. This is also disputed by Henkel.

17. According to Henkel, *Deutsches Museum,* 80.

18. *Hubbard 1965,* 25, n. 24, wonders if Zenti himself introduced the bentside spinet into France and England during his travels.

19. Even Wraight's method of comparing moldings and other decorative elements of known and unknown instruments cannot completely solve attribution problems. For example, Robert Greenberg, reporting his use of Wraight's techniques in *Greenberg 1993,* believed that an instrument he was restoring might have been by Giusti. Shortly after, however, he published a supplement to his report, *Greenberg 1995,* in which he stated that after conferring with Denzil Wraight he was no longer certain that Giusti was the builder. *Wraight 1997,* part II, 176, thinks it might have been made by Giusti, but will go no farther than that.

20. The Basil instrument is now a two manual, probably transformed by Franciolini; see *Wraight 1984b,* 20.

21. One of these, long thought to be anonymous (Vermillion, Shrine to Music Museum), has recently been ascribed to Ridolfi by John Koster on the basis of the similarity of its moldings to the other Ridolfi instruments, particularly the 1682 (New Haven, Yale Collection of Musical Instruments); see *Boalch III,* 541.

22. *Wraight 1997,* part II, 355–56, observes that the harpsichord must have been built between 1656 and 1676, since Todini claimed that he spent those years completing his *galleria. Pollens 1990* is a detailed article on the "golden harpsichord."

23. From the position of Galatea's arms and hands, it has been assumed that she was playing a lute, now missing. Even though she would have been playing the instrument left-handed, there is no reason to dispute this assumption, particularly since one of the figures on the bas-relief of the case is also playing a left-handed lute.

24. As Homer tells it in the *Odyssey,* Polyphemus was the giant cyclops blinded by Odysseus. Seeking food and water while returning home after the Trojan War, Odysseus and his men dropped anchor in an unknown land. Not far from shore they found a cave with provisions, to which they helped themselves. Soon, however, the cave's owner returned: it was Polyphemus, the one-eyed monster, who began eating Odysseus's men, one by one. Finally Odysseus drugged the

cyclops by plying him with wine, and while he was sleeping, drove a red-hot stake into his eye. With the cyclops blinded, the travelers were able to escape. Centuries later Polyphemus (his eye miraculously restored) fell in love with the beautiful sea nymph Galatea. She rejected the hideous and pitiful giant in no uncertain terms, and he spent his days singing love songs, hoping she would hear and take pity.

25. *Kircher,* 167–70.

26. *Todini,* cited in *Boalch III,* 776.

27. This combination is pictured in *Bonanni,* plate 33.

28. *Burney 1771,* 393. It is likely that Burney saw the machine that Todini described in his *Dichiarazione.*

29. *Todini.*

30. Cited in *Winternitz,* 113–14.

31. *Winternitz,* chapter 7, "The Golden Harpsichord and Todini's *Galleria Armonica.*"

32. *Boalch III,* 705, lists more than thirty Florentine builders who practiced in the seventeenth century.

33. *Wraight 1992a,* 128–32. All the Vincentius instruments have been authenticated by Wraight.

34. "Survive" is a relative term here. A 1614 harpsichord that was in Berlin survived for more than four hundred years, but it did not survive World War II.

35. See *Wraight 1997,* part II, 243–45.

36. *Hubbard 1965,* 270, quotes from *Sprengel,* 265, in which the author describes this sort of stop and identifies it as a *Cornettzug.* He noted that the stop "shortened the strings," but by the time of his writing had gone out of fashion.

37. Cited in *Boalch III,* 133.

38. These instruments are listed in Ferdinand's 1700 inventory; see *Gai,* 11 ff., cited in *Libin 1987,* 383.

39. This may be the Mondini previously known only through a notice in a 1988 sales catalog; see *Boalch III,* 510.

40. See *Libin 1987,* 378–79, for details.

41. Migliai may have had a tie to Cristofori: a 1702 inner-outer harpsichord (Leipzig, Musikinstrumenten-Museum der Universität Leipzig) has an incipient form of A-frame bracing, a construction adopted by Cristofori; see *Sutherland 1998–99,* 29, and *Schwarz.* Preprints of these two articles were made available to me by their authors, both scholars as well as builders. I very much appreciate their helpful assistance.

42. Some insight into this conservatism can be gleaned from *Chiesa.* Chiesa, who examined documents in the Milan city archives, tells of an otherwise unknown builder named Giovanni Antonio Brena who applied to the city for a patent for a transposing device he claims to have in-

vented. The state asked other builders for comments, and a number of them, including Annibale dei Rossi, claimed to have seen such devices elsewhere and recommended that the patent be refused. The patent was not issued; if it had, Brena would have been the only maker allowed to use this invention for the next ten years.

43. See *Russell Collection* 8–9; *Boalch III,* 248; and *Wraight 1997,* part II, 65–73. *O'Brien 2000* is an exhaustive study of the instrument, and a fascinating bit of detective work.

44. The sound of a virginal constructed in this manner will be somewhat different from the usual Italian, although not as much as might be expected. Acoustical tests have demonstrated that either one side or the other of a virginal's soundboard responds to a particular frequency (see *Kottick 1985,* 64). But deadening one side of the board creates an entirely different set of boundary conditions, and the vibrating portion of the board will respond to all normal modes.

45. See *Nocerino 1998,* 95–98, for documentary information on Guarracino. The article is full of information on Neapolitan builders and instruments.

46. The 1651 was signed by Guarracino, and the Berlin instrument has been tentatively assigned to him by Denzil Wraight. I thank both John Koster and Grant O'Brien for this information. O'Brien believes that several other unsigned harpsichords can be attributed to Guarracino.

47. See *Koster 1997.* The 1694 octave virginal is listed in neither *Boalch III* nor *Wraight 1997.* Koster, private communication, thinks it a genuine Guarracino.

48. John Koster, private communication, suggests that it might have been made by a builder coming between Fabri and Guarracino.

49. See *Nocerino 2000.*

50. *Boalch III* states that the compass is C/E–d³, and the picture of this instrument, plate 2 of *Russell 1959/1973,* indeed shows d³ as the highest note. However, when I saw the instrument, in the early 1990s, it ascended only to c³. The photo in *Russell* shows that the d³ touch plate was made by slicing the tail of the c³ down the middle (to make room for the c♯³) and using the discarded section as part of the d³. It also shows that the keyboard has a natural-wood end block in the bass, but not the treble. Clearly the instrument was returned to its original compass during its last restoration, which had taken place shortly before my visit. *Wraight 1997,* part II, 157, lists c³ as the top note.

51. Sgraffito is a technique whereby a solid material is incised and the scratches filled with color. Scrimshaw, the decoration of whale bone by this technique, is a particular form of sgraffito.

52. See *Wraight 1988b.*

53. See *Wraight 1992a,* and *Wraight 1997,* part II, 322–97. The latter is a catalog of anonymous Italian instruments.

54. *Wraight and Stembridge,* 159, note that split-sharp instruments appear to have come primarily from the shops of Poggio, Bolcioni, and Boni, between the years 1610 and 1640.

7. SEVENTEENTH-CENTURY INTERNATIONAL STYLE

1. The word "intermediate" will be used to describe the thickness of the sides of International-style harpsichords, implying bentside, cheek, and tail thicker than the thin sides of Italian inner-outers, but thinner than the heavy case walls of Flemish instruments. That same word will be used to describe scales, denoting a c² string length of more than 11″, but less than 14″. The word is not meant to suggest that International-style instruments represented an averaging, or combining, of Italian and Flemish practices.

2. The composer Michel Corrette (1709–95) made an interesting observation in *Corrette,* 82. Referring to seventeenth-century instruments, he noted that "When c³ is only five *pouces* it is necessary to string the harpsichord with yellow (i.e., brass) wire." Five *pouces* are about $5^{17}/_{64}$″, making c² slightly more than 10½″. Clearly, Corrette is saying that short-scaled instruments were strung in brass, and long-scaled in iron. The passage is cited in *Hubbard 1965,* 90, and *Koster 1994,* 44–45.

3. There are some extant 2×8′ seventeenth-century French harpsichords, such as the 1683 Nicholas Du Four (Vermillion, Shrine to Music Museum), all single-manual instruments. For more information see *Anderson.*

8. FRANCE

1. His other instruments were a clavichord and two virginals; cited in *Hubbard 1965,* 88. The inventory can be found in *Lesure,* 45–46.

2. *Mersenne,* 212.

3. *Boalch III,* 696–98.

4. See *Boalch III,* 695–98.

5. *Hubbard 1965,* 93–95, devotes nearly two pages to disputing Mersenne's "twenty-five folio pages of slippery ambiguities."

6. *Mersenne,* 155–56.

7. *Mersenne,* 155.

8. *Mersenne,* 155.

9. 1681 is an early date for cabriole legs, and it is possible that they may not be original with the instrument.

10. Material for this section is taken from *Hubbard 1965*, 84–86, and *Hunt 1998*.

11. *Hubbard 1965*, 89.

12. *Hubbard 1965*, 106, observes that an inventory was also taken at the death of Jacquet's son, Claude (1605–before 1675). It is clear that Claude also ran a three-man shop, and Hubbard wonders if the "three bad benches" mentioned in the inventory were the same ones noted in 1632.

13. *Hubbard 1965*, 86.

14. *Hubbard 1965*, 101–4, knew of only four seventeenth-century French harpsichords, all doubles (actually, he *described* only four, which he characterized as the "most representative specimens," suggesting that he knew of others as well). These were the 1652 Claude Jacquet, the 1678 or 1679 Desruisseaux, the 1679 Vincent Tibaut, and an anonymous instrument. This last, at one time thought to be German (see *Nobbs 1991*), has since been attributed to Claude Labrèche of Carpentras and dated 1699 (see *Anselm 1996d*, 228). Twenty years later *Scheibert*, 218, n. 16, mentioned that William Dowd reported to her that he knew of fifteen survivors, one of which was a single. Ten years after that *Koster 1994*, 44, reported twenty-five extant seventeenth-century French harpsichords. The latest inventory I have seen, in *Amselm 1996d*, 228, lists thirty-three known instruments, of which seven are singles. The Anselms also list an additional eleven instruments which, though built at the beginning of the eighteenth century, are seventeenth century in concept and style. Five of these, all constructed between 1700 and 1715, are *clavecins brisés*, or folding harpsichords, by Jean Marius. None of these lists include virginals and spinets, although I have been able to identify nine spinets and two octave spinets (but no virginals) from the late 1600s. With an average of seven or eight instruments coming to light each year over the last forty years, it is certainly possible that more harpsichords from this important school may yet appear.

15. Meaning "broken style." The name is modern. *Ledbetter* gives an excellent account of the relationship between lute and harpsichord music in seventeenth-century France.

16. The Denis dynasty is described in several places, notably in *Samoyault-Verlet*, 29–37; see also *Denis*, 5–6. Various members of the Denis family are discussed in *Hubbard 1965*, 84–132.

17. The 1674 is not in *Boalch III*, but is listed in *Anselm 1996d*, 228. The 1674 in *Boalch III*, 291, is misdated and misattributed to Pierre II: it is by Louis, and the correct date is 1658. *Thomas 1974*, 73, attributes it to Philippe, but *Koster 1994*, 45, n. 4, says that he examined the instrument and that Thomas misattributed it. It is correctly listed in *Anselm 1996d*. Parenthetically, Philippe is also known as an inventor, and in 1708 presented to the *Académie* his plans for a *vis-à-vis* harpsichord, with a keyboard at each end. See *Hubbard 1965*, 323.

18. See *Hunt 1998*.

19. Cited in *Hubbard 1965*, 225.

20. See *Denis* for a translation and commentary.

21. See *Denis*, 103–5.

22. See *Denis*, 106–7.

23. See *Denis*, 68.

24. *Mersenne*, 165. It is possible that Mersenne was referring to Ruckers two-manual harpsichord-virginal combinations. Such instruments do have three manuals.

25. See *Ledbetter*, 8–11.

26. *Jonckbloet and Land*, cxlix, cited in *Hubbard 1965*, 232–33.

27. Most of these harpsichords now have shove couplers, but they have been worked over and rebuilt so many times it is nearly impossible to know their original states.

28. This distinction of tone color would not be possible with adjacent 8' jacks. Their plucking points would be too close to make any but a negligible difference.

29. *Denis*, 69–70.

30. A two-manual 2×8', 1×4' harpsichord need not have the ability to couple keyboards in order to play *pièces croisées*. John Koster (private communication) suspects that some of the earliest French doubles were made without couplers. These harpsichords would likely have been thought of as combining a conventional 1×8', 1×4' instrument, as illustrated by *Mersenne*, with a separate 1×8' — the upper manual.

31. Manual couplers first appeared on French organs early in the sixteenth century; see *Dufourcq*, 47, cited in *Denis*, 70, n. 36.

32. John Koster (private communication) notes that there are several thick-case early French harpsichords extant: the 1648 and 1658 by Denis, and the 1652 Jacquet (Sarasota, N.Y., John and Mable Ringling Museum). This suggests that thick-case instruments might have been an earlier part of the International style.

33. The bottoms of the sides of the 1681 Vaudry are rabbeted, and the case bottom fits into these cuts. Hence, the bottom is attached in a way that combines sides that both overlap the bottom and sit on it. My thanks to harpsichord builder Owen J. Daly for pointing this out to me in a private communication.

34. At least, it is today's conventional wisdom that these instruments are not as powerful and complex in tone; but it should be remembered that thirty years ago we regarded the eighteenth-century French harpsichord as somewhat weak sounding.

35. The only identifiable member of the fam-

ily is Jean Antoine Vaudry (ca. 1680–1750). Obviously, he could not have made this 1681 harpsichord.

36. The story of the restoration is told in *Adlam 1976*. The ensuing description draws heavily on this article.

37. This bit of insight is gleaned from *Thomas 1974*, 73.

38. A 1683 single by Nicholas Du Four (Vermillion, Shrine to Music Museum) is braced by three "U"s, each made from three pieces of wood about 3″ square. This "post and beam" construction is found in a few other International-influenced instruments as well. There are also three thin upper braces, and two diagonal struts. Du Four was probably from Lyons, and perhaps related to the Lyonnaise builder Claude Du Four.

39. Owen J. Daly, private communication, suggests that the instrument was originally finished in natural walnut, with the chinoiserie coming later. His point is well worth consideration.

40. Twist-turned legs are quite common in International style, but they are rarely of this quality.

41. This is the conventional wisdom, although certainly the Duchesse Du Maine had the means to hire an excellent decorator to redo the lid's interior. Nevertheless, stuck in the wine fields of Burgundy, she probably was not able to find a local artist worthy of her instrument and may not have been able to import someone from Paris. Still, it is strange that she would allow shoddy work on such a stunning instrument.

42. *Adlam 1976, 265*. Indeed, having heard the Vaudry myself on record, I must say that its unusual reedy vowel quality is quite striking. *Hubbard 1965*, 104, had just the opposite opinion, characterizing seventeenth-century French harpsichords as "Percussive and thin with very little sustaining power or majesty of effect." But the few examples known to him were poorly restored.

43. *Adlam 1976, 265*.

44. Date according to *Pussiau*, 162. This informative article uncovers much information about Desruisseaux's life, and discusses the decoration of his instrument in great detail.

45. Another harpsichord by Desruisseaux, also with a curved tail, is in private ownership.

46. *Pussiau*, 158, identified the garlic.

47. *Pussiau*, 158–59, suggests that the lid painter was influenced by the work of the Flemish artist Paul Potter (1625–54).

48. What little is known of Tibaut is summed up in *Gétreau 1996b*.

49. For more information on this instrument see Alain and Marie-Christine *Anselm 1996c*.

50. *Boalch III* lists a fourth possible Tibault (1689, ownership and whereabouts unknown),

but *Anselm 1996a*, disputes this, as does *Anselm 1996b*.

51. The three extant Tibauts are compared in detail in *Anselm 1996a*.

52. The rose of the 1681 Tibaut shown in *Anselm 1996a*, 203, is upside down. The same rose is depicted in *Mercier-Ythier*, 73, but is reversed left to right. The 1691 Tibaut appears to have lost its rose; see *Mercier-Ythier*, 213.

53. I thank John Nothnagle, professor emeritus of French and Italian at the University of Iowa, for this insight.

54. See *Mercier-Ythier*, 73.

55. See *Gétreau 1996b*, 197, for a discussion of the marquetry.

56. *Anselm 1996d*, 228, list eleven French instruments in seventeenth-century style built after the turn on the century. Excluding the folding harpsichords of Jean Marius, which are really outside the normal harpsichord tradition, the list mentions six instruments, four of which are undated and anonymous, and two, dated 1704 and 1707, by the Parisian builder Nicolas Dumont.

9. GERMANY AND AUSTRIA

1. *Boalch III*, 698–703.

2. See, e.g., *Smith 1980*, 40–41.

3. *Praetorius*.

4. *Hubbard 1965*, 166, and plate XXV. Hubbard also believed the oblong virginal to be Flemish, and that almost all the keyboard instruments Praetorius showed were of foreign origin.

5. See *Ripin 1972*.

6. This is indeed how *Van der Meer 1991b*, 42, classifies it.

7. *Mersenne*, 212. Henry VIII had an automatic spinet, but it could not have been by one of the known Bidermans; Samuel was only seven years old when Henry died.

8. *Hubbard 1965*, 167, and plate XXIV.

9. It must be admitted that the appearance of expansion could be nothing more than an exaggerated attempt at perspective. However, Sheridan Germann informs me (private communication) that she has analyzed the vanishing points on Praetorius's drawing and is convinced that the artist intended showing a jackrail wider at the bass end.

10. This information and Meyer's dates come from *Birsak*, 47. *Boalch III*, 127, mistakenly calls Meyer a Salzburg builder.

11. For a description of this instrument see *Van der Meer 1991a*. Van der Meer thought this harpsichord dated from ca. 1700, but *Koster 1999*, n. 48, reports that further evidence, discovered by Sabine Klaus (and dealt with in *Klaus*), suggests the earlier date. My thanks to Professor Koster for making a preprint of this article available to me.

12. The lid no longer exists, but the spine shows signs of hinges.

13. Conventional wisdom has it that because it distorted their facial features, women did not play wind instruments. Sheridan Germann also reminds me (private communication) that from Medieval times wind instruments had a strongly phallic association, and that a painting showing a woman playing a recorder probably invited viewers to seek allegorical meanings. It is likely that even in real life it was considered to be somewhat indelicate for a woman to play a wind instrument. A festival book produced for the marriage of Cosimo de' Medici in 1539 notes that after the nuptial feast "Apollo" himself appeared, with his lyre, surrounded by the nine Muses playing various instruments, among them trombone, dulcian, recorder, cornetto, and crumhorn (cited in *Bowles 2000*, 426); but the Muses were goddesses and presumably above such earthly associations. Still, wind playing among women in domestic situations might not have been as rare as supposed.

14. See *Germann 1978a*, 87–88.

15. It is equally possible that the BB♭ could have been an early manifestation of the special Austrian form of the short octave, to be discussed in Chapter 15.

16. Its lid may not be original. *Van der Meer 1991a*, 8, believes the instrument to have been an inner-outer, with the lid a later addition. However, Koster (private communication), who also examined the instrument, notes that the hinges extend almost the full depth of the case, undoubtedly in an effort to provide enough holding surface. Also, the lid is thin, perhaps no thicker than the case walls, which means that it would not provide much burden on the spine. Although this evidence does not prove that the instrument was originally supplied with a lid, Koster further reports that its hinges are identical to those on an anonymous Hamburg instrument to be discussed shortly. This instrument also has a rather thin spine, indicating that there may have been some thin-spined integral-case seventeenth-century German harpsichords.

17. This same half-U-brace construction is also seen in a late-seventeenth- (or possibly eighteenth-) century 2×8′ South German harpsichord (Basel, Historisches Museum); see *Klaus and Rose*.

18. *Van der Meer 1991a*, 8.

19. The 1691 Tibaut (discussed in the previous chapter) has a wrestplank partially hollowed out under the bass half of the two nuts. While this is literally "hollowed out," it does not fit the normal narrow-plank definition.

20. See *Klaus and Rose*, 259.

21. So little soundboard remains that it is impossible to tell, but the disposition might have been 2×8′, 1×4′.

22. *Praetorius*, 67.

23. *Virdung* also says that the one clavicytherium he saw was strung in gut.

24. *Praetorius*, 62.

25. *Praetorius*, 63.

26. *Mersenne*, 165.

27. I thank John Koster for this insight.

28. See *Smith 1980*, 41.

29. There is one other extant clavicytherium built in this way, a seventeenth-century anonymous Italian instrument (Rome, Museo Nazionale degli Strumenti Musicali). It is thought to have been made by Cristofori.

30. Austria and Germany were not separate countries at this time, but were both part of the Habsburg empire.

31. According to *Klaus and Rose*, 270–72.

10. ENGLAND

1. See *Boalch III*, 694.

2. Two other grands, dated 1623 and 1634, were built in England and for years thought to be of seventeenth-century origin (see, e.g., *McGeary 1973*, 12–15). It has now been established that they were built nearly a century later than their given dates and were intended to be passed off as Flemish instruments. See *O'Brien 1994*, 3.

3. See *Boalch III*, 83–84.

4. *Boalch III*, 660.

5. *Hubbard 1965*, 150–51. "Like a platoon of marching soldiers they burst into view in 1641. Seventeen dated examples are found in the thirty-eight years between that date and 1679. There are no stragglers, no prototypes, and few variants." A few other instruments have been uncovered since Hubbard wrote those words, with the earliest dated 1638. For an almost complete list see *Boalch III*, 714. See also *Martin 1996*, 98–99.

6. While the evidence suggests that coffering might have been a characteristic of most sixteenth-century virginal lids north of the Alps, only in England was that feature retained into the seventeenth.

7. Darryl Martin (private communication) disagrees. He believes that these virginals were strung in iron, and played at a pitch ca. 1½ semitones higher than a = 440 Hz.

8. Two exceptions start on FF, without FF♯: a 1664 Robert Hatley (London, Benton Fletcher Collection), and a 1668 Stephen Keene (Edinburgh, Russell Collection). The Hatley ascends to c^3, the Keene to d^3. I thank Darryl Martin for this attribution (private communication), which is misattributed in *Boalch III* to Thomas White, Cardiff, Welsh Folk Museum.

9. The AA is a frequent requirement of English music as early as the first decades of the seventeenth century. For more on this see *Luckett 1974*.

10. *Germann 1978a,* 99.

11. *Germann 1978a,* 97. This suggests that the virginals were carted off to a decorating shop after they were built, and then back to the builder for stringing, jacking, and tonal finishing.

12. *Martin 1996* holds that rather than a Flemish derivation, the origins of the seventeenth-century English virginal are to be sought in Naples, by way of Spain, through Catherine of Aragon, Henry VIII's first wife, and Catherine's daughter, Mary Tudor, who reigned from 1553 to 1558 (the last four of those years as the wife of Philip, the son of Holy Roman Emperor Charles V, who became Philip II of Spain in 1556). If the Spanish connection is clear, the Neapolitan one is less so, and political connections do not necessarily influence conservative instrument makers. Nevertheless, Martin's thesis is provocative and serves to indicate once again our imperfect understanding of the earlier years of the history of plucked keyboard instruments.

13. *Russell 1959/1973,* 69.

14. *Hubbard 1965,* 151.

15. *Germann 1978a,* 97.

16. *NGEKI,* 129.

17. *Van der Meer 1991b,* 49–50.

18. See her article on decoration in the forthcoming *The Clavichord and Harpsichord,* vol. 2 of *Encyclopedia of Keyboard Instruments,* ed. Igor Kipnis and Robert Palmieri (New York: Garland Publishing).

19. The earliest dated extant English virginal, a 1638 octave instrument by Thomas White (London, private ownership), indicates that in at least one respect the English followed the Flemish. The slots in its bottom offer proof that at one time it was part of a mother and child combination. With evidence of an Italian mother and child as well (see Chapter 6), it is clear that the construction of these combination instruments was not the exclusive domain of Low Country builders.

20. For example, we have the evidence of Flemish instruments built with chromatic basses for export to England. An exchange of letters in 1638 between Balthazar Gerbier, an English painter living in Antwerp, and Sir Francis Windebank, King Charles I's secretary of state, is also enlightening. Writing from Brussels, Gerbier tells Windebank of a Ruckers harpsichord for sale (with a flap painting by Rubens, which doubled its cost). Windebank asks Gerbier to buy it for him, but when it arrives he complains that it lacks six or seven notes. Although Windebank's statement has often been interpreted as a complaint about the "missing" notes of a Flemish nonaligned double, *O'Brien 1990,* 229, observes that seven notes would have filled out the Ruckers short octave and extended the range down to AA. The correspondence can be found in *Russell 1959/1973,* 161–62; *Hubbard 1965,* 231–32; and *O'Brien 1990,* 304.

21. *Melville,* cited in *Russell 1959/1973,* 67.

22. A spinet by Thomas Hitchcock (d. 1700) bearing the legend 1660 may be the earliest of these, although it is thought that this may well be a serial number, rather than a date. Hitchcock's second surviving spinet seemed to be dated 1664, but this instrument has disappeared, and it is believed that the date has been misread; see *Boalch III,* 386.

23. See Sheridan Germann's article on decoration in the forthcoming *The Clavichord and Harpsichord.*

24. Skunktail sharps were either an ebony insert between two pieces of ivory or bone or, less often, the reverse. In the next century the keyboard changed to ivory naturals and ebony sharps. Some spinets also had the embossed key fronts seen on virginals, but in black or red.

25. *Hubbard 1965,* 152, did not think these spinets had a very good tone, but this misses the point. If these domestic instruments had neither the resources nor the depth and brilliance of the grands, neither did they have the cost or upkeep of the larger instruments. But they did provide the middle and upper classes with harpsichords of a sort, capable of playing the contemporary literature.

26. Nevertheless, as late as 1691, the title page of a song book entitled *The Banquet of Musicke* shows a woman playing an old-fashioned virginal. This also appears to be yet one more example of an instrument reversed by the printer, but the accompanying violinist is pictured correctly, indicating that the artist unwittingly copied an already reversed virginal.

27. The attribution to Hasard is fairly recent. For years the difficult-to-read signature was interpreted as Hayward, Haward, Asard, Issard, or Izzard by various investigators, but the now accepted Hasard was arrived at by Ann and Peter Mactaggart and discussed in *Mactaggart.*

28. Translation from *McGeary 1981,* 24–25. The instrument is described in some detail in *Koster 1980,* 54–64.

29. *Hubbard 1965,* 140–42; *McGeary 1981,* 9–12; *Koster 1980,* 54–64.

30. The name may have belonged to the builder, a former owner, or someone who repaired the instrument at one point; see *Boalch III,* 265.

31. See, e.g., *McGeary 1973,* 17, and *Boalch III,* 265.

32. The top four keys are different from the others, and the key bed has been tampered with; nevertheless, given the English insistence on the low AA, it could be the original range.

33. *McGeary 1973,* 15.

34. See *Boalch III,* 84; *Hubbard 1965,* 146–47; and *Russell 1959/1973,* 71–72.

35. *Mace,* 235–36. *Hubbard 1965,* 147, calcu-

lates from Mace's description that his harpsichord had a single manual and was disposed 2×8′, 1×4′ plus lute, plus hand-operated buff.

36. The composer Henry Purcell (ca. 1659–95) was "Keeper, maker, mender, repayrer and tuner of the regalls, organs, virginals, flutes and recorders" for the king from 1673 until his death.

37. The invention was in use for at least twenty years; see *Hubbard 1965*, 147–48, for documentation.

38. See, e.g., *Troeger 1987*, 194–96.

39. Other harpsichords will be seen with rounded tails in the beginning of the next century, and English bentside spinets with rounded tails were made before 1683.

40. A drawing of the internal structure can be seen in *Hubbard 1965*, plate XIX.

41. The Haward harpsichord is illustrated in *Russell 1959/1973*, plate 61.

11. THE DECLINE OF THE ITALIAN HARPSICHORD

1. *Boalch III*, 704–8.

2. *Wraight 1997*, part I, 130 ff., counts thirty-two virginals and spinets and eighty-two harpsichords. To put these numbers in context, his catalog of all extant Italian instruments (145) numbers 748.

3. It is often stated that Cristofori was also a maker of lutes and bowed instruments, but this is based on the evidence of labels in instruments bearing Cristofori's name; see, e.g., *Montanari*. *Pollens 1995*, 51, notes that the instruments themselves do not exhibit the level of workmanship of his stringed keyboards, that there is no evidence that Cristofori ever worked on a bowed instrument during his stay in Florence, and that the labels were likely cut from documents that Cristofori headed with his name.

4. *Pollens 1995*, 47, holds that there is no evidence to support this story, which was first stated in an 1874 article by an Italian musicologist, Leto Puliti. Nevertheless, it is a good tale.

5. See *Restle*, 59.

6. Nevertheless, Cristofori is reported to have let it be known that he did not wish to leave Padua, upon which the duke replied that he would make him go, whether he wished it or not. The story may be apocryphal, but the force behind the duke's threat would have been quite real. See *Och.*

7. Cited in *Montanari*, 384. Montanari's article should not be read without reference to *Wraight 1992b*, in which he suggests several corrections and additions.

8. Cited in *Montanari*, 385. These archival documents are preserved in the *Archivio di Stato di Firenze*.

9. The "Inventario di diverse sorti d'instru-menti musicali in proprio del Serinissimo Sig. Principe Ferdinando di Toscana" (Inventory of different types of musical instruments belonging to His Highness Prince Ferdinand of Tuscany). The Medici inventories have been published by *Gai* and *Puliti*. See *Montanari*, 385, and *Russell 1959/1973*, 125–30.

10. The inventory, found in *Russell 1959/1973*, 125, reveals that the prince owned thirty-six jack-action instruments (twenty harpsichords and sixteen spinets), seven of which had been made by Cristofori.

11. The principal secondary sources for information on Cristofori and his instruments are *Henkel 1992*, *Montanari*, *Pollens 1995*, *Restle*, *Schwarz*, *Sutherland 1998–99*, and *Sutherland 2215*. I thank Kerstin Schwarz and David Sutherland for generously providing me with preprints of their articles.

12. *Henkel 1992*, 15.

13. See *Wraight 1997*, part II, 110–16. Other instruments have been attributed to Cristofori but have not been absolutely authenticated.

14. The Museo Nazionale degli Strumenti Musicali, Rome, has a clavicytherium they suspect might be by Cristofori; see *Cervelli*, 328. *Sutherland 1998–98*, 69–75, offers some convincing reasons why the instrument was probably made by Cristofori.

15. The outer case of the 1693 and its matching stand were lost sometime around 1910. *Boalch III*, 280–81, reports that the 1690 was lost sight of after 1878, so it may still exist in the hands of some secretive private collector.

16. See, e.g., *Henkel 1992*, 3. Evidently, it has been called an oval virginal (or spinet) from its first mention in the inventory of 1700; see *Montanari*, 388.

17. Elsewhere (*Kottick and Lucktenberg*, 99), I have described these projections as "half ovals"; but *Boalch III*, 280, characterizes them more accurately as Gothic arches.

18. A description of this mechanism can be found in *Henkel 1992*, 18–19.

19. The question of Cristofori's stringing practices is dealt with at some length in *Wraight 2229*.

20. *Sutherland 2000*, 50, notes that the instrument was probably used in the Pratolino opera theater for more than a century.

21. My thanks to David Sutherland (private communication) for this perceptive description of the instrument's probable usefulness; his help throughout this chapter has been invaluable.

22. The most complete information on these instruments is found in *Schwarz*.

23. Both the harpsichord and piano of 1726 have outer cases (they also had stands, but these were destroyed or lost during World War II). The Leipzig Musikinstrumenten-Museum believed them to have belonged to other instruments, and

the fact that both of the 1726's were constructed with heavy cases with lids of their own would seem to confirm that. But *Sutherland 2000,* 10, notes that the cases fit the instruments perfectly, which would be unlikely if they were intended for some other pair. Furthermore, they are elaborately decorated in chinoiserie and constitute a matched pair. This leads him to suggest that the cases were made for the instruments after they were completed, and the ensembles were intended as luxury items for a wealthy patron.

24. Both *Henkel 1992,* 15, and *Sutherland 1998–99,* 21–22, are of the opinion that it was around the last decade of the seventeenth century that Cristofori abandoned thin-case inner-outer construction and began making integral-case instruments.

25. A 1740 harpsichord by Hieronymus Hass and a 1760 by Johann Adolph Hass both have 2′ choirs, but these are designed to brighten the sound of the ponderous 16′ rank also present in both, and are really outside the normal tradition of German harpsichord building.

26. A detailed description of the operation of the stop levers can be found in *Henkel 1992,* 20–23. *Sutherland 2000,* 36–43, goes into even more detail and offers an explanation of why Cristofori set up the stops as he did.

27. *Sutherland 2000* discusses this instrument in great detail. His perceptive analysis is well worth reading.

28. See *Schwarz,* illustration 8.

29. At present there are three bars in the treble, but *Schwarz* does not believe them to be original; see also *Sutherland 1998–99,* 20.

30. These elements of the 1726 harpsichord are covered in detail in *Sutherland 2000.*

31. Maffei's original notes still exist; see *Pollens 1995,* 232–37, for original and English translation.

32. Scipione Maffei, "Nuova invenzione d'un gravicembalo col piano e forte . . . ," *Giornale de' letterati d'Italia* 5 (1711), 144–59. An English translation is found in *Pollens 1995,* 57–62. The original text is also given, 238–43. Maffei's article covered most, but not all, of the information in the interview.

33. Exactly the same principle is used in the hammer head of the modern piano, which is made of wood and covered with an inner layer of hard felt and an outer layer of softer felt.

34. Cited in *Pollens 1995,* 61.

35. Cited in *Pollens 1995,* 60.

36. See *Kottick, Marshall, and Hendrickson, Kottick 1991,* and *Savage et al.*

37. Cited in *Montanari,* 388.

38. The Antwerp builder Johann Daniel Dulcken also used an inner bentside, perhaps because he heard of Cristofori's similar invention. But as *Sutherland 1998–99,* 27, n. 51 observes,

Dulcken's inner bentside was weight bearing and heavily framed, quite unlike his Italian colleague's work.

39. Cristofori left most of his estate to the Del Mela sisters "for their continued assistance lent to him during his illnesses and indispositions." To Giovanni Ferrini he left only 5 scudi; see *Pollens 1995,* 55.

40. The *spinettone* and the harpsichord-piano, plus the 1666 Zenti harpsichord restored by Ferrini, are described in *Pollens 1991;* see also *Tagliavini.*

41. This instrument was turned into a three-manual harpsichord by Franciolini.

42. See *Rice 1993* for more information about Italian piano making in the late eighteenth century.

43. See *Koster 1998e.* Again, I am in Professor Koster's debt for making a preprint of this paper available to me.

44. The instrument is dated 1799 on the bottom of the soundboard. The S-shaped bentside would be more consistent with the later date, which likely makes it the last known Italian grand harpsichord.

45. A 1792 (Leipzig, Musikinstrumenten-Museum der Universität Leipzig) was destroyed in World War II.

46. See *Van der Meer 1986,* 399.

47. It is possible that the Taskin jacks are not original. Aside from these limited uses, the device did not become popular, perhaps because of the need to maintain rather close tolerances.

48. The information in this paragraph was taken from *Jensen.*

49. *Jensen,* 73, notes that it was not possible to determine if the bentsides were kerfed.

50. The information in this paragraph was taken from *Sutherland 1998–99,* 35–44.

51. *Sutherland 1998–99,* 47–49.

52. The last is described in *Pollens 1991.*

53. This instrument was formerly in London, Royal Academy of Music. *Brauchli 1998,* 138, suggests that it might have been converted from an early square piano to a clavichord.

54. See *Boalch III,* 39.

55. See *Boalch III,* 348 and 472. The instruments are a suspect 1753 by Hadrianus (whereabouts unknown) and a 1773 Giovanni Paolo Leoni (New York, Metropolitan Museum of Art).

56. In 1997 Sheridan Germann decorated the case of a modern copy of the 1697 Grimaldi in this manner. It is eye-catching and quite elegant.

57. *Boalch III,* 331–32, notes that the instrument was in Franciolini's hands, and thus suspect. *Deutsches Museum,* 112–14, is not willing to assign it to Goccini and lists it as anonymous, second half of the seventeenth century.

58. See *Boalch III,* 332.

59. Although Goccini's use of this octave-

doubling device was probably unique to the harpsichord, it was occasionally found on Italian organs, where it was appropriately called the *terza mano*. I thank John Koster (private communication) for this information.

60. See *Augelli* for an account of the event and a detailed description of the instrument.

61. *Wraight 1997*, part II, 180, raises a question about the date of 1797, given by Finchcocks. If correct, Gregori would have had a working life of at least sixty-one years which, although possible, is doubtful. Wraight believes the date should read 1779. He also lists a few other instruments attributed to Gregori, but without validating them. A harpsichord dated 1740 and attributed to Nicolas de Gregori (St. Paul, Schubert Club) is probably spurious. See *Boalch III*, 340–41.

12. THE IBERIAN PENINSULA

1. Eight extant harpsichords supposedly of seventeenth-century Spanish origin, and two claiming a Portuguese pedigree — one seventeenth, the other eighteenth, century — are known to me and have not been discussed here. Critical examination of these instruments suggests that they may be counterfeits with false attributions, and until authorities with better credentials than mine have come to some degree of unanimity, it is impossible to do more than simply mention them. Six of these are discussed in *Beurmann 1999*, and three, with transposing keyboards, in *Beurmann 1998*. The instruments cited by Beurmann, and their attributions, consist of three unaligned double-manual harpsichords: "Fray Raymundo et Fray Antonio, 1624," "Fray Pedro Luis de Berganos, 1629," and "Fray Bartomeu Angel Risueño, 1664." Two are singles: "Ludovicus Muñoz, 1644" and "Domingo de Carvaleda, 1676." The sixth is a *vis à vis*, "Roque Blasco, 1691." *Knighton* warns against citing the *Beurmann 1999* article until the question of authenticity is resolved. *Koster 2000c* closely examined another suspect instrument, one dated "1641" and signed "Luis de Carballeda." To anyone interested in the techniques of discovering such forgeries, this article is required reading. The eighth suspect harpsichord is attributed to "Fr. Ant. L . . . , 1716." The "Portuguese" instruments are both singles, by "Jeronimo Bocaro, ca. 1650" and "Antonio Oliveres, ca. 1740."

2. See *Kenyon de Pascual 1992*, 614.

3. *Kenyon de Pascual 1992*, 614.

4. *Kenyon de Pascual 1991*.

5. See *Kenyon de Pascual 1982*, 66.

6. *Kenyon de Pascual 1992*, 611, citing the 1989 edition of the *Diccionario manual e ilustrado de la lengua española*, notes that modern Spanish still has not resolved the confusion in terminology.

7. Cited in *Brauchli 1998*, 88–89.

8. *Bordas* discusses this phenomenon at some length.

9. *Cerone*, ch. 53, cited in *Kenyon de Pascual 1992*, 614.

10. There are fourteenth-century references to the Chekker; see *Ripin 1975*, 16–17.

11. See *Bowles 1977*, plate 27b. *Kenyon de Pasqual 1992*, 629, n. 33, mentions two additional late-fifteenth-century Spanish carvings, one of a harpsichord, the other of a keyed psaltery.

12. See *Gestoso*, cited in *Boalch III*, 53–54.

13. See *Calahorra*, cited in *Boalch III*, 13.

14. Brahem Mofferriz (d. 1513), also a builder and also from Saragossa, may have been his brother.

15. The event was mentioned in Gonzalo Fernández de Oviedo y Valdés, *Libro de la cámera real de Don Juan*. The author was a servant of Prince John, and his manuscript book was written a half century after the prince's death. Cited in *Kenyon de Pascual 1992*, 611.

16. See *Kenyon de Pascual 1992*, 611.

17. See *Kenyon de Pascual 1992*, 611–30.

18. The reference is in *Van der Straeten*, vol. 7, 248.

19. See *Kenyon de Pascual 1992*, 612.

20. See *Kenyon de Pascual 1992*, 612. The inventory, in Spanish, with translation and commentary in English, is given on pp. 625–26.

21. See *McLeish*.

22. Jobernardi described the instrument (but evidently never built it) in a manuscript he presented to the king in 1634 and which now resides in the Biblioteca Nacional, Madrid. The contents of the manuscript are discussed in *Kastner*, cited in *Boalch III*, 99, and *Russell 1959/1973*, 116.

23. See *Boalch III*, 31.

24. *Nassarre*, 612, cited in *Kenyon de Pascual 1992*, 612; see also *Brauchli 1998*, 127–28.

25. For further information on Scarlatti see *Boyd* and *Kirkpatrick*.

26. This is, in fact, the thesis of *Van der Meer 1997*.

27. The inventory is in Madrid, Royal Palace Library VII E 4 305. For the original Spanish see *Kirkpatrick*, 361. English translations appear in many sources, including *Russell 1959/1973*, 185.

28. It has been assumed that this was done because the Spanish technicians, unable to cope with the unfamiliar and fairly complex Cristofori action, turned two otherwise unusable pianos into functioning, even if not ideal, *clavicordios de plumas* (quilled harpsichords). However, *Sutherland 1995* suggests that those pianos may have been either early, outmoded examples of Cristofori's work that were converted to keep them useful, or pianos that had simply failed because of the heavy string tensions required, and were rescued by substituting the lighter stringing more suitable for jack-action instruments. Another expla-

nation is offered by *Van der Meer 1997*, 154–55, who suggests that these instruments were combined harpsichord-pianos, like the one made in 1746 by Ferrini, and that the piano portion of the action was simply removed.

29. One might suspect that this large instrument was a North German double disposed 1×16′, 2×8′, 1×4′ with lute stop, and in fact, that description matches the specifications of an extant two-manual GG–d³ Hieronymus Hass of 1734 (Brussels, Musée Instrumental). The other two walnut instruments had three sets of strings, presumably 2×8′, 1×4′, and could have been either singles or doubles—again, dispositions common to North German harpsichords. However, walnut was not a case wood known to have been used by those builders, so despite the similarity of dispositions, it is unlikely that the instruments came from Hamburg or anywhere else in Germany.

30. Fernández was made court builder in 1747, charged with the care and repair of the harpsichords in the royal household, as well as the building of new instruments; see *Kenyon de Pascual 1985*, 36.

31. *Sacchi*, 29 ff.

32. See *Kenyon de Pascual 1982*, 69, n. 6.

33. This instrument is listed as number four in the 1609 inventory of Philip II's holdings; see *Kenyon de Pascual 1992*, 625–26.

34. *Kenyon de Pasqual 1986* offers evidence that Diego Fernández was the builder of some of the queen's harpsichords, including the three five-octave instruments mentioned in the inventory.

35. *Burney 1771*, 211–12. It would seem clear from Burney's language that these were true inner-outers, but the Southern insistence of the appearance of an inner instrument in an outer case was so pervasive that even if he recognized them as false inner-outers he might still have used those words.

36. See *Kenyon de Pascual 1985*.

37. See *Kenyon de Pascual 1985*, 39.

38. *Kenyon de Pasqual 1986*, 125, offers archival evidence supporting this view.

39. Most of this information comes from *Heriot*, 95–110.

40. It is likely that this was by Bull, Dulcken, or one of their contemporaries. As *Van der Meer 1997*, 143, notes, the queen liked to keep her instruments up to date.

41. See *Shevaloff* for more information.

42. This question is discussed by *Kenyon de Pasqual and Van der Meer*; see also *Van der Meer 1986*.

43. The contents of this paragraph come from *Kenyon de Pascual 1985*.

44. *Kenyon de Pascual 1986*, 504, comes to the same conclusion about the rounded tail, calling it "a feature of the Andalusia school of keyboard instrument construction in the 18th century."

45. *Byne and Stapely*, plate 192; see *Pollens 1995*, 124–35, for a detailed description of this instrument.

46. *Kenyon de Pascual 1987*. The picture of the 1754 harpsichord appears on p. 504; it is likely that this was the instrument pictured in *Byne and Stapely*.

47. Both are also decorated with chinoiserie. In fact, from its picture, the 1754 Pérez Mirabal, with its rounded tail, large bottom molding, vague inner-outer reference in the keywell, and table stand with four turned legs on a low frame, could easily be mistaken for an eighteenth-century German harpsichord. Such instruments were certainly to be found in Spain. *Kenyon de Pascual 1982*, 69, notes that a harpsichord advertised for sale in Madrid in 1789 was described as having five registers, inlaid keys, and chinoiserie decoration.

48. *Kenyon de Pascual 1987*, 504–5. *Pollens 1995*, 125–26, notes that these pianos have cases derived from German models combined with a Cristofori-like action.

49. This last instrument can be seen in *Russell 1959/1973*, plate 102A, where it is identified as a "harpsichord, probably of eighteenth century Spanish origin," but *Kenyon de Pascual and Law* identify it as a piano.

50. *Kenyon de Pascual 1991*, 96, notes that at least three harpsichords claiming to be of Spanish origin have a scroll-sawn decoration of unique design glued to the interiors of the cheeks.

51. See *Kenyon de Pascual 1982* for some indication of the non-Spanish instruments in Madrid.

52. *Kenyon de Pascual 1991*, 94, claims that as of 1991 at least fourteen harpsichords laying claim to Spanish origin were known, although she admits that some of those claims are arguable, since the great diversity among the claimants makes it impossible to define a clear-cut building style.

53. See *Boalch III*, 711.

54. *Pollens 1995*, 121, believes that Joachim José was probably Manuel's son.

55. *Boalch III*, 222, and *Russell 1959/1973*, 118 and plate 99, date this instrument at 1758, which is certainly possible; but Robert Greenberg (private communication), who examined the instrument, dated it at 1785.

56. Tulip is a Brazilian wood and was shipped to Portugal in large quantities.

57. The Finchcocks Antunes has two pedals, one to take off the back 8′ and the other to activate the buff stop. Christopher Nobbs (*Nobbs Unpublished*), who was involved in the restoration of the instrument, believes that this feature is original.

58. See *Nobbs Unpublished*.

59. *Clinkscale*, 6, attributes the instrument to José Joachim, but *Koster CD* believes it to be by Manuel. Koster notes that in 1760 Manuel "had obtained the exclusive right to make 'harpsi-

chords with hammers' in Portugal for a period of ten years."

60. The piano has a much more elaborate exterior, but much of that was applied later, probably in the late nineteenth or early twentieth century.

61. See *Pollens 1985*. The van Casteel instrument has inverted-heart bench stands, but they are modern; see *Pereira 1983*.

62. See *Nobbs Unpublished*. The fourth piano is by Bostem, 1777.

13. HARPSICHORD BUILDING IN FRANCE UP TO THE REVOLUTION

1. *Dowd 1984*, 45, observes that it was these early *ravalements* that so profoundly influenced the course of French harpsichord building.

2. *Bemetzrieder*, 13, cited in *O'Brien 1990*, 207, n. 1.

3. Although the process of *ravalement* is well known and has been described many times, no one has done this as clearly as *O'Brien 1990*, 207–17. This section depends heavily on his work.

4. *Gétreau 1998*, 124, reports that while a new harpsichord cost between 300 and 400 livres, a Ruckers or Couchet *ravalement* could command 600 to 1,000 livres. If the rebuilding was carried out by a famous maker, and if the instrument boasted a lid painting by a well-known artist, the price could rise to between 2,000 and 5,000 livres.

5. *Dowd 1978*.

6. See *O'Brien 1990*, 209.

7. *Van Blankenburg*, 142, cited in *O'Brien 1990*, 297, 98. The term "Van Blankenburg problem" is O'Brien's.

8. *O'Brien 1990*, 215–16, notes that outside France the dogleg was most often used to couple the keyboards, and all four registers of the unaligned doubles' jacks were often retained.

9. See *Clarke* for a detailed account of a Ruckers harpsichord that underwent *petite ravalement* twice.

10. *Germann 1980, 1981*, part 2, 193, notes that the artists she identifies as the "Blanchet painters" were skilled at imitating Flemish-style soundboard decoration, but can be identified easily because their normal French style kept creeping back in.

11. *O'Brien 1990*, 211, notes that many of the single to double conversions omit the low GG♯ or use a GG/BB short octave.

12. *O'Brien 1974* holds that the instrument had been built either by Taskin himself or by Taskin and Blanchet together. *Germann 1979a*, a fine bit of detective work, is responsible for the Goermans attribution.

13. See *Germann 1979a*. Germann calls Taskin's disregard for other builders' work "ruthless."

14. See *O'Brien 1990*, 158–65 and 186–87,

for detailed information on the rose castings of the various members of the Ruckers and Couchet families.

15. This instrument must have been built sometime before 1749. Originally GG–d³, it was increased to FF–e³ in 1749, the date on the jacks. In 1784 another builder, Joachim Swanen, added the top f³.

16. It was suggested to me by an official of the Musée de la Musique (private communication) that by putting Ruckers's name on the harpsichord, Goujon — or any other French builder, for that matter — did not intend to deceive, but merely to pay tribute to an illustrious predecessor.

17. *Dowd 1978*, 112.

18. One more Goujon instrument is extant, a 1753 bentside spinet (Paris, Musée de la Musique). This one has his name on it. Goujon was also responsible for a number of *ravalements*, including 1627 and 1632 Ioannes Ruckers harpsichords done in 1745 and 1753.

19. *O'Brien 1990*, 207–8 gives more detail.

20. See *Libin 1987*.

21. See *Elste 1988*, 253.

22. At least, what is generally accepted to be his first. *Watson 1983–84*, 67, reports the discovery of Blanchet's signature on a 1686 bentside spinet (Charleston, Charleston Museum). According to *Boalch III*, 243, this instrument is thought to be (1) by Blanchet, although he would not have been a master at that date, and hence not free to sign instruments, (2) spurious, or (3) by some other, hitherto unknown member of the Blanchet family. In this last regard, *Dowd 1984*, 22, n. 5, cites entries in *Documents du Minutier Central concernant l'histoire de la musique (1600–1650)* (Paris, 1974), vol. 1, that deal with an earlier Nicolas Blanchet (b. 1598), a Paris builder who may well have been an ancestor — perhaps even the grandfather — of the later Nicolas Blanchet. In any event, the instrument in question is thoroughly seventeenth-century French in appearance.

23. *Dowd 1984*, 29, tremblingly suggests that the long c² scaling was a layout error on Blanchet's part, since the rest of the scale seems fairly normal. It is likely that before the twentieth century, builders were not as concerned with the accuracy of scale to the extent that we are.

24. *Dowd 1984*, 27–30. Most of the information in this section on Blanchet's work is derived from Dowd's valuable monograph.

25. See *Dowd 1984*, 38–39. The painting on the wrestplank, which is original, was identified by Sheridan Germann as coming from the hand of the "early Blanchet painter," who also painted the 1709 and 1710 spinets. For more on the painter see *Germann 1980, 1981*, part 2.

26. *Dowd 1984*, 59–60, thinks that this instrument and a similar one from 1733 were built from nonstandard cases for which Blanchet could

find no other use. He suggests that they may have been originally intended for claviorgana.

27. See *Hubbard 1965*, 120, table 11.

28. See *Hubbard 1965*, 122, table 13.

29. See *Hubbard 1965*, 122, table 13.

30. These measurements were taken from *Dowd 1984*, 85–86.

31. *Dowd 1984*, 91, notes that this standard French soundboard ribbing only becomes so on instruments built after the middle of the century.

32. Most of this section is derived from the work of Sheridan Germann, particularly *Germann 1978a* and *Germann 1980, 1981*, as well as her extensive article on decoration in the forthcoming *Clavichord and Harpsichord*, and her forthcoming monograph on harpsichord decoration which will be vol. 4 of *The Historical Harpsichord*, ed. Howard Schott (New York: Pendragon Press). Germann has shared the manuscripts of these last two with me, and I thank her for her generosity.

33. For information on the place of harpsichord decoration as an expression of aristocratic taste see *Gétreau and Herlin 1996, 1997*, vol. 2, 83–88.

34. Germann observes that the bird scene as a resurrection symbol first appears in a 1683 single-manual harpsichord by Nicolas Dufour (see *Koster 1996b*). Germann was the first to understand this symbolism and wrote about it in *Germann 1978b* and *Germann 1979a*.

35. A possible floral plan for a French soundboard is found in *Mercier-Ythier*, 190.

36. In *Germann 1980, 1981*, vol. 1, 440–42, the author provides a map pinpointing the locations of 170 Parisian harpsichord builders, tuners and regulators, and musicians, as well as the decorator Monsieur Doublet.

37. The letter is quoted in Ernest Closson, "Pascal Taskin," *Sammelbände der Internationalen Musikgesellschaft* (1910–11), 234, cited in *Hubbard 1965*, 217. The customer's inquiry must have involved the exterior only, since Taskin says nothing about the interior colors. He does mentions the gold bands, however.

38. Most of the information for this section comes from *Hardouin*, a valuable article that reproduces the inventories taken at the marriages and deaths of the Blanchet builders and their wives. Additional information comes from *Boalch III, Dowd 1984, Clinkscale*, and especially, *Hunt 2000*.

39. Also in that year his daughter Elizabeth Antoinette, herself reputed to be a remarkable keyboard player, married the great organist and composer Armand Louis Couperin (1725–89).

40. *Germann 1978a*, 79–80. In note 42 she reports that the present owner said that he still retained a bill of sale from Huet, for the decoration.

41. *Dowd 1984*, 51–60, describes this instrument in unusual detail.

42. *Dowd 1984*, 61, says, "I suspect it [the joint] is either a scarf or a half-lap, and I certainly hope it is a long one."

43. *Dowd 1984*, 68.

44. *Dowd 1984*, 77–80.

45. Sheridan Germann, who restored the soundboard painting on this instrument in 1975, reports (private correspondence) that the buff-stop was added over the painted soundboard borders, but was definitely original, since the wood underneath had never darkened from exposure to light.

46. The advantages worked both ways. The widow kept her intangible but substantial investment in her deceased husband's affairs, her children would be supported and trained in the craft, and she was assured of the continuation of the comfortable life style afforded a prosperous harpsichord maker's wife.

47. Armand had a son, Nicolas, who also became a builder, but by this time the Blanchet firm was building nothing but pianos.

48. In 1777 Pascal-Joseph II married François-Etienne Blanchet II's daughter Marie-Françoise-Julie. Their son Henri-Joseph (1779–1852) became a maker of pianos. Presumably, the dynasty died with him.

49. *Brauchli 2000*, 26–27, suggests that Taskin's building fell into the following categories: new harpsichords, signed by the builder; *ravalements* of older instruments, particularly Flemish; and new harpsichords, with or without the incorporation of parts from older instruments, sold as antiques, and "signed" by Ruckers or some other older builder. An example of the last is found in the "1612 Hans Ruckers" (Brussels, Musée Instrumental), an instrument made by Taskin, but with parts of old virginal and harpsichord soundboards. For a description see *Awouters*.

50. A well-known example of the latter not yet mentioned is the 1697 Nicolas Dumont (Paris, Musée de la Musique) rebuilt and enlarged in 1789 by Taskin.

51. Evidently the harpsichords at Versailles had their quills replaced on a three-month schedule; see *Benoit*, 215, cited in *Germann 1980, 1981*, part 1, 451, n. 18.

52. See *Dictionnaire des facteurs*, 397. According to *Hunt 2000*, 54–55, the musical instrument maker's guild, first established in 1599, was combined with other guilds in 1776. The guilds were abolished in 1791.

53. See *Germann 1980, 1981*, part 2, 198–200. Germann notes that his style is more sophisticated than that of most other French soundboard decorators.

54. *Burney 1971*, 38.

55. *Dowd 1984*, 87–88.

56. It has also been noted that these jacks may not be original.

57. *Seeing Double* reports that the Paris spinet was loaned to the Yale collection in order to study and compare the two side by side. The article contains a picture of both instruments and notes that "nowhere else in the world are there two French harpsichords by the same builder, made in the same year over the same drawing and in original condition."

58. *O'Brien 1990,* 282.

59. All these innovations can be seen in *Dowd 1984,* 105, fig. 3; see also *Hubbard 1965,* plate XII.

60. See *Hubbard 1965,* 301–2, for a translation of the inventory taken at the death of Henri Hemsch.

61. The exact date is somewhat in doubt. The original date on the soundboard was overpainted in the nineteenth century, and for years had been read as 1756 (see *Hubbard 1965,* plate XI); but in a recent restoration, John Koster compared this Hemsch to the other survivors and to the extant harpsichords of Antoine Vater, Hemsch's teacher. He concluded that this instrument was closer to the work of Vater, and therefore the earliest of the Hemsches. See *Koster 1994,* 91.

62. See *Germann 1980, 1981,* part 2, 193.

63. According to Sheridan Germann; see also *Koster 1994,* 94.

64. A large share of Parisian harpsichord builders were either born in Germany or could claim German parentage.

65. Another octave instrument of his, of unknown date, is reported to be in Lisbon.

66. For more information on the 1774 see *Anselm 1996c.*

67. According to *Boalch III,* 334.

68. *Hardouin,* 22. Hardouin's sources are the various inventories and records still extant in Paris. *Hubbard 1965,* 84, who consulted many of the same documents, notes that "The French genius for red tape has provided archives of unequaled richness." *Samoyault-Verlet* is another valuable source of documents concerning Parisian harpsichord builders.

69. Swanen is known for his EE–a³ harpsichord of 1786 (Paris, Musée des Arts et Métier). This is an unusually wide range for a harpsichord at any time, and it is not known why Swanen extended the compass to that high a³, four notes higher than the usual French compass, and two notes more than the g³ to which some English and Irish instruments ascend. Only the 1789 harpsichord by Manuel Antunes, with an F–a³ compass, reaches that height. At some later date Swanen's was given a two-octave set of 16′ strings, which are struck by hammers operated by a pedal board.

70. Coincidentally, Jean Phillipe Rameau worked as an organist in Lyons in 1713–14, and he and Pierre undoubtedly rubbed shoulders on more than one occasion.

71. This could have been a peculiarity of Lyonnais musical life, but is likely no more than a coincidence.

72. This is also true of a small number of other eighteenth-century French harpsichords, including the 1680 Couchet/1758 Blanchet/1781 Taskin, and the 1746 and 1754 Hemsches.

73. See *Boalch III,* 111.

74. Strasbourg could just as easily have been discussed in the forthcoming chapter on Germany. The city was part of France at that time, but was heavily populated by Germans, and Silbermann's work is derived from that tradition, not France's.

75. Sheridan Germann (private communication) rightly points out that Strasbourg was (and still is) a city with a duel culture, and Silbermann was under no pressure to modify his German training to suit a French taste. He brought his German traditions to France and went on working in the style he learned from his uncle.

76. "Basse" may well have been a variant spelling for "Bas."

77. *Thomas 1974,* 83, claimed to have examined instruments by Louis Bas, Colesse, and Kroll and reported that the cases were made of pine, and that the internal structure consisted of U-braces and diagonal struts.

78. *Histoire de l'Académie Royale des Sciences,* Année MDCCLIX (Paris, 1765), 241–42, cited in *Ripin 1970c,* 21.

79. A 1779 harpsichord by Sébastien Érard (Paris, Musée de la Musique) has a combined pedal and knee-lever mechanism, different from Taskin's.

80. There is some evidence to suggest that credit for inventing the *peau de buffle* stop should go to Claude Balbastre, rather than Taskin; see *Hubbard 1965,* 130.

81. *Diderot and d'Alembert 1785,* translated by and cited in *Hubbard 1965,* 252.

82. *Diderot and d'Alembert 1785,* cited in *Hubbard 1965,* 253.

83. See *Ripin 1970c,* 22 ff., for a detailed explanation of the operation of the French machine stop. A picture of a stand with its pommels exposed is on p. 28. For an excellent diagram of the operation of the machine stop see *Brauchli 2000,* 29.

84. The pommels were labeled as follows: "G" (*grand*) for the lower-manual 8′; "OC" (*octave*) for the 4′; "B" (*peau de buffle*); and "D" (*decrescendo*) for the machine stop. The pommel that raised the *peau de buffle* jacks, normally not labeled, was sometimes marked "E" (*élévateur*). The *genouillère* for the coupler, when present, was labeled "PC" (*petit clavier*).

85. *Hubbard 1965,* 127.

86. See *Ripin 1970c,* 24.

87. *Diderot and d'Alembert 1785*, cited in *Hubbard 1965*, 260.

88. Some of this music actually calls for dynamics as well as the use of the *peau de buffle*. See *Ripin 1970c*, 23, for an example by the composer Jean François Tapray, written around 1784. Ripin also cites a ca. 1772 piece by Armand-Louis Couperin.

89. *Dictionnaire portatif*, vol. 2, 7, cited in *Russell 1959/1973*, 59.

14. THE LOW COUNTRIES IN THE POST-RUCKERS ERA

1. *Burney 1773*, 28.

2. As usual, these numbers are gleaned from the lists in *Boalch III*, 708–9.

3. See *Boalch III*, 709–10. There are fewer than ninety builders from all the Low Countries listed for the eighteenth century.

4. The members of the Dulcken family and their extant instruments are discussed in detail in *Tournay 1987*.

5. *Burney 1773*, 28, mistakenly thought that Dulcken was German (Hessian).

6. *Clinkscale*, 90–91, is of the opinion that it could have been Johan Lodewijk the younger, rather than his father, who was the Louis Dulcken working in Paris between 1783–93; if so, he would not have gone to Munich until after that period; see also *Gug*.

7. *Boalch III*, 302, notes that the ca. 1745 double (Brussels, Musée Instrumental) has a case made of oak. The use of this wood is quite unusual not only for Dulcken, but for any Low Country builder at any time. This has led to questions about its authenticity, but *Tournay 1987* accepts it as genuine. Given the traditional frugality with which builders viewed their materials, it is possible that Dulcken found himself with a supply of oak which, while not suitable for wrestplanks, could be made into case sides.

8. Dulcken may have come to the conclusion that this experimental device either was not worth the trouble or was ultimately of no use. According to *Tournay 1987*, beginning with the 1755 double (Brussels, Musée Instrumental), he no longer used the inner bentside. Cited in *Boalch III*, 302–3.

9. The ca. 1740 single (Edinburgh, private collection) has no soundboard painting, although it may have had one in the past. In addition, its rose, with a harp-playing angel, is different from the normal Dulcken device. Nevertheless, *Tournay 1987* believes it to be authentic.

10. In a bit of serendipitous symmetry, two of the extant singles and two of the doubles have ebony naturals and bone- or ivory-topped sharps, while three of each have the reverse.

11. There is another Dulcken in America, in a private collection.

12. *Burney 1773*, 28.

13. *Van der Meer 1998c*, 45, notes that van den Elsche introduced knee levers to the harpsichord before Taskin.

14. *Tournay 1980*, 148, notes that although Delin was supposed to have apprenticed in Antwerp with Antoine Dulcken (d. 1763), who may have been the father of Johann Daniel, there is no proof.

15. *Tournay 1980* authenticates ten instruments by that maker. *Boalch III*, 287, lists eleven but indicates that a 1738 bentside spinet (Paris, Musée de la Musique) "is not mentioned by Tournay, and may perhaps be spurious."

16. *Boalch III*, 289, is in error in assigning the compass of GG–e^3 to the 1765 spinet. He also reports a C–f^3 compass for the 1763, but if that is true it is likely to have been changed in one of its many restorations.

17. The ca. 1760 clavicytherium now has a compass of AA–f^3, but that is not original.

18. According to *Tournay 1980*, 162, who cites a laboratory analysis of the wood. Tournay devotes nine pages of description, photographs, and drawings to this instrument, and also includes a fold-out plan.

19. See the table in *Tournay 1980*, 181.

20. The 1770 has a cutoff bar as well.

21. *O'Brien 1990*, 206.

22. The ca. 1760 clavicytherium does not seem to have had any upper braces.

23. Although its decor is not original, the ca. 1760 is one of the more spectacular sights in The Hague's Gemeentemuseum. An account of the restoration of this instrument can be found in *Scheuerwater and van Acht*, 50–62; see also *Tournay 1980*, 216, fig. 93.

24. The endblocks of the 1750 harpsichord are painted the same green as the case, but that is probably not original. The spinets and the virginal have no endblocks at all.

25. According to *NGEKI*, 94.

26. *Boalch III*, 498, notes that it is a single, dated 1732, with a DD–d^3 compass. *NGEKI*, 94, presumes that this strange compass resulted from a rebuilding of the original FF–f^3 keyboard.

27. See *O'Brien 1990*, 282.

28. See *Boalch III, 124*.

29. *Gierveld*, 122, claims that half of the instrument makers in Amsterdam were born in Germany, that most of them were also organ builders, and that there was a brisk business in house organs.

30. The enlarging of an anonymous harpsichord dated "1669" and bearing the name of "Petrus Ioannes Couchet" is attributed to Laescke; see *Libin 1975*, 48, and *Libin 1998b*, 185. Laescke

also enlarged a 1599 double by Ioannes Ruckers; see *O'Brien, Ehricht, and Rieche*.

31. *Libin 1998b*, 183, notes that this conservative compass was found on contemporary Dutch chamber organs as well.

32. The information on Laescke's instrument is drawn from *Libin 1975* and *Libin 1998b;* see also *Gierveld*, 144.

33. *Boalch III*, 147, suggests that the second soundboard may have been the bottom of the harpsichord, and that the jacks worked upside down. If so, the jacks would have to have been mounted in some sort of cradle, with mechanical linkage between them and the keys, since gravity insists that jacks work right side up.

34. See *Hubbard 1965*, 320–21, for a more complete list of Plenius's inventions.

35. Cited in *Boalch III*, 148. The lyrichord was the subject of *Halfpenny 1950*.

15. GERMANY, SCANDINAVIA, AUSTRIA, AND SWITZERLAND

1. *Jacobsson*, 766, stated that organ makers, not joiners, were the "true" harpsichord and clavichord builders, involving themselves in that activity when they had no organ commissions or repairs to carry out. Cited in *Hubbard 1965*, 172.

2. *Boalch III*, 698–703.

3. *Boetius*, quoted in *Geiringer*, 5, and cited in *Koster 1999*. My thanks to Professor Koster for providing me with a preprint of this informative article.

4. *O'Brien 1990*, 204. This is O'Brien's observation.

5. This view is contrary to that of *O'Brien 1990*, 204, who states that the Ruckers influence was strong in Saxon instruments in general and Dresden harpsichords in particular. My statements are based on detailed examination of the extant Gräbner instruments by John Phillips, who graciously shared his research with me in private communications as well as in an unpublished monograph written in 2000, "The Surviving Harpsichords of the Gräbner Family." See also *Phillips*.

6. *Pollens 1995*, 171, raises the interesting point that the actions of Silbermann's earliest pianos might have been based on the work of Christoph Gottlieb Schröter (1699–1782), a musician and theorist who claimed to have invented the hammer action before Cristofori.

7. Silbermann was also the inventor of the *Cembal d'Amour*, which he completed in 1721. This was a large—one might say enormous—clavichord whose strings were touched in the middle and were therefore free to vibrate on both sides of the tangent. A few were made by other builders,

but the unwieldy instrument never achieved any real success, perhaps because, since struck at their centers, the strings were too liable to stretching, thereby sharping the pitch; and although louder than a conventional clavichord, it did not produce the volume level of a piano.

8. The description and most of the information on the *Pantalon* come from *Cole 1998*, 26 ff.

9. *Leipziger Post-Zeitung*, October 23, 1731, cited in *Cole 1998*, 28.

10. *Adlung 1758*, 559, cited in *Cole 1998*, 29. Cole perceptively remarks that although the keyed *Pantalon* was undoubtedly capable of dynamics by finger pressure, it did not share this aesthetic with the piano; instead, like the harpsichord, it was expected to produce terraced dynamics and varied tonal effects.

11. According to *Cole 1998*, 195, but there is some controversy here. *Clinkscale*, 271, holds that the tangent piano was invented by Christoph Gottlieb Schröter (1699–1782), and that Späth was building them as early as 1751, but Cole disputes this. *Pollens 1995*, 168, notes that Schröter's drawing describes a *Tangentenflügel*, but he adds that Schröter may have come up with the idea through a misunderstanding of Maffei's drawing of the early Cristofori action.

12. *Cole 1998*, 196.

13. *Cole 1998*, 196.

14. *Adlung 1758*, vol. 2, 133 ff., cited in *Hubbard 1965*, 330. *Hubbard 1965*, 329–30, gives a translation of Adlung's discussion of the *Lautenwerk*.

15. *NGEKI*, 191, reports that a copy of that suite owned by Johann Ludwig Krebs (1713–80), a student of Bach's for nine years, indicates on the title page that it is to be performed on a *"Lauten Werck."*

16. One in Florence and one in Dresden; see *NGEKI*, 196.

17. See *Koster 1993, 1994* for further discussion of some of these instruments.

18. *Koster 1998b* concludes that the instruments sound at chamber pitch, at about a = 415 Hz, or perhaps a little lower. Once again, my thanks to Professor Koster for sharing his research with me.

19. Hans Christoph Fleischer's sister Catherina married the famed lute maker Joachim Tielke (1641–1719).

20. According to the periodical *Sammlung von Natur und Medicin* (winter quartal, 1718), Johann Christoph built a *Lauten-Clavessin*, a 2×8' gutstrung harpsichord; and a *Theorbenflügel*, a 2×8' keyboard lute with an additional set of strings in metal. Cited in *Boalch III*, 60.

21. See *Boalch III*, 60.

22. This harpsichord has the same disposition as the 1679 Ioannes Couchet, where the 4'

jacks separate the two 8′ sets. It is possible that, when new, the two 8′ sets of jacks of the Fleischer were also separated by the 4′ jacks. *O'Brien 1994,* 31, n. 45, doubts that the present disposition is original.

23. *Germann 1978a,* 91–92, notes this similarity.

24. As with so many aspects of harpsichord decoration, this is an insight I received from Sheridan Germann.

25. The instrument was purchased from a collector in New York, and it is claimed that it may have been in America since the middle of the eighteenth century. According to *Berlin,* 91, the lid was left behind when the museum acquired the instrument and supposedly is still somewhere in New York.

26. I am indebted to *Koster 1999,* 65, for this piece of information.

27. The gap of the 1716 Fleischer also slants in the bass, but only slightly.

28. *Whitehead* compares many of the measurements of the extant Hass harpsichords.

29. *Whitehead,* 98, believes that the width of the octave spans of the Hass harpsichords is related to the number of registers. Another theory holds that the rears of the keys were laid out with a rule, while the fronts were spaced by simply dividing the available space by the number of keys. This could vary slightly from instrument to instrument.

30. *Whitehead,* 97–100.

31. *Whitehead,* 101.

32. See *Koster 1999,* 70.

33. *Hubbard 1965,* 332, mistakenly claimed that the coupler has on, off, and intermediate positions. George Lucktenberg and I, in *Kottick and Lucktenberg,* 49, erred in saying that all four registers could be played from the lower manual.

34. See *Whitehead,* 99, for a cross section of the 1723 nut.

35. See *Koster 1999,* 67.

36. *Koster 1999,* 69.

37. I thank Lance Whitehead and Göran Grahn for information about this instrument. *Whitehead,* 101, suggests that the 1721 double was probably converted into a piano, thereby saving it from oblivion, because its lovely chinoiserie lid was perceived to have some value.

38. See *Lunde.*

39. According to *Hubbard 1965,* 176. Actually, oak makes more sense than pine for a bentside, since it bends more easily and is the bending wood that would have been most familiar to ship builders and other craftsmen in that mighty seaport. *Adlung 1768,* vol. 2, 103, says that cases were sometimes made of softwood, but that hardwood was more stable.

40. I thank Sheridan Germann for pointing this out to me.

41. There is some anecdotal evidence that the woman may be Catherine the Great of Russia. *Eigeldinger* reports that Wanda Landowska saw the 1740 Hass at an international exposition in 1900 and identified the woman as Catherine. Marie Antoinette has also been mentioned as a candidate for the lady's identity.

42. For years the date of this instrument was thought to be 1710, but a recent restoration determined its date to be 1760.

43. Frank Hubbard examined this instrument, and a drawing of its internal structure appears in *Hubbard 1965,* plate XXVIII.

44. *Hubbard 1965,* 191. Hubbard's statement was refuted as long ago as 1971. *Williams 1971,* 278, noted that other German builders gave no indication of adapting tonal concepts appropriate to the organ. Furthermore, in Hass's time Hamburg organ building was not in very high repute, and the new organ for Matheson's church, made in 1762, was built by a Saxon. Finally, the German organ at this time featured ranks of unison 8′ reed and flue stops, rather than the octave stops the Hasses built into these two instruments. Williams believes that the presence of 16′, 4′, and 2′ stops probably reflects a proclivity for experimentation, the same predilection that led to the various forms of the German piano in the second half of the century. But *Koster 2000,* 104, takes exception with Williams, holding that Hamburg organ building was in the highest repute in the early decades of the eighteenth century, and points to the popularity of Arp Schnitger and his sons during this time.

45. *Adlung 1768,* vol. 2, 110.

46. See *Krickeberg and Rase,* and *Restle and Aschenbrandt,* both cited in *Koster 1999;* see also *Stauffer,* 311.

47. *Strassburger Gelehrte Nachrichten* (1783), 178; cited in *Hubbard 1965,* 175.

48. See *Stengel,* 76; cited in *Germann 1985,* 138.

49. The ad appeared in the *Leipziger Intelligenz-Blatt* on April 19, 1766; see *Anthon.*

50. See *Koster 1999,* 70. An instrument such as this, which must have been between 10′ and 12′ long, staggers the imagination. As Koster notes, it would have allowed most of the harpsichord literature to be played at 16′, 8′, or 4′ pitch.

51. See *Heyde,* 76; translated by and cited in *Koster 1999,* 71.

52. *Germann 1978a,* 95

53. *Hubbard 1965,* 182.

54. *Koster 1999,* 67.

55. *Hubbard 1965,* 185.

56. *Koster 1999,* 67.

57. *Hubbard 1965,* 191. At least one eighteenth-century authority thought differently. *Gerber* observed that "the Hasses, father and son . . .

made excellent harpsichords and clavichords"; cited in *Russell 1959/1973*, 104. Hubbard's tables listing the characteristics of selected eighteenth-century German harpsichords are extremely valuable; see *Hubbard 1965*, 176–81.

58. Crenelated nameboards are not uncommon in eighteenth-century German instruments and are found on pianos well into the nineteenth.

59. I am quoting myself here; see *Kottick and Lucktenberg*, 93.

60. See *Skowroneck 1974*.

61. See *Helenius-Öberg 1986* for information on Roos and all the Swedish makers.

62. Gottlieb Silbermann is likely to have been the "Silbermann, in Dresden" referred to in *Thon;* see *Brauchli 1983*.

63. A picture of this harpsichord can be seen in *Nordenfelt-Åberg*, 53.

64. Nevertheless, around 1770 Pehr Lundborg and Pehr Lindholm, two of Rosenau's workmen, left him and set up on their own as clavichord builders, claiming that their former employer's workmanship was poor and his wood of second quality; see *Boalch III*, 158

65. The gap for the lute register is now closed up.

66. *Proceedings of the Royal Academy of Science,* 1739; cited in *Brauchli 1998*, 177.

67. Most of this information on Brelin and Faggot was taken from *Boalch III*, 23–24 and 57. For further information see *Helenius-Öberg 1986* and *1987*.

68. According to *Boalch III*, 257; but I was told the same thing by the museum staff when I saw the instrument in 1992.

69. *Boalch III*, 257, mistakenly identifies the disposition as 2×8′, 1×4′ with lute.

70. See *Dahl 1969*.

71. *Dahl 1969*, 13. Whether or not that was the original finish is unclear.

72. For more information on the Swedish clavichord see *Helenius-Öberg 1986* and *Brauchli 1998*, 176–84.

73. *Helenius-Öberg 1986*, 63, shows a photograph of this instrument.

74. See *Boalch III*, 693. One of these, Cornelis Hoornbee(c)k (1766/67–22), found greener pastures in Amsterdam, where he settled down and married a Dutch woman in 1706; see *Gierveld*, 142.

75. See *Boalch III*, 695, 710.

76. See *Boalch III*, 699.

77. See *Walther* and *Gerber.*

78. See *Krickeberg and Rase;* cited in *Stauffer*, 293, n. 12.

79. The definitive work on Mietke is *Krickeberg.*

80. See *Fremdschriftliche*, no. 95; cited in *Germann 1985*, 121, and *Stauffer*, 293.

81. See *Fremdschriftliche*, no. 627. For a complete list of the instruments in the inventory see *Russell 1959/1973*, 183.

82. *Stauffer*, 304.

83. See *Kilström 1991* and *Kilström 1994*. The attribution of this instrument, formerly thought to have been a Swedish-built anonyme, has only recently come to light, when Kilström discovered Mietke's signature and the date written on the top key lever. One would think that Mietke's name would appear in similar positions on the other two instruments, but in both cases the compasses were enlarged later in the eighteenth century, and identifying marks, if there were any, were removed.

84. Chinoiserie and japanning are complex terms to describe, with the former having to do with a fantasy-like imitation of oriental style, and the latter with an imitation of gold-on-black lacquer work. Obviously, chinoiserie can also include japanning, and in casual parlance the terms can almost be interchanged. Not entirely accurately, the application of either or both was called "japanning."

85. Nevertheless, some of the instruments of the Gräbner family in Dresden had veneered soundwells and painted keywells.

86. Mietke was said to have aped the French style, and given that all things French were fatuously admired at the Berlin court, this is not surprising. However, it seems that the builder claimed that his instruments were French imports and sold them for more than two to three times the amount he could charge for an instrument of German origin. He was eventually found out and forced to lower his prices. This anecdote, with its somewhat elusive sources, is cited in *Germann 1985*, 134, n. 51.

87. Johann Rost (ca. 1670–ca. 1747) was the only known student of Mietke. There is the supposition that he worked on Mietke's instruments after the latter's death, and it has been suggested that there is an unlikely possibility that the white and black instruments decorated by Dagly were actually made by Rost. Otherwise, none of his instruments have survived. See *Germann 1985*, 135, and *Krickeberg.*

88. One of the people responsible for this change of view was the musicologist J. Murray Barbour, who saw the history of temperament as an evolution from Pythagorean tuning with its undivided comma, through the mean-tone temperaments of the Renaissance, to the sixth-comma revolving temperaments of the Baroque, to the twelfth-comma equal temperament of the present day; see *Barbour.*

89. See, e.g., *Rasch.*

90. I suspect that most eighteenth-century harpsichord owners probably paid little attention to theoretical discussions of temperament. They were taught a way to tune, whatever it was, and

that is what they used. Then, as now, their major concern probably was setting a usable temperament, and only the most skillful and ambitious among them would be likely to consider learning to set something different.

91. The harpsichord portion of a 1712 claviorganum by Hermann Willenbrock (dates unknown) (New York, Metropolitan Museum of Art) is also from Hannover. Unfortunately the instrument has been rebuilt so many times (and finally turned into a piano) that it is difficult to say anything about it, other than that its keywell is highly decorated and its exterior is in chinoiserie. See *Boalch III*, 682–83.

92. See *Schröder 1928;* cited in *Boalch III*, 193.

93. In the 1782 edition of *Forkel.*

94. *Lemme;* see also *McGeary 1990.*

95. The case was repainted in black sometime prior to 1800. Later, just before the turn of the twentieth century, it was returned to gray, but around 1900 it was once again painted black. All the paint was removed in 1959; see *Berlin*, 102.

96. To be more precise, the heads of the natural touch plates are of ebony, while the tails are of black-stained wood.

97. See *Krickeberg and Rase.* This instrument has a modern history that will be discussed in Chapter 18.

98. *Adlung 1768*, vol. 2, 110.

99. *Adlung 1768*, vol. 2, 110.

100. *Koster 1999*, 67, alludes to this. Koster further points out that both Johann Lorenz Albrecht and Johann Friedrich Agricola, who edited the work, did not dispute Adlung's words.

101. See *Adlung 1758*, note to paragraph 246, cited in *Hubbard 1965*, 169.

102. See *Sprengel*, 265, cited in *Hubbard 1965*, 169–70.

103. When in Dresden, Burney took the trouble to remark on the elegant Dresden china on which he was served dinner at the home of Count Sachen, the minister for foreign affairs; see *Burney 1773,* 62–63.

104. *Boalch III*, 700.

105. The other son, Christian Heinrich (1704–69), was not a builder, but studied organ with J. S. Bach at Leipzig.

106. According to some other sources, Karl August went off on his own.

107. See *Boalch III*, 338.

108. John Phillips, private communication, notes that these modifications probably all took place in 1885, when the instrument was "renovated." I am exceedingly grateful to Mr. Phillips for his generous assistance with Gräbner harpsichords.

109. So claims *Hirt*, 37. John Phillips, private communication, disputes this.

110. *Boalch III* erroneously reports the date of this instrument as 1744.

111. John Phillips, private communication, cautiously believes that this unique scaling, reminiscent of the rising scales found early in the instrument's history, is characteristic of all Saxon harpsichords.

112. *Boalch III* erroneously reports the instition as the Museum für Kunsthandwerk. I thank John Phillips for this clarification.

113. *Boalch III*, 339, states that it is by either the father or the son, but John Phillips, who has examined the instrument closely, is convinced that it is by the younger. In a private communication he noted that the elder Gräbner retired from active building in 1735, when his son took his position as court builder, and that "there are some fundamental differences in the scale design, framing, soundboard ribbing and keyboards which suggest the work of a different member of the same tradition." Bohuslav Čižek is also of this opinion; see *Stauffer*, 312, n. 60; see also *Phillips.*

114. A photograph of the 1774 Gräbner can be seen in *Hirt*, 155.

115. See *Ernst*, 73–74.

116. An instrument possibly by Karl August, of unknown date and compass, thought to be in Brunswick, Germany, is disposed 2×8′. Even at this late date that disposition was not unknown in Germany and was standard in Vienna. *Ernst*, 73–74, had trouble accepting this as a bona fide German disposition; he thought it exclusively Italianate.

117. Another instrument in the Dresden tradition is an undated two-manual harpsichord by Jacob Hartmann (Eisenach, Bach-Haus). It is very much in the Gräbner style, with a disposition of 2×8′, 1×4′, shove coupler, a compass of FF–f³, and ebony naturals with ivory-topped sharps. Although now painted blue, it was originally painted or stained brown. See *Boalch III*, 364.

118. Although within the borders of France, Strasbourg has been a German city (Strassburg) for a substantial part of its history.

119. The current fame of Gottfried Silbermann's clavichords rests chiefly on Charles Burney's account in *Burney 1773*, 269–71, of C. P. E. Bach playing his Silbermann clavichord for him in 1772: "M. Bach was so obliging as to sit down to his *Silbermann clavichord,* and favorite instrument, upon which he played three or four of his choicest and most difficult compositions, with the delicacy, precision, and spirit, for which he is so justly celebrated among his countrymen. In the pathetic and slow movements, whenever he has a long note to express, he absolutely contrived to produce, from his instrument, a cry of sorrow and complaint, such as can only be effected upon the clavichord, and perhaps by himself."

In 1781 Emanuel Bach sold his Silbermann clavichord, immortalizing the occasion by composing a rondo, *Abschied vom meinem Silber-*

mann'schen Clavier ("Farewell to my Silbermann Clavier").

120. See *Clinkscale*, 266.

121. Actually, it was not Maffei's article he saw, but a German translation of that article by the Dresden poet Johann Ulrich König; see *König*, cited in *Pollens 1995*, 278. A facsimile of König's translation can be found in *Restle*, 401–8.

122. See *Pollens 1995*, 159 ff.

123. *Adlung 1768*, vol. 2, 116–17.

124. Nevertheless, it would be an exaggeration to suggest that Bach ended his life as a piano salesman.

125. *Clinkscale*, 265–66.

126. This is the museum's dating. The instrument could be later, by Johann Heinrich.

127. The rose of the 1785 Silbermann spinet (Vermillion, Shrine to Music Museum) is gilded.

128. For further information see *Hummel*.

129. See *Fontana*.

130. *Schubart*, 175, cited in *Cole 1998*, 193.

131. Stein's notebook, which still exists (Vienna, private ownership), itemizes those instruments; see *Latcham 1998*, 118, which also includes (123) a list of all Stein's surviving instruments (excluding clavichords). Latcham suggests that the survivors represent only 3 percent of Stein's output of harpsichords and pianos. If this pitiful representation is all that is left of a builder recognized as one of the greatest of his time, we can easily surmise that the survivors from all of eighteenth-century German harpsichord building total far less than 1 percent of the production. How many of these instruments spent their last days on a wood pile?

132. The instrument was described in the October 5, 1769, edition of the *Augsburger Intelligenzblatt*, cited in *Boalch III*, 183; see also *Rice 1995*, 36.

133. In fact, *Russell 1959/1973*, plate 95, mistakenly identifies it as a buff stop. *Koster 1994*, 143, seems to be the only authority to mention this stop.

134. See *Clinkscale*, 265–66; see also *Pollens 1995*, 181–82, with picture on p. 182. This device is a wooded batten with an ivory edge which, when pulled forward, contacts the strings. Supposedly, the effect was meant to imitate the harpsichord.

135. See *Latcham 1993*, 36.

136. *Latcham 1993*, 37, suggests that Stein omitted hammer leathers in order to give that end of the *vis-à-vis* the louder sound it needed to balance with the harpsichord. Both square and grand pianos around this time can be found with bare-wood hammers, perhaps attempting to reproduce a sound closer to that of the harpsichord.

137. *Rice 1995*, 61, reproduces some correspondence between the Austrian diplomat Norbert Hadrava and a friend of his concerning what is likely this *vis-à-vis*, in which Hadrava notes that Stein called it the *Büffel* stop. Hadrava refrained

from translating this stop into Italian, claiming that *dei buffali* was too humorous; therefore, he christened the stop "the harmonica."

138. "Sehr elastische Materie," described in the *Musikalsche Realzeitung*, 1759, and cited in *Boalch III*, 184.

139. See, e.g., *Koster 1994*, 142–43, and *Cole 1998*, 184.

140. *Koster 1996a*, 163.

141. *Reichardt*, vol. 1, cited in *Koster 1994*, 141.

142. Any sign of a plucking mechanism has long since disappeared; see *Koster 1994*, 133–46.

143. See *Cole 1998*, 179.

144. For example, the 1792 instrument by Johann Christoph Oesterlein.

145. See *Maunder*, 198–221. Maunder's groundbreaking study forms the basis for almost all the ensuing discussion on Viennese harpsichords. *Boalch III*, 692, lists only nine Viennese builders active in the century, but since three of the extant instruments are anonymous, it is likely there may have been more. Since Boalch documents only those builders who made harpsichords, for our purposes his figure may be more realistic than Maunder's.

146. See *Maunder*, 17–33.

147. *Maunder*, 17–33.

148. However, that rule was relaxed in 1781, when Emperor Joseph II (1741–90) issued his act of toleration, giving the same rights to Protestants and Greek Orthodox.

149. *Maunder*, 19.

150. The ensuing description is taken from *Maunder*, 35–38.

151. It will be remembered that slanted (but not reinforced) cheeks were found on two German instruments from the previous century, an anonyme from 1620 in Munich, and another, dated "early seventeenth century," in Hamburg.

152. Maunder's term; see *Maunder*, 35.

153. The existence of the Viennese short octave was first described in *Huber 1988* and *Huber 1991b*. Huber also describes it in *Huber 1991a*, and it is found in *Maunder*, 35–37, as well.

154. Contrary to all the other split notes, the apparent E is divided so that the C, rather than the BB, is in front; evidently, it was felt that the note most likely to be used should be handiest. This was also true of the placement of the accidentals in chromatic instruments with split sharps.

155. *Maunder*, 42, n. 14, observes that a change from white naturals and black sharps to the reverse occurred in Vienna between ca. 1710 and 1740.

156. Evidently, such stands were not uncommon. *Maunder*, 46–47, reports finding advertisements in Viennese newspaper for harpsichords with such chests under them.

157. *Maunder*, 40, n. 9, reports that the Mal-

lek instrument had been only just discovered, probably in 1998, the date his book was published.

158. See the chapter on "Viennese Keyboard-Instrument Makers" in *Maunder,* 17–33.

159. Not all of these instruments have been opened and examined internally, but *Maunder,* 44, believes that they were all constructed in a similar manner.

160. The soundboard of the Händel-Haus instrument has been replaced, so its scale is by no means certain. Originally it may have been brass.

161. See *Boalch III,* 712–13.

162. Most of our information on Swiss builders comes from *Rindlisbacher.*

163. For information on the Brosis see *Gutmann.*

164. *Bruggmann* describes an instrument found in Toggenburg, Switzerland, in 1949. It is an interesting harpsichord, but no evidence is advanced that would indicate a Swiss origin.

165. See *Bierdimpffl,* 54, 56, cited in *Boalch III,* 71.

166. *Gerber,* cited in *Boalch III,* 64.

167. *Adlung 1768,* vol. 2, 139.

168. Cited in *Boalch III,* 64.

169. Cited in *Boalch III,* 64. Both C. P. E. Bach and the Mozart family owned Friederici clavichords. Bach liked them because they did not have 4′ strings in the bass, as the North German clavichords did.

16. GREAT BRITAIN AND AMERICA

1. *Burney 1771,* 288.

2. *Hubbard 1965,* 162. But Hubbard went on to damn English harpsichords with faint praise, saying that they were so good that their luxurious tone almost interfered with the music. Few today would agree with that assessment.

3. There are at least two other English instruments extant from this period, but they were built to pass as Ruckers harpsichords and therefore are out of the mainstream of English building: a "1646 Andreas Ruckers" (England, private collection), and a "1634 Ioannes Ruckers" (London, Ham House). There is also a "1623" anonymous instrument (formerly Michael Thomas collection) that *O'Brien 1994,* 3, thinks may have come from the same workshop as the above fakes. O'Brien suggests that all three instruments were built in London, between 1725 and 1735.

James Talbot, an eighteenth-century professor at Cambridge University, gathered information about harpsichords between 1685 and 1701, seemingly in preparation for a book. He took measurements of an English harpsichord that belonged to a woman named Jenny, but since he did not appear to be particularly knowledgeable about the instrument, the descriptions are not very helpful. Nevertheless, it seems clear that Talbot was describing an English harpsichord with an International pedigree. See *Hubbard 1965,* 260–64, for a transcription of the manuscript. *Martin 1995* attempts to date the instrument and speculates that it might have been built by John Player. See also *Baines* for information about the rest of the contents of the manuscript.

4. *Boalch III,* 193, suggests that Tisseran was not a native of England, and that the instrument is an "amalgam of continental and English practice." *Hubbard 1965,* 153, was so convinced that this instrument was made by a Frenchman working in London that he does not even discuss it. If true, these opinions would seem to contradict our notion that no matter where the builder comes from, harpsichords are usually built according to local tradition. More likely, what Boalch and Hubbard were seeing were International, rather than foreign, traits. *Hubbard 1965,* 152–53, goes on to discuss instead an instrument by the builder John Player mentioned in a letter of 1712. After describing the harpsichord, Thomas Day, the letter writer, remarks that it comes with a leather cover. He may have meant a dust or carrying cover, but it is also possible that he was talking about a leather-covered outer case, although this seems farfetched.

5. See *Mould 1974.*

6. See *Cole 1993,* 108.

7. *Hubbard 1965,* 155, seems to have been the first to advance this explanation, albeit he offered it for the ca. 1725 Hitchcock, rather than the Smith, which he did not know.

8. Interestingly, Michael Cole, who restored the instrument in 1990, noted some resemblance between this instrument and one depicted in a portrait of Handel painted by the French artist Philip Mercier (1689–1760) around 1720; see *Cole 1993* for the author's argument. A reproduction of the Mercier portrait of Handel is on the cover of this issue of *Early Music.*

9. See *O'Brien 1994,* 2.

10. *O'Brien 1994,* 4, suggests that the Tisseran and the Coston soundboards were painted by the same artists.

11. According to a report in the *Newsletter* of the Friends of St. Cecilia's Hall and the Russell Collection of Early Keyboard Instruments (December 1999), the hinges, hardware, and stop knobs were originally gilded.

12. See *Victoria and Albert,* 69.

13. See *Broadwood.*

14. *Hubbard 1965,* 157–58, was not convinced that there was a genuine connection between Tabel and the Ruckers tradition, thinking that Tabel's two famous students, Burkat Shudi and Jacob Kirkman, fabricated the story in an

effort to bask in the reflected glory of the Ruckers name. As Hubbard put it (158), "it seems likely that the traditional role ascribed to Tabel and his posthumous fame were the fabrication of both Kirckman [*sic*] and Shudi in their dotage, a reminiscence of the good old days and a shrewd effort to claim descent from the Ruckers in order to share their eternal glory." Mould examined the 1721 instrument closely and takes exception to this view.

15. Photographs of Tabel's harpsichord can be seen in *Mould 1977*, plates 46–52.

16. Cited in *Mould 1977*, 59.

17. Cited in *Mould 1977*, 59–60.

18. What little is known of Tabel is covered in *Boalch III*, 188–89. Editor Charles Mould suggests that Tabel's fame may not have been as great as he would have had his contemporaries believe, and that his Ruckers-derived instruments were so different from the indigenous product that there was little demand for them before the 1740s, by which time he was dead.

19. *Dale*, 15, reports that in Shudi's case we have records of his family going back to the ninth century.

20. *Burney 1819*.

21. "Questo cimbalo è del^a Sig^ra Anna Strada, 1731, London," cited in *Dale*, 33.

22. Cited in *Wainright*, 23.

23. As reported by *Dale*, 31.

24. Evidently that royal warrant continued for at least as late as 1903. See *Wainright*, 257. Many of Shudi's customers must have purchased his instruments for political reasons, since the Prince of Wales supported him, while the king, his estranged father, supported Kirkman.

25. The battle of Prague was an early engagement in the Seven Years' War (1756–63), yet another conflict fought to achieve political dominance in central Europe. It pitted England and Prussia against Austria, France, Russia, Saxony, Sweden, and Spain. Frederick was unable to sustain his early triumph, and by 1763 all seemed lost. At the last moment however, when Frederick was surrounded by his enemies and defeat seemed inevitable, Peter III, an enthusiastic admirer of the Prussian emperor, succeeded to the Russian throne. He withdrew his forces, thereby giving Frederick the victory he so desperately sought. The whereabouts of the 1745, if it still exists, are unknown. Of the other four, the first, dated 1765, Shudi's number 496, is believed to have been in Poland before World War II. It has since disappeared. The second and third, dated 1766 and numbered 511 and 512, are in Potsdam and Moscow (Muzei Muzykal'noi Kul'tury imeni M. I. Glinki). The number and location of the fourth are unknown. See *Wainright and Mobbs*, which includes photographs of numbers 496, 511, and 512.

26. That painting, now believed to have been by Marcus Tuscher, hangs in the National Portrait Gallery, London. See *Wainright*, insertion between pages 104–5, for a color reproduction.

27. The story of nephew Joshua's insertion into Burkat's life is rather dramatic. According to *Dale*, 51–53, Burkat's older brother Nicholas (1700–1760), a cavalry soldier, fought with a local butcher in Schwanden. Neither man was severely injured, but a bystander who attempted to keep the men apart was killed. To avoid prosecution, Nicholas fled Schwanden and went to London, to his brother's home, taking his son Joshua with him. Evidently his welcome there was not a warm one, and his stay was short. From London he went to Holland, and then to America. It is not known when Joshua joined Burkat's household, and it is possible that Burkat raised him. He would have been only three years old when Nicholas brought him to London.

28. The exchange is cited in *Dale*, 53–55.

29. The affidavit is cited in *Russell 1959/1973*, 169.

30. *Public Advertiser*, 1775, cited in *Dale*, 56.

31. See *Ripin 1970c*, 20, for details on the workings of the Venetian swell; see also *Halffpenny 1946*.

32. In order for the swell to operate effectively a special music desk or solid plank of wood was supplied, one that completely covered the area between the jackrail and the nameboard, to prevent any leakage of sound. Many instruments equipped with a swell are today missing that accoutrement, thus presenting a false impression of their effectiveness.

33. The two Ruckers harpsichords, both rebuilt doubles, were finally sold in 1790 and 1792. The buyers paid very little for them, probably acquiring them as curios rather than for any intrinsic value as useful instruments.

34. *Cole 1998*, 132 ff., holds that these early piano sales refer to squares, not grands. He notes that it is not until 1785 that a grand piano was sold by Broadwood.

35. See *Wainright*, 60. *Boalch III* notes that the firm averaged twenty harpsichords a year from 1740–90, with averages of thirteen a year from 1740–59, fifteen from 1750–69, twenty-three from 1770–79, and twenty-five from 1780–89.

36. *Burney 1819* referred to both Shudi and Kirkman as foremen of Tabel.

37. *Boalch III*, 103, notes that from 1755 on the builder signed official documents with "Kirkman," and that is the spelling adopted here. Nevertheless, many modern sources spell the name as "Kirckman."

38. *Engel*, 356, reported that the younger Joseph Kirkman remembered that he and his father built a harpsichord in 1809. *Koster 1994*, from which this information is cited, notes on p.

184 that by that date harpsichords had fallen into such disfavor that second-hand instruments could be had for next to nothing. Koster suggests that it was vanity on the part of the buyer, who required a new, rather than a used, instrument.

39. *Burney 1819.*

40. See *Boalch III*, 104–5, who quotes the omnipresent Charles Burney.

41. Smith seemed to be interested in several aspects of the harpsichord, including stringing material. He was opposed to the use of equal temperament (which in any case probably would not have been generally practiced in England at this early a date), noting in his *Harmonics* that it produced a "harmony extremely course and disagreeable." Cited in *Helmholtz,* 548.

42. Shudi and Snetzler must have been fairly good friends, since Shudi named him one of the executors of his estate, and bequeathed his Frederick the Great ring to him.

43. See *Williams 1977.*

44. See the exchange of letters between Hopkinson, Jefferson, and Burney, in *Russell 1959/1973,* 177–82.

45. There was no love lost between the king and his son William.

46. See *Mobbs and MacKenzie.* The instruments discussed in the article were made for Longman and Broderip; but no matter the signature, they are magnificent harpsichords.

47. *Boalch III,* 57–58.

48. It will be remembered that the soundboards of the Coston and Smith instruments were also barred in this manner, and it may have represented an earlier practice still used by some.

49. Cited in *James,* 67.

50. *Mould 1976.*

51. See *Boalch III,* 107.

52. See *Good,* 118 ff. It is a commentary on the conservative nature of instrument building that, prior to that point, English makers seemed to make no attempt to strengthen that joint and avoid the repeated failures of their harpsichords and pianos.

53. *Koster 1994,* 103, remarks on the conservative nature of English harpsichord decoration. He notes that the Boston Museum's 1758 Kirkman is veneered in walnut, even though mahogany veneer had been fashionable in furniture for about twenty-five years. He also observes (132) that walnut veneers were used by English builders as late as the 1780s.

54. *Koster 1994,* 103, makes a similar remark about the large strap hinges, as well as the balustrade legs, which by 1758 had been out of style for more than fifty years.

55. See *Russell 1959/1973,* 163, for a list of these.

56. *Hubbard 1965,* 162, thought the French disposition more musical.

57. See *Barnes 2001* for more information on the use of leather in late English harpsichords.

58. It is not clear where the machine stop came from, but *Boalch III,* 176, thinks that Shudi may have invented it specifically for the harpsichords he supplied to Frederick the Great.

59. One is immediately reminded of the pedal-operated register-changing device described by Mace a century earlier. Although there is no evidence for it, it is possible that copies of this earlier machine were preserved, to be resurrected and adapted to the newer instrument by Shudi.

60. *Mobbs and MacKenzie,* 43, perceptively observes that although the change on the lower manual is one of dynamics, on the upper manual it is more a question of tonal contrast.

61. See *Ripin 1970c,* 18–19, for a detailed explanation of the workings of the English machine.

62. *Mobbs and MacKenzie.*

63. The Venetian swell appeared on a few pianos, but generally speaking, once the production of harpsichords came to an end, it lost any significance to stringed keyboards. Shudi's friend Snetzler, however, adapted the device to the organ, where it became standard.

64. Backers is considered to be the father of the English grand piano. Originally from the Netherlands, he invented the English grand action with the assistance of his apprentice Robert Stodart and his friend John Broadwood, who was then still working with Shudi. Charles Burney thought highly of his pianos. In his famous statement about German builders doing better work outside their country than in it, he cited the excellent pianos of Backers as an example. On the other hand, in *Burney,* he thought Backers to be "a harpsichord maker of the second rank."

65. See *NGEKI,* 198, for an engraving of Plenius's lyrichord.

66. Cited in *Russell 1959/1973,* 84.

67. The entire correspondence, the originals of which are in the Library of Congress, is found in *Russell 1959/1973,* 177–82.

68. Cited in *Russell 1959/1973,* 180.

69. Merlin's down-striking piano action was comparatively simple and could be retrofitted to existing harpsichords. In 1779 he converted a 1758 Kirkman single into a harpsichord-piano (Boston, Museum of Fine Arts) by fitting it with this action and also supplied it with the machine stop and pedals he devised for his "compound harpsichord."

70. According to *Boalch III,* 505, this harpsichord may have been owned by Catherine the Great.

71. The device is pictured in *Deutsches Museum,* 100–101.

72. Cited in *Scholes,* 202.

73. In England the wheelchair is still occasionally known as the "Merlin chair."

74. *Dalyell*, 147, cited in *Scholes*, 206.

75. *Busby*, 137, cited in *Scholes*, 206.

76. For more on Merlin see *Mould 1973* and *Mould 1985*.

77. *Boalch III*, 693–95.

78. Cited in *Boalch III*, 359.

79. A 1770 (whereabouts unknown) might be a spinet rather than a harpsichord; a 1774 double (Birmingham, England, private ownership) is of dubious authenticity; and a 1780 double (Wildbad, Germany, private ownership) might have been either a Baker Harris single converted to a double by someone else, or a single by someone else converted to a double by Harris.

80. See *Boalch III*, 711.

81. See *Boalch III*, 173.

82. See *Boalch III*, 704.

83. *Thomas 1979*.

84. According to *Wells 1984*, 6–7, the swell was added at the end of the eighteenth century. At the same time the soft leather plectra that Weber had used for the front 8′ jacks were replaced by quill.

85. *Russell 1959/1973* pictures this clavicytherium in plates 77 and 78 and erroneously states that the disposition is 2×8′, 1×4′. *Boalch III*, 677, repeats the error.

86. The soundboard on this instrument was replaced by Michael Thomas in the 1960s.

87. This may not be completely true. In *Lloyds Evening Post and British Chronicle* of July 1771, the York builder Thomas Haxby advertised upright harpsichords for sale. However, it is not clear that the instruments are by him, or even that they were made in Britain. Cited in *Boalch III*, 85–86. I thank Peter Bavington for bringing this citation to my attention.

88. In fact, the instrument deconstructed in *Hubbard 1965*, plate XXIII, that Hubbard thought to be an anonymous English bentside spinet, is actually a 1771 John Harris (Boston, Museum of Fine Arts), built in Boston. Hubbard did not suspect that it was made in America.

89. Tannenberg is of some importance to the clavichord world, since his design for one, along with instructions for building it, still exist; see *McGeary 1982*.

90. Dunlap and Claypools's *American Daily Advertiser*, no. 4600, January 8, 1794, cited in *Watson 1997*, 134.

91. In the nineteenth century the harpsichord was turned into a piano, with part of the front of the case cut off. The American maker John Challis rebuilt it as a single, then as a double. See *Watson 1997*, 130–35, and *Haney 1974a*, 12.

92. Hopkinson's letters and some of his diagrams are given in *Russell 1959/1973*, 170–76, and plates 52a and b.

93. *Recreations and Studies of a Country Clergy-man of the Eighteenth Century, Being Selections from the Correspondence of the Rev. Thomas Twining . . .* (London, 1882), 25–26, cited in *Ripin 1970c*, 20.

94. *Schott 1985b*, 34, notes that only a small minority of harpsichords had these expressive accessories. Nevertheless, the devices were available, and if one had the funds to purchase a grand harpsichord, they were not prohibitively expensive. If harpsichords so fitted out had served the music better, or even as well as the piano, they would have been far more common.

17. THE HARPSICHORD HIBERNATES

1. By 1842 production was up to twenty-five hundred pianos a year, and Broadwood was one of London's twelve largest employers. The Broadwood factory, on Horseferry Road, consisted of four groups of buildings, each with three stories. The total work space measured more than a half mile in length; see *Wainright*, 150–51.

2. The railroad revolutionized music in other ways as well. When Mozart and his mother toured Europe in the 1770s they moved in the time-honored fashion, by horse-drawn coach; but eighty years later, when Brahms and the Hungarian violinist Eduard Reményi toured, they traveled by train.

3. Cited in *Ellis*, 382.

4. Cited in *Ellis*, 383.

5. For more on this theme see *Robbins Landon*.

6. *Boalch III*, 252–53, expresses slight reservations about this, but a group of instruments whose compasses all commence with BB or E leaves one with suspicions.

7. Many of them have retained this temperament to the present day.

8. See *Sween*, 92.

9. *Devrient* remarked that he and Mendelssohn called on Zelter in 1829 and found him playing his harpsichord. The Berlin Museum claims that its 1792 Oesterlein double is the instrument in question; see *Berlin*, 96, 242–43.

10. *Palmer 1989*, 12, reports that this harpsichord was later exhibited in the St. Louis World's Fair of 1904.

11. *Kilvert*, 255, cited in *Palmer 1989*, 2. Palmer relates this anecdote, others mentioned here, and yet others in *Palmer 1983*.

12. *Koster 1994*, 94, n. 5, includes an informative mini-essay on redecoration by Sheridan Germann, who identified the 1709 Blanchet spinet, the ca. 1736 Hemsch, the 1643 Andreas Ruckers, the 1737 Jean-Louis Bas, the 1765 François-Etienne Blanchet II, and the 1770 Pascal Taskin harpsichords as redecorated products of that workshop.

13. See *Victoria and Albert,* 102–3.

14. A list of instruments restored by Tomasini can be found in *Elste 1991,* 245. Elste's monograph is particularly valuable for information on the harpsichord in the late nineteenth and early twentieth centuries.

15. See *Boalch III,* 489.

16. *Moscheles,* 236–37, cited in *Palmer 1989,* 2–3.

17. *Wainright,* 217–18.

18. In *Steinert,* the author related the details of his passion for collecting.

19. The instrument was not passed down through the Taskin family to Émile-Alexandre; rather, the singer specifically sought to purchase a harpsichord made by his illustrious ancestor and found the 1769 in a provincial furniture store; see *Boalch III,* 652.

20. These works are cited by *Palmer 1989,* 5, who has an 1893 program of the Société des Instruments Anciens in his possession. Recital fare today is meatier, and such pieces, while still heard from time to time, are more likely to be considered as "fluff," suitable mainly as encores.

21. For more information on French collectors see *Gétreau 1995.*

22. This harpsichord had been on loan to the collection of the conservatoire, and now to the Musée de la Musique.

23. For a list of sixty-two harpsichords and spinets confiscated from the nobility and wealthy bourgeois during the French Revolution, see *Hess.* Unfortunately most of those listed were subsequently disposed of in one way or another.

24. The story of this collection from its beginnings through the establishment of the Musée de la Musique is told in *Gétreau 1996a.*

25. This abbreviated description of collectors and collections is not meant to be complete, but simply to indicate how the activity was carried out. For a more complete list of collections see *Boalch III,* ix–xxxii.

26. This information comes from *Hoover.*

27. *Sween* describes how Franciolini made his genuine instruments as well as his counterfeits resemble the romanticized nineteenth-century ideal of the harpsichord.

28. See *O'Brien 2000* for an account of the probable original state of this instrument.

29. *Schott 1974,* 88, cites the case of Wilhelm von Bode, one of the founders of modern art history, who purchased a wax bust falsely attributed to Leonardo da Vinci.

30. *Ripin/Franciolini,* ix. In 1890 Franciolini published the first of several sales catalogs listing his inventory. Some of these included drawings of the instruments, and these have been such invaluable aids in identifying bogus harpsichords that Ripin republished them.

18. THE HARPSICHORD REVIVAL FROM THE PARIS EXPOSITION TO WORLD WAR II

1. The harpsichord revival is dealt with in a number of standard sources. The entry in *NGEKI,* 97–110, is a succinct but valuable account. *Palmer 1989* gives considerably more detail but deals mostly with the United States. *Russell 1955–56* provides a fascinating account by an astute observer. *Schott 1974* is a genuinely informative article, and the present account owes much to it. *Elste 1991* is also quite useful, as well as quite complete. *Zuckermann* is a retrospective work of incalculable value. All these sources were consulted in the preparation of this chapter.

2. National pride may also have played a part in their decision to revive the harpsichord. These instruments, and the one made by Tomasini, also exhibited at the Exposition, are now in Berlin, Staatliches Institut für Musikforschung.

3. The first of these was the London Exposition of 1851, for which the Crystal Palace was erected. Other famous examples were the Paris Exposition of 1867, the Philadelphia Centennial Exhibition of 1876, and the Chicago Columbian Exhibition of 1893.

4. The 1889 Tomasini has never been opened, so neither its soundboard thickness, its barring, nor its internal structure is known; nevertheless, some beams can be seen through the rose hole, and given Tomasini's piano background, it is unlikely that the soundboard was barred in the traditional eighteenth-century French manner.

5. For more information on the 1889 Tomasini harpsichord see *Berlin,* 279–83.

6. For more information on the 1889 Érard harpsichord see *Berlin,* 284–88.

7. Two Taskin spinets from 1788 have rococo curves, but they are the only examples I know of.

8. For more information on the 1889 Pleyel harpsichord see *Berlin,* 289–93.

9. It could be argued that these instruments were more influenced by English models than by French. In fact, this is the conclusion of *NGEKI,* 98.

10. De Falla was Spanish, but lived in Paris from 1907 to 1914 and was much influenced by Debussy, Ravel, and Impressionism. Nevertheless, the two works mentioned here are neoclassical in outlook and use the harpsichord to evoke earlier times.

11. Even after World War II their instruments continued to be revered in some quarters. See, e.g., *Richard,* which calls for a revival of this instrument.

12. Fairly or not, De Wit does not seem to have had a good reputation as a dealer. *Russell 1959/1973,* 123, calls him "unreliable."

13. The Berlin Staatliches Institut now attributes it to the workshop of Johann Heinrich Harrass and dates it ca. 1700.

14. As noted in an earlier chapter, Adlung mentioned the possibility of removing a set of 8′ strings from a 2×8′, 1×4′ instrument, and replacing it with overwound 16′ strings. Although such occurrences undoubtedly took place, it would have been a compromise, and not a very satisfactory one, since 16′ strings need their own soundboard area and bridge. Hence, the twentieth-century builders who emulated this practice did not choose the most effective method of providing their instruments with the 16′ sound, and the tone quality of the 8′ was compromised as well. Furthermore, there seems to have been a prejudice against long harpsichords, probably because it was feared that potential buyers would not be able to fit them into their apartments and homes. As a result, instruments that barely had the length to sustain a 2×8′, 1×4′ stringing were also saddled with a set of overwound 16′ strings. Nevertheless, even with their longest models, the 16′ was still treated in what must have originally been a crude although usable attempt to increase a harpsichord's resources. Still, with few well-restored antiques with which to compare, the early keyboard world, such as it was, was well pleased with its new versions of the old harpsichord.

15. Much of the preceding paragraph was extracted from *Schott 1974*.

16. *Neupert*, 59.

17. From the viewpoint of our superior knowledge it is easy to denigrate these *Serien* instruments; but it should be remembered that there were few antiques in playing condition, and most of those had been poorly restored. From a cultural standpoint, it made no sense to those builders merely to copy what had been done before; that was not progress, that was antiquarianism, a concept that had no place in modern instrument building. Furthermore, the same drive for modernity could be seen in the revival of the gamba, the recorder, and other obsolete music-making devices. To be viable in the twentieth century it had to be a twentieth-century instrument. *Rutledge* is an enlightening account of the revival of the gamba, a story that has some of the same characters and follows the same path as the harpsichord.

18. Several books have been written about Dolmetsch. The earliest, by the British musicologist Robert Donington, was *Donington*. Mabel Dolmetsch wrote the sympathetic *Dolmetsch 1958*. *Campbell* is probably the most thorough and accurate account of the man. *Dolmetsch 1981*, a rather one-sided, although endearingly personal, view of Dolmetsch's work written by his son, Carl Dolmetsch, is found in *Paul*, 57–72. For a more balanced account see *Palmer 1989*, 14–45. All these sources were consulted in this section on Dolmetsch's life and works.

19. Dolmetsch eventually wrote a ground-breaking book, *Dolmetsch 1915*.

20. Dolmetsch built six clavichords after the Hass. He built many clavichords over his career and has been recognized as a fine designer of that instrument.

21. For a more detailed account of the Arts and Crafts movement and its influence on Dolmetsch, see *Adlam 1996*.

22. *Schott 1974*, 87, suspects that Dolmetsch had intended the instrument to be disposed 2×8′, but gave it only one 8′ because he was in a rush to get it ready for the exhibition.

23. According to *Russell 1955–56*, 66.

24. See *Troeger 1996*, 213. Troeger got his numbers from the Chickering Archives, available on microfilm through the Smithsonian Institution.

25. *Schott 1974*, 92.

26. Gaveau continued to produce harpsichords—grands and spinets, and clavichords as well—until the Great Depression of the 1930s.

27. In his short monograph about his father, *Dolmetsch 1981*, 68–70, insists that the invention failed only because those outside of Haslemere lacked the skill to adjust it, and suggests that the same argument was heard about the complexity of the piano in the eighteenth century. When the Dolmetsch shop resumed the production of harpsichords after World War II the device was abandoned.

28. *Dolmetsch 1958*, 28–29, tells of a visit she and Arnold made to Franciolini's shop in Florence in 1897 or 1898 (it is clearly Franciolini, although she does not mention his name). She relates that in contradistinction to most people who visited the old reprobate, Dolmetsch had a pretty good idea of Franciolini's chicanery and was able to spot his forgeries.

29. The limerick was written by Grant O'Brien. The term "stifle bar" was coined by John Barnes, who was, in fact, the "old man with a beard," and who was responsible for the reverse restoration of many instruments that had been "Dolmetsched."

30. In the forty or so years in which he was active Hodsdon claimed to have made seven hundred instruments, most of them spinets, virginals, and clavichords. That would be an average of seventeen or eighteen a year, which does not seem likely, since he essentially worked alone; see *Zuckermann 1969a*, 130. By the time Zuckermann's book appeared Hodsdon seemed to have lost interest in harpsichord building.

31. See *Wardman*.

32. Lambert's book, *Studio Portrait Lighting*, published in 1930, is still in print at this writing.

33. According to Ruth Dyson, in liner notes

to her 1981 recording of Herbert Howells's "Lambert's Clavichord" and eight pieces from "Howells' Clavichord," played on a Goff clavichord, cited in *Wardman*.

34. *Paul,* 120–23.

35. For more information about Thomas Goff see *Paul,* 120–23, and *Wardman*.

36. By the end of her life Woodhouse owned five Goff and three Dolmetsch clavichords. See *Troeger 1997*.

37. Woodhouse was among the very first artists to make a commercial recording of the harpsichord, in 1920. Her recordings were rereleased on CD in the late 1990s by Pearl Records, PEACD9242.

38. In view of Beecham's widely publicized witticism that a harpsichord sounded like a bird cage played with a toasting fork (another, perhaps later, version has it that a harpsichord sounded like two cats copulating on a tin roof), one wonders how sympathetic he really was toward Woodhouse's playing.

39. *Douglas-Home.*

40. Andrea, not Andreas as reported in *Zuckermann 1969a,* 121–23. Zuckermann was undoubtedly thinking he was named after Andreas Ruckers; but Andrea was named after his godfather, Andrea Pallis. It would appear that Zuckermann also erred in identifying Robert Goble as "George" Goble in captioning a picture of him (122), probably confusing Robert with a popular midcentury American television comedian, George Gobel; but in a letter to the editor, *The Harpsichord* 3, no. 2 (May–July 1970), 18, he explains that he had to leave for London before the book was done and thus never saw the final proofs. Many of the captions, he said, were written by the publisher.

41. Even so, these measures were not sufficient to prevent hangers.

42. In practice, the coarse adjustment was only used when a string was replaced by a new one.

43. In her interview with Harold Haney, *Haney 1974b,* Restout recalls that Landowska required all her students to go to the Pleyel factory for instruction on maintenance.

44. I speak here not only from written accounts, but from personal experience as well.

45. Pleyel never did turn out harpsichords in large numbers. *Dahl 1973* estimated their production at about one per year.

46. In her memoirs *Harich-Schneider,* 81–83, the German harpsichordist and Landowska student Eta Harich-Schneider describes Lew as a Communist (not unusual for an intellectual in those days), the marriage to Landowska as "tragic," and his death as "murder by right-wing terrorists." There are also allusions that Landowska's sexual orientation was bisexual. It is possible, if not likely, that Landowska's reputation has

been polished by her biographers. The excerpt is translated by and cited in *Palmer 1989,* 57–58.

47. *Haney 1974b.* December 7 was the day the Japanese attacked the American naval base at Pearl Harbor, Hawaii. Restout's interview and her description of her life with Landowska is gripping, and her account of Landowska's death and its aftermath is particularly beautiful.

48. Landowska is reported to have told the great cellist Pablo Casals, "You play Bach *your* way and I'll play him *his* way."

49. *Musical Courier,* November 19, 1923, 20, cited in *Palmer 1989,* 47. This was during her first American tour.

50. *Thomson,* 203. Thomson's review, entitled "A Shower of Gold," made it clear that he was utterly taken with Landowska as an artist, and the fact that she was playing a harpsichord was distinctly secondary. Harpsichordist and pianist Rosalyn Tureck, in *Haney 1975,* 19, expressed the same thought almost thirty years later, saying "I feel that [Landowska] was the greatest harpsichord player I have ever heard, or ever expect to hear, as an artist who understood the instrument. There is still no one who can touch her toe for the understanding of the instrument."

51. *Haney 1969,* 15.

52. Challis was hypoglycemic most of his life, and in his later years had to confine himself to finishing work only.

53. See *Haney 1972b,* 7.

54. Almost all the information in this paragraph and the next was extracted from the informative *Palmer 1989*.

55. He seemed to have been quite successful in his lecture-recitals, since it was reported that a Yale-Princeton basketball game was postponed because a Whiting recital was taking place that evening; see *Palmer 1989,* 32–36. Palmer's account goes a long way to resurrect the name of this important American pioneer of the harpsichord.

56. *Palmer 1989,* 42, reports that van Buren had a harpsichord on order from Dolmetsch for years, but the builder was so far behind that he returned her deposit. Nevertheless, she was able to buy the Dolmetsch-Chickering that had belonged to Busoni, after his death in 1924.

57. He was the assistant director of Herbert Hoover's Belgian Relief effort.

58. *Palmer 1989,* 76, reports that when the duo, rather than Landowska, had been given a particular concert engagement, she grumbled that "these children are taking the food out of my mouth."

19. THE MODERN HARPSICHORD

1. Wolfgang Zuckermann's book by this name (*Zuckermann 1969a*), cited so often in the previous

chapter, is a primary source of information about the various builders discussed here. Unless specific factual material is involved, the book is not expressly cited. Larry Palmer's *Harpsichord in America* (*Palmer 1989*) was also an invaluable reference. The periodical *The Harpsichord* is a unique source that chronicled the shift from the revival harpsichord to the historically informed instrument. It was conceived, edited, typed, and published by Harold L. Haney, a dedicated amateur harpsichordist who worked for the Colorado Chamber of Commerce. In evenings and on weekends, as a labor of love, he produced *The Harpsichord,* for which he also wrote, supplied photos, and on occasion supported financially. The magazine was published quarterly from 1968 to 1976, the years in which the center of gravity shifted from revival instruments with heavy cases and metal frames to lightly built modern harpsichords based on classical models. Although Haney did not intend to chart this shift, *The Harpsichord*'s thirty-two issues were nevertheless snapshots of the early keyboard scene during those years, and in that sense invaluable historical documents.

2. To the amazement of all concerned, more than thirty thousand albums of Landowska's RCA Victor recording of Bach's *Goldberg Variations* (first issued on 78 rpm disks) were sold in 1976. It was named one of the year's outstanding recordings by the *Review of Recorded Music.* Landowska's playing still holds up, particularly since through electronic means her Pleyel harpsichord is given a depth and resonance it lacked in real life.

3. *Time,* February 3, 1947, 46.

4. *Zuckermann 1969a,* 47, also devised six categories, which are somewhat different from mine: "(1) faithful individual copies of historic instruments; (2) faithful copies in production; (3) free copies; (4) commercial production; (5) new designs; and (6) complete break with tradition." My classification of these building practices has the advantage of the clarity gained from thirty years' distance from events that were still in progress while Zuckermann was writing.

5. *Zuckermann 1969a,* 127.

6. They may also have started a trend. Many of today's builders have gone through graduate work—more than a few hold the Ph.D. or some other doctoral title, but like Hubbard and Dowd, they decided that the life of a builder would be more fulfilling. Although I was never tempted to give up the academic life for a career as a harpsichord builder, I was profoundly affected by the kit harpsichord, which led to my present involvement with the instrument as a scholar and part-time builder.

7. The Serviceman's Readjustment Act, popularly known as the GI Bill of Rights or simply the GI Bill, was enacted by Congress in 1944. Part of its purpose was to aid any serviceman or woman

who wished to do so to obtain a college education. It was still in effect during the Korean conflict, in which I served, and I am forever grateful for its assistance, which saw me through to the completion of my doctorate.

8. *Hubbard 1984,* 7–8. This is a transcription by Thomas McGeary of a lecture given by Hubbard on June 28, 1974, at the School of Music of Indiana University. *The Historical Harpsichord,* cited many times in this work, is a monograph series commemorating and building on the work of Frank Hubbard.

9. *Hubbard 1984,* 10.

10. The 1637 Ruckers had belonged to Hugh Gough, and Hubbard had an opportunity to study it when he worked with him.

11. Although all were based on that Ruckers single, one was a double.

12. *Haney 1972a,* 17.

13. *Haney 1971a,* 13.

14. *Hubbard 1984,* 10–11. In view of his and Dowd's achievements, Hubbard is rather hard on himself as he writes, "We, of course, thought to temper the manifest eccentricities of the past by choosing the best, judiciously adding obvious modern technological improvements, and employing certain materials unknown to earlier ages. This was an error which has taken many years partially to overcome. . . . Our harpsichords, by their very choice of model, the use of materials such as screws and plywood, music wire and machined brass parts, showed their age and our fatal knowledge of what came after our model in the development of the instrument. Although they were more useful in the performance of old music than the modernist concoctions of Pleyel and Dolmetsch, they testified to our failure to enter into the world of the past. Although they pretended to follow seventeenth-century Flemish models, they would not have seemed very familiar to Froberger or Chambonnières."

15. At least at first. All new construction expands and contracts more at first, then settles down after a few seasonal cycles.

16. Many of today's builders use a lightweight bottom screw, but this is a far cry from the long, heavy, metal screws of the past.

17. With seasonal changes the case may expand or shrink in height, and on larger instruments it may be necessary to raise or lower all the jacks by raising or lowering the back end of the keyframe.

18. If the stigma of instability placed on the antiques and their reproductions was unfair, there was more than a core of truth to it when the harpsichord was transplanted to the New World. The instrument was developed in Western Europe, where a fairly stable humidity without great temperature extremes is found throughout the year. But the North American climate is not quite so

temperate, and much of the continent sees far greater extremes in temperature and humidity. The twentieth-century phenomenon of central forced-air heating compounded the situation, ensuring that a harpsichord traversing the continent with its artist would be exposed to extreme heat and humidity in the South, extreme heat and dryness in the Southwest, extreme cold and dryness in the northern parts of the United States and Canada, and all of the above in the Midwest. Fortunately, the move to more historically oriented harpsichords coincided with the adoption of air conditioning and central heating systems with humidity control. The interior climate on the North American continent is much more benign than it was fifty years ago, and historically informed harpsichords stand a much better chance of survival now than they did when radiant heating and the lack of means to regulate humidity were the rule.

19. *Russell 1955–56.*

20. *Zuckermann 1969a,* 60–64, 67.

21. *McClew.* At the Boston Early Music Festival of 2001 I struck up an acquaintance with a gentleman named Peter Martin who, after learning of my involvement with this book, related that his 1958 Hubbard and Dowd French double was the first to be quilled in Delrin. Mr. Martin maintained that he was the one responsible for getting Hubbard, Dowd, Dupont, and Delrin together, through an uncle whose work dealt with the strength of plastics and who knew everyone in the plastics industry. Finally, he told me that in the intervening years the instrument has suffered only three or four broken plectra.

22. *Hubbard 1984,* 14.

23. As, e.g., in *Dowd 1984.* Dowd retired from active building around 1990.

24. In 1968 Skowroneck wrote an article, *Skowroneck 1974,* in which he attempted to influence his fellow German makers, almost all of whom were still deeply committed to the building practices and tonal resources of the *Serien* instruments. His words fell on mostly deaf ears.

25. David Way, who was just beginning his career as a harpsichord builder, depended heavily on Hyman, whom he had retained as a consultant. At Hyman's death Way took over his order list and, with the help of two Hyman apprentices, eventually filled them all. In design, materials, joinery, and sound, these instruments were quite different from the kit harpsichords that were then Way's stock-in-trade.

26. Michael Thomas, a presence on London's early keyboard scene rather than an important builder, influenced many of today's English makers. He ran a "Harpsichord Centre" and filled the pages of the *English Harpsichord Magazine* with articles dealing with his restorations and the lessons purportedly learned from them. Collector, restorer, dealer, teacher, and performer,

Thomas was an erratic individual. While his speculative writings need to be taken with a grain of salt, he did help spread the word about the beauties of the antiques and the wisdom of building instruments like them.

27. See, e.g., *Schütze.*

28. *Zuckermann 1969a,* 170.

29. Rutkowski and Robinette have been the restorers for the instruments in the Yale collection for many years.

30. *Haney 1974c,* 18.

31. The name of the firm is Robert Morley and Co., Ltd. The Morleys have been building instruments for at least six generations.

32. By 1969, the year of publication of *Zuckermann 1969a,* de Blaise had produced some eight hundred instruments.

33. *Zuckermann 1969a,* 107.

34. *Zuckermann 1969a,* 172.

35. *Zuckermann 1969a,* 174.

36. *Haney 1973–74,* 17.

37. Ammer and one other firm, Lindholm, were the main producers of harpsichords for the postwar Communist world and supplied countries from Poland to China with *Serien* instruments.

38. Cited in *Zuckermann 1969a,* 154.

39. *Adlam 1994.*

40. In 1965 the harpsichordist Fernando Valenti, who then owned a large Challis, told me the following story (which may be apocryphal). He was to play a recital at the University of Wisconsin, in Madison. Arriving late at night, without realizing it he parked his vehicle, with the harpsichord inside, just a few feet from Lake Mendota. He rounded up some workmen to unload his Challis, and as they were getting it out the back of the van the heavy instrument got away from them and plunged into the lake. According to Valenti, after it dried out it was found to be in perfect tune and in concert-ready condition.

41. *Haney 1969,* 21.

42. Letter from John Challis to John Brodsky, January 22, 1967. I thank Dr. Brodsky for sharing a copy of this letter with me more than thirty years ago.

43. Cited in *Challis.*

44. See *Zuckermann 1969a,* 158.

45. That feedback is an important but poorly understood element of harpsichord sound. For more information see *Kottick, Marshall, and Hendrickson;* see also *Kottick 1991,* and *Savage et al.*

46. *Paul,* 269.

47. This was also the claim of the early Zuckermann kit harpsichord. The construction manual claimed—albeit somewhat tentatively—that "openings in the bottom increase the volume somewhat and perhaps enhance the bass tone." See *Zuckermann 1963,* 7.

48. *Zuckermann 1969a,* 197.

49. *Haney 1968–69,* 19.

50. Duo harpsichordists Philip Manuel and Gavin Williamson reported in an article in *Time*, October 30, 1939, 36, that they were disturbed at Pessl's sacrilege; cited in *Palmer 1989*, 74.

51. *Haney 1971b*, 7. Marlowe's stint at the Rainbow Room with her blue Dowd inspired her friend Francis Steegmuller to write the mystery novel (under the nom de plume of David Keith) *Blue Harpsichord* (New York: Dodd, Mead, 1949). After reading Steegmuller's book, scholar and decorator Sheridan Germann built a kit harpsichord, intending to paint it "the robin's egg–blue with rosebuds and bosoms all over it, which was my image of the delicate rococo 'blue harpsichord' of this book." When Germann realized that the shape of her 5′ Zuckermann slantside bore little resemblance to Marlowe's deep-blue Dowd, she abandoned the idea and simply oiled the walnut case (Germann, personal communication). By strange coincidence, years later Germann's slantside came into my shop for repair, brought in by a former student to whom the instrument had been given by the college at which she was teaching. The college had received it as a gift from a piano technician in Ohio, to whom it had been sold by Germann.

52. See *Palmer 1989*, 156–61, for many other instances of jazz on the harpsichord. Perhaps the ultimate crossover event of those days took place at Frances Cole's harpsichord festival held at Westminster Choir College in Princeton, New Jersey, in June 1973, when ragtime great Eubie Blake appeared and played — on the harpsichord — the *Charleston Rag* he had composed in 1899. Blake, then ninety-two years old, also appeared in Cole's next festival, in June 1975, at the College of Mount St. Vincent-on-Hudson, in Riverdale, New York; see *Cole 1975*.

53. *Zuckermann 1969a*, 199.

54. *Zuckermann 1969a*, 201.

55. The kit cost $150.00 exclusive of the plywood and remained at that figure for years, with inflation offset by increasing economies of production. Later a set of precut case parts was also offered, and 2×8′ and 1×8′, 1×4′ versions became available.

56. An interesting anecdote was told by a Dr. W. Schröder, a proud owner of a *Serien* harpsichord, who described his amazement on hearing his instrument share a stage with an American model. Schröder, who likened his ignorance of the historically informed early keyboard movement to a "Sleeping Beauty–like oblivion," purchased and constructed a Hubbard kit and declared the result incomparably superior to the factory instruments available in Germany; see *Schröder 1968*, viii.

57. As a result of his experience in writing the book and the introspection it engendered, Zuck-ermann decided to stop producing his less-than-ideal instrument and sold his kit business to David Way.

58. *Zuckermann 1968*. As the developer and purveyor of the world's first and most successful harpsichord kit, Zuckermann had his own opinion of the societal shift that moved so many to undertake the transcendental experience of building a harpsichord. He offered this bleak comment on the zeitgeist of the 1960s: "The do-it-yourself phenomenon is allowing thousands of people who are caught up in the innumerable dead-end activities of modern society to find in a small measure, that which really should have filled their lives. In letter after letter, people say that putting the harpsichord together was the most meaningful project they had ever been engaged in. Rather than taking this as a flattering comment on my kit, I take it as a devastating comment on their lives."

59. See *Bedford*.

60. In a sense, builders have been too successful. With the large number of good to excellent instruments now in circulation, demand has declined and the sale of used harpsichords has increased. Builders still make new instruments, but many of them spend a considerable amount of time repairing and refurbishing older ones. The situation may not be unlike the one that took place in eighteenth-century Italy.

61. In *Zuckermann 1971*, the author undertook a study of the key spans of forty-four antiques. He showed that while the keys of the French, German, English, Flemish, and Italian schools grouped themselves into distinctly different average octave spans, there was no standard key span for the historical harpsichord as there was for the modern piano. In fact, he maintained that some of the historical measurements were closer to modern piano dimensions than they were to the French span, which was just coming into acceptance as the "correct" octave span for harpsichords. For several reasons, Zuckermann's research was flawed: first, his sample was rather small; second, he averaged together the spans of seventeenth- and eighteenth-century French harpsichords; and third, he had not realized that at least some of the keyboards in his sample were replacements for the originals. Nevertheless, his overall conclusion was not without merit, and the information was useful.

62. Of course, that is exactly what happened when the Viennese fortepiano was revived in the 1960s.

63. As with every change, not everyone was convinced it was for the better. Brahms was adamantly opposed to the sound of the valved horn, and had he the power to do so, might well have banned its use in his works.

Bibliography

Adlam 1976
Adlam, Derek. "Restoring the Vaudry." *Early Music* 4, no. 3 (1976): 255–65.

Adlam 1994
———. "Magnano Clavichord Symposium." *Early Music* 22, no. 3 (1994): 533.

Adlam 1996
———. "Arts & Crafts and the Clavichord: The Revival of Early Instrument Building in England." In *De Clavicordio*, vol. 2, 202–12.

Adlung 1758
Adlung, Jacob. *Anleitung zu der musikalischen Gelahrtheit*. Erfurt: Jungnicol, 1758; 2nd ed., 1783. Reprint ed., ed. Hans J. Moser. Kasel: Bärenreiter, 1958.

Adlung 1768
———. *Musica mechanica organoedi*. 2 vols. Berlin: F. W. Birnstiel, 1768. Facsimile reprint, Kasel: Bärenreiter, 1961.

Agricola
Agricola, Martin. *Musica instrumentalis deudsch*. Wittenberg: Rhaw, 1529.

Anderson
Anderson, R. Dean. "Extant Harpsichords Built or Rebuilt in France during the Seventeenth and Eighteenth Centuries: An Overview and Annotated List, Part 1." *Early Keyboard Journal* 19 (2001): 69–171.

Anselm 1996a
Anselm, Alain. "Bref regard sur les trois clavecins de Vincent Tibaut." *Musique, Images, Instruments* 2 (1996): 203–9.

Anselm 1996b
Anselm, Marie-Christine. Review of *Boalch III*. *Musique, Images, Instruments* 2 (1996): 271–72.

Anselm 1996c
Anselm, Alain, and Marie-Christine Anselm. "La Collection Yannick Guillou." *Musique, Images, Instruments* 2 (1996): 117–48.

Anselm 1996d
———. "Petit prélude à l'étude des clavecins français du XVIIᵉ siècle." *Musique, Images, Instruments* 2 (1996): 227–30.

Anthon
Anthon, Carl G. "An Unusual Harpsichord." *Galpin Society Journal* 37 (March 1984): 115–16.

Apel
Apel, Willi. *Keyboard Music of the Fourteenth and Fifteenth Centuries. Corpus of Early Keyboard Music*, vol. 1. Rome: American Institute of Musicology, 1963.

Augelli
Augelli, Francesco. "Indagini conoscitive sul clavicembalo mozartiano di Antonio Scotti." In *Strumente per Mozart*, 193–208. Milan: Longo Editore, 1991.

Awouters
Awouters, Mia. "The Ruckers/Taskin Harpsichord in the Brussels Museum of Musical Instruments." In *Kielinstrumente*, 294–304.

Baines
Baines, Anthony. "James Talbot's Manuscript." *Galpin Society Journal* 1 (March 1948): 9–26.

Barbieri
Barbieri, Patrizio. "Cembalaro, organaro, chittararo e fabbricatore di corde armoniche nella *Polyanthea technica* di Pinaroli (1718–32)." In *Recercare*, vol. 1, 123–210. Lucca: Libreria Musicale Italiana Editrice, 1989.

Barbour
Barbour, J. Murray. *Tuning and Temperament: A Historical Survey*. East Lansing, Mich.: St. Coll Press, 1951; 2nd ed., 1953.

Barnes 1965
Barnes, John. "Pitch Variations in Italian Keyboard Instruments." *Galpin Society Journal* 18 (March 1965): 110–16.

Barnes 1973
———. "The Stringing of Italian Harpsichords." In *Beiträge zur Aufführungspraxis 2: Der klangliche Aspekt beim Restaurieren von Saitenklavieren*, ed. Vera Schwarz, 35–39. Graz: Akademische Druck, 1973.

Barnes 1977
———. "The Specious Uniformity of Italian Harpsichords." In *Keyboard Instruments*, 1–22.

Barnes 2001
———. "Boxwood Tongues and Original Leather Plectra in Eighteenth-Century English Harpsichords." *Galpin Society Journal* 54 (May 2001): 1–15.

Barry 1982
Barry, Wilson. "The Keyboard Instruments of King Henry VIII." *Organ Yearbook* 13 (1982): 31–45.

Barry 1985
———. "Henri Arnaut de Zwolle's *Clavicordium* and the Origin of the Chekker." *Journal of the American Musical Instrument Society* 11 (1985): 5–13.

Barry 1990
———. "The Lodewyk Theewes Claviorganum and Its Position in the History of Keyboard Instruments." *Journal of the American Musical Instrument Society* 16 (1990): 5–41.

Barry 1991
———. "The Scaling of Flemish Virginals and Harpsichords." *Journal of the American Musical Instrument Society* 17 (1991): 115–31.

Bavington
Bavington, Peter. "An Early Clavicytherium Reconstructed." *English Harpsichord (and Fortepiano) Magazine* 3, no. 6 (1984): 106–11.

Bedford
Bedford, Frances. *Harpsichord and Clavichord Music of the Twentieth Century.* Berkeley: Fallen Leaf Press, 1993.

Bemetzrieder
Bemetzrieder, Anton. *Leçons de clavecin, et principes d'harmonie.* Paris: Bluet, 1771.

Benoit
Benoit, Marcelle. *Versailles et les musiciens du roi: 1661–1733: Étude institutionnelle et sociale.* Paris: Presses Universitaires de France, 1971.

Berlin
Van der Meer, John Henry, et al. *Kielklaviere: Cembali, Spinette, Virginale.* Berlin: Preussischer Kulturbesitz, 1991.

Beurmann 1990
Beurmann, Andreas. "Ein weiterer 'Celestini' in Hamburg: ein Beitrag zur Geschichte der Tasteninstrumente." In *Musikkulturgeschichte, Festschrift für Constantin Floros zum 60. Gerburtstag,* 587–92. Wiesbaden: Breitkopf & Härtel, 1990.

Beurmann 1998
———. "Drei Spanische Transpositions-Cembali des 17. Jahrhunderts." In *Kielinstrumente,* 104–13.

Beurmann 1999
———. "Iberian Discoveries: Six Spanish 17th-Century Harpsichords." *Early Music* 27, no. 2 (1999): 183–208.

Beurmann and Pilipczuk
———, and Alexander Pilipczuk. "Eine Rarität der Cembalobaukunst: das Virginal des Venetianers Celestini von 1594." *Das Musikinstrument* 40, no. 9 (1991): 32–38.

Bierdimpffl
Bierdimpffl, K. A. *Die Sammlung der Musik-Instrumente im Baierischen Nationalmuseum.* Munich, 1883.

Birkett and Jurgens
Birkett, Stephan, and William Jurgens. "Geometrical Methods in Stringed Keyboard Instrument Design: Why Didn't Historical Makers Need Drawings? Part I: Practical Geometry and Proportion." *Galpin Society Journal* 54 (May 2001): 242–84.

Birsak
Birsak, Kurt. "Klaviere im Salzburger Museum Carolino Augusteum." *Salzburger Museum Carolino Augusteum Jahresschrift* 34 (1988): 7–148.

Boalch II
Boalch, Donald H. *Makers of the Harpsichord and Clavichord, 1400–1840.* 2nd ed. Oxford: Clarendon Press, 1974.

Boalch III
———. *Makers of the Harpsichord and Clavichord, 1400–1840.* 3rd ed. Ed. Charles Mould. Oxford: Clarendon Press, 1995.

Boetius
Boetius, August. *Merkwürdige und auserlesene Geschichte von der berühmten Landgrafschaft Thüringen.* Gotha, 1684.

Bonanni
Bonanni, Filippo. *Gabinetto armonico.* Rome, 1723. Modern edition, *The Showcase of Musical Instruments.* Ed. Frank Lloyd Harrison and Joan Rimmer. New York: Dover Publications, 1964.

Bonza and O'Brien
Bonza, Augusto, and Grant O'Brien. "The 'H. Ruckers' Double Virginal in Milan: Two Important Discoveries." *Galpin Society Journal* 52 (April 1999): 314–23.

Bordas
Bordas, Cristina. "The Double Harp in Spain from the 16th to the 18th Centuries." *Early Music* 15, no. 2 (1987): 148–63.

Bowles 1966
Bowles, Edmund A. "On the Origin of the Keyboard Mechanism in the Late Middle Ages." *Technology and Culture* 7 (1966): 152–62.

Bowles 1977
———. "A Checklist of Fifteenth-Century Representations of Stringed Keyboard Instruments." In *Keyboard Instruments,* 11–17 and plates 1–31.

Bowles 2000
———. "Music in Court Festivals of State: Festival Books as Sources for Performance Practices." *Early Music* 28, no. 3 (2000): 421–43.

Boyd
  Boyd, Malcolm. *Domenico Scarlatti: Master of Music.* London: Weidenfeld and Nicolson, 1986.
Brauchli *1983*
  Brauchli, Bernard. "The Clavichord in Christian Friedrich Gottlieb Thon's Keyboard Manual, *Ueber Klavierinstrumente* (1817)." *Journal of the American Musical Instrument Society* 9 (1983): 68–88.
Brauchli *1998*
  ———. *The Clavichord.* Cambridge: Cambridge University Press, 1998.
Brauchli *2000*
  ———. "The 1782 Taskin Harpsichord, Colares, Portugal." *Galpin Society Journal* 53 (April 2000): 25–50.
Broadwood
  Broadwood, Henry Fowler, ed. *Some Notes Made by J. S. Broadwood, 1838, with Observations and Elucidations by H. F. Broadwood.* London, 1862.
Bruggmann
  Bruggmann, Will. "A Harpsichord from Switzerland." *English Harpsichord (and Fortepiano) Magazine* 2, no. 2 (1978): 40–44.
Burney *1771*
  Burney, Charles. *The Present State of Music in France and Italy.* London: T. Becket, 1771.
Burney *1773*
  ———. *The Present State of Music in Germany, the Netherlands, and United Provinces.* 2 vols. London: T. Becket, 1773.
Burney *1819*
  ———. "Jacob Kirckman." In *The Cyclopaedia,* ed. Abraham Rees. London: Longman, Hurst, Rees, Orn, Brown, 1819.
Busby
  Busby, Thomas. *Concert Room and Orchestra Anecdotes.* London: Clementi, 1825.
Byers
  Byers, Reid. "A New Solution to the Ruckers Transposing Double Puzzle." *Continuo* 21, no. 2 (1997): 5–7.
Byne and Stapely
  Byne, Arthur, and Mildred Stapely. *Spanish Interiors and Furniture.* New York: W. Helburn, 1922.
Calahorra
  Calahorra, Pedro Martínez. *La Música en Zaragoza en siglos XVI y XVII.* Vol. 1: *Organistas, organeros, organos.* Zaragoza: Institución Fernando el Católico, 1977.
Campbell
  Campbell, Margaret. *Arnold Dolmetsch: The Man and His Work.* London: Hamish Hamilton, 1975.
Cerone
  Cerone, Domenico Pietro. *El Malopeo y Mae-stro, tractado de música teórica y práctica.* Naples: I. B. Gargano and L. Nucci, 1613.
Cersne
  Cersne, Eberhard. *Der Minne Regal.* Ed. Franz Xaver Wöber. Vienna: Willhelm Braumüller, 1861.
Cervelli
  Cervelli, Luisa. *La Galleria armonica: catalogo del museo degli strumenti musicali di Roma.* Rome: Istituto Poligrafico e Zecca dello Stato, 1994.
Challis
  Challis, John. "Letters." *The Harpsichord* 3, no. 2 (1970): 18.
Chiesa
  Chiesa, Carlo. "Milanese Keyboard Makers: 16th Century." *Fellowship of Makers and Restorers of Historical Instruments Quarterly* 74 (January 1994): 79–81.
Clark
  Clark, J. Bunker. *Transposition in Seventeenth Century English Organ Accompaniments and the Transposing Organ.* Detroit Monographs in Musicology, vol. 4. Detroit: Information Coordinators, 1974.
Clarke
  Clarke, Christopher. "The Restoration of the 1624 Joannes Ruckers, Now at Unterlimden Museum, in the Atelier *Les Tempéraments inégaux,* Paris 1979–80." In *Kielinstrumente,* 270–78.
Clavichord and Harpsichord
  The Clavichord and Harpsichord: Encyclopedia of Keyboard Instruments, vol. 2. Ed. Igor Kipnis and Robert Palmieri. New York: Garland Publishing. Forthcoming.
Clinkscale
  Clinkscale, Martha Novak. *Makers of the Piano 1700–1820.* Oxford: Oxford University Press, 1993. Reprinted with corrections, 1995.
Cole *1975*
  Cole, Francis. "Francis Cole Announces 3rd Annual Harpsichord Festival." *The Harpsichord* 8, no. 1 (1975): 6.
Cole *1993*
  Cole, Michael. "A Handel Harpsichord." *Early Music* 21, no. 1 (1993): 99–109.
Cole *1998*
  ———. *The Pianoforte in the Classical Era.* Oxford: Clarendon Press, 1998.
Corrette
  Corrette, Michel. *Le Maître de clavecin.* Paris, 1753; modern ed., New York: Broude Brothers, 1976.
Curtis
  Curtis, Alan. "Dutch Harpsichord Makers." *Vereniging voor Nederlands Muziekgeschiedenis* 19, nos. 1–2 (1960–61): 44–66.

Dahl 1969
Dahl, Bjarne. "Harpsichord of Note." *The Harpsichord* 2, no. 1 (1969): 10–15.

Dahl 1973
———. "The Ehler's Pleyel." *The Harpsichord* 6, no. 2 (1973): 3.

Dale
Dale, William. *Tschudi the Harpsichord Maker.* London: Constable and Company, 1913.

Dalyell
Dalyell, Sir John Graham. *Musical Memoirs of Scotland.* Edinburgh: Constable, 1849.

Debenham
Debenham, William. "The Compass of the Royal College of Music Clavicytherium." *Fellowship of Makers and Restorers of Historical Instruments Quarterly* 11 (April 1978): 9–21.

De Clavicordio
De Clavicordio: Proceedings of the International Clavichord Symposium. Ed. Bernard Brauchli et al. Vol. 1, Torino: Istituto per i Beni Musicali in Piemonte, 1994; vols. 2, 3, Magnano: Musica Antica a Magnano, 1996, 1998.

Denis
Denis, Jean. *Traité de l'accord de l'espinett.* Paris: Robert Ballard, 1650. Trans. and ed. Vincent J. Panetta, Jr., as *Treatise on Harpsichord Tuning.* Cambridge: Cambridge University Press, 1987.

Deutsches Museum
Kataloge der Sammlungen: besaitete Tasteninstrumente. Ed. Hubert Henkel. Frankfurt am Main: Verlag Erwin Bochinsky, 1994.

Devrient
Devrient, Eduard. *Meine Erinnerungen an Felix Mendelssohn-Bartholdy und seine Briefe an mich.* Leipzig, 1869.

Dictionnaire des facteurs
Dictionnaire des facteurs d'instruments de musique en Wallonie et à Bruxelles du 9ᵉ siecle à nos jours. Ed. Malou Haine and Nicolas Meeùs. Liège: Pierre Margdaga, 1986.

Dictionnaire portatif
Dictionnaire portatif des arts et métiers. Yverdon, 1767.

Diderot and d'Alembert 1785
Diderot, Denis, and Jean le Rond d'Alembert. *Encyclopédie méthodique, ou par ordre de matières par une societé de gens de lettres.* Volumes entitled *Arts et metiers.* Paris: Braisson, 1785.

Diderot and d'Alembert 1791
———. *Encyclopédie méthodique, ou par ordre de matières par une societé de gens de lettres.* Vol. 4: *Instruments de musique et lutherie . . . (Musique).* Paris: Braisson, 1791 and 1818.

Dixon
Dixon, Graham. "The Performance of Palestrina." *Early Music* 22, no. 4 (1994): 667–75.

Dolmetsch 1915
Dolmetsch, Arnold. *The Interpretation of the Music of the XVII and XVIII Centuries.* London: Novello & Co., 1915.

Dolmetsch 1958
Dolmetsch, Mabel. *Personal Recollections of Arnold Dolmetsch.* New York: Macmillan, 1958.

Dolmetsch 1981
Dolmetsch, Carl. "Arnold Dolmetsch and the Harpsichord Revival." In *Paul,* 57–72.

Donington
Donington, Robert. *The Work and Ideas of Arnold Dolmetsch.* Haslemere: Dolmetsch Foundation, 1932.

Douglas-Home
Douglas-Home, Jessica. *Violet: The Life and Loves of Violet Gordon Woodhouse.* London: Harvill, 1996.

Douwes
Klaas Douwes. *Grondig onderzoek van de toonen der muzyk.* Franeker: A. Heins, 1699. Facsimile ed., Amsterdam: F. Knuf, 1970.

Dowd 1978
Dowd, William. "A Classification System for Ruckers and Couchet Double Harpsichords." *Journal of the American Musical Instrument Society* 4 (1978): 106–13.

Dowd 1984
———. "The Surviving Instruments of the Blanchet Workshop." In *The Historical Harpsichord,* vol. 1, 17–107.

Downing
Downing, John. "Bogwood Again." *Fellowship of Makers and Restorers of Historical Instruments Quarterly* 74 (January 1994): 88.

Dufourcq
Dufourcq, Norbert. *Le Livre de l'orgue français. Tome III: la facture.* Paris: Picard, 1975.

Eigeldinger
Eigeldinger, Jean-Jacques. "Pérennité de Wanda Landowska." *Revue Musicale de Suisse Romande* 3 (1979): 2–3.

Ellis
Ellis, Katherine. "Female Pianists and Their Male Critics in Nineteenth-Century Paris." *Journal of the American Musicological Society* 50, nos. 2–3 (1997): 353–85.

Elste 1988
Elste, Martin. "Einsichten und Ansichten: Musik en détail." In *100 Jahre Berliner Musikinstrumenten-Museum 1888–1988,* 135–279. Berlin: Staatliches Institut für Musikforschung Preussischer Kulturbesitz, 1988.

Elste 1991
———. "Nostalgische Musikmaschinen: Cembali im 20. Jahrhundert." In *Berlin,* 239–77.

Engel
Engel, Carl. "Some Account of the Clavi-

chord with Historical Notices." *Musical Times* (1879): 356–59, 411–15, 468–72.

Ernst

    Ernst, Friedrich. *Der Flügel Johann Sebastian Bachs.* Frankfort: C. F. Peters, 1955.

Esch

    Esch, Doris. "Die früheste Erwähnung des Clavicymbalum in italienischer Sprache." In *Studien zur italienisch-deutschen Musikgeschichte* 12 (*Analecta Musicologica* 19, 1979): 378–79.

Fletcher, Blackham, and Stratton

    Fletcher, H., E. D. Blackham, and R. Stratton. "Quality of Piano Tones." *Journal of the Acoustical Society of America* 36 (1962): 749–61.

Fontana

    Fontana, Eszter. "Mozarts 'Reiseclavier.'" In *Klangwelt*, 73–78.

Ford 1984

    Ford, Terence. "Andrea Sacchi's 'Apollo Crowning the Singer Marc Antonio Pasqualini.'" *Early Music* 12, no. 1 (1984): 79–84.

Ford 1997

    Ford, Karrin. "The Pedal Clavichord and the Pedal Harpsichord." *Galpin Society Journal* 50 (March 1997): 161–79.

Forkel

    Forkel, Johann Nikolaus. *Musikalischer Almanach für Deutschland: Fremdschriftliche.* Leipzig: Schwickert, 1782.

Fremdschriftliche

    Fremdschriftliche und gedruckte Dokumente zur Lebensgeschichte Johann Sebastian Bachs, 1685–1750. Ed. Werner Neumann and Hans-Joachim Schulze. *Bach-Documente*, vol. 2. Kassel: Bärenreiter, 1969.

Gai

    Gai, Venicio. *Gli strumenti musicali della corte Medicea e il museo del Conservatorio 'Luigi Cherubini' di Firenze.* Florence: Licosa, 1969.

Geiringer

    Geiringer, Karl. *The Bach Family: Seven Generations of Creative Genius.* London: Oxford University Press, 1954.

Gerber

    Gerber, Ernst Ludwig. *Historisches-biographisches Lexicon der Tonkünstler.* Leipzig: J. G. Breitkopf, 1790–92. 2nd ed., 1812, 1814. Facsimile reprint, Graz: Akademischer Druck, 1966.

Germann 1978a

    Germann, Sheridan. "Regional Schools of Harpsichord Decoration." *Journal of the American Musical Instrument Society* 4 (1978): 54–105.

Germann 1978b

    ———. "La Décoration des clavecins italiens et flamands." *Musique et Loisirs, Paris* 5 (November 1978): 15–22.

Germann 1979a

    ———. "'Mrs Crawley's Couchet' Reconsid-

ered." *Early Music* 7, no. 4 (October 1979): 473–81.

Germann 1979b

    ———. "La Décoration des clavecins français, allemands et anglais." *Musique et Loisirs, Paris* 7 (May 1979): 17–25.

Germann 1980, 1981

    ———. "Monsieur Doublet and His *confrères:* The Harpsichord Decorators of Paris, Parts 1 and 2." *Early Music* 8, no. 4 (1980): 435–53; 9, no. 2 (1981): 192–207.

Germann 1985

    ———. "The Mietkes, the Margrave and Bach." In *Bach, Handel, Scarlatti: Tercentenary Essays,* ed. Peter Williams, 119–48. Cambridge: Cambridge University Press, 1985.

Gestoso

    Gestoso, José y Pérez. *Ensayo de un diccionario de los artifices que florecièron en esta ciudad de Sevilla desde al siglo XIII hasta XVIII.* Seville: La Andalucía Moderna, 1899.

Gétreau 1995

    Gétreau, Florence. "Images de patrimoine: collectionneurs d'instruments anciens et ensembles de musique ancienne en France (1850–1950)." *Musique, Images, Instruments* 1 (1995): 35–47.

Gétreau 1996a

    ———. *Aux origines du musée de la musique: les collections instrumentales du Conservatoire de Paris.* Paris: Éditions Klincksieck / Éditions de la Réunion des Musées nationaux, 1996.

Gétreau 1996b

    ———. "Vincent Tibaut de Toulouse, ébéniste et facteur de clavecins." *Musique, Images, Instruments* 2 (1996): 197–202.

Gétreau 1998

    ———. "The Fashion for Flemish Harpsichords in France: A New Appreciation." In *Kielinstrumente,* 114–35.

Gétreau and Herlin 1996, 1997

    ———, and Denis Herlin. "Portraits de clavecins et de clavecinistes français I, II." *Musique, Images, Instruments* 2 (1996): 89–114; *Musique, Images, Instruments* 3 (1997): 64–88.

Gierveld

    Gierveld, Arend Jan. "The Harpsichord and Clavichord in the Dutch Republic." *Tijdschrift van de Vereniging voor Nederlandse Muziekgeschiedenis* 31, no. 2 (1981): 117–66.

Good

    Good, Edwin M. *Giraffes, Black Dragons, and Other Pianos.* Stanford: Stanford University Press, 1982. 2nd. ed., 2001.

Goodman

    Goodman, W. L. "Musical Instruments and Their Makers in Bristol Apprentice Register, 1536–1643." *Galpin Society Journal* 27 (May 1974): 9–14.

Goodway and Odell
  Goodway, Martha, and Scott Odell. *The Metal-lurgy of 17th- and 18th-Century Music Wire*. Vol. 2 of *The Historical Harpsichord*.

Greenberg 1993
  Robert Greenberg. "Restoration Report, Seventeenth-Century Italian Harpsichord at *MusicSources, 1993*." *Fellowship of Makers and Restorers of Historical Instruments Quarterly* 74 (January 1994): 64–72.

Greenberg 1995
  ———. "Withdrawal of Ascription." *Fellow-ship of Makers and Restorers of Historical Instru-ments Quarterly* 80 (July 1995): 52.

Gug
  Gug, Rémy. "Le Zelé de 'Monsieur Dulcken' en 1815." In *Musique, Images, Instruments* 1 (1995): 187–88.

Gutmann
  Gutmann, Veronica. "Zum Schaffen der 'In-strument und Orgelmacher' Peter Fridrich Brosi und Johann Jacob Brosy." Vol. 11 of *Basler Jahrbuch für Historische Musikpraxis*. Basel: Amadeus, 1987.

Halfpenny 1946
  Halfpenny, Eric. "Shudi and the 'Venetian Swell.'" *Music and Letters* 27 (1946): 180–84.

Halfpenny 1950
  ———. "The Lyrichord." *Galpin Society Jour-nal* 3 (March 1950): 46–49.

Hamel
  Hamel, Christopher de. *A History of Illumi-nated Manuscripts*. London: Phaidon Press, 1994.

Hammond
  Hammond, Frederick. "Some Notes on Gio-vanni Battista Boni da Cortona, Girolamo Zenti, and Others." *Galpin Society Journal* 40 (December 1987): 37–47.

Haney 1968–69
  Haney, Harold. "Interview with Isolde Ahl-grimm." *The Harpsichord* 1, no. 4 (1968–69): 4–7, 9, 12, 19.

Haney 1969
  ———. "Portrait of a Builder." *The Harpsi-chord* 2, no. 3 (1969): 14–23.

Haney 1971a
  ———. "Portrait of a Builder." *The Harpsi-chord* 4, no. 1 (1971): 8–19.

Haney 1971b
  ———. "Interview with Sylvia Marlowe." *The Harpsichord* 4, no. 3 (1971): 6–11, 18–20.

Haney 1972a
  ———. "Portrait of a Builder." *The Harpsi-chord* 5, no. 1 (1972): 5–9, 14–17.

Haney 1972b
  ———. "Conversation with Builder-Harpsichordist Claude Jean Chiasson." *The Harpsichord* 5, no. 3 (1972): 4–9, 12, 20.

Haney 1973–74
  ———. "Harpsichord of Note." *The Harpsi-chord* 6, no. 4 (1973–74): 10–19.

Haney 1974a
  ———. "Harpsichord of Note." *The Harpsi-chord* 7, no. 4 (1974–75): 8–12.

Haney 1974b
  ———. "Conversation with Harpsichordist Denise Restout." *The Harpsichord* 7, no. 1 (1974): 6–11, 14–23.

Haney 1974c
  ———. "Conversation with Harpsichord Maker Richard Jones." *The Harpsichord* 7, no. 2 (1974): 10–21.

Haney 1975
  ———. "Conversation with Harpsichordist Rosalyn Tureck." *The Harpsichord* 8, no. 1 (1975): 8–11, 14–22.

Hardouin
  Hardouin, Pierre J. "Harpsichord Making in Paris Part I, Eighteenth Century." With in-troduction, translation, and notes by Frank Hubbard. *Galpin Society Journal* 10 (May 1957): 10–29.

Harich-Schneider
  Harich-Schneider, Eta. *Charaktere und Katas-trophen*. Berlin: Ullstein, 1978.

Helenius-Öberg 1986
  Helenius-Öberg, Eva. *Svenskt Klavikordbygge 1720–1820*. Stockholm: Almqvist & Wiksell, 1986.

Helenius-Öberg 1987
  ———. "Kyrkoherden Nil Brelin: mechani-cus och klaverälskare." *Svensk Tidskrifft för Musikforskning* (1987): 91–114.

Hellwig 1974
  Hellwig, Friedemann. "Lute-Making in the 15th and 16th Century." *The Lute* 16 (1974): 24–38.

Hellwig 1977
  ———. "The Single-Strung Italian Harpsi-chord." In *Keyboard Instruments*, 29–38.

Helmholtz
  Helmholtz, Hermann. *On the Sensations of Tone*. Trans. Alexander Ellis from the Ger-man edition of 1877. New York: Dover Pub-lications, 1954.

Henkel 1979
  Henkel, Hubert. *Beitrage zum historischen Cem-balobau*. Band 2: *Kielinstrumenten*. Leipzig: Deutscher Verlag für Musik, 1979.

Henkel 1990
  ———. "Sechszenfuss-Register im italien-ischen Cembalobau." *Das Musikinstrument* 39 (1990): 6–10.

Henkel 1992
  ———. "Bartolomeo Cristofori as Harpsi-chord Maker." In *The Historical Harpsichord*, vol. 3, 1–58.

Heriot

Heriot, Angus. *The Castrati in Opera*. London: Martin Secker & Warburg, 1956. Reprint ed., New York: Da Capo Press, 1975.

Hess

Hess, Albert G. "The Transition from Harpsichord to Piano." *Galpin Society Journal* 6 (July 1953): 75–87.

Heyde

Heyde, Herbert. "Der Instrumentenbau in Leipzig zur Zeit Johann Sebastian Bachs." In *300 Jahre Johann Sebastian Bach*. Exhibition catalog, Internationale Bachacademie, Staatsgalerie, Stuttgart, 1985. Tutzing: Hans Schneider, 1985.

Hipkins

Hipkins, Alfred J. *A Description and History of the Pianoforte, and of the Older Keyboard Stringed Instruments*. London: Novello, 1896.

Hirt

Hirt, Franz Joseph. *Stringed Keyboard Instruments*. Trans. M. Boehme-Brown. Zurich: Urs Graf-Verlag Dietikon, 1981. Originally published in 1955 as *Meisterwerke des Klavierbaus*.

The Historical Harpsichord

The Historical Harpsichord. Ed. Howard Schott. Stuyvesant, N.Y.: Pendragon Press. Three vols. to date: 1, 1984; 2, 1987; 3, 1992.

Hoover

Hoover, Cynthia Adams. "Hugo Worch." In *The New Grove Dictionary of Music and Musicians*, ed. Stanley Sadie, vol. 20, 528. London: Macmillan, 1980.

Howell 1979–80

Howell, Standley. "Paulus Paulirinus of Prague on Musical Instruments." *Journal of the American Musical Instrument Society* 5–6 (1979–80): 9–36.

Howell 1990

———. "Medical Astrologers and the Invention of Stringed Keyboard Instruments." *Journal of Musicological Research* 10 (1990): 1–17.

Hubbard 1965

Hubbard, Frank. *Three Centuries of Harpsichord Making*. Cambridge, Mass: Harvard University Press, 1965.

Hubbard 1984

———. "Reconstructing the Harpsichord." In *The Historical Harpsichord*, vol. 1, 1–16.

Huber 1988

Huber, Alfons. "Saitendrahtsysteme im Wiener Klavierbau zwischen 1780 und 1880." *Das Musikinstrument* 37, no. 9 (1988): 84–94.

Huber 1991a

———. "Der Österreichische Klavierbau im 18. Jahrhundert." In *Klangwelt*, 47–72.

Huber 1991b

———. "The Short Broken Contra Octave: An Austrian Speciality?" *Das Musikinstrument* 40, no. 8 (1991): 74–77.

Hullmandel

Hullmandel, Nicolas. "Musique." In vol. 1 of *Encyclopédie méthodique*, 2 vols. Paris: Chez Panckoucke, 1791.

Hummel

Hummel, Jörg Dieter. *Friedrich Ring, Der vergessene Instrumentbauer*. Augsburg: J. P. Himmer, 1976.

Hunt 1998

Hunt, John N. "Jurors of the Guild of Musical Instrument Makers of Paris." *Galpin Society Journal* 51 (July 1998): 110–13.

Hunt 2000

———. "The Blanchets: Parisian Musical Instrument Makers of the Seventeenth and Eighteenth Centuries." *Early Keyboard Journal* 18 (2000): 53–93.

Jacobsson

Jacobsson, Johann Karl. *"Flügelmacher."* In vol. 1 of *Technologisches Wörterbuch oder alphabetische Erklärung aller nützlichen mechanischen Künste, Manufacturen, Fabriken und Handwerken*. Berlin: Bey Friedrich Nicolai, 1781–94.

James

James, Philip. *Early Keyboard Instruments from Their Beginnings to the Year 1820*. London: Peter Davies, 1930.

Jensen

Jensen, David P. "A Florentine Harpsichord: Revealing a Transitional Technology." *Early Music* 26, no. 1 (1998): 70–85.

Jonckbloet and Land

Jonckbloet, W. J. A., and J. P. N. Land, eds. *Musique et musiciens au XVIIe siècle: correspondance et œuvre musicales de Constantin Huygens*. Leiden: E. J. Brill, 1882.

Karl Marx University Clavichords

Henkel, Hubert. *Musikinstrumenten-Museum der Karl-Marx Universität, Leipzig Katalog*, Band 4: *Clavichorde*. Frankfurt am Main: Verlag das Musikinstrument, 1981.

Karl Marx University Harpsichords

———. *Musikinstrumenten-Museum der Karl-Marx Universität, Leipzig Katalog, Band 2, Kielinstrumente*. Leipzig: Deutscher Verlag für Musik, 1979.

Karpiak

Karpiak, Robert. "Researching Early Keyboards in Russia." *Continuo* 20, no. 1 (February 1995): 2–6.

Kastner

Kastner, Santiago. "Los manuscritos musicales nos. 48 y 242 de la Biblioteca General de la Universidad de Coimbra." *Anuario musical* (1950): 193–209.

Kaufmann 1966

Kaumann, Henry W. *The Life and Works of Nic-*

ola Vicentino. Rome: American Institute of Musicology, 1966.

Kaufmann 1970
———. "More on the Tuning of the *Archicembalo.*" *Journal of the American Musical Instrument Society* 23, no. 1 (spring 1970): 84–94.

Kaufmann 1980
Kaufmann, Martin M. "Le Clavier à balancier du clavisimbalum (XVᵉ siècle): un moment exceptionnel de l'évolution des instruments à clavier." In *Mercier,* 9–57.

Kenyon de Pascual 1982
Kenyon de Pascual, Beryl. "Harpsichords, Clavichords and Similar Instruments in Madrid in the Second Half of the Eighteenth Century." *Research Chronicle* 1 (1982): 66–84.

Kenyon de Pascual 1985
———. "Diego Fernández — Harpsichord Maker to the Spanish Royal Family from 1722 to 1775 — and His Nephew Julián Fernández." *Galpin Society Journal* 38 (April 1985): 35–47.

Kenyon de Pascual 1986
———. "Queen Maria Barbara's Harpsichords." *Galpin Society Journal* 39 (September 1986): 125–27.

Kenyon de Pascual 1987
———. "Francisco Pérez Mirabel's Harpsichords and the Early Spanish Piano." *Early Music* 15, no. 4 (1987): 503–13.

Kenyon de Pascual 1991
———. "Two Features of Early Spanish Keyboard Instruments." *Galpin Society Journal* 34 (March 1991): 94–102.

Kenyon de Pascual 1992
———. "*Clavicordios* and Clavichords in 16th-Century Spain." *Early Music* 20, no. 4 (1992): 611–30.

Kenyon de Pascual and Law
———, and David Law. "Another Early Iberian Grand Piano." *Galpin Society Journal* 48 (March 1995): 68–93.

Kenyon de Pasqual and van der Meer
———, and John Henry van der Meer. "The Five-Octave Compass in 18th-Century Spanish Harpsichords." *Early Music* 15, no. 1 (1987): 74–76.

Keyboard Instruments
Keyboard Instruments: Studies in Keyboard Organology, 1500–1800. Ed. Edwin M. Ripin. 2nd ed. New York: Dover Publications, 1977.

Kielinstrumente
Kielinstrumente aus der Werkstatt Ruckers: zu Konzeption, Bauweise und Ravalement sowie Restaurierung und Konservierung; Bericht über die Internationale Konferenze vom 13. bis 15. September 1996 im Händel-Haus Halle (Schriften des Händel-Hauses in Halle 14). Ed. Christiane Rieche. Halle: Händel-Haus, 1998.

Kilström 1991
Kilström, Andreas. "A Signed Mietke Harpsichord." *Fellowship of Makers and Restorers of Historical Instruments Quarterly* 64 (July 1991): 59–62.

Kilström 1994
———. "The Hudiksvall Mietke." *English Harpsichord (and Fortepiano) Magazine* 5, no. 1 (1994): 15–18.

Kilvert
Kilvert, Rev. Francis. *Selections from the Diary.* Ed. William Plomer. London: J. Cape, 1938–40.

Kinsela 1998
Kinsela, David. "The Capture of the Chekker." *Galpin Society Journal* 51 (July 1998): 64–85.

Kinsela 2001
———. "A Taxonomy of Renaissance Keyboard Compass." *Galpin Society Journal* 54 (May 2001): 352–96.

Kircher
Kircher, Althanasius. *Phonurgia nova.* Kempton: Rudolphum Dreherr, 1673.

Kirkpatrick
Kirkpatrick, Ralph. *Domenico Scarlatti.* Princeton: Princeton University Press, 1953.

Klangwelt
Die Klangwelt Mozarts. Vienna: Kunsthistorisches Museum, 1991.

Klaus
Klaus, Sabine Katharina. *Studien zur Entwicklungsgeschichte besaiteter Tasteninstrumente bis etwa 1830, unter besonderer Berücksichtigung der Instrumente im Musikinstrumentenmuseum im Münchner Stadtmuseum. Band 1: Quellen und Studien zur technischen Entwicklung.* Tutzing: Hans Schneider, 1997.

Klaus and Rose
———, and Malcolm Rose. "An Unsigned South-German Harpsichord in the Historisches Museum Basel. *Galpin Society Journal* 53 (April 2000): 254–73.

Knighton
Knighton, Tess. Editorial. *Early Music* 27, no. 4 (1999): 516.

König
König, Johann Ulrich. "Musicalische Merckwürdigkeiten: des Marchese, Scipio Maffei, Beschreibung eines neuerfundenen Claviceins, auf welchem das *piano* und *forte* zu haben, nebst einigen Betrachtungen über die musicalische Instrumente, aus dem Welschen ins Teutsche übersetzt." In *Critica Musica,* ed. Johann Mattheson, vol. 2, 335–42. Hamburg, 1722–25.

Koster 1977
Koster, John. "The Mother and Child Virginal and Its Place in the Culture of the Sixteenth and Seventeenth Centuries." In *Collo-*

quium: *Ruckers klavecimbels en copieën: universele instrumenten voor de interpretatie van de muziek uit Rubens tijd,* 78–96. Antwerp: Ruckers Genootschap, 1977.

Koster 1980
———. "The Importance of the Early English Harpsichord." *Galpin Society Journal* 33 (March 1980): 45–73.

Koster 1981
———. "Italian Harpsichords and the Fugger Inventory." *Galpin Society Journal* 34 (March 1981): 149–51.

Koster 1982
———. "A Remarkable Flemish Transposing Harpsichord." *Galpin Society Journal* 35 (March 1982): 45–53.

Koster 1992
———. Review of *O'Brien 1990. Journal of the American Musical Instrument Society* 18 (1992): 109–24.

Koster 1993, 1994
———. "Pianos and Other 'Expressive' *Claviere* in J. S. Bach's Circle." *Early Keyboard Studies Newsletter* 7, no. 2 (1993): 1–11; 8, no. 1 (1994): 1–7.

Koster 1994
———. *Keyboard Musical Instruments in the Museum of Fine Arts, Boston.* Boston: Museum of Fine Arts, 1994.

Koster 1995
———. "Conservator Unravels Mystery . . . Keyboard Instruments Traced Back to 16th-Century Naples." *Shrine to Music Museum Newsletter* 23, no. 1 (1995): 1–3.

Koster 1996a
———. "The 'Still, Small Voice' and the Exploration of Inner Musical Space." In *De Clavicordio,* vol. 2, 155–65.

Koster 1996b
———. "From the Age of Louis XIV . . . Rare French Harpsichord Enters Museum's Collections." *Shrine to Music Museum Newsletter* 23, no. 4 (1996): 1–3.

Koster 1997
———. "Discovered Near Paris . . . Museum Acquires Rare 17th-Century Italian Virginal." *Shrine to Music Museum Newsletter* 24, no. 3 (1997): 1–2.

Koster 1998a
———. "The Origin of Hans Ruckers's Craft." In *Lambrechts-Douillez 1998a,* 53–64.

Koster 1998b
———. "The Scaling and Pitch of Stringed-Keyboard Instruments in J. S. Bach's Environs." Paper delivered at the American Bach Society meeting in 1998.

Koster 1998c
———. "Pitch and Transposition before the Ruckers." In *Kielinstrumente,* 73–94.

Koster 1998d
———. "Toward the Reconstruction of the Ruckers' Geometrical Methods." In *Kielinstrumente,* 22–47.

Koster 1998e
———. "Three Grand Pianos in the Florentine Tradition." *Musique, Images, Instruments* 4 (1998): 94–116.

Koster 1999
———. "The Harpsichord Culture in Bach's Environs." In *Bach Perspectives: The Music of J. S. Bach — Analysis and Interpretation,* vol. 4, ed. David Schulenberg, 57–77. Lincoln: University of Nebraska Press, 1999.

Koster 2000a
———. "A Netherlandish Harpsichord of 1658 Re-examined." *Galpin Society Journal* 53 (April 2000): 117–39.

Koster 2000b
———. "Cathedrals, Cabinetmaking, and Clavichords, Part I." *Clavichord International* 4, no. 1 (2000): 6–13.

Koster 2000c
———. "A Contemporary Example of Harpsichord Forgery." *Early Music* 28, no. 1 (2000): 91–97.

Koster 2000d
———. "Some Remarks on the Relationship between Organ and Stringed-Keyboard Instrument Making." *Early Keyboard Journal* 18 (2000): 95–137.

Koster CD
———. Liner notes to "Treasury of Iberian Keyboard Music on the Antunes Fortepiano (1767): Susanne Skyrm, fortepiano." Berkeley: Music and Arts CD 985.

Koster Forthcoming
———. *Early Netherlandish Harpsichord Making from Its Beginnings to 1600.* Forthcoming.

Kottick 1985
Kottick, Edward L. "The Acoustics of the Harpsichord: Response Curves and Modes of Vibration." *Galpin Society Journal* 38 (April 1985): 55–71.

Kottick 1991
———. "Basic Harpsichord Acoustics." *Early Keyboard Journal* 9 (1991): 21–50.

Kottick and Lucktenberg
———, and George Lucktenberg. *Early Keyboard Instruments in European Museums.* Bloomington: Indiana University Press, 1997.

Kottick, Marshall, and Hendrickson
———, Kenneth D. Marshall, and Thomas J. Hendrickson. "The Acoustics of the Harpsichord." *Scientific American* 264, no. 2 (February 1991): 110–15.

Krickeberg
Krickeberg, Dieter. "Michael Mietke: ein Cembalobauer aus dem Umkreis von Johann Sebastian Bach." In *Cöthener Bach, Hefte 3:*

Sonderheit zur Bach-Händel-Schütz-Ehrung der DDR, 47–56. Köthen: Historisches Museum, 1985.

Krickeberg and Rase

———, and Horst Rase. "Beiträge zur Kenntnis des mittel- und norddeutschen Cembalobaus um 1700." In *Studia organologica: Festschrift für John Henry van der Meer,* ed. Friedemann Hellwig, 285–93. Tutzing: Hans Schneider, 1987.

Kukelka

Kukelka, Peter. "Der Kielflügel B13/4: 'Versuch einer Funktionsdeutung.'" In *Salzburger Museum Carolino Augusteum, Jahresschrift,* vol. 34 (1988), 151–58. Salzburg: Museum Carolino Augusteum, 1990.

Lambrechts-Douillez 1973

Lambrechts-Douillez, Jeannine. "Hans Ruckers and His Workshop." In *Beiträge zur Aufführungspraxis 2: der Klangliche Aspekt beim Restaurieren von Saitenklavieren,* ed. Vera Schwarz, 41–45. Graz: Akademische Druck, 1973.

Lambrechts-Douillez 1977

———. "Documents Dealing with the Ruckers Family and Antwerp Harpsichord-Building." In *Keyboard Instruments,* 39–43.

Lambrechts-Douillez 1998a

———, ed. *Hans Ruckers: Stichter van een klavecimbelatelier van wereldformaat in Antwerpen.* Peer: Alamire Muziekuitgeverij, 1998.

Lambrechts-Douillez 1998b

———. "Ruckers Instruments in Antwerp: Principles of Restoration around 1970 and the New Historic Research about the History of the Ruckers-Couchet Family." In *Kielinstrumente,* 14–21.

Lambrechts-Douillez and Bosschaerts-Eykens 1986

———, and M. J. Bosschaerts-Eykens. "De Familie Couchet." Vol. 5 of *Mededelingen van het Ruckers-Genootschap.* Antwerp: Ruckers Genootschap, 1986.

Lambrechts-Douillez and Bosschaerts-Eykens 1987

———. "Hans Bos." In *Mededelingen van het Ruckers-Genootschap,* vol. 6, 8–13. Antwerp: Ruckers Genootschap, 1987.

Latcham 1993

Latcham, Michael. "The Check in Some Early Pianos and the Development of Piano Technique around the Turn of the 18th Century." *Early Music* 21, no. 1 (1993): 28–42.

Latcham 1998

———. "Mozart and the Pianos of Johann Andreas Stein." *Galpin Society Journal* 51 (July 1998): 114–53.

Latcham 2000

———. *The Stringing, Scaling, and Pitch of Hammerflügel Built in the Southern German and Viennese Traditions, 1780–1820.* Vol. 1: *Text.*

Munich and Salzburg: Musikverlag Katzbichler, 2000.

Le Cerf and Lebande

Le Cerf, G., and E. R. Lebande, eds. *Instruments de musique du XVe siècle: les Traités d'Henri Arnaut de Zwolle et de divers anonymes.* Paris: August Picard, 1932.

Ledbetter

Ledbetter, David. *Harpsichord and Lute Music in 17th-Century France.* Bloomington: Indiana University Press, 1987.

Lemme

Lemme, Karl Friedrich Wilhelm. *Anweisung und Regeln zu einer Zweckmässigen Behandlung englischer und deutscher Pianofortes und Klaviere.* Brunswick, 1802.

Leonhardt

Leonhardt, Gustav. "In Praise of Flemish Virginals of the Seventeenth Century." In *Keyboard Instruments,* 45–48.

Leppert

Leppert, Richard D. *The Theme of Music in Flemish Paintings of the Seventeenth Century.* Munich and Salzburg: Emil Katzbichler, 1977.

Lester

Lester, John, "The Musical Mechanisms of Arnaut de Zwolle." *English Harpsichord (and Fortepiano) Magazine* 3, no. 3 (1982): 35–41.

Lesure

Lesure, François. "La Facture instrumentale à Paris au seizième siècle." *Galpin Society Journal* 7 (April 1954): 11–52.

Libin 1975

Libin, Laurence. "A Dutch Harpsichord in the United States." *Galpin Society Journal* 28 (April 1975): 43–49.

Libin 1987

———. "Folding Harpsichords." *Early Music* 15, no. 3 (1987): 379–83.

Libin 1989

———. *Keyboard Instruments: The Metropolitan Museum of Art Bulletin* (summer 1989).

Libin 1998a

———. "Remarks on the 1581 Hans Ruckers Virginal at the Metropolitan Museum of Art." In *Lambrechts-Douillez 1998a,* 77–84.

Libin 1998b

———. "Carel Fredrik Leascke and Ruckers in Amsterdam." In *Kielinstrumente,* 182–86.

Libin and Shanks

———, and Kathryn L. Shanks. "A Harpsichord from Sorrento." *Early Music* 18, no. 2 (1989): 216–18.

Luckett

Luckett, Richard. "The English Virginals: I." *English Harpsichord (and Fortepiano) Magazine* 1, no. 3 (1974): 69–72.

Lunde

Lunde, Nanette G. "Harpsichord of Note." *The Harpsichord* 4, no. 4 (1971–72): 10–13.

Mace

Mace, Thomas. *Musick's Monument.* London, 1676.

Mactaggart

Mactaggart, Ann, and Peter Mactaggart. "The Knole Harpsichord: A Reattribution." *Galpin Society Journal* 31 (May 1978): 2–8.

Marcuse

Marcuse, Sibyl. "Transposing Keyboards on Extant Flemish Harpsichords." *Musical Quarterly* 38, no. 3 (1952): 414–25.

Martin 1984

Martin, Lynn Wood. "The Colonna-Stella *Sambuca lincea,* an Enharmonic Keyboard Instrument." *Journal of the American Musical Instrument Society* 10 (1984): 5–21.

Martin 1995

Martin, Darryl. "The Identification of the Talbot Manuscript Harpsichord." *Galpin Society Journal* 48 (March 1995): 46–51.

Martin 1996

———. "The Spanish Influence on the English Virginal." *Early Keyboard Journal* 14 (1996): 85–99.

Martin 2000

———. "Two Elizabethan Virginals?" *Galpin Society Journal* 53 (April 2000): 156–67.

Maunder

Maunder, Richard. *Keyboard Instruments in Eighteenth-Century Vienna.* Oxford: Clarendon Press, 1998.

McClew

McClew, Ray. "The 'Delrin' Biography." *The Harpsichord* 4, no. 2 (1971): 18–19.

McGeary 1973

McGeary, Thomas. "Early English Harpsichord Building: A Reassessment." *English Harpsichord (and Fortepiano) Magazine* 1, no. 1 (1973): 7–19.

McGeary 1980

———. "Harpsichord Decoration: A Reflection of Renaissance Ideas about Music." *Explorations in Renaissance Culture* 6 (1980): 1–27.

McGeary 1981

———. "Harpsichord Mottoes." *Journal of the American Musical Instrument Society* 7 (1981): 5–35.

McGeary 1982

———. "David Tannenberg and the Clavichord in Eighteenth-Century America." *Organ Yearbook* 13 (1982): 94–106.

McGeary 1990

———. "Karl Lemme's Manual on Fortepiano and Clavichord Maintenance (1802)." *Early Keyboard Journal* 8 (1990): 111–29.

McLeish

McLeish, Martin. "An Inventory of Musical Instruments at the Royal Palace, Madrid, in 1602." *Galpin Society Journal* 21 (March 1968): 108–28.

Meeùs 1980

Meeùs, Nicolas. "Le Diapason authentique: quelques réflexions àpropos du clavecin transpositeur des Ruckers." In *Mercier,* 79–87.

Meeùs 1986

———. "Ruckers Doubles: The 'Sixth Hypothesis.'" *Fellowship of Makers and Restorers of Historical Instruments Quarterly* 42 (January 1986): 50–55.

Meeùs 1998

———. "The Musical Purpose of the Ruckers Transposing Harpsichord." In *Kielinstrumente,* 63–72.

Melville

Melville, James. *Memoirs of Sir James Melville.* Ed. George Scott. Edinburgh: T. and W. Ruddimans, 1735.

Mercier

La Facture du clavecin du XVᵉ au XVIIIᵉ siècle. Ed. Philippe Mercier. Louvain-la-Neuve: Institut Súperieur d'Archéologie et d'Histoire de l'Art, Collège Érasme, 1980.

Mercier-Ythier

Mercier-Ythier, Claude. *Les Clavecins.* Paris: Éditions Vecteurs, 1990.

Mersenne

Chapman, Roger E. *Harmonie universelle: The Books on Instruments.* Trans. of Marin Mersenne, *Harmonie universelle,* 3 vols. (Paris, 1636–37). The Hague: Martinus Nijhoff, 1957.

Mitchell

Mitchell, Nicholas. "Pitch in Viols and Harpsichords in the Renaissance." *Galpin Society Journal* 54 (May 2001): 97–115.

Mobbs and MacKenzie

Mobbs, Kenneth, and Alexander MacKenzie of Ord. "The 'Machine Stop' and Its Potential on Full-Specification One-Manual Harpsichords Made by Thomas Culliford in 1785." *Galpin Society Journal* 47 (March 1994): 33–46.

Moens

Moens, Karel. "Klavierinstrumenten als Moraliserende Metaforen in de Beeldende Kunsten uit de Nederlanden Tijdens de 16de den 17de Eeuw." In *Lambrechts-Douillez 1998a,* 95–119.

Montanari

Montanari, Giuliana. "Bartolomeo Cristofori: A List and Historical Survey of His Instruments." *Early Music* 19, no. 3 (1991): 383–96.

Moscheles

Moscheles, Charlotte. *Life of Moscheles.* Adapted from the original German by A. D.

Coleridge. London: Hurst and Blackett, 1873.

Mould 1973
Mould, Charles. "The Ingenious Mechanician." *Antique Collector* (June 1973): 165–69.

Mould 1974
———. "An Early-Eighteenth-Century Harpsichord by Thomas Barton." *English Harpsichord (and Fortepiano) Magazine* 1, no. 2 (1974):36–38.

Mould 1976
———. "The Development of the English Harpsichord with Particular Reference to the work of Kirkman." Ph.D. thesis, Oxford University, 1976.

Mould 1977
———. "The Tabel Harpsichord." In *Keyboard Instruments*, 46–52.

Mould 1985
———. "The Ingenious Mechanik." In *Exhibition Catalogue, Iveagh Bequest, Kenwood*. London: Greater London Council, 1985.

Nassarre
Nassarre, Pablo. *Escuela Música segun la Práctica Moderna*. Zaragoza: Diego de Larumbe, 1723. Facsimile ed., Zaragosa: Institución Fernando el Católico, 1980.

Neupert
Neupert, Hanns. *Harpsichord Manual*. Trans. Frank E. Kirby. Kassel: Bärenreiter Verlag, 1960. First edition 1932, with revisions in 1946 and 1955.

Neven
Neven, Armand. "L'Arpicordo." *Acta Musicologica* 42, nos. 3–4 (1970): 230–35.

NGEKI
Edwin M. Ripin, et al. *The New Grove Early Keyboard Instruments*. New York: W. W. Norton, 1989.

Nixon
Nixon, Paul. "Keyboard Instruments in Dublin, c. 1560–1860." *Early Music* 27, no. 2 (2000): 253–68.

Nobbs Unpublished
Nobbs, Christopher. "Two Portuguese Pianos and a Harpsichord." Undated and unpublished manuscript.

Nobbs 1991
———. "A Seventeenth-Century French Harpsichord?" *Fellowship of Makers and Restorers of Historical Instruments Quarterly* 63 (April 1991): 65–73.

Nocerino 1998
Nocerino, Francesco. "Arte cembalaria a Napoli: documenti e notizie su costruttori e strumenti napoletani." In *Ricerche sul' 600 napoletano: saggi e documenti 1996–1997*, 85–109. Naples: Electa Napoli, 1998.

Nocerino 2000
———. "Evidence for Italian Mother-and-Child Virginals: An Important Document Signed by Onofrio Guarracino." *Galpin Society Journal* 53 (April 2000): 317–21.

Nordenfelt-Åberg
Nordenfelt-Åberg, Eva. "The Harpsichord in 18th-Century Sweden." *Early Music* 9, no. 1 (1981): 47–54.

O'Brien 1974
O'Brien, Grant. "The 1764/83 Taskin Harpsichord." In "A Clavichord, a Harpsichord, and a Chamber Organ in the Russell Collection, Edinburgh." *Organ Yearbook* 5 (1974): 91–102.

O'Brien 1979
———. "Ioannes and Andreas Ruckers: A Quatercentenary Celebration." *Early Music* 7, no. 4 (1979): 453–66.

O'Brien 1990
———. *Ruckers: A Harpsichord and Virginal Building Tradition*. Cambridge: Cambridge University Press, 1990.

O'Brien 1994
———. "The Double-Manual Harpsichord by Francis Coston, London, c. 1725." *Galpin Society Journal* 47 (March 1994): 2–32.

O'Brien 1998
———. "Ruckers Double-Manual Harpsichords and Details of Them Relevant to the 1599 Ioannes Ruckers Double-Manual Harpsichord, Händel-Haus, MS-65." In *Kielinstrumente*, 48–62.

O'Brien 1999
———. "The Use of Simple Geometry and the Local Unit of Measurement in the Design of Italian Stringed Keyboard Instruments: An Aid to Attribution and to Organological Analysis." *Galpin Society Journal* 52 (April 1999): 108–71.

O'Brien 2000
———. "Towards Establishing the Original State of the Three-Manual Harpsichord by Stefano Bolcioni, Florence, 1627, in the Russell Collection of Early Keyboard Instruments, Edinburgh." *Galpin Society Journal* 53 (April 2000): 168–200.

O'Brien, Ehricht, and Rieche
———, Stefan Ehricht, and Christiane Rieche. "The Original State and Later Alterations of the Double-Manual Harpsichord, Antwerp 1599/Originalzustand un spätere Veränderungen des zweimanualigen Ruckers-Cembalos, Antwerpen 1599." In *Kielinstrumente*, 187–230.

Och
Och, Laura. "Bartolomeo Cristofori, Scipione Maffei e la prima descrizione del 'Gravicembalo col piano e forte.'" *Il Flauto Dolce* 14–15 (April–October 1986): 21–22.

Page 1978
Page, Christopher. "String-Instrument Mak-

ing in Medieval England and Some Oxford Harpmakers 1380–1466." *Galpin Society Journal* 31 (May 1978): 44–67.

Page 1984
———. "In the Direction of the Beginning." In *The Historical Harpsichord,* vol. 1, 111–25.

Page and Jones
———, and Lewis Jones. "Four More 15th-Century Representations of Stringed Keyboard Instruments." *Galpin Society Journal* 31 (May 1978): 151–55 and plates 11–12.

Palmer 1983
Palmer, Larry. "Some Literary Influences on the Harpsichord and Clavichord." *Diapason* 74, no. 9 (September 1983): 18–19.

Palmer 1989
———. *Harpsichord in America: A Twentieth-Century Revival.* Bloomington: Indiana University Press, 1989.

Paul
Paul, John. *Modern Harpsichord Makers.* London: Victor Golancz, 1981.

Pereira 1978
Pereira, L. A. Esteves. "An Octave Harpsichord at the Instrumental Museum—Lisbon." *English Harpsichord (and Fortepiano) Magazine* 2, no. 2 (1978): 30–32.

Pereira 1983
———. "A Forte-piano at the Instrumental Museum—Lisbon." *English Harpsichord (and Fortepiano) Magazine* 3, no. 4 (1983): 67–70.

Phillips
Phillips, John. "The 1739 Johann Heinrich Gräbner Harpsichord—An Oddity or a *Bach-Flügel?*" In *Das deutsche Cembalo: Symposium im Rahmen der 24. Tage alter Music in Herne 1999,* ed. Christian Ahrens and Gregor Klinke, 123–39. Munich and Salzburg: Musikverlag Katzbichler, 2000.

Pollens 1985
Pollens, Stuart. "The Early Portuguese Piano." *Early Music* 13, no. 1 (1985): 18–38.

Pollens 1990
———. "Michele Todini's Golden Harpsichord: An Examination of the Machine of Galatea and Polyphemus." *Metropolitan Museum of Art Journal* 25 (1990): 33–47.

Pollens 1991
———. "Three Keyboard Instruments Signed by Cristofori's Assistant, Giovanni Ferrini." *Galpin Society Journal* 44 (March 1991): 77–93.

Pollens 1995
———. *The Early Pianoforte.* Cambridge: Cambridge University Press, 1995.

Pollens 1998
———. "Early Alterations Made to Ruckers, Couchet, and Grouwels Harpsichords in the Collection of the Metropolitan Museum of Art." In *Kielinstrumente,* 136–70.

Praetorius
Michael Praetorius. *De Organographia. Syntagma Musicum,* vol. 2. Wolfenbüttel: Elias Holwein, 1618.

Puliti
Puliti, Leto. "Della vita del Serinissimo Ferdinado dei Medici Granprincipe di Toscana e della origine del pianoforte: cenne storici." *Atti dell'Accademia del R. Istituto Musicale di Firenze* 12 (1874): 101–7.

Pussiau
Pussiau, Vincent. "Gilbert Desruisseaux, facteur de clavecins lyonnais." *Musique, Images, Instruments* 2 (1996): 151–67.

Rasch
Rasch, Rudolph. "Does 'Well-Tempered' Mean 'Equal-Tempered'?" In *Bach, Handel, Scarlatti: Tercentenary Essays,* ed. Peter Williams, 293–310. Cambridge: Cambridge University Press, 1985.

Reichardt
Reichardt, Johann Friedrich. *Vertraute Briefe aus Paris geschrieben in der Jahren 1802 und 1803.* Hamburg: B. G. Hoffmann, 1804.

Restle
Restle, Konstantin. *Bartolomeo Cristofori und die Anfänge des Hammerclaviers.* Munich: Editio Maris, 1991.

Restle and Aschenbrandt
———, and Susanne Aschenbrandt, eds. *Das Berliner "Bach-Cembalo": Ein Mythos und seine Folgen.* Exhibition catalog. Berlin: Musikinstrumenten-Museum des Staatlichen Instituts für Musikforschung Preussischer Kulturbesitz, 1995.

Reynvann
Reynvann, Joos Verschuere. "Harpsichord." In *Muzijkaal Kunst-Woordenboek,* 111. Amsterdam: W. Brave, 1795.

Rice 1993
Rice, John R. "The Tuscan Piano in the 1780s: Some Builders, Composers, and Performers." *Early Music* 21, no. 1 (1993): 4–26.

Rice 1995
———. "Stein's 'Favorite Instrument': A Vis-à-Vis Piano-Harpsichord in Naples." *Journal of the American Musical Instrument Society* 21 (1995): 30–64.

Richard
Richard, J. A. "The Pleyel Harpsichord." *English Harpsichord (and Fortepiano) Magazine* 2, no. 5 (1979): 110–13.

Rindlisbacher
Rindlisbacher, Otto. *Das Klavier in der Schweiz: Geschichte der schweizerischen Klavierbaus 1700–1900.* Bern and Munich: Francke Verlag, 1972.

Ripin 1968
Ripin, Edwin M. "The Two-Manual Harpsi-

chord in Flanders before 1650." *Galpin Society Journal* 21 (March 1968): 33–39.

Ripin 1970a
———. "Antwerp Harpsichord-Building: The Current State of Research." In *Colloquium: Restauratieproblemen van Antwerpse klavecimbels*, 12–23. Antwerp: Ruckers Genootschap, 1970.

Ripin 1970b
———. "A 'Three-Foot' Flemish Harpsichord." *Galpin Society Journal* 23 (August 1970): 35–39.

Ripin 1970c
———. "Expressive Devices Applied to the Eighteenth-Century Harpsichord." *Organ Yearbook* 1 (1970): 16–31.

Ripin 1972
———. "A Suspicious Spinet." *Metropolitan Museum of Art Bulletin* (February/March 1972): 196–202.

Ripin 1973
———. "The Surviving *Oeuvre* of Girolomo Zenti." *Journal of the Metropolitan Museum of Art* 7 (1973): 71–87.

Ripin 1975
———. "Towards an Identification of the Chekker." *Galpin Society Journal* 28 (April 1975): 11–25.

Ripin 1977
———. "On Ioes Karest's Virginal and the Origins of the Flemish Tradition." In *Keyboard Instruments*, 67–75 and plates 53–61.

Ripin/Franciolini
———, ed. *The Instrument Catalogs of Leopoldo Franciolini*. Hackensack: Joseph Boonin, 1974.

Robbins Landon
Robbins Landon, H. C. "The Dawn of the Romantic Period." In *Essays on the Viennese Classical Style: Gluck, Haydn, Mozart, Beethoven*. New York: Macmillan, 1970.

Robinson
Robinson, Thomas. *The School of Musicke*. London: S. Waterson, 1603.

Rueger
Rueger, Christoph. *Musikinstrument und Dekor*. Leipzig: Verlag für Kunst und Wissenschaft, 1982.

Russell 1955–56
Russell, Raymond. "The Harpsichord since 1800." *Proceedings of the Royal Music Association* (1955–56): 61–74.

Russell 1959/1973
———. *The Harpsichord and Clavichord*. London: Faber and Faber, 1959. 2nd ed., ed. Howard Schott. New York: W. W. Norton, 1973.

Russell Collection
Newman, Sidney, and Peter Williams. *The Russell Collection of Early Keyboard Instruments*.

Edinburgh: Edinburgh University Press, 1968.

Rutledge
Rutledge, John B. "Late 19th-Century Viol Revivals." *Early Music* 19, no. 3 (1991): 409–18.

Sacchi
Sacchi, Giovanali. "Vita del Cav. Don Carlo Broschi." In *Raccolta Ferrarese di opuscoli*, vol. 15. Vinegia: Coleti, 1784.

Samoyault-Verlet
Samoyault-Verlet, Colombe. *Les Facteurs de clavecins parisiens*. Paris: Société Française de Musicologie, Heugel, 1966.

Savage et al.
Savage, William R., Edward L. Kottick, Thomas J. Hendrickson, and Kenneth D. Marshall. "Air and Structural Modes of a Harpsichord." *Journal of the Acoustical Society of America* 91, no. 4 (1992): 2180–89.

Scheibert
Scheibert, Beverly. *Jean-Henry D'Anglebert and the Seventeenth-Century Clavecin School*. Bloomington: Indiana University Press, 1986.

Scheuerwater and van Acht
Scheuerwater, W., and R. van Acht. *Oude Klavecimbels — Old Harpsichords — Kijkboekjes van het Haags Gemeentemuseum*. The Hague: Gemeentemuseum, 1977.

Scholes
Scholes, Percy. *The Great Dr. Burney*. London: Oxford University Press, 1948.

Schott 1974
Schott, Howard. "The Harpsichord Revival." *Early Music* 2, no. 2 (1974): 85–95.

Schott 1985a
———. *Victoria and Albert Museum, Catalog of Musical Instruments*. Vol. 1: *Keyboard Instruments*. London: Her Majesty's Stationery Office, 1985.

Schott 1985b
———. "From Harpsichord to Pianoforte: A Chronology and Commentary." *Early Music* 13, no. 1 (1985): 28–38.

Schröder 1928
Schröder, Hans. *Verzeichnis der Sammlung alter Musikinstrumente im . . . Museum Barunschweig*. Brunswick: Appelhans, 1928.

Schröder 1968
Schröder, W. "Ausprüche eines Cembalisten." *Das Musikinstrument* 17, no. 7 (1968): vii–x.

Schubart
Schubart, Christian Friedrich Daniel. *Ideen zu einer Aesthetik der Tonkunst*. Vienna: Mörschner und Jasper, 1806.

Schütze
Schütze, Rainer. "Die Unterschiede in der akustischen und musikalischen Qualität bei

alten und modernen Cembali." *Das Musikinstrument* 14 (1965): 1071–73.

Schwarz
Schwarz, Kerstin. "Die Hammerflügel und Cembali Bartolomeo Cristoforis im Vergleich." In *Scripta Artium,* vol. 3. Leipzig: University of Leipzig, forthcoming.

Seeing Double
"Seeing Double." *Newsletter of the Yale University Collection of Musical Instruments* 21 (spring 1999).

Segarizzi
Segarizzi, Arnaldo. "La Corrispondenza familiare d'un medico erudito del quattrocento (Pietro Tomasi)." *Atti della R. Accademia di scienze, lettere ed arti degli Agiati, Rovereto* 13 (1907): 219–28.

Segerman
Segerman, Ephraim. "A Survey of Pitch Standards before the Nineteenth Century." *Galpin Society Journal* 54 (May 2001): 200–218.

Shann 1984
Shann, Richard. "Flemish Transposing Harpsichords: An Explanation." *Galpin Society Journal* 37 (March 1984): 52–71.

Shann 1985
———. "Ruckers Doubles: A Survey of the Theories." *Fellowship of Makers and Restorers of Historical Instruments Quarterly* 41 (October 1985): 69–75.

Shevaloff
Shevaloff, Joel. "The Keyboard Music of Domenico Scarlatti: A Re-evaluation of the Present State of Knowledge in the Light of the Sources." Ph.D. dissertation, Brandeis University, 1970.

Shortridge 1960
Shortridge, John. "Italian Harpsichord Building in the 16th and 17th Centuries." *Contributions from the Museum of History and Technology: United States National Museum Bulletin* 225 (1960): 93–107.

Shortridge 1985
———. "Ruckers 'Transposing' Double Harpsichords." *Fellowship of Makers and Restorers of Historical Instruments Quarterly* 40 (July 1985): 23.

Shuman
Shuman, Jack C. " 'Reversed' Portatives and Positives in Early Art." *Galpin Society Journal* 19 (July 1971): 16–21.

Skowroneck 1968
Skowroneck, Martin. "Probleme des Cembalobaus aus historischer Sicht." *Hi Fi Stereophonie* 9, 10, 11 (1968): 700–711, 781–84, 875–78.

Skowroneck 1974
———. "Das Cembalo von Christian Zell, Hamburg 1728, und seine Restaurierung." *Organ Yearbook* 5 (1974): 79–87.

Smith 1759
Smith, Robert. *Harmonics.* London, 1759. 2nd ed., 1766–67.

Smith 1980
Smith, Douglas Alton. "The Musical Instrument Inventory of Raymund Fugger." *Galpin Society Journal* 33 (March 1980): 36–44.

Sprengel
Sprengel, Peter. *Handwerk und Künste in Tabelen.* Berlin, 1773.

Stauffer
Stauffer, George B. "J. S. Bach's Harpsichords." In *Festa Musicologica: Essays in Honor of George J. Buelow,* ed. Thomas J. Mathiesen and Benito V. Rivera, 289–318. Stuyvesant, N.Y.: Pendragon Press, 1995.

Steiner
Steiner, Thomas Friedmann. "Clavichords No. 2 and 3 in the Leipzig Collection: Some Complementary Thoughts about Their Origins." In *De Clavicordio,* vol. 1, 41–46.

Steinert
Steinert, Morris. *Reminiscences.* Compiled by Jane Marlin. New York: Putnam's, 1900.

Stellfield
Stellfield, J. A. "Bronnen tot de geschiedenis der Antwerpsche clavecimbel—en orgelbouwers in de XVIᶜ en XVII eeuwen." In *Vlaamsch jaarboek voor muziekgeschiedenis,* vol. 4, 3–110. Antwerp: Drukkeri Gresseler, 1942.

Stembridge 1992
Stembridge, Christopher. "Music for the *Cimbalo cromatico* and Other Split-Keyed Instruments in Seventeenth-Century Italy." *Performance Practice Review* 5, no. 1 (1992): 5–43.

Stembridge 1993
———. "The *Cimbalo cromatico* and Other Italian Keyboard Instruments with Nineteen or More Divisions to the Octave (Surviving Specimens and Documentary Evidence)." *Performance Practice Review* 6, no. 1 (1993): 33–59.

Stengel
Stengel, W. *Alte Wohnkultur in Berlin.* Berlin, 1958.

Stradner
Stradner, Gerhard. "Bemerkungen zu den Tasteninstrumenten in Sebastian Virdungs 'Musica getutsch.' " *Beiträge zur Aufführungspraxis* 2 (1974): 80–81.

Strohm
Strohm, Reinhardt. "Die privat Kunst und das öffentliche Schicksal von Hermann Poll, dem Erfinder das Cembalos." In *Musica privata: die Rolle der Musik im privaten Leben. Festschrift zum 65. Geburtstag von Walter Salmen.* Innsbruck: Edition Helbling, 1991.

Sutherland 1995
Sutherland, David. "Domenico Scarlatti and

the Florentine Piano." *Early Music* 23, no. 2 (1995): 243–56.

Sutherland 1998–99
———. "The Florentine School of Cembalo-Making Centered in the Works of Bartolomeo Cristofori." *Early Keyboard Journal* 16–17 (1998–99): 7–75.

Sutherland 2000
———. "Bartolomeo Cristofori's 1726 Cembalos." *Journal of the American Musical Instrument Society* 26 (2000): 5–56.

Sween
Sween, P. "The Nineteenth-Century View of the Old Harpsichord." *English Harpsichord (and Fortepiano) Magazine* 2, no. 4 (1979): 92–95.

Tagliavini
Tagliavini, Luigi Ferdinando. "Giovanni Ferinni and His Harpsichord 'a penne e a martelletti.'" *Early Music* 19, no. 3 (1991): 398–408.

Thomas 1974
Thomas, Michael. "Early French Harpsichords." *English Harpsichord (and Fortepiano) Magazine* 1, no. 3 (1974): 73–84.

Thomas 1976
———. "The Harpsichord at the Courtauld Institute." *English Harpsichord (and Fortepiano) Magazine* 1, no. 7 (1976): 194–97.

Thomas 1979
———. "The Upright Harpsichord." *English Harpsichord (and Fortepiano) Magazine* 2, no. 4 (1979): 84–92.

Thomas and Rhodes 1967
Thomas, W. R., and J. J. K. Rhodes. "The String Scales of Italian Keyboard Instruments." *Galpin Society Journal* 20 (March 1967): 48–62.

Thomas and Rhodes 1979
———, and ———. "Harpsichords and the Art of Wire Drawing." *Organ Yearbook* 10 (1979): 126–39.

Thomson
Thomson, Virgil. *The Musical Scene*. New York: Alfred Knopf, 1947.

Thon
Thon, Christian Friedrich Gottlieb. *Ueber Klavierinstrumente*. Sondershausen: Bernhard Friedrich Voight, 1817.

Tiella
Tiella, Marco. "The Archicembalo of Nicola Vicentino." *English Harpsichord (and Fortepiano) Magazine* 1, no. 5 (1975): 134–44.

Todini
Todini, Michele. *Dichiarazione della Galleria armonica*. Rome: Tirroni, 1676.

Tournay 1980
Tournay, Jean. "Á propos d'Albertus Delin, 1712–1771: petite contribution à l'histoire du clavecin." In *Mercier*, 139–232.

Tournay 1987
———. *Archives Dulcken*. Vol. 1. Brussels: Musée Instrumental, 1987.

Troeger 1987
Troeger, Richard. *Technique and Interpretation on the Harpsichord and Clavichord*. Bloomington: Indiana University Press, 1987.

Troeger 1996
———. "The Dolmetsch/Chickering Clavichords and Their Model." In *De Clavicordio*, vol. 2, 213–24.

Troeger 1997
———. "A New Light on Violet Gordon Woodhouse." *Continuo* 21, no. 2 (April 1997): 2–4.

Tyre
Tyre, Philip. Review of Girolamo Frescobaldi, *Il primo libro di capriccii (1624)*: John Butt, organ; and Girolamo Frescobaldi, *Partite e toccate*, Pierre Hantaï, harpsichord. *Continuo* 21, no. 2 (1997): 34–35.

Van Blankenburg
Van Blankenburg, Quirinus. *Elementa musica, of nieuw licht tot het welverstann van de musiec en de bas continuo*. The Hague: Laurens Berkoske, 1739. Facsimile ed., Amsterdam, 1972.

Van der Meer 1965
Van der Meer, John Henry. "A Flemish 'Quint' Harpsichord." *Galpin Society Journal* 18 (March 1965): 117–21.

Van der Meer 1966a
———. "Beiträge zum Cembalobau im deutschen Sprachgebiet bis 1700." In *Anzeiger des germanisches national Museums*, 103–33. Nuremberg, 1966.

Van der Meer 1966b
———. "Flämische Cembali in italienischem Besitz." *Analecta Musicologica* 3 (1966): 114–21.

Van der Meer 1977
———. "More about Flemish Two-Manual Harpsichords." In *Keyboard Instruments*, 49–58.

Van der Meer 1978
———. "A Contribution to the History of the Clavicytherium." *Early Music* 6, no. 2 (1978): 247–59.

Van der Meer 1986
———. "A Curious Instrument with a Five-Octave Compass." *Early Music* 14, no. 3 (1986): 397–400.

Van der Meer 1991a
———. "A Little-Known German Harpsichord." *Early Keyboard Studies Newsletter* 5, no. 2 (1991): 8–13.

Van der Meer 1991b
———. "Die Geschichte der Zupfklavire bis 1800, ein Überblick: regional Schulen." In *Berlin*, 16–53.

Van der Meer 1997
    ———. "The Keyboard String Instruments at the Disposal of Domenico Scarlatti." *Galpin Society Journal* 50 (March 1997): 136–60.
Van der Meer 1998a
    ———. "Types of Transposing Harpsichords, Mainly Outside the Netherlands." In *Kielinstrumente*, 95–103.
Van der Meer 1998b
    ———. "The Position of Harpsichord-Making in the Northern Netherlands." In *Kielinstrumente*, 171–81.
Van der Meer 1998c
    ———. "Der Zuid-Nederlandse Klavecimbelbau." In *Lambrechts-Douillez 1998a*, 35–52.
Van der Straeten
    Van der Straeten, Edmond. *La Musique aux pays-bas avant le XIXe siècle.* Brussels: C. Mucquart, 1867–88. Reprint ed., New York: Dover Publications, 1968.
Van Roey
    Van Roey, Jan, "Antwerpen: Vanaf de 15de Tot in de 17de Eeuw." In *Lambrechts-Douillez 1998a*, 30–33, 136.
Verlet
    Verlet, Colombe. "Jalons pour une recherche de la facture de clavecins en province." *Recherches* 4 (1964): 101–4.
Victoria and Albert
    Schott, Howard, ed. *Victoria and Albert Museum, Catalogue of Musical Instruments.* Vol. 1: *Keyboard Instruments.* London: Her Majesty's Stationery Office, 1985.
Virdung
    Virdung, Sebastian. *Musica getutscht: A Treatise on Musical Instruments ([Basel], 1511) by Sebastian Virdung.* Ed. Beth Bullard. Cambridge: Cambridge University Press, 1993.
Wainright
    Wainright, David. *Broadwood by Appointment: A History.* London: Quiller Press, 1982.
Wainright and Mobbs
    ———, and Kenneth Mobbs. "Shudi's Harpsichords for Frederick the Great." *Galpin Society Journal* 49 (March 1996): 77–94.
Walther
    Walther, Johann Gottfried. *Musikalisches Lexicon oder musikalische Bibliothek.* Leipzig: Wolfgang Deer, 1732. Facsimile reprint, *Documenta musicologica,* 1, no. 3. Kassel: Bärenreiter, 1953.
Wardman
    Wardman, Judith. "Thomas Goff and His Clavichords: A Brief Introduction." *British Clavichord Society Newsletter* 15 (October 1999): 18–20.
Watson 1983–84
    Watson, John. "A Catalogue of Antique Keyboard Instruments in the Southeast." *Early Keyboard Journal* 2 (1983–84): 64–82.

Watson 1997
    ———. "A Catalog of Antique Keyboard Instruments in the Southeast, Part V." *Early Keyboard Journal* 15 (1997): 93–158.
Wells 1978
    Wells, Elizabeth. "An Early Stringed Keyboard Instrument: The Clavicytherium in the Royal College of Music, London." *Early Music* 6, no. 4 (1978): 568–71.
Wells 1984
    ———. *The Royal College of Music Museum of Instruments Guide to the Collection.* London: Royal College of Music, 1984.
Whitehead
    Whitehead, Lance. "An Extraordinary Hass Harpsichord in Gothenburg." *Galpin Society Journal* 49 (March 1996): 95–102.
Williams 1971
    Williams, Peter. "Some Developments in Early Keyboard Instruments." *Music and Letters* 52 (1971): 272–86.
Williams 1977
    ———. "The Earl of Wemyss' Claviorgan and Its Context in Eighteenth-Century England." In *Keyboard Instruments,* 77–87.
Williams 1980
    ———. *A New History of the Organ from the Greeks to the Present Day.* London: Faber and Faber, 1980.
Winternitz
    Winternitz, Emanuel. *Musical Instruments and Their Symbolism in Western Art.* New Haven: Yale University Press, 1979.
Woods
    Woods, Paula. "The Gerbier-Windebank Letters: Two Ruckers Harpsichords in England." *Galpin Society Journal* 54 (May 2001): 76–89.
Wraight 1984a
    Wraight, Denzil. "Italian Harpsichords." *Early Music* 12, no. 1 (1984): 151.
Wraight 1984b
    ———. "Italian Two-Manual Harpsichords." *Fellowship of Makers and Restorers of Historical Instruments Quarterly* (July 1984): 19–22.
Wraight 1986
    ———. "Vincentius and the Earliest Harpsichords." *Early Music* 14, no. 4 (1986): 534–38.
Wraight 1988a
    ———. "Strong Iron Wire and Long Scales in Italian Harpsichords." *Fellowship of Makers and Restorers of Historical Instruments Quarterly* 50 (January 1988): 37–40.
Wraight 1988b
    ———. "The 1605 Celestini Harpsichord: Another Misleading Instrument." *Organ Yearbook* 19 (1988): 91–103.
Wraight 1990
    ———. "The Early 16th-Century Italian

Short Octave." *Fellowship of Makers and Restorers of Historical Instruments Quarterly* 59 (April 1990): 17–23.

Wraight 1991
———. "A Zenti Harpsichord Rediscovered." *Early Music* 19, no. 1 (1991): 99–101.

Wraight 1992a
———. "The Identification and Authentication of Italian String Keyboard Instruments." In *The Historical Harpsichord,* vol. 3, 59–161.

Wraight 1992b
———. "Cristofori's Instruments." *Early Music* 20, no. 4 (1992): 701.

Wraight 1993
———. "Two Harpsichords by Giovanni Celestini." *Galpin Society Journal* 46 (March 1993): 120–36.

Wraight 1997
———. "The Stringing of Italian Keyboard Instruments, c. 1500–c. 1650." Part I: "Discussion and Bibliography." Part II: "Catalogue of the Instruments." Ph.D. dissertation, Queens University of Belfast, 1997.

Wraight 2000
———. "Principles and Practice in Stringing Italian Keyboard Instruments." *Early Keyboard Journal* 18 (2000): 175–238.

Wraight and Stembridge
———, and Christopher Stembridge. "Italian Split-Keyed Instruments with Fewer than Nineteen Divisions to the Octave." *Performance Practice Review* 7, no. 2 (1994): 150–81.

Zarlino
Zarlino, Gioseffe. *Le Istituzioni harmoniche.* Venice: F. Senese, 1558.

Zuckermann 1963
Zuckermann, Wolfgang Joachim. *Build Your Own Harpsichord: Construction and Maintenance Manual.* New York: Zuckermann Harpsichords, 1963.

Zuckermann 1968
———. "Sympathetic Vibrations: The Do-It-Yourself Phenomenon." *The Harpsichord* 1, no. 2 (1968): 2, 19.

Zuckermann 1969a
———. *The Modern Harpsichord: Twentieth-Century Instruments and Their Makers.* New York: October House, 1969.

Zuckermann 1969b
———. "Sympathetic Vibrations: Dilemma Italian Style." *The Harpsichord* 2, no. 1 (1969): 2, 17.

Zuckermann 1971
———. "Sympathetic Vibrations." *The Harpsichord* 4, no. 3 (1971): 3–5.

Index

Page numbers for illustrations and photographs are italicized.

Mass-produced harpsichords, 416, 518n17. *See also Serien* instruments
Massenet, Jules, 414
Materials
  to add stability to harpsichord frames, 445–446
  in Baffo's 1574 harpsichord, 87
  Challis all-metal harpsichord, 451
  cypress wood, 79–80, 142, 479n27, 485n22
  decoration, 85 (*see also* Decoration)
  in Dulcken's instruments, 286, 287, 507n7
  ebony, 84, 86, 149
  in English bentside spinets and virginals, 201
  in Flemish decoration, 480n32
  Italian harpsichords, 98
  ivory, 84 (*see also* Ivory)
  in Ioes Karest's virginals, 480nn38–39
  keys, 84
  mahogany, 368
  Neapolitan harpsichords, 97
  oak wood, 314, 507n7, 509n39
  in soundboards, 478n70
  in Spanish instruments, 237–238
  for strings, 485n48
  tortoise shell, 313
  walnut wood, 167, 368 (*see also* Walnut wood)
  wood movement, 440
Mattmann, Louise, 392
Maunder, Richard, 342, 343, 512n145
Mayer, Johann, 179, 182, 183, 185
  1619 harpsichord by, pl. 13
Mayone, Asciono, 89
Meantone temperament, 88, 487n73
  described by Pietro Aron, 487n72
  on double-manual harpsichords, 119–120
  and equal temperament, 326
  quarter-comma, 487n72
Medici family, 66
  Cosimo, 498n13
  Ferdinand de', 144, 210, 500nn6,9–10
  Florentine Camerata under, 133
  Girolamo Zenti serving, 137
Meeùs, Nicolas, 122
Meidting, Anton, 181
Mendelssohn, Felix, 469, 516n9
Menuisiers, 265
Mercator, Michael, 31
Mercier, Philip, 513n8
Merlin, John Joseph, 315, 366, 376
  down-striking piano action of, 515n69
  inventions by, 379
  wheelchair invention, 515n73
Mersenne, Marin, 24, 44
  on automated spinets, 180
  Harmonie universelle, 161

on harpsichord construction in France, 164
octave virginal, *162*
on virginal construction in France, 163
Merulo, Claudio, 52
Merzdorf, Walter, 446
Messina, Italy, 227–228
Metallurgy, 15, 17
Metastasio, Pietro, 238
Metsys, Jan, 54
Metsys, Quentin, 54
Micanon, 12, 476n16
Michelangelo, 66, 484n2
Middelburg, Johann, 305
MIDI (Musical Instrument Digital Interface), 458
Mietke, Michael, 323–325, 510n83
  1702 harpsichord by, pl. 23
  charging for harpsichords, 510n86
  decoration of 1702, 314
  16' harpsichord, 315
Migliai, Antonio, 144, 494n41
Miklis, Johannes, 299
Milan, Italy, 94–97, 227
Minden Cathedral, 13
  carving in, *15,* 64
Minne Regal (Rules of Love) (Eberhard Cersne), 11–12
The Modern Harpsichord (Zuckermann), 459, 461
Moermans, Hans, 62, 130, 484n43
Mofferriz, Brahem, 502n14
Mofferriz, Mohama, 234, 235, 237
Moldings, 479n31, 493n10, 494n19. *See also* Decoration
  on English virginals, 197
  in French harpsichords, 167
  International style, 158
Mondini, Giuseppe, 144
  1701 harpsichord, *146*
  folding harpsichords, 258
Mongin, Marie, 392
Monochords, 12–13
Monodic style, 133
Monteverdi, Claudio, 132
Moor of Saragossa, 234
Moorish design, 74, 483n25
Moors, Antonius, 31
Morel, Marie, 418
Morley, John, 448–449
Morley, Thomas, 200
Morris, William, 419
Moscheles, Ignaz, 398
Moser, Anton, 342
Moshak, Moritz Georg, 322
Mother and child spinett, 59–60
Mother and child virginals, *61,* 110–111
  possibly from Naples, *150*
  piece by Sweelinck for, *116*
  purpose of, 483n36
  (Hans) Ruckers 1581 instrument, 60–62, pl. 6
  Van der Biest 1580 mother and

child spinett virginal, 489n12, pl. 5a–b
Mottoes, 127, 128, 486n62, 492n82
Mould, Charles, 366, 368
Mozart, Wolfgang Amadeus, 92, 230, 332
  Friederici clavichord owned by, 351, 513n169
  piano sonatas, 388
  playing a Shudi harpsichord, 361
  studying works of Bach, 397
Muffat, Georg, 189
Müller, Hans, 29, 33–37
  1537 harpsichord, *34,* 110, 117
  comparison between Ioes Karest's virginals, 37–38
  comparison between Lodewijk Theewes's 1579 claviorganum, 49–50
  influence on German harpsichord making, 176
  as representative of German style, 50–51
  soundboard construction, 216
The Mulliner Book, 200
"Multiple-broken" short octave, 344–345
Musée de la Musique (Paris), 401–402
Muselar virginals, 60, 61, 110
  1614 instrument by Ioannes Ruckers, *112*
  in Flemish terminology, 112, 483n39
  sound of, 111
Museum of Fine Arts (Boston), 402
Musica getutscht (Virdung), 23
Musical Instruments and Their Symbolism in Western Art (Winternitz), 142
Musick's Monument (Mace), 204
My Ladye Nevells Book, 200

Nag's-head swells, *375*
Naples
  16th century, 97–98
  17th century, 144, 146–148, 150–151, 495n44
  influence on English virginals, 499n12
Nassarre, Pablo, 235
Natoire, Charles, 265
Neri, Francesco, 488n95
Neupert, Hanns, 416, 450, 451
Nineteenth century, 391–406
  attitude toward harpsichord, 391–394
  building in early part of century, 394–395
  collecting harpsichords during, 400–403
  historicism and antiquarianism, 397–400
  Paris exposition of 1889, 409–414
  preservation of harpsichord, 396–397

Instrument maker, scholar, researcher, author, and lecturer, musicologist **ED KOTTICK** built his first harpsichord in 1963. He has investigated the instrument's acoustical properties as well as its historical aspects and has published articles on the harpsichord in both scientific and scholarly journals. His collection of more than three thousand slides, a product of his visits to the major museums in the United States and Europe, keeps him in demand as a speaker.

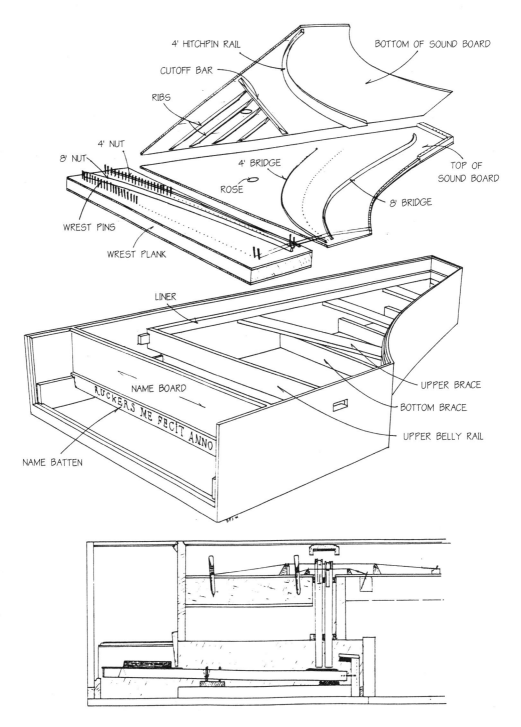

4' HITCHPIN RAIL

BOTTOM OF SOUND BOARD

CUTOFF BAR

RIBS

4' NUT

8' NUT

4' BRIDGE

ROSE

TOP OF
SOUND BOARD

8' BRIDGE

WREST PINS

WREST PLANK

LINER

NAME BOARD

RUCKERS ME FECIT ANNO

UPPER BRACE

BOTTOM BRACE

UPPER BELLY RAIL

NAME BATTEN

17ᵗʰ-CENTURY FLEMISH HARPSICHORD
EXPLODED VIEW AND SECTION